PASSENGERS WHO ARRIVED IN THE U.S.
SEPTEMBER 1821 - DECEMBER 1823

PASSENGERS
WHO ARRIVED
IN THE UNITED STATES

SEPTEMBER 1821 - DECEMBER 1823

From

Transcripts made by

The State Department

WITH INDEX

CLEARFIELD

Originally published
from transcripts made by
The State Department

Reprinted with permission for
Clearfield Company, Inc. by
Genealogical Publishing Co., Inc.
Baltimore, Maryland
2005

International Standard Book Number: 0-8063-5287-6

Made in the United States of America

CONTENTS

INTRODUCTION

In the National Archives in Washington repose eight volumes, in an unknown hand, of copies of lists of passengers who arrived at American ports during the years 1819 to 1832. These were copied by order of the State Department from the lists of passengers which the ship captains were ordered to deposit with the Customs Collectors of the American ports upon arrival.

It is believed that the government ordered this to be done with a view to supervising conditions on the ships bringing in immigrants, for a law of 1819 stated that ships were to carry no more than two passengers for every five tons burden. The crowded emigrant ships of colonial days, bringing in cargoes of indentured servants and transported malefactors, were often so overcrowded and unsanitary that many of the passengers died on the voyage. Remembering those grim days, the State Department included in its printed forms a column for "died on the voyage"; but owing to the improvement in shipping conditions and the restrictions upon overcrowding the column was barely necessary. During the two years covered by the present volume, only seven people died on the voyage, three of them by an unlucky mishap in the river at New Orleans. (See pages 54, 134, 180, 332).

When ordering these transcripts to be made from the original documents, the State Department evidently intended them for publication, and in fact they did publish the first volume, under the title LETTER FROM THE SECRETARY OF STATE WITH A TRANSCRIPT OF THE PASSENGERS WHO ARRIVED IN THE U. S. FROM THE 1st OCTOBER, 1819 TO THE 30th SEPTEMBER, 1820. Whether a flash of foresight revealed that future years would bring a flood of immigrants too great to publish, or whether the printers could not decipher the transcribers' writing, we do not know; but the remaining transcripts, bound into volumes, did not fulfill the purpose for which they were made until the present publication of the third and part of the fourth volumes, covering a few names from the end of 1821 and the whole of the years 1822 and 1823. It does not follow on immediately from the first published volume, as the second volume of the transcripts has been lost; which means that, since some of the originals are missing also, certain names for 1820 and 1821 are lost forever.

It is certain that the faded and inconsistent handwriting is daunting and it is believed that some of the more difficult names were not copied correctly by the State Department scribes. Comparison with some of the original captains' returns make it appear that some names are left out altogether, but closer scrutiny seems to point to the fact that they are put in further down the page where the name of the same vessel, at the same port appears again. Every name in the transcripts has been checked off in a contemporary hand, as though it had been compared with the originals.

Other areas for error are created by the scribe's passion for dittoes, which he has often thoughtlessly copied down an entire page, quite regardless of what the top word might be. These give rise occasionally to such phenomena as a shipload of passengers arriving at an American port from several different European origins, all bound for Portugal; or a load of working folk from England, intending to return to England and settle there; and in one or two cases, a female stone mason, although perhaps one can forgive the occasional lapse where a wife is dittoed under her husband's occupation. And if he copied several portions down twice, who among us has not done the same? (Where noticed, these duplications have been removed). But, what was not his fault at all, the binders managed to bind a few of the names into the binding of the books, so that they are lost forever; but there are very few of these. Neither was it his fault that the collectors at Baltimore usually failed to write down the names of the ships, thus defeating the very purpose for which the lists were kept, namely to check on the number of passengers per ton burden. All he could do for Baltimore was to write down "vessel not mentioned".

However, there are times when we cannot forgive the non-crossing of ts, thus presenting us with such interpretations as CULLING, CUTTING or CULTING; the reader must sometimes take his choice   I and J are often confused, although J usually has a longer tail; but the first initial has usually been interpreted as J where there is some doubt. Many of the names were spelled phonetically, of course, which is quite forgiveable, but the poor handwriting caused the greatest confusion between e and i, and even between n and r.

Perhaps, aware of his shortcomings as an amanuensis, he rejoiced that the government had decided against printing the work; so let criticism be restrained more than a century after his death and may he continue to sleep in peace.   For it is usually possible to see where the dittoes should have ended and reverted to the proper sex, place of origin or destination.   It is almost certain that where a long string of dittoes appears under some other destination, that the United States is really intended.

In spite of some shortcomings, however, the lists are practical for publication, unlike the originals, and are valuable also, since they contain many names for which the originals no longer exist for this period, such as those for Baltimore.

It seems that very little research has been done for this early period of what the sociologists call "The Old Immigration".   Much has been written about the period from the 1830s to 1882, when the first restrictions began to be placed upon immigrants; but the immigrants of the 1820s were among the first to feel the lure of the New World when immigration once more became possible after the hostilities.   Marcus Lee Hanson, in his book THE ATLANTIC MIGRATION, 1607-1860, calculates that the cost of steerage passage from British ports to the United States cost between ten and twelve pounds, a large sum for an ordinary family to find.   By 1832, accomodation could be obtained in the regular New York Packet Boats at six pounds and on ordinary trading vessels at about four pounds, thus bringing the voyage within reach of many more laboring people.

The passengers in the present list are, as always, of every age, from babes in arms to George Baley on p. 88, who was 83 years old, and they are from all walks of life, including the butcher, the baker and the candlestick maker (only in this case he is denominated a tallow chandler).   Occupations range through a comedian, a tragedian, several consuls with their secretaries, several Parisian hairdressers and pastry cooks, a few ladies and gentlemen of leisure, merchants, naval and military personnel, a twenty year old nephew of Napoleon and the inevitable dancing master.

Some of the passengers are not of the emigrant breed, but if we can believe the dittoes, are visiting only, or are Americans returning from visits to Europe, usually described under the catch-all appellation of "merchant". Several names can be identified as making several visits to and from Europe, perhaps merchants on buying trips, perhaps couriers or diplomats.   One of the so-called merchants was David Douglas, who sailed from Liverpool on June 5th, 1823, arriving in New York on August 4th, aboard the Anna Maria.   Douglas was a member of the Royal Horticultural Society, sent over by them to make a study of the flora and fauna of the United States.   His Journal was published by the Society in 1914 and besides his description of 33 species of American oaks and 18 species of pine trees, there is an interesting account of his arrival at New York, recording his detention in quarantine at Staten Island for 14 days on account of an outbreak of smallpox, etc.   He records that he was the first one off the ship, and sure enough, in the State Department records of this ship, his name leads all the rest.   No doubt many other passengers can also be identified.

As in most immigrant lists, there is a predominence of single young men, but there are also large numbers of husbands and wives, frequently young, but often middle aged, with families of all sizes.   In the original lists, it is possible to find the names of all the children, but in these transcripts, only the numbers of children are usually given.   Occasionally we meet a woman travelling alone with children, perhaps to join her husband, or to deliver the children to somebody.   In the winter months, it is noted that the number of single men is larger in proportion to the numbers of women and children.

As might be expected at this time, the greatest number of immigrants is from the British Isles, followed by other Western European countries.   No attempt has been made to list the numbers arriving from each country, but on p. ix will be found a list of countries of origin, while a list of ports of entry appears on page x.

The ships bringing in the passengers are of all sizes, carrying anywhere from a crowd to a single passenger, in addition to the cargo.   The names of the ships are often troublesome to decipher and the names of the captains often missing or illegible.   Often it is impossible to know whether a vessel of the same name but with a different captain on a different voyage, is or is not, the same vessel.   The index of vessels is an addition which the State Department's printed volume did not have and it is believed that this is the first time a list of vessels has been compiled for this period.

PLACES OF ORIGIN

Aberdeen
Amsterdam
Antigua
Armoy (Amoy in China)
Austria
Baden
Bahama
Barbadoes
Bayonne
Bengal
Bermuda
Bordeaux
Brazil
Bremen
Brussels
Buenos Ayres
Cadiz
Canada
Canary Isles
Cape de Verde
Cape Hatien
Catalonia
Chile
Columbia
Copenhagen
Cuba
Curraco
Currecoa
Darien
Demerara
Denmark
Dominica
Edinburgh
England
Flanders
Florida
France
Geneva
Genoa

Germany
Great Britain
Guadaloupe
Guernsey
Halifax
Hamburgh
Hanover
Havana
Hayti (Hayte)
Holland
Honduras
Ireland
Italy
Jamaica
Jaqumel
Kingston
Leghorn
Lima
Liverpool
Louisiana
Lubeck
Madiera
Malanzes
Mantanzas
Maragalante
Marseilles
Martinique
Mexico
Montreal
Naples
Neiuvetos
Netherlands
New Brunswick
New Foundland
New Providence
Nova Scotia
Oporto
Orleans
Paris

Piedmont
Poland
Porte Au Prince
Porto Rico
Portugal
Prince Edward Island
Prussia
Quebec
Rome
Russia
St. Barts
St. Croix
St. Domingo
St. Eustatia
St. Helena
St. Jage de Cuba
St. Johns
St. Martin's
Sardinia
Scotland
Sicily
Smyrna
South America
South Wales
Spanish Main
Spain
Stockholm
Surinam
Sweden
Switzerland
Tenneriffe
Trinidad
Turkey
Upper Canada
Vera Cruz
Wales
West Indies

PORTS OF ENTRY

Alexandria, Va.
Baltimore, Md.
Barnstable, Mass.
Belfast, Maine
Boston, Mass.
Boston and Charlestown, Mass.
Bristol, R.I.
Bristol and Warren, R.I.
Charleston, S.C.
Edgartown, Mass.
Frenchman's Bay, Maine
Kennebunk, Maine
Marblehead, Mass.
Nantucket, Mass.
New Bedford, Mass.
New Bern, N.C.
Newburyport, Mass.
New Haven, Conn.
New London, Conn.
Newport, R.I.
New Orleans, La.
New York, N.Y.
Norfolk, Va.
Oswegatchie, N.Y.
Passamaquoddy, Maine
Petersburg, Va.
Philadelphia, Pa.
Plymouth, Mass.
Portland, Maine
Portland and Falmouth, Maine
Portsmouth, N.H.
Providence, R.I.
Richmond, Va.
St. Augustine, Fla.
Salem and Beverly, Mass.
Savanna(h), Ga.
South Carolina
Waldoboro, Maine

1822

EDITORS' NOTE

The passengers' names are arranged firstly by the date of the quarter on which they disembarked, except in one case, where the first and second quarters of 1823 are grouped together for New Orleans. Under each quarter they are grouped by port and then by vessel. It is believed that Passamaquoddy on p. 326 should be Philadelphia.

After the vessel's name, it can be assumed that all passengers were on that vessel until the next vessel's name appears. However, there are several instances, such as at the port of Baltimore, where nearly all the vessels are omitted. This is usually obvious from the unduly long gap which appears between vessels.

Spelling of names is so erratic that searchers are advised to look under every possible variation of spelling, likely or unlikely, bearing in mind the following peculiarities in the original handwriting:

Ts were rarely crossed, so there are many instances where t and l might have been transposed through error.

Lower case e and i may have been confused, since the writer frequently omitted the dots on the i's.

Lower case n and r are often indistinguishable; also s and r.

Capital J and capital I are often indistinguishable. Where this is initial only, J has usually been assumed.

Many times, O'Brien and perhaps other names starting with O have been written as O. Brien.

Note that there are several types of vessels, sch. being the abbreviation for schooner.

* denotes that there was some difficulty in reading the writing and it is not certain whether the names are correctly transcribed.

/ denotes alternative interpretations of the writing, either of a whole word or a part.

( ) denotes that this word or letter does not appear on the work from which this was copied, but does appear on another version in the National Archives.

PASSENGERS WHO ARRIVED IN THE U.S.
SEPTEMBER 1821 - DECEMBER 1823

Names of passengers	Age	Sex	Occupation	Country to which they belong	Country of which they intend becoming inhabitants	Ship or vessel with the name of the master or commander
NEW YORK						
Q. E. Sept. 30, 1821						
Richd. Jenkins	30	M	Merchant	England	U. States	Ship Amity. Maxwell.
Wm. Milne	25	M	"	Scotland	Havana	
Thos. C. Walker	23	M	"	U. States	U. States	
Nathan Hunt	63	M	"	"	"	
Alexr. Stansber	58	M	"	England	"	
Edwd. Wilson & son	48	M	"	U. States	"	
J. Hudson	27	M	"	"	"	
John Bower	50	M	"	"	"	
Wm. Chadwick	42	M	"	England	"	
John Bennington	21	M	"	"	"	
Benj. Lucas	17	M	"	U. States	"	
David Henderson	21	M	"	England	"	
Alexr. McCulloch	18	M	"	"	"	
James McLeod	51	M	"	U. States	"	Ship Stephanian. Bunker.
Samuel Lamb	38	M	"	"	"	
F. Taylor	18	M	"	"	"	
J. B. Viole	27	M	Physician	France	"	
R. A. Barba	24	M	"	"	"	
Edwd. Gosselin	26	M	Merchant	Canada	"	
Francis Salmon	24	M	Student	France	"	
Theodore Page	22	M	"	"	"	
Francis Ganohl	20	M	Clerk	Germany	Germany	
Samuel Henderson	22	M	"	England	England	
Joseph Dryfaus	28	M	Merchant	U. States	U. States	
P. L. Jane	25	M	"	France	"	
J. P. Hill	28	M	Doctor	U. States	"	
John Willig	55	M	Merchant	Germany	"	
Lewis Vallice	20	M	"	Switzerland	"	
M. L. Fretagert *	41	M	"	"	"	
James Cox	29	M	Miller	England	England	
J. Spoker	18	M	Watchmaker	Switzerland	Switzerland	
John Stat	20	M	"	"	"	

Names of passengers	Age	Sex	Occupation	Country to which they belong	Country of which they intend becoming inhabitants	Ship or vessel with the name of the master or commander
George Black	35	M	Merchant	England	U. States	Schooner Native. Bidell
M. Aldrick •	34	M	Mariner	U. States	"	Brig Louisa Ann. Bassett.
Mr. Crowry •	29	M	Merchant	St. Martins	St. Martins	Brig Matilda. McGown
John Nichols	22	M	Servant			
John Park	60	M	Labourer	Scotland	U. States	Ship Camillas. Peck
Letitia " & 6 ch.	45	F		"	"	
Mary Finnie & 4 ch.	40	F		"	"	
Wm. Johnston & 5 ch.	30	M	Labourer	"	"	
Jane Gamble & 4 ch.	36	F		"	"	
Archibald McKuen	34	M	Labourer	"	"	
Wm. Stephenson	28	M	Carpenter	"	"	
Wm. Neilson & 2 ch.	40	M	Merchant	"	"	
Mary Ann Swan & ch.	24	F		"	"	
John Cunningham	40	M	Labourer	"	"	
Cath. P. Carr	30	F		"	"	
Samuel Laird	20	M	Labourer	"	"	
Martha Moore	40	F		"	"	
James McAllister	20	M	Labourer	"	"	
Allen Lee	45	M	"	"	"	
Peter McOwen	25	M	"	"	"	
Robt. Minzies	40	M	Farmer	"	"	
Christian "	35	M	"	"	"	
George Currie	22	M	Labourer	"	"	
John Hood	38	M	Farmer	"	"	
James "	34	M	"	"	"	
Peter "	28	M	"	"	"	
J. S. Fowler	35	M	Merchant	U. States	"	Sch. General Jackson. Nicholas.
J. L. Nichlauf	35	M	"	"	"	
Peter Dodely	28	M	"	France	"	Brig Mentor. Pratt.
Francis Corbail	36	M	"	"	"	
Mary Taylor	34	F		U. States	"	
Saml. B. Phillips	25	M	U. S. Navy	"	"	
Moses Mills	35	M	Mariner	"	"	
George Gordon	31	M	Gent.	St. Croix	G. Britain	Ship Chase. Baxter.
Jas. McCann	35	M	Gent.	"	"	
Thomas Hinders	41	M	Gent.	"	"	
Thomas Wilson	45	M	Gent.	"	"	
E. W. Waring	46	M	Merchant	U. States	U. States	Ship Musidora. Hiller.
D. Borlock	36	M	"	"	"	
Mrs. " & child	22	F		"	"	Brig Catharine. Barnard.
Thomas Murray	33	M	Merchant	Scotland	"	
Mrs. "	26	F		"	"	
James Robe	35	M	Planter	England	"	
E. Armstrong	55	M	"	"	"	
Elizabeth Bowlins	38	F		"	"	Brig. Jas. Lawrence. Copeland.
Wm. Rawlins	38	M	Merchant	U. States	"	
John M. Barry	28	M	"	England	"	Sch. Carpenter. Barnes.

Names of passengers	Age	Sex	Occupation	Country to which they belong	Country of which they intend becoming inhabitants	Ship or vessel with the name of the master or commander
F. Arolly	27	M	Merchant	Spain	Spain	
NEWBERN Q. E. Sept. 30, 1821						
Desire Mowley & 3 ch.	32	F		U. States	U. States	Brig Jason. Willis.
James Barry	32	M		Spain	S. America	
Joseph Pell	32	M	Mechanic	U. States	U. States	
EDGARTOWN Q. E. Dec. 31, 1821						
Nicholas Pabiona	35	M	Cook	Genoa	U. States	Brig Levant. Cock
Antonio Gandell *	29	M	Merchant	Italy	"	Sch. Caleb. Jaques.
Majel Cavellary	15	M	Gent.	Porto Rico	"	Sch. New Packet. Bailey.
Nathanal Kingsbury	22	M	Gent.	U. States	"	Brig Planter. Lopham.
Henry Ingraham	26	M	Mariner	"	"	
John D. Gore/Gove	33	M	Mariner	"	"	Sch. Hannah & Susan. Jaque.
ALEXANDRIA Q. E. Dec. 31, 1821						
John Cammel	54	M	Labourer	Ireland	U. States	Sch. Thetis. Newcombe.
Margaret "	24	F		"	"	
Catharine "	54	F		"	"	
Agnes "	19	F		"	"	
Cornelius "	22	M	Labourer	"	"	
Mary Ann "	23	F		"	"	
John "	15	M	Labourer	"	"	
Thomas "	13	M	Labourer	"	"	
Neil McNeck	21	M	"	"	"	
Sarah "	19	F		"	"	
B. McAllister	21	M		"	"	
Mary Cammel & ch.	56	F		"	"	
B. Whitney & ch.	60	M	Labourer	England	"	Ship Boston. Fenly.
Sarah Seabrook	32	F	Weaver	Ireland	"	
M. Gee	24	M		"	"	
Mary Murphy & 2 ch.	38	F		"	"	Sch. Southern Trader. Simpson.
Kitty Derby & 2 ch.	29	F		"	"	
RICHMOND Q. E. Dec. 31, 1821						
Wm. Henderson	46	M	Weaver	Ireland	U. States	Sch. Emerald.
Martha " & 5 ch.	44	F		"	"	
R. "	50	M	Farmer	"	"	
Mary " & 5 ch.	38	F		"	"	
Mary Mitchell & ch.	36	F		"	"	

Names of passengers	Age	Sex	Occupation	Country to which they belong	Country of which they intend becoming inhabitants	Ship or vessel with the name of the master or commander
RICHMOND						
Q. E. Dec. 31, 1821						
Sally Davelin	26	F		Ireland	U. States	
F. McKlenen	28	F?	Mason	"	"	
Lydia "	28	F		"	"	
Bell " & 3 ch.	24	F		"	"	
John Gibbon	22	M	Labourer	"	"	
Wm. Bradley	22	M	"	"	"	
Hugh Balin	25	M	"	"	"	
James Diver	18	M	"	"	"	
WALDBORO						
Q. E. Dec. 31, 1821						
John Gray	38	M	Gent.	Scotland	"	Ship Lydia Adams.
Ann McGuirk	19	F		Ireland	"	
James Orr & 3 ch.	40	M	Farmer	"	"	
M. Tolerton	20	M	"	"	"	
John Sergeant	20	M	"	"	"	
James Mullen	23	M	Shoemaker	"	"	
Rebecca Scott & 2 ch.	43	F		"	"	
Peter C. Quinn	18	M	Farmer	"	"	
Matthew Denning	42	M	"	"	"	
Michael O'Donnell	40	M	"	"	"	
Mary "	35	F		"	"	
Henry Adams	40	M	Farmer	"	"	
P. Fitzpatrick	22	M	"	"	"	
Wm. Park	21	M	"	"	"	
Hugh McCreasy	40	M	Weaver	"	"	
Susanna " & ch.	30	F		"	"	
Thomas Nesbitt	50	M	Farmer	"	"	
James Farmer	21	M	"	"	"	
Anthony March	19	M	"	"	"	
Hugh Miller	19	M	"	"	"	
Edwd. Fletcher	48	M	"	"	"	
Wm. Boyd	28	M	"	"	"	
Samuel "	23	M	"	"	"	
David Wilson	35	M	"	"	"	
Eleanor " & 2 ch.	28	F		"	"	
Nancy "	67	F		"	"	
Margt. McLaughlin & 2 ch.	28	F		"	"	
BRISTOL						
Q. E. Dec. 31, 1821						
Ann Bolt & ch.	48	F		U. States	U. States	Brig Collector. Rawson.
Jane Jackson & 3 ch.	43	F		"	"	

Names of passengers	Age	Sex	Occupation	Country to which they belong	Country of which they intend becoming inhabitants	Ship or vessel with the name of the master or commander
CHARLESTON S. C. Q. E. Dec. 31, 1821						
Andw. McMillen	67	M	Farmer	G. Britain	U. States	Brig George.
Mrs. " & 8 ch.	67	F		"	"	
Margt. McCay & 5 ch.	33	F		"	"	
John O'Neil	25	M		"	"	
Mary " & 3 ch.	34	F		"	"	
Peter Sharp	24	M		"	"	
Jane " & 2 ch.	26	F		"	"	
Wm McWhirr *	64	M		"	"	
James Shannon	22	M		"	"	
John Printer	60	M		"	"	
Stephen Miller	20	M	Merchant	"	"	Sloop Cherub
John Cattell	24	M	Confectioner	"	"	Sch. Emily
Townson Moore	30	M	Merchant	"	"	Sch. Liberty
Archibald Watson	20	M	Clerk	"	"	Ship Thos. Gelston
Lewis Flemming	26	M	Merchant	"	"	Sch. Col. Ramsay
Mrs. "	20	F		"	"	
Thomas Donathan	28	M	Merchant	"	"	
Joseph Hogson	35	M	Taylor	"	"	Brig Harmony
Margaret " & 4 ch.	30	F		"	"	
James Ross	31	M	Mariner	"	"	Sch. Jane
Anthony Aymat	33	M	Trader	"	"	
Alfred Woodhouse	24	M	Merchant	"	"	Ship So. Boston
John Makle	36	M	"	"	"	
Mrs. Dalton & child	21	F		Holland	"	Ship Isabella.
Campbell Douglass	40	M	Grocer	"	"	
Henry Middleton	19	M		Britain	"	
R. O. Anderson	26	M	Trader	"	"	
Robert Whitfield	25	M	"	"	"	
Thomas Jones	23	M	"	"	"	
Thomas Simmons	20	M	"	"	"	
John Torrington	25	M	"	"	"	
Wm. Cox	20	M	"	"	"	
John Rose	50	M	Carpenter	"	"	
Eliza "	40	F		"	"	
Mrs. Topham & 5 ch.	40	F		"	"	
Edward Honeywell	33	M		"	"	Ship Hunter
Eliza " & 2 ch.	28	F		"	"	
David Meyer	35	M	Musician	"	"	
George Pritchard	24	M	Merchant	"	"	Sch. Louisa
Joseph Veason	26	M	"	"	"	
T. H. Findley	40	M		"	"	Ship Mary & Susan
T. B. Clough	33	M		"	"	
P. Fitzsimmons	21	M		"	"	
L. Moffat	32	M		"	"	

Names of passengers	Age	Sex	Occupation	Country to which they belong	Country of which they intend becoming inhabitants	Ship or vessel with the name of the master or commander
CHARLESTON S. C. **Q. E. Dec. 31, 1821**						
Alfred Huger	33	M	Planter	G . Britain	U. States	Brig Catharine.
Lewis Preiss •	30	M	Watch maker	"	"	
M. Richard	40	M		"	"	
Mrs. " & child	45	F		"	"	
M. Sosie •	45	M	Tinner	"	"	
Mrs. " & 6 ch.	45	F		"	"	
M. E. Levy	45	M	Trader	"	"	
M. Rutant	27	M	Merchant	"	"	
James Miller	26	M	"	"	"	
M. Brush & child	20	M	Tailor	"	"	
John Lowden	34	M	Merchant	"	"	Ship Corsair
Don Diago Carrare	47	M		Spain	"	
Mrs. "	30	F		Britain	"	
Andw. McDowall	31	M	Merchant	"	"	
Mrs. "	24	F		"	"	
Andw. Henderson	25	M	Merchant	"	"	
Joseph Harrison	21	M	Mechanic	"	"	
Stephen Watson	24	M	"	"	"	
George Grairson	22	M	"	"	"	
- Matthewson	24	M	"	"	"	
S. Domingo	35	M	Trader	Portugal	"	Sloop Ann
Lousa Vensey & ch.	33	F		Spain	"	
B. Gonsalves	38	M	Trader	"	"	Sch. Mary Ann
J P. Barre	28	M	"	France	"	
E. Chisolme	16	M	Mariner	U . States	"	
Samuel Corman	22	M	"	"	"	
Edwd. Buckler	24	M	Merchant	"	"	Sch. Endora
J. Stanter •	35	M	Clerk	"	"	
Manuel Fernandez	39	M	Trader	Portugal	"	Sch. Betsy & Peggy
George Welden	23	M	Labourer	Britain	"	Ship Hornet
Niel McDuffee	24	M	Labourer	"	"	
John Patterson	22	M	"	"	"	
Niel McPhail	26	M	"	"	"	Brig Phoebe
James "	40	M	"	"	"	
Janett McNair & 4 ch.	40	F		"	"	
Maria Douglass	23	F		"	"	
James Wilson	25	M	Labourer	"	"	
Eliz. Marshal & 3 ch.	28	F		"	"	
William Shields	35	M	Labourer	"	"	
R. Cheves	34	M	"	"	"	Ship Adriana
H . N. Vest	35	M	"	"	"	
Jonathan Cooper	20	M	Planter	"	"	Sch. Decatur
John Noga	36	M	Mariner	"	"	
John Salter	35	M	"	U. States	"	

Names of passengers	Age	Sex	Occupation	Country to which they belong	Country of which they intend becoming inhabitants	Ship or vessel with the name of the master or commander
CHARLESTON S.C. Q. E. Dec. 31, 1821						
James L. Brown	35	M	Merchant	G. Britain	U. States	Sloop General Washington
Mrs. "	38	F		"	"	
Wm. Welsh & child	35	M	Tailor	"	"	
Joseph Delamore	22	M	Planter	"	"	Sch. Comet
Thomas Marx *	19	M	"	"	"	
C. M. Dumoulin	22	M	Merchant	"	"	
J. Ross	27	M	Mariner	"	"	
Dr. Richardson	50	M	Physician	U. States	"	Ship S. Carolina
Mrs. " & child	35	F		"	"	
Miss Coffin	19	F		"	"	
Miss Field	30	F		"	"	
Dr. Hannah	24	M	Physician	"	"	
John Paul	37	M	Merchant	"	"	
John McKenzie	41	M		"	"	
Charles Goodshie	21	M	Shoemaker	G. Britain	"	Sch. Eliza
Edwd. Phillips	21	M	Farmer	"	"	Ship James Bailey
Samuel Adams	36	M	"	"	"	
Robert Wilson	30	M	"	"	"	
John Adams	24	M	"	"	"	
Mrs. "	25	F		"	"	
Isaac Walker	14	M	Farmer	"	"	
Samuel Ewart *	23	M	"	"	"	
Wm. Kennedy	22	M	"	"	"	
Saml. McCohet	21	M	"	"	"	
Wm. Dunlop	19	M	"	"	"	
Thomas Boggs	32	M	"	"	"	
Martha " & 3 ch.	32	F		"	"	
James McClure	60	M	Apothecary	"	"	
Mrs. " & 4 ch.	60	F		"	"	
Jane Harper & 6 ch.	45	F		"	"	
Betty McFee	24	F		"	"	
Robert Irvin	47	M	Labourer	"	"	
James Irvin	22	M	Labourer	France	U. States	
Daniel McClowell	20	M	"	"	"	
Wm. Charles	23	M	"	"	"	
John Houtain	25	M	"	"	"	
Thomas Kennedy	27	M	"	"	"	Ship Jane
Richd. "	21	M	"	"	"	
Henry McGrahagan	22	M	"	"	"	
James Haslett	20	M	"	"	"	
Margt. Davidson & 3 ch.	44	F		G. Britain	"	
James Carlisle	36	M	Labourer	"	"	
Mary " & 4 ch.	53	F		"	"	
Wm. Martin	25	M	Labourer	"	"	

Names of passengers	Age	Sex	Occupation	Country to which they belong	Country of which they intend becoming inhabitants	Ship or vessel with the name of the master or commander
CHARLESTON, S. C.						
Q. E. Dec. 31, 1821						
Susanna Martin	23	F		G. Britain	U. States	
Andw. Dool	42	M	Labourer	"	"	
Philip McClery	25	M	"	"	"	
Alexr. Henderson	21	M	"	"	"	
Philip Kaney	21	M	"	"	"	
Mary Burns & 3 ch.	42	F		"	"	
Robt. McMaster	26	M	Labourer	"	"	
Wm. Owens	25	M	"	"	"	
Wm. Dunn & 5 ch.	30	M	"	"	"	
Wm. Fullerton	21	M	"	"	"	
Henry Caulfield	20	M	"	"	"	
Robert Dobbin	20	M	"	"	"	
John Blair	60	M	"	"	"	
Jane " & 3 ch.	55	F	"	"	"	
P. Mannock	49	M	Labourer	"	"	
Mrs. " & 5 ch.	45	F		"	"	
James McNeilly	20	M	"	"	"	
Wm. Riddon	26	M	"	"	"	
Wm. White	18	M	"	"	"	
Wm. Scott	24	M	"	"	"	
Ellen "	26	F		"	"	
Wm. McGowan	20	M	Labourer	"	"	
John McKissick	25	M	"	"	"	
Robert Larney	67	M	"	"	"	
Mrs. " & 3 ch.	53	F		"	"	
David McCallish	18	M	Labourer	"	"	
Wm. Hugh	26	M	"	"	"	
James "	47	M	"	"	'	
Wm. " & 5 ch.	29	M	"	"	"	
PHILADELPHIA						
Q. E. Dec. 31, 1821						
J. B. McIlvaine	30	M	Merchant	U. States	"	Brig Com. Barry. Thos. Lyle
Joseph Pacy	23	M	"	"	"	Brig Caroline. Midlen.
John Taylor	68	M		G. Britain	"	Ship Bainbridge. Berry.
Betty Miner & 6 ch.	38	F		"	"	
Charles Jones	31	M	Trader	U. States	"	Ship Electra. Robinson
John Manter	32	M	"	England	"	
Edward Hayward	32	M	"	"	"	
Mrs. " & 4 ch.	32	F		"	"	
Richd. B. "	32	M	Trader	"	"	
Charles Caldwell	46	M	Physician	U. States	"	
Joseph Klyser •	21	M	Trader	England	"	

Names of passengers	Age	Sex	Occupation	Country to which they belong	Country of which they intend becoming inhabitants	Ship or vessel with the name of the master or commander
PHILADELPHIA Q. E. Dec. 31, 1821						
T. W. Spencer	21	M	Trader	England	U. States	
James Martin	45	M	Farmer	"	"	
Sarah " & 4 ch.	40	F		"	"	
Robert Pratt	35	M	Cooper	"	"	
Mrs. "	25	F		"	"	
Joseph Waghorn	40	M	Farmer	"	"	
Mary "	39	F		"	"	
Fredk. Marganthal	58	M	Farmer	"	"	
Wm. Strawbridge	65	M	Preacher	U. States	"	
Dennis Driscoll	20	M	Shoemaker	England	"	
Richd. Denicord	23	M	Carpenter	"	"	
John Leary	25	M	Shoemaker	"	"	
Ellen " & 2 ch.	40	F		"	"	
Cath. Peters	20	F		"	"	
Joseph Rigney	30	M	Labourer	"	"	
Wm. Porter	45	M	Farmer	Ireland	"	
Jane "	43	F		"	"	
Sarah M. " & 6 ch.	25	F		"	"	
John Ferguson	38	M	Farmer	"	"	
Eliz. " & 4 ch.	36	F		"	"	
Jane "	31	F		"	"	
Martha Briton	20	F		"	"	
John Larkin	60	M	Farmer	"	"	
Jane "	30	F		"	"	
Edwd. Murkledowne	30	M	Farmer	"	"	
Margt. " & 5 ch.	28	F		"	"	
Pat. McCan	40	M	Labourer	"	"	
Charles Cassady	28	M	"	"	"	
Robt. Carthwood	28	M	"	"	"	
H. Henry	30	M	"	"	"	
James Stafford	32	M	Gent.	"	"	
Gustavus Durand	28	M		France	"	Brig Mary & Aschsah. Bouquet
Philip M. Carl	32	M		Ireland	"	Schooner Telegraph. Blanchard
Ann M. " & ch.	30	F		"	"	
Wm. Mackman	25	M		"	"	
Ellen " & child	20	F		"	"	
Jane Armstrong	20	F		"	"	
Margaret Coulter	18	F		"	"	
Robert Greaton	18	M		"	"	
George M. Eyre	21	M	Merchant	U. States	"	Brig George. Sharp.
Edwd. W. Robinson	25	M	"	"	"	
Eliza Watts & child	28	F		G. Britain	"	Ship Jane. Luberg.
H. Dougherty	45	M	Labourer	"	"	
Jane "	56	F		"	"	

Names of passengers	Age	Sex	Occupation	Country to which they belong	Country of which they intend becoming inhabitants	Ship or vessel with the name of the master or commander
PHILADELPHIA **Q. E. Dec. 31, 1821**						
Joseph Solms	34	M	Merchant	U. States	U. States	Ship Columbia. Kurby.
M. " & 3 ch.	26	F		"	"	
Charles Nirinckz •	59	M	Clergyman	"	"	
P. Freislman •	24	M	"	Flanders	"	
Francis Mastley •	26	M	Student	"	"	
P. "	21	M	"	"	"	
Felix Zerudt	23	M	"	"	"	
Joseph Van Horsey	24	M	"	"	"	
John P. Smitz	20	M	"	"	"	
John Elet	19	M	"	"	"	
Francis Van Acke	20	M	"	"	"	
Peter J. de Smith	20	M	"	"	"	
Wm. Huaff •	16	M	Printer	"	"	
John Gilbert	26	M	Joiner	G. Britain	"	
Gotlieb Sheerer	23	M	Shoemaker	Baden	"	
Wm. Schaffer	24	M	Traveller	"	"	
Wm. Wallace	30	M	Merchant	U. States	"	Brig Margaret. Hall
W. Winebrener	35	M	"	"	"	
Samuel Talbot	28	M		Ireland	"	Sch. Lydia. Reid.
Ellen " & 2 ch.	25	F		"	"	
N. Durand	41	M	Confectioner	U. States	"	Brig Junius. Dunton
George Follin	27	M	Merchant	"	"	
L. Nordman	35	M	Farmer	Germany	"	Brig Hibernia. Hutchinson
J. Jacobson	22	M	Merchant	"	"	
F. Margaret •	35	M	Farmer	"	"	
Charlotte " & 3 ch.	25	F		"	"	
F. Wickman	35	M	Farmer	"	"	
Cath. " & 4 ch.	30	F		"	"	
F. Boleast •	34	M	Shoemaker	"	"	
Johanna " & 2 ch.	33	F		"	"	
G. Hagen	30	M	Merchant	"	"	
H. Hock	35	M	Farmer	"	"	
J. Wendt	35	M	"	"	"	
C. Mahn	40	M	"	"	"	
Eliz. " & 4 ch.	45	F		"	"	
Mr. Destouet	22	M	Merchant	France	U. States	Schooner Argo. Hovey
Thomas B. Tooker	35	M	Mariner	G. Britain	"	Brig Antelope. Hardy
Wm. Leybert	40	M	"	"	"	
Stephan Cabot	40	M	Merchant	U. States	"	Ship Howard
Alexr. Hagle	25	M	"	"	"	
Henry Maitre	31	M	"	"	"	
L. Bernard & child	30	M	"	France	"	
Samuel Blair	22	M	Clerk	"	"	
John More	20	M	Tailor	Ireland	"	Brig Betsey

Names of passengers	Age	Sex	Occupation	Country to which they belong	Country of which they intend becoming inhabitants	Ship or vessel with the name of the master or commander
PHILADELPHIA						
Q. E. Dec. 31, 1821						
Edwd. Maine	20	M	Tailor	Ireland	U. States	
James Wilson	25	M	Carpenter	"	"	
Joseph "	19	M	Farmer	"	"	
Andw. Kennedy	20	M	"	"	"	
Thomas Kaver	20	M	"	"	"	
Samuel McCouglin	24	M	Carpenter	"	"	
James King	55	M	Farmer	U. States	"	
George McDintock	24	M	Weaver	"	"	
John King	14	M	Farmer	"	"	
Lawrence Donelly	31	M	Tailor	"	"	
Michael "	30	M	Weaver	"	"	
Thomas Hogun	29	M	Shoemaker	"	"	
Patrick Heyland	27	M	Carpenter	"	"	
David Fleming	32	M	Weaver	"	"	
Jane " & 2 ch.	27	F		"	"	
M. Seminall	44	M	Merchant	"	"	Schooner Baltimore. Read.
John Baker	30	M	"	England	"	Ship Warren. Webber.
Richd. Dentor	27	M	Taylor	"	"	
Gracia Gamble & 3 ch.	28	M ?		"	"	
Chas. Montgomery	23	M	Farmer	Ireland	"	Brig Rising Sun. Prince.
Joseph "	15	M	"	"	"	
George White	20	M	"	"	"	
George Paterson	23	M	"	"	"	
James Brown	20	M	"	"	"	
Ann Moody & 2 ch.	42	F		England	"	Ship Wm. & Jane. Brown.
John K. Hassinger	25	M	Merchant	"	"	
David "	25	M	Lawyer	"	"	
Thomas Orr	33	M	Merchant	"	"	
Thomas Fletcher	43	M	"	"	"	
Elizabeth Hamilton & child	55	F		"	"	
Patrick Quinlan	52	M	Farmer	"	"	
Mary "	40	F		"	"	
John Horney	35	M	Farmer	"	"	
Hannah " & child	28	F		"	"	
Edwd. McLean	22	M		"	"	
Wm. Taggert	29	M	Farmer	Ireland	"	
Francis Cassady	22	M	Labourer	"	"	
Patrick "	25	M	"	"	"	
Jonas Newell	40	M	Shoemaker	"	"	
Mary " & 8 ch.	37	F		"	"	
James Murphy	21	M	Accomptant	"	"	Brig Jane. Richard.
Edwd. Green	25	M	Bookbinder	"	"	
John Kelly	23	M	Carpenter	"	"	

Names of passengers	Age	Sex	Occupation	Country to which they belong	Country of which they intend becoming inhabitants	Ship or vessel with the name of the master or commander
PHILADELPHIA						
Q. E. Dec. 31, 1821						
John Bligh	26	M	Baker	Ireland	U. States	
Andw. Mulligan	21	M	Cooper	"	"	
Nicholas Baden	23	M	Distiller	"	"	
Philip Collan	22	M	Farmer	"	"	
Ph. Coulson	40	M	Chapman	"	"	
Robt. Moore	19	M	Clerk	"	"	
Francis S. Coxe	30	M	Merchant	U. States	"	Brig Superior. Dixon.
S. Casamajor *	26	M	"	"	"	Sch. Little G. Eyre. Collison.
A. S. C. Nichols	35	M	"	"	"	
John F. Ohl	28	M	"	"	"	
F. Silva	40	M	"	"	"	
R. Gray	37	M	Mariner	"	"	
J. B. Caulcan *	20	M	Merchant	"	"	
Victor Vassaise	44	M	Jeweller	France	"	Brig Richard & Sally. Erwin.
J. Lusyana	24	M	Tailor	Italy	"	Brig Jos. Eastburn. Earle.
A. J. Bernard	24	M	Cooper	"	"	
N. Patterson	21	M		Ireland	"	Brig Hal. Grant.
Robt. Cummins	24	M	Farmer	"	"	
Francis Mitchell	26	M	Weaver	"	"	
Wm. Wright	24	M	"	"	"	
Joseph Jenny & ch.	53	M	Merchant	U. States	"	Ship Hunter. Davis
Michael J. Gueberry *	30	M	"	"	"	
Joseph Sallier	31	M	"	"	"	
John Durand	25	M	"	"	"	
Louis Lay & child	37	M	"	"	"	
Richd. Paxon	39	M	"	"	"	
John Bass	32	M	"	"	"	
Thomas Dellaway	23	M	"	"	"	
J. L. F. Macy	22	M	Weaver	France	"	
Prosper "	21	M	Gilder	"	"	
J. C. Campardon	16	M	Tailor	"	"	
F. D. Zynsiki	44	M	Priest	Poland	"	Jno. & Adam. Knight.
P. B. Sculchi	33	M	"	Italy	"	
Francis Mazas	24	M	Merchant	U. States	"	
Alexr. Lopez	25	M	"	"	"	
E. Brise *	35	M	"	"	"	
John Fernandez	39	M		Spain	Spain	Ship Halcyon. Wooster
Mary Burns & child	30	F		Ireland	U. States	
J. Peldes	28	M	Merchant	Spain	"	Brig Joseph & Lewis. Caldwell.
P Kintana	20	M	"	"	"	
Wm. Cogden	25	M	Mechanic	Ireland	"	Schooner Eagle. Soule.
Thomas Nones	26	M	"	"	"	
J. E. Jackson	46	M	Merchant	G. Britain	"	Ship Jane. Ferguson.
H. "	30	F		"	"	

PASSENGERS WHO ARRIVED IN THE U.S. SEPTEMBER 1821 - DECEMBER 1823

Names of passengers	Age	Sex	Occupation	Country to which they belong	Country of which they intend becoming inhabitants	Ship or vessel with the name of the master or commander
PHILADELPHIA						
Q. E. Dec. 31, 1821						
Thomas Ellis	48	M	Merchant	G. Britain	U. States	
John Park	34	M		"	"	
Thomas Bailey	28	M	Farmer	"	"	
Hannah " & ch.	30	F		"	"	
Thomas Burgess	20	M	Farmer	"	"	
Wm. Burrows	45	M	"	"	"	
Wm. Pearson	21	M	"	"	"	
Revd. Dr. Harrold	50	M	Minister	"	"	
Joseph Belbrough	40	M	Merchant	"	"	
James Moody	45	M	Labourer	"	"	Ship Kensington. Hamilton.
Mary " & 3 ch.	42	F		"	"	
John Lowerly	23	M	Farmer	"	"	
Maria Fitgerald & ch.	39	F		"	"	
Wm. Taylor	25	M	Farmer	"	"	
Wm. Owen	39	M	"	"		
Wm. Dodd	36	M	"	"	"	
Wm. Holland	25	M	Joiner	"	"	
Abraham Springer & 2 children	49	M	Butcher	Holland	"	Ship Govr. Hawkins. Bowen.
J. Brand	29	M	"	"	"	
A. C. Find	29	M	Farmer	"	"	
W. F. Pix	44	M	Broker	"	"	
S. L. Klosser	29	M	Porter	"	"	
N. Heydemand	21	M	Pedlar	"	"	
J. Lemon	22	M	"	"	"	
L. Helger	34	M	Merchant	"	"	
E. George	50	M	"	"	"	
L. D. Carpinter	24	M	"	U. States	"	Ship America. Aldridge.
Ligna	44	M	"	France	"	Brig Savannah Packet.
David Jeffreys	24	M	Labourer	G. Britain	"	Ship Tuscarora. West.
Margaret " & 4 ch.	48	F		"	"	
Rachel Jones & 2 ch.	29	F		"	"	
Sarah Taylor & 2 ch.	30	F		"	"	
Richd. Smith	38	M	Merchant	"	"	
Wm. Williams	54	M	"	"	"	Ship Reaper. Yorke.
Thomas Johnson	29	M	"	"	"	
Denis Casey	34	M	Farmer	"	"	
Philip Merchant	55	M	Merchant	G. Britain	U. States	
Edwd. B. Hanson	24	M	Musician	Denmark	"	Brig Mary. McPherson.
John Stace	45	M	Physician	England	"	Ship Ruth & Mary. Mickle.
Galley	40	M	"	France	"	
G. B. Philipps	28	M	Merchant	U. States	"	Brig Edwd. D. Douglass. Morgan

c.W.

13

Names of passengers	Age	Sex	Occupation	Country to which they belong	Country of which they intend becoming inhabitants	Ship or vessel with the name of the master or commander
NEW ORLEANS **Q. E. Dec. 31, 1821**						
C. Mendiburn	45	M	Merchant	U. States	U. States	Schooner Brisk. Paillet.
Ant. Chs. Lefevere	30	M	Watchmaker	"	"	
A. Chardon	29	M	Merchant	France	"	Brig Neptune. Lutzere.
J. M. " & child	28	F		"	"	
Pierre Hurtel	26	M		"	"	
J. B. Daubut	40	M		"	"	
G. DelaValette	37	M		"	"	
E. Durand	20	M	Butcher	U. States	"	
B. Lacoste	30	M	Merchant	France	"	Ship Transit. Greig.
Guillard	22	M	Physician	"	"	
Leguyer	28	M	Merchant	"	"	
Menard	28	M	Sailor	"	"	
E. Le (Grastin)	28	M	Cooper	"	"	
James Bernard	25	M	Saddler	"	"	
---Vial	30	M	"	"	"	
---Azar	23	M	Clerk	"	"	
---(Brimare)	23	M	"	"	"	Ship Venus. Proctor.
F. Monez	24	M	Merchant	Spain	"	Sch. Little Sally.
B. Sileasa	28	M	"	"	"	
O. Sara	18	M	"	"	"	
J. M. Silva	30	M	"	"	"	
Sarrliege Castelez	61	M	Mason	"	"	Ship Highlander. Welch.
Baptiste Romeo	61	M	"	"	"	
John Brady	50	M	Priest	U. States	"	
Joseph Fernandez	45	M	"	Spain	"	
Joseph Carrion •	30	M	Clerk	U. States	"	
Louis Danney	37	M	Span. Officer	Spain	"	
Samuel Paxton	30	M	Merchant	U. States	"	
John Betz	28	M	Butcher	England	"	Brig Brothers. Ekin.
Samuel Stokes	29	M	Carpenter	England	"	
---Wallace	22	M	Stone cutter	"	"	
John Kelham	27	M	Merchant	"	"	
---Malcum	18	M	Clerk	Scotland	"	Brig Thornton. Holmes.
F. St. Amant	23	M	Planter	U. States	"	Sch. Elizabeth. Fougard.
Mrs. "	26	F		"	"	
Edwd. Herbault	27	M	Merchant	France •	"	Galliot Anacreon.
M. Peat	33	M	Clerk	England	".	
F. Nadolsky	27	M	"	Poland	"	
A. Belgarrie	24	M	"	France	"	
G. M. Michoux	26	M	Hat maker	"	"	
A. Lafferranderie	26	M	Clerk	U. States	"	Sch. Louisiana.
Nelson Peychant	23	M	"	"		
Limasin	21	M	Mason	"	"	
Navarre	27	M	Shop keeper	France	"	

Names of passengers	Age	Sex	Occupation	Country to which they belong	Country of which they intend becoming inhabitants	Ship or vessel with the name of the master or commander
NEW ORLEANS						
Q. E. Dec. 31, 1821						
J. Chesse	28	M	Block maker	U. States	U. States	
Mrs. " & 2 ch.	22	F		"	"	
T. Hibbert	25	M	Merchant	England	"	Brig Rollo. Downing.
F. Spicer	20	M	"	U. States	"	Schooner Bee. Bacon.
Samuel Woodberry	28	M	"	"	"	
J. Basque	26	M	"	"	"	
D. Morceau	18	M	Printer	"	"	
John Abbott	40	M		Germany	"	Brig Hugh Wallace. McClure.
Charles Starr	35	M	Painter	England	"	
Ann " & 5 ch.	26	F		"	"	
L. Kane	22	M	Clerk	Ireland	"	Brig Parker & Sons. Hodgson.
John Hunter	18	M	"	"	"	
John Watt	17	M	"	"	"	
A. Kirken	22	M	"	"	"	
Mrs. Caslow & 4 ch.	50	F		"	"	
M. Olliver	28	M	Farmer	"	"	
Jaques Pressoir	23	M	Shoemaker	France	"	Brig Alabama.
P. M. Nicot	33	M	Clerk	"	"	
N. Hilten	50	M	Ship carpenter	U. States	"	Sch. Emeline.
J. "	38	M	"	"	"	
N. Page	35	M	"	"	"	
Isaac Nelson	35	M	Shoemaker	"	"	
John Lovejoy	24	M	Brickmaker	"	"	
Ab. Thusto	36	M	Shoemaker	"	"	
David Morgan	22	M	Cabinetmaker	"	"	
John Priscott	23	M	Carpenter	"	"	
Thos. Cucullin *	29	M	Merchant	"	"	
A. G. Aldrich	24	M	"	"	"	
Wm. Johnson	30	M	"	"	"	
J. Walker	24	M	Clerk	"	"	Schooner Eagle. King
Thomas Warren	20	M	Merchant	"	"	Brig Julia. Cole.
David Wyer	40	M	"	"	"	
J. Bougain & ? ch.	43	F		"	"	Brig Mary Anne. Humphrey.
---Linary	36	M	Carpenter	"	"	
---Latimore	33	M	"	Scotland	"	
P. Lison	70	M	Sugar maker	France	"	
P. Ferrel	27	M	Farmer	Ireland	"	Brig Williamson. Windes.
Joseph Cook	27	M	Carpenter	"	"	
G. Robinson	32	M	Wheelwright	"	"	
Edwd. Gibson	44	M	Joiner	"	"	
Hugh McIntire	28	M	Mariner	"	"	
---Serrin	32	M	Perfumer	France	N. Orleans	Ship Concordia. Davis.

15

Names of passengers	Age	Sex	Occupation	Country to which they belong	Country of which they intend becoming inhabitants	Ship or vessel with the name of the master or commander
---Reynez	31	M	Merchant	France	N. Orleans	
Mrs. " & child	25	F		"	"	
---Lefebre	38	M	Farmer	"	"	
---Fouché	46	M	Teacher	"	"	
---Layotte	45	M	"	"	"	
J. F. Gaubert & child	34	F		"	"	
---Bointersat	48	M	Merchant	"	"	
---Languerille	21	M	"	"	"	
A. Pitot	17	M	Student	"	"	
L. Guisnard & child	48	M	Merchant	"	"	
---Bougnan	45	M	"	"	"	
---Marlut	34	M	"	"	"	
Boulemat	18	M	Farmer	"	"	
G. Pritchard	19	M	Clerk	U. States	"	Ship Ganges. Chapman.
Wm. Ferriday	26	M	Broker	England	"	
James Frenet/Freret	55	M	Merchant	"	"	
J.P. "	22	M		"	"	
A. Porter	45	M	Judge S. Ct. Louisiana	U. States	"	
Jno. White	17	M	Broker	Ireland	"	
Geo. Lloyd	35	M	Merchant	U. States	"	
O. Nagle	44	M	"	"	"	
Wm. Frazer	60	M	Farmer	"	"	
Wm. " Jr.	20	M	"	"	"	
Walter Williams	35	M	Merchant	"	"	Brig Martha. Parker.
F. Martinez	32	M	Secy. Sp. Consul	Spain	"	Brig Sarah Ann. Giranda
F. Coquet	28	M	Mariner	France	"	
Thomas Good	40	M	"	"	"	
James Connor	32	M	Merchant	Ireland	"	Brig Forest. Morgan.
Daniel Brown	23	M	Farmer	U. States	"	
Horace W. Robbins	34	M	Merchant	"	"	
C. Calvin	30	M	Clockmaker	"	"	
---Chamout	30	M	Teacher	France	"	Sch. Elizabeth. Lapham.
S. Perrin	55	M	Mariner	"	"	
T. Mitlu	38	M	"	"	"	
John Crawford	38	M	Baker	Scotland	"	Ship Mars. Mitchell.
Wm. Liddle	20	M	"	"	"	
Thos. Bogle	30	M	Merchant	"	"	
---Christi	38	M	"	U. States	"	Ship Despatch. Urann.
Jno. P. Bassemant	30	M	Hatter	France	"	Brig Leopard. Fearson.
J. Baldez	50	M	Mariner	Spain	"	
H. Bettrineux	35	M	Printer	France	"	
T. Bruninull *	38	M	Merchant	"	"	Brig Bel dame ? Samson.
C. Moreau	50	M	"	"	"	
Wm. Runditch	35	M	Merchant	Austria	"	
S. Jahn	35	M	Mariner	"	"	

Names of passengers	Age	Sex	Occupation	Country to which they belong	Country of which they intend becoming inhabitants	Ship or vessel with the name of the master or commander
NEW ORLEANS						
Q. E. Dec. 31, 1821						
B. De Vanssel	41	M	Merchant	France	U. States	Brig Baltic. Gillis.
A. Senecal	32	M	"	"	"	
J. B. Harpen	52	M	"	"	"	
J. B. Tissun/Tesseur	35	M	Goldsmith	"	"	
---Gary	18	M	Clerk	"	"	
---Lothaly	35	M	Shoemaker	Germany	"	
P. Garseau	35	M	Saddler	France	."	
---Romain	22	M	Clerk	"	"	
---Adam	31	M	Shoemaker	Germany	"	
---Harny & child	25	M	"	France	"	
---Ozuit	26	M		"	"	
---Dehl	38	M	Shoemaker	"	"	
---Marcotte	31	M	Merchant	"	"	
N. Baudousque	20	M	Planter	"	"	Ship Warrington. Dothingham.
A. Tessier	26	M	Farmer	France	"	
C. Calombe	49	M	"	"	"	
J. J. H. Duval	26	M	Druggist	"	"	
J. Nabat	45	M		"	"	
Louis Daquin	45	M	Baker	"	"	
Mrs. " & 2 ch.	38	F		"	"	
J. Demming	22	M	Trader	"	"	
J. Fritte	20	M		"	"	
G. Dayson	57	M	Shop keeper	U. States	"	
---Biana	20	M	Farmer	France	"	
---Magourau	22	M	"	"	"	
Mrs. Roy & 3 ch.	45	F		"	"	
---Ridou	24	M	Butcher	"	"	
---Rouchard	25	M	Candle mkr.	"	"	
John Dulan	28	M	"	"	"	
Piot ---	24	M	Butcher	"	"	
P. Dutihl *	14	M		"	"	
---Borward	35	M	Farmer	"	"	
L. Bayer	25	M	Joiner	"	"	
P. Uzera	22	M	Farmer	"	"	
NEW YORK						
Q. E. Dec. 31, 1821						
George Gill	53	M	Labourer	G. Britain	"	Brig Kate. Anderson.
James Camerson *	18	M	"	"	"	
James Fleming	19	M	"	"	"	
James Camerson	41	M	Surveyor	"	"	
Mrs. "	38	F		"	"	
Wm. Blair	18	M	Weaver	"	"	

Names of passengers	Age	Sex	Occupation	Country to which they belong	Country of which they intend becoming inhabitants	Ship or vessel with the name of the master or commander
NEW YORK						
Q. E. Dec. 31, 1821						
Israel H. Lewis	28	M	N. Officer U. S.	U. States	U. States	Ship Venus. Chandler.
Matthew H. Shepherd	22	M	Gent.	G. Britain	G. Britain	
Wm. H. Wilson	23	M	Doctor	"	"	
Matthew B. Minds	31	M	Attorney	"	"	
4 children						
F. Coventry	22	M		"	"	
John Wordswoth	34	M	Farmer	U. States	U. States	
Mary " & 2 ch.	34	F		"	"	
Joseph Russell	47	M		"	"	
S. " & child	37	F		"	"	
Wm. Greenland	27	M	Tailor	England	"	
Sarah " & child	22	F		"	"	
John Stiles	30	M	Joiner	"	"	
Jane "	21	F		"	"	
Wm. Harland	27	M	"	"	"	
Wm. Lawbard	30	M	Springmaker	"	"	
John Jolley	57	M	Tailor	"	"	
Maria " & child	31	F		"	"	
E. S. Drelawn	25	M	Mechanic	U. States	"	
Richd. Bailley	23	M	Farmer	"	"	
Wm. Cook	19	M	Tailor	"	"	
James Robertson	31	M	Merchant	England	"	
Charles Watts	30	M	Brewer	"	"	
Daniel Poland & child	26	M				
A. Lasuse	42	M	Shipmaster	France	France	Sloop Packet. Russell
S. Felix	40	M	Merchant	Portugal	U. States	
Emanuel G. Easen	28	M		Spain	"	Brig Ambuscade. Bryan
Madam Seas & child	31	F		France	"	
Calisto Gonzales	25	M	Merchant	Spain	"	
Francisco Fundora	41	M	Planter	"	"	
S. Christania	30	M	Painter	Portugal	Portugal	Sch. Dart. Van Dine.
R. Castillo	18	M	Merchant	Spain	Spain	Brig Victory. Wilson.
F. Fernandez	23	M	"	"	"	
G. Estano	28	M	"	"	"	
Moses Bailey	35	M	Farmer	Ireland	U. States	Sch. Independence. Hopkins.
John Charlton	30	M	Weaver	"	"	
Mr. La Forest	40	M	Barber	France	"	Sch. Neptune.
James Cant	26	M	Shoemaker	G. Britain	"	Brig Superb. Conner.
Wm. Drigham & 4 ch.	46	M	Farmer	"	"	
Wm. Stack	17	M	Clerk	"	"	
Margaret Hunter	36	F		"	"	
Helen Pinvil & 2 ch. *	22	F		"	"	
Alexr. Gregory	17	M	Merchant	"	"	

Names of passengers	Age	Sex	Occupation	Country to which they belong	Country of which they intend becoming inhabitants	Ship or vessel with the name of the master or commander
NEW YORK						
Q. E. Dec. 31, 1821						
Wm. (Gardner)	20	M	Merchant	G. Britain	U. States	
John Robinson	24	M	"	"	"	
John Perrit	26	M	"	"	"	
Peter Fisher & 2 ch.	45	M	Farmer	"	"	
S. M. Whitering	25	M	Merchant	Surinam	"	Brig C. Rogers. Barnard
Chev de Andivago	35	M	Min. to U. S.	Spain	?	Ship Albion. Williams.
James Arrott & 2 ch.	44	M	Merchant	U. States	U. States	
J. H. Read	32	M	Planter	"	"	
Stephen Price	38	M	Attorny	"	"	
F. Maule	20	M	Military	G. Britain	"	
N. Roskill	22	M	Merchant	"	"	
A. Belloc	27	M	"	France	"	
Wm. Gaston	35	M	"	"	"	
A. Wilkinson	27	M	"	U. States	"	
A. Monteith	19	M	"	G. Britain	"	
A. Wood	40	M	"	"	"	
Thos. Phillips	41	M	Prof. of music	"	"	
Catharine "	26	F		"	"	
John Wild	28	M	Farmer	"	"	
Ann " & child	26	F		"	"	
Wm. Bacon	16	M	Farmer	"	"	
H. Ray	35	M	"	"	"	
Mrs. " & 4 ch.	29	F		"	"	
Joseph Rhode & ch.	22	M	Farmer	"	"	
David Anderson	22	M	Merchant	"	"	Brig Spring.
Edwd. Willey	64	M	Planter	"	"	
Edward Wright	30	M	Planter	"	"	
A. Thomas	21	M	Carpenter	"	"	
Isaac Daniels	19	M	"	"	"	
Wm. Stephens	32	M	Blacksmith	"	"	
Robt. Groom	36	M	Clothier	"	"	
Wm. Roberts	26	M	Shoemaker	"	"	
Wm. Mortimer	42	M	"	"	"	
Mary " & 5 ch.	41	F		"	"	
Wm. Thomas	28	M		"	"	
Jno. De Wolf	40	M	Mariner	U. States	"	Brig Balance. Bennett
George Palmer	23	M	Merchant	G. Britain	"	Brig Bordeaux. Butman.
D. K. Rodgers	21	M	"	U. States	"	Brig Atlanta. Goldsmith.
Fredk. Platt	33	M	Blockmaker	Curraco	"	Brig Vigilant. Brown.
Daniel Coffin	33	M	Merchant	U. States	"	Brig Lady's Delight. Scribner.
L. Billaby.	36	M	"	"	"	Sch. Betsy Ann. Driggs.
Henry Augustine	35	M	Mariner	"	"	Brig Jane. Fowler.
Samuel Leavitt	42	M	Merchant	England	England	Sch. Hope. Lewis.

PASSENGERS WHO ARRIVED IN THE U.S. SEPTEMBER 1821 - DECEMBER 1823

Names of passengers	Age	Sex	Occupation	Country to which they belong	Country of which they intend becoming inhabitants	Ship or vessel with the name of the master or commander
NEW YORK						
Q. E. Dec. 31, 1821						
John White	27	M	Merchant	England	England	Schooner Hope. Lewis.
O. Pendergrass	36	M	"	"	"	
J. Alexander	26	M	Joiner	U. States	U. States	
D. Tucker	26	M	Mariner	"	"	Schooner Atlantic. Richardson.
A. Frazier	22	M	"	"	"	
Henry Grut	25	M	Doctor	England	"	Sch. Eliza Piget. Waterman.
John Martin	35	M	Storekeeper	Guadeloupe	France	Sch. James Monroe. Harker.
James Newell	35	M	Miller	Ireland	U. States	Sch. Lady Washington. Eaton.
Margaret " & 4 ch.	51	F		"	"	
Thos. Tumblety	54	M	Cooper	"	"	
Catharine " & 4 ch.	50	F		"	"	
Jacob Randal & child	45	M	Ship carptr.	"	"	
Munson Hinman	39	M	Mariner	U. States	"	Schooner Jane. Gibbs.
Benj. Johnson	49	M	"	"	"	
Manuel R. Fritas	22	M	Merchant	Oporto	Portugal	Brig Eliza. Waring.
John Wood.	55	M	Planter	Porto Rico	Porto Rico	Brig Commerce. Funk.
Lewis Du Canarc(r)y	21	M	Merchant	"	Spain	Schooner Harmony. Thomas.
Mary Mason	40	F		"	"	
Daniel Hafer & 3 ch.	26	M	Planter	Germany	U. States	(Juffraw Johanna)
T. Piron & 7 ch.	44	M	"	"	"	
Joseph Sigris	35	M	"	"	"	
Maria " & 3 ch.	30	F		"	"	
Jacob Smit	54	M	Planter	"	"	
Catharine Smit & 5 ch.	40	F		"	"	
Fredk. Hoffinger	40	M	Planter	"	"	
Cath. "	38	F		"	"	
Fredk. Kutcher	58	M	Farmer	"	"	
Maria " & ch.	40	F		"	"	
Michael Noel	28	M	Farmer	"	"	
Charlotte "	24	F		"	"	
Peter Haffener	36	M	Farmer	"	"	
Charlotte " & 5 ch.	24	F		"	"	
Jacob "	27	M	Farmer	"	"	
Eliz. " & 2 ch.	29	F		"	"	
George Wing	23	M	Farmer	"	"	
Fredk. Foller	24	M	"	"	"	
Charlotte " & 2 ch.	28	F		"	"	
Adam Geldebretch	26	M	Farmer	"	"	
Dorothea " & 5 ch.	26	F		"	"	
Conrad M. Smit	27	M	Farmer	"	"	
E. Smit & child	27	F		"	"	
Joseph Churbech & ch.	21	M	Farmer	"	"	
Sebastian Weber	24	M	"	"	"	
Barbara "	22	F		"	"	

Names of passengers	Age	Sex	Occupation	Country to which they belong	Country of which they intend becoming inhabitants	Ship or vessel with the name of the master or commander
NEW YORK						
<u>Q. E. Dec. 31, 1821</u>						
L. Kyzer	22	M		Germany	U. States	
Adam Morgenster	20	M		"	"	
Christian Forgo	37	M		"	"	
Catharine Moorster & 3 ch.	26	F		"	"	
Jacob Klein	34	M		"	"	
Louisa Smit & 6 ch.	34	F		"	"	
Ludwig Mondinger & 4 ch.	58	M		"	"	
Jacob Luther	33	M	Shoemaker	"	"	
Louisa Landering & 4 ch.	27	F		"	"	
Adam Pacter & 4 ch.	34	M	Weaver	"	"	
Martin Scharpenter & 2 ch.	45	M		"	"	
Jacob Ringer	21	M		"	"	
Joachim Schilk	26	M		"	"	
J. Meyer	25	M		"	"	
N . Smit	28	M		"	"	
Peter Towrany	27	M		"	"	
Daniel Cornlower	18	M		"	"	
Christian Stallie	36	M		"	"	
J. G. Heinoshier	28	M		"	"	
L. Stansois	40	M		"	"	
G. H. Mangal	36	M		"	"	
Jacob Hawpt	49	M		"	"	
Job Hanchamp	25	M		"	"	
Antonio Gevir	40	M		"	"	
James Morits	40	M		"	"	
Philip Wassem	26	M		"	"	
G. Ruelles	36	M		"	"	
A. Bouner	31	F		"	"	
J. F. Grape	26	M	Gent.	France	France	Brig Superb. (Hamilton)
G. M. Liebunsad	32	M	Merchant	Holland	Holland	
W. D. Patton	19	M	"	U. States	U. States	
James Laws & child	28	M	Mariner	"	"	Brig Harriet Smith. Tafts.
John Scofield	50	M	Clothier	"	"	Schooner Nancy. Crowell.
Thomas Hamford	21	M	Merchant	"	"	
John Whitehead	40	M	Teacher	"	"	
Wm. B. Webster	22	M	Doctor	St. Johns	St. Johns	
Allen Duncan	20	M	Labourer	Ireland	U. States	
Thomas Ervin & ch.	35	M	"	"	"	
Fredk. Burns	25	M	Farmer	"	"	
Charles Maguire	25	M	"	"	"	

Names of passengers	Age	Sex	Occupation	Country to which they belong	Country of which they intend becoming inhabitants	Ship or vessel with the name of the master or commander
NEW YORK						
Q. E. Dec. 31, 1821						
Francis Maguire	22	M	Farmer	Ireland	U. States	
Francis Cumin	20	M	"	"	"	
James Dugan	22	M	"	"	"	
Mary "	25	F		"	"	
Mary Logan & 2 ch.	30	F		"	"	
A. Philipson	19	M	Merchant	Holland	"	Brig Resign. Schnyder
Edwd. Holden	26	M	"	England	"	Ship Robert Fulton. Holdridge.
Wm. Syers	32	M	Farmer	England	"	
Martha " & 4 ch.	22	F		"	"	
P. Egan	28	M	Book keeper	Ireland	"	
Thomas Everand	70	M	Preacher	G. Britain	"	
Charles Bayles	36	M	Farmer	"	"	
James Bell	54	M	"	Ireland	"	
Jno. B. Phythean	25	M	Surgeon	G. Britain	"	
Wm. Miller	32	M	Clerk	"	"	
Geo. Cross	26	M	Shoemaker	"	"	
Mary " & 2 ch.	29	F		"	"	
James Maxwell	45	M	Shop keeper	"	"	
Joseph J. Leca	35	M	Ship master	Portugal	"	Ship Andes. Fleming.
F. M. Zegnago	18	M	Merchant	"	"	
Joseph Garrett	25	M	Gent.	Ireland	"	Ship Dublin Packet. Newcomb.
Fredk. "	19	M	"	"	"	
Edwin "	17	M	"	"	"	
James Carberry	22	M	Farmer	"	"	
Edwin McCorry	22	M	"	"	"	
John Brady	23	M	"	"	"	
Daniel Kenifeck	22	M	"	"	"	
Michael Daley	21	M	"	"	"	
John Mullins	17	M	"	"	"	
Wm. Kerney	20	M	"	"	"	
Matthew Hanlen	23	M	"	"	"	
Thomas Brady	18	M	"	"	"	
John Murphy	19	M	Clerk	"	"	
John Doyle	36	M	Labourer	"	"	
Patrick Ward	34	M	Farmer	"	"	
Thomas Bishop	23	M	Clerk	"	"	
Francis W. Cassach	23	M	Merchant	Germany	"	Ship Merchant. Aymar.
James Holeryhead	25	M	"	England	"	
James Adams	40	M	"	U. States	"	
John Smith	35	M	Merchant	"	"	Ship Ganges. Tomkins.
Wm. Langsden	31	M	"	G. Britain	"	Ship Hercules. Cobb.
Thomas Stead	24	M	Manufactr.	"	"	
John Mountford	38	M	Merchant	"	"	
John Cox	26	M	"	"	"	

Names of passengers	Age	Sex	Occupation	Country to which they belong	Country of which they intend becoming inhabitants	Ship or vessel with the name of the master or commander
NEW YORK						
Q. E. Dec. 31, 1821						
John Herst	35	M	Merchant	G. Britain	U. States	
J. North	26	M	"	"	"	
Saml. J. Burdon	27	M	Military	"	"	
Fredk. Bradley	26	M	"	"	"	
John D. Jones	26	M	Merchant	"	"	
Robt. Masters	24	M	"	"	"	
Alexr. Thompson	42	M	"	"	"	
George P. Trimble	28	M	"	"	"	
James Rushton	45	M	"	"	"	
Hugh Dale	28	M	Merchant	"	"	
John McDonough	40	M	"	"	"	
James Spur	38	M	"	"	"	
Edwd. Maxwell	31	M	Mechanic	"	"	
Robt. Lee	32	M	"	"	"	
Robt. Sutton	24	M	Farmer	"	"	
Eliza White & ch.	37	F		"	"	
Mary Meadowcraft & 2 ch.	34	F		"	"	
Martha Gillespie & & 3 ch.	56	F		"	"	
John Lumey	29	M	Mechanic	"	"	
Sarah Wright & 3 ch.	27	F		"	"	
Ann Fenton & child	37	F		"	"	
Owen Littleton	32	M	Mechanic	"	"	
Hannah Hutchman & child	45	F		U. States	"	Schooner Lewes. Sears.
John Kent	35	M	Comedian	England	England	Ship Thames. Marshall.
Joseph Cowall & ch.	29	M	Artist	"	"	
Sarah Ganling & ch.	28	F		"	"	
Richd. Atkinson & ch.	39	M	Merchant	"	"	
James Arbuckle	33	M	Minister	"	"	
Arnos Scrowell	30	M		"	"	
John Cheeseman	22	M	Wheelwright	England	England	
Joseph Stickland	33	M	Blacksmith	"	"	
Emma " & 4 ch.	28	F		"	"	
Stephen Jeffrey	23	M	Farmer	"	"	
Mary Ann " & 2 ch.	22	F		"	"	
Thomas Justine	19	M		"	"	
Thomas Potter	35	M		"	"	
Ann "	28	F		"	"	
Thomas Cranch	25	M		"	"	
George Oliver	23	M	Blacksmith	"	"	
John Scarborough & ch	23	M	Painter	"	"	
Thomas Cade	38	M	Farmer	"	"	Ship Cadmus. Whitlock.

Names of passengers	Age	Sex	Occupation	Country to which they belong	Country of which they intend becoming inhabitants	Ship or vessel with the name of the master or commander
NEW YORK **Q. E. Dec. 31, 1821**						
Edwd. Pendergrast	23	M	Book keeper	G. Britain	England	
Wm. Bulmer	40	M	Farmer	"	"	
Wm. McClere	50	M	Draper	"	"	Ship Criterion. Avery.
Jacob Walton	50	M	Capt. H. B. M. Navy	"	"	
Sarah " & 6 ch.	30			"	"	
Charles Thompson	26	M	Gent.	"	"	
Thomas Smith	55	M	"	"	"	
Wm. Smith	23	M	Farmer	"	"	
Thomas Pool	46	M	Math. Instrument maker	"	"	
Alice " & 4 ch.	45	F		"	"	
George Phillips	39	M	Gent.	"	"	
Mary " & 3 ch.	33	F		"	"	
Samuel Howsworth	44	M	Gent.	G. Britain	U. States	
Thomas Hogg	43	M	Gardner	"	"	
Mary " & 3 ch.	33	F		"	"	
Alfred Harrison	29	M	Farmer	"	"	
James Vasser	60	M	"	"	"	
Wm. Atkinson	30	M	Gent.	"	"	
Wm. Beeny & 2 ch.	27	M	Miller	"	"	
James Bissen	26	M	Cordwainer			
Francis Lilly	31	M	Tailor	"	"	
Wm. Sargeant	43	M	Farmer	"	"	
Mary " & 2 ch.	26	F		"	"	
Wm. Holland	26	M	Farmer	"	"	
James Nevins	18	M	"	"	"	
Walter Wren	22	M	Miller	"	"	
Wm. Eales	28	M	Grocer	"	"	
Frances " & 2 ch.	25	F		"	"	
Augustine Moggio	26	M	Barber	Italy	"	Brig Neptune. Minro
George How	29	M	Supercargo	U. States	"	
H. Godfrey	32	M	Mariner	"	"	Sch. Eliza Jane. Weldon.
H. P. Price	27	M	"	"	"	
John Johnson	23	M	Merchant	G. Britain	"	
A. Perry	50	M	"	Spain	Spain	Brig Volant. Wiley.
S. Lowth	50	M	Mariner	U. States	U. States	Brig Abeona. Folger.
Wm. Hollingsworth	36	M	Merchant	"	"	Schooner Cherub. Webster.
Nathanl. Young	35	M	Merchant	Ireland	"	Ship Orion. Davis.
Ann Young & 3 ch.	29	F		"	"	
Ellen McNight	20	F		"	"	
Matthew Whitmarsh	26	M	Mariner	U. States	"	Sloop Jay. Thompson.
J. B. Nones	22	M	Merchant	"	"	Sch. Fair Play. Kimball.
Valand	32	M	"	Hayti	Hayti	

24

Names of passengers	Age	Sex	Occupation	Country to which they belong	Country of which they intend becoming inhabitants	Ship or vessel with the name of the master or commander
NEW YORK						
Q. E. Dec. 31, 1821						
David Moffett	32	M	Mariner	U. States	U. States	Ship S. Carolina Packet. Guill.
D. Anderson	36	M	"	"		
J. W. McCulloch	34	M	Physician	England	"	Brig Ann Maria. Summers.
Joseph Gauthier	32	M	Merchant	U. States	"	
Robert Tudant	30	M	"	England	"	Ship Erin. Bunker.
G. Whitney	30	M	Labourer	Ireland	"	
Thomas Rein	24	M	Book binder	England	"	
Mary Rich & 5 ch.	40	F		"	"	
Thomas Barks	43	M	Farmer	"	"	
James Shanton	32	M	Mason	"	"	
Ellen Robinson	20	F		"	"	
A. Gracias	54	M	Mariner	Spain	"	Sch. Sally. McLaughlin.
N. G. Hatch	34	M	Accomptant	Ireland	"	Brig Hannah. Cullen.
Rosanna Malone & ch.	21	F		"	"	
Abel North	20	M	Gent.	"	"	
J. Irvin	45	M	Painter	"	"	
Stephen Stephens	44	M	Merchant	G. Britain	"	Ship Euphrates. Stoddard.
Mary "	30	F		"	"	
P. Lawton	27	M	Merchant	"	"	
Alexr. Davidson	38	M	"	"	"	
A. W. Deckner	29	M	Grocer	"	"	
Stephen Lyster	31	M	Merchant	"	"	
Virgil Peck	25	M	"	U. States	"	Sch. Combine. Dunham.
Lewis Chollen	18	M	Farmer	"	"	
Thomas R. Ford	32	M	"	"	"	Brig Catharine. Clark.
Wm. Pommer	24	M	Cab. maker	Hamburgh	"	Sch. Rebecca & Sally. Scull.
Luke Pemilent	41	M	"	France	"	
James Jack	55	M	Merchant	U. States	"	Ship Magnet. Ogdon.
George Witherspoon	25	M	"	G. Britain	"	
Joseph Harpham	38	M	"	"	"	
G. B. Fisk	28	M	"	"	"	
Mrs. Mawby & 4 ch.	27	F		"	"	
Thomas Chamberlin	29	M	Shoemaker	"	"	
Jno. Knare	20	M	Merchant	U. States	"	Ship Mohawk. Lawrence.
D. Bascome	40	M	Salt baker	Bermuda	"	
Wm. Randel	24	M	Physician	N. Scotia	"	
Mrs. "	20	F		"	"	
John Milwain	21	M	Labourer	England	"	Ship Alexr. Mansfield. Hamilton.
Lucy Bock & 4 ch.	30	F	Housekeeper	"	"	
Lewis Stanley	25	M	Merchant	Germany	"	Brig Martha. Nile
Wm. Chisholm	74	M	Blacksmith	Scotland	"	Sch. Hunter. Sears.
Donald "	30	M	"	"	"	
H. Phillips	37	M	Farmer	G. Britain	"	Ship Cortes. De Cost.
Sophia Phillips	34	F		"	"	

Names of passengers	Age	Sex	Occupation	Country to which they belong	Country of which they intend becoming inhabitants	Ship or vessel with the name of the master or commander
NEW YORK						
Q. E. Dec. 31, 1821						
James Gardiner	50	M	Merchant	G. Britain	U. States	
Wm. Mackie	40	M	"	"	"	
Wm. Calder	40	M	"	"	"	
Henry Birkett	30	M	"	"	"	
Thomas Smith	22	M	"	"	"	
John Johnson	25	M	"	"	"	
John McAdams	24	M	"	"	"	
Wm. Holdworth	23	M	"	"	"	
Joshua Robyn	32	M	"	U. States	"	
Fredk. Brandt	?	M	"	Hamburg	Hamburg	Sch. Swan. Skinner.
Alfred Seaton		M	"	U. States	U. States	
M. Baria	38	M	"	France	"	Brig Fortune. Clark.
Antonio M. Hermandez	24	M	"	Trinidad	"	
M. J. Del Castello	25	M	"	"	"	
R. Byard	27	M	"	U. States	"	Ship Marmion. Hawkins
E. " & child	20	F		"	"	
M. Alexander	40	M	Merchant	France	"	
G. W. Smith	22	M	"	U. States	"	
G. Vogel	35	M	"	France	"	
Mrs. " & 3 ch.	35	F		"	"	
A. Mi(c)helon	25	M	Barber	"	"	
J. Vignadome	32	M	"	"	"	
J. James	30	M	Carpenter	England	"	
Elizabeth Pringle	40	F		Canada	"	Ship Juno. Doak.
Robt. Reppery	42	M		England	"	
John Ingals	58	M		U. States	"	
James Nock	33	M		"	"	
Elizabeth Nock & 2 ch.	32	F		"	"	
John Richards	53	M	Merchant	G. Britain	"	Ship Cincinnatus. Champlin.
Fredk. W. Payne	33	M	"	U. States	"	
J. P. J. Cambridge	28	M	Physician	"	"	
E. K. Price	24	M	Lawyer	"	"	
Chas. Lee	45	M	Merchant	"	"	
Eleazor Parmley	23	M	Dentist	"	"	
J. Parmley	21	M	"	"	"	
Charles Bond	23	M	Merchant	England	"	
Joseph Turnly	54	M	"	"	"	
Matthew Swift	40	M	"	"	"	
Wm. J. Nunns	27	M	"	"	"	
Wm. Corne	26	M	"	"	"	
R. S. Herring	26	M	"	"	"	
Joseph Fordham	24	M	Miller	"	"	
John Holden	19	M	"	"	"	
Edwd. Mun	23	M	Carpenter	"	"	

Names of passengers	Age	Sex	Occupation	Country to which they belong	Country of which they intend becoming inhabitants	Ship or vessel with the name of the master or commander
NEW YORK						
Q. E. Dec. 31, 1821						
Robt. Smith	26	M	Farmer	England	U. States	
James Gowan	23	M	Tailor	"	"	
Henry Turner	39	M		"	"	
Rebecca " & 3 ch.	33	F		"	"	
Stephen Butler	19	M	Farmer	"	"	
H. Eartham	48	M	Merchant	"	"	
Stephen Jennings	17	M	Farmer	"	"	
Richd. "	23	M	"	"	"	
Sarah Jones & 2 ch.	29	F		"	"	
W. Arundell	41	M	Carpenter	"	"	
Eliz. " & 5 ch.	41	F		"	"	
Mary Jones & 2 ch.	34	F		"	"	
John Thorn	30	M	Farmer	"	"	
Emma Langton	31	F		"	"	
Wm. Stuart	26	M	Merchant	"	"	Ship Nestor. Macy.
Henry Cadmore & ch.	23	M	Shoemaker	Ireland	"	
Christopher Romancie	40	M	Mariner	Russia	"	
Mary Romancie	30	F		"	"	
Ab. Mansfield	21	M	Merchant	England	"	
G. H. Walker	32	M	Farmer	"	"	
J. Insinger	28	M	Merchant	Amsterdam	"	
James Dunlop	58	M	"	Scotland	"	
Ezra Weeks	48	M		U. States		
Vinct. Noble	41	M	Merchant	Leghorn	"	
Eliza Thornton & 5 ch.	35	F		England	"	
Wm. Liddle	39	M	Merchant	U. States	"	
Samuel Thompson	25	M	"	"	"	
James Smith	21	M	"	"	"	
George Trotter	34	M	"	"	"	
John McPherson	24	M	Farmer	"	"	
Edwd. "	17	M	"	"	"	
Saml. Nivens	31	M	Merchant	"	"	
Thomas H. Leggett	33	M	"	"	"	
J. W. Wallack	27	M	Tragedian	England	"	
James Drobble	38	M	Merchant	"	"	
Robert Lyons	25	M	"	"	"	
W. Belcher	22	M	Rule maker	"	"	
Martha Belcher	20	F		"	"	
Alexr. Purlands	26	M	Merchant	Scotland	"	
John Moorhead	38	M	"	"	"	
Rebecca " & child	21	F		"	"	
John Steel	35	M	Merchant	"	"	
W. J. Hunter	20	M	"	U. States	"	Ship Romulus. Lovett.
G. Shillabar	25	M	Mariner	"	"	

Names of passengers	Age	Sex	Occupation	Country to which they belong	Country of which they intend becoming inhabitants	Ship or vessel with the name of the master or commander
NEW YORK **Q. E. Dec. 31, 1821**						
Benj. Johnson	52	M	Mariner	U. States	U. States	Sch. Amazon. Hamor.
Eli Wainwright	37	M	Merchant	England	"	Ship Rockingham. Holdridge.
Mary " & 2 ch.	31	F		"	"	
Richd. March	22	M	Farmer	"	"	
George Brown & ch.	23	M	"	"	"	
James McLane	25	M	Farmer	"	"	
Agnes " & ch.	22	F		"	"	
D. S. Kennedy	31	M	Merchant	U. States	"	Ship Ann Maria. Graham.
John Francis	21	M	Physician	"	"	
George Law	33	M	Merchant	"	"	
James Sloane	38	M		"	"	
J. Maitland	20	M		"	"	
Thomas Adair	19	M		"	"	
James Riddle	30	M		"	"	
James Wilkinson	40	M	Farmer	G. Britain	"	
Wm. "	19	M	"	"	"	
Robert Martin	22	M	Dyer	"	"	
Wm. Hilton	22	M	Grocer	"	"	
R. Par	25	M	Labourer	"	"	
John Snow	22	M	Tailor	"	"	
Matilda Snow & 2 ch.	20	F		"	"	
Pat. McMalron	36	M	Labourer	"	"	
James "	32	M	"	"	"	
Joseph Howe	40	M	Farmer	"	"	
Sarah " & child	32	F		"	"	
John "	33	M	Farmer	"	"	
Eliz. " & 3 ch.	32	F		"	"	
Benj. Bulland	48	M	Farmer	"	"	
Elizabeth " & 8 ch.	48	F		"	"	
John Rowell	44	M		"	"	
Ann " & 3 ch.	26	F		"	"	
Wm. Charlesworth	26	M		"	"	
John Howard	29	M		"	"	
Martha " & 2 ch.	28	F		"	"	
Mary Shirley	48	F	Spinster	Ireland	"	Brig Hibernia. Wattling.
Ellen Gorman	22	F	"	"	"	
Ellen Reiley & 2 ch.	30	F	"	"	"	
Daniel Soragan	23	M	Farmer	"	"	
John Wood	24	M	"	"	"	
Timothy Phelan	23	M	"	"	"	
James Cocker	21	M	"	"	"	
Wm. Patterson	24	M	"	"	"	
W. Branscour	45	M	"	U. States	"	Sch. Nancy. Crowell.
James Lewes	18	M	Mariner	St. Johns	"	

Names of passengers	Age	Sex	Occupation	Country to which they belong	Country of which they intend becoming inhabitants	Ship or vessel with the name of the master or commander
NEW YORK						
Q. E. Dec. 31, 1821						
Alexr. Anderson	25	M	Mariner	Ireland	U. States	
David Linch	28	M	"	"	"	
A. Crawford	40	M	"	"	"	
Sarah " & 2 ch.	38	F		"	"	
B. O'Brien	25	M	"	"	"	
John Flinn	20	M	"	"	"	
P. Burnes	24	M	"	"	"	
Lewis Harrison	35	M	"	"	"	
Wm. Givans	22	M	Farmer	"	"	
Betsey Conklin & 2 ch.	35	F		"	"	
Margt. Mays & 2 ch.	30	F		"	"	
Betsey Foy & child	25	F		"	"	
D. Rice	40	M	Mariner	U. States	"	Brig Neptune. Keating
R. Beelbez	50	M	Merchant	G. Britain	"	Ship Orbit. Macy.
Jas. Mills	60	M	"	"	"	
Wm. Woodvill	28	M	"	U. States	"	
James Stool	47	M	"	G. Britain	"	
Arthur Hurst	27	M	"	"	"	
Ann "	25	F		U. States	"	
Wm. Mallet	40	M	Merchant	England	"	Sloop Elizabeth. Clark.
Jos. Sisler	47	M	"	U. States	"	Sloop Morgiana. Taylor.
James Masfield	35	M	Mariner	"	"	Brig Hope. Hatch.
John White	37	M	"	"	"	
Jose Antonio Pasquel	24	M	Merchant	Spain	"	
John M. Southgate	24	M	"	U. States	"	Ship Constitution. McRea.
J. W. Story	44	M	Mariner	"	"	
Wm. Rice	35	M	"	"	"	
M. Parker	36	M	Mariner	"	"	Sch. Mary Jane. Barnard.
C. Franceton	24	M	Merchant	Switzerland	"	
J. S. Baker	37	M	Mariner	U. States	"	Sch. McDonough. Auger.
James Buckley	22	M	Merchant	"	"	Sloop Wave. Harper.
Henry Boyce	25	M	"	Ireland	"	
C. Savage	31	M	Carpenter	England	"	Ship Illinois. Funk.
Thos. Martin	50	M	Merchant	Spain	"	Ship Fair American. Dugan.
Wm. Akin	50	M	"	"	"	
Bernard Castela	25	M	"	"	"	
C. Rochet	35	M	Coppersmith	France	"	
---Escondon	21	M	Merchant	Havana	Spain	
G. C. Thornville	40	M	"	England	U. States	Ship Comet. Griswold.
S. "	32	F		"	"	
C. F. Valz	50	M	Merchant	Germany	"	
G. C. Joynt	58	M	Farmer	England	"	
Mary "	40	F		"	"	
John McCall	52	M	Merchant	"	"	
Spencer West & 7 ch.	55	M	Farmer	"	"	

Names of passengers	Age	Sex	Occupation	Country to which they belong	Country of which they intend becoming inhabitants	Ship or vessel with the name of the master or commander
NEW YORK						
Q. E. Dec. 31, 1821						
John Morris	28	M	Shoemaker	England	U. States	
John Powell	20	M	Clerk	"	"	
George Prince	45	M	Mariner	U. States	"	
John P. Keely	21	M	Clerk	Canada	"	Brig Commerce. Fink.
C. G. Ekiland	23	M	Mariner	Sweden	"	Ship Anna Christina. Pagarda.
V. O. Tero	25	M	Tailor	Spain	Spain	Sch. Betsey Ann. Fisher.
Henry Mohr	35	M	Merchant	Germany	U. States	Ship Ann. West.
D. Dyson	18	M	"	Scotland	"	
John Shearman	29	M	Farmer	G. Britain	"	
Wm. Patterson	27	M	Manufactr.	"	"	
Janett " & ch.	25	F		"	"	
Wm. Martin/Merlin	27	M	Farmer	"	"	
Wm. Boothby	24	M	Watchmaker	"	"	
James Croop	21	M	Joiner	U. States	"	
Harnet Stanbirg & 2 ch.	23	F		"	"	
Wm. Hodgson	28	M	Miller	G. Britain	"	
Margt. " & 6 ch.	29	F		"	"	
John Thompson	21	M	Farmer	"	"	
James White	23	M	Ropemaker	"	"	
Thomas Lee	27	M	Printer	"	"	
John Perry	27	M	Merchant	"	"	
Margt. " & child	28	F		"	"	
Jane Lee & child	26	F		"	"	
B. Belgardo	30	M	Merchant	Spain	"	Brig Hippomanes. Bourne.
Geo. O. Sampson	22	M	Mariner	U. States	"	
Jaques Rudin	23	M	Merchant	"	"	Brig Fox. Wheeler.
Charles Graile	30	M	"	Port au Prince	"	
J. Mazias	23	M	"	Spain	"	Brig Alfred. Calder.
R. De la Seinna	26	M	"	"	"	
R. Shepherd & child	45	M	Attorney	England	"	Brig Bee. Wilson.
Jno. Fenokea	27	M	Merchant	"	"	
C. G. Caravasa	22	M		Spain	"	
James Ridgway	41	M	Mariner	U. States	"	Ship Chase. Baxter.
C. D. Rhodes	28	M	Merchant	"	"	
A. C. Runteaux	26	M	"	"	"	
E. Sheel	27	M	"	Ireland	"	
John Mansfield	48	M	Gent.	U. States	"	Brig Orleans. Brown.
J. T. Conrad	34	M	Cabinet mkr.	Russia	"	
L. " & 3 ch.	34	F		"	"	
Wm. F. Meyer	45	M	Merchant	U. States	"	Ship Focus. Moran.
Eliza Moran & child	30	F	Spinster	"	"	
Wm. Newton	23	M	Tailor	G. Britain	"	Ship Laburnum. Taylor.
James Widney	44	M	Merchant	U. States	"	Sch. Huntress. Morgan.
Peter Revaris	25	M	Mariner	"	"	

Names of passengers	Age	Sex	Occupation	Country to which they belong	Country of which they intend becoming inhabitants	Ship or vessel with the name of the master or commander
NEW YORK						
Q. E. Dec. 31, 1821						
John Barclay	26	M	Clergyman	G. Britain	Canada	Ship James Monroe. Rogers.
Benj. Donald	24	M		U. States	U. States	
Benj. Delveldt	41	M	Merchant	"	"	
Matthew Steel	21	M	"	G. Britain	"	
P. Colleson	36	M	"	U. States	"	
John Welsh	18	M	Shoemaker	G. Britain	"	
Thomas Doyle	22	M	Farmer	"	"	
Simon "	38	M	"	"	"	
Robert Stevenson	31	M	"	"	"	
Margaret " & 2 ch.	25	F		"	"	
E. Beynon	36	M		U. States	"	
John C. Green	22	M		"	"	
---De la forest	42	M	Consul	France	France	Ship Imperial. Deslebiche.
D. (Espenville)	18	M	Secretary	"	"	
---Fessert	36	M	Merchant	U. States	U. States	
---Lacorte	45	M	"	"	"	
M. Fernade	32	M	"	"	"	
---Sounalot	34	M	"	France	"	
---Duhamel	48	M	"	"	"	
---Fuillet	32	M	"	"	"	
---Motimer	30	M	"	"	"	
---Philip	26	M	Flour dresser	U. States	"	
M. Labardier	30	M	Merchant	"	"	
---Bentley	28	M	Farmer	England	"	
Mrs. " & 2 ch.	28	F		"	"	
Mr. Barber	24	M	Merchant	"	"	
Jose Maria Arguillous	34	M	Soldier	Spain	Spain	Sch. Mary & Betsey. Hall.
E. W. Waring	24	M	Merchant	U. States	U. States	Brig Cannon. Ryan.
J. Lesqua	25	M	"	France	"	
F. Garriel	25	M	"	"	"	
J. G. Duant *	25	M	Tailor	U. States	"	
C. Matthews	24	M	Gent.	G. Britain	"	Brig Clarence. Walker.
F. Lantrom	20	M	"	"	"	
W. Park	30	M	Joiner	"	"	
Mrs. " & 2 ch.	28	F		"	"	
Thomas C. Smith	25	M	Merchant	U. States	"	Brig Laura. Holman.
John Dias	35	M	"	"	"	Sch. Patty & Sally. Stenman.
F. A. D'Peyster	32	M	Ship master	"	"	Ship Augustia. Giles.
Henry Cutting	14	M	Mariner	"	"	
P. Woodhouse	32	M	B. Officer	England	England	Ship Elizabeth. Sebor.
C. Jones	24	M	"	"	"	
John Crisfield	24	M	Merchant	"	"	
Jane " & child	20	F		"	"	
J. Austin	50	M	Merchant	"	"	
Wm. Simpson	36	M	Brasier	"	"	

Names of passengers	Age	Sex	Occupation	Country to which they belong	Country of which they intend becoming inhabitants	Ship or vessel with the name of the master or commander
NEW YORK						
Q. E. Dec. 31, 1821						
Henry Fowler	31	M	Merchant	Scotland	U. States	
Jane " & child	30	F		"	"	
John Wise	19	M	Whitesmith	U. States	"	
Charlotte Cleadon * & 3 ch.	32	F		"	"	
Wm. Munn	24	M	Baker	England	"	
Richd. Matthews	22	M	"	"	"	
Wm. Hickman	18	M	Carpenter	"	"	
James Wood	60	M	Saw filer	U. States	"	
Wm. Moore	56	M	Guilder	"	"	
Eliz. Laswell & 8 ch. *	41	F		England	England	
Mordecai Frois	26	M	Merchant	Holland	Holland	Brig Rebecca Ann. Becker.
Thos. B. Donovan	20	M	Planter	England	W. Indies	Ship Robt. Burns. Coffin.
Ann "	45	F		"	"	
Johanna " & ch.	22	F		"	"	
Wm. W. Hughes	25	M	Merchant	U. States	U. States	
John Lupton	25	M	Farmer	"	"	
John Leonard	20	M	"	England	"	
John Williams	29	M	" ·	"	"	
Wm. Clark	49	M	Tallow chandler	"	"	
G. " & 7 ch.	49	F		"	"	
Wm. Philips & 6 ch.	41	M	Farmer	"	"	
Uriah Lampert	21	M	"	"	"	
H. F. Smith	32	M	Merchant	U. States	"	Sch. Musquito.
Silas Kellog	21	M		"	"	
Wm. Frampton	23	M		England	"	Ship Irene. Williams.
Peter Hurtel	49	M	Merchant	U. States	"	
Anthony Bonasset	47	M	"	"	"	
Jerome L. Roy	23	M	Cooper	France	"	
Moses Boget	54	M	Merchant	"	"	
Aaron "	19	M	"	"	"	
J. L. Spinola	40	M	"	Madeira	"	Brig Pomona. Bright.
John Welsly	24	M		England	"	Ship Braganza. Rogers.
A. Welch & child	40	F		Ireland	"	Brig Prince Edward. Sears.
Wm. Murray	21	M		"	"	
James Hannerbury	23	M	Mariner	N. Scotia	"	
E. Preble	30	M	"	U. States	"	
A. Pollard	35	M	"	"	"	
Andw. Glondon	24	M	Merchant	"	"	Sch. Diana
F. Seavers	29	M	Druggist	Germany	"	Ship Louisa Matilda. Turner.
Wm. Schlrip	35	M	Merchant	"	"	
D. S. Cook	32	M	Mariner	U. States	"	
Wm. H. Macomb	25	M	Merchant	"	"	Brig Mary. Noyes.

Names of passengers	Age	Sex	Occupation	Country to which they belong	Country of which they intend becoming inhabitants	Ship or vessel with the name of the master or commander
NEW YORK						
Q. E. Dec. 31, 1821						
Susan Macomb & ch.	24	F		U. States	U. States	
L P. Barre	27	M	Merchant	France	France	
Stephen Purdy	38	M	Shipwright	U. States	U. States	Sch. Loire. Bassett.
George Mansfield	26	M		"	"	
Wm. Johnson	20	M	Clerk	"	"	
Adolphus Brown	24	M	Mariner	"	"	
Elizabeth " & 2 ch.	25	F		"	"	
James Smith	27	M	Servant	England	N. Brunswick	
Geo. Vandlame	31	M	Merchant	St. Johns	St. Johns	
M. C. Hailes	25	M	Attorney	"	"	
John Chame *	29	M	Merchant	Ireland	U. States	Ship Globe. Brittan.
Chas. S. Murray	28	M	"	Scotland	Canada	
Samuel D. Moor	27	M	"	"	U. States	
Wm. Douglass	22	M	Merchant	Scotland	"	
Robert Henry	28	M	Farmer	Ireland	"	
James Galldley & ch.	27	M	"	Scotland	Canada	
Wm. Bowden	56	M	"	Ireland	U. States	
Margt. " & 5 ch.	45	F		"	"	
Alexr. "	24	M	Farmer	"	"	
James C. Neal	21	M	"	"	"	
Robert Murdoch	17	M	"	"	"	
David Kennedy	28	M	"	"	"	
H. McDonald	26	M	Merchant	G. Britain	"	Brig Finchot. Webster
Mrs. "	26	F		"	"	
Samuel C. Nichols	42	M	Mariner	U. States	"	Ship Genl. Brown.
Josiah Cowper	50	M	"	"	"	
Augustus Contee *	38	M	"	"	"	
William Cothen	38	M	Planter	Denmark	Denmark	Ship Elias Burger. Jennings.
Lewis P. De Conder	45	M	"	U. States	U. States	Ship Minerva.
Benj. Barstow	25	M	Merchant	"	"	
Jno. D. Bates	22	M	"	"	"	
Lewis Corell *	18	M	Planter	"	"	
Francis D. Smith	45	M	"	"	"	
Laura Purley	18	F	Spinster	"	"	
Joseph Green	33	M	Merchant	England	"	Ship Lycurgus.
E. Toderherst	40	M	"	Germany	"	
D. McCormick	50	M	Mariner	U. States	"	
Walter McFarland	45	M	"	"	"	
Antonio Hasel	35	M	Planter	Germany	"	
H. "	35	M	"	"	"	
C. Aug. Holst	25	M	"	"	"	
G. W. Clark	28	M	Mariner	U. States	"	Brig Helecon. Johnson.
John Riddle	22	M	Labourer	Ireland	"	Ship Grand Turk. O'Hara.
Eliz. Coglin & child	27	F		"	"	

PASSENGERS WHO ARRIVED IN THE U.S. SEPTEMBER 1821 - DECEMBER 1823

Names of passengers	Age	Sex	Occupation	Country to which they belong	Country of which they intend becoming inhabitants	Ship or vessel with the name of the master or commander
NEW YORK						
Q. E. Dec. 31, 1821						
Willet Hicks	52	M	Merchant	U. States	U. States	Ship Atlantic. Taylor.
Thomas Purser	50	M	"	"	"	
Joshua Milner	24	M	"	G. Britain	"	
Jas. "	18	M	"	"	"	
Thomas Lee	23	M	"	"	"	
R. Griffith	24	M	Surgeon	U. States	"	
Wm. Horner	28	M	"	"	"	
Peter Hathrick	60	M	Merchant	"	"	
Mrs. " & child	50	F		"	"	
Joshua Yates & child	45	M	"	"	"	
James Ferguson	35	M	"	"	"	
Matthew Jackson	34	M	"	"	"	
John Dick	30	M	Farmer	"	"	
OSWEGATCHIE						
Q. E. Dec. 31, 1821						
Henry Jenkinson	32	M	Labourer	Ireland	Kingston	Boat Huron. Graham.
Ann " & ch.	28	F		"	"	
John Forsyth	30	M	Weaver	"	Lisbon St. Law	
Catharine " & 4 ch.	27	F		"	"	
Joseph Winshall	30	M	Carpenter	"	U. States	
Fanny " & ch.	24	F		"	"	
Joseph Wilson	25	M	Labourer	"	"	
NEWPORT						
Q. E. Dec. 31, 1821						
Joseph B. Fox	20	M	Physician	U. States	U. States	Ship Fisher Ames. Seabury.
Rachel Ray	67	F		G. Britain	"	Sch. Abigail Elwell.
Mary Clark	22	M		U. States	"	
Wm. Leavitt	25	M	Merchant	G. Britain		
J. H. Fowler	24	M	"	"	"	
Thomas Nugent	26	M	Trader	"	"	
James Grant	45	M	Merchant	"	"	Ship Belle Savage. Russell.
Thomas Johnson	50	M	"	"	"	
Thomas Fernside	30	M	Labourer	"	"	
Jane Perry	30	F	Spinster	Ireland	"	
Mary Andrews	17	F	"	"	"	
Jane Ross & 4 ch.	40	F		"	"	
John Morehead	32	M	Merchant	Scotland	"	
Margt. "	25	F		"	"	
John P. Wall	46	M	Merchant	Ireland	Canada	Brig Monitor. Whitton.

Names of passengers	Age	Sex	Occupation	Country to which they belong	Country of which they intend becoming inhabitants	Ship or vessel with the name of the master or commander
NEWBURYPORT Q. E. Dec. 31, 1821						
Robert Storey	37	M	Weaver	England	U. States	Vessel not mentioned.
Ann " & 5 ch.	43	F		"	"	
M. McKinny & 3 ch.	30	F		Ireland	"	
Patrick McGowen	23	M	Labourer	"	"	
Patrick Collins	25	M	Fisherman	"	"	
John Welsh	25	M	Teacher	"	"	
Joseph D. Gore/Gove	32	M	Mariner	U. States	"	
MARBLEHEAD Q. E. Dec. 31, 1821						
David Stonehouse	52	M	Farmer	England	Canada	Sch. Good Exchange. Leran.
Robert "	23	M	Joiner	"	"	
Jane " & 7 ch.	37	F		"	"	
John Bellamy	46	M	Farmer	"	"	
SAVANNAH Q. E. Dec. 31, 1821						
James Wood	45	M	Merchant	Scotland	U. States	Ship Pallas. Land.
John McKenzie	40	M	"	"	"	
Duncan "	27	M	"	"	"	
Robert Gantt •	22	M	"	"	"	
George Relph	35	M	"	U. States	"	Ship Oglethorpe. Rawson.
James Maguire	28	M	"	"	"	
Robt. Isaac	42	M	"	"	"	Ship Georgia. Varnum.
Lucy " & 2 ch.	35	F		"	"	
John Miller	43	M	Planter	"	"	
David Johnston	53	M		Scotland	"	
Michael O'Dwyer	26	M	Teacher	"	"	
John P. Hunt	19	M	Clerk	Ireland	U. States	
Patrick Higgins	23	M	Labourer	G. Britain	"	
Margt. Egan	26	F		"	"	
Wm. Hutchins	21	M	Merchant	Scotland	"	
Richd. W. Stiles	20	M	"	U. States		
R. N. How	22	M	"	"	"	
J. C. Hanahan	23	M	"	"	"	
N. M. Peterson	35	M	"	Denmark	"	
Mrs. Lewis & child	22	F		Ireland	"	
Robert Howman	22	M	Mason	G. Britain	"	Sch. Greyhound. Peck.
Antonio Silvara	22	M	Barber	Portugal	"	
Antonio Lewis	24	M	Carpenter	"	"	
Francisco Joseph	18	M	Cooper	"	"	
A. L. Molyneux	26	M	Merchant	England	"	Ship Dorset. Dixon.

PASSENGERS WHO ARRIVED IN THE U.S. SEPTEMBER 1821 - DECEMBER 1823

Names of passengers	Age	Sex	Occupation	Country to which they belong	Country of which they intend becoming inhabitants	Ship or vessel with the name of the master or commander
SAVANNAH						
Q. E. Dec. 31, 1821						
W. C. Molyneux	24	M	Merchant	England	U. States	
Wm. Heifren •	36	M	Labourer	Ireland	"	
Robt. McIntosh	40	M	Merchant	G. Britain	"	Ship Three Sisters. Bell.
Helen " & ch.	42	F		"	"	
Catharine Reid	30	F	Spinster	"	"	
Robert Burns	28	M	Labourer	"	"	
Mary " & child	35	F		"	"	
Robert Hampsead	26	M	Labourer	"	"	
Agnes "	27	F		"	"	
Archibald McLaren	20	M	Merchant	"	"	
Hugh Alexander	26	M	Labourer	"	"	
John C. Ross	23	M	Merchant	"	"	
John Frazer	30	M	"	"	"	
Ann " & 2 ch.	26	F		"	"	
James McLea	30	M	Merchant	"	"	
John Dreghorn	25	M	"	"	"	
Thomas Bertram	19	M	Clerk	"	"	
Robt. McHenry	40	M	Merchant	"	"	
Alexr. McGrey	23	M	"	"	"	
BOSTON, CHARLES-						
TOWN DISTRICT						
Q. E. Dec. 31, 1821						
James McDonald	27	M	Merchant	Honduras	"	Brig Two Brothers. Tuckey.
George A. Usher	24	M	"	"	"	
Peter H. Symms	30	M	Mariner	U. States	"	
James Berry	22	M	"	"	"	
Wm. Lighter •	38	M	Merchant	Ireland	"	Ship Charles. Presson.
Charles Howe	40	M	Mariner	U. States	"	Sch. Susan. Baxter.
G. Moore	30	M	Labourer	Scotland	"	Sch. Thetis. Newcombe.
Catharine Moore & 2 ch.	25	F		"	"	
J. B. James	31	M	Merchant	Cuba	Cuba	Sch. Jane. Miller.
Patrick Hough	34	M	"	Halifax	Halifax	Sch. Cherub. Sheffield.
James Weatherston	24	M	Farmer	"	U. States	
Daniel Campbell	24	M	Sailor	Halifax	U. States	
James Sampler	25	M	Mechanic	"	"	
James M. Grath	30	M	"	"	"	
Peter Leshman	24	M	Tailor	"	"	
Wm. Nook	22	M	Merchant	"	"	
J. A. Tolland	25	M	"	U. States	"	
N. "	23	M	"	"	"	
G. W. Crielman	35	M	"	Halifax	"	

Names of passengers	Age	Sex	Occupation	Country to which they belong	Country of which they intend becoming inhabitants	Ship or vessel with the name of the master or commander
BOSTON, CHARLESTOWN DISTRICT **Q. E. Dec. 31, 1821**						
Ellen Bard *	25	M ?	Mantua mkr.	Halifax	U. States	
G. Whipper	30	M	Mariner	"	"	
James Sullivan	20	M	Trader	"	"	
James Armed	35	M	Carpenter	Wales	"	
Richd. Thornbery	27	M	Labourer	Ireland	"	Sch. Two Friends. Laker.
Elizabeth " & 4 ch.	29	F		"	"	
Edwd. Conway	24	M	Labourer	"	"	
Patrick Cary	25	M	"	"	"	
Michael Murison	26	M	"	"	"	
Catherine " &2 ch.	25	F		"	"	
M. Moore	38	M	Painter	N. Scotia	"	Sch. Com. Penn. Foster.
Nicholas Daunas	48	M	Chemist	France	"	Sch. Virginia Packet. La Forette.
John Wright	22	M	Mariner	England	"	
D. J. B. Francois	22	M	"	France	"	Ship Charles. Coffin.
Jean B. "	17	M	"	"	"	
James Colmell	36	M	Farmer	U. States	"	Sch. Rising States.
Wm. Blakely	42	M	"	"	"	
James Perry	25	M	"	"	"	
Robert Henderson	28	M	"	Ireland	"	
Robert Hughly *	28	M	"	"	"	
S. "	45	M	"	"	"	
Jame McAster	25	M	"	"	"	
Betsey "	33	F		"	"	
S. Naton	65	M	Merchant	U. States	"	Sch. St. Croix. Brooks.
W. Lowell	29	M	"	Lubeck	Lubeck	
C. McOnerry	24	M	Mechanic	St. Johns	U. States	
---Riley	29	M	Labourer	"	"	
---La Crown & ch.	31	M	Merchant	"	"	
---Kelly	28	M	"	"	"	
---Foster	25	M	"	"	"	
James Curtis	21	M	Mariner	U. States	"	Sch. Pilgrim. Soule.
Wm. Kidfield	44	M	Farmer	"	"	Brig Victory. Barker.
Rebecca "	44	M ?		"	"	
J. Ferguson & ch.	33	F		"	"	
R. C. D. Trango	20	M	Merchant	Madeira	Madeira	
Wm. Bowman	20	M	"	England	England	
Joseph Spink	39	M	Farmer	Halifax	Halifax	
G. Shaw	29	M		"	"	
Lawrence Doyle	25	M	Shoemaker	Ireland	U. States	
Benj. Coats	23	M	Tailor	England	"	
Michael Henning	26	M	Farmer	Ireland	"	
James Power	38	M	Fisherman	"	"	
Philip	29	M	"	"	"	

PASSENGERS WHO ARRIVED IN THE U.S. SEPTEMBER 1821 - DECEMBER 1823

Names of passengers	Age	Sex	Occupation	Country to which they belong	Country of which they intend becoming inhabitants	Ship or vessel with the name of the master or commander
BOSTON, CHARLESTOWN DISTRICT. **Q. E. Dec. 31, 1821**						
James Martin	23	M	Millwright	Ireland	U. States	
W. Clark	27	M	Weaver	"	"	
J. D. Bliss	17	M	Farmer	"	"	
P Bandry	28	M	Cab. Maker	France	"	Brig Packet. Campbell.
B. H. Bardnell	30	M	Missionary	U. States	"	Ship Franklin. O'Lear.
Mrs. R. " & 2 ch.	29	F		"	"	
Jeremiah C. Cook	35	M	Mariner	"	"	Brig Vancouver. Leach
Thomas Moterfield	28	M	Engineer	Scotland	"	Brig Missionary. Sears
Archibald Scott	26	M	Butcher	"	"	
Joseph Blake	26	M	Farmer	"	"	
Robert Mitchell	18	M	Butcher	"	"	
Jonathan Bowler	33	M	Mariner	St. Johns	"	
Amos Pomeroy	33	M	Merchant	U. States	"	Ship Cadmus. Ires.
James Welsh	25	M	M ? Dresser	"	"	Ship Triton. Bassey.
Joseph Marsh	25	M	Glass blower	England	"	
B. Goscar *	21	M	Ship master	U. States	"	Brig George. Harding.
A. Gracie	26	M	Merchant	"	"	Ship Mercury. Nichols.
P. C. Brook Jn.	22	M	"	"	"	
A. S. Wellington	42	M	"	"	"	
Saml. McNeil	40	M	"	"	"	
Mrs. Carter & 2 ch.	33	F		"	"	
John Ires	37	M	Labourer	G. Britain	"	Ship Glide. Adams.
Jane " & child	30	F		"	"	
Peggy Hogan & 3 ch.	30	F		"	"	
Robert Graves	27	M	Merchant	U. States	"	Brig Cornelia. Hammond.
Edmund Baylies	30	M	"	"	"	
James D. Hubbard	23	M	Printer	N. Scotia	"	Sch. Independence. Hopkins.
James Doyle	24	M	Labourer	Ireland	"	
John Candy	26	M	"	"	"	
Pat. Unokee *	22	M	"	"	"	
Nicholas Carter	23	M	"	"	"	
Andw. Shay	26	M	"	"	"	
Mary "	20	F		"	"	
Michael Webb	22	M	Mariner	U. States	"	Ship American Hero. Atkins.
Moses Roesch	20	M	Glass blower	Holland	"	
Jacob Bucks	25	M	Brewer	"	"	
Wm. Bustle *	29	M	Merchant	U. States	"	
James Hamilton	27	M	Physician	"	"	Sloop Katy Ann. Fisher.
Wm. King	27	M	Trader	"	"	
Winslow Corbett	24	M	Blacksmith	Ireland	"	
James McNaughton	21	M	Labourer	"	"	
David Pollock	33	M	Physician	Scotland	"	
Luke Knowles	33	M	Cooper	"	"	

Names of passengers	Age	Sex	Occupation	Country to which they belong	Country of which they intend becoming inhabitants	Ship or vessel with the name of the master or commander
BOSTON, CHARLES- TOWN DISTRICT. Q. E. Dec. 31, 1821						
James Reid	30	M	Labourer	Ireland	U. States	
James Hogan	30	M	Mariner	U. States	"	
Geo. W. Randell & neice	25	M	Farmer	"	"	
Peter Kodschild	21	M	Mechanic	Denmark	"	
Joseph Swett	28	M	Trader	U. States	"	
Joseph King	28	M	"	"	"	
M. Wills & 6 ch.	29	F		"	"	
Antonio P. Mancil *	32	M	Merchant	Portugal	Portugal	Ship Deborah. Gray.
I. S. D. Avila	28	M	Mariner	"	"	
John Burk	35	M	Clerk	Ireland	U. States	
Wm. Hardyman	25	M	Tailor	"	"	
Wm. Griffin	30	M	"	"	"	
Thomas Walker	20	M	Labourer	"	"	
James Verong * & ch.	55	M	Baker	France	"	Sch. Catharine. Doane.
A. " & ch.	36	F		"	"	
Thomas Phillips & ch.	25	M	Cooper	"	"	
C. Toss *	40	M	Mariner	U. States	"	Brig Phoenix.
Wm. Goodman	22	M	Merchant	"	"	
Wm. Beroan	29	M	Farmer	"	"	
Daniel Moore	19	M	Baker	Ireland	"	Sch. Cherub. Shepperd.
John Shaffer	40	M	Gardner	Holland	"	
John N. Connell	30	M	"	Ireland	"	
John Milvil	18	M	"	Scotland	"	
Michl. Williams	22	M	"	Ireland	"	
J. A. Pollard	28	M	Silversmith	U. States	"	
George Innes	40	M	Merchant	Halifax	Halifax	
Henry Hammond	38	M	"	Ireland	U. States	
Mrs. "	36	F		"	"	
Mr. Buchanan	32	M	Gent.	Jamaica	Jamaica	
Mr. Hinds	34	M	"	England	Quebec	
Mr. Henderson	28	M	Merchant	Scotland	U. States	
Mr. Full	25	M	Carpenter	Halifax	Halifax	
Mr. Ward	19	M	Farmer	U. States	U. States	
Mr. Dulany	21	M	"	"	"	
Mr. Irvin	50	M	"	England	"	
Mrs. " & child	40	F		"	"	
Mr. Peat	22	M	Merchant	Scotland	"	
J. G. Hill	35	M	"	U. States	"	Brig Betsey. Eells.
Samuel M. Lowell Jr.	35	M	"	England	"	Brig Margaret. Page.
Joseph Askin	35	M	"	U. States	"	Brig Rapid. Lincoln
M. M. Verby *	36	M	"	France	"	Ship Two Brothers. Henchman.
Mr. Pringle	36	M	"	Scotland	Scotland	Sch. Albion. Ward.

Names of passengers	Age	Sex	Occupation	Country to which they belong	Country of which they intend becoming inhabitants	Ship or vessel with the name of the master or commander
BOSTON, CHARLESTOWN DISTRICT. Q. E. Dec. 31, 1821						
Mrs. Pringle & 2 ch.	27	F		Scotland	Scotland	
Chas. G. Boyd	34	M	Sailmaker	Halifax	U. States	
James Harrington	23	M	Physician	"	"	
J. Boyle	25	M	Labourer	"	"	
Fredk. Kerr	25	M	"	"	"	
S. Field	45	M	Blacksmith	"	"	
Mrs. "	25	F		"	"	
Michael Shield	35	M	Blacksmith	"	"	
James McKer	25	M	Labourer	"	"	
John Hagarty	27	M	Farmer	"	"	
Danl. Moriarty	25	M	Labourer	"	"	
Danl. Sullivan	27	M	"	"	"	
Edwd. Cully	25	M	"	"	"	
John Harfell	22	M	"	"	"	
Jno. L. Taylor	23	M	Merchant	U. States	"	Brig Cyprus. Dickson.
Chas. C. Rice	20	M	"	"	"	
Saml. J. Armstrong	38	M	Bookbinder	"	"	Ship Partheon. Mackay.
Mrs. "	28	F		"	"	
Thomas Little	34	M	Clerk	England	"	
Mrs. R. Moreland & ch	28	F		U. States	"	Ship Eagle. Davis.
S. A. Smith	40	M	Merchant	"	"	
Wm. Spearony	23	M	Mariner	"	"	
Saml. Bradley	39	M	Carpenter	"	"	Brig Lion. Humphrey.
Amelia " & 4 ch.	34	F		"	"	
Samuel Gibson	17	M	"	"	"	
D. Burns	28	M	Clergyman	Scotland	Scotland	Sch. Victory. Leavet.
G. W. Critnan	34	M	Farmer	"	"	
D. Spencer	34	M	Bookbinder	Halifax	Halifax	
Isaac Winslow	18	M	Merchant	U. States	U. States	
James Combs	26	M	Servant	England	"	
B. " & child	25	F	"	"	"	
George Buchan	39	M	Carpenter	"	Canada	
Anthony Beacher	40	M	Farmer	U. States	U. States	Sch. Rising States. Wasket.
John Saunders	45	M	"	"	"	
Edmund Williams	25	M	Merchant	"	"	Brig Fame. Zelder.
Wm. Palmer	21	M	"	"	"	
John Haney	35	M	"	"	"	Sch. Margaret. Bradford.
Samuel Thatcher	23	M	"	"	"	
Thomas Rogers	34	M	"	"	"	
Thomas Rogers	34	M	Mariner	"	"	
Isaac Morton	22	M	"	"	"	
Mary "	21	F		"	"	
Wm. Williams	34	M	Merchant	"	"	Brig Jane. George.

Names of passengers	Age	Sex	Occupation	Country to which they belong	Country of which they intend becoming inhabitants	Ship or vessel with the name of the master or commander
BOSTON, CHARLES-TOWN DISTRICT **Q. E. Dec. 31, 1821**						
Alexr. Mitchell	21	M	Trader	U. States	U. States	Sch. Gen. Greene. Bears.
Robt. Danton	38	M	"	N. Scotia	N. Scotia	
Thomas Laraby	36	M	Shoemaker	G. Britain	U. States	
Thomas Cushing	33	M	Trader	U. States	"	
M. Murphy	24	M	Sailmaker	Ireland	"	
Randal Russell	21	M	Coachman	U. States	"	
John Patterson	29	M	Merchant	"	"	Ship Jasper. Crocker.
T. H. Patterson	30	M	Officer	Scotland	"	
George Purdy	35	M	Tailor	U. States	"	
John Sullivan	30	M	"	G. Britain	"	
Thomas Morgan	20	M	"	"	"	
Charles Purdy & 2 ch.	30	M	"	"	"	
Robt. Huddson	49	M	Mariner	U. States	"	Brig Margt. Ford.
Robert Kelly	35	M	"	"	"	
P. Sanderson	50	M	Merchant	Halifax	"	Sch. Cherub. Shepherd.
N. Upham & child	25	M	"	"	"	
M. Noble	30	M	"	"	"	
A. Emerson	30	M	"	U. States	"	
Edwd. Dugan	21	M	Gardner	Ireland	"	
N. R. Burchhill	21	M	Farmer	Scotland	"	
M. Quigley	25	M	Gardner	England	"	
M. Foster	24	M	"	"	"	
Wm. Lorey	26	M	Farmer	"	"	
Wm. C. Akin	23	M	"	"	"	
Michl. Nowlen	29	M	B. Smith	Ireland	"	
Jno. Terence	63	M	Merchant	U. States	"	Sch. Volant. Greenlaw.
Danl. Mills	28	M	"	"	"	
Augustus Contee	26	M	"	"	"	Brig Abeona. Porter
Andw. McCall	38	M		"	"	
Thomas Shea	24	M	Cordwainer	Germany	"	Sch. Two Sisters. Laureston.
BARNSTABLE **Q. E. Dec. 31, 1821**						
John Gaul	35	M	Labourer	Scotland	U. States	Sch. Alert. Pearse.
Alexr. Downy	36	M	"	"	"	
Ann Martin & child	49	F		"	"	
Wm. Nott	65	M	"	"	"	
Frances Nott	55	F		"	"	
Wm. " & child	28	M	Labourer	"	"	
Thomas Moran	30	M		"	"	
Joseph Kingston	40	M	Labourer	"	"	
Margaret " & 2 ch.	35	F		"	"	

Names of passengers	Age	Sex	Occupation	Country to which they belong	Country of which they intend becoming inhabitants	Ship or vessel with the name of the master or commander
BARNSTABLE						
Q. E. Dec. 31, 1821						
Wm. Agin	30	M	Tailor	Ireland	U. States	
Catharine Agin & ch.	35	F	"	"	"	
Thomas Bates	24	M	Labourer	"	"	
Francis McMann & 2 children	38	M	Mason	"	"	
Thomas Kelley	24	M	Labourer	Ireland	U. States	
Thomas Glaney	29	M	Cobler	England	"	Sch. Mary. Crowell.
Mary " & 3 ch.	30	F		"	"	
Noble McClinton	40	M	Mason	"	"	
Eleanor " & 4 ch.	35	F		"	"	
Margaret Hanny	25	F		"	"	
Pat. Gallaghan	24	M	Labourer	"	"	
PORTLAND AND						
FALMOUTH DISTRICT						
Q. E. Dec. 31, 1821						
B. Bascomb	35	M	Missionary	U. States	U. States	Ship Liverpool. McLeland.
Daniel Howe	26	M	Merchant	"	"	Sloop President. Collins.
Benjamin Lincoln	19	M	"	"	"	Sloop Govr. Knight
James Bickford	23	M	Mechanic	"	"	Sch. Dolphin. Blanchard.
Abraham Ireland	24	M	"	"	"	
Nathan Blackstone	24	M	"	"	"	
James Roberts	29	M	"	"	"	
James Porter	37	M	Gent.	G. Britain	G. Britain	Brig Nimrod. Alden.
Nathaniel Knight	22	M	"	U. States	U. States	
Jesse Sparrori	25	M		"	"	
NORFOLK						
Q. E. Dec. 31, 1821						
Thomas Underhill	25	M	Mariner	U. States	U. States	Sloop Amy & Polly. Macomber.
James Paul	25	M	"	"	"	
Wm. White	27	M	Planter	England	England	Sloop Anna. Laycock.
Roger Goodrich	28	M	Mariner	U. States	U. States	
Wm. Anderson	32	M	"	"	"	Brig Only Son. Green.
Henry Peters	43	M	Ship master	"	"	Sch. Star. Lawrence.
Oliver Brooks	27	M	"	"	"	Sch. Lively. Swain.
James A. Bell	21	M	Merchant	England	Bermuda	Sch. Lottery. Tyler.
Thomas Moore	27	M	Butcher	U. States	U. States	
Christian Hartell	23	M	"	"	"	
Benj. Fisher	35	M	Mariner	"	"	Brig Margt. Wright. Choate.
Benj. Clark	22	M	Merchant	"	"	Sch. Wickes. Ward.
Francis M. Wells	33	M		"	"	Sch. Mary & Ann. Gales.

Names of passengers	Age	Sex	Occupation	Country to which they belong	Country of which they intend becoming inhabitants	Ship or vessel with the name of the master or commander
NORFOLK						
Q. E. Dec. 31, 1821						
G. I. West	23	M	Merchant	U. States	U. States	
James Clarkson	35	M	Ship master	"	"	
A. B. Nones	25	M	Merchant	"	"	
Henry Warren	27	M	Ship Master	"	"	Eliza Jane. Pearson.
John B. Osborne	26	M	Supercargo	"	"	
Edmund March	24	M	Mariner	"	"	
John Fibbets	23	M	"	"	"	
Wm. Miller	18	M	"	"	"	
James Noble	21	M	"	"	"	
D. Stannaford	21	M	"	"	"	
David Loring	28	M	"	"	"	
Jeremiah Prince	55	M	"	"	"	
Wm. Love	44	M	"	"	"	
James Smith	27	M	"	"	"	
Adolphus Denison	24	M	"	"	"	
B. or G. Glasure	40	M	Mariner	"	"	
J. Franklin	35	M	"	"	"	
M. Stowe	22	M	"	"	"	
Jos. Minor	27	M	"	"	"	
J. Holland	25	M	"	"	"	
Wm. Fordon	20	M	"	"	"	
ALEXANDRIA						
Q. E. Dec. 31, 1821						
Andw. Adams	25	M	Merchant	U. States	U. States	Sch. Rose in Bloom. Soule.
C. Chapman	25	M	Mariner	"	"	
BRISTOL						
Q. E. April 1, 1822						
David Stevenson	35	M	Merchant	Canada	Canada	Brig Clarissa. Church.
Stephen Cady	25	M	Baker	U. States	U. States	
RICHMOND						
Q. E. April 1, 1822						
Abigail Shannon & ch.	24	F		Ireland	U. States	Brig
Patrick Hurley & ch.	27	M	Labourer	"	"	
John Kenny	23	M	"	"	"	
David Broderick	20	M	"	"	"	
John Eagan	21	M	"	"	"	
Thomas Hart	16	M	"	"	"	

Names of passengers	Age	Sex	Occupation	Country to which they belong	Country of which they intend becoming inhabitants	Ship or vessel with the name of the master or commander
PORTSMOUTH AND FALMOUTH Q. E. April 1, 1822						
Wm. C. Sears	20	M	Merchant	N. Brunswick	N. Brunswick	Sch. Caseo. York.
Michael Reilly	55	M	"	Jamaica	W. Indies	
Jas. Moorcroft	24	M	Farmer	N. Brunswick	N. Brunswick	
BOSTON Q. E. April 1, 1822						
John Suter	42	M	Mariner	U. States	U. States	Ship Alert. Nye.
Andw. Blanchard	38	M	"	"	"	
Thomas Holman	28	M	Physician	"	"	
Lucy " & ch.	26	F		"	"	
Levi Cook	24	M	Merchant	"	"	Sch. Ann. Dunn.
Wm. Hill	22	M	Mariner	"	"	
James Ingersoll	42	M	Merchant	"	"	Ship Pearl. Leach
F. A. Bunham	34	M	Mariner	"	"	Bark Garland. Wilson
James Middleton	21	M	"	"	"	
M. Hoffman	40	M	Physician	Halifax	Halifax	Brig Nile. Hatchings.
Wm. Lowell	29	M	Shipmaster	U. States	U. States	Brig Diligence. Jones.
Isaac Peabody	22	M	Mariner	G. Britain	G. Britain	Brig Levant. Crockett.
Wm. Ryan	46	M	"	U. States	U. States	
J. S. Soper	33	M	Trader	"	"	Sch. Cherub. Sheffield.
John Storey	28	M	"	Halifax	Halifax	
Jonas Smith	29	M	Merchant	"	"	
Chas. Gronard	18	M	Trader	"	"	
Jas. Roach	32	M	"	Ireland	U. States	
Robert Dunton	34	M	"	"	"	
George Leval	33	M	"	Halifax	"	
A. Mitchell	29	M	"	"	"	
Wm. Wright	22	M	Merchant	Canada	Canada	
Elizabeth Ryan & ch.	44	F		Ireland	U. States	
A. Trickling	30	M	Weaver	Halifax	"	
A. Archibald	28	M	Mariner	"	"	
John Wright	22	M	Labourer	"	"	
W. Lewis	30	M	"	Ireland	"	
Philip Stickney	19	M	"	"	"	
Peter Coral	23	M	"	"	"	
Patrick Neal	33	M	"	"	"	
Joshua Gerard & 4 ch.	50	M	Manufactr.	England	"	Sch. Victory. Barker.
H. Clark	26	M	Merchant	U. States	"	
Thomas Benett	31	M	Mariner	"	"	
John Henry	24	M	Merchant	"	"	
Christopher Carrot	26	M	"	"	"	
Lewis Thatcher	26	M	Mariner	"	"	Brig Draco. Atwood.

Names of passengers	Age	Sex	Occupation	Country to which they belong	Country of which they intend becoming inhabitants	Ship or vessel with the name of the master or commander
PORTSMOUTH AND FALMOUTH Q. E. April 1, 1822						
James Stoney	31	M	Farmer	Ireland	U. States	Sch. Tornas. Bradford.
Patrick Troy	23	M	Labourer	"	"	
David Mulin	36	M	Merchant	U. States	"	Brig Adriana. Baker.
George Osborn	25	M	"	"	"	
Samuel Johnston	28	M	"	"	"	Brig Lark. Lee.
Caleb Luther	21	M	Carpenter	"	"	Sch. Rapid. Haff.
NEW YORK Q. E. April 1, 1822						
Philip Hone	41	M	Merchant	U. States	U. States	Ship Amity. Maxwell.
B. P. Tilden	26	M	"	"	"	
Alexr. Disman	17	M	"	Scotland	"	
Mary Jane Pritchard	30	F		England	"	
A. Crighton	32	M	Dyer	Scotland	"	Brig Hind. Boyal.
Agnes " & 2 ch.	30	F		"	"	
Joseph Spear	34	M	Mariner	U. States	"	Ship Adonis. Bramley.
Jno. S. Wood	28	M	"	"	"	
Wm. S. Bawson	26	M	"	"	"	
U. H. Priest	32	M	Super cargo	"	"	
Alexr. Todd	50	M	Mariner	"	"	Brig Trident. Bunham.
D. Davis	25	M	Carpenter	"	"	
Chas. Pettit	28	M	Merchant	"	"	Brig Catherine. Clark.
Jno. McDonald	24	M	"	"	"	
Robert Musten	28	M	"	Antigua	G. Britain	Sch. Eliza Pigott. Waterman.
P. Austin	26	M	"	U. States	U. States	Brig Nymph. Smith.
Edmund Telfair	40	M	"	"	"	
Wm. Banker	38	M	"	England	"	
P. D. Loria	46	M	"	Spain	Spain	Sch. Martha. Driggs.
Charles Ferry	45	M	Priest	Ireland	U. States	Sch. Nancy. Crowell.
Jno. Hasting	20	M	Merchant	"	"	
Wm. Morrison	25	M	Farmer	"	"	
Ann "	22	F		"	"	
James Brown	18	M	Farmer	"	"	
O. Newcombe	34	M	Carpenter	U. States	"	Brig Ambuscade. Bryan.
Domingo Parora	37	M	Mariner	Portugal	"	
J. D. Corey	27	M	Merchant	U. States	"	
Jacob J. Stade	35	M	Gent.	"	"	Ship Orozimbo. Nichols.
Thos. H. Mason	25	M	Merchant	England	"	
Andw. T. Hull	21	M	"	U. States	"	
B. Horton	30	M	Farmer	England	"	
B. Haynes	27	M	"	"	"	
Robt. Wood	22	M	"	"	"	

Names of passengers	Age	Sex	Occupation	Country to which they belong	Country of which they intend becoming inhabitants	Ship or vessel with the name of the master or commander
NEW YORK						
Q. E. April 1, 1822						
Thos. J. Mills	25	M	Glass blower	England	U. States	
John Murphy	25	M	Farmer	"	"	
John Ross	40	M	"	"	"	
Wm. Pope	30	M	"	"	"	
Samuel Sack	35	M	Farmer	G. Britain	U. States	
Saml. Iver •	31	M	"	"	"	
Mrs. Ross & 4 ch.	25	F		"	"	
Robt. Henry	35	M	Mariner	U. States	"	Brig Aginora. Stanley
Lyman Nichols	14	M	"	"	"	
F. Files	25	M	Merchant	Jaqumel	Hayti	Brig Re-Union. Douglass.
L. Boironnet	27	M	"	"	"	
Jno. H. Dickson	30	M	"	U. States	U. States	Brig Jas. Murdoch. Fortescue.
James Morris	28	M	"	· Ireland	"	Brig Decatur. Brownell.
A. U. Searle	28	M	"	England	"	
Joseph Lasalle	34	M	"	Germany	"	Ship Otho. Gifford.
Peter Lunsan	45	M	"	"	"	
Louis Frugeser •	23	M	"	France	"	
John Martin	35	M	"	U. States	"	Ship Hope. Shippen.
Felix Amites •	53	M	"	Sardinia	"	Brig Exchange. Jenkins.
A. Cheneletti •	50	M	"	U. States	"	
Jno. Cossel	25	M	Farmer	Genoa	"	
C. G. Carvagal	25	M	Merchant	Spain	Spain	Brig Prince Edwd. Sears.
E. S. Yaselan	25	M	"	"	"	
C. Roderego	27	M	"	"	"	
A. Bragas	25	M	"	"	"	
Joseph Dunit	40	M	"	U. States	U. States	
John Perry	18	M	"	"	"	
G. Jacobus	22	M	"	"	"	
Francis Anna	30	M	"	"	"	
L. Rebala	40	M	"	Italy	"	Sch. Patty & Sally. Stennan.
C. Smith	22	M	"	U. States	"	Ship Liverpool Packet. Riding.
John Lamount	42	M	"	France	"	Brig Fame. Clark.
H. "	34	M	"	"	"	
W. Kimball	27	M	Mariner	U. States	"	
John Carr	28	M	Merchant	England	"	Ship Charlotte. Appleton.
John Brown	38	M	Cooper	"	"	
Mrs. " & 2 ch.	30	F		"	"	
Wm. Blusk	20	M	Clerk	"	"	
Wm. Wilson	32	M	Merchant	U. States	"	
Mary Geary & 2 ch.	30	F		Ireland	"	Sch. Enterprise. Shaw.
Ellen Blake & 4 ch.	35	F		"	"	
Ann Swift & ch.	30	F		"	"	
Margt. Graham & 3 ch.	40	F		"	"	
Pat. Flannary	22	M	Labourer	"	"	

Names of passengers	Age	Sex	Occupation	Country to which they belong	Country of which they intend becoming inhabitants	Ship or vessel with the name of the master or commander
NEW YORK						
Q. E. April 1, 1822						
Saml. Simpson	21	M	Shoemaker	Ireland	U. States	
Chas. Conway	20	M	Labourer	"	"	
Michael Kent	25	M	"	"	"	
Isaac Ludd & child	26	M	"	"	"	
Sarah Massey & child	29	F		England	"	Ship Emulous. Selvin.
Joseph Prosser	21	M	Farmer	"	"	
Wm. Greben	30	M	Labourer	"	"	
Simon Fowler & 7 ch.	38	M	Farmer	"	"	
Mary "	25	F		"	"	
John Kemp	31	M	Tailor	"	"	
Ann Lilly & child	28	F		"	"	
Richd. Culling	24	M	Farmer	"	"	
Mary "	20	F		"	"	
Thomas "	20	M	Carpenter	"	"	
John Holmes	36	M	Farmer	"	"	
Jno. Jackson	35	M	Carpenter	"	"	
Wm. Wright	35	M	Farmer	"	"	
Mary " & child	26	F		"	"	
James Hamilton	30	M	Merchant	Scotland	"	Brig Ossian. Black.
Andw. "	24	M	"	"	"	
Jas. Kerr	18	M	Clerk	"	"	
Robt. Ferguson	30	M	Merchant	"	"	
Fredk. Bower	26	M	Chemist	U. States	"	Ship Fredk. Davis.
M. Lavelle & child	30	F	Lady	France	"	Sch. Exchange. White.
Wm. M. Power	50	M	Soldier	Ireland	"	
James W. Ripley	30	M	"	"	"	
E. Montague	23	M	Physician	"	"	
Asa Killpatrick	31	M	Mariner	"	"	
Benj. Lord	26	M	Merchant	U. States	"	
Mrs. "	20	F		"	"	
A. Zimmerman	19	M	Merchant	Germany	"	Brig Ohio. Carman.
Robt. Ross	23	M	"	England	"	Sch. Sandford Wm. Chase.
W. Hogan	28	M	"	Ireland	"	
Wm. B. Boardman	25	M	"	U. States	"	Sch. Rambler. Sage.
John Peshaw	36	M		"	"	Ship Hercules. Gardiner.
Martin Moult	33	M	Merchant	"	"	
George Latter	27	M	"	"	"	
Sarah "	26	F		"	"	
John Holmes	30	M	Labourer	"	"	
Saml. Lord	62	M	Farmer	"	"	
Saml. " Jn.	21	M	"	"	"	
Wm. Taylor	24	M	Prof. of Music	"	"	
A. Painter	25	M	Gent.	"	"	
Thomas Holines	25	M	Merchant	"	"	Sch. Duclett. Williams.

Names of passengers	Age	Sex	Occupation	Country to which they belong	Country of which they intend becoming inhabitants	Ship or vessel with the name of the master or commander
NEW YORK						
Q. E. April 1, 1822						
James L. Mountindwert	29	M	Merchant	U. States	U. States	
Robert Pack	27	M	Mechanic	"	"	
James Swan	22	M	Hatter	"	"	
James "	28	M	"	"	"	
Charles Chinn	35	M	Mariner	"	"	Brig Robt. Read. Smith.
Fredk. Straw	27	M	"	"	"	
J. H. Eldridge	25	M	"	"	"	
Joseph Pendreas	29	M	Merchant	Havana	Havana	
Peter Quintava	22	M	"	"	"	
Francis Manns	23	M	"	"	"	
James Riley	26	M	"	U. States	U. States	Brig Radius. Granger.
Joshua Walker	31	M	"	"	"	
John Moor	40	M	"	"	"	
George Murray	23	M	"	"	"	Brig Helen. Patterson.
Robert Shaw	21	M	"	"	"	
John Crozier	24	M	Farmer	Ireland	"	
Phebe "	26	F	Spinster	"	"	
H. Gillespie	26	M	Farmer	"	"	
James Green	25	M	"	"	"	
Nancy " & ch.	22	F		"	"	
I. I. Himley	26	M	Merchant	U. States	"	Ship Randl. Stenhaver.
H. B. "	22	M	"	"	"	
R. Clessy	66	M	"	"	"	
H. Pallet	23	M	"	"		
Charles Hughes	30	M	"	England	"	Ship Panther. Eldridge.
Henry J. Sharp	25	M	"	"	"	
Thos. Tomlinson	40	M	Farmer	"	"	
Saml. Fletcher	25	M	"	"	"	
Robt. Fletcher	25	M	"	"	"	
Robt. Craven	23	M	"	"	"	
Joseph Crawsha	40	M	"	"	"	
Thomas Rostan	28	M	"	"	"	
E. B. Squires	38	M	Gent.	G. Britain	"	Ship Wm. Penn. Hamilton.
Wm. Strickland	36	M	Architect	U. States	"	
Jno. B. Horsford	32	M	Physician	"	"	
John Coates	40	M	Shop keeper	G. Britain	"	Ship Martha. Gifford.
Ann "	35	F		"	"	
Philip McCardle	20	M	Labourer	"	"	
Peter Regrart *	64	M	Merchant	U. States	"	Brig Ann Maria. Leemming.
P. Peabody	30	M	"	"	"	
Wm. Darrach	24	M	Physician	"	"	Ship Albion. Williams.
Edwd. Holbrook	25	M	"	"	"	
F. S. Waldberg	27	M	Merchant	Denmark	"	
S. Maxwell	26	M	Mariner	U. States	"	

Names of passengers	Age	Sex	Occupation	Country to which they belong	Country of which they intend becoming inhabitants	Ship or vessel with the name of the master or commander
NEW YORK						
Q. E. April 1, 1822						
Danl. Armstrong	25	M	Mariner	U. States	U. States	
Janet Pierson & 3 ch.	36	F		England	"	
M. Debroux	30	M	Merchant	France	"	Sloop Plato. Smith.
P. Schuran	22	M	"	Germany	"	Ship Protection. Tyson.
R. R. Coates	21	M	"	U. States	"	Ship Govr. Griswold. Snow.
N. G. Ingraham	34	M	"	"	"	Ship Manhattan. Crocker.
Matthew Woodhead	25	M	"	"	"	
Matthew Wragg	24	M	"	"	"	
Jon. R. Winn	36	M	Mariner	"	"	Ship Virginia. Newman.
Jacob Cobert	40	M	Merchant	"	"	Ship Beaver. Jennings.
O. Huse	26	M	Physician	"	"	Brig Hannah. Mason.
John Brick	30	M	Officer	"	"	
Joseph Williams	25	M	"	"	"	Brig Buck. Hutchinson.
P. Sidney	28	M	Tailor	"	"	
Jerry Vernick	30	M	Mariner	"	"	
John Lupton	48	M	Merchant	England	"	Ship Martha. Baslow.
Jane " & 2 ch.	25	M		"	"	
W. J. Hughes	37	M		"	"	
Wm. Morrison	24	M		Scotland	"	
Reuben Brinson	24	M	Mason	U. States	"	Brig Planter. Pratt.
Joshua Thruitt	29	M	Merchant	England	Buenos Ayres	Brig Perseverance. Shaw.
Wm. Gillman	23	M	"	"	"	
Jno. W. Rathine	38	M	Planter	St. Croix	St. Croix	Ship S. C. Packet. Cartwright.
Edwd. Codwise	24	M	Clerk	U. States	U. States	
M. Nagel	28	M	Farmer	Germany	"	Brig Anna Dorothea. Hardez.
James Duprey	40	M	Gent.	France	"	Sloop Wave. Harper.
Joshua Rathbone	53	M	Mariner	U. States	"	Brig Pelham. McIntire.
Isaac Citchen	25	M	Merchant	"	"	Sch. Nancy. Crowell.
Benj. Chandler	45	M	"	"	"	
Aaron Foot	35	M	"	"	"	
Isaac Holmes	30	M	"	"	"	Brig Yamacraw. Bates.
G. R. G. Hill	24	M	Clergyman	Jamaica	Jamaica	Brig Peruvian. Hall
T. L. Page	42	M	Merchant	U. States	U. States	
Reuben Eldridge	27	M	Mariner	"	"	
Saml. Page	28	M	"	"	"	
Mr. L. Feder	27	M	Clergyman	England	"	Ship Robt. Edwd. Sherborne.
Mr. Gibson	27	M	Merchant	"	"	
Mr. Macks	65	M	Farmer	"	"	
D. Hart	40	M	Physician	"	"	
Mr. Foster	25	M	Merchant	"	"	
Mr. Nicholas	40	M	Carpenter	U. States	"	
A. Mezer *	45	M	Merchant	France	"	
C. Martin	30	M	"	"	"	
Thomas Bell	26	M	"	England	"	Sch. Endymion. Hathaway.

Names of passengers	Age	Sex	Occupation	Country to which they belong	Country of which they intend becoming inhabitants	Ship or vessel with the name of the master or commander
NEW YORK **Q. E. April 1, 1822**						
John Lewis	22	M		U. States	U. States	
Saml. Groves	30	M	Mariner	"	"	Sloop Income. Brown.
B. Boldora	47	M	"	Spain	"	
G. Sullivan	30	M	Merchant	U. States	"	
Stephen Collins	35	M	Mariner	"	"	
Ann Murray & 6 ch.	41	F		England	"	Ship Radius. Deland.
Thomas Puling	32	M		"	"	
Ann " & 4 ch.	25	F		"	"	
Joseph Sutcliff	32	M	Merchant	"	"	
Alexr. Barton	35	M	"	U. States	"	Ship Alexr. Taylor.
A. F. De Casta	48	M	Portuguese Legation	Portugal	Portugal	
Charles "	18	M	"	"	"	
Jose Habier •	24	M	Merchant	"	"	
B. Ballott	23	M	"	"	"	
Ebenr. Meacon & ch.	45	M	Mariner	U. States	"	Brig Perseverance. Bray
Wm. Cacken Jr.	25	M	Carver & Guilder	England	"	Ship Cadmus. Whitlock.
P. Millan	22	M	Dealer	Ireland	"	
Wm. Dillon	22	M	Mason	"	"	
Wm. Prinle •	24	M	Farmer	Scotland	"	
David Ray	26	M	Farmer	"		
Gilbert Miller	35	M	Mechanic	U. States	"	Brig Despatch. Wrann.
Stephen West	23	M	Mariner	"	"	
Richd. Graves	63	M	Admiral	England	America	Ship Liverpool Packet. Coffin.
Arthur Lupton	39	M	Merchant	"	"	
P. I. Becar & child	27	M	"	France	"	
John Passware	32	M	"	"	"	
Charles Reade	50	M	"	U. States	"	Sch. Andw. Jackson. Gold.
Charles " Jn.	26	M	"	"	"	
Francis Sawyer	22	M	Pilot	"	"	
John Morrison	26	M	Mechanic	"	"	Brig Hippomanes. Bourne.
James L. Foote	33	M	Mariner	"	"	Brig Abigail. Satcomb.
A. M. Arcost	44	M	Merchant	Spain	"	Sch. Huntress. Morgan.
Geo. Pride	21	M	"	U. States	"	
Jno. Ganchill & child	42	M	"	"	"	
S. Smith	45	M	"	"	"	Brig Jno. Lindon. Barber.
L. Ruggles	45	M	"	"	"	
P. Willin	33	M	Physician	Germany	"	
P. Moran	20	M		N. Orleans	"	
S. Roney	28	M	Merchant	St. Domingo	"	
Jas. Renworthy Jr.	28	M	"	G. Britain	G. Britain	Ship Jno. Cropper. Boune.
Saml. Hall	29	M	Teacher	"	U. States	
Esther "	22	F		"	"	

Names of passengers	Age	Sex	Occupation	Country to which they belong	Country of which they intend becoming inhabitants	Ship or vessel with the name of the master or commander
NEW YORK Q. E. April 1, 1822						
Thomas Barnwell	26	M	Farmer	G. Britain	U. States	
V. Cropper	22	M	Joiner	Ireland	"	
Arthur Johnson	44	M	Farmer	"	"	
F. Brown	44	M	Grocer	"	"	
Francis Sherman	30	M	Gent.	Scotland	"	
Thomas Martin	40	M	Merchant	U. States	U. States	Sch. Emerald. Bradford.
M. R. D. Friters	22	M	"	"	"	
Elisha Wills	45	M	"	"	"	Sch. Morning Star. Manta.
John E. Wadsworth	25	M	"	"	"	Ship Pacific. Hood.
Geo. A. Owen	22	M	"	"	"	
David Finch	25	M	"	"	"	
PHILADELPHIA Q. E. April 1, 1822						
V. A. Silva	30	M	Merchant	Portugal	Madeira	Brig Spartan. Chapman.
Julius "	21	M	"	"	"	
John Halberstadt & ch.	28	M	"	U. States	U. States	Sch. Favourite. Rogers.
Isaac Joseph	50	M	Tobacconist	England	"	Sch. Telegraph. Blanchard.
Rebecca " & 2 ch.	44	F		"	"	
John Solomon	31	M		"	"	
F. Fox	42	M	Captain	U. States	"	Sch. Bellemore. Rea.
R. Sandiford	68	M	Coachmaker	"	"	Ship Electra. Robinson.
U. "	19	M	Printer	"	"	
C. Trimmer	30	M	Farmer	"	"	
NORFOLK Q. E. April 1, 1822						
Thomas McCarty	21	M	Seaman	"	"	Sch. Larine. Howland.
James Goodall	26	M	"	Scotland	Madeira	Ship Edward. Hayward.
John Freelov/Freetos	25	M	Merchant	Madeira	"	
Thomas Nickworth	23	M	Mariner	U. States	U. States	
Asa Crosby	30	M	Saddler	"	"	Sch. Decatur. Ballard.
J. S. Raphel	30	M	Merchant	"	"	Sch. Alpha. Hall.
D. Owens	21	M	Farmer	England	"	
Jno. N. Cassancave	21	M	Merchant	Spain	Spain	Brig Beaver. Patterson.
Wm. Rudder	35	M	Ship master	U. States	U. States	Sch. Wm. & Frederick. Butler.
Lewis Lathen	16	M	Mariner	"	"	
EDGARTOWN Q. E. April 1, 1822						
Wm. Haff	32	M	Mariner	U. States	U. States	Sch. Only Son. Drew.

Names of passengers	Age	Sex	Occupation	Country to which they belong	Country of which they intend becoming inhabitants	Ship or vessel with the name of the master or commander
EDGARTOWN Q. E. April 1, 1822						
Ebenezer Perkins	35	M	Mariner	U. States	U. States	Sch. Climax. Simpson.
Samuel Collins	28	M	"	"	"	Sch. Julia Ann. Higgins.
Stephen Gibson	21	M	"	"	"	Sch. Catharine. Cheeves.
John F. Powell	18	M	"	"	"	
Edward Foster	25	M	Merchant	Jamaica	Jamaica	Brig Clarissa. Piper.
Alexr. Coffin	32	M	Mariner	U. States	U. States	Ship Boston. Foy.
George Drew	26	M	"	"	"	
George Gibson	22	M	Mariner	"	"	Brig Edward. Clark.
John Brown	20	M	"	"	"	
ST. AUGUSTINE Q. E. April 1, 1822						
I. Sanchez	45	M	Officer	Spain	Florida	Sch. Opposition. Martinly.
Joseph Ximines •	29	M	Pilot	"	"	
Robt. G. Barde	30	M	Merchant	U. States	"	
Barbara Somila	40	F		Spain	Spain	
R. Fuertes	60	M	Apothecary	"	"	
Juan Ravero	60	M	Merchant	"	"	
Joseph Barinque	22	M	Gardner	"	"	
Pedro Rodriques	24	M	Baker	"	"	
John Cavedo	30	M	Clark	Spain	U. States	Brig Soldado. Montu.
B. M. Mestor	40	M		"	Florida	
Manuel Vasquez	35	M		"	"	Sloop Aimable. Herbert.
Felix Fiutis •	40	M		"	"	
Josiah Smith	45	M	Merchant	U. States	"	
Antonio Cala	40	M	"	Spain	"	
Louis La Truche	35	M	"	France	"	Sloop Leopard. Story.
Madame "	25	F		"	"	
John Huertos	35	M	Merchant	Spain	"	
Martin Lopez	40	M	"	"	"	
John P. Salar	30	M	Planter	"	"	
Antonio Mier	42	M	Merchant	"	"	Sch. St. Augustine. Lopez.
M. Pons	30	M	Mariner	"	"	
John Manes	22	M	"	"	"	
M. Andreo	29	M	"	"	"	
SOUTH CAROLINA Q. E. April 1, 1822						
Joseph Urban	30	M	Merchant	France	U. States	Sloop Ann.
Peter Manguld •	32	M	"	Britain	"	
Henry Goldsmith	16	M	"	U. States	"	
John Dash	20	M	"	"	"	
George Phillips	18	M	"	"	"	

Names of passengers	Age	Sex	Occupation	Country to which they belong	Country of which they intend becoming inhabitants	Ship or vessel with the name of the master or commander
SOUTH CAROLINA						
Q. E. April 1, 1822						
John Damon	40	M	Mariner	G. Britain	U. States	Sch. Mary Ann
John Shegog *	28	M	Merchant	"	"	Sch. Comet
B. Gonsally	30	M	"	Spain	"	
John Howard	25	M	Cab. Maker	U. States	"	Sch. Sarah Ann.
John F. Ohl	30	M	Merchant	Hamburgh	"	Brig Philadelphia.
Wm. Phillpot	30	M	"	G. Britain	"	
Wm. C. Kausler	40	M	"	Germany	"	
Mary Ann Magnan	35	F		W. Indies	"	
A. Segar	30	M	Trader	U. States	"	
L. C. Gross	40	M	"	Germany	"	
Charles Meyo	30	M	Mariner	U. State	"	Brig Ann
E. C. Brire	28	M	Merchant	Holland	"	Brig Govr. Brooks.
John Oaks	25	M	"	U. States	"	Sch. Sampson.
Wm. Hall	24	M	Mariner	"	"	
Baldwin M. Halsey	24	M	Merchant	"	"	Sch. Larch.
Thomas Barnett	28	M	Engineer	G. Britain	"	Sch. Eliza & Polly.
Henry Brookins	50	M	Mariner	U. States	"	
John Anthony	25	M	"	"	"	
Roger Harriet & 2 ch.	58	M	Merchant	"	"	Sch. Saml. Smith
Daniel Allen	30	M	Physician	"	"	
S. C. Potter	26	M	Merchant	"	"	
J. Matthews	50	M	"	"	"	Brig Catharine.
A. Forsyth	52	M	Mariner	"	"	
Adam McClaren	45	M	Merchant	G. Britain	"	Ship Jane.
Agnes McClaren & 8 ch.	45	F		G. Britain	"	
George Shaw	28	M	Butcher	"	"	
James Phillips	35	M	"	"	"	
* Thomas Hemmernysway	21	M	Baker	"	"	
Pat. McBriet	27	M	Lawyer	"	"	Ship Bayard.
Mary "	22	F		"	"	
Thomas Lates *	24	M	Farmer	"	"	
James Carroll	28	M	"	"	"	
Edmund Dyer	44	M	"	"	"	
Ann Dyer & 2 ch.	36	F		"	"	
John Duffy	34	M		"	"	
Ellen " & 4 ch.	35	F		"	"	
Wm. Lamb	24	M	Farmer	"	"	
B. Sweeny	20	M	"	"	"	
Michl. Smith	22	M	"	"	"	
Pat. Naughton	27	M	"	"	"	
James Phalen	22	M	"	"	"	
Pat. Lahy	39	M	"	"	"	
Michl. Carroll & ch.	30	M	"	"	"	
Charles Freebody	23	M	"	"	"	Brig Mary.

Names of passengers	Age	Sex	Occupation	Country to which they belong	Country of which they intend becoming inhabitants	Ship or vessel with the name of the master or commander
SOUTH CAROLINA						
Q. E. April 1, 1822						
Stephen Singleton	36	M	Mariner	U. States	U. States	Ship Johanna.
David Canter	42	M	"	"	"	Sch. Content.
Nathan Bacon	43	M	Trader	"	"	Sch. Philander
Hugh Graham	30	M		G. Britain	"	Brig Leopold
Mary "	25	F		"	"	
Edwd. "	25	M	Grocer	"	"	
Alexr. Holstrum	19	M	Clerk	"	"	
James Logan	30	M	Baker	"	"	
Margt. Larman & 2 ch.	28	F		"	"	
P. Macalette	55	M	Mariner	Portugal	"	Brig Neptune's Barge.
Lewis "	28	M	"	"	"	
D. Bolston	25	M	Physician	U. States	"	Ship Lucius
Francis de Castro	44	M	Planter	Spain	"	
G. W. de Roche	40	M	Merchant	France	"	
M. Gouche	19	M	"	"	"	
John Oates	60	M	Publican	U. States	"	
John Urban	28	M	Tailor	France	"	Sch. Bee
Fredk. Monquet	35	M	"	"	"	
Abel Harris	60	M	Merchant	U. States	"	Sch. Roxby.
Saml. Snoddy	20	M	Labourer	G. Britain	"	Sch. Grace.
Jane McIrish	35	F	Spinster	"	"	
Martha "	29	F	"	"	"	
M. Montanden	52	M		France	"	Sch. Comet.
M. Brandt	40	M		"	"	
John Dunscomb	40	M	Merchant	G. Britain	"	Sch. Industry.
C. Baker	50	M	Mariner	"	"	
Joseph Hammond	24	M	Mercht.	"	"	
Thomas Williams	26	M	Broker	"	"	Ship Portia.
L. Monseur	50	M	Trader	France	"	Sch. Mary Ann
---Lyebodiere	28	M	Merchant	"	"	* Died 13th March
Robt. Wallace	63	M	Farmer	G. Britain	"	Ship Jesse & Flora.
Mrs. " & 5 ch.	45	F		"	"	
Joan Robinson	30	M	Farmer	"	"	
Mary " and 2 ch.	28	F		"	"	
Alexr. McPhaul	18	M	"	"	"	
David Brown	25	M	"	"	"	
Wm. Snoddy	68	M	"	"	"	
Mrs. " & 2 ch.	62	F		"	"	
John McKeown	23	M	Farmer	"	"	
John Shaw	35	M	"	"	"	
Mrs. " & ch.	30	F		"	"	
Adam Wallace	24	M		"	"	
John McCormick	36	M		"	"	
Mrs. " & 5 ch.	35	F		"	"	

Names of passengers	Age	Sex	Occupation	Country to which they belong	Country of which they intend becoming inhabitants	Ship or vessel with the name of the master or commander
SOUTH CAROLINA						
Q. E. April 1, 1822						
Thomas McCoy	50	M		G. Britain	U. States	
Mrs. " & 3 ch.	40	F		"	"	
Thomas Hart	27	M	Merchant	U. States	"	Ship Trojan.
Simeon Barthe *	66	M	"	"	"	Sch. Col. Ramsay.
James Lawson	20	M	"	"	"	
Wm. R. Faber	27	M	"	"	"	
A. Gerald	30	M	Mariner	"	"	
John Langenette	27	M	Merchant	Spain	"	
Wm. Eckel	28	M	"	U. States	"	Sch. Jane.
John Dominique	40	M	"	Italy	"	Sch. Sarah Ann.
Robt. McFannen	24	M	Farmer	G. Britain	"	Brig Ann.
James Kinsey	25	M	Farmer	"	"	
Ann "	22	F		"	"	
James McCann	30	M	Farmer	"	"	
Isabella " & child	21	F		"	"	
Saml. McKey	20	M		"	"	
Robert Harret	30	M		"	"	
Mrs. Balker & child	42	F		"	"	Ship Bern.
Henry Dreffren *	35	M		"	"	
Maria " & ch.	20	F		"	"	
Samuel M. Smith	36	M	Trader	U. States	"	Sloop Emily.
Peter "	24	M	"	"	"	
Charles Hawkins	28	M	"	"	"	
Bernard "	26	M	"	"	"	
George Beale	25	M	"	"	"	
Otho Lawrence	38	M		U. States	U. States	Ship Perfect.
Charles Maxwell	25	M	Teacher	G. Britain	"	
Bernard Chinn *	28	M		France	"	Brig Deux Freres.
John J. Appleton	30	M	Secy. of Legation	U. States	"	Brig Standard.
Nicholas Aquilar	26	M	Merchant	"	"	
St. Jago Tabara	29	M	"	Spain	"	
Herman H. Green	23	M	"	U. States	"	
Thomas Munroe	27	M	"	"	"	
Peter Barrett	37	M	Mariner	"	"	
Samuel Stimson	30	M	"	"	"	
John Nolan	27	M		"	"	
Josiah Calliona	35	M		"	"	
Michael Praya	29	M	Mariner	Spain	"	
R. Pease	25	M	"	U. States	"	
Wm. Fox	30	M	"	"	"	
Charles Gidding	19	M	"	"	"	
---Huger	30	M	Physician	"	"	Brig Catharine.
M. Simonton	34	M	Merchant	"	"	

Names of passengers	Age	Sex	Occupation	Country to which they belong	Country of which they in-tend becoming inhabitants	Ship or vessel with the name of the master or commander
SOUTH CAROLINA						
Q. E. April 1, 1822						
---Keith	24	M	Merchant	U. States	U. States	
---Depass	25	M	"	"	"	
---Alexander	28	M	"	"	"	
BALTIMORE						
Q. E. April 1, 1822						
J. D. Daniels	40	M	Mariner	Columbia	Columbia	Brig Fabius.
---Blanchart	32	M	Miller	England	England	
---Wilson	34	M	Farmer	"	"	
Nicholas Bouston	24	M	Mariner	U. States	U. States	Sch. Genl. Jackson.
John Patrick	21	M	Supercargo	"	"	Sch. Congress.
Wm. H. Sinclair	20	M	"	"	"	
F. M. Wells	38	M	Bookbinder	"	"	Sch. Mary Ann.
Geo. G. West	28	M	Supercargo	"	"	
Lewes Zadino	23	M	Gent.	Italy	"	Sch. Iris.
---Walstrum	30	M	Mariner	U. States	"	
R. W. Garritson	33	M	Supercargo	"	"	Brig Canada
Wm. Colesburg	38	M	Physician	"	"	Brig Homer.
Aug. J. Laass	32	M	Farmer	Prussia	"	Ship Graaf Zenzendarff.
Fred. Pestlien	36	M	Carpenter	"	"	
Henry Armstrong	28	M	Gent.	U. States	"	Sch. Dart.
John Beckett	22	M	Barber	"	"	Sch. Nancy.
Stephen Lawson	28	M	Merchant	"	"	Brig Oswego.
Gustavus Harrison	28	M	"	"	"	
Wm. M. Milroy	25	M	Manufactr.	"	"	Sch. William.
John Gainard *	22	M	Tailor	"	"	Brig Harriet.
Edwd. Garraud *	25	M	Confectioner	"	"	
E. Cortes	25	M	Officer	Spain	Temporary	Sch. Segunda.
J. D. Bradkurn	35	M	"	U. States	U. States	
J. J. Bustemante	38	M	Military	Spain	Temporary	
J. M. Allen	30	M	Merchant	"	"	
E. Arne	31	M	"	U. States	U. States	
Juan Regallon	28	M	Servant	Spain	"	
J. R. Reuz	22	M	Soldier	U. States	"	Sch. Lucy.
Wm. Wade	45	M	Mariner	"	"	Sch. Dick.
Saml. Winchester	22	M	"	"	"	
James Ryan	36	M	Farmer	England	"	Brig True Blue.
Mary " & 4 ch.	33	F		"	"	
John Maynard	26	M	Farmer	"	"	
Gabriel "	24	M	"	"	"	
Daniel Jennings	35	M	"	"	"	
Benj. Blanchard	32	M	"	"	"	
John Morton	33	M	Tailor	"	"	
Joseph Southward	23	M	Farmer	"	"	

Names of passengers	Age	Sex	Occupation	Country to which they belong	Country of which they intend becoming inhabitants	Ship or vessel with the name of the master or commander
BALTIMORE						
Q. E. April 1, 1822						
John Magee & 2 ch.	26	M	Weaver	England	U. States	
Griffith Williams	28	M	Merchant	"	"	
John Levin	22	M	Farmer	"	"	
John Wilson	47	M	"	"	"	
Joseph Karrick	50	M	Merchant	U. States	"	Sch. Lapwing.
Wm. King	55	M	"	England	"	Brig Jno. ?
Matthew Kelly	43	M	Mariner	U. States	"	
Thomas W. Bell	28	M	Merchant	"	"	Sch. Who d'thought it.
Joshua P. Clark	34	M	Mariner	"	"	Sch. Carolina.
Wm. G. Bolgiano	22	M	Merchant	"	"	Sch. Arrengeon.
Wm. P. Matthews	25	M	"	"	"	
Wm. Helhause	25	M		"	"	Brig Doris.
James Stanbury	28	M	Merchant	"	"	Sch. Wasp.
James Merchant	22	M	Farmer	England	"	Sch. James Monroe.
John Kelly	35	M	Teacher	Ireland	"	
J. T. Atkinson	36	M		U. States	"	Brig Mary.
B. Nicolan	37	M		Darien	"	
Fred. Donop	40	M	Military	Germany	Temporary	Sch. Adeline.
NEWBERN						
Q. E. April 1, 1822						
Robert M. Harrison	10	M		St. Barts.	U. States	Sch. Industry. Jenkins.
George "	7	M		"	"	
PROVIDENCE						
Q. E. June 30, 1822						
John P. Froding	22	M	Merchant	Sweden	U. States	Ship Patterson. Pearce.
D. S Britto & ch.	40	M	"	Surinam	Surinam	Sch. Leander. McFoy.
James Wood	24	M	"	Honduras	Honduras	Sch. Experiment. Paine.
BRISTOL						
Q. E. June 30, 1822						
Danl. Haywood	27	M	Carpenter	U. States	U. States	Brig Orozimbo. Dearth.
Samuel Goodridge	25	M	Cooper	"	"	Sch. Shepherdess. Frink.
Benj. Howard	31	M	"	"	"	
Basil Crow	55	M	Planter	Louisiana	"	Brig Friendship. Gladding.
H. S. Newcomb	57	M	U. S. Navy	U. States	"	Sch. Zephyr. Barton.
Wm. Savage	42	M	Merchant	"	"	Brig ? Jones.
Charles Mitchell	35	M	"	Prussia	"	
H. Nolt	35	M	Merchant	Germany	"	
G. S. Dominberg	32	M	"	"	"	

Names of passengers	Age	Sex	Occupation	Country to which they belong	Country of which they intend becoming inhabitants	Ship or vessel with the name of the master or commander
BRISTOL Q. E. June 30, 1822						
J. W. Mitchell	37	M	Merchant	England	U. States	
Thomas Hanson	31	M	"	U. States	"	
NEWPORT Q. E. June 30, 1822						
Charles Freebody	27	M	Mechanic	"	"	Brig John. Burdick.
RICHMOND Q. E. June 30, 1822						
John Bailey	45	M	Merchant	U. States	U. States	Ship Comet.
Wm. Brown	22	M	"	"	"	
---Parker	40	M	"	England	"	
ALEXANDRIA Q. E. June 30, 1822						
Samuel B. Harper	22	M	Merchant	U. States	U. States	Sch. Dash. Cunningham.
Ebenezer Bishop	29	M	Mechanic	"	"	
Joshua Yeaton	30	M	Merchant	Bermuda	"	Brig Columbia. Marbury.
J. C. P. Eaton	26	M	Physician	"	"	
PLYMOUTH Q. E. June 30, 1822						
John Lockhert	28	M	Merchant	Nova Scotia	Nova Scotia	Sch. Albion. Hall.
John Bull	27	M	Weaver	"	"	
Joseph Rice	30	M	"	Ireland	U. States	
James Coleman	26	M	Mechanic	Nova Scotia	"	
John McDonnell	23	M	"	Scotland	"	
Peter Hogg	24	M	"	Ireland	"	
Ellen Fannell & 3 ch.	25	F		N. Scotia	"	
Joseph "	22	M	Mariner	Ireland	"	
Michael Wall	23	M	Labourer	"	"	
Patrick Ennis	30	M	"	"	"	
Michael Kelly	27	M	"	"	"	
Pat. Sullivan	19	M	"	"	"	
John Bradley	26	M	"	"	"	
Patrick Orman	22	M	"	"	"	
Dennis Sweeny	26	M	"	"	"	
Miles "	30	M	"	"	"	
Daniel " & ch.	23	M	"	"	"	
Thomas Williams	35	M	Farmer	England	"	Sch. Morning Star Faller.

Names of passengers	Age	Sex	Occupation	Country to which they belong	Country of which they intend becoming inhabitants	Ship or vessel with the name of the master or commander
PLYMOUTH Cont. Q. E. June 30, 1822						
Cornelius O'Brien & ch.	43	M	Cordwainer	Ireland	U. States	
NEWBURYPORT Q. E. June 30, 1822						
Thomas Hall	43	M	Mariner	U. States	U. States	Vessel not mentioned.
Wm. Nichols	21	M	Merchant	"	"	
John M. Bossieux	42	M	Teacher	France	"	
Mrs. " & 2 ch.	27	F		"	"	
BOSTON Q. E. June 30, 1822						
Jose Adela	30	M	Physician	Lima	Peru	Brig Olive. Lunt.
Jose Mayo	32	M	"	"	"	
James Haskell	40	M	Ship master	U. States	U. States	
W. Wernchwolman	18	M	Merchant	Sweden	"	Ship Ariadne. Gytt.
W. C. Ward	41	M	Farmer	Ireland	"	Brig Flora. Smith.
Mary C. Ward & 2 ch.	38	F		"	"	
Thomas Conyn	24	M	Farmer	"	"	
Hugh Collins	22	M	"	"	"	
John Russell	34	M	"	"	"	
Mrs. " & child	30	F		"	"	
Martin Hough	27	M	Farmer	Ireland	U. States	
Bridget Carol	22	F	Servant	"	"	
Mary Kennedy	21	F	"	"	"	
Honora Vear	21	F	"	"	"	
Dennis O'Brien	35	M	Labourer	"	"	
Michael Bolin	24	M	"	"	"	
John Adams	68	M	Farmer	"	"	
L. "	17	M	"	. "	"	
R. Smith	22	M	"	"	"	
C. " & ch.	22	F		"	"	
Mary Johnston	20	F	Servant	*	"	
Lewis Auriane	40	M	Farmer	France	"	Brig Albert. Robertson.
Robert Harris	45	M	Physician	U. States	"	Sch. Atlantic. Richardson.
Richd. Hancott	28	M	Planter	W. Indies	"	
A. V. Macuin	25	M	Merchant	Portugal	"	Ship Deborah. Fleming.
George Lucas	19	M	Mariner	U. States	"	Brig Jane. Bishop.
Thomas Bennett	30	M	"	"	"	
Mary Gulliver	23	F	Mantua mkr.	Ireland	"	Sch. Enterprize. Waters.
John Rasander	32	M	Mariner	Switzerland	"	
Joseph West	30	M	Baker	England	"	Ship Alert. Hutchinson.
John Greene	20	M	"	"	"	

Names of passengers	Age	Sex	Occupation	Country to which they belong	Country of which they intend becoming inhabitants	Ship or vessel with the name of the master or commander
BOSTON Cont.						
Q. E. June 30, 1822						
M. Mackaroy	19	M	Weaver	Ireland	U. States	
Wm. Inglis	21	M	Farmer	"	"	
Hugh Oglan	22	M	Weaver	"	"	
Saml. Johnson	29	M	Merchant	U. States	"	Sch. Ann. Bury
Charles Cunningham	30	M	"	"	"	Brig Wave. Norton.
Mrs. "	23	F		"	"	
Chas. W. Darby	26	M	Merchant	"	"	
Mrs. " & 3 ch.	25	F		"	"	
Nancy Hicks	43	F	Servant	"	"	
Mary Ward	23	M	"	"	"	
Sally Cannal	20	M	"	"	"	
Geo. M. Goulart	40	M		"	"	
Antonio Pereira	22	M		"	"	
James Perkins	30	M	Weaver	Scotland	"	Sch. Three Brothers. Young
Joseph Thompson	25	M	"	"	"	
Eliz. Reed & 3 ch.	43	F		"	"	
Eliz. Dixon & 2 ch.	29	F		"	"	
E. Noland	24	M	Tailor	N. Scotia	"	Sch. Dollar. Mayo.
Wm. Collins	23	M	Shoemaker	"	"	
Wm. Brophy	26	M	Pedlar	"	"	
Mrs. " & 2 ch.	25	F		"	"	
Kitty Noland	24	F		"	"	
John Coleman	22	M	Carpenter	"	"	
Mrs. Tonahoe *& 3 ch.	36	F		"	"	
John McDant	23	M	Shoemaker	Ireland	"	
Mrs. McFail & 2 ch.	20	F		"	"	
Thomas Buns	30	M	Mechanic	N. Scotia	N. Scotia	Sch. Margaret. Bradford.
John Manly	33	M	"	"	"	
Joseph Budon & 6 ch.	39	M	Cooper	"		Sch. Caroline. Susbury.
Thomas Nelson	30	M	Shoemaker	Ireland	U. States	
Mrs. Nelson & 2 ch.	25	F		"	"	
A. Pickette	40	M	Confectioner	Genoa	"	Brig Forester. Sade
Edward Allen	21	M	Merchant	U. States	"	Sch. Plato. Treadwell.
W. H. Gaines	34	M	Mariner	"	"	Sch. Carpenter. Harding.
T. L. Tinman	37	M	Mariner	"	"	
W. Ryan	14	M	"	"	"	
Joseph Major	30	M	Manufactr.	Ireland	"	Sch. Stork. Bray.
Mary " & 3 ch.	27	F		"	"	
J. F. Page	22	M	Turner	U. States	"	Brig Venus. Atwood.
Phil. Taylor	22	M	Merchant	"	"	Brig Cyprus. Dickson.
Christopher Salimus	29	M	Gent.	Sicily	Sicily	
Thomas Boggs & ch.	32	M		Halifax	Halifax	Sch. Billow. Parker.
A. G. Boggs	22	M		"	"	
W. Runnacks	25	M	Officer	"	"	
John Seaton	25	M	Labourer	Ireland	U. States	

Names of passengers	Age	Sex	Occupation	Country to which they belong	Country of which they intend becoming inhabitants	Ship or vessel with the name of the master or commander
BOSTON Cont.						
Q. E. June 30, 1822						
Edwd. Hayley	18	M	Labourer	Ireland	U. States	
Michael Bowland	30	M	"	"	"	
M. Cunningham	22	M	"	"	"	
David Ruffle	36	M	"	"	"	
Robt. Griffin	23	M	"	"	"	
John Blanch	26	M	"	"	"	
Mary "	21	F		"	"	
Eliz. Jervis	36	F		"	"	
Abigl. McLeland	24	F		"	"	
Alexander Caldwell	32	M	Merchant	U. States	"	Brig Caspian. Guyer
John Moore	29	M	Mariner	"	"	Ship Coral. Treadwell.
Isaiah Randall	32	M	Carpenter	N. Scotia	Canada	Sch. Enterprise. Mater.
Mrs. " & 4 ch.	30	F		"	"	
N. D. Hutton	23	M		"	"	
M. "	20	F		"	"	
W. Bray	32	M	Mariner	Lubec ?	"	
Thos. Tenley	32	M	"	Halifax	U. States	
Danl. Darick	29	M	"	"	"	
Mrs. "	24	F		"	"	
R. Seller	38	M	Mariner	"	"	
John Jones	35	M	Shoemaker	"	"	
Sophia Clark	15	F		"	"	
Thomas Draper	24	M	Blacksmith	"	"	
Joseph Blakely	30	M	Merchant	"	"	Govr. Henck.
Mary Trumbull & 2 ch.	22	F	Lady	Canada	Canada	Brig Swiftsure. Baker.
Joseph Siddons & 2 ch.	30	M	Joiner	"	U. States	
Thomas M. Kelly	45	M	Mariner	G. Britain	"	
John Alley	35	M	Merchant	U. States	"	Brig Friends. Wilson.
Mrs "	26	F		"	"	
F. Mitter	25	M	Carpenter	"	"	Brig Washington. Gale.
Joseph Philips	27	M	Mariner	"	"	Sch. Zealous. Baker.
Bartholomew Regarda	28	M		Italy	"	Brig Mary & Eliza. Lufkins.
John Barroca	35	M	Mariner	France	"	Sch. Caravan. Swietser.
Robert Luschnan	22	M	Labourer	Halifax	"	Sch. Cherub. Andrews.
Mrs. " & ch.	23	F		"	"	
John Kehoe	28	M	Labourer	Ireland	"	
C. Harrington	29	M	"	"	"	
John Wheeler	27	M	"	"	"	
Michael Conway	29	M	"	"	"	
Wm. Thompson	22	M	"	"	"	
Michael McGrath	40	M	"	"	"	
Michael Morrison	30	M	"	"	"	
Daniel Sullivan	22	M	"	"	"	
Richd. Haskell	23	M	"	"	"	

Names of passengers	Age	Sex	Occupation	Country to which they belong	Country of which they intend becoming inhabitants	Ship or vessel with the name of the master or commander
BOSTON Cont.						
Q. E. June 30, 1822						
John O'Brien	30	M	Labourer	Ireland	U. States	
Richd. Keating	25	M	"	"	"	
Thomas Steward	23	M	"	"	"	
Robert Brown	25	M	"	"	"	
J. T. Wild	26	M	Merchant	"	"	
Peter Murphy	30	M	Labourer	"	"	
Timothy Barrington	30	M	"	"	"	
Michl. Butler	29	M	"	"	"	
Michl. Carver	40	M	"	"	"	
John Miller	30	M	"	"	"	
Matthew Colcorthy	26	M	Shoe maker	"	"	
John Mills	21	M	Baker	England	"	
Thomas Quigly	25	M	Labourer	Ireland	"	
H. Carter	30	M	"	"	"	
Matthias Cusha	33	M	Merchant	Madeira	Madeira	Brig Shanmel. Luce.
P. Burke	21	M	"	Sicily	U. States	Brig Aurora. Warner
Jacob Lindly	24	M	Carpenter	U. States	"	Brig Hope & Polly. Vaughan.
Ebenr. Lee	21	M	"	"	"	
James Usher	34	M	Merchant	"	"	
Nicholas L. Dana	25	M	"	"	"	Sch. Active. Drummond.
B. Ward	21	M	"	G. Britain	"	
Maria Ward	18	F	Lady	"	"	
Alex. Ross	60	M	Carpenter	U. States	"	Brig Leo. Green.
John Barrett	41	M	Ship master	"	"	
Arloff Delahar	32	M	Merchant	Sweden	Sweden	Sch. Greyhound. Peck.
M. D. Sehora	30	M	"	Portugal	Portugal	
Mary Ann Cliffen *	22	F		England	U. States	
Enos Futel	20	M	Carpenter	Portugal	"	
John Jeffrey	63	M	Blacksmith	N. Scotia	Canada	Sch. Enterprise. Morton.
Miss "	60	F		"	"	
John "	40	M	Blacksmitn	"	"	
Mrs. " & 6 ch.	34	F		"	"	
Andw. "	30	M	Blacksmith	"	"	
Miss "	22	F		"	"	
Amos "	18	M	Blacksmith	"	"	
H. Hallam	19	M	"	"	"	
John Ingalls	29	M	"	"	"	
Mrs. Wilby & 4 ch.	62	F		England	England	Ship Mary & Catharine. Pace.
Geo. W. Rogers	22	M	Seaman	U. States	U. States	Brig Howard. Blackner
A. Hughes	32	M	Seaman	"	"	
John Koof	39	M	"	"	"	
John Pollard	12	M	"	"	"	
A. Pollock	57	M	Manufactr.	"	"	Ship Mercury. Nichols.
Henry Smith	35	M	"	"	"	

Names of passengers	Age	Sex	Occupation	Country to which they belong	Country of which they intend becoming inhabitants	Ship or vessel with the name of the master or commander
BOSTON Cont.						
Q. E. June 30, 1822						
Mrs. Smith & 2 ch.	36	F		U. States	U. States	
Stephen Foster	28	M	Mariner	"	"	Sch. Diomide. Snow.
Caval. Jewit	34	M	Gent.	St. Johns	St. Jons	Ship Castlerough. Garrison.
James Burroughs	25	M	Merchant	U. States	U. States	Brig Anson. Gorham.
Louis V. Mansar	19	M	"	France	"	
P. Punchward •	23	M		"	"	Brig Duxburgh. Drew.
M. Stanislaw	22	M		"	"	
John Galbraith	28	M	Slater	Scotland	"	Brig H. More. Heinn.
O. Hughes	26	M	Labourer	Wales	"	
Elizabeth Donald	20	F	Lady	N. Foundland	"	Sch. Alert. Williams.
John McCracken	38	M	Gent.	"	"	
Andw. "	35	M	Joiner	"	"	
Wm. Bancroft	35	M	T. Chandler	N. Scotia	Halifax	
James Newill	30	M	Farmer	"	"	
T. McGrath	23	M	"	"	"	
John Sinter	29	M	"	"	"	
Mary "	22	F		"	"	
James Linch & 3 ch.	50	M	Farmer	"	"	
James Sullivan	30	M	"	"	"	
Thomas "	20	M	"	"	"	
Dennis Harrington	39	M	"	"	"	
Jonathan Chase	32	M	Mariner	U. States	"	Brig Eliza. Bowen.
Wm. Shaw	32	M	Merchant	"	"	
Abraham Cole	56	M	Mariner	"	"	Brig Sarah Maria. Williams.
A. W. Wittimore	30	M	"	"	U. States	Brig Falcon. Merritt.
John Lewis	30	M	"	"	"	
Charles Lawrence	25	M	Merchant	"	"	Ship Mary. Smith.
Edwd. Fitzgerald	29	M	Currier	Ireland	"	Sch. Hero. Burr.
H. N. Pollard	22	M	Jeweller	U. States	"	
Wm. Pettigrew	21	M	Baker	"	"	
Jas. McGrath	30	M	Trader	Ireland	"	
Geo. W. Tiffin	25	M	"	U. States	"	
Thos. Cushing	24	M	"	"	"	
Lorenzo Draper	31	M	Merchant	"	"	Ship London Packet. Tracy.
Wm. C. Hall	35	M	"	"	"	
George Bord	23	M	"	"	"	
Saml. Hammond Jr.	20	M	"	"	"	
Saml. Stickney	31	M	"	"	"	
Susan " & 2 ch.	29	F		"	"	
J. Sherburne & ch.	29	F		"	"	
Sarah Nott	25	F		"	"	
Hugh G. Mann	22	M		Ireland	"	Sch. Favorite. Rogers.
John Neal	24	M	Stone cutter	U. States	"	
Nancy " & 2 ch.	23	F		"	"	

Names of passengers	Age	Sex	Occupation	Country to which they belong	Country of which they intend becoming inhabitants	Ship or vessel with the name of the master or commander
BOSTON Cont.						
Q. E. June 30, 1822						
H. Buckley	22	M	Merchant	England	U. States	Ship Herald. Fox.
James Ward	34	M	"	"	"	
Ephraim Wilcox	40	M	Mariner	U. States	"	
H. J. Williams	21	M	Merchant	"	"	
David Brown	26	M	Farmer	"	"	
M. Rodin	28	M	"	"	"	
Edwd. Robinson	25	M	"	"	"	
Francis Joseph	27	M	Merchant	"	"	
Ab. Duff	28	M	Cooper	"	"	
J. Topliff	21	M	Merchant	"	"	Brig Caroline. Bodfish
John Campbell	35	M	"	"	"	
Stephen Binney	24	M	Mariner	"	"	Brig Confidence. Stevenson.
Wm. Trusty	30	M	Mariner	"	"	
Thomas Bruce	38	M		"	"	Ship Susan. Wallis.
Louis B. Grosvernor	30	M	Merchant	"	"	Ship Champion. Levis.
E. T. Clark	30	M	"	"	"	
Elizabeth Francis	35	F		G. Britain	"	
Maria Collins & 3 ch.	29	F		"	"	
James W. Little	26	M	Manufactr.	"	"	
Charles Allen	25	M	Turner	"	"	
Charles Collins	25	M	Mill wright	"	"	
John Ashmuth	26	M	Fuller	"	"	
John Richmond	30	M	Potter	"	"	
Peter Ruddy	22	M	Labourer	"	"	
J. R. Taylor	35	M	Merchant	U. States	"	
Edwd. Clark	30	M	"	"	"	
George Dolever	35	M	"	"	"	
Silas Lee	17	M	Supercargo	"	"	Sch. Galaxy. Kid.
Jacob Weis	34	M	Merchant	"	"	Brig Fortune. Hatch.
R. T. Hubbard	31	M	Mariner	"	"	
Felix Izmayer	21	M	Gent.	Spain	"	
A. M. Hernandos	21	M	"	"	"	
Caroline Robinson	22	F		"	"	
Isaac W. Courdy	38	M	Mariner	U. States	"	Brig Hornet. Page.
Wm. Lane	29	M	"	"	"	
George Smith	23	M	"	"	"	
Moses Fetyman	38	M	"	"	"	
Abraham Rich	27	M	"	"	"	Ship Mt. Vernon. Howes.
G. Henchman	33	M	"	"	"	Brig Philo. Grindall.
NEW ORLEANS						
Q. E. June 30, 1822						
John Kerr	30	M	Merchant	Scotland	"	Ship Liverpool Packet Ricker.

Names of passengers	Age	Sex	Occupation	Country to which they belong	Country of which they intend becoming inhabitants	Ship or vessel with the name of the master or commander
NEW ORLEANS Cont.						
Q. E. June 30, 1822						
A. D. Whitehead	26	M	Merchant	Scotland	U. States	
Abel Sterns	27	M	"	U. States	"	
John Bernard	25	M	"	Russia	"	
--- Cabance	24	M	"	Spain	"	
Henry Doubretier	23	M	"	France	"	Sch. Louisiana. Mailer.
--- Duval	25	M		"	"	
--- Cole	45	M	Planter	U. States	"	
J. Ganzales	70	F		Spain	"	
---Jaques	37	M		Italy	"	
---Martin	28	M	Planter	U. States	"	
Joseph Arans	40	M	Silversmith	Spain	"	
Fleury Soubercase	37	M	Merchant	U. States	"	Brig Two Friends. Chote.
Francis Calice	37	M	"	Spain	"	
Frederick H. Goodwin	24	M	Supercargo	U. States	"	Sch. Aurora. Baker.
F. L. A. Heuse	32	M	Lawyer	France	"	Brig Plant. Williams.
F. G. Marins	18	M	Clerk	"	"	
A. C. Julius	24	M	Baker	"	"	
Abraham Schoolfield	27	M	Engineer	England	"	Brig Constitution. Dixon.
John Watson	40	M	"	"	"	
John Brock	31	M	Merchant	"	"	Brig William. Hall.
Mad. Paysant & ch.	30	F		France	"	Brig Brothers. Hill.
L. W. Maul	22	M	Clerk	Germany	"	Brig Fortuna. Wassels.
Charles de Bensche	29	M	Gent.	Poland	Poland	Brig Diomide. Harris.
John Dusseau	26	M	Sugar refiner	France	U. States	
Felix Carre	28	M	Merchant	"	"	Sch. Bee. Baron.
S. Amoris	25	M	"	Germany	"	Brig Idris. Evans,
J. Cleding	45	M	Joiner	"	"	
Jeremiah Sullivan	40	M	Merchant	U. States	"	Sch. Geo. Washington.
Leonti	55	M	Merchant	"	"	Brig Phebe. Proctor.
Isoard	28	M	Currier	"	"	
Arnold-- -	26	M	Bricklayer	France	"	
---Jaugon	23	M	Miller	Spain	"	
James Holland	23	M	Engineer	England	"	Ship Braganza. Oberry.
Wm. Hughs *	24	M	"	"	"	
John Simpson	19	M	Baker	"	"	
William Wilkinson	45	M	Merchant	"	"	Brig. Genl. Phipps. Robson.
James Todd	30	M	"	Ireland	"	
John Groves	20	M	"	"	"	
J. Williams	38	M	"	U. States	"	Ship Robt. Fulton. Barnard.
J. Reasques	20	M	"	Cuba	"	
Vincent Rainos	36	M	"	"	"	
Francis Brunetto	44	M	"	U. States	"	Sch. Brisk. Morant.
John B. Passment	26	M	"	"	"	
Philip C. Homan	34	M	Mariner	"	"	

Names of passengers	Age	Sex	Occupation	Country to which they belong	Country of which they intend becoming inhabitants	Ship or vessel with the name of the master or commander
NEW ORLEANS Cont.						
Q. E. June 30, 1822						
Oliver Brown	27	M	Mariner	U. States	U. States	
E. Mandeburn	42	M	Merchant	Spain	"	
Juan Gonzales	17	M	Tailor	"	"	
Antonio Robles	34	M	Merchant	Italy	"	
Mrs. Reynard & ch.	48	F		France	"	Brig Wm & Emeline.
Mrs. Sagory & ch.	30	F		"	"	Ship Nestor. Beamis.
J. Bertrand	25	M	Clerk	"	"	
---Roland	35	M	Gardner	"	"	
Prullard	32	M	Cooper	"	"	
---Martin	24	M	"	"	"	
---Peau	26	M	Farmer	"	"	
--- Duclos	23	M	Hatter	"	"	
Joseph Pecond	28	M	Merchant	"	"	Ship Vermont.
S. "	25	M	Merchant	"	"	
Augusta Baumier	30	M	Trader	"	"	Sch. Little Sally. Quese.
Louis Martin	38	M	Shop keeper	"	"	
Wm. Kinslow	45	M	Farmer	U. States	"	Sloop Only Son. Ellison
Caleb Fellows	50	M	Trader	"	"	Brig Messenger. Bassett.
D. C. Borrow	45	M	Merchant	"	"	
Jesse Andrews	25	M	Mechanic	"	"	
Wm. Moody	27	M	Merchant	"	"	
Daniel Green	47	M	"	"	"	Sch. Cygnet. Kimbal.
Jose O. Beneditos	45	M	Physician	Spain	Spain	Sch. Louisiana. Mailer
Adelaid Champion & child	30	F		U. States	U. States	Sloop Good Hope. Hague.
M. Desbordes & ch.	36	F		"	"	
Daniel Clark	20	M	Merchant	"	"	
Victor Harrel	28	M	Pedlar	"	"	
Francois Borde	35	M	Saddler	"	"	
Peter Pechin •	23	M	Sigar Maker	"	"	
Joseph Grasset	37	M		"	"	
Vincent Perraults	38	M		"	"	
Francois Julien	60	M	Merchant	France	"	Sch. Tartar. Dennett.
--- Jose	25	M	Mariner	"	"	
Henry Wilkinson	15	M		England	"	Brig Isabella. Dugnia.
John Leecock	40	M	Merchant	"	. "	
James Newman	36	M	Mariner	U. States	"	Sch. Two Brothers. Webber.
T. M. Tuski	30	M	Merchant	Holland	"	
P. Luziana	30	M	Shoemaker	"	"	
Edmund Maler/Maden	25	M	Mariner	France	"	
H. J. Marigny	21	M	Tailor	"	"	
Peter Lambert	50	M	Gent.	U. States	"	Brig Fame. Adams.
Madame " & ch.	42	F		"	"	
S. Soumelet	35	M	Gent.	"	"	

Names of passengers	Age	Sex	Occupation	Country to which they belong	Country of which they intend becoming inhabitants	Ship or vessel with the name of the master or commander
NEW ORLEANS Cont.						
Q. E. June 30, 1822						
S. Legard	25	M		U. States	U. States	
W. Wheeler	30	M		"	"	
Sebastian Esleban	60	M	Merchant	"	"	Sch. Minerve. Bayan.
James Morgan	36	M	Mariner	"	"	Brig Belvedere. Lamson.
Thomas Bremell	35	M	Merchant	England	"	
Thomas Davis	20	M	Seaman	"	"	
--- Moore	20	M	Clerk	U. States	"	
-- Mitchen	30	M	Farmer	"	"	
Anderson	38	M	Mariner	"	"	
Mrs. Arsenaux & 4 ch.	50	F		"	"	
L. Delaporte	25	M	Merchant	France	"	Brig Forest. Morgan.
J. G. Hawley	25	M	Trader	Scotland	"	
N. Bezel	38	M	Ship master	U. States	"	
R, Salice	23	M	Merchant	Mexico	"	
F. Belly	23	M	Merchant	"	"	
Wm. Brown	25	M	"	"	"	
Samuel Leamore	28	M	Mariner	"	"	
M. Andre	49	M	Merchant	Spain	"	
B. Treignes	27	M	"	"	"	
P. Treirnges/Treignes?	27	M	"	"	"	
Antonio Mandas	29	M	"	"	"	
P. Garcia	36	M	"	"	"	
Richd. Purse	30	M	"	U. States	"	
Jean Guerin	29	M	Play actor	France	"	Ship Jane. Ferguson.
Joseph Dwyer/Devyer	25	M	Physician	Ireland	"	Ship Flora. Mildrum.
John "	19	M		"	"	
Christopher Jardine	50	M	Labourer	"	"	
H. Findlay	40	M	"	"	"	
Robt. Higgins	31	M	Merchant	England	"	Brig Hotspur. Bragg.
Richard Clague	22	M	Farmer	U. States	"	
Louis Laporte	31	M	Merchant	"	"	Sch. Elizabeth Nartique.
Seth W. Wye	38	M	"	"	"	
P. R. Bertrand	28	M	"	"	"	
Antonio Certiles	38	M	"	France	"	
C. J. St. Clair	32	M	Mariner	U. States	"	
M. Eells	44	M	"	"	"	
Mrs. Vergies & 5 ch.	44	F		"	"	
D. Luba	35	M	Mariner	Spain	"	Sch. Resource. Ritolona.
D. J. Russell	34	M	"	Portugal	"	
J. Marquese	32	M	"	Sweden	"	
A. Pane	36	M	"	France	"	

Names of passengers	Age	Sex	Occupation	Country to which they belong	Country of which they intend becoming inhabitants	Ship or vessel with the name of the master or commander
PORTLAND & FALMOUTH Q. E. June 30, 1822						
Simon Raymond	45	M	Brick maker	U. States	U. States	Brig Echo. Jordan.
Wm. Currey	27	M	Mason	Ireland	"	
Thos. Trask	30	M	Consul U. S. at Surinam	U. States	"	Brig Francis. Preble.
Preston Fosler	33	M	Merchant	"	"	Sloop Liberty. Pollup.
J. Y. Thompson	35	M	Mariner	Scotland	"	
Daniel Brooks	19	M	Mechanic	U. States	"	
Thos. Brundage	39	M	"	"	"	
Samuel Whitcomb	30	M	Merchant	"	"	
Alexr. Law	33	M	Mariner	England	"	Sch. Ospra. Harding.
Oliver Stoddard	35	M	"	U. States	"	
Ezek. Souther	24	M	Mechanic	"	"	Brig Amazon Harward.
Aaron Riley & child	40	M	Planter	W. Indies	"	Brig Susan & Sarah. Robinson.
PORTSMOUTH Q. E. June 30, 1822						
Robert Richie	27	M	Labourer	England	"	Ship John. Taylor.
Alexr. Rees	25	M	"	"	"	
J. Smilie	22	M	"	"	"	
Wm. Peters	30	M	"	"	"	
CHARLESTON Q. E. June 30, 1822						
W. R. Smith	28	M	Merchant	Havana	U. States	Sch. Eliza & Polly.
John Halden	35	M	"	Trinidad	"	Sch. Col. Geo. Armstead.
M. Stevenson	38	M	Carpenter	Germany	"	
Jacon Gilbert	25	M	"	U. States	"	
Sarah "	20	F		"	"	
John W. Trott	40	M	Merchant	England	"	Sch. Betsy & Peggy.
Henry Goldsmith	77	M	"	"	"	
John Norga	45	M	Mariner	Portugal	"	
Antonio Pannell	15	M	"	Spain	"	
H. Eymar	30	M	Shop keeper	"	"	Sch. Comet.
H. Debal	21	M	"	"	"	
Augustus Linguart	30	M	Merchant	Austria	"	Sch. Neptune.
Frances Prioze	32	M	"	"	"	
E. Emenes	60	M		Denmark	"	
John Wurner	23	M	Merchant	U. States	"	Sch. Emeline.
Mrs. "	21	F		"	"	
--- Piene	30	M	Merchant	"	"	
D. Montgomery	40	M	Planter	"	"	

Names of passengers	Age	Sex	Occupation	Country to which they belong	Country of which they intend becoming inhabitants	Ship or vessel with the name of the master or commander
CHARLESTON Cont.						
Q. E. June 30, 1822						
G. W. Giddes	22	M	Lawyer	U. States	U. States	
John Gill	25	M	Planter	"	"	
Manuel Piera	38	M	Mariner	Spain	"	
Fredk. Polles	27	M	"	"	"	
P. Reynal	46	M	Merchant	U. States	"	Brig Commerce.
John Chartran	35	M	Planter	France	"	Sch. Mary.
Louisa " & child	20	F		"	"	
--- Monquoit	35	M		"	"	
Wm. Sullivan	25	M		England	"	
Jose A. Iswoga	26	M	Merchant	Spain	"	Sch. Louisa.
F. Delahanka	25	M	"	"	"	
Benj. Buchanan	45	M	"	Scotland	"	Sch. Jane.
P. J. Lorent	60	M	"	Germany	"	Ship Boston.
H. J. Faber	23	M	"	U. States	"	
Henry Rolando	28	M	"	"	"	Brig Catharine
Joseph Matthews	25	M	"	"	"	
Charles Mugridge	20	M	Blacksmith	Britain	"	Ship Isabella.
Claude Rache	20	M	Sugar baker	"	"	
John Anderson	21	M	"	"	"	
C. Vigue *	18	M	"	"	"	
Henry Shorelts *	24	M	"	"	"	
John Loconro *	22	M	"	"	"	
Wm. Callender	38	M	Merchant	U. States	"	Ship Sally.
Townsend Moore	36	M	"	"	"	Sloop Liberty.
John Coleman	24	M	Watch makr.	"	"	Sch. Fama.
Patrick McClevanty	34	M	Shoe maker	G. Britain	"	
David Mitchell	32	M	Farmer	"	"	Ship Triton.
James I. Lawson	20	M	Merchant	U. States	"	Sch. Sally.
Morgan Jones	52	M	"	"	"	
B. Gonsales	29	M	"	Spain	"	Sch. Eliza & Polly.
J. Cardoza	35	M	Trader	"	".	
James Todd	40	M	Farmer	G. Britain	"	Ship Bayard.
Wm. Stewart	45	M	Mariner	U. States	"	Sch. Comet.
Francis Falio	35	M	Merchant	Spain	"	
Patrick Gilmore	28	M	"	G. Britain	"	
J. A. Barelli	21	M	"	Italy	"	
Lewis Pilalugner	35	M	"	"	"	
N. Rutal & 2 ch.	40	F		France	"	
John Basello	40	M	Trader	"	"	
C. H. Riley	40	M	Merchant	U. States	"	Sch. Bee
D. Canton	40	M	Mariner	"	"	Sch. Mechanic.
P. Munoz	30	M	Traveller	"	"	
John Dill	35	M	Shoemaker	"	"	
Mrs. "	18	F		"	"	

Names of passengers	Age	Sex	Occupation	Country to which they belong	Country of which they intend becoming inhabitants	Ship or vessel with the name of the master or commander
CHARLESTON Cont.						
Q. E. June 30, 1822						
Timothy White	19	M	Planter	U. States	U. States	Sch. Joseph.
C. Pevaso	35	M	Merchant	Spain	"	
John Chaves	22	M	"	"	"	
Francesci Fernandez	28	M	"	"	"	
Francis Mearandez	25	M	"	"	"	
SAVANNAH						
Q. E. June 30, 1822						
James D. Hamilton	30	M	Merchant	England	U. States	Sloop Packet.
James Pennet	23	M	"	"	"	Brig Penelope. Chisholme.
Wm. Hare	60	M	Gent.	U. States	"	Ship L. Packet. Barkiss.
John L. Hopkins	30	M	Lawyer	"	"	Ship Georgia. Varnum.
Wm. Crothers	28	M	Mariner	"	"	Ship Dorset. Dixon.
John Ferguson	17	M	Clerk	Scotland	"	Brig Traveller. Goldie.
John Turner	24	M	Merchant	England	"	Ship Blucher. Potter
Eliza "	19	F		"	"	
E. E. Peterson	21	M	Merchant	Denmark	"	
John Goff	42	M	"	England	"	
Thomas Jones	65	M	Mechanic	"	"	
Wm. "	25	M	"	"	"	
George Oates	28	M	Merchant	"	"	
Thos. "	26	M	"	"	"	
Alex McIver	22	M	"	"	"	
Colin Mackenzie	21	M	"	"	"	Brig Oriel. Ritchie.
Wm. Man	55	M	"	U. States	"	Ship Oglethorpe. Jayon.
John Milburn	34	M	"	England	"	
Gabriel Murray	22	M	"	"	"	
Saml. C. Magowan	36	M	"	Ireland	"	Ship Endeavor. Carter.
John Haughty	20	M	Farmer	"	"	
Jane " & child	25	F		"	"	
Rodk. McLeod	45	M	Merchant	U. States	"	Ship Comet. Boag.
David McIntire	30	M	Gardner	G. Britain	"	
NEWHAVEN						
Q. E. June 30, 1822						
George Watts	45	M	Merchant	G. Britain	U. States	Sch. Lottery. Tyler.
James Gardener	30	M	"	"	"	
Mary Ann Needham	36	M ?		"	"	
Amos Thomas	40	M	Mariner	"	"	
Noah Tuel	39	M	Merchant	U. States	"	
Hannah "	24	F		"	"	

Names of passengers	Age	Sex	Occupation	Country to which they belong	Country of which they intend becoming inhabitants	Ship or vessel with the name of the master or commander
NEW YORK						
Q. E. June 30, 1822						
Ezra W. Waring	24	M	Merchant	U. States	U. States	Sch. Ann Maria. Hunt.
William Wallace	50	M	Planter	"	"	
James F. Uhlhorn	37	M	Merchant	"	"	Brig Ant. Lane.
Harriet " & 5 ch.	30	F		"	"	
Ann Shattuck	27	F		"	"	
Henrietta Overman	22	F		"	"	
Judith Daniel	30	F		"	"	
Sarah Barkman	26	F		G. Britain	"	Brig Albert.
M. Jones & child	52	M		"	"	
Alexr. Ross	26	M	Merchant	"	"	
George McCauley	30	M	"	"	"	
L. De Caudey	26	M	"	Havana	Spain	Ship William. Moffat
Peter Rivers	26	M	"	U. States	U. States	
M. Fontinall	22	M	Gent.	Havana	Spain	
Saml. G. Muson	30	M	Joiner	U. States	U. States	
Geo. Tucker	25	M	Merchant	G. Britain	"	Ship Nestor. Macy.
Andw. Ripanti	25	M	"	Italy	"	
Samuel Crookes	25	M	Stationer	G. Britain	"	Ship Euphrates. Stoddard.
Hetty Hilyer	34	F		U. States	"	Sch. Prospect. Perkins.
Chas, Bissell	45	M	Mariner	"	"	
E. Brunell	28	M	Merchant	France	"	Brig Fair American. Dugan.
Chas. B. Allen	23	M	"	U. States	"	Sch. Dart. Vandine.
J. Sagerdolph	27	M	Carpenter	"	"	
J. W. Brower	31	M	Mariner	"	"	
Jno. R. Latimer	23	M	Merchant	"	"	Ship China ? Dondall.
Wm. C. McCall	26	M	"	"	"	
Joseph E. Whitall	23	M	"	"	"	
C. Van Houtenberg & ch	45	M		"	"	Brig Mattewan. Scribner.
Betsey Stokes	35	F		"	"	
Daniel Coffin	33	M	Merchant	"	"	
James Scott	50	M	Farmer	Scotland	"	Sch. Richmond Packet. Boardman.
Thomas Backus	37	M	Merchant	U. States	"	Ship Prudence. Jenkins.
Edwd. Whiting	40	M	"	"	"	
John Van Clark	44	M	Mariner	"	"	Sch. Craven. Sparrow.
James Welsh	41	M	Merchant	"	"	Ship Frances Henrietta. Dickson.
John Shaw	25	M	Comedian	"	"	Brig. Genl. Jackson. Bidell.
James Lapres	25	M	Merchant	France	"	
B. Bean	27	M	"	"	"	
Francis Platt	57	M	"	England	"	Ship Cortes. De Cost.
James Rangeley	48	M	"	"	"	
Charles Bird	43	M	"	"	"	
Abraham Broadhurst	24	M	"	"	"	
Joseph Gerrard	22	M	"	"	"	
James Lawton	21	M	"	"	"	

Names of passengers	Age	Sex	Occupation	Country to which they belong	Country of which they intend becoming inhabitants	Ship or vessel with the name of the master or commander
NEW YORK Cont.						
Q. E. June 30, 1822						
Jos. R. Panson	33	M	Merchant	U. States	U. States	
George Delins	34	M	"	Germany	"	
Edward Clarke	31	M	"	U. States	"	
Fredk. White	49	M	"	G. Britain	G. Britain	Ship Columbia. Rogers.
Samuel Gordon	18	M	"	"	U. States	
W. "	22	M	"	"	"	
James Fox	25	M	"	"	"	
L. McGillveray	30	M	"	"	"	
James McTavish	32	M	"	"	"	
Thomas Newbold	24	M	"	"	"	
Benj. L. Peters	30	M	"	St. Johns	St. Johns	Sch. Nancy. Crowell.
Peter Hatfield	30	M	"	"	"	
Thomas H. Mason	25	M	"	"	"	
Mrs. Blood & child	28	F		"	"	
Harriet H. Thompson	16	F		"	"	
James Aslo	18	M	Merchant	"	"	
Joseph Hughes	20	M	"	"	"	
Edwd. Fitzpatrick	30	M	Tailor	U. States	U. States	
Wm. Quinn	20	M	"	"	"	
Antonio Fernando	28	M	Merchant	Spain	"	Sch. Ariadne. Swain.
Peter Bashan	35	M	Hairdresser	Italy	"	
Mrs. "	35	F		"	"	
Paul Barnard	30	M		France	"	
Jesse Taylor	28	M		U. States	"	
James Comps	48	M	Merchant	France	"	Ship Maria Theresa. Smith.
John L. Besse	18	M		"	"	
C. F. Gozon	17	M		"	"	
George Western	32	M	Ship master	U. States	"	
James Beard	30	M	Mariner	"	"	
M. Joagrum	35	M	Officer Portuguese Navy	" ?		
D. Gallagher	48	M	Physician	"	"	Brig Emma. Fosdick.
Mrs. "	34	F		"	"	
E. W. Sage	31	M	Merchant	"	"	
J. Smith	56	M	Mariner	"	"	
B. Hannah	24	M	Merchant	"	"	
Thomas Stow	43	M	"	"	"	Brig Orion. Crawford.
R. Castelo	21	M	"	Spain	"	
E. H. Mix	46	M	Mariner	U. States	"	Brig Seneca. Dutch.
S. Serperte & child	40	M	Merchant	Porto Rico	Spain	Sch. New Packet. Rayley.
Julian Mortordean	33	M	Watchmaker	Switzerland	U. States	Sch. Dolphin. Nichols.
Elijah Farington	28	M	"	U. States	"	
Thomas B. Crowell	24	M	Chairmaker	"	"	
Diego Dortole	50	M	Merchant	G. Britain	"	

PASSENGERS WHO ARRIVED IN THE U.S. SEPTEMBER 1821 - DECEMBER 1823

Names of passengers	Age	Sex	Occupation	Country to which they belong	Country of which they intend becoming inhabitants	Ship or vessel with the name of the master or commander
NEW YORK Cont.						
Q. E. June 30, 1822						
Joseph F. Rattenberry	35	M		G. Britain	U. States	Sch. Venus. Mount.
Mrs. "	28	F		"	"	
Thomas Forbes	35	M	Merchant	"	"	
Mary " & 4 ch.	26	F		"	"	
John Stewart	24	M	Merchant	"	"	
Joseph Warrell	22	M	"	"	"	
Jasper Hurston	14	M	"	"	"	
John Rutley	26	M	"	"	"	
Sarah Rutley & child	24	F		"	"	
John Hyland	23	M	Printer	"	"	
Rebecca " & ch.	20	F		"	"	
Elizabeth Moreman & 5 ch.	32	F		"	"	
David Groves	31	M	Farmer	"	"	
Thomas Jones	27	M	Composer	"	"	
John Frevackiss & ch.	38	M	Tailor	"	"	
Joseph Tynan	20	M	Druggist	Ireland	"	
Wm. Williams	28	M	Mechanic	U. States	"	
Mary Green	21	F	Spinster	"	"	
Wm. Fapp	47	M	Farmer	"	"	
James Nash	40	M	"	"	"	
Henry "	25	M	"	"	"	
Alexr. Henderson	48	M	Merchant	Scotland	"	Ship Camillas. Peck.
Wm. K. Kidd	26	M	"	"	"	
Alexr. Nicol	26	M	Clergyman	"	"	
Thomas Baird	30	M	Mariner	"	"	
James Hill	28	M	Farmer	"	"	
George "	30	M	Shoemaker	"	"	
Robt. Ferguson	24	M	"	"	"	
Hugh McLean	40	M	Weaver	"	"	
John McVenar	24	M	Shoemaker	"	"	
Donald "	22	M	"	"	"	
Jane Cunningham & 3 ch.	33	F		"	"	
J. Wilson	24	M	Mariner	"	"	
John P. Jennison	26	M	"	"	"	
F. Tangrena	18	M	Gent.	Spain	U.S.for a time	Brig Lucy Ann. Davis.
F. La Roser	23	M	"	"	"	
J. Balano	18	M	"	"	"	
Alexr. Coldwell	31	M	Capt. Army	G. Britain	G. Britain	Brig Betsey. Donkin.
Wm. Blyth	28	M	Merchant	"	"	
Richd. Radley	42	M	Mason	"	"	
Mrs. "	40	F		"	"	
Daniel Nichols	42	M		"	"	

Names of passengers	Age	Sex	Occupation	Country to which they belong	Country of which they intend becoming inhabitants	Ship or vessel with the name of the master or commander
NEW YORK Cont.						
Q. E. June 30, 1822						
S. Dymake	30	M	Joiner	G Britain	G. Britain	
T. Jenner	40	M	Farmer	"	"	
Ann " & 8 ch.	44	F		"	"	
James Lidfind	25	M	Farmer	"	"	
Ann " & 3 ch.	23	F		"	"	
H. Wilson	30	M	Farmer	"	"	
Francis Cox	29	M	Painter	"	"	
Lewis Moor	22	M	Farmer	Ireland	U. States	Brig Wilson. Britton.
Margt. Brenner & 4 ch.	30	F		"	"	
Morgan Dougharty	22	M	Farmer	"	"	
John Bradbury	29	M	Merchant	England	England	Ship Meteor. Cobb.
James Mornpisson *	27	M	Officer	"	"	
Andw. Porteus	36	M	Merchant	Montreal	Montreal	
S. W. Potter	25	M	"	Scotland	U. States	
Enoch Beaumont	20	M	Manfactr.	G. Britain	"	
George Wilson	28	M	"	"	"	
Wm. Brewer	17	M	Mariner	"	"	
Wm. Reynolds	28	M	Gent.	Ireland	"	Ship Dublin Packet. Newman
Catharine Cassady & ch	40	F		"	"	
James McKean	18	M	Farmer	"	"	
Wm. Bates	20	M	"	"	"	
Philip Kehoe	18	M	Clerk	"	"	
Patrick Liddy	50	M	Farmer	"	"	
Miles McCarter	35	M	"	"	"	
Robt. Barsley	24	M	"	"	"	Ship Merchant. Aymer.
Wm. Garlan	20	M	"	G. Britain	"	
P. Hagarty	28	M	Teacher	"	"	
Hugh Downs	26	M	Farmer	"	"	
James "	18	M	"	"	"	
George Taylor	27	M	"	"	"	
Wm. Dillon	44	M	"	"	"	
John Kain	27	M	"	"	"	
John Hurst	41	M	"	"	"	
J. Brownswent	25	M	Grocer	"	"	
Wm. Whitehead	35	M	Merchant	"	"	Ship Natchez. Cook.
Alexr. P. Gregg	45	M	"	"	"	
Margt. " & 2 ch.	45	F		"	"	
James Livingston	22	M	Farmer	"	"	
Alexr. Dall	30	M	"	"	"	
Helen "	25	F		"	"	
Wm. Johnston	23	M	Tailor	Ireland	"	Sch. Gleaner. Saunders.
Geo. G. Gardiner	37	M	Mariner	U. States	"	Brig Charles. Haskell.
Robt. Andrews	47	M	Merchant	"	"	Ship Stephanea. Burke
Margt. " & 5 ch.	36	F		"	"	

Names of passengers	Age	Sex	Occupation	Country to which they belong	Country of which they intend becoming inhabitants	Ship or vessel with the name of the master or commander
NEW YORK Cont.						
Q. E. June 30, 1822						
Felix La Coste	29	M	Merchant	France	U. States	
Emily　　"	22	F	Chambermd.	"	"	
S. Croix Caumont	44	M	Merchant	"	"	
Louis S. Serrion	35	M	"	"	"	
Paul Dupene	24	M	"	"	"	
John Marshall & ch.	35	M	"	England	"	
Louis Grillet	32	M	"	France	"	
Thomas Morris	25	M	"	U. States	"	
John Renault	42	M	"	France	"	
Edward Low	19	M	"	England	"	
James Morin	50	M	Shoemaker	Ireland	"	Sch. Albion.　Hall.
Sarah Hines & 2 ch.	25	F		"	"	
Lawrence Kehoe	22	M	Merchant	"	"	
John Sheak	35	M	Gardner	Germany	"	Brig Fanny.　Baker.
R. F. Muller	65	M	Merchant	Holland	"	Sch. Eliza Pigott.　Waterman.
C. F. Vogel	53	M	"	"	"	
J. S. Brandon	29	M	"	"	"	
J. B. Jones	26	M	"	U. States	"	
M. Carmichael	28	M		G. Britain	"	Sch. Jas. Monroe.　Lee.
J. Bristed	43	M		"	"	
W. Blackwood	34	M		"	"	
N. Bethune	33	M		"	"	
J. McLaughlin	37	M		"	"	
Jno. E. Smith	44	M		"	"	
Edwd. Holt	36	M	Merchant	"	"	
John Bulger	43	M	Mariner	"	"	
John Haywood	36	M	Merchant	"	"	
David Carne	26	M	"	"	"	Brig Henry Clay.　Fosdick.
Thomas　　"	28	M	"	"	"	
Catherine " & 4 ch.	40	F	Spinster	"	"	
Jane Blair	40	F	"	"	"	
Mary Orr & 2 ch.	34	F	"	"	"	
E. Hunter & 4 ch.	38	F		"	"	
Thomas Reed	19	M	Farmer	"	"	
David Blair	23	M	"	"	"	
John　　"	26	M	"	"	"	
James Clark	39	M	Merchant	N. Scotia	"	Sch. Tantamount.　Allen.
Frances Hunter	35	M	"	"	"	
Thomas Cook	38	M	"	G. Britain	"	Ship Atticus.　Wescott.
John Holmes	19	M	"	"	"	
Wm. Wagstaff	36	M	Farmer	"	"	
S.　　" 　 & ch.	35	F		"	"	
R. S. Worth	25	M		"	"	
Wm. Taylor	25	M		"	"	

PASSENGERS WHO ARRIVED IN THE U.S. SEPTEMBER 1821 - DECEMBER 1823

Names of passengers	Age	Sex	Occupation	Country to which they belong	Country of which they intend becoming inhabitants	Ship or vessel with the name of the master or commander
NEW YORK Cont.						
Q. E. June 30, 1822						
Wm. Allen	26	M		G. Britain	U. States	
Ann " & child	28	F		"	"	
Mary Dunbar	22	F		"	"	
F. Watson	23	M		"	"	
Geo. Stanfield	24	M		"	"	
James "	20	M		"	"	
Robt. Darby	24	M		"	"	
John Bennett & 2 ch.	36	M	Glass maker	"	"	Ship Pierson. Terry
S. Macomb	40	M	Planter	Cuba	Cuba	Brig Romulus. Allen
Wm. H. De Wolf	37	M	Gent.	U. States	U. States	
J. Lovett	40	M	Merchant	"	"	
Wm. Savage	30	M	Carpenter	"	"	
Geo. Pollard	24	M	Merchant	"	"	Ship Ann Maria. Graham.
C. Rodieu	24	M	"	Montreal	Montreal	
James Maury	24	M	"	Liverpool	Liverpool	
J. S. Platt	28	M	"	U. States	U. States	
Joseph Sanders	48	M	Carpenter	"	"	
Thomas Bontes	48	M	Farmer	England	"	
Wm. Bishop	37	M	Tailor	"	"	
Wm. Hutchinson	30	M	"	"	"	
J. Kurnan •	38	M	Farmer	"	"	
Wm. Sewall	46	M	"	"	"	
John Wakes	26	M	"	"	"	
Geo. Cox	32	M	Smith	"	"	
Elizabeth Cox & 2 ch.	32	F		"	"	
Thomas Hanes	43	M	Mason	"	"	
Wm. Egglesfield	44	M	Farmer	"	"	
James Wood	28	M	Engraver	"	"	
John Ealing	26	M		"	"	
Moses H. Morferugo •	40	M	Teacher	Amsterdam	"	Brig Richd. Mead. Barnard.
Mrs. " & 5 ch.	38	F		"	"	
J. Bingham	35	M	Engineer	U. States	"	
Thomas Betts	46	M	Mariner	"	"	Brig New Packet. Chase
Wm. Taylor	30	M	"	"	"	
J. S. Cromony	30	M	Planter	W. Indies	"	Brig Matilda, Kown.
Geo. Reynolds	28	M	Merchant	"	"	
Thos. Deromy	19	M	"	"	"	
Edmund Ray	17	M	"	"	"	
Michl. Denny	30	M	"	G. Britain	"	Ship Orbit. Macy.
John Jones	25	M	"	"	"	
John Mullins	27	M	"	"	"	
D. Arratt	21	M	"	"	"	
Geo. Bennett	23	M	"	"	"	
Joseph Barabet	26	M	Farmer	"	"	

Names of passengers	Age	Sex	Occupation	Country to which they belong	Country of which they intend becoming inhabitants	Ship or vessel with the name of the master or commander
NEW YORK Cont.						
Q. E. June 30, 1822						
John Penny	29	M	Farmer	G. Britain	U. States	
Wm. Parker	40	M	"	"	"	
John Holmes	45	M	"	"	"	
Wm. Williamson	34	M	Merchant	U. States	"	Ship India. Hatch.
J. J. Astor & child	59	M	"	"	"	Ship Cincinnatus. Champlin.
J. Hoffman	40	M	"	"	"	
P. Petinas	31	M	"	"	"	
J. Del Vechio	20	M	"	"	"	
John Bouchette	19	M	Merchant	Canada	"	
Robert Nunns	30	M	"	England	"	
Eleanor " & 5 ch.	24	F		"	"	
Wm. Hanna	53	M	Farmer	"	"	
Jennet " & 8 ch.	51	F		"	"	
Mary Barney & 6 ch.	45	F		"	"	
Jas. Bridger	20	M	Farmer	"	"	
Geo. Parker	20	M		"	"	
John West	50	M		"	"	
Elias Gilbert	56	M		"	"	
Eliz. " & 8 ch.	50	F		"	"	
Geo. Wilcox	30	M		"	"	
Rebecca "	27	F		"	"	
Wm. "	22	M		"	"	
Mary Bishop	28	F		"	"	
R. W. Higgins	30	M	Merchant	Bermuda	"	Sloop Wave. Harker.
John Sate	34	M	Shoemaker	U. States	"	Sch. Patty & Sally. Hinman.
Wm. Batist	38	M	Merchant	"	"	
Wm. Casey or Carey	21	M	"	France	"	Sch. Fair Play. Kimball.
Robt. Kerr	32	M	"	U. States	"	Sch. Jane. Gibbs.
M. " & child	25	F		"	"	
N. Franklin	20	M	Gent.	"	"	
Jacob Curtis	50	M	Mariner	"	"	
L. Fox	35	M	Merchant	"	"	
Andw. Thompson	50	M	"	Scotland	G. Britain	Ship Friends. Choate.
Pat. McAuly	35	M	Clergyman	Ireland	"	
Thomas Farrar	28	M	Farmer	Scotland	"	
Geo. McNelly	26	M	Baker	"	"	
Robt. Ken	28	M	Clerk	"	"	
R. N. J. Sepman *	40	M	Trader	"	"	
Fredk. Platt	28	M	Merchant	U. States	U. States	Brig Magnolia. Root.
J. J. Brown	24	M	Saddler	"	"	
G. Saunders	25	M	Merchant	"	"	
James Yates	33	M	Tailor	G. Britain	"	Ship Wm. Thompson.
Martha " & 5 ch.	30	F		"	"	
John Harris	17	M	Merchant	"	"	

Names of passengers	Age	Sex	Occupation	Country to which they belong	Country of which they intend becoming inhabitants	Ship or vessel with the name of the master or commander
NEW YORK Cont.						
Q. E. June 30, 1822						
Edwd. Thompson	26	M	Mariner	U. States	U. States	Ship Atlantic. Taylor.
S. Sanderson	42	M	"	"	"	
Wm. Rider	46	M	Painter	Ireland	"	
Judith Ewing & 4 ch.	26	F		"	"	Sch. John Dickinson. Baush.
Joseph Cunin	38	M	Physician	"	"	
Danl. Carmichael	55	M	Merchant	U. States	"	
James Irvine	24	M	"	Ireland	"	
Geo. McCann	19	M	Farmer	"	"	
David Crossley	26	M	"	"	"	
Joseph Canning	28	M	"	"	"	
Wm. Black	23	M	Weaver	"	"	
Thomas Kirkpatrick	24	M		"		
Robt. Patterson	28	M	Farmer	"	"	
Ann " & 3 ch.	24	F		"	"	
James Cleland	24	M		"		
John McCherry	20	M	Tailor	"		
Alexr. Thompson	23	M	Weaver	"		
Catharine Steele & ch.	27	F		"		
Robert Shields	28	M	Merchant	"		
Wm. G. Patterson	19	M	"	"		
John Burkett	24	M	Farmer	"		
Thomas Brown	66	M	Merchant	U. States	U. States	Brig Transit. Gillet.
James Victory	42	M	Physician	"	"	Sch. Mona. West.
Mrs. " & 2 ch.	25	F		"	"	
John Shutt	38	M	Farmer	England	"	Ship Comet. Moore.
Ab. Taylor	32	M	"	"	"	
Sarah " & 3 ch.	24	F		"	"	
Robt. Loader	34	M	Farmer	"	"	
Thomas Fowler	27	M	"	"	"	
Ephraim Morris	22	M	"	"	"	
Wm. Morgan	22	M	"	"	"	
David "	21	M	"	"	"	
Richd. Combes	40	M	"	"	"	
Elizabeth " & 5 ch.	32	F		"	"	
Edwd. Landsten	27	M	Saddler	"	"	
Henry Gore	23	M	Planter	"	"	
Alex. Cakery •	21	M	Wood stapler	"	"	
John Middleton	22	M	Cooper	"	"	
Wm. Manning	23	M	Silversmith	"	"	
F. F. Kenny & child	24	M	Merchant	U. States	"	Ship Sally. Gladden.
J. Kittell	34	M	"	"	"	
Thomas Butler & 2 ch.	44	M	Planter	"	"	Ship Robt. Fulton. Holddrige.
Louis Martelly	42	M	Merchant	France	"	
S. McGillivray	38	M	"	U. States	"	

Names of passengers	Age	Sex	Occupation	Country to which they belong	Country of which they intend becoming inhabitants	Ship or vessel with the name of the master or commander
NEW YORK Cont.						
Q. E. June 30, 1822						
Duncan Kennedy	37	M	Merchant	G. Britain	U. States	
Robert Frost	36	M	"	"	"	
Maria "	28	F		"	"	
Thos Bruyers	24	M	Offr. Eng- ineers ?	"	"	
Joseph Raphael	35	M	Farmer	"	"	
Wm. Gooday	21	M	"	"	"	
Charles Atkinson	19	M	"	"	"	
Luke Hinchcliffe	20	M	"	"	"	
Fernando Rhodes	36	M	Merchant	U. States	"	Brig Venus. Ferris.
Robert Morrell	33	M	Physician	"	"	
John Dillet	28	M	Gent.	St Domingo		Brig John. Barber.
John Mallet	26	M		France	"	
Peter Moren	22	M		"	"	
W. J. Johnston	63	M	Merchant	Ireland	"	Brig Abigail. Martin.
S. A. Powers	30	M	"	"	"	
M. Hogan	30	M	"	"	"	
J. Hitchcock	30	M	"	U. States	"	
E. Winterbotham	45	M	"	England	"	
E. Doran	28	M	Farmer	Ireland	"	
J. "	32	M	"	"	"	
James Behan	26	M	"	"	"	
Mrs. "	24	F		"	"	
John Donahoe	26	M	Merchant	"	"	
Patrick Cunningham	26	M	Farmer	"	"	
James Perry	22	M	"	"	"	
John A. Deansfield *	75	M	"	"	"	Brig L. M. Belham. Hatch.
A. S. Buchanan	25	M	"	"	"	
James McCates	32	M	"	"	"	
S. McAllister	20	M	Weaver	"	"	
James Haddock	37	M	Farmer	"	"	
M. Kran	28	M	"	"	"	
John McLaughlin	27	M	"	"	"	
Wm. Haddock	24	M	"	"	"	
Wm. Hamilton	28	M	"	"	"	
John Sinclair	22	M	Baker	Scotland	"	Brig Morning Star. Stevens.
Wm. Jackson	46	M	Labourer	"	"	
John Cross	21	M		"	"	
Charles Killan	25	M		"	"	
W. R. Robinson	26	M		"	"	
James "	19	M		"	"	
Saml. Asser	32	M	Merchant	Hayti	"	Sch. Sarah Ann. Vinson.
F. Lally	35	M	"	"	"	
F. Clark	23	M	"	"	"	

Names of passengers	Age	Sex	Occupation	Country to which they belong	Country of which they intend becoming inhabitants	Ship or vessel with the name of the master or commander
NEW YORK Cont.						
Q. E. June 30, 1822						
Patrick Fletcher	27	M	Farmer	Ireland	U. States	Brig Cuba. Cushing.
Mary "	23	F		"	"	
S. Lolen & 4 ch.	40	M	Farmer	"	"	
Martin Donald	24	M	"	"	"	
E. Casey	30	M	"	"	"	
Mary Casey	25	F		"	"	
John Ray	27	M	Farmer	"	"	
M. Corbett	20	M	"	"	"	
M. Gice •	30	M	"	"	"	
Michael Wiggins	25	M	Farmer	"	"	
Ellen "	20	F		"	"	
Martin Caine	21	M	Farmer	"	"	
Michael Corey	42	M		"	"	
George Sandham	28	M		"	"	
Thomas McCormick	28	M		"	"	
Michael Taraty	25	M		"	"	
John Thompson	27	M		"	"	
Thomas B. Lynch	26	M		"	"	
John Derand	50	M		"	"	
Mary " & 3 ch.	50	F		"	"	
Martin Green & child	30	M		"	"	
J. B. Duffue	38	M	Merchant	France	"	Brig Rapid. Nichols.
Joseph Renault & 3 ch.	58	M	Musician	"	"	Brig Magnet. Thaxter.
P. Petit	37	M	Merchant	U. States	"	Brig Emma. Fosdick.
G. Timmons	37	M	"	"	"	
Wm. A Slocum	38	M	"	"	"	
B. F. Willard	24	M	"	"	"	
C. Madon & 4 ch.	23	M	"	"	"	
P. G. Judson	19	M	"	"	"	Sch. Martha. Townes.
Philip Stagg	20	M	"	"	"	Brig Hippomanes. Bourne.
George Danford	31	M	Counsellor	"	"	Ship S. Carolina. Cartwright.
Wm. H. Vining	28	M	"	"	"	
James Veitch	26	M	Planter	"	"	
George Lyons	42	M	Merchant	England	"	Brig Rebecca & Sally. Thatcher.
Wm. Rae	30	M	Farmer	"	"	Sch. Huldah & Judah. Thomas
M. "	25	M	"	"	"	
Elizabeth Rae & 3 ch.	30	F		"	"	
Samuel Course	21	M		"	"	
Edwd. Reid	37	M	Planter	Jamaica	"	Sch. Indus. Smith.
A. Thorndike	38	M	Merchant	U. States	U. States	Ship Draper. Cary.
P. McSoiley	25	M	Labourer	Ireland	"	Ship Robt. Burns. Coffin.
Ann O'Donnell	66	F	Spinster	"	"	
Mary "	70	F		"	"	
Owen McColgen	20	M	Labourer	"	"	

Names of passengers	Age	Sex	Occupation	Country to which they belong	Country of which they intend becoming inhabitants	Ship or vessel with the name of the master or commander
NEW YORK Cont.						
Q. E. June 30, 1822						
Nancy McColgen	17	F		Ireland	U. States	
Mary Crawford & 2 ch.	36	F		"	"	
Mary Ann Reid & ch.	21	F		"	"	
Henry Moore	20	M	Labourer	"	"	
Smith Osborn	20	M	Merchant	"	"	
Edwd. Fitzsimmons	16	M	Tailor	"	"	
Wm. Holmes	20	M	Merchant	"	"	
Andw. Sommerville	20	M	Coppersmth	"	"	
Matthew Sommerville	20	M	Labourer	"	"	
John Groves	20	M	Shoemaker	"	"	
Robt. Russell	56	M	Farmer	"	"	
M. "	21	M	"	"	"	
Geo. McCauley	65	M	"	"	"	
Jane. "	55	F		"	"	
Joseph "	35	M	"	"	"	
Rebecca "	30	F		"	"	
Susanna "	27	F		"	"	
Mary "	26	F		"	"	
Jane " & 3 ch.	21	F		"	"	
James Lawson	25	M	Merchant	"	"	
Joseph Wiley	28	M		"	"	
Paul "	78	M	Farmer	"	"	
Wm. "	30	M	"	"	"	
Mary Clark & 2 ch.	40	F		"	"	
Robt. Risk	40	M	Grocer	"	"	
M. " & 3 ch.	35	M		"	"	
John Knox	18	M	Clerk	"	"	
John Smith	21	M	Merchant	"	"	
Wm. B. Hart	24	M	Gent.	U. States	"	Ship Panther. Bennett.
B. "	24	M		"	"	
Robt. D. Handyside	32	M	Merchant	G. Britain	"	
James Mauran	30	M	Leather dresser	U. States	"	
B. Daley	30	M	Tailor	G. Britain	"	
Thos. Daley	30	M	"	"	"	
James Fottinghaul	46	M	Farmer	"	"	
Janet " & 5 ch.	40	F		"	"	
Richd. Wells	34	M	Merchant	U. States	"	Brig Aginora. Mauran.
Wm. Copeland	26	M	"	"	"	
Wm. Biander	30	M	"	"	"	
George Mitchell	26	M	"	"	"	
Robt. Ross	35	M	Mason	Scotland	"	Ship Iris. Smith.
Wm. Tabbs	36	M	Merchant	U. States	"	Sch. Augustus. Button.
James Smith	26	M	Grocer	"	"	Brig Sprightly. Canon.

Names of passengers	Age	Sex	Occupation	Country to which they belong	Country of which they intend becoming inhabitants	Ship or vessel with the name of the master or commander
NEW YORK Cont.						
Q. E. June 30, 1822						
Geo. Emsham *	25	M	Weaver	U. States	U. States	
N. Fulson	27	M	Ship master	"	"	Ship Zodiac. Burnes.
Samuel Fox	46	M	Merchant	"	"	
Thomas Pitts	51	M	"	"	"	
Wm. Brewer	38	M	Farmer	G. Britain	"	
Emanuel Wilson	21	M	Collar mkr.	"	"	
Thomas Trout	25	M	Coachman	"	"	
John Paul	22	M	Farmer	"	"	
John Parks	21	M	"	"	"	
Wm. Roberts	27	M	Shoemaker	"	"	
Ch. Hespindale & 4 ch.	37	M	Farmer	G. Britain	"	
Benj. Stokes	35	M		"	"	
Mary " & ch.	41	F		"	"	
John Croft	32	M		"	"	
Wm. Smith	54	M		"	"	
Robt. Jefferson	60	M	Shoemaker	"	"	
Eliz. " & 3 ch.	50	F		"	"	
S. Bolson	21	M	Tailor	"	"	
Thomas Wells	32	M	Farmer	"	"	
Sarah Wood & 6 ch.	38	F		"	"	
Wm. Tayler	28	M	Mechanic	Ireland	"	Sch. Sukey. Haskall.
Mrs. "	28	M ?		"	"	
Samuel Ballard	22	M	Clerk	"	"	
N. Burgger	30	M	Gent.	Sweden	"	Brig Neptune. Hagbey.
C. Lofggert	46	M	"	"	"	
Charles Johnson	22	M	Mariner	England	"	
L. Bulkley	30	M	Merchant	U. States	"	Sch. Haytian. Smith.
E. Meanans	21	M	"	"	"	
Thos. Higham	40	M	"	"	"	Ship Seine. Williams.
C. Kershaw	55	M	"	"	"	
Ann Lamb & 3 ch.	40	F		"	"	
Cornelius Broadway	68	M	Farmer	"	"	
James Clark	27	M	"	"	"	
Frances " & 3 ch.	27	F		"	"	
John Perry	22	M	Farmer	"	"	
John Bartlett	34	M	"	"	"	
Hester " & 5 ch.	30	F		"	"	
Philip Arnold	19	M	Labourer	"	"	
Joseph Jones	24	M	Farmer	"	"	
Eliz. " & 2 ch.	24	F		"	"	
Richd. "	36	M	Tanner	"	"	
John Walsh	28	M	Mechanic	"	"	
Henry Young	36	M	Farmer	"	"	
James Trumble	35	M	Blacksmith	England	"	Sch. Champion. Anderson.

Names of passengers	Age	Sex	Occupation	Country to which they belong	Country of which they intend becoming inhabitants	Ship or vessel with the name of the master or commander
NEW YORK Cont.						
Q. E. June 30, 1822						
Margt. Trumble & 5 ch.	36	F		England	U. States	
John L. Spinolla	38	M	Merchant	Madeira	"	Barque Sarah & Louisa. Colver
M. Known	30	M	Mechanic	Ireland	"	Sch. P. Franscisco. Rierson.
Mrs. "	20	F		"	"	
J. Fowler	28	M	Merchant	U. States	"	
Geo. Blany	26	M	Officer	"	"	Ship Chase. Baxter.
John Platt	30	M	Physician	"	"	
D. Buchanan	42	M	"	Scotland	"	
W. Douglass	32	M	Merchant	"	"	
C. Muir	33	M	"	U. States	"	Brig Constitution.
Susanna Austin & 2 ch.	60	F		England	"	Ship Orozimbo. Mayell.
John Death	19	M	Baker	"	"	
Elizabeth Death	49	F		"	"	
Charlotte " & 8 ch.	40	F		"	"	
John Coupland	50	M	Farmer	"	"	
Henry "	30	M	"	"	"	
George "	22	M	"	"	"	
Sarah " & 6 ch.	30	F		"	"	
Joseph Taylor	56	M		"	"	
Rachel " & 5 ch.	41	F		"	"	
Ann Whalley & 5 ch.	65	F		"	"	
Hannah Sykes & 3 ch.	35	F		"	"	
Diana Searce & child	23	F		"	"	
Edwd. Quinn & 2 ch.	51	M	Farmer	"	"	
Henry Roberts	22	M	"	"	"	
Thomas Pierce	30	M	Labourer	"	"	
John "	25	M	"	"	"	
Thomas Hearson	28	M	"	"	"	
Wm. Lindsley	22	M	"	"	"	
John Hallison	26	M	"	"	"	
John Metcalf	23	M	"	"	"	
James Burton	27	M	"	"	"	
Nehemiah Merrit	50	M	Merchant	U. States	"	Sch. Nancy. Crowell.
John H. Pratt	22	M	"	St. Johns	St. Johns	
Wm. Leafrey	25	M	Labourer	Ireland	U. States	
Robt. White	24	M	"	"	"	
Ann "	20	F		"	"	
Wm. Eaven	25	M	Labourer	"	"	
Robt. Nicholls	22	M	"	"	"	
Alexr. Maclay	22	M	"	"	"	
Ann Green	24	F		"	"	
Eliza "	22	F		"	"	
Robt. Lorrey	20	M	Labourer	"	"	
James Salter	56	M	Printer	England	"	Sch. Resolution. Corlias.

PASSENGERS WHO ARRIVED IN THE U.S. SEPTEMBER 1821 - DECEMBER 1823

Names of passengers	Age	Sex	Occupation	Country to which they belong	Country of which they intend becoming inhabitants	Ship or vessel with the name of the master or commander
NEW YORK Cont.						
Q. E. June 30, 1822						
James Cantalo	57	M	Gunsmith	P. Edwd. Isl.	U. States	
Wm. Ewing	53	M	Farmer	Scotland	"	
Thomas "	22	M		"	"	
Christiana " & ch.	24	F		"	"	
Thomas Drum	24	M	Labourer	Ireland	"	
Wm. Wells	18	M	Butcher	Halifax	"	
Mrs. De La Forest & 3 ch.	33	F		France	France	Sch. Six Brothers. Williams.
G. W. Irvine	50	M	Merchant	U. States	U. States	
A. W. Sheldon	25	M	"	"	"	
Henry Sampson	26	M	"	"	"	
A Borg	23	M	Farmer	G. Britain	"	Brig Trafalgar. Henderson.
Lewis Gordon	20	M	"	"	"	
M. Young	19	M	"	"	"	
George Hutson	32	M	"	"	"	
Helen "	30	F		"	"	
John Marshall	40	M	Paper mfr.	"	"	
Janet " & 2 ch.	30	F		"	"	
Wm. More	28	M	Baker	"	"	
John McLouchton	18	M	Clerk	"	"	
Walter Colton	38	M	Merchant	U. States	"	Sch. Rampart. Graham.
F. W. Dominick	35	M	Mariner	"	"	
B. Enuigh	19	M	Printer	Ireland	"	Sch. Union. Patterson.
V. Daley	24	M	Shoemaker	"	"	
Margt. Dempsey	27	F		"	"	
Michael J. Sullivan	15	M		"	"	
W. C. Connor	32	M	Carpenter	"	"	
Thomas More	20	M	Printer	"	"	
Thomas Edwards	57	M	Farmer	U. States	"	Ship Illinois. Funk.
Mary " & 7 ch.	47	F		"	"	
John Robertson	50	M		England	"	
Sarah " & 6 ch.	51	F		"	"	
Isaac Killing	46	M		"	"	
Ellen " & 7 ch.	51	F		"	"	
James Carter	45	M	Farmer	"	"	
Susanna " & 3 ch.	37	F		"	"	
Henry. Dodd	41	M	Farmer	"	"	
Margt. " & 2 ch.	38	F		"	"	
George Vickers	23	M		"	"	
E. "	22	F		"	"	
George Gillespie	46	M		"	"	
Ann "	37	F		"	"	
George Cook	24	M		"	"	
Wm. Wallace	21	M		"	"	
Peter Nelson	42	M		"	"	

Names of passengers	Age	Sex	Occupation	Country to which they belong	Country of which they intend becoming inhabitants	Ship or vessel with the name of the master or commander
NEW YORK Cont.						
Q. E. June 30, 1822						
John Sutherland	27	M	Painter	England	U. States	
Mary "	34	F		"	"	
Wm. Deagan	35	M	Farmer	"	"	
H. Deagan	21	F		"	"	
Pat. Murphy	20	M		"	"	
Ellen "	22	F		"	"	
John Norman	37	M	Wheelwright	"	"	
Wm. Dedley	40	M	Blacksmith	"	"	
Wm. Chapman	20	M	"	"	"	
John Burton	30	M	"	"	"	
Wm. Melloes	25	M	Farmer	G. Britain	"	
Geo. Good	26	M	"	"	"	
Robt. Robertson	28	M	"	"	"	
Wm. Atkinson	21	M	"	"	"	
Wm. Harris	19	M	"	"	"	
James Mell	26	M	Carpenter	"	"	
James Faddington	30	M	Farmer	"	"	
Thomas Morton	24	M		"	"	
Samuel Waisden	25	M		"	"	
Wm. Spence	23	M		"	"	
John Lowe	22	M		"	"	
Robt. Cheslyn	15	M		"	"	
Thomas Strawson	25	M		"	"	
Samuel Oglesby	24	M		"	"	
Thomas Newton	38	M		"	"	
Joseph Blow *	23	M		"	"	
James Hall Senior	72	M	Merchant	"	"	Brig Margaret. Cray.
James Hall Junior	47	M	"	"	"	
John "	31	M	"	"	"	
Jane "	26	F		"	"	
Ann "	24	F		"	"	
Helen "	23	F		"	"	
Mary "	18	F		"	"	
John Henderson	38	M		"	"	
Jane "	22	F		"	"	
James Baird	60	M		"	"	
John Loring	26	M	Barber	"	"	
J. Henderick	40	M	Printer	"	"	
Joanna " & 7 ch.	34	F		"	"	
John Sutherland	42	M	Merchant	"	"	
James Reddie *	26	M	Clerk	"	"	
H. Harvey	23	M	Merchant	U. States	"	Sch. Benjamin. Smith.
W. Wells	24	M	"	"	"	
L. Hands	22	M	"	"	"	

Names of passengers	Age	Sex	Occupation	Country to which they belong	Country of which they intend becoming inhabitants	Ship or vessel with the name of the master or commander
NEW YORK Cont.						
Q. E . June 30, 1822						
O. Buckley	22	M	Merchant	U. States	U. States	
S. Hammer	24	M	"	"	"	
Jos. Choate	27	M	"	"	"	
Jas Rhodes	24	M	"	"	"	
D. Halcomb	20	M		"	"	
Jos. Lewis	28	M		"	"	
L. Fils	30	M	Merchant	St Domingo	"	Sch. Diana. McPherson.
W. H. Cutchen	40	M	"	U States	"	
John Chicoll	22	M	Lawyer	"	"	
--- Dupont	26	M	Mechanic	"	"	
F G Schneider	25	M	Merchant	Prussia	"	
B. Thrasher	28	M	Baker	U States	"	Brig Mary Ann. Martin.
Wm Hancock	26	M	Merchant	"	"	
Robt. Norris & child	60	M	Manfactr.	Ireland	"	Sch. Alexr. Mansfield. Hamilton
Thomas Barber	28	M	Farmer	"	"	
Eliza "	22	F		"	"	
C. Foster	19	M	Clerk	"	"	
F. Evans	14	M	"	"	"	
Jos. Supple	24	M	"	"	"	
D. "	17	M	"	"	"	
M. Gavey	33	M	Merchant	"	"	
Pat. Rice	26	M	"	"	"	
Wm. Byrn	32	M	Mechanic	"	"	
Wm. Seatley	25	M	Farmer	"	"	
Wm. Ryan	15	M	"	"	"	
M. Cheanly	18	M	Mason	"	"	
Pat Clack	20	M	"	"	"	
John Faggan	22	M	Labourer	"	"	
J. C. Cannon	19	M	Farmer	"	"	
Matthew Lymburn	60	M	Merchant	England	England	Ship Amity. Maxwell.
John Davis	32	M	"	"	"	
Mary "	26	F		"	"	
Albert Davy	21	M		"	"	
D. Hadden	48	M		"	"	
Ann "	36	F		"	"	
L. F. Burton	54	M		"	"	
Robt. Layfield	27	M		"	"	
Jno. I. Walker	25	M	Merchant	U. States	U. States	
Robt. Arrott	21	M		"	"	
Saml. Lowney	20	M		"	"	
John Forsyth	55	M		"	"	
John Miller	40	M		"	"	
John Hame	37	M		"	"	
Edward Nicol	32	M		"	"	

Names of passengers	Age	Sex	Occupation	Country to which they belong	Country of which they intend becoming inhabitants	Ship or vessel with the name of the master or commander
NEW YORK Cont.						
Q. E. June 30, 1822						
I. Townshend	27	M		U. States	U. States	
Lavielle Du Berceau	29	M	Planter	Guadaloupe	"	Brig Horace. Hatch.
Mrs. " "	28	F		"	"	
W. Matilda "	25	F		"	"	
& 2 ch.						
Mrs. L. Luzent & ch.	30	F		"	"	
Edwd. Cornette	20	M	Planter	"	"	
Geo. W. Smith	24	M	Farmer	England	"	Ship Criterion. Lebor.
Ann " & 3 ch.	53	F		"	"	
Henry J. Grace	23	M		"	"	
Wm. Martin	45	M		"	"	
Eliza Wheeler & 5 ch.	36	F		"	"	
James Apps	22	M		"	"	
Henry D. Chatterton	42	M	Navy offcr.	France	U. States	Sch. Huntress. Morgan.
Henry Golfs	21	M	Sugar baker	Bremen	"	
George Schnider	26	M	"	"	"	
Henry King	38	M	Mariner	U. States	"	Ship Martha. Sketchly.
John James Hall	25	M	Merchant	England	"	Sch. Abigail. Duggs.
Sarah Willis	28	F		"	"	Brig Pomona. Handyside.
James Truelove	38	M	Engineer	"	"	
Mrs. " & 3 ch.	36	F		"	"	
M. Summerville	27	M	Mason	"	"	
Mrs. "	23	F		"	"	
Eliz. Hails	38	F		"	"	
Sarah "	22	F		"	"	
Albert Lopkin	26	M	Sugar baker	Germany	"	
Henry Rosinburgh	23	M	"	"	"	
James Fitzgerald	23	M	"	"	"	
Wm. Leider	25	M	Miller	U. States	"	Brig. Elizabeth. Williams.
John Saaman	23	M	"	Amsterdam	"	
Joseph Refford	30	M	Merchant	Ireland	"	Ship Xenophon. Aiken.
Mary " & 2 ch.	30	F		"	"	
Nancy Phillips & 4 ch.	36	F		"	"	
Wm. Johnson	40	M	Farmer	"	"	
Grace " & 3 ch.	35	F		"	"	
Sarah Gibson & 2 ch.	36	F		"	"	
John Patterson	18	M	Farmer	"	"	
Isabella McCormich	31	F		"	"	
Ann " & ch.	30	F		"	"	
James Banter	24	M	Farmer	"	"	
Alexr. McTillop	23	M	Merchant	"	"	
A. Klovenhousen	35	M	Mariner	Bremen	"	Sloop Jay. Smith.
A. Slater	43	M	Merchant	U. States	"	Ship Hannibal. Watkinson.
Isabella Slater & ch.	25	F		"	"	

Names of passengers	Age	Sex	Occupation	Country to which they belong	Country of which they intend becoming inhabitants	Ship or vessel with the name of the master or commander
NEW YORK Cont.						
Q. E. June 30, 1822						
Ab. Kintzing	28	M	Merchant	U. States	U. States	
W. S. Copper	24	M	"	"	"	
E. U. Johnson	23	M	"	"	"	
Wm. Bryan	62	M	"	"	"	
Thomas Wright	46	M	"	"	"	
E. C. Ward	23	M	"	"	"	
H. S. Bloodgood	29	M	"	"	"	Brig. Commerce. Funk
John Hinde	30	M	Farmer	England	"	Ship Thames. Marshall.
Elizabeth Hinde & 3 ch.	54	F		"	"	
James Collane	20	M	Blacksmith	"	"	
Mary "	20	F		"	"	
John Bastock	44	M	Farmer	"	"	
Mary " & 5 ch.	37	F		"	"	
John Hoden	49	M	Farmer	"	"	
Mary " & 7 ch.	46	F		"	"	
George Baley	83	M	Farmer	"	"	
Wm. Warrick	28	M	"	"	"	
Elizabeth " & 2 ch.	33	F		"	"	
Richd. Lawson	22	M	Farmer	"	"	
Roger Moods	32	M	"	"	"	
James Baldwin	25	M	"	"	"	
Wm. Thelbourn	30	M	"	"	"	
Nichl. "	20	M	"	"	"	
Wm. Dobbs	24	M	Wheelwright	"	"	
J. Walker	33	M	Farmer	"	"	
Vincent Doase	40	M	"	"	"	
Mary " & 9 ch.	40	F		"	"	
Vincent Cottane	48	M	Farmer	"	"	
Catharine " & 4 ch.	53	F		"	"	
Walter King & 3 ch.	42	M	Farmer	"	"	
Henry Hatfield	33	M	"	"	"	
Ann " & 6 ch.	32	F		"	"	
M. Porter	35	M	Merchant	U. States	"	Brig Laura Ann. Bassett.
M. Harper	34	M	Mariner	"	"	
G. Dayton	23	M	"	"	"	
Samuel De Forest	38	M	Merchant	"	"	Brig Jason. Marshall.
Wm. McBonnery	27	M	Carpenter	"	"	
Timothy Wood	22	M	Mechanic	"	"	Brig Albeona. Blinn.
J. Cottrell	23	M	"	"	"	
Robt. Fitzgerald	40	M	Merchant	Ireland	"	Sch. Jane. Copeland.
Peter Gombault	30	M	"	"	"	
Manuel Puga	37	M	"	Spain	Spain	Brig Brilliant. Begona.
I. De La Cerna	42	M	"	"	"	
Pedro Mather	20	M	"	"	"	

Names of passengers	Age	Sex	Occupation	Country to which they belong	Country of which they intend becoming inhabitants	Ship or vessel with the name of the master or commander
NEW YORK Cont.						
Q. E. June 30, 1822						
Jos. Pinaldi	42	M	Merchant	Spain	Spain	Sch. Anna. Dominique.
John Tayler	34	M	"	England	U. States	Ship Manhattan. Crocker.
John A. James	18	M	"	"	"	
John Wheely	30	M	"	"	"	
Arthur Shaaff	18	M	"	U. States	"	
Arthur Newbold	16	M	"	"	"	
James Ratcliff	36	M	"	"	"	
Wm. Powell	27	M	Planter	England	"	
Sarah " & 4 ch.	26	F		"	"	
Stephen Kennedy	40	M	Merchant	U. States	"	
Jeremiah Jones	31	M	"	"	"	
Wm. Fenner	40	M	Clergyman	Switzerland	"	Ship Manchester. Lambert.
B. Carren	30	M	Merchant	"	"	
M. Maillard	29	M	"	France	"	
L. Bugard	30	M	"	"	"	
E. "	25	M	"	"	"	
J. K. Grovenor	30	M	"	U. States	"	Brig Mary. Noyes.
D. F. Squire	23	M	"	"	"	
I. M. Noyes	33	M	"	"	"	
Thomas Bell	28	M	"	England	"	Sch. Endymion. Hathaway.
T. M. Taylor	20	M	"	U. States	"	
T. Denna	45	M	"	Spain	"	
S. Key	19	M	"	"	"	
Reuben Leonard	25	M	Gardner	G. Britain	"	Sch. Two Friends. Adams.
Simeon "	22	M	"	"	"	
James L. Suett	18	M	Gent.	"	"	Brig Columbia. Loring.
Wm. Jackson	19	M	Labourer	"	"	Brig Maria. Hewitt.
John Scott	22	M	"	"	"	
John Richardson	19	M	"	"	"	
John W. Carter	22	M	"	"	"	
T. Holme	30	M	"	"	"	
James Watson	28	M	"	"	"	
Robert Witkins	47	M	"	"	"	
Joseph Cox	23	M	"	"	"	
Samuel Hadden	24	M	Druggist	"	"	
Charles Dutton	27	M	Farmer	"	"	
Thos. K. Grape	20	M	Brick layer	"	"	
T. Rutley	21	M	"	"	"	
James Smith & son	39	M	"	"	"	
James Boxer	40	M	"	"	"	
James Hadden & ch.	36	M	"	"	"	
Paul Joff	31	M	"	"	"	
Charles Baslock	38	M	"	"	"	
James Linley	21	M	"	"	"	

Names of passengers	Age	Sex	Occupation	Country to which they belong	Country of which they intend becoming inhabitants	Ship or vessel with the name of the master or commander
NEW YORK Cont.						
Q. E. June 30, 1822						
Francis Hernandez	58	M	Gent.	Spain	U. States	Ship Madison. Norris.
Mrs. " & 5 ch.	38	F		"	"	
Joseph Pacy	23	M		"	"	
D. Pexolto/Pexotto	23	M	Physician	U. States	"	Brig Clio. Langdon.
B. Oliver	28	M	Mariner	N. Scotia	"	Sch. F. Miller. Henderson.
Thomas Talbot	45	M	Gent.	G. Britain	Canada	Ship Maria. Fowler.
John Tilby	28	M	Surgeon	"	U. States	
Wm. Wallace	30	M	Merchant	"	"	
Walter Stevenson	41	M	"	"	"	
Wm. Coffin	30	M	Gent.	"	"	
Joseph Freeman	40	M	Merchant	"	"	
Caroline " & ch.	28	F		"	"	
H. Hoole & 7 ch.	48	F		"	"	
C. Ingraham & ch.	28	F		"	"	
Augusta Beckett	22	F	Lady	"	"	
Hannah Hoole & 7 ch.	48	F		"	"	
David Best	24	M	Mechanic	"	"	
Eliza "	23	F		"	"	
Thos. Forbes	58	M	Weaver	"	"	
Mary " & 4 ch.	49	F		"	"	
Wm. Robinson	38	M	Farmer	"	"	
James Wood	26	M	Grocer	"	"	
Edwd. Faraby	21	M	Farmer	"	"	
Cath. Ganch & 2 ch.	23	F		"	"	
Adolphus Frisby	26	M	Labourer	"	"	
Wm. Fullager	27	M	Carpenter	"	"	
Sarah "	20	F		"	"	
Edwd. Shirley	31	M	Farmer	"	"	
Esther " & 3 ch.	27	F		"	"	
Saml. Cooper	39	M	Merchant	"	"	
Joseph Joy	24	M	Farmer	"	"	
Sarah " & 2 ch.	22	F		"	"	
Thomas Addison	23	M	Groom	"	"	
Andw. Thomas	25	M	Farmer	"	"	
John Russell	25	M	Merchant	U. States	"	Brig Leno. Slade.
J. Ballestier	35	M	"	"	"	
Joseph Oliver	32	M	"	France	France	Sch. Atlantic. Davies.
P. Marietta	34	M	"	"	"	
John B. Casto	19	M	Carpenter	Itlay	Italy	
Manuel " & ch.	36	M	"	"	"	
Alexr. Brown	48	M	Gent.	G. Britain	U. States	Ship Mt. Vernon. Rawson.
Wm. Neve & child	45	M	Farmer	"	"	
Stephen Stafford	30	M	Mason	"	"	
George Rage	27	M	"	"	"	
			"			

Names of passengers	Age	Sex	Occupation	Country to which they belong	Country of which they intend becoming inhabitants	Ship or vessel with the name of the master or commander
NEW YORK Cont.						
Q. E. June 30, 1822						
Jonas Littlewood	22	M	Mason	G. Britain	U. States	
John Rumett	24	M	Weaver	"	"	
Wm. Wheston	39	M	"	"	"	
J. Rage	29	M	Mason	"	"	
Edwd. Tinling	52	M	"	"	"	Brig Orient. Gallilie.
J. G. Petman	29	M	Merchant	U. States	"	Ship Savannah. Hughes.
Wm. Scallack	35	M	Gent.	England	England	Brig Elizabeth. Smail.
Geo. Conteur	20	M	Surgeon	"	"	
F. Giles	34	M	Labourer	"	U. States	
Sarah Giles & 6 ch.	34	F		"	"	
Sarah Church & 3 ch.	30	F		"	"	
U. H. Morton •	26	M		"	"	Ship Ann. Williams.
James Goodwin	42	M		"	"	
C. Savage	35	M		"	"	
T. Hewitt	30	M		"	"	
Geo. Jaggers	25	M		"	"	
Walter Scott & child	28	M		"	"	
Wm. Richardson	22	M		"	"	
Charles Bonn	21	M		"	"	
Wm. Shannon	25	M	Navy officer	"	"	Brig Dalmanock. Cummings.
James Simpson	30	M	Cooper	"	"	
Samuel Croes •	30	M	Merchant	U. States	"	Sch. Ranger. Lawrence.
Schuyler Colfax	29	M	Accountant	"	"	Brig Catharine. Clark.
James Pitkin	26	M	Supercargo	"	"	Brig Prize. Ball.
Charles Magra	35	M	Mariner	"	"	Ship Ajax. Hubbell.
T. Cow •	30	M	Merchant	Armoy	China	
R. Knowland	50	M	Clergyman	Halifax	Halifax	Brig Albert. Walworth.
Mrs. " & child	42	F		"	"	
Mrs. Walloughby & ch.	50	F		"	"	
Mrs. Mason & 3 ch.	28	F		"	"	
Mrs. Anderson & ch.	38	F		"	"	
E. Samuel	26	M		"	"	
Noah Disbrow & ch.	52	M	Merchant	G. Britain	"	Sch. Constitution. Spurling.
Thomas Johnson	30	M	"	"	"	Sch. Globe. Hill.
Elizabeth "	28	F		"	"	
John McCaltice	47	M	Merchant	Scotland	U. States	Brig Helen. Erskin.
James Pullar	24	M	"	"	"	
Robert Dilling	22	M	Labourer	St. Johns	G. Britain	Sch. Nancy. Crowell.
Thomas H. Davis	25	M	Merchant	"	U. States	
John Lane	20	M	Labourer	"	"	
Lucy Dawson	18	F		"	"	
S. Steeling	35	M	Merchant	U. States	"	Sch. Madison. Jones.
Joseph Shuter	38	M	"	England	Canada	Ship Florida. Matlack.
Peter McGill	30	M	"	"	"	

PASSENGERS WHO ARRIVED IN THE U.S. SEPTEMBER 1821 - DECEMBER 1823

Names of passengers	Age	Sex	Occupation	Country to which they belong	Country of which they intend becoming inhabitants	Ship or vessel with the name of the master or commander
NEW YORK Cont.						
Q. E. June 30, 1822						
Robt. Bertledge	28	M	Merchant	U. States	U. States	
Samuel Jones	24	M	"	"	"	
H. B. Barowell	17	M	"	"	"	
Phebe Blackburn & 2 ch.	30	F		England	"	
Wm. Dawson	37	M	Saddler	U. States	"	Brig Frances Jarvis. Sheed.
W. H. Lawrence	32	M	Mariner	"	"	
J. G. Bernard	31	M	Merchant	Prussia	"	Brig Ann Maria. Summers.
Mrs. Bernard	26	F		.	"	
Peter Bayor	42	M	Merchant	France	"	
P. Hansen	32	M	"	U. States	"	Brig Wm Smith. McClellan.
Mrs. "	24	F		"	"	
D. Austin	45	M	Merchant	"	"	
M. Watkins	29	M	"	"	"	
James Smith	38	M	"	"	"	
M. Vinerin	20	M	"	"	"	Ship America. Wallace
Ann Moore	21	F		G. Britain	"	Ship Weser. Jenkins.
Henry Ruckell	30	M	Farmer	"	"	
Catharine " & 7 ch.	28	F		"	"	
Pat. Redden	30	M	Farmer	"	"	
B. "	25	F		"	"	
Mary "	20	F		"	"	
Daniel Buckley	30	M	Farmer	"	"	
Wm. Slattery	30	M	"	"	"	
John Dever	22	M	Merchant	U. States	"	Brig Caroline. Hubbs.
A. Boorasdris	25	M	"	Cuba	"	
J. Paine	30	M	Mariner	U. States	"	Sch. Bolena. Houston.
Justus Hunsun •	38	M	Merchant	"	"	Brig Shepherdess. Stores.
John R. Thompson	22	M	"	"	"	
A. Bertrand & child	30	M	"	Spain	Spain	
L. Debour	25	M	"	"	"	
J. Del Bais	20	M	"	"	"	
J. F. Meliaus	23	M	"	"	· "	
John Raymond	34	M	"	U. States	"	Brig Planter. Edes.
L. Prentice	34	M	Mariner	"	"	
Antonio Gundell	29	M	Merchant	Italy	"	Sch. Dolphin. Colby.
Edwd. Weir	35	M	"	Ireland	"	Brig Vigilant. Stewart.
Eliza " & 2 ch.	25	F		"	"	
James Archibald '	20	M	Merchant	"	"	
Wm. Wantyn	19	M	"	"	"	
Mary Fallen & 3 ch.	30	F		"	"	
Wm. Crystal & 2 ch.	29	M	Labourer	"	"	
M. Gill & 3 ch.	30	F		"	"	
Wm. W. Horoland	24	M	Merchant	U. States	"	Brig Louisa. Smith.
E. A. Smith	27	M	Mariner	"	"	

Names of passengers	Age	Sex	Occupation	Country to which they belong	Country of which they intend becoming inhabitants	Ship or vessel with the name of the master or commander
NEW YORK						
Q. E. June 30, 1822						
A. L. Lawrence	25	M	Mariner	U. States	Spain	
L. C. Weivel	22	M	Merchant	"	"	
L. Renaud	38	M	"	France	France	Sch. Abigail. Ewell
W. Fletcher	34	M	"	"	"	
John Payson	31	M	Cordwainer	G. Britain	U. States	Brig Margt. Ann. Bowman.
Jane "	32	F		"	"	
John Atkinson	28	M	Farmer	"	"	
James Atkinson	19	M	Farmer	G. Britain	U. States	
James Bratt	19	M	"	"	"	
Joseph Young	25	M	"	"	"	
John Bircham	29	M	"	"	"	
Richd. "	20	M	"	"	"	
E. Ellerby	27	M	Miller	"	"	Brig Wellington. Eyre.
Jno. Brathworth	20	M	Grocer	"	"	
George Scott	19	M	Baker	"	"	
George Miln	28	M	Merchant	"	"	Brig Resign. Clements.
S. Moore	40	M	"	U. States	"	Brig Radius. Granger.
J. Harris Jr.	20	M	"	"	"	
Peter Gerard	40	M	Cab. Maker	Paris	"	Sch. Harriet. Rogers.
Victor Dantillac	23	M	Hairdresser	"	"	
M. Calala	21	M	Pastry cook	"	"	
B. Jascon	24	M	"	"	"	
W. I. Powell	35	M	Cotton Pltr.	Louisiana	Louisiana	
John McKeen	35	M	Carpenter	U. States	U. States	
Thomas Davis	33	M	"	"	"	
Robt. Furnes	43	M	"	"	"	
D. Donahoe	40	M	"	"	"	
John Gilbert	37	M	Farmer	England	"	Ship Ulysses. Stone.
Mary " & 4 ch.	33	F		"	"	
Wm. Broadford	35	M	Distiller	"	"	
John Griffin & child	32	M	Labourer	"	"	
Wm. "	22	M	"	"	"	
Michael Burnes	35	M	"	"	"	
ST. AUGUSTINE						
Q. E. June 30, 1822						
Moses E. Levy	45	M	Planter	U. States	U. States	Sch. Content. Small.
James Robinson	28	M	Mariner	"	"	
Francis Lorano	40	M	"	Spain	"	
Antonio Maceshe	25	M	Tailor	"	"	
C. Hernandez	32	F		"	"	
D. "	26	F		"	"	

Names of passengers	Age	Sex	Occupation	Country to which they belong	Country of which they intend becoming inhabitants	Ship or vessel with the name of the master or commander
EDGARTOWN						
Q. E. June 30, 1822						
Wm. P. Dean	26	M	Mariner	U. States	U. States	Sch. Ruby. Shute.
John Russell	24	M	"	"	"	
John Tucker	49	M	"	"	"	
Martin Russell	21	M	"	"	"	
Peter Smith	32	M	"	"	"	
John Collins	30	M	"	"	"	
Manuel Antonio Romas	18	M	"	Cape de Verd	Cape de Verd	
Charles Papunee	35	M	"	Marseilles	U. States	Brig Neutrality. Thompson
BARNSTABLE						
Q. E. June 30, 1822						
Andw. Redman	21	M	Labourer	Ireland	U. States	Sch. Mary. Crowell.
James Dearmand	25	M	"	"	"	
Joseph Lernan •	29	M	"	"	"	
Wm. Palk	21	M	Malster	England	"	
Andw. Noulden	24	M	Mariner	Ireland	"	Sch. Betsey & Eliza. Baker.
Philip Phalen	20	M	Farmer	"	"	
Joseph Purcel	23	M	"	"	"	
Michael Thatcher	24	M	"	"	"	
John Callon	28	M	Labourer	"	"	Sch. Jas. Monroe. Simmons.
Wm. Rodgers	30	M	"	"	"	
Edwd. McDermott	17	M	"	"	"	
Ambrose Clapp	50	M	Farmer	Wales	"	Sch. Hunter. Sears.
Sarah "	42	F		"	"	
David Bowen	45	M	Farmer	"	"	
Margaret "	38	F		"	"	
John Perry	38	M	Farmer	"	"	
Lewis Laurence	26	M	Blacksmith	"	"	
Wm. Bell	33	M	Farmer	England	"	
James "	25	M	"	"	"	
Samuel Davis	22	M	Trader	"	"	
David Langley	23	M	"	"	"	
Henry Logan	25	M	Weaver	"	"	
OSWEGATCHIE						
Q. E. June 30, 1822						
Thomas B. Cowen	27	M	Surgeon	U. States	U. States	Boat Buran. Brandy.
Mary "	21	F		"	"	
Wm. Watson	25	M	Labourer	England	"	
Hannah "	22	F	Spinster.	"	"	
Alexander Hyndman	21	M	Farmer	"	"	
Esther "	21	F		"	"	

Names of passengers	Age	Sex	Occupation	Country to which they belong	Country of which they intend becoming inhabitants	Ship or vessel with the name of the master or commander
OSWEGATCHIE Con.						
Q. E. June 30, 1822						
James McOnell	47	M	Farmer	"	"	
Agnes " & 7 ch.	43	F		"	"	
David Patterson	50	M	Farmer	"	"	
Mary " & 6 ch.	40	F		"	"	
Thomas Simpson	27	M	Farmer	"	"	
Margaret " & 3 ch.	26	F		"	"	
Robt. Armstrong	30	M	Labourer	Ireland	"	Boat Cherub. Johnson.
Thomas "	30	M	"	"	"	
Sidney "	28	M	"	"	"	
Ellen " & 7 ch.	25	F		"	"	
James McGrath	20	M	Labourer	"	"	
Samuel Milligan	30	M	Weaver	Scotland	"	Boat Fair Trader. Ballantine.
Margaret " & ch.	20	F		"	"	
George White	23	M	Farmer	Ireland	"	
Wm. Graham & 5 ch.	32	M	"	"	"	
Wm. Tracy	30	M	Surveyor	"	"	
Ann "	20	F		"	"	
John Kelly	26	M	Farmer	"	"	
Wm. Davis	30	M	"	"	"	
Mary " & 3 ch.	27	F		"	"	
Michael McAboy	25	M	Farmer	"	"	
Wm. Armstrong	25	M	"	"	"	
Margt. Armstrong & 2 children	24	F		"	"	
Jane Staples	43	M	Farmer	"	"	
Mary " & 9 ch.	34	F		"	"	
NORFOLK						
Q. E. June 30, 1822						
Hickman	30	M	Mariner	U. States	U. States	Brig Nautilus. Blair.
N.P. Wilkinson	35	M	Ship master	"	"	Sch. Lavine. Howland.
John Davenport	60	M	Physician	England	"	Ship Philip Tabb. Wheeler.
John Mollyneux	19	M	Farmer	"	"	
Wm. Williamson	19	M	"	"	"	
Thomas Mollyneux	18	M	"	"	"	
John McFarden	15	M	"	Ireland	"	
Ellen Johnson & 5 ch.	40	F		"	"	
Catharine Wadly	21	F		"	"	
Robt. Watson & ch.	34	M	Farmer	"	"	
Wm. Sands	22	M	"	"	"	
Jane Mages *	22	F		"	"	
Nancy Kenny	22	F		"	"	
Samuel Campbell	21	M	Labourer	"	"	

Names of passengers	Age	Sex	Occupation	Country to which they belong	Country of which they intend becoming inhabitants	Ship or vessel with the name of the master or commander
NORFOLK						
Q. E. June 30, 1822						
Stephen Trowbridge	40	M	Shipmaster	U. States	U. States	Sch. Independence. Ames.
Cesar Carpenter	39	M	"	France	France	
F. "	47	M	"	"	"	
Pierre Lubart	21	M	Mariner	"	"	
J. B. Dupray	50	M	"	"	"	
N. A. Fromentin	46	M	"	"	"	
E. F. Le Blond	36	M	"	"	"	
B. Japin	26	M	"	"	"	
C. Mastel	36	M	"	"	"	
Louis Nicol	40	M	"	"	"	
Pierre Happiday	18	M	"	"	"	
S. Corden	17	M	"	"	"	
C. Gugnon	15	M	"	"	"	
George White	25	M	"	"	"	
John Welch	35	M	"	"	"	
Jas. L. Maxwell	21	M	Farmer	U. States	U. States	Sch. Star. Bacci.
M. Lopez	25	M	Supercargo	"	"	Brig Only Daughter. Forsyth.
John Francis	40	M	Merchant	"	"	
Thomas Shepherd	22	M	Farmer	"	"	Ship Eliza & Abby. Drummond.
Mary "	22	F		"	"	
John Raisonby	62	M	Farmer	"	"	
Robert Walker	26	M	"	"	"	
Harriot "	21	F		"	"	
Joseph Curtis	27	M	Carpenter	"	"	
Mary " & child	27	F		"	"	
James Burrill	31	M	Farmer	England	"	
George Skerritt	21	M	"	"	"	
Evans Watkins	25	M	"	"	"	
John "	20	M	Carpenter	"	"	
Margaret " & 6 ch.	49	F		"	"	
BELFAST						
Q. E. June 30, 1822						
Joshua L. Cordon	23	M	Farmer	U. Canada	U. Canada	Sch. Venus.
Nathaniel Tapley	23	M	"	"	"	
A. Campbell	45	M	"	U. States	U. States	
John Wood	42	M	Mariner	"	"	
Moses Merrill	24	M	Farmer	"	"	
Charles Harris	32	M	Mariner	"	"	
Asa Miller	42	M	"	"	"	
Alexander Carter	15	M	"	"	"	
Jonathan Boles	33	M	"	"	"	
Aaron Warden	16	M	"	G. Britain	"	

Names of passengers	Age	Sex	Occupation	Country to which they belong	Country of which they intend becoming inhabitants	Ship or vessel with the name of the master or commander
BELFAST Q. E. June 30, 1822						
Sarah Boles	34	F		G. Britain	U. States	
Joseph Wabeston	28	M	Mariner	U. States	"	
Nathaniel Philbrick	28	M	Farmer	"	"	
E. Varney	24	M	"	"	"	
Richd. Dow	23	M	Blacksmith	"	"	
Wm. Hamilton	22	M	Farmer	"	"	
B. "	22	F		Ireland	"	
John Rorick	27	M	Farmer	"	"	
Ann Turnbull	46	F		N. Scotia	N. Scotia	
NEWBURN Q. E. Sept. 30, 1822						
John Hay	40	M	Seaman	U. States	U. States	Sch. Nancy. Rich.
F. Eules	35	M	"	"	"	Sch. Milo. Skidmore.
S. Legendre & 2 ch.	36	F		France	"	Sch. Mary. Shaw.
Francis J. Avice	28	M	Merchant	U. States	"	Sch. Mentor. Lane.
P. M. Boutan	31	M	Mechanic	France	"	
PORTSMOUTH Q. E. Sept 30, 1822						
Charles Rahn	30	M	Mechanic	England	U. States	Sch. Fox. Churchill.
Wm. "	22	M	"	"	"	
Timothy J. Kelly	22	M	Studt. at Law	"	"	Sch. Cordelia. Mayo.
MARBLEHEAD Q. E. Sept. 30, 1822						
Charles W. Brown	23	M	Mariner	U. States	"	Sch. America.
NEWPORT Q. E. Sept. 30, 1822						
Charles Langloir	52	M		France	Unknown	Brig Hiram. Easton.
Clemt. Gerard	24	M		"	"	
Maurice O'Conner	19	M	Studt. of Physc.	St. Helena	U. States	Brig. Catherine. Smith.
Cornelius Fowlay	35	M	Carpenter	"	"	
Pat. McQuaid	36	M	"	"	"	
BRISTOL Q. E. Sept. 30, 1822						
John Wood	52	M	Mariner	U. States	"	Brig Bowdoin. Carr.

Names of passengers	Age	Sex	Occupation	Country to which they belong	Country of which they intend becoming inhabitants	Ship or vessel with the name of the master or commander
BRISTOL Cont. Q. E. Sept. 30, 1822						
A. M. Oliver	28	M	Mariner	U. States	U. States	
Saml. Berrie	24	M	"	"	"	
W. E. Colliser	31	M	"	"	"	
Thos. D. Brown	25	M	"	"	"	
Saml. Emery	35	M	"	"	"	
Wm. M. White	21	M	"	"	"	
Catherine Minot & 3 children	35	F	Seamstress	"	"	Brig Jacob. Eddy.
PROVIDENCE Q. E. Sept. 30, 1822						
Charles Preble	26	M	Mariner	U. States	U. States	Ship Superior. Snow.
Thomas Shaw	30	M	Carpenter	"	"	
James F. Jackson	19	M	Gent.	"	"	Sch. Maria. Rhodes.
Benj. Shaw	70	M	Merchant	"	"	Sch. Experiment. Steel.
James Cunningham	23	M	"	"	"	
Edwd. Fernandez	21	M	Gent.	Cuba	Cuba	Brig Argus. Bowers.
Mrs. Gray & child	24	F		"	"	
Joseph Emanuel	35	M	Cooper	"	"	Brig. Govr. Hopkins Wilkinson.
BOSTON Q. E. Sept. 30, 1822						
B. W. Chase	27	M	Merchant	U. States	U. States	Ship Mount Vernon. Howes.
John Riley	26	M	Mariner	"	"	
Ann " & 3 ch.	26	F		"	"	
A. Whitehead	35	M	Trader	"	"	
E. Hillen	40	M		"	"	
John Lighton	53	M	Farmer	"	"	Ship London Packet. Tracy.
Jas. A. Dickson	48	M	Merchant	"	"	
Edwd. Baylis	33	M	"	"	"	
Henry Richards	17	M	"	"	"	
Frances "	17	M	"	"	"	
Sarah Ann Owen	28	F		G. Britain	"	
Henry Conner	39	M	Cab. Maker	"	"	
Wm. Smith	17	M	"	"	"	
Felix C. Ellis	23	M	Merchant	U. States	"	Brig Havre Packet. Miller.
Wm. M. Townshend	18	M	Mariner	"	"	Brig Independence. Low.
Oliver Finney	24	M	"	"	"	
M. Londigan	40	M	Merchant	Halifax	Halifax	Sch. Cherub. Andrews.
M. Gough	35	M	"	"	"	
George Shiel •	40	M	"	U. States	U. States	

Names of passengers	Age	Sex	Occupation	Country to which they belong	Country of which they intend becoming inhabitants	Ship or vessel with the name of the master or commander
BOSTON						
Q. E. Sept. 30, 1822						
Rufus Shiel *	19	M	Merchant	U. States	U. States	
Wm. Kens	22	M	Tailor	Halifax	Halifax	
Nicholas Mussoon *	28	M	Labourer	"	"	
Mary Kennison	25	F		"	"	
Ann "	19	F		"	"	
Miss Porter	23	F		"	"	
Sarah Ross & child	26	F		"	"	
George Sewell	30	M	Merchant	"	"	
George Pindar	45	M	Mariner	U. States	U. States	Brig Mary. Hooper.
John Singleton	50	M	Cooper	"	"	Brig Superior. Mavorach.
Franklin Chase	30	M	Mariner	"	"	
John Dagie *	35	M	Cooper	France	"	
George Williams	23	M	Trader	England	"	Brig Oak. Oaks.
C. C. Dargor	39	M		France	France	
John Robertson	26	M	Merchant	England	England	Sch. Billow. Barker.
Wm. Prior	50	M	"	Halifax	Halifax	
G. Brown	45	M	"	England	England	
H. E. Way	25	M	Merchant	"	"	
Thomas Ridgway	27	M	"	"	"	
Dalton Deblois	22	M	"	U. States	U. States	
Melchior Pramer	29	M	Mechanic	Germany	"	Sch. James. Holmes.
Joseph Wall	30	M	Farmer	U. States	"	Sch. Abigail. Elwell.
Hugh Hill	23	M	"	"	"	
Betsy "	20	F		"	"	
John Smith	36	M	Mariner	"	"	Ship Mercury. Nichols.
James Lees	62	M	Manufactr.	England	"	
Robt. Dalgell	45	M		"	"	
Samuel Sage	45	M	Mechanic	"	"	
Mary Wilson	48	F		"	"	
George "	22	M	Manufactr.	"	"	
James Walker	41 ·	M	Book keeper	"	"	
Thomas Pratt	58	M	Merchant	U. States	"	Sch. Plant. Stackpole.
Geo. W. Dorsett	25	M	Mariner	"	"	Brig Independence. Bartlett.
John McCarty	35	M	"	England	"	Brig Confidence. Stevenson.
Wm. Green	63	M	"	Scotland	"	Sch. Elizabeth. Bakenor.
Mary " & 2 ch.	28	F		"	"	
Wm. Hutchinson	25	M	Mariner	"	"	
Margaret "	24	F		"	"	
Patrick Dana	22	M	Mechanic	"	"	
John Stears *	38	M	Mariner	N. Scotia	Halifax	Sch. Harriet. Kennard.
S. King	27	M	"	"	"	
John McFarlane	16	M	"	"	"	
Joseph Miller	37	M	"	U. States	U. States	Sch. Zealous. Baker.
Wm. Thompson	28	M	Trader	"	"	

Names of passengers	Age	Sex	Occupation	Country to which they belong	Country of which they intend becoming inhabitants	Ship or vessel with the name of the master or commander
BOSTON						
Q. E. Sept. 30, 1822						
Anthony Zahr	38	M	Merchant	U. States	U. States	Brig Mary Howe. Wister.
J. R. Matthews	40	M	Planter	"	"	Ship Champion. Lewis.
W. "	17	M		"	"	
Wm. Langton	36	M	Merchant	"	"	
James Boot	26	M	"	"	"	
L. Dexter	28	M	"	"	"	
B. C. Ward	36	M	"	"	"	
J. Clark	28	M	"	"	"	
W. Lee	45	M	"	"	"	
J. Bottomly	23	M	"	"	"	
P. Smith	21	M		"	"	
John Richards	36	M	Mariner	"	"	Brig Betsy. Pratt.
John Bradley	45	M	"	"	"	
Edmund Hasteny	45	M	Merchant	"	"	
A. Saggert	25	M	Weaver	Ireland	"	Sch. Boston. Cox.
Wm. Robertson	25	M	Miller	"	"	
David Clark	20	M	Weaver	"	"	
Matthew Conally	22	M	"	"	"	
Peter McGinnes	24	M	Weaver	"	"	
George James	19	M	"	"	"	
Soloman Barnes	20	M	"	"	"	
Eleanor Robinson	20	F		"	"	
Isabella Taggert	25	F		"	"	
John Sears	40	M	Barber	U. States	"	Sch. Hope. Lassell.
John S. Demore *	23	M	Merchant	C. Hayteen ?	C. Hateen ?	
Mr Young	50	M	"	Halifax	U. States	Sch. Cherub. Andrews.
Mrs. "	48	F		"	"	
Mr. " Jr.	35	M	Merchant	"	"	
Mrs " & 3 ch.	34	F		"	"	
--- Stickle	65	M	Physician	"	"	
L. Belcher	25	M	Navy officer	"	"	
Lt. Butler	25	M	"	"	"	
Mr. Mitt	29	M	Merchant	U. States	"	
Mr. Alport	37	M	"	"	"	
Mr. Burnes	27	M	"	"	"	
Patrick Lynch	33	M	Farmer	Halifax	"	
James Forlay	39	M	"	"	"	
Dennis Sullivan	42	M	Servant	"	"	
Ann Collins & 2 ch.	46	F	Tailoress	"	"	
James Trader	42	M		"	"	
Mary "	46	F		"	"	
Joseph Martin	35	M	Cigar maker	Spain	"	Brig Delegate. Davis.
C. A. Crawley	23	M	Gent.	N. Scotia	N. Scotia	Sch. Billow. Barker.
I. S. "	25	M	"	"	"	

Names of passengers	Age	Sex	Occupation	Country to which they belong	Country of which they intend becoming inhabitants	Ship or vessel with the name of the master or commander
BOSTON Cont.						
Q. E. Sept. 30, 1822						
--- Payor	17	M	Gent.	N. Scotia	N. Scotia	
--- Perley	33	M	Mariner	"	"	
--- Oliver	30	M	Merchant	U. States	U. States	
---Osborn	23	M	"	"	"	
--- Castrail	38	M	"	"	"	
--- Turnluff	26	M	"	"	"	
R. Mano	37	M	Tailor	Ireland	"	
John Clyson	28	M	"	"	"	
Edwd. Murphy	40	M	Fisherman	"	"	
James Hammessy	37	M	"	"	"	
John Simpson	18	M	Clerk	U. States	"	
Thomas Dunn	30	M	Labourer	Ireland	"	
John Height	26	M	"	"	"	
Horace Steel *	35	M	Sail master	U. States	U. States	Ship Lion. Greene.
Francis Deper	24	M	Gent.	"	"	
John May	40	M	"	"	"	
Wm. Heath	40	M	Mariner	"	"	
Joseph Fenner	40	M	"	"	"	
Thomas Davis	20	M	Merchant	"	"	Sch. Resolution. Mye.
Edmund Martin	25	M	Mechanic	"	"	Sch. Brocksville. Grove.
John Barnes	22	M	Mariner	"	"	
H. Gray	20	M	"	"	"	Ship Courier. Eaves.
John Hallett & ch.	50	M	Farmer	England	"	Sch. Bristol Trader. Peterson.
Thomas Mack & ch.	24	M	Blacksmith	"	"	
George Brown	20	M		U. States	"	
Susan Armstrong	42	F	Seamstress	St. Croix	St. Croix	Brig Washington. Fisher.
L. G. Shaw	28	F	"	"	"	
Wm. Jackson	24	M	Merchant	Ireland	U. States	Brig Tom. Spear.
Mary Ann " & 2 ch.	24	F		"	"	
John McLane	23	M	Labourer	"	"	
P. McGuinn	31	M	Whitesmith	"	"	
Edwd. McLane	40	M	Labourer	"	"	
M. McElroy	16	M	"	"	"	
J. S. Kelly	17	M	"	"	"	
E. D. "	21	M	"	"	"	
Michael Gill	28	M	"	"	"	
Edwd. Quelton	40	M	"	"	"	
Bernard Eager *	30	M	"	"	"	
Mary McEvin & ch.	60	F		"	"	
Ann Collins	26	F		"	"	
Ann Reilly	26	F		"	"	
Mary Egar	24	F		"	"	
Grace Patten	18	F		"	"	
C. Fitzpatrick & 2 ch.	35	F		"	"	

Names of passengers	Age	Sex	Occupation	Country to which they belong	Country of which they intend becoming inhabitants	Ship or vessel with the name of the master or commander
BOSTON Cont. Q. E. Sept. 30, 1822						
James Doyle	29	M	Labourer	Ireland	U. States	
Ann "	30	F		"	"	
Patrick "	30	M	Labourer	"	"	
Catharine "	20	F	Spinster	"	"	
Thomas Kane	21	M	Labourer	"	"	
Wm. Brown	33	M	"	"	"	
M. McGratch	24	M	"	"	"	
Henry Booth	29	M	Merchant	"	"	
Pat. Cogen	42	M	Labourer	"	"	Sch. Resolution. Collier.
Edwd. Welsh	23	M	"	"	"	
Eliza "	18	F		"	"	
James Burk	18	M	Labourer	"	"	
Andw. Falerty *	29	M	"	"	"	
Mrs. "	19	F		"	"	
Thomas Magee	21	M	Labourer	"	"	
Mary Rodgers	25	F		"	"	
Patrick Colin	22	M	Labourer	"	"	
John Malary	30	M	"	"	"	
Mrs. "	25	F		"	"	
Mat. "	33	M	"	"	"	
James Dunn	25	M	"	"	"	
John Tuel *	30	M	"	"	"	
Saml. Pepper	16	M	"	"	"	
B. Kelty & 11 ch.	33	F		"	"	
Mary Jaques	60	F		U. States	"	Sch. Hero. Beers.
Sarah Mosely & 2 ch.	27	F		"	"	
Edwd. A. Free	18	M	Student	"	"	
Richd. Mollyman	25	M	Farmer	Ireland	"	
Edmund Kearroy	30	M	Merchant	"	"	
Wm. Jones	40	M	Farmer	"	"	
John Bigh- *	30	M	Labourer	"	"	
Ann " & 3 ch.	30	F		"	"	
Wm. Gardner	19	M	Groom	"	"	
Edwd. Powers	34	M	Labourer	"	"	Sch. Two Brothers. Young.
Mary Ann " & child	24	F		"	"	
T. Harby	30	M	Labourer	"	"	
D. F. Patrick	29	M	"	"	"	
Wm. Baldwin	20	M	"	"	"	
P. Murphy	29	M	Cooper	"	"	
Mary "	21	F		"	"	
M. Gardner	25	M	Weaver	"	"	
Jane " & ch.	26	F		"	"	
John T. Ross	55	M	Mariner	U. States	"	Brig Echo. Thompson.

Names of passengers	Age	Sex	Occupation	Country to which they belong	Country of which they intend becoming inhabitants	Ship or vessel with the name of the master or commander
BOSTON Cont.						
Q. E. Sept. 30, 1822						
P. Rovero	30	M	Mariner	U. States	U. States	
Danl. Skillings	50	M	Carpenter	"	"	
Henry S. Gibson	21	M	Supercargo	"	"	
Henry William	40	M	Barber	"	"	
Nicholas Gibart	50	M	Merchant	France	"	Sch. Little Sarah. Lincoln.
Isaiah C. Whitmore	29	M	"	St. Croix	St. Croix	Brig St. Clair. Whitmore.
Eliz. A "	17	F		"	"	
Eliz. Wally * & ch.	44	F	Lady	U. States	U. States	Brig Exchange. Perkins.
Thomas Walley *	21	M	Gent.	"	"	
Mark Ryan	30	M	Blacksmith	Halifax	"	Sch. Billow. Barber.
John "	28	M	Labourer	"	"	
Michael "	25	M	"	"	"	
Patrick Girk	29	M	"	Ireland	"	
Thomas Walsh	26	M	"	"	"	
Thomas Toblar	29	M	"	"	"	
Wm. Harrison	50	M	"	"	"	
Thomas Cleary	21	M	"	"	"	
Pat. Murphy	30	M	"	"	"	
Edwd. Burke	21	M	"	"	"	
Bridget Ryan	26	F		"	"	
Ann "	28	F		"	"	
Joseph Pope Jr.	25	M	Merchant	U. States	"	Brig Caroline. Turner.
Wm. Bowles	22	M	"	"	"	Ship Ceres. Gardner.
John Wood	67	M	Iron founder	G. Britain	"	
Rosanna "	67	F		"	"	
Saml. "	19	M	Brickmaker	"	"	
Wm. " & 2 ch.	22	M	"	"	"	
Robert Wilson	32	M	Farmer	"	"	
Saml. C. Nichols	40	M		"	"	Ship Cadmus. Larcom.
Nicholas Sharp	28	M	Engineer	U. States	"	
A. D. Mallo	31	M	Merchant	Portugal	"	Brig Eliza. Griffith.
T. M. Teal	47	M	"	"	"	
Manuel J. de Matte	24	M	"	"	"	
John Demford	31	M	"	U. States	"	Brig Leo. Perkins.
B. Sarcher & 4 ch.	31	M	"	Havana	"	
B. J. Usher	18	M	"	France	"	Brig Ann Maria. Pope
Eliza Hayden	28	F	Lady	England	"	Ship Triton. Bassey.
George Barker	34	M	Mariner	Smyrna	"	
Mrs. Bussey	31	F		"	"	
N. Niles	25	M	Merchant	Halifax	"	Sch. Lingan. Haskell.
Daniel Collins	25	M	Butcher	Ireland	"	
John Morrison	21	M	Labourer	"	"	
Arthur Lowrey	21	M	Weaver	"	"	
Patrick Collins	20	M	Labourer	"	"	

Names of passengers	Age	Sex	Occupation	Country to which they belong	Country of which they intend becoming inhabitants	Ship or vessel with the name of the master or commander
BOSTON Cont.						
Q. E. Sept. 30, 1822						
John Corsican	48	M	Merchant	Turkey	U. States	
Mrs. " & 2 ch.	38	F		"	"	
Isaac W. Lord	30	M	Merchant	U. States	"	Sch. Franklin. Foster.
Wm. Kelly	18	M	Mariner	"	"	Brig Ant. Lane
L. M. Goldsmith	29	M	Trader	"	"	Sch. Eliza. Hopkins.
M. S. Nevin	25	M	"	"	"	
Danl. Knox	45	M	Supercargo	Ireland	Ireland	Sch. Stork. Bray.
Thomas More	40	M	Weaver	"	"	
Joseph Stuart	25	M	Shoemaker	"	"	
Eleanor " & ch.	25	F		"	"	
Patrick McLaughter	30	M	Shoemaker	"	"	
Mrs. " & ch.	25	F		"	"	
Danl. Winer	28	M	Labourer	"	"	
Ebenezer "	25	M	Farmer	"	"	
Pat. Gallers	30	M	Weaver	"	"	
Eben "	50	M	Farmer	"	"	
James Buckner	50	M	"	"	"	
Mary " & ch.	45	F		"		
Elisha Small	30	M	Teacher	U. States	"	Sch. Thomas. Burgess.
Darius Clapp	23	M			"	
Mr. Freeman	30	M	Merchant	Halifax	Halifax	Sch. Billow. Barker.
Mrs. Freeman	29	F		"	"	
Mr. Young	24	M	Merchant	N. Foundland	U. States	
Miss "	18	F		"	"	
Mrs. Henderson	35	F		"	"	
Mr. Osborn	22	M	Merchant	U. States	"	
M. Pollard	24	M	"	"	"	
John Murphy	26	M	Labourer	Ireland	"	
Wm. Daniel	30	M	"	"	"	
Thos. Byrne	23	M	"	"	"	
James Mayo	26	M	"	"	"	
Bridget "	21	F		"	"	
M. Burnes	19	F		"	"	
Thos. Flanagan	19	M	Labourer	"	"	
Th. Dorshan	20	M	"	"	"	
Mary "	19	F		"	"	
John Doyle	31	M	Labourer	"	"	
Thomas Trull	26	M	"	"	"	
Charles Condor	18	M	"	"	"	
Ann "	18	F		"	"	
Wm. Regan	40	M	Labourer	"	"	
Mary "	40	F		"	"	
John Haley	27	M	Labourer	"	"	
M. Caney	24	M	"	"	"	

Names of passengers	Age	Sex	Occupation	Country to which they belong	Country of which they intend becoming inhabitants	Ship or vessel with the name of the master or commander
BOSTON Cont.						
Q. E. Sept. 30, 1822						
Mary Michael	23	F		Ireland	U. States	
J. Bowes	31	M	Labourer	"	"	
John Dalton	17	M	"	"	"	
John Carter	18	M	"	"	"	
S. Hatfield	18	M	"	"	"	
Wm. Haver	45	M	Gent.	England	"	Ship S. Boston. Campbell.
A. S. Weldberg	23	M	Merchant	Sweden	"	Ship Saco. Woodberry.
J. A. Allen	47	M	"	Matanzas	"	Brig Augustus. Wise.
James Robertson	21	M	Mariner	"	"	Sch. Govr. Brooks. Snow.
Antonio Hernandez	24	M	Merchant	Cuba	"	Brig Turk. Rice.
Francisco Enteria	27	M	Planter	"	"	
E. G. Scudder	31	M		U. States	"	Brig Henry. Atwood.
Geo. F. Barnard	27	M	Mariner	"	"	Sch. Mary & Susan. Curtis.
Chas. Cooper	26	M	Merchant	"	"	Brig Draco. Bishop.
Donarto Gerardi	22	M	"	Italy	"	
Martin Callan	22	M	Marble wkr.	"	"	
Juan Bautisbe	38	M	Merchant	Havana	Havana	Brig Anson. Bignall.
Thomas Read	25	M	Engineer	England	England	
Saml. Beck	28	M	Carpenter	U. States	U. States	Brig Sarah Maria. Williamson.
Joshua Frost	33	M	"	"	"	
Francis Denval	31	M	Merchant	Spain	Spain	
Edward Dove	22	M	"	U. States	U. States	Sch. Lucretia. Fernis.
Anthony Dixon	22	M	"	Scotland	"	Ship Milo. Carelle.
John Smith	70	M	Farmer	"	"	Ship Charles. Brown.
Jane "	60	F		"	"	
Robt. "	25	M	Farmer	"	"	
Duncan McFarland	30	M	"	"	"	
Charlotte "	24	F		"	"	
Robt. McDonald	17	M	Farmer	"	"	
Robt. Black	24	M	"	"	"	
Jane " & ch.	24	F		"	"	
Lewis Grosmer	29	M	Merchant	U. States	"	Ship Herald. Fox.
Saml. Lawrence	22	M	"	"	"	
Wm. Rhodes	34	M	"	England	"	
Mrs. Fox	22	F		U. States	"	
Wm. Hitchey	19	M	Merchant	England	"	Brig Ally ? Nichols.
S J Duport	19	M	Offcr. of U. S. Navy	U. States	"	Sch. Sally Ann. Coles.
A. R. Bogardas	24	M		"		
Mrs. Essom & child	46	F		Halifax	Halifax	Sch. Cherub. Andrews.
Mr. Power	28	M	Merchant	"	"	
Mr. Curtis	19	M	Farmer	"	"	
Mr. Walker	30	M	"	"	"	

Names of passengers	Age	Sex	Occupation	Country to which they belong	Country of which they intend becoming inhabitants	Ship or vessel with the name of the master or commander
RICHMOND Q. E. Sept. 30, 1822						
Henry Braddish	29	M	Farmer	England	Halifax	Brig Laura.
James "	29	M	Clerk	"	"	
NORFOLK Q. E. Sept. 30, 1822						
Edwd. Hudson	35	M	Merchant	U. States	Halifax	Sch. Lorine. Howland
C. J Morris	32	M	Mariner	"	"	Sch. Francis. Seaward.
Donald Chester	22	M	Clerk	"	"	
James Ogilvie	28	M	Merchant	"	"	Brig Hunter. Doggitt.
John Mussen	23	M	Barrister	England	England	Sch. Mary. Bagley.
Thomas Phillips	40	M	Officer	"	"	
George Smith	29	M	Merchant	"	"	
E. J. Teasdale	30	M	"	U. States	U. States	
Wm. W. Lewis	44	M	Farmer	"	"	Sch. Ceres. Brown.
John Smith	30	M	Merchant	England	England	
Thomas Parker	35	M	Farmer	U. States	U. States	
S. J. Bacci	23	M	Ship master	"	"	Brig Only Daughter. Wilkinson.
Michael Rogers	27	M	Shoemaker	"	"	Sch. Columbus. Ross.
Isaac Smith	27	M	Merchant	Bermuda	Bermuda	
John G. Gray	48	M	Farmer	U. States	U. States	Ship Georgiana. Cornick.
Robt. Cruit	27	M	"	England	"	
Catharine Cruit & ch.	25	F		"	"	
James B. Haley	26	M	Merchant	Bermuda	England	Sch. Rose in Bloom. Soule.
James Taylor.	36	M	"	"	"	
--- Boucher	43	M	"	France	France	Ship Felicity. Delaruche.
Andrew Scott	42	M	Merchant	U. States	U. States	Brig Alexr. Kenny.
Mary " & ch.	35	F		"	"	
ALEXANDRIA Q. E. Sept. 30, 1822						
Henry M. Janners	24	M	Merchant	U. States	U. States	Brig Jas Monroe Tobey.
Wm. Waite	31	M	Brick layer	England	"	Ship Boston. Finley.
Mary " & 2 ch.	23	F		"	"	
Wm. Currie	57	M	Farmer	"	"	
Mrs. " & 7 ch.	46	F		"	"	
John Waite	23	M	Farmer	"	"	
Robt. Currie	25	M	"	"	"	
John Milligan	23	M	"	"	"	
Mrs "	21	F		"	"	
Thomas Taylor	30	M	Tailor	"	"	
Thomas Spreid	25	M	Farmer	"	"	
Wm. Patterson	25	M	"	"	"	

Names of passengers	Age	Sex	Occupation	Country to which they belong	Country of which they intend becoming inhabitants	Ship or vessel with the name of the master or commander
ALEXANDRIA Cont.						
Q. E. Sept. 30, 1822						
Hugh Clark	30	M	Farmer	England	U. States	
Mrs. " & 2 ch.	25	F		"	"	
Mary Carroll	26	F		"	"	
Wm. Tunnicliff *	30	M		U. States	"	
Thomas Pursell	21	M	Packer	England	"	Brig Missionary. Downing.
Robt. H. Miller	23	M	Merchant	U. States	"	
PORTLAND & FAL-						
MOUTH						
Q. E. Sept. 30, 1822						
Wm. Gallaghen	40	M	Shoemaker	Ireland	U. States	Ship Tryall. Farnsworth.
Mary " & ch.	38	F		"	"	
Alexander Ballack *	31	M	Surgeon	England	"	
John Graham	30	M	Labourer	Scotland	"	
John Hounam	31	M	Weaver	"	"	
Charles Collins	30	M	Cab. maker	Ireland	"	
Juba " & 5 ch.	26	F	Milliner	"	"	
Jacob Evans	34	M	Roller	S. Wales	"	
R. Bujon	24	M	Peddlar	"	"	
Joseph Carroll & 2 ch.	50	M	Labourer	Ireland	"	
Elizabeth Frazer & 6 ch.	42	F		"	"	
Joseph Menders	27	M	Mariner	Italy	Havana	Brig Amazon. Harward.
Thomas Twiner	25	M	Carpenter	U. States	U. States	Sloop President. Poland.
Nathanl. Carlton	35	M	"	"	"	
Benj. Jewett	25	M	Farmer	"	"	
Orchard Reasly *	27	M	Carpenter	"	"	
Isaac Hosses	23	M	"	"	"	
Vincent Gurzman	15	M		Havana	"	Brig Hind. Prince.
R. Parmer	36	M	Farmer	U. States	"	Sch. Solon. Johnson.
Ephraim Pomroy	21	M	Mariner	"	"	
Henry A. Davis	22	M	Merchant	"	"	
KENNEBUNK						
Q. E. Sept. 30, 1822						
Maria L. Treadwell	29	F		U. States	U. States	Sch. Rapid. Huff.
Mary T. Freeman	27	F		"	"	
P. Constant	31	M	Merchant	France	"	Brig Ospray. Perkins.
PORTSMOUTH						
Q. E. Sept. 30, 1822						
Eliz. Brown & 2 ch.	38	F		England	U. States	Ship Maria. Kennard.

Names of passengers	Age	Sex	Occupation	Country to which they belong	Country of which they intend becoming inhabitants	Ship or vessel with the name of the master or commander
ST. AUGUSTINE Q. E. Sept. 30, 1822						
Francis Gice	30	M	Blacksmith	Florida	Florida	Sch. Opposition. Martinely.
M. Pontremuly	20	M	Scrivener	Spain	"	
Theodore Clinginbies	48	M	Tailor	Poland	"	
Antonio Jose	51	M	Farmer	Canary Isles	"	
Fernandez Gonzales	25	F	Lady	Florida	"	
Maria Fuentes	50	F	"	"	"	
NEWBURYPORT Q. E. Sept. 30, 1822						
John Forrister	32	M	Merchant	Porto Rico	Porto Rico	Vessel not mentioned.
James Golden	19	M	Husbandman	U. States	U. States	
Harding Bradish	22	M	Mariner	"	"	
Joseph Newhause	33	M	"	Cadiz	Havana	
NEW HAVEN Q. E. Sept. 30, 1822						
James Robarts	34	M	Farmer	U. States	U. States	Sch. Industry. Bordington.
G. Bartlett	32	M	"	"	"	
Robert Curtis	34	M	"	"	"	
Mrs. " & 5 ch.	27	F		"	"	
Wm. H. Steer	34	M	Mariner	England	"	Sch. Julia & Laura. Trowbridge
Theodore Duboas	33	M	"	France	"	
Henry Taintor	29	M	Merchant	U. States	"	
BELFAST Q. E. Sept. 30, 1822						
Patrick Costican	30	M	Shoemaker	Ireland	U. States	Sch. Prospect. Perkins.
Laurence "	28	M	Labourer	"	"	
L. Riley	22	M	"	"	"	
M. Harbell & 4 ch.	39	F		Canada	"	Sch. Venus. Emery.
Ann Rourk & ch.	23	F		"	"	
Jude McMann	30	F		"	"	
Alexr. "	28	M		"	"	
Patrick McShea	24	M	Farmer	"	"	
John Mitchell	21	M	"	"	"	
Wm. Tilden	26	M	Painter	U. States	"	
Benjamin Lewis	31	M	Farmer	"	"	
Samuel Spiller	26	M	Blacksmith	"	"	
John Mackey	19	M	Saddler	"	"	
James Clark	20	M	Tanner	"	"	
Geo. M. McDonald	19	M	Brick maker	"	"	

Names of passengers	Age	Sex	Occupation	Country to which they belong	Country of which they intend becoming inhabitants	Ship or vessel with the name of the master or commander
BELFAST Cont.						
Q. E. Sept. 30, 1822						
Wm. Pelcher	46	M	Farmer	U. States	U. States	
Chas. L. Adams & ch.	32	M	Saddler	"	"	
Elizabeth "	30	F		"	"	
Israel Huff	36	M	Mariner	"	"	
Josiah "	37	M	"	"	"	
Christopher Morsey	38	M	Farmer	Ireland	"	
Patrick "	26	M	"	"	"	
Dennis "	23	M	"	"	"	
Mary " & 2 ch.	38	F		"	"	
Wm. Dunlap	22	M	Farmer	"	"	
Nancy "	60	F		"	"	
Elizabeth Dunlap	28	F		"	"	
Jane Dunlap	26	F		"	"	
Margaret Dunlap	24	F		"	"	
John Howard	23	M	Shoemaker	"	"	
Joseph Worener	22	M	Carpenter	"	"	
James McMillan	22	M	Farmer	"	"	
Thomas Morrison	27	M	Blacksmith	"	"	
Patrick Croall	22	M	Mat maker	"	"	
John Joy	23	M	Farmer	"	"	
Nathan Dawes	46	M	Wheelwright	U. States	"	
Edmund Barnes	34	M	Stage driver	"	"	
Wm. Pitcher	46	M	Farmer	"	"	
James Houston	38	M	"	"	"	
Simon Hamilton	27	M	"	"	"	
Elias Cragie	21	M	Blacksmith	"	"	
David Bloomfield	23	M	Clothier	"	"	
George Miller	25	M	Farmer	"	"	
Elijah Elden	24	M	"	"	"	
Jeremiah Mills	25	M	"	"	"	
Samuel "	21	M	"	"	"	
Asa Paine	20	M	"	"	"	
Henry Davis	24	M	"	"	"	
John Fairfield	23	M	Blacksmith	"	"	
Robert Tilden	13	M		. "	"	
Edwd. Samuel	49	M	Mariner	N. Brunswick	"	
Margaret " & 2 ch.	29	F		"	"	
NEW YORK						
Q. E. Sept. 30, 1822						
A. Bowne	50	M	Mariner	U. States	U. States	Brig Belvedere. Hawthorn.
Wm. Sheffield	25	M	"	"	"	
G. Head	35	M	"	G. Britain	"	Brig Robt. Quagle.

Names of passengers	Age	Sex	Occupation	Country to which they belong	Country of which they intend becoming inhabitants	Ship or vessel with the name of the master or commander
NEW YORK Cont.						
Q. E. Sept. 30, 1822						
Sarah Head & 2 ch.	32	F		G. Britain	U. States	
Edward Black	30	M	Clergyman	"	"	
Elizabeth "	27	F		"	"	
David Hearson	30	M	Farmer	"	"	
George "	40	M	Merchant	"	"	
Eliz. " & ch.	32	F		"	"	
Wm. Cooper	28	M	Farmer	"	"	
Charles Cummings	30	M	"	"	"	
James Robson	24	M	"	"	"	
Elizabeth " & 2 ch.	30	F		"	"	
Joseph Cook	34	M		"	"	
Sarah " & 2 ch.	44	F		"	"	
Wm. Thompson	27	M		"	"	
John Page	52	M	Gent.	U. States	"	Brig Assiduous. Lovelass.
Eliz. Phillips & 4 ch.	45	F		G. Britain	"	
Mary McTeeler • & 3 ch.	30	F		Ireland	"	Sch. Huldah & Judah. Thomas.
Samuel Marsh	34	M	Merchant	U. States	"	Ship Nestor. Macy.
James E. Smith	22	M	"	Halifax	Halifax	
Stephen Benney	27	M	"	"	"	
Stanislaus D'Laveduque	30	M		France	U. States	
Robt. McRobb	31	M		Halifax	"	
Eliza. "	25	F		"	"	
L. E. L. Briton	46	M	Merchant	France	"	
James Scott	33	M	Farmer	G. Britain	"	
Jonathan "	26	M		"	"	
Elizabeth " & ch.	25	F		"	"	
L. King	23	F		"	"	
Hugh Ainsley	30	M	Farmer	"	"	
James Willeston	31	M	"	"	"	
Conrad Willet	33	M		Germany	"	
John Haskett	31	M		"	"	
P. Nagle	22	M	Gent.	Ireland	"	Ship Justinia. Aling
L. G. Morsing	25	M	Lawyer	Stockholm	"	Ship Commerce. Apelssen.
W. Morris .	22	M	Silversmith	U. States	"	Brig Helicon. Dayton.
James Lorman	60	M	Farmer	"	"	Brig Fame. Adams.
D. M. Miles	39	M	Mariner	"	"	Brig New Packet. Chase.
J. B. West	42	M		"	"	
L. C. Lutton	40	M		"	"	
Joseph Peircy	27	M	Engineer	"	"	Sloop Wave. Harper.
P. Chardon	24	M	Merchant	Netherlands	"	Brig La Voltigern. Raytes.
H. J. Damey •	36	M	Farmer	"	"	
Henry "	36	M	"	"	"	
H. Sewell	20	M	Surgeon	England	"	Brig Sceptre. Smith.

Names of passengers	Age	Sex	Occupation	Country to which they belong	Country of which they intend becoming inhabitants	Ship or vessel with the name of the master or commander
NEW YORK Cont.						
Q. E. Sept. 30, 1822						
Jane Simpson & 3 ch.	29	F		Scotland	U. States	
Wm. Douglass	25	M	Teacher	"	"	
Rachel Hilloch	29	F		"	"	
Stephen "	30	M	Labourer	"	"	
David Low	25	M	"	"	"	
George McComb	32	M	Merchant	U. States	"	Brig Planter. Pratt.
Nicholas Sarah	30	M	"	"	"	
John Edwards	24	M		"	"	
S. Hanan & child	23	M	Merchant	"	"	
H. C. Desmoulins	30	M	"	France	France	Brig Fair American.
M. F. Alexis	35	F		"	"	
Wm. Dawson	48	M	Merchant	U. States	U. States	Sch. Ariadne.
Pascal Riccardo	35	M		France	"	
Mrs. "	32	F		"	"	
James Guibart	31	M		"	"	
P. Livingston	25	M	Merchant	U. States	"	
John McCall	30	M	Farmer	Ireland	"	Brig Emigrant. Baker.
Wm. McCloy	38	M	Weaver	"	"	
Margt. " & 4 ch.	33	F		"	"	
John Hunter	33	M		"	"	
Jane " & 6 ch.	41	F		"	"	
John Rutherford	38	M	Labourer	G. Britain	"	Brig Ariel. Ritcher.
Mary "	24	F		"	"	
Jane Scobie	31	F		"	"	
John Fraser	20	M	Labourer	"	"	
John Bradley	25	M	"	"	"	
John S. Barnard	22	M	Merchant	U. States	"	Brig Mary. Burns.
Thomas Ratcliff	26	M	Wheelwright	England	"	Sch. Wm. Henry. Drew.
Elizabeth " & 2 ch.	28	F		"	"	
Wm. "	21	M	Tailor	"	"	
Joseph Learson	22	M		Ireland	"	
Charles Conway	36	M	Farmer	"	"	
Martha "	34	F		"	"	
Thomas Banks	37	M		"	"	
Wm. Blanchard	27	M		"	"	
Elizabeth " & ch.	25	F		"	"	
Michael Malady	22	M	Labourer	"	"	
Bridget "	20	F		"	"	
John Newman	24	M		"	"	
James Neivel	26	M		"	"	
Thomas Leny	28	M		"	"	
Joseph Johnson	26	M	Tailor	England	"	
Ann "	24	F		"	"	
James Gray	22	M	Clerk	Ireland	"	

Names of passengers	Age	Sex	Occupation	Country to which they belong	Country of which they intend becoming inhabitants	Ship or vessel with the name of the master or commander
NEW YORK Cont.						
Q. E. Sept. 30, 1822						
Richd. McQuillan	23	M	Labourer	Ireland	U. States	
Thomas Baker	28	M	"	"	"	
Mary "	25	F		"	"	
Dominic Cassady	28	M		"	"	
Robt. McNellan	29	M	Farmer	"	"	
James McCleland	32	M		"	"	
Wm. Phillips	72	M	Stonecutter	Wales	"	
Susanna "	66	F		"	"	
Maria " & ch.	24	F		"	"	
Jacob Highman	20	M	Pedlar	Prussia	"	
John Prime	29	M	Farmer	England	"	
Francis McMurray	35	M	Butcher	Ireland	"	
John McCavin	22	M		"	"	
John Bennet	26	M		England	"	
Mary "	19	F		"	"	
Thomas Hatwell	35	M	Farmer	"	"	
John Riley	27	M	"	Ireland	"	
William Smith	50	M	Clerk	England	"	
James Lunley	20	M	Farmer	"	"	
Jeremiah Lawton	21	M	Captain	U. States	"	
S. Driggs	32	M	Doctor	"	"	Brig Hannah. Mason.
N. Roome	15	M	Clerk	"	"	
Saml. H. Smith	21	M	Merchant	England	"	
Wm. "	19	M		"	"	
Bridget "	50	F		"	"	
Mary " & ch.	24	F		"	"	
A. B. Swift	49	M	Distiller	U. States	"	
J. Hamilton	18	M	Gent.	G. Britain	"	Brig Herton. Webster.
Wm. S. Johnson	18	M	Clerk	"	"	
Charles Huchell	50	M	Merchant	France	"	Ship John & Edwd. Webb.
Mrs. " & 2 ch.	50	F		"	"	
Thomas Owen	23	M	Merchant	U. States	"	Sch. Gleaner. Saunders.
Antonio ---	50	M	"	Spain	"	
John Adams	21	M	"	U. States	"	Sch. Selina. Sislan.
Peter Croniesa	40	M	"	England	"	Brig Mary. Schyler.
Joseph Lammer *	35	M	"	U. States	"	Ship Eagle. Mix.
John C. Delohne *	38	M	"	Geneva	"	
Isaac Metcalf	24	M	Carpenter	Ireland	"	Sch. Abigail. Elwell.
Jane "	50	F		"	"	
Elizabeth "	22	F		"	"	
Jane "	20	F		"	"	
Ann " & 3 ch.	25	F		"	"	
John Jackson	25	M	Farmer	"	"	
James "	22	M	Shoemaker	"	"	

Names of passengers	Age	Sex	Occupation	Country to which they belong	Country of which they intend becoming inhabitants	Ship or vessel with the name of the master or commander
NEW YORK Cont.						
Q. E. Sept. 30, 1822						
Thomas Langton	35	M	Tailor	Ireland	U. States	
James Clency	24	M	Carpenter	"	"	
Elizabeth "	20	F		"	"	
Peter Mains	25	M		"	"	
Eliz. McGowan	35	F		"	"	
Wm. Earle	26	M	Blacksmith	England	England	Sch. Hazard. Higgins.
Margt. Bunton	25	F		"		
James Savage	24	M	Farmer	St. Johns	U. States	Sch. Lingan. Haskell.
P. Slown	23	M		Ireland	"	
Mrs. " & child	20	F		"	"	
Joseph Russell	53	M	Merchant	U. States	"	Ship Acarta. Griswold.
Saml. Humphries	43	M	Mechanic	"	"	
Benj. Wills	40	M	Merchant	"	"	
Mrs. " & child	35	F		"	"	
Samuel McCown	49	M		"	"	
John "	17	M		"	"	
Margt. "	38	F		"	"	
Susanna House	53	F		England	"	
Samuel Wilsford	34	M		"	"	
F. W. "	38	M		"	"	
Edwd. Wadington	27	M		"	"	
Joseph Sills	28	M		"	"	
Wm. Wood	23	M	Stationer	"	"	
Sarah "	55	F		"	"	
Ann "	40	F		Scotland	"	
Margt. Sebballa	55	F		Italy	"	
James Balls	44	M	Merchant	France	"	
Joseph Testi	22	M	Gilder	"	"	
Ferdinand Mea	28	M	Basket maker	"	"	
Richd. F. Damon	18	M	Clock maker	"	"	
Bernd. Beha	30	M	Look. glass maker	"	"	
C. Reckley	39	M	Apothecary	Italy	"	
George Handel	26	M	Farmer	England	"	
Jon. Leslie	28	M	Mason	Scotland	"	Brig James & Margt. Milne.
James Gray	42	M	Farmer	"	"	
Mrs. " & 5 ch.	49	F		"	"	
Thomas Levins	30	M	Clergyman	England	"	Ship Mary. West.
James Bolton	30	M	Merchant	"	"	
Wm. Graham	24	M	Cooper	"	"	
John Thompson	22	M	Tailor	"	"	
John Hoolkins	35	M	Lacksmith	"	"	
Sarah "	30	F		"	"	
J. Fletcher	40	M		"	"	

Names of passengers	Age	Sex	Occupation	Country to which they belong	Country of which they intend becoming inhabitants	Ship or vessel with the name of the master or commander
NEW YORK Cont.						
Q. E. Sept. 30, 1822						
Elizabeth Fletcher & 2 ch.	35	F		England	U. States	
Thos. McRusk	30	M		"	"	
Lawrence McKirk	34	M		"	"	
Owen Martin	45	M	Labourer	"	"	
M. Roodhame *	48	M	Farmer	"	"	
F. Quigley	30	M	Shoemaker	"	"	
Ann "	25	F		"	"	
Joseph Wolnesley	50	M	Farmer	"	"	
Rachel " & ch.	48	F		"	"	
Betsey Harbinson & 4 children	35	F		"	"	
Eliz. Rutherfd. & 8 ch.	30	F		"	"	Brig Cannon. Ryan.
Sarah E. Gibson & 5 ch.	33	F		"	"	
Benj. Burns	43	M	Labourer	"	"	Brig Robert. Mackey.
Thomas Griffith	43	M	"	"	"	
Mary " & 2 ch.	38	F		"	"	
E. Walker	48	M		"	"	
Ann " & 4 ch.	30	F		"	"	
John Lewes	33	M		"	"	
Jane " & 3 ch.	33	F		"	"	
Thomas Williams	25	M		"	"	
Samuel L. Noch	18	M	Brewer	Halifax	U. States	Brig Almira. Bears.
James B. Loveland	18	M	Mariner	"	"	
D. Hannington	30	M	"	"	"	
Mary "	30	F		"	"	
Thomas Welch	40	M	Farmer	"	"	
Margt. "	42	F		"	"	
G. Andrews	36	M	Merchant	"	"	
Edmund Le Duc	45	M	Physician	France	"	
John McAlley	35	M	Teacher	Halifax	"	
Margt. "	43	F		"	"	
Mary Wilkinson	27	F		U. States	U. States	
Catharine Smith	23	F		"	"	
Arnold Manet	24	M	Gent.	Switzerland	"	Ship Hercules. Gardner.
Thomas Wilkinson	26	M	Farmer	England	"	
Cath. Shepherd & 4 ch.	38	F		"	"	
Edmund Robbins	22	M	Merchant	"	"	
James Watson	23	M		"	"	
Geo. Moore	25	M	Cab. Maker	"	"	Ship Pallas. Center.
L. Muchead	25	M	Merchant	Holland	"	
Sarah Shaw & 2 ch.	48	F		G. Britain	"	Ship Euphrates. Stoddard.
John S. Feltus	32	M	Planter	U. States	"	
Charles Pellet	30	M	Merchant	"	"	Brig Eliza. Folger.

NEW YORK Cont.
Q. E. Sept. 30, 1822

Names of passengers	Age	Sex	Occupation	Country to which they belong	Country of which they intend becoming inhabitants	Ship or vessel with the name of the master or commander
Peter Tregent	30	M	Merchant	England	U. States	Ship James Cropper. Rudd.
A. La Branche	68	M	"	N. Orleans	N. Orleans	
Isaac Packard	48	M	"	U. States	U. States	
Mary A. "	18	F		"	"	
Thos. L. Hosman	45	M	Merchant	"	"	
John S. Cray	39	M	"	"	"	
Isaac U. Coles	30	M	"	"	"	
S. Bailie	38	M	"	"	"	
F. Golstanstall	35	M	"	France	"	
Chas. H. Harriman	23	M	"	U. States	"	
Joseph Dodge	30	M	Consul at Marseilles	"	"	
John Sharpe	23	M	Merchant	England	"	
Mary " & child	22	F		"	"	
Joel Root	49	M	Merchant	U. States	"	
John Fernanda	30	M	"	Cape Hatien	"	Brig Eugene. Foster.
G. Vashie	41	M	"	France	"	
E. W. Wild	38	M	"	U. States	"	Ship Eliza Jane. Burger.
Wm. Newbold	22	M	"	England	"	
Don A. Burcid	28	M	"	Spain	"	
Charles Leon	19	M	"	"	"	
Wm. Bordenow	40	M	"	Port au Prince	"	Sch. Nile. Aldrich.
James Irish	25	M	"	Scotland	"	
J. Jacobs	32	M	"	"	"	
Wm. Hewlet	24	M	"	"	"	
D. Tuttle	45	M		U. States	"	Brig Actress. Anderson.
Wm. Wright	40	M	Mariner	St. Johns	"	Sch. Nancy. Crowell.
Fredk. Clement	35	M	Captain	"	"	
Bridget Guthery	38	F		"	"	
James Lears	25	M	Printer	"	"	
A. W. Gillis	22	M	Merchant	"	"	
John Day	20	M		"	"	
Charles Kelly	25	M		Ireland	"	
John Forsyth	45	M		"	"	
Rachael " & 2 ch.	43	F		"	"	
Andw. Forbes	25	M		"	"	
Thomas Bard	28	M	Mariner	"	"	
Rachel "	18	F		"		
Benj. Marshall	20	M		"		
Thos. R. Bockles	30	M		"		
Margaret Gibbons	26	F		"		
George Hamilton & 3 ch	40	M		"		
Daniel La Rey	24	M		"		
Hugh Ganin	30	M		"		

Names of passengers	Age	Sex	Occupation	Country to which they belong	Country of which they intend becoming inhabitants	Ship or vessel with the name of the master or commander
NEW YORK Cont.						
Q. E. Sept. 30, 1822						
A. Smith	58	M		Ireland		
B. " & 4 ch.	40	F		"		
M. Lasqua	45	M	Upholsterer	U. States	U. States	Sch. Andw. Jackson. Loyd.
Mrs. "	30	F		"	"	
W. B. Hardington	25	M	Merchant	"	"	
J. Martins	34	M	"	France	"	
I. Delbrut	23	M	Tailor	"	"	
Lewis Brown	37	M	Merchant	"	"	
Christopher Robert	72	M	Farmer	U. States	"	Ship Alfred. Tuoll.
R. Alverton	25	M	Merchant	France	"	
Mrs. "	25	F		"	"	
J. Gauelet	33	M	Merchant	"	"	Brig Soldade Espard. Tarquin.
George "	30	M	"	"	"	
B. "	28	M	"	"	"	
F. "	40	M	"	"	"	
Ann Adams	38	F		U. States	"	Brig Alciopes. Adams.
J. G. Chamberlain	38	M	Merchant	"	"	
Thos. B. Goslett	23	M	"	"	"	
Martin Areoss	40	M	"	Spain	"	Brig Abeona. Bryan
R. Castello	25	M	"	"	"	
Martin Hall	28	M	"	Ireland	"	
Polly Vandervoort	22	F		U. States	"	
Jane C. Bryan	25	F		"	"	
S. H. Monson	21	M	Merchant	"	"	Ship Amphion. Blann.
H. E. O'Brien	23	M	"	"	"	
A. Belany	40	M	"	"	"	Brig Ambuscade. Skidmore.
A. Hawkins	28	M	Carpenter	"	"	
John Cameron	25	M	Merchant	"	"	
E. G. Gibbs	30	M	Mariner	"	"	
James Murphy	28	M	Merchant		"	Brig Astria. Baker.
Geo. Pinet	35	M	"	France	"	Sch. Traveller. Frost.
Dennis Phelany	22	M	"	"	"	
P. Hawthorn	30	M	Mariner	U. States	"	
M. A. Bolivar & 2 ch.	37	F		Carracoa	"	Sch. Virginia Packet. Allen.
J. Boyr *	52	M	General	Russia	"	Brig Balance. Bennett.
Antonio Moles	17	M	Merchant	"	"	
James Bellamly *	25	M	"	England	"	Ship America. Wallace.
Benj. Johnston	50	M	"	U. States	"	Brig McHope. Allen.
Richd. Peach	50	M	Jeweller	"	"	Sch. Mary. Crowell.
Sally "	45	F		"	"	
J. Goodall	26	M	Merchant	Madiera	"	Brig Factor. Gray.
E. Lawsige	28	M	"	France	"	Brig Aimable. Matilda.
E. Myers	25	M			"	
W. Hall	44	M	Merchant	England	"	Ship Friends. Choate.

Names of passengers	Age	Sex	Occupation	Country to which they belong	Country of which they intend becoming inhabitants	Ship or vessel with the name of the master or commander
NEW YORK Cont.						
Q. E. Sept. 30, 1822						
J. Green & child	38	M	Ship master	U. States	U. States	
John Taylor	40	M	Carpenter	Scotland	"	
John Bee	25	M	Merchant	England	"	
Adam Jamison	20	M	Farmer	Scotland	"	
W. Gillespie	25	M	Tailor	"	"	
Francis "	26	M	Labourer	"	"	
A. H. Judson	32	F		U. States	"	Ship Amity. Maxwell.
Eben Wooster	26	M	Merchant	"	"	
Robt. Rainey	45	M	"	Scotland	"	
John H. Reid	25	M	"	"	"	
Robert Garside	22	M	Manfactr.	England	"	
Robt. Lees	22	M	"	"	"	
George W. Limes	22	M	Mariner	U. States	"	
P. G. Judson	17	M	Merchant	"	"	Sch. Martha. Carlisle.
James Steel	27	M	Gent.	England	"	Ship Elizabeth. Delano.
Mrs. "	24	F		"	"	
Wm. Worrell	37	M		"	"	
J. Guacadin *	42	M		U. States	"	
F. C. Labe	38	M	Professor	"	"	
E. Spencer	31	M	Shoemaker	"	"	
Mrs. " & child	34	F		"	"	
Edgar Higginson	24	M	Farmer	England	"	
C. Dennis	27	M	"	"	"	
B. D. Dessance	22	M	Dyer	"	"	
Richd. Simpson	21	M	Farmer	"	"	
Sarah "	48	F		"	"	
Sarah " Jr.	30	F		"	"	
Mary "	25	F		"	"	
Thomas Drake	27	M	Physician	"	"	
Mrs. "	23	F		"	"	
Isaac Green	45	M	Farmer	U. States	"	Brig Prize. Talbot.
N. Robinson	23	M	Distiller	"	"	
Horace Beckworth	27	M	Merchant	"	"	
Thomas Backus	38	M	"	"	"	
P. Baker & child	33	M	Merchant	England	"	Brig Louisiana. Bugan.
L. Zenisi *	45	M		Tenneriffe	Spain	
Joseph Veires *	17	M		"	"	
Charles Rugan	30	M		U. States	U. States	
Samuel A. Lawrence	40	M	Merchant	"	"	Sch. Brandt. Steinhauer.
Benj. A. Stevens	26	M	"	"	"	
Wm. Peterson	25	M	"	"	"	
Edwd. Penill	21	M	Watchmaker	France	"	Ship Benlomond. Rattray.
John Vyss	24	M	Mill wright	"	"	
G. G. Cookman	21	M	Gent.	G. Britain	G. Britain	Ship Ann. Williams.

Names of passengers	Age	Sex	Occupation	Country to which they belong	Country of which they intend becoming inhabitants	Ship or vessel with the name of the master or commander
NEW YORK Cont.						
Q. E. Sept. 30, 1822						
Richard Hay	24	M	Gent.	G. Britain	G. Britain	
James Banks	47	M	Farmer	"	"	
Wm. Gray	49	M	Glassblower	U. States	"	
Ann " & 4 ch.	44	F		"	"	
David Dunlap	28	M	Merchant	"	"	
Alexr. Davidson	22	M	Mechanic	G. Britain	"	
Geo. Thompson	35	M	"	"	"	
Mary Ann "	30	F		"	"	
Richd. Mahin & 2 ch.	33	M	Farmer	"	"	
James Braimont	42	M	Manfactr.	"	"	
Wm. H. Allen	27	M	Attorney	U. States	"	
Michl. Hudson	35	M	Mechanic	G. Britain	"	
Josiah Cook	23	M	Brewer	"		
Mary "	19	F		"		
Elizabeth Cook	17	F		"		
Edwd. McClary	20	M	Merchant	U. States	U. States	Brig Bordeaux. Balman.
Theodore Claws	35	M	"	"	"	Sch. Nancy. Crowell.
John Dounam	28	M		"	"	
John Spatman	18	M	Labourer	Ireland	"	
S. H. Cox	24	M	Gent.	"	"	Ship John & Adams. Faber.
Henry "	20	M		"	"	
F. Craigh & 4 ch.	27	F		"	"	
Patrick Sullivan	35	M	Merchant	"	"	
E. Hagerty & 4 ch.	55	F		"	"	
Richd. Barry	26	M		"	"	
W. O'Leary	29	M		"	"	
W. Baley	26	M		"	"	
Ellen Sullivan & 4 ch.	34	F		"	"	
Danl. Cosby	20	M		"	"	
J. Dowing	26	M		"	"	
Danl. McNaman	24	M		"	"	
Pat. McCarty	27	M		"	"	
E. Murphey	26	M		"	"	
A. Sullivan	34	M		"	"	
John Finn	21	M		"	"	
M. Collins & child	28	F		"	"	
James Wright	21	M	Gent.	England	England	Ship Manhatten. Croker.
Saml. C. Graves	34	M	"	"	"	
John G. Chapman	25	M	Army	"	"	
W. W. Daulby	28	M	Merchant	"	"	
J. Kenworthy Jr.	21	M	"	"	"	
Wm. Tuly	22	M		"	"	
Pat. Cassady	30	M		"	"	
Wm. Larenby	59	M	Farmer	"	"	

Names of passengers	Age	Sex	Occupation	Country to which they belong	Country of which they intend becoming inhabitants	Ship or vessel with the name of the master or commander
NEW YORK Cont.						
Q. E. Sept 30, 1822						
Joseph Clark	22	M	Farmer	England	England	
John Stansfield	36	M	Linen draper	"	"	
Jane "	42	F		"	"	
Maria " & 4 ch.	37	F		"	"	
John Whitehead & 2 ch.	42	M		"	"	
James Weaton	43	M	Tailor	"	"	
Joseph Lord	19	M		"	"	
Wm. Jackson	27	M	Farmer	"	"	
M. Constantia	38	M	Clergyman	Portugal	"	Sch. Phocion. Duplex.
Mrs. "	45	F		"	"	
James Grogan	20	M	Merchant	Ireland	"	
Marg. Mansfield & ch.	25	F		"	"	
Lucy Ogsburg & 3 ch.	39	F		U. States	"	Sch. Thomas & Sarah. Gay.
John Abrams	31	M	Merchant	"	"	Ship Alfred. Zuille.
Owen Evans	41	M	"	Ireland	"	
Mrs. Kenny	23	F		W. Indies	"	
C. D. Rhodes	28	M	Merchant	U. States	"	
John Dunlap	46	M	Mariner	"	"	
John Riley	31	M	Merchant	England	"	Sch. Mary Ann. Denis.
Robt. Barry	40	M	"	Ireland	"	
Jacob Anderson	30	M	"	Scotland	"	
J. Conton	35	M	Printer	U. States	"	Sch. Abigail. Driggs.
John Marshall	25	M	"	"	"	
John M. Goldrick	41	M	Merchant	"	"	
P. R. Schenck	26	M	"	Italy	U. States	
Louisa McPherson	22	F		England	"	Ship Elias Burger. Disney.
Ann "	24	F		"	"	
Cath. Babcock	27	F		W. Indies	"	
Amos "	34	M	Planter	"	"	
Henry Miller	50	M	"	England	"	
Thomas Nugent	45	M	"	Ireland	"	
F. J. Hanschell	45	M	Merchant	Denmark	"	
J. Cumming	45	M	Planter	Ireland	"	
P. Cruger	45	M	"	W. Indies	"	
J. G. McCant *	34	M	Merchant	Scotland	"	
M. Dyell	28	M	"	"	"	
I. P. Genands *	22	M	Physician	W. Indies	"	
L. Redwood	40	M	Gent.	England	"	Ship Radius. Fanning.
M. Owen	21	M	Gent.	"	"	
W. J. Rutgers	26	M	Merchant	Holland	"	Brig Hippomanes. Bourne.
C. Newcomb	23	M	"	U. States	"	Brig Orleans. Brown.
W. B. Nolan	37	M	Mariner	England	U. Canada	Brig Loyalty. Metcalf.
W. Davidson	20	M	Merchant	"	U. States	
Thomas Hardy	45	M	Teacher	"	"	

Names of passengers	Age	Sex	Occupation	Country to which they belong	Country of which they intend becoming inhabitants	Ship or vessel with the name of the master or commander
NEW YORK Cont.						
Q. E. Sept. 30, 1822						
P. McManus	21	M	Teacher	England	U. States	
Wm. Dick	22	M	Labourer	"	"	
Thomas Willoughby	24	M	Painter	"	"	
Wm. Boardman	27	M	Lawyer	"	"	
Wm. Dunn	30	M	Distiller	"	"	
Wm. Gordon	65	M	Farmer	Scotland	"	Ship Camillus. Peck.
Peter Neilson	26	M	Merchant	"	"	
Eliza " & child	22	F		"	"	
Jane Gordon & 5 ch.	39	F		"	"	
Eliza McPherson & 3 ch.	37	F		"	"	
Jennet McCleod	35	F	Spinster	"	"	
Hugh Barclay	24	M	Farmer	"	"	
Margaret Bell	34	F		"	"	
Wm. Chalmers	43	M	Weaver	"	"	
James Bau	40	M	Millwright	"	"	
D. M. Taulain	39	M	Gardener	"	"	
Jane Taylor & ch.	19	F		"	"	
James Paud *	22	M	Labourer	"	"	
S. Sawyer	33	M		"	"	
C. " & 3 ch.	30	F		"	"	
Jane Blair & 5 ch.	30	F		"	"	
Patrick Bradley	23	M	Labourer	Ireland	"	
Helen "	26	F		"	"	
Thomas R. Anderson	30	M		Scotland	"	
Isabella Ferguson	22	F	Spinster	"	"	
John Jark	19	M	Labourer	"	"	
James Chapman	17	M	"	"	"	
D. McFarlain	17	M	"	"	"	
Wm. McIntire	24	M	"	"	"	
J. M. Kittera	24	M	Merchant	U. States	"	Ship Antelope. Berrien.
Hugh Salsbury	29	M	Farmer	Ireland	"	Sch. Loire. Bassett.
M. Farrow	20	M	Labourer	"	"	
Mary "	20	F		"	"	
B. McLaughlin	20	M	Farmer	"	"	
Nancy "	19	F		"	"	
Maria Orton *	16	F		"	"	
B. Carman	20	M		"	"	
Jane Orton *	26	F		"	"	
Helen Miller & ch.	30	F		"	"	
Danl. McLaughlin	19	M	Tailor	"	"	
James Morin	22	M	Farmer	"	"	
Chas. Douglass	36	M	Merchant	U. States	"	Brig Betsey. Cunningham.
Maria " & ch.	23	F		"	"	

Names of passengers	Age	Sex	Occupation	Country to which they belong	Country of which they intend becoming inhabitants	Ship or vessel with the name of the master or commander
NEW YORK Cont.						
Q. E. Sept. 30, 1822						
J. M. Pintado	35	M	Merchant	Spain	U. States	Brig Dolphin. Tissett.
D. I. A. Abeille	24	M	Physician	U. States	"	Sch. Ann Eliza Jane. Abeille.
M. Duperius	26	M	Merchant	France	"	
P. Cavalrey	17	M	"	Porto Rico	"	
Stephen Price	39	M	Gent.	U. States	"	Ship Wm. Thompson.
W. Livingston	23	M	"	"	"	
Thos. Barclay	70	M	"	"	"	
Robt. Hunt	20	M	"	"	"	
B. Jackson	28	M	Merchant	"	"	
Chas. Matthews	45	M	Comedian	London	G. Britain	
John Holmes	45	M	Merchant	"	"	
I. P. Phoenix	25	M	"	U. States	U. States	
I. P. Taylor	25	M	"	"	"	
I. R. Angell	27	M	"	"	"	
F. H. Reynolds	33	M	"	"	"	
L. Broughton	21	M	"	"	"	
James Lanchez	45	M	"	Spain	Spain	Brig Lucy Ann. Davis.
Mrs. " & ch.	35	F		"	"	
S. Hartman	30	M	Planter	St. Croix	U. States	Ship S. Carolina. Cartwright.
D. Buslock	20	M	Merchant	U. States	"	
R. Rogers & child	56	F		St. Croix	"	
A. G. Limberg	40	M	Merchant	Denmark	"	
James Hobson	52	M	Farmer	G. Britain	"	Brig Jamaica. Bates.
Eliz. " & 6 ch.	42	F		"	"	
Margt. Black & 5 ch.	48	F		"	"	
John Armstrong	34	M	Farmer	"	"	
Geo. Beatty	37	M	Farmer	"	"	
Isaac Richardson	33	M	"	"	"	
Eliza " & ch.	29	F		"	"	
Jerry "	36	M	Farmer	"	"	
Christian Bell	50	M	"	"	"	
Hugh Scanler	20	M	"	"	"	
Thos. McCornell	21	M	"	"	"	
Thomas Powers	25	M	"	"	"	
Wm. Williams	20	M	"	"	"	
J. Stilman	18	M	Carpenter	U. States	"	Sch. Almira. Bears.
Mary "	40	F		"	"	
Margt. Hallet	25	F		"	"	
Peggy "	20	F		"	"	
Sarah "	38	F		"	"	
David Ormster	23	M	Merchant	Scotland	"	Sch. Rufus King. Badger.
Nancy " & child	24	F		"	"	
Thomas Melleger	47	M	Iron founder	U. States	"	
Mary " & ch.	25	F		"	"	

NEW YORK Cont.
Q. E. Sept. 30, 1822

Names of passengers	Age	Sex	Occupation	Country to which they belong	Country of which they intend becoming inhabitants	Ship or vessel with the name of the master or commander
Jas. Ormster	37	M	Merchant	Scotland	U. States	
Jane Craig	24	F	Seamstress	"	"	
R. Green	37	M	Farmer	England	"	
R. Nash	22	M	Shoemaker	"	"	
Wm. Hearsay	30	M	Mariner	U. States	"	Brig Thomas. Sampson.
Anthony Rolla	37	M	Merchant	Switzerland	"	
Margt. Norris	65	F	Lady	Ireland	"	Sch. Dublin Packet. Newcomb.
Catharine Egless *	40	F		"	"	
Wm. James	24	M	Clergyman	U. States	"	
John McEneroe *	26	M	"	Ireland	"	
James Harris	24	M	Merchant	England	"	
J. F. Tray	54	M	"	Ireland	"	
Saml. P. Monns *	22	M	"	"		
Wm. Pentland	19	M	Farmer	"		
Dennis McManns	26	M	"	"		
Mary Jones	60	F	Spinster	"		
Jane Brown	21	F	"	"		
Michael Stephens	22	M	Farmer	"		
John Foderhorst & 4 ch.	40	M	Merchant	Hamburgh	U. States	Ship Maria Elizabeth. Hamburg
F. Janicke	35	M	"	"	"	
I. I. Wance	23	M	"	"	"	
C. Haskell	30	M	"	"	"	
Wm. McCall	38	M	"	England	"	Ship Favorite. Bearns.
John Robson	59	M	Farmer	"	"	
A. Hunt or Hurst	29	M	Weaver	"	"	
Thomas Greenhoff	23	M		"	"	
Wm. Bournot	35	M	Manufactr.	"	"	
Thomas Johnson	28	M	"	"	"	
J. O'Brien	40	M	Blacksmith	Ireland	"	
Esther "	30	F		"	"	
A. Wilkins	23	M	Brewer	"	"	
Andw. Gray	24	M	Merchant	G. Britain	"	Ship Florida Mattock.
Joseph Sands	26	M	"	"	"	
Jeremiah Rhodes	30	M	"	"	"	
Wm. Banaclough	30	M	"	"	"	
Abraham Wrigley	40	M	"	"	"	
Robt. Parker	35	M	"	"	"	
John Welds	21	M	"	"	"	
Robt. I Kerr	28	M	Gent.	England	"	Ship William. Moffat.
Mary Ann "	22	F		"	"	
Thos. Farley	25	M		"	"	
H. Bonnet & 6 ch.	38	F		"	"	
George Cross & ch.	40	M	Mechanic	"	"	
M. Skinman	31	M	Merchant	U. States	"	Brig Prince Edwd. Searl.

Names of passengers	Age	Sex	Occupation	Country to which they belong	Country of which they intend becoming inhabitants	Ship or vessel with the name of the master or commander
NEW YORK Cont.						
Q. E. Sept. 30, 1822						
I. B. Isambartle	28	M	Merchant	Switzerland	U. States	Brig Leonidas. Lord.
Adolphus Dunan	24	M	Doctor	U. States	"	Ship Elbe. Syme.
Edwd. Chanou	19	M	Artist	France	"	
G. Duclese	20	M	Clerk	"	"	
F. Canolo	28	M	Architect	"	"	
Madam Canoto	25	F		"	"	
John Steinere	30	M	Farmer	Switzerland	"	
Jacob Coseti	40	M	"	"	"	
J. Cobratt	35	M	"	"	"	
Michl. Stunock	30	M	"	"	"	
John Venzer	29	M	"	"	"	
Christr. Hindrick	32	M	"	"	"	
Saml. Vise	35	M	Shoemaker	"	"	
Christian Besege	52	M		"	"	
Michael Gaver	58	M	Clock maker	"	"	
W.	39	M	Weaver	"	"	
Antonio Herman	38	M	Farmer	"	"	
John Gaeber	42	M	Weaver	"	"	
John Basager	30	M	"	"	"	
Ulsch ? "	24	M	Farmer	"	"	
Peter Vise	22	M	"	"	"	
Joseph Romsey	27	M	"	"	"	
Jacob "	30	M	Weaver	"	"	
Jacob Smoker	21	M	Miller	"	"	
Christian Onett *	38	M	Farmer	"	"	
Joseph Sintor/Suitor	15	M	Shoe maker	"	"	
Jacob Newspond *	20	M	Farmer	"	"	
Joseph Rumsey	20	M	Weaver	"	"	
Christian "	18	M	Farmer	"	"	
Fred. Vangar *	22	M	"	"	"	
Ulrick Steiner	24	M	"	"	"	
W. Geger	32	M	"	"	"	
Jacob Gaeber	30	M	Weaver	"	"	
Ulrick Nashwan	26	M	"	"	"	
Danl. Cosett	18	M	Farmer	"	"	
Christian Gasler	19	M	"	"	"	
H. Gronever *	24	M	Teacher	"	"	
John Bezleir *	28	M	Weaver	"	"	
Matthew Miller	18	M	Cooper	"	"	
John Gaeber	18	M	Joiner	"	"	
Fred. Jont *	26	M	Brewer	"	"	
P. "	25	M	Wheelwright	"	"	
Fred. Balliard	26	M	Brewer	"	"	
John Chander	28	M	Farmer	"	"	

Names of passengers	Age	Sex	Occupation	Country to which they belong	Country of which they intend becoming inhabitants	Ship or vessel with the name of the master or commander
NEW YORK Cont.						
Q. E. Sept. 30, 1822						
A. Hasthers	26	M	Watchmaker	Switzerland	U. States	
Mary Baseger	28	F		"	"	
Eliz. "	22	F		"	"	
Francis "	20	F		"	"	
Barbara Garbaca	44	F		"	"	
Susan Botick	29	F		"	"	
Barbara Garbaca	23	F		"	"	
Cath. Vice & 3 ch.	23	F		"	"	
Mrs. Cosset & 6 ch.	24	F		"	"	
A. Musson	41	M	Merchant	Bermuda	"	Sch. Lucan. Chace.
Mrs. " & 2 ch.	27	F		"	"	
George Gibson	22	M	Merchant	"	"	
Saml. Turner	33	M	"	U. States	"	Brig S. Carolina. Johnson.
Mrs. "	22	F		"	"	
P. Benjamin	53	M	Merchant	"	"	
Mary " & 3 ch.	40	F		"	"	
George Carter	50	M		"	"	
Peter Newman	35	M	Mariner	"	"	
James Miller	37	M	Physician	Scotland	Halifax	Sch. Hunter. Sears.
James Ellis	23	M	Merchant	"	"	
Lewis Knout	40	M	"	Hanover	U. States	Brig Perseverence. Bray.
Robt. Walhewson •	30	M	"	England	"	Sch. Dart. Van Dene.
Archibald Hope	20	M	"	"	"	
James Russell	25	M	"	U. States	"	Brig Intrepid. Jason.
Thomas Brown	47	M	Farmer	G. Britain	"	
Thomas Cochrane	27	M	Merchant	"	"	
Wm. Forrester	30	M	Labourer	"	"	
James McIntire	36	M	Farmer	U. States	"	
Mary " & 3 ch.	26	F		"	"	
A. McAustin	26	M	Farmer	G. Britain	"	
John Hay	24	M	"	"	"	
Wm. Stevenson	24	M	Labourer	"	"	
Alexr. Rodgers	20	M	Merchant	U. States	"	
James Buchanan	19	M		"	"	
Mrs. Rolin & Son	32	F		"	"	Ship Belle. Wibray.
Edwd. Vedde	25	M	Gent.	France	"	
Charles Harvick	21	M	"	U. States	"	
Geo. Barcroft	21	M	Student	"	"	
C. Panrin •	18	M	Mechanic	France	"	
H. Cort	22	M	"	"	"	
Geo. W. Lee	45	M	Merchant	"	"	
G. W. Lyman	35	M		U. States	"	Ship Cortes. De Cost.
Eliz. " & 2 ch.	29	F		"	"	
J. Smith	67	M	Merchant	"	"	

Names of passengers	Age	Sex	Occupation	Country to which they belong	Country of which they intend becoming inhabitants	Ship or vessel with the name of the master or commander
NEW YORK Cont.						
Q. E. Sept. 30, 1822						
Wm. D. Powell	66	M	Chief Justice	G. Britain	Canada	
John Connell	37	M	Merchant	U. States	U. States	
George Machie	29	M	"	"	"	
R. H. Height	23	M	"	"	"	
John Ryan	40	M		"	"	
F. Platt	21	M	Clerk	G. Britain	"	
Samuel Armstrong	35	M	Farmer	"	"	
J. H. Holmes	22	M	"	"	"	
John Augustine & ch.	45	M	Merchant	Spain	Porto Rico	Brig Otter. Bayley.
Antonio Belliand	30	M	"	"	U. States	Brig Packet. Penn.
John Roberts	35	M	"	U. States	"	
H. B. Wolf	32	M	"	"	"	Brig Upton. Sampson.
D. Scainsborough	25	M	Shoemaker	Ireland	"	Sch. Climax. Prince.
Hannah " & 2 ch.	22	F		"	"	
Felix Surseau	35	M	Merchant	U. States	"	Brig Buck. Hutchinson.
F. Lawing	30	M	"	France	"	
Peter E. Devral *	30	M	"	"	"	
J. Varrick	30	M	"	"	"	
W. D. Patlin	19	M	"	U. States	"	Ship Adriana. Quercian.
N. W. Whitencoth	28	M	"	"	"	
H. J. Hulson	34	M	Carpenter	"	"	
John Griffin & ch.	35	M	Confectioner	France	"	Brig Chatham. Harding.
A. Delitant	55	M	Supercargo	"	"	
A. " Jr.	20	M	Gent.	"	"	
J. Peters	45	M	Mariner	U. States	"	Sch. Diana. McPherson.
Wm. Voyart	37	M	"	"	"	
Wm. Peters	21	M	"	"	"	
M. J. Collins	26	M	Mility. Offr.	England	England	Sch. Almira.
Rebecca " & child	25	F		"	"	
Wm. Thompson	37	M	Merchant	U. States	U. States	
Joseph Paiz	42	M	"	France	"	Brig Commerce. Funk.
Richd. Harris	33	M	Labourer	G. Britain	"	Ship Comet. Boag.
Mary " & 2 ch.	27	F		"	"	
John Bates	39	M		"	"	
Thomas Baker	31	M		"	"	
M. "	28	M		"	"	
P. Williams	40	M	Labourer	"	"	
Robt. Hibbit	29	M	Gardner	"	"	
Susan " & ch.	27	F		"	"	
Henry Mitchell	22	M		"	"	
W. W. Priest	27	M	Farmer	"	"	
Wm. Goodbehr	22	M	"	"	"	
Paul Riche	53	M	Cooper	"	"	
Wm. Lowry	20	M	Labourer	"	"	

PASSENGERS WHO ARRIVED IN THE U.S. SEPTEMBER 1821 - DECEMBER 1823

Names of passengers	Age	Sex	Occupation	Country to which they belong	Country of which they intend becoming inhabitants	Ship or vessel with the name of the master or commander
NEW YORK Cont.						
Q. E. Sept. 30, 1822						
H. Haslin	45	M	Labourer	G. Britain	U. States	
John Cleary	20	M	Farmer	"	"	
Geo. Shaw	24	M	"	"	"	
Saml. "	60	M	"	"	"	
Jane " & 3 ch.	28	M		"	"	
M. Ennis	24	M	Coachmaker	"	"	
Jno. Askin	26	M	"	"	"	
Thomas Evans	42	M	Labourer	"	"	
John Buly	52	M	Farmer	"	"	
Ann " & 4 ch.	53	F		"	"	
Thomas Elwood	64	M	Farmer	"	"	
Ann "	26	F		"	"	
Thomas Medlar	48	M	Farmer	"	"	
Susan " & 3 ch.	54	F		"	"	
Saml. "	25	M	Farmer	"	"	
Jno. "	27	M	"	"	"	
Alexr. Read	32	M	Clerk	"	"	
Eliza " & 3 ch.	32	F		"	"	
James Little	26	M	Clerk	"	"	
Cath. "	22	F		"	"	
John Levin	26	M	Blacksmith	"	"	
P. "	30	M	Farmer	"	"	
Catharine Levin	25	F		"	"	
John Shaw	35	F ?		"	"	
C. Cleary	50	F ?		"	"	
S. Blane	26	F ?	Merchant	U. States	"	Ship Columbia. Rogers.
Wm. Everhart	36	F ?	"	"	"	
John McCracken	47	M	"	"	"	
C. H. Russell	25	M	"	"	"	
John P. Wilson	32	M	"	"	"	
Isaac Coffin	50	M	B. Navy	G. Britain	G. Britain	
James Erving	30	M	Merchant	"	"	
Archibald Gordon	20	M	"	"	"	
Thos Watkinson	40	M	Comedian	"	"	
James Gallagher & 3 ch.	30	M		"	"	
Richd. Jennings	28	M	Lawyer	"	"	
Thomas " & ch.	26	M		"	"	
Moses Tryon	38	M	Merchant	U. States	U. States	Brig Radius. Granger.
L. Haff	27	M	"	"	"	
Joseph Randal	28	M	Farmer	"	"	Brig Mount Hope. Alex. Allen.
Isabella " & 4 ch.	49	F		"	"	
A. B. Vanhorn	28	M	Merchant	"	"	Brig Betsey. Waly.
Thomas Robertson	40	M	Mariner	"	"	Ship Glenthorne. K. Lewis.
H. G. D. Schmidtz	32	M	Gent.	Germany	"	Ship Debby & Eliza.

Names of passengers	Age	Sex	Occupation	Country to which they belong	Country of which they intend becoming inhabitants	Ship or vessel with the name of the master or commander
NEW YORK Cont.						
Q. E. Sept. 30, 1822						
Edwards Williams	30	M	Gent.	Germany	U. States	
Jas. J. Wesbits	41	M	"	"	" "	Sch. Olive Branch.
Robt. Patterson	23	M	Merchant	Wales	"	
Rufus Evans	23	M	"	U. States	"	Sch. Weymouth.
A. Roberts	35	M	"	"	"	
F. Sureas	25	M	"	"	"	
J. Mantier	26	M	"	Spain	"	
Rufus Gens	27	M	"	"	"	
A. Foster	22	M	"	U. States	"	Brig Francis. Boyer.
John Durato & child	31	M	Planter	St. Martins	"	Brig Matilda. McKown.
M. Monroe & child	24	F		U. States	"	
H. W. Plant	25	M	Merchant	G. Britain	St. Johns	Sch. Nancy. Crowell.
Wm. Sudlin	40	M	Officer	"	Canada	
W. Ogden	40	M	Merchant	U. States	U. States	
M. Mulich	22	M	"	St. Johns	St. Johns	
Rachel Crow	28	F		U. States	U. States	
Isabella Nicolls	35	F		"	"	
Geo. Petchin	40	M	Merchant	St. Johns	St. Johns	
Wm. Hay	25	M	Baker	U. States	U. States	
Eliza. "	20	F		"	"	
B. Adkins	30	M	Merchant	"	"	
John Meised	30	M	"	"	"	
Wm. McNamar	30	M	Farmer	Ireland	"	
James "	20	M	"	"	"	
Wm. "	18	M	"	"	"	
Eliz. Kelly	35	F		"	"	
Esther Swann	20	F		"	"	
Margt. Swan & 3 ch.	18	F		Ireland	"	
Rebecca Long	25	F		"	"	
James Mills	18	M		"	"	
John Black	25	M	Labourer	"	"	
Jane "	20	F		"	"	
Eliz. Brittain	30	F		"	"	
Martha Quig	28	F		"	"	
Wm. McGughy *	25	M		"	"	
Wm. Cromby	30	M		"	"	
Sarah "	28	F		"	"	
R. Hurley	25	M		"	"	
Ellen " & child	25	F		"	"	
John Cross	30	M		"	"	
Sarah "	28	F		"	"	
N. McNames	18	F		"	"	
Ellen McGuire	15	F		"	"	
Catharine "	16	F		"	"	

Names of passengers	Age	Sex	Occupation	Country to which they belong	Country of which they intend becoming inhabitants	Ship or vessel with the name of the master or commander
NEW YORK Cont.						
Q. E. Sept. 30, 1822						
Rose Buchanan	16	F		Ireland	U. States	
Ann "	15	F		"	"	
Mary Wright	14	F		"	"	
Margt. "	18	F		"	"	
Isabella "	17	F		"	"	
Henry Forsyth	16	M		"	"	
John Steward	25	M		"	"	
Thompson Steward	20	M		"	"	
Mary McGee	18	F		"	"	
Isabella Johnston	18	F		"	"	
Thomas Swan	30	M		"	"	
Thomas Hegan	25	M		"	"	
Thomas Riley	20	M		"	"	
John Shudder	20	M		"	"	
B. Brady	25	M		"	"	
R. McDonald	30	M		"	"	
Joseph Dealy	25	M		"	"	
Thos. McCask	28	M		"	"	
A. McAllister	25	M		"	"	
F. M. McCurger *	20	M		"	"	
R. Palmer	20	M		"	"	
John Glass	24	M		"	"	
C. Dawson & child	21	M		"	"	
Mary Conelly	20	F		"	"	
Ann Burns & 2 ch.	25	F		"	"	
Mary Cross	16	F		"	"	
Mary Sheridan	18	F		"	"	
John Thorpe	29	M	Merchant	England	"	Ship Indian Chief. Humphrey.
Thos. Holmes	30	M	"	"	"	
Robt. Cummings	25	M	"	"	"	
James Baynes	46	M	Farmer	Ireland	"	
Eliz. " & 9 ch.	46	F		"	"	
Michael Akins ?	45	M		England	"	
Eliz. " & 3 ch.	37	F		"	"	
An O'Neil & 5 ch.	56	F		"	"	
Edwd. Wardell	25	M	Farmer	"	"	
Mary "	19	F		"	"	
Geo. Beron	18	M	Labourer	"	"	
Thos. Whitross	47	M	Farmer	"	"	
Cath. " & 6 ch.	42	F		"	"	
Thomas Johnson &2 ch.	32	F	Flax dresser	"	"	
H. Murgeturd	26	F		"	"	
E. Howell & 3 ch.	31	F		"	"	
Jas. Pemberton	35	M	Gardner	U. States	"	

Names of passengers	Age	Sex	Occupation	Country to which they belong	Country of which they intend becoming inhabitants	Ship or vessel with the name of the master or commander
NEW YORK Cont.						
Q. E. Sept. 30, 1822						
Thomas Pemberton	18	M	Gardner	U. States	U. States	
John James	45	M	Labourer	"	"	
Isaac Gancaster	30	M	Weaver	"	"	
George Rudford	39	M	Gardner	"	"	
Anthony Jones	34	M	Physician	Scotland	"	
Thomas Tinker	34	M	Farrier	England	"	
Wm. Young	30	M	Cordwainer	"	"	
Pat. Bryan	51	M	Teacher	Ireland	"	
P. McClosky	34	M	Labourer	"	"	
Thomas Millain	30	M	"	"	"	
James Gordon	28	M	"	"	"	
Sarah Donaghey	25	F		Ireland	"	
Grace Mastersan	27	M	Labourer	"	"	
Thomas Brady	19	M	"	"	"	
Pat. Drum	24	M	"	"	"	
Pat. McGuire	21	M	"	"	"	
Francis Magahy	24	M	"	"	"	
P. McCabe	27	M	"	"	"	
John "	22	M	"	"	"	
John Robinson	21	M	"	"	"	
David Fergus	60	M	Clergyman	G. Britain	"	Brig Natchez. Cook.
Jannit "	60	F		"	"	
Mary "	26	F		"	"	
A. Langland	40	M	Farmer	"	"	
Jennit " & 4 ch.	27	F		"	"	
John Turner	28	M		"	"	
Agnes "	55	F		"	"	
Robert Porter	26	M	Farmer	G. Britain	U. States	
Robt. Culbertson	30	M	"	"	"	
John "	23	M	"	"	"	
Peter McMecachy	23	M	"	"	"	
Jean "	50	F		"	"	
Mary " & 8 ch.	44	F		"	"	
Margt. Reed	60	F		"	"	
Alexr. "	52	M	Farmer	"	"	
Margt. " Jr.	25	F		"	"	
Elizabeth "	17	F		"	"	
Jennet Watson & 5 ch.	35	F		"	"	
C. J. FitzManus	30	M	B. Army	Ireland	"	Sch. Exchange. Davis.
M. Tadquin	26	M	Planter	Scotland	"	
M. Pinto	55	M	Merchant	U. States	"	
A. Milne	22	M	Farmer	Scotland	"	
B. Johnston	49	M	Mariner	U. States	"	Brig Harmony. Lewis.
Mrs. " & child	35	F		"	"	

Names of passengers	Age	Sex	Occupation	Country to which they belong	Country of which they intend becoming inhabitants	Ship or vessel with the name of the master or commander
NEW YORK Cont.						
Q. E. Sept. 30, 1822						
Henry Bau •	60	M	Merchant	U. States	U. States	Sch. June Ann. Colley.
James Anners •	25	M		G. Britain	"	Brig Magnet. Mount.
Ann "	24	F		"	"	
Mary Fox & 2 ch.	26	F		"	"	
L. Leverick	23	M	Mariner	U. States	"	
James Pearl	23	M	Farmer	"	"	
Michl. Redding	40	M	"	G. Britain	"	
Charles Hickland	44	M	Weaver	"	"	
B. Glerney	42	M	"	"	"	
P. McKay	22	M	"	"	"	
John U. Castle	60	M	Notary	France	"	Brig Little John. Willis.
M. Guibert	30	M		U. States	"	
E. Gemming	29	M	Merchant	England	"	
M. Jessop & 2 ch.	40	F		"	"	
Wm. Achers	45	M	Merchant	"	"	
John Aldum	38	M	"	"	"	
Wm. C. Shaw	35	M	Mariner	"	"	Brig Fame. Ross.
James E. James	36	M	Farmer	"	"	Ship Meteor. Cobb.
Lydia " & 2 ch.	34	F		"	"	
F. Witherall & 9 ch.	28	F		"	"	
Saml. Parris	23	M	Butcher	"	"	
Wm. Shepherd	35	M	Merchant	"	"	
J. Robinson	35	M	"	"	"	
Wm. Whitten	20	M	"	U. States	"	Ship Wm. John. Ebbets.
Thomas Gregory	40	M	"	"	"	
Theodore Kimbal	19	M	"	"	"	Brig Indian Chief. Nye.
S. Sherriff	36	M	Labourer	Scotland	"	Brig Margaret. Mitchell.
Elizabeth Sherriff	20	F		"	"	
Geo. Benton	23	M	Labourer	"	"	
Peter "	30	M	"	"	"	
Jane "	25	F		"	"	
Alexr. Maxton	22	M	Clerk	"	"	
Matthew Lemartin	24	M	Labourer	"	"	
R. McGregor	22	M	"	"	"	
James Whitlane	52	M	"	"	"	
Jane " & 6 ch.	41	F		"	"	
Mary Renton	20	F		"	"	
Elizabeth Muar •& 4 ch.	40	F		"	"	
John M. Read	35	M	Merchant	St Croix	"	Brig Condor. Goodrich.
J. W. Alsop	48	M	"	U. States	"	
P. A. Krug	25	M	Mariner	Denmark	"	
John Coningham	26	M	Merchant	Ireland	"	Brig Magnet. Levenart.
Ann Cally & 2 ch.	30	F		"	"	
Thomas John	55	M	Farmer	England	England	Ship Rockingham. Coffin.

Names of passengers	Age	Sex	Occupation	Country to which they belong	Country of which they intend becoming inhabitants	Ship or vessel with the name of the master or commander
NEW YORK Cont.						
Q. E. Sept. 30, 1822						
Jno. F. John	22	M	Farmer	England	England	
Eleanor "	21	F		"	"	
Wm. Cove	56	M	Farmer	"	"	
Eliz. "	16	F		"	"	
Rosanna Lunch	21	F		"	"	
James Oaldfield *	16	M		"	"	
Thos. Bridges & ch.	48	F		"	"	
David Hine	24	M	Carpenter	"	"	
Wm. Fiurguard	21	M	Merchant	"	"	
Simon Coleman	47	M	"	"	"	
Nicholas Hopkins	59	M	"	"	"	
J. Brown	34	M	Baker	U. States	"	
Charles Townsend	54	M	Grocer	"	"	
J. A. Bruce	32	M	Merchant	"	"	Ship Jas. Monroe. Marshall.
E. J. Forstace	26	M	"	"	"	
John Newton	22	M	"	England	"	
James Manks	40	M	"	"	"	
Ann Brookes	43	F		"	"	
Margt. Gibson	27	F		"	"	
N. Hadden & 3 ch.	31	F		"	"	
Chas. Henlquesen *	25	M	Merchant	Germany	Germany	Brig Vorwatz.
Thomas Mountion	51	M	Gent.	Denmark	Denmark	Ship Chase. Baxter.
Chas. Rasmusson	44	M	"	"	" "	
G. Van Schmidler	37	M	"	"	"	
N. H. Thildt	28	M	Army	"	"	
R. W. Lawson	23	M	"	England	England	
John Gibes	38	M	Gent.	"	"	
Peter James	29	M		Denmark	Denmark	
Richd. Hathamon	39	M	Farmer	G. Britain	U. States	Brig Laburnan. Taylor.
F. " & 4 ch.	37	F		"	"	
J. Comforth & child	23	M	Ganger	"	"	
Thomas Brown	45	M	Merchant	U. States	"	Sch. Patty & Sally. Rawson.
Jas. McKibbin	36	M	Shoemaker	Ireland	"	Sch. Jas. Monroe. Gibs.
Eliza " & 4 ch.	34	F		"	"	
Gordon Savage	22	M		"	"	
Margt. Whiteside & 6 ch.	40	F		"	"	
Thomas Watson	38	M	Gent.	G. Britain	G. Britain	Ship Ductile. Williams.
Asa W. Welden	43	M	Mariner	U. States	U. States	
M. Terth	27	M	Shoemaker	England	"	Ship Ann Maria. Gale.
Mrs. " & 6 ch.	25	F		"	"	
Isabella Gunton & ch.	50	F		"	"	
Wm. Wriott	26	M	Farmer	"	"	
Sarah " & 3 ch.	25	F		"	"	

Names of passengers	Age	Sex	Occupation	Country to which they belong	Country of which they intend becoming inhabitants	Ship or vessel with the name of the master or commander
NEW YORK Cont.						
Q. E. Sept. 30, 1822						
John Farmer	24	M		England	U. States	
James Sheinks	25	M		"	"	
John Gallagher	23	M		"	"	
John Francis	25	M		"	"	
James Murphy	30	M	Trader	"	"	
John Halwood	21	M	"	"	"	
John Olman	25	M	Merchant	"	"	
Samuel Reforce	25	M	"	Ireland	"	Sch. Ospray. Rice
Alex. McNaugton	31	M	Physician	Scotland	"	Ship Cadmus. Whitlock.
L. J. Salargnac	25	M	Merchant	U. States	"	
John David	60	M	"	France	"	
Mrs. "	26	F	Seamstress	"	"	
Jno. Mortimer	47	M	Gent.	U. States	"	
Sarah "	45	F		"	"	
Charlotte "	23	F		"	"	
P. A. Philippe	34	F	Seamstress	France	"	
A. T. Hognet	51	M	Merchant	U. States	"	
K. J. Lequin	34	M	Physician	England	"	
B. C. Tutler *	23	M	"	"	"	
E. M. Bardy	21	M	"	"	"	
Thomas Searle	26	M	Merchant	U. States	"	
Francis B. Rhodes	21	M	"	"	"	
Joseph Duprie	28	M	"	France	"	
Louis A. Delancenville	29	M	"	"	"	
Thos. Fitzgibbon	49	M	" "	England	"	
Mrs. Dorothy (" ?)	40	F		"	"	
Fred. W. Roussel	37	M	Blacksmith	Swiss	"	
H. Luvy *	27	M	Merchant	France	"	
C. Cahn	23	M	Merchant	"	"	
Eliz. Mount	53	F	Seamstress	"	"	
Benj. Thompson	49	M	Druggist	England	"	Ship Packet. Boggs.
Wm. Grant	40	M		"	"	
Ann " & ch.	38	F		"	"	
Charles Cudlip	18	M	Barber	"	"	
Robt. Linsted	42	M	Upholsterer	"	"	
Saml. Brewer		M	Farmer	"	"	
George White	65	M	Mariner	"	"	
S. Linsted & 8 ch.	28	F		"	"	
Benj. Bovinson *	30	M	Farmer	"	"	
Sarah " & 3 ch.	26	F		"	"	
John Horman	25	M		"	"	
Sophia " & ch.	24	F		"	"	
E. Lemanovsky	46	M		"		
Christiana " & ch.	27	F		"		

Names of passengers	Age	Sex	Occupation	Country to which they belong	Country of which they intend becoming inhabitants	Ship or vessel with the name of the master or commander
NEW YORK Cont.						
Q. E. Sept. 30, 1822						
Chas. Featherston	38	M		England		
Mrs. " & 5 ch.	37	F		"		
Thomas Jenkins	28	M	Mariner			
Joseph Williams & ch.	43	M	Barber	U. States	U. States	Sch. Atalanta. Gorsuch.
Wm. A. Weaver	31	M	Merchant	"	"	Sch. Franklin. Gorsuch.
T. Eldridge	23	M	"	"	"	
Wm. Baquinan	38	M	Mariner	"	"	
Saml. McKay	60	M	Army	England	"	Ship Foster. Moran.
James Reshey	24	M	Merchant	"	"	
C. S. Williams	25	M	Clerk	"	"	
E. Reily	50	M	Drover	"	"	
Saml. Inap *	36	M	Army	"	"	
Emily Williams &2 ch.	21	F		"	"	
Geo. Lancaster	27	M	Farmer	"	"	
James Hughes	59	M	Merchant	U. States	"	Brig Wilson. Britton.
John Carton	18	M	"	Ireland	"	
S. S. J. Aughworthy	21	M	"	"	"	
Mary Young & 5 ch.	30	F	Spinster	"	"	
John McCornill	29	M	Labourer	"	"	
Alexr. Wilson	42	M	"	"	"	
E. Clannon	21	F		"	"	
John Campbell	30	M	Cooper	Aberdeen	"	Brig Gowan. Mearns.
James Johnston	26	M	Blacksmith	"	"	
James Mount	30	M	Farmer	Ireland	"	Sch. Eliza. Nelson.
Cath " & 3 ch.	30	F		"	"	
James Medole	28	M	Farmer	"	"	
Cath. " & 3 ch.	28	F		"	"	
Wm. Kenny	26	M	Farmer	"	"	
Benj. Gibson	26	M	"	"	"	
Francis Mulligan	26	M		"	"	
Mary " & ch.	26	F		"	"	
Grace Brown	16	F	Servant	"	"	
Chas. Dollen	40	M	Farmer	"	"	
Ann " & ch.	30	F		"	"	
Michl. Corcoran	28	M	Farmer	"	"	
Thomas "	22	M	"	"	"	
James Kelly	26	M	Carpenter	"	"	
James McMonagle	25	M	Farmer	"	"	
Danl. C. Donald	25	M	"	"	"	
James Daily	30	M	"	"	"	
Thomas Feagan	26	M	Teacher	"	"	
Cath. "	50	F	Spinster	"	"	
Wm. McGowan	22	M	Farmer	"	"	
L. Cox	36	M	"	"	"	

Names of passengers	Age	Sex	Occupation	Country to which they belong	Country of which they intend becoming inhabitants	Ship or vessel with the name of the master or commander
NEW YORK Cont. **Q. E. Sept. 30, 1822**						
Rach. Cox & 4 ch.	34	F		Ireland	U. States	
Mary Dorsey	22	F	Seamstress	"	"	
J. S. Avellar	21	M	Gent.	Portugal	"	Brig New Packet.
Fred. Engles	24	M	Merchant	Prussia	"	Brig Horizon. Smith.
John Beall	21	M	"	U. States	"	Brig Betsey. Simonton.
John A. Frith	32	M	"	Bermuda	Hayti	Sch. Pacificator.
Wm. Sharp & 2 ch.	40	M	"	U. States	U. States	
J. A. Labats	35	M	"	Portugal	"	Ship Daphne. Kohler.
Jno. Smith	21	M	Miller	England	"	Ship Solon. Joy.
L. Fraser	35	M	Gent.	Edinburgh	"	Brig Orbit. Macy.
J. Brown	57	M	Merchant	"	"	
S. H. Jackson	45	M	"	"	"	
ORLEANS **Q. E. Sept. 30, 1822**						
Wm. Mallett	40	M	Merchant	England	N. Orleans	Sloop Elizabeth. Clark.
Samuel H. Turner	25	M	"	U. States	"	Sch. Miller. Slocum.
P. H. Tuyes	29	M	"	France		Died in the fever *
Bernard Prieto	45	M	Span. Officer	Spain	Havana	
A. Villiers	25	M	"	"	"	
Thomas Cucullin	35	M	Merchant	"	N. Orleans	
John Mager	40	M	"	U. States	"	
Le Morce	27	M	"	France	"	Died at quarantine ground *
F. Mossey & ch.	45	M	"	"	"	
Mrs. "	33	F		"	"	
Miss Teringire	50	F		"	"	
Mrs. Nartian	28	F		"	"	
M. Brouard	24	M	Merchant	"	"	
R. Ganger	24	M	"	"	"	
--- Ostin	24	M	Priest	"	"	
Mnr. Michaud	23	M	"	"	"	
--- Blanc	22	M	"	"	"	
--- Caretta	23	M	"	"	"	
--- Pieretto	23	M	"	"	"	
--- Aniago	24	M	"	"	"	
C. Philips	24	M		U. States	"	Brig Two Friends. Snow.
A. Prenuil	19	M		"	"	
A. Manifee	24	M	Merchant	"	"	Sloop Only Son. Ellison.
James Dixon	27	M	"	"	Charleston	
O. H. Zecooly *	26	M	Engineer	"	N. Orleans	Sch. Tartar. Dennett.
F. Swatt	40	M	Clerk	"	"	
J. D. Arnaud	25	M		France	"	
J. Beebe	25	M	Mariner	"	"	

Names of passengers	Age	Sex	Occupation	Country to which they belong	Country of which they intend becoming inhabitants	Ship or vessel with the name of the master or commander
ORLEANS						
Q. E. Sept. 30, 1822						
F. Merino	30	M	Soldier	Mexico	N. Orleans	Sch. Maria Ann. Anderson.
J. Passment	28	M	Hatter	France	"	Sloop Susan. Rogers.
F. Cassassus	45	M	Merchant	Spain	Campeachy	
J. Mitchell	42	M	Musician	U. States	N. Orleans	
D. Smith	25	M	Mariner	"	"	
R. Wilson	20	M	"	England		) These belonged to
R. Robinson	21	M	"	"		) an English ship
Thomas Hall	14	M	"	"		) cast away.
James Kennedy	25	M	"	Bengal		
--- Molot	30	M	Merchant	France	N. Orleans	
--- Sarriague	20	M	"	Spain	?	
Eugene McCarty	50	M	Planter	N. Orleans	U. States	Sch. Spartan. Mastigue.
Mrs. Hutris & 4 ch.	34	F		"	"	
Mrs. Thelbrut & 2 ch.	25	F	Lady			
Mr. McMullen	34	M	Farmer	"	"	Sloop Good Intent. Weightman.
Thomas Francis	24	M	Mariner	U. States	"	
Benj. Stark	32	M	Sea captain	"	"	Brig Bull Dog. Graham.
P. Guidenet	40	M	Gent.	"	"	
Mary Ann Moore & ch.	25	F		"	"	
C. Souteyran	28	M	Merchant	"	"	Sch. Ceres. Marchand.
Lorenzo Garcia	30	M	Mariner	Spain		
Augustine "	15	M	"	"		
P. Amonsitto	53	M	Merchant	Italy	?	Sch. Ranger. Arnoux.
G. Bertole	34	M	Sculptor	Switzerland	"	
P. Felix	19	M	Clerk	France	N. Orleans	
Jose Garcia	40	M	Mariner	Spain	"	
Francois Larosa	30	M	"	"	"	
P. Carrion	28	M	Farmer	"	"	Brig Sarah Ann. Terandel.
F. "	40	M	"	"	"	
J. Tirean	53	M	Carpenter	"	"	
Juan Alsina	45	M	Mariner	"	"	
J. B. L. Marsin	36	M	"	"	"	
S. P. Moyon	20	M	"	France		
J. Cleart	22	M	"	Ireland		
H. Pedesclaud	25	M		U. States	N. Orelans	Sch. Elizabeth. Hasle.
Christopher Megel	44	M	Trader	"	"	
--- Tcheclurin	28	M	Mexican officer	Russia	"	
D. A. Negra & 2 ch	44	F		Spain	"	Sch. Thorn. Greaves.
Joseph Fraza	44	M	Merchant	"	"	
M. Freisa	40	M	Mariner	"	"	
Joseph Oliver	44	M	"	U States	"	
Arnaud Guilbert	23	M	Merchant	France	"	Sch. Tom Shields. Saxtor.
Geo. Singleton	34	M	"	Ireland	"	

Names of passengers	Age	Sex	Occupation	Country to which they belong	Country of which they intend becoming inhabitants	Ship or vessel with the name of the master or commander
ORLEANS						
Q. E. Sept. 30, 1822						
A. D. Morant	24	M	Mariner	U. States	N. Orleans	Polaese Protegeda. Gastenaga
A. Casus	28	M	Merchant	Spain	"	
Ma. Del C. Lines	25	F		"	"	
E. Mandebused	45	M	Merchant	"	"	
F. Calico	36	M	"	"	"	
Juan Casse	30	M	"	France	"	
B. Proux & ch.	35	F		U. States	"	Sloop Volant. Salier.
J. Burgham	36	M		Hamburgh	"	
F. Dorrivigney	36	M	Merchant	"	"	
Thos. Huguenot	50	M	"	France	"	?
J. B. Volmar	21	M	Farmer	Louisiana	"	
A. Alexenau	18	M	Mariner	"	"	
Thos. Gibson	32	M	"	"	"	
W. Bogart	31	M	Merchant	U. States	"	Sch. G. Washington. Newman.
E. Laserre	20	M	Clerk	"	"	
Charles Perrot	64	M	Barber	France	"	Ship Ceres. McLean.
Leonard Poulot	22	M		"	"	Brig Graff Katchrusth. Salin.
M. Geraud	23	M	Tailor	"	"	
A. Veal	27	M	Apothecary	"	"	
J. Lesparre	23	M	Mechanic	"	"	
--- Dominique	23	M	"	"	"	
P. Tougent	23	M	"	"	"	
Mrs. Cader	30	F		England	"	
Peter Lightburn & ch.	26	M	Pilot	"	"	Brig Penn. Halsey.
John Chase	30	M	Merchant	U. States	"	Sloop Only Son. Ellison.
--- Francis	28	M	Mariner	France	"	
A. Ernin	42	M	Planter	U. States	U. States	Sch. Eliza. Nailique.
F. de Armas	26	M	Clerk	"	"	
John D. Martin	28	M	Planter	"	"	
Soloman S. Livegrive	30	M	Merchant	"	"	
M. Burdet	23	M		"	"	
J. K. Dubart	18	M	Tailor	"	"	
C. W. Spilia	28	M	Merchant	Hanover	Hanover	Ship Americas. Kleene
L. Hogedorn	22	M	Merchant	Bremen	Bremen	
Peter Dispan	57	M	Planter	U. States	?	Ship Warrington. Haskins.
Edwd. "	18	M	"	"	"	
A. Senniace	34	M	"	France	Louisiana	
B. Binos *	25	M	Baker	"	"	
F. Carsine	21	M	"	"	"	
PHILADELPHIA						
Q. E. Sept. 30, 1822						
John Dikeman	25	M	Merchant	U. States	U. States	Ship Missouri. Baush.

Names of passengers	Age	Sex	Occupation	Country to which they belong	Country of which they intend becoming inhabitants	Ship or vessel with the name of the master or commander
PHILADELPHIA Cont.						
Q. E. Sept. 30, 1822						
James Robinett	26	M	Merchant	U. States	U. States	
Mary Harper	21	F		G. Britain	"	Sch. Horatio. Hallett.
M. Bello	20	M	"	Spain	"	Sch. Infanta. Clark.
M. Jaques	25	M	"	U. States	"	
Wm. Irvin	20	M	Carpenter	G. Britain	"	Brig Sisters. Dobie.
Phineas Moses	30	M	Merchant	"	"	Ship Crisis. Mead.
Saml. Jones	15	M	"	"	"	
M. Brown	25	M	Carver	"	"	
Mrs. " & child	22	F		"	"	
Wm. Cornell	40	M	Farmer	"	"	
Mrs. " & ch.	35	F		"	"	
Wm. Thorn	28	M	Farmer	"	"	Brig Highlander. Moor.
Geo. "	25	M	"	"	"	
John Taylor	40	M	"	"	"	
John M. Jackson	57	M		"	"	Ship Hector. Gillander.
Andw. B. Huncket	25	M	Physician	U. States	"	
William Tate & ch.	27	M	Merchant	England	"	
Nancy Hardman & ch.	30	F		"	"	
Jonathan Watmorgh & 3 ch.	30	M	Druggist	"	"	
John Hudson	26	M	"	"	"	
Martha Bickerton & 2 ch.	55	F		"	"	
Wm. Bickerton	34	M	Druggist	"	"	
Joseph Fletcher	29	M	Grocer	"	"	
Patrick Divan	25	M	Drover	Ireland	"	
John D. Bradburn	33	M	Col. in Mex. Army	U. States	"	Sch. Highlander. Gibson.
Wm. Thompson	30	M	Capt. in " "	"	"	
John F. Ohle	27	M	Merchant	"	"	Brig Alabama. Stoneman.
John Donougher	40	M	"	"	"	
--- Mecel	30	M	"	Spain	"	
Mr. Johns	20	M	U. S. Navy	U. States	"	Brig Margaret. Furlong.
Chas. Esnard	21	M	Merchant	"	"	
Thomas Nobles	20	M	"	Switzerland	"	Brig Jas. Laurence. Hunter.
E. C. Delapaine	21	M	"	U. States	"	Brig Mary. McPherson.
Henry Wooldridge	22	M	"	"	"	
Alexr. Hunter	23	M	Farmer	Ireland	"	Sch. Climax. Prince.
Thomas Gardiner	19	M	"	"	"	
John "	20	M	"	"	"	
Wm. McIntire	15	M	Farmer	"	"	
James Story	21	M	Weaver	"	"	
M. Ferris	21	M	"	"	"	
Wm. McCarra	22	M	"	"	"	

Names of passengers	Age	Sex	Occupation	Country to which they belong	Country of which they intend becoming inhabitants	Ship or vessel with the name of the master or commander
PHILADELPHIA						
Q. E. Sept. 30, 1822						
Hugh Boyle	22	M	Weaver	Ireland	U. States	
Danl. "	24	M	"	"	"	
R. Megonigal	32	M		"	"	
Jane " & ch.	24	F		"	"	
Pat. Donover	39	M		"	"	
Eleanor " & 4 ch.	38	F		"	"	
Hugh Cavinaugh	24	M	Farmer	"	"	
Archibald Mason	25	M	"	"	"	
Oliver Husser	22	M	Weaver	"	"	
John Erwin	19	M	"	"	"	
Robt. Campbell	22	M	"	"	"	
Thos. Manly	26	M	"	"	"	
M. M. Nalley	22	M	"	"	"	
Ann Dougherty	20	F		"	"	
Mary Storry	20	F		"	"	
Joseph "	15	M	Tailor	"	"	
James Bau	18	M	Weaver	"	"	
James Porter	25	M	"	"	"	
James Scanlor	18	M	"	"	"	
Geo. McFarland	19	M	"	"	"	
Edwd. Kelly	26	M	"	"	"	
Saml. Erwing	22	M	"	"	"	
David Esler	22	M	Farmer	"	"	
Ann "	30	F		"	"	
Wm. Cochran	26	M	Farmer	"	"	
Nancy "	28	F		"	"	
Joseph Ross & ch.	60	M	Farmer	"	"	
Wm. McCormick	22	M	"	"	"	
Wm. Woods	22	M	"	"	"	
Pat. Micken	22	M	"	"	"	
Hugh Osborne	38	M	"	"	"	
Michael Knap	41	M	"	"	"	
John Duncan	25	M	"	"	"	
Deborah "	25	F		"	"	
Levi Parrent	22	M		"	"	
Mary "	24	F		"	"	
Arthur Beattie	50	M	Farmer	G. Britain	"	Sch. Julia Ann. Higgins.
Robt. "	20	M	Clockmakr.	"	"	
Sarah " & 6 ch.	44	F		"	"	
John Withers	61	M	Farmer	"	"	
John Withers Jr.	25	M	Shoemaker	"	"	
Jane " & 4 ch.	59	F		"	"	
David Craig	25	M	Blacksmith	"	"	
James Golley	25	M	"	"	"	

Names of passengers	Age	Sex	Occupation	Country to which they belong	Country of which they intend becoming inhabitants	Ship or vessel with the name of the master or commander
PHILADELPHIA Cont.						
Q. E. Sept. 30, 1822						
L. Golley	22	M	Blacksmith	G. Britain	"	
Mr. Snodgrass	55	M	Weaver	"	"	
Wm. "	25	M	"	"	"	
Mrs. " & ch.	55	F		"	"	
John Wilson	25	M	Weaver	"	" "	
Sarah " & 2 ch.	22	F		"	" "	
John Patterson	23	M	Weaver	"	"	
Margaret "	22	F		"	"	
John Craig	22	M	Weaver	"	"	
Jane " & ch.	22	F		"	"	
Samuel Howard	25	M	Weaver	"	"	
David Turner	22	M	"	"	"	
John Abiot	24	M	"	"	"	
Wm. Patten	22	M	"	"	"	
Andw. McEllerey	35	M	Farmer	"	"	
Isabella " & 2 ch.	35	F		"	"	
Alexr. Forsyth	23	M	Farmer	"	"	
George Nixon	23	M	"	"	"	
Richd. Goldsmith	30	M	Miner	"	"	
N. McIntire	26	M	Mechanic	"	"	
George Nock	56	M	rewer	"	"	
L. Posunchas	23	M	Merchant	U. States	"	Brig Jas. Coulter. Hill.
F. Mazas	22	M	"	"	"	
John Wright	24	M	Labourer	Ireland	"	Sch. Iceplant. Bunker.
Walter Stewart	26	M	"	"	"	
Wm. Bradley	40	M	Farmer	"	"	
Ann " & 7 ch.	35	F		"	"	
Charles McGlade	21	M	Labourer	"	"	
Peter "	22	M	Weaver	"	"	
Edwd. Devlin	18	M	Labourer	"	"	
Henry Donnelly	20	M	"	"	"	
Wm. Henderson	70	M	Farmer	"	"	
F. Stewart	25	M	"	"	"	
Eliz. Henderson	62	F	Spinstress	"	"	
Alexr. "	23	M	Sawyer	"	"	
David "	19	M	Labourer	"	"	
John McCutchin	40	M	Chandler	"	"	
Ann " & 4 ch.	38	F		"	"	
John McAllister	68	M	Farmer	"	"	
Robert "	18	M	"	"	"	
Robt. McFadden	21	M	Weaver	"	"	
Wm. Getty	25	M	"	"	"	
Wm. McPherson	20	M	"	"	"	
Robt. McMullin	45	M	"	"	"	

Names of passengers	Age	Sex	Occupation	Country to which they belong	Country of which they intend becoming inhabitants	Ship or vessel with the name of the master or commander
PHILADELPHIA Cont.						
Q. E. Sept. 30, 1822						
Hugh Glass	21	M	Weaver	Ireland	U. States	
James McGonagle	24	M	Labourer	"	"	
Robert Aikin	43	M	Farmer	"	"	
Letitia " & 6 ch.	35	F		"	"	
Samuel McCormick	24	M	Weaver	"	"	
Samuel Jack	21	M	"	"	"	
Wm. Moore	20	M	"	"	"	
John Connor	23	M	"	"	"	
Wm. Smith	24	M	Tailor	"	"	
Wm. Lockart	21	M	Weaver	"	"	
Mary McLaughlin	28	F		"	"	
Wm. McCollum	21	M	Labourer	"	"	
Mary "	18	F		"	"	
David McFarland	25	M	Farmer	"	"	
Mary "	21	F	Seamstress	"	"	
Sarah Scott	55	F	"	"	"	
I. George	23	M	Weaver	"	"	
Jane "	21	F	Seamstress	"	"	
Mary McIlvaine	24	F	"	"	"	
Wm. "	20	M	Labourer	"	"	
Samuel Arey	30	M	Merchant	U. States	"	Brig Philadelphia. Hall.
Mrs. " & ch.	30	F		"	"	
Thomas Wood	30	M	Mariner	Holland	Holland	
A. Alequa	35	M	Merchant	Spain	Spain	
Hugh Branner	40	M	Tailor	G. Britain	U. States	Ship Lancaster. Buckhart.
Sarah Hesketh & ch.	30	F		"	"	
James Preston	32	M	Broker	"	"	
Isabella " & 2 ch.	30	F		"	"	
Mary Hesketh & ch.	25	F		"	"	
James Reddock	33	M	Merchant	"	"	Ship Stranger. Fisher.
Samuel Mabberly '	47	M	Farmer	"	"	
Thomas Royston	29	M	Cordwainer	"	"	
Andw. Williams	28	M	Labourer	"	"	
Richd. Robinson	32	M	Farmer	"	"	
Robert Kirk	26	M	"	"	"	
Joshua Cockcroft	13	M		"	"	
Thomas Hall	31	M	Farmer	"	"	
Thomas Morgan	27	M	"	"	"	
Edward Wyler	25	M	"	"	"	
Joseph Aykerora	28	M	Brewer	"	"	
Lewis Howard	50	M	Merchant	France	"	Sch. Catharine. Davis.
John Delmonico	50	M	"	Swiss	U. States	
Joseph Fourtanico	28	M	"	France	"	
Wm. Young	40	M	"	U. States	"	Ship Columbia. Kurtz.

Names of passengers	Age	Sex	Occupation	Country to which they belong	Country of which they intend becoming inhabitants	Ship or vessel with the name of the master or commander
PHILADELPHIA Cont.						
Q. E. Sept. 30, 1822						
Nicholas Devrenier	50	M	Traveller	France	U. States	
E. E. Pintary	22	M	U. S. Army	U. States	"	Brig Jas. Coulter. Hill.
H. Arsola	28	M	Merchant	Havana	Havana	
P. Alvans	35	M	"	"	"	
P. Louitana	23	M	"	"	"	
Sophia Reading	45	F		Russia	"	Brig Com. Perry. Selby.
F. Mazas	23	M	Merchant	Spain	"	
J. Scott	33	M	"	U. States	"	
F. C. Bartou	46	M	"	"	"	
John Hefferman	50	M	"	"	"	Brig Timandra. Yamall.
G. W. Bedwell	35	M	"	"	"	
F. R. Backus	20	M	"	"	"	
X. A. Prena	46	M	"	Spain	Havana	
B. F. Johnson	26	M	"	U. States	U. States	
Oliver Le Chevalier	30	M	Physician	"	"	Brig George. Kean.
F. De Lhomaca	39	M	Merchant	"	"	
Edwd. W. Robinson	27	M	"	"	"	
Francis Markal	48	M	"	"	"	Brig Com. Porter. Bell.
A. Nichols	49	M	"	"	"	Brig Mary Ann. Thorp.
P. Coken	56	M	"	"	"	
J. Turell	51	M	"	"	"	
Joseph Cobbett	45	M	Farmer	G. Britain	"	Ship Unicorn. McKown.
James Jackson	30	M	"	"	"	
John Boothman	25	M	"	"	"	
W. Warren	27	M	"	"	"	
John Hanop	20	M	"	"	"	
James Hyde	24	M	"	"	"	
Wm. Watkins	25	M	"	"	"	
James Sarpham * & 2 ch	45	M	"	"	"	
Ann Bamber	45	F		"	"	
Esther " & 5 ch.	21	F		"	"	
Priscilla Bury & 4 ch.	29	F		"	"	
Priscilla Cochran	70	F		"	"	
Edmund Shaw	22	M		"	"	
Eustace Davis	29	M	Farmer	"	"	
James Kirby	62	M	"	"	"	
Wm. Shipley	21	M	Shoemaker	"	"	
Richd. Haworth	62	M	Teacher	"	"	
B. "	33	F		"	"	
John Clark	50	M	Weaver	"	"	Ship Warren. Webb.
Mrs. " & 6 ch.	45	F		"	"	
Edwd. Riley	45	M	Weaver	"	"	
Mrs. " & 7 ch.	32	F		"	"	
Mary Sheridan & 3 ch.	28	F		"	"	

Names of passengers	Age	Sex	Occupation	Country to which they belong	Country of which they intend becoming inhabitants	Ship or vessel with the name of the master or commander
PHILADELPHIA Cont.						
Q. E. Sept. 30, 1822						
Barney Chune & 2 ch.	22	M	Weaver	G. Britain	U. States	
Thos. Dolan	22	M	"	"	"	
John Schale	50	M	"	"	"	
James Schofield	34	M	"	"	"	
Mrs. " & 3 ch.	30	F		"	"	
Abraham "	26	M	Weaver	"	"	
B. C. White	32	M	Merchant	U. States	"	Brig Ontario. Erwin.
G. W. Miller	38	M	"	"	"	
James Scull	30	M		"	"	
John Frier	30	M	Goldbeater	England	"	Brig Robert. Steele.
Nathanl. Fellows	42	M	Gent.	U. States	"	Brig Margaret. Eldridge.
Alexr. Lewis	26	M	"	"	"	
A. Pelayo	25	M	"	"	"	
L. De Forrest	38	M	"	"	"	
Francis Silver & ch.	40	M	"	"	"	
Andw. S. Gar	40	M	"	"	"	
George Lawson	74	M	Farmer	Scotland	Scotland	Ship Sachem.
James Ricketts	30	M	"	U. States	U. States	
John Taylor	25	M	Merchant	Scotland	"	
Wm. McHaig	22	M	"	"	"	
Robert Cook	26	M		"	"	
H. Mair & 3 ch.	28	F		"	"	
J. Mason & 3 ch.	31	F		"	"	
J. Steel & 2 ch.	31	F		"	"	
Wm. Black	18	M	Farmer	"	"	
James Baird	20	M	"	"	"	
Benj. Carman	22	M	Merchant	U. States	"	Brig Decatur. Bell.
Robert Jones	45	M	"	"	"	
Walter Brush	28	M	"	"	"	
D. Bachong	45	M	Physician	France	"	Sch. Good Friends
--- Brown	25	M	Labourer	U. States	"	
J. B. Clement	37	M	Merchant	"	"	Brig Pilot Wing.
R. R. Stewart	33	M	"	"	"	
Chevalr. Bernabeau	49	M	Consul	"	"	Ship Hunter. Davis.
L. Chastaul	31	M	Merchant	France	"	
B. Cadit	20	M	"	"	"	
A. Gardere	49	M	"	"	"	
Thomas Hibbert	37	M	Farmer	England	"	Ship Franklin. Garrard.
Mary " & 2 ch.	28	F		"	"	
D. C. Lever	26	M	Farmer	"	"	
James "	20	M	"	"	"	
John Jackson	26	M	Labourer	"	"	
Wm. Corbett	17	M	"	"	"	
M. Armour	67	M	Carpenter	U. States	"	

Names of passengers	Age	Sex	Occupation	Country to which they belong	Country of which they intend becoming inhabitants	Ship or vessel with the name of the master or commander
PHILADELPHIA Cont.						
Q. E. Sept. 30, 1822						
H. Pace	55	M	Merchant	U. States	U. States	
Hugh Alexander	39	M	"	"	"	
John Berry	20	M	Farmer	Ireland	"	Ship Ceres. Patterson.
Joseph Hare	24	M	"	"	"	
Francis Short	24	M	Weaver	"	"	
Robt. Dewady *	35	M	Farmer	"	"	
Rebecca Wilson & 4 ch.	44	F		"	"	
Michael Campbell	25	M	Farmer	"	"	
Mary "	30	F		"	"	
H. McCoy	22	M	Farmer	"	"	
Wm. Agnew	25	M	"	"	"	
Robt. Little	20	M	"	"	"	
James McAdam	16	M	"	"	"	
Robert Lenton	31	M	"	"	"	
Patrick Roney	30	M	Merchant	"	"	
Thomas Grier	22	M	Farmer	"	"	
James Wilson	28	M	Merchant	"	"	
Neal Mullen	26	M	Labourer	"	"	
Thomas Dodson	30	M	"	"	"	
E. Richards	26	M	Lawyer	St. Domingo	"	Brig Wm. & Thos. Dobson.
S. Portes	25	M	"	"	"	
W. N. Waskell	22	M	Cab. maker	U. States	"	
J. Stevenson	22	M	Shoemaker	"	"	
Geo. Burge	56	M	Confectioner	G. Britain	"	Brig Emerald. Gray.
Sarah "	52	M		"	"	
Jos. Fisher	32	M	Farmer	"	"	
Jos. Naffer	22	M	"	"	"	
Robt. Dale	23	M	Shoemaker	"	"	
Margt. Ford & 2 ch.	45	F		"	"	
Wm. Baldwin	28	M	Shoemaker	"	"	Ship Bengal. Pearce.
Mary " & 3 ch.	29	F		"	"	
Julia Watson & 5 ch.	34	F		"	"	
C. Smith & ch.	40	M	Merchant	"	"	Brig Philadelphia. Hall.
D. Niar	35	M	"	Spain	Spain	
L. D. Carpenter	23	M	"	U. States	U. States	Sch. Jane. Corson.
J. P. Wolfe	26	M	Mariner	"	"	
M. Aiken	40	M	Merchant	. "	"	
A. Hertill	23	M	Mariner	` France	"	Sch. Lively. Groves.
Andrew Fleming	27	M	"	U. States	"	
John Hurdle	27	M	"	"	"	
H. Radcliff	17	M	"	"	"	
James Knox	21	M	Farmer	G. Britain	"	Brig Collector. Telcombe.
Nancy "	21	F		"	"	
Madame Roper * & ch.	40	F		Havana	"	Brig Alonzo. Murphy.

Names of passengers	Age	Sex	Occupation	Country to which they belong	Country of which they intend becoming inhabitants	Ship or vessel with the name of the master or commander
PHILADELPHIA Cont.						
Q. E. Sept. 30, 1822						
F. Gint	23	M	Merchant	Germany	Germany	Brig Maria Elizabeth.
H. Schliephake *	22	M	Farmer	"	"	
F. W. Binderman	32	M	Merchant	"	"	
F. W. Weiss	20	M	"	"	"	
M. Hatch	29	M	"	G. Britain	U. States	Sch. Mt Vernon.
David Correy	30	M	"	U. States	"	Brig Junius. Danton
J. Woolen	28	M	Mariner	"	"	
A. Webler	32	M	Merchant	Denmark	"	
J. R. Lawrence	34	M	"	U. States	"	Brig Harriet Clark.
M. Stevens	33	M	"	"	"	
D. B. Nones	43	M	"	"	"	Brig Edwd D. Douglass.
F. Hanson	33	M	"	"	"	
B. H. Kentzing	35	M	"	"	"	
John Bancroft	47	M	Farmer	G. Britain	"	Ship Tuscarora. West.
Eliz. " & 9 ch.	45	F		"	"	
James Wood	27	M	Merchant	"	"	
Jane " & 2 ch.	25	F		"	"	
Mary Dodgson & ch.	22	F		"	"	
Thomas Atkinson	27	M	Gardner	"	"	
H. Thos. Hobson	25	M	Merchant	"	"	
Wm. Worrell	38	M	"	"	"	
L. Moore & 4 ch.	40	F		"	"	
Margt. Pratt & 3 ch.	27	F		"	"	
Archibald Carrier	45	M	Farmer	"	"	
Flora " & 2 ch.	40	F		"	"	
Eliz. Head & 2 ch.	33	F		"	"	
Sarah Smith & 3 ch.	39	F		"	"	
EDGARTOWN						
Q. E. Sept. 30, 1822						
A. Richardson	39	M	Farmer	Ireland	U. States	Sch. Planter. Fisher.
Bradshaw Hancock	30	M	Merchant	"	"	
David Horthorn	25	M	Farmer	"	"	
John Stewart	30	M	"	"	"	
Henry McCoult	24	M	"	"	"	
Edwd. Milligan	25	M	"	"	"	
John Hort	26	M	"	"	"	
Ezek. Roddy	30	M	"	"	"	
Wm. Osborn	22	M	"	"	"	
Saml. Stewart	21	M	"	"	"	
Rachl. "	24	F		"	"	
Eliz. Morrow & 4 ch.	49	F		"	"	
Eliz. Osborn & ch.	20	F		"	"	

Names of passengers	Age	Sex	Occupation	Country to which they belong	Country of which they intend becoming inhabitants	Ship or vessel with the name of the master or commander
EDGARTOWN Cont. Q. E. Sept. 30, 1822						
Jane Dixon	20	F		Ireland	U. States	
SOUTH CAROLINA Q. E. Sept. 30, 1822						
G. Del Roches	37	M	Farmer	France	France	Brig Mary.
--- Urban	30	M	Trader	Malanzes	"	Sch Sally & Polly.
Madame Tournassen*	31	F		"	"	
J. H. Magwood	27	M	Merchant	"	"	
Jno. Routledge	27	M	Mariner	U. States	U. States	Sloop Victory.
Mrs. Hamilton & ch.	30	F		Havana	G. Britain	Brig Catharine.
John Rodrigues	30	M	Trader	Porto Rico	"	Sch. Felix.
Samuel Withington	35	M	Merchant	G. Britain	U. States	
David Tirundale *	30	M	"	"	"	Sch. Fame.
Charles Delorme	18	M		U. States	"	
J. J. Vollee/Vottee	13	M		"	"	
Isaac Wolf	38	M	Trader	"	"	Ship S. Carolina
Mrs. " & 5 ch.	28	F		"	"	
E. Morris	25	M	Merchant	"	"	Sch. Louisa.
Antonio Ramarez	35	M	Planter	Spain	Spain	
Thomas Legium	30	M	Trader	France	U. States	Sch. Eliza & Polly.
Lewis Vegin	29	M	Carpenter	"	"	
Anthony Bragas	30	M	Merchant	Spain	"	Brig Neptune's Barge.
Joaquim Savater	33	M	"	"	"	
Thos. Srain *	35	M	Mariner	"	"	
Archibald McFarlan	54	M	Farmer	G. Britain	"	Ship Jane.
Mary " & ch.	29	F		"	"	
George "	29	M	Cooper	"	"	
John Watson	27	M	Mariner	"	"	Sloop Endeavour
John Noga	40	M	"	Spain	"	Sch. Sarah Ann.
John Lomis	22	M	Millwright	G. Britain	"	Ship Ceres.
John Davis	41	M	Shopkeeper	"	"	
John C. Beale	46	M	"	U. States	"	Ship Perfect.
Henry Noyes	32	M	Mariner	"	"	
John Geddes	50	M	Lawyer	"	"	Sch. Betsey & Peggy.
G. H. Geddes	17	M		"	"	
H. ":	19	F		"	"	
M. Montg'omery	40	M	Planter	"	"	
Henry Goldsmith	19	M	Trader	"	"	
John B. Rogers	28	M	Merchant	"	"	
Hugh Shannon	36	M	Mechanic	G. Britain	"	Sch. Mechanic.
John Arthur	32	M	"	"	"	
Robt. Holberton	30	M	Hozier	"	"	Ship Fame.
Ch. McDonlad	19	M	Farmer	"	"	

Names of passengers	Age	Sex	Occupation	Country to which they belong	Country of which they intend becoming inhabitants	Ship or vessel with the name of the master or commander
SOUTH CAROLINA Q. E. Sept. 30, 1822						
--- Gallagher	32	M	Trader	G Britain	U States	
Mrs " & 2 ch.	28	F		"	"	
John C. Ross	27	M	Merchant	"	"	
Mrs. " & ch.	20	F		"	"	
L. Y. Abrahams	45	M	Trader	"	"	Ship Charles & Henry
H. J. Janke	22	M		Amsterdam	"	
Jennet De Wolf	30	F		"	"	
James Ross	36	M	Mariner	G. Britain	"	Sch. Felix.
James Green	25	M	Merchant	"	"	Sch. Fate.
J. Flint	40	M	"	"	"	
Thomas McCreidy	24	M	"	"	"	
BARNSTABLE Q. E. Sept. 30, 1822						
Edwd. M. Purcell	45	M	Merchant	Jamaica	"	Sch. Mark. Small.
Ann " & 2 ch.	40	F		"	"	
Lewis Charles	35	M	Servant	"	"	
Wm. Little	35	M	Labourer	Ireland	"	
Jno. M. C. Govern	20	M	"	"	"	
Thomas Fogarty	25	M	"	"	"	
James Finly	25	M	"	"	"	
Peter Cochran	25	M	"	"	"	
Richd. McGowan	25	M	"	"	"	
Owen Gillman	33	M	Farmer	"	"	
Margt. " & 3 ch.	35	F		"	"	
Wm. Powers	28	M	Cooper	"	"	Sch. Betsey & Eliza. Baker
Michael "	21	M	Tanner	"	"	
John Nighland	25	M	Cooper	"	"	
John Welch	30	M	Tailor	"	"	
Margt. "	30	F		"	"	
James Powers	25	M	Cooper	"	"	
Wm. M. Brown	26	M	Tailor	"	"	
Wm. M Hall	30	M	Carpenter	U States	"	
Francis Kelly	24	M	Farmer	N. Scotia	"	Sch. Lewes. Sears
Hugh Biggs	25	M	Millwright	"	"	
Thomas Rotch	28	M	Farmer	"	"	
Wm. Griffin	23	M	"	"	"	
Susan McLanin	24	F		"	"	
Thomas Wright	23	M	Labourer	Ireland	"	
James Forsyth	20	M	"	"	"	
Peter Danhorke	25	M	"	"	"	
Wm. Johnson	19	M	"	"	"	
Wm. Ryan	18	M	"	"	"	

Names of passengers	Age	Sex	Occupation	Country to which they belong	Country of which they intend becoming inhabitants	Ship or vessel with the name of the master or commander
BARNSTABLE Cont						
Q. E Sept 30, 1822						
Charles Mullen	23	M	Tailor	Ireland	U. States	
Daniel "	25	M	"	"	"	
John Harkin	17	M	Labourer	"	"	Sch. Financier. Crowell.
John McTolgin	22	M	"	"	"	
Mary Polter/Potter	17	F		"	"	
George Creland	24	M	Labourer	"	"	
Thomas Shields	25	M	Butcher	"	"	
Edwd Leverty	26	M	Labourer	"	"	
James Patchet	32	M	Farmer	"	"	
Margaret "	25	F		"	"	
John Marson	38	M	Labourer	"	"	
D. McOuby *	20	M	Blacksmith	Scotland	"	
R A. Camring	29	M	"	N. Scotia	"	
Robert McCleson	24	M	"	Ireland	"	
Edward Colge	22	M	Weaver	"	"	
James Moors	18	M	"	"	"	
Alex Kelly	22	M	Shoemaker	"	"	
David McLane	23	M	Dyer	"	"	
Martha "	23	F	"	"	"	
John Ilderchase	38	M	Weaver	"	"	
Eliz. " & ch.	30	F		"	"	
Ann Cummings	20	F		"	"	
Barney Martin	45	M	Labourer	"	"	
Nancy " & 7 ch.	42	F		"	"	
Samuel Baird	18	M	Labourer	"	"	Sch. Nancy. Eldridge.
M. McCarnan	26	M	"	"	"	
Sarah "	18	F		"	"	
John Hickat *	27	M	Labourer	"	"	
John Anderson	16	M	"	"	"	
Hugh Cummins	18	M	"	"	"	
David Pollock	20	M	"	"		
James Farney	24	M	Mariner	"	"	
Sally McCaver	21	F		"	"	
Mary Kelly	18	F		"	"	
Biddy "	17	F		"	"	
Martin Pollock	18	F		"	"	
Rebca "	16	F		"	"	
George Kaulbach	27	M	Tailor	Halifax	"	
Sarah " & 2 ch.	30	F		"	"	
Edwd Hagerty	32	M	Tailor	"	"	
Rachel " & ch.	25	F		"	"	
James Bulger	25	M	Tailor	"	"	Sch. Hunter. Sears.
Robt. Southerland	28	M	Labourer	"	"	
Pat. Fitzgerald	32	M	Carpenter	"	"	

Names of passengers	Age	Sex	Occupation	Country to which they belong	Country of which they intend becoming inhabitants	Ship or vessel with the name of the master or commander
BARNSTABLE Cont.						
Q. E. Sept. 30, 1822						
John P. Bigelow	25	M	Attorney	U. States	U. States	
Daniel O'Neal	26	M	Labourer	England	"	
Margt. "	24	F		"	"	
Thos. Thomas	31	M	Labourer	"	"	Sch. Mark. Small.
David Furnham	30	M	Mariner	"	"	
Margt. Lee	30	F	Tailoress	Ireland	"	
Rosanna Kearns	24	F	Spinster	"	"	
Roger Nott	34	M	Painter	Halifax	Halifax	
Eleanor " & ch.	21	F		"	"	
George Nolk *	20	M	Farmer	"	"	
Ann " & 4 ch.	47	F		"	"	
Timothy Danny	21	M	Tailor	"	"	
John " & 2 ch.	24	M	"	"	"	
Moris Murphy	34	M	Labourer	"	"	Sch Alert Bearse
Allan Danny	45	M	"	"	"	
Philip Fogerty	24	M	"	"	"	
John Pengley	26	M	"	"	"	
Thomas McDonald	24	M	"	"	"	
Timothy Hearn	35	M		"	"	
Mary Sterling & ch.	46	F		"	"	
John Patrick	45	M	Labourer	"	"	
Mary " & ch.	40	F		"	"	
OSWEGATCHIE						
Q. E. Sept. 30, 1822						
John Kown	21	M	Farmer	Ireland	U States	Vessel not mentioned.
Thomas "	18	M	"	"	"	
Mary "	63	F	Spinster	"	"	
James "	24	M	Farmer	"	"	
Eleanor "	32	F	Spinster	"	" "	
Mary McCard	23	F	"	"	"	
James Shankey	27	M	Farmer	"	"	
John "	33	M	"	"	"	
Catharine " & 3 ch.	24	F	Spinster	"	"	
Robert Miller	33	M	Farmer	"	"	
Jno. McBride	26	M	"	"	"	
Margt. Gordon & ch.	24	F	Spinster	"	"	
John Wilson	36	M	Farmer	"	"	
Wm. " & 4 ch.	30	M	"	"	"	
Andw. Backhuse	35	M	"	England	"	
Mary " & 4 ch.	25	F		"	"	
Richd. Hudson	22	M	Farmer	"	"	
Hannah " & ch.	24	F		"	"	

Names of passengers	Age	Sex	Occupation	Country to which they belong	Country of which they intend becoming inhabitants	Ship or vessel with the name of the master or commander
BARNSTABLE Cont.						
Q. E. Sept. 30, 1822						
Wm. Pick	44	M	Farmer	England	U. States	
John Ellent	40	M	"	"	"	
Richd. Hudson	27	M	"	"	"	
H. Ellent & 2 ch.	26	F		"	"	
Mary Hudson	21	F		"	"	
Robt. Preston	25	M	Farmer	"	"	
Jas. Douthwrait	35	M	"	"	"	
Richd. Thornton	22	M	"	"	"	
John Preston	28	M	"	"	"	
Joseph Elmherd	31	M	"	"	"	
Mary " & 5 ch.	31	F		"	"	
Wm. Lang	26	M	Farmer	"	"	
Samuel Milligan	30	M	Weaver	Scotland	"	
Susannan " & ch.	20	F		"	"	
Wm. Graham & 4 ch.	32	M	Farmer	Ireland	"	
Geo. White	23	M	"	"	"	
Wm. Tracy	30	M	Surveyor	"	U. Canada	
Ann "	20	F		"	"	
John Kelly	26	M	Farmer	"	"	
Wm. Davis	26	M	"	"	"	
Mary " & 3 ch.	27	F		"	"	
M. McAbay	25	M	Farmer	"	"	
Wm. Armstrong	25	M	"	"	"	
Cath. " & 2 ch.	24	F		"	"	
John Staples	43	M	Farmer	"	"	
Mary " & 9 ch.	34	F		"	"	
Margt. Kenney	30	F		"	"	
James Wilson	65	M	Blacksmith	"	"	
John "	17	M	"	"	"	
John Cray	25	M	Farmer	"	U. States	
John " Jr.	18	M	"	"	"	
Jane Wilson	24	F	Spinster	"	"	
Martha "	21	F	"	"	"	
Martha "	18	F	"	"	"	
Cath. "	18	F	"	"	"	
Mary "	60	F	"	"	"	
Ann Newell & 2 ch.	43	M	"	"	"	
Joseph Taylor & 2 ch.	45	M	Farmer	"	"	
James Stevenson	34	M	"	"	"	
Esther " & 2 ch.	30	F		"	"	
James Delston	17	M	Farmer	"	"	
Margt "	24	F		"	"	
Joseph Greer	52	M	Weaver	"	"	
Jane "	52	F		"	"	

Names of passengers	Age	Sex	Occupation	Country to which they belong	Country of which they intend becoming inhabitants	Ship or vessel with the name of the master or commander
BARNSTABLE Cont.						
Q. E. Sept. 30, 1822						
Wm. Greer	24	M	Weaver	Ireland	U. States	
Nancy " & 2 ch.	21	F		"	"	
Hugh Goligar & 4 ch.	45	M	Farmer	"	"	
Francis Barnes	24	M	"	"	"	
Joseph Berk	40	M	"	"	"	
Eliza " & 2 ch.	34	F		"	"	
James Trowbridge	24	M	Farmer	"	"	
James "	24	M	"	"	"	
George "	28	M	"	"	"	
Margt. "	24	F		"	"	
John Pollock	20	M	Farmer	"	"	
Alexr. Dolan	24	M	Farmer	"	"	
Wm. Phillips	21	M	"	"	"	
John Sprand	20	M	Farmer	"	"	
John Marshall & 3 ch.	55	M	Shoemaker	"	"	
Wm. Bunett & ch.	45	M	Weaver	"	"	
James "	55	M	"	"	"	
James Wilson & ch.	25	M		"	"	
Alexr. Baggs	28	M	Reed maker	"	"	
Archibald "	24	M	Farmer	"	"	
Isaac "	20	M	"	"	"	
Charles Wilson	20	M	Blacksmith	"	"	
Nancy Marshall & ch.	45	F		"	"	
Eliz. Bunatt & 4 ch.	45	F		"	"	
Agnes Wilson	30	F		"	"	
Susan Baggs	22	F		"	"	
Mary "	22	F		"	"	
Rachel "	25	F		"	"	
Mary Truisdale & ch.	25	F		"	"	
Joseph Kilgour	56	M	Labourer	"	"	
Wm. "	20	M	Farmer	"	"	
Martha " & 4 ch.	50	F	Spinster	"	"	
Robt. Park	21	M	Farmer	"	"	
Margt. Jobson *	28	F	Spinster	Scotland	"	
Nancy " & 2 ch.	20	F	"	"	"	
Margt. McMatt	25	F	"	"	"	
Robt. Sampson	19	M	Cab. Maker	"	"	
Daniel Taylor	29	M	Farmer	"	"	
Mary " & 3 ch.	25	F	Spinster	"	"	
Thomas Graham	40	M	Weaver	"	"	
Ann " & 5 ch.	30	F		"	"	
Wm. Cisay *	20	M	Weaver	"	"	
M. Caldwell	60	M	"	"	"	
Eliz. "	58	F		"	"	

Names of passengers	Age	Sex	Occupation	Country to which they belong	Country of which they intend becoming inhabitants	Ship or vessel with the name of the master or commander
BARNSTABLE Cont.						
Q. E. Sept. 30, 1822						
Hugh Best	47	M	Weaver	Scotland	U. States	
Eliz. McFarland	20	F	Spinster	"	"	
Jane McBride	22	F	"	"	"	
Catharine "	65	F	"	"	"	
Robt. "	35	M	Farmer	"	"	
Robt. Smith	23	M	"	"	"	
Robt. Templeton	40	M	Weaver	"	"	
Isabella " & 3 ch.	36	F	Spinster	"	"	
Robt. McGee	26	M	Weaver	"	"	
Martha " & 5 ch.	26	F	Spinster	"	"	
James Toll	28	M	Weaver	"	"	
Andw. McLane	63	M	Farmer	"	"	
Margt. "	50	F	Spinster	"	"	
E. McLan & 6 ch.	50	F	Spinster	"	"	
Robt. Tagut	25	M	Labourer	"	"	
Sarah " & ch.	24	F	Spinster	"	"	
Thomas Conich	32	M	Blacksmith	"	"	
Cath. " & 4 ch.	32	F	Spinster	"	"	
Sampson Moore	40	M	Farmer	"	"	
Jane " & 6 ch.	31	F	Spinster	"	"	
John Allen	18	M	Weaver	"	"	
Margaret Grier	18	F	Spinster	"	"	
Edwd. Jones	40	M	Farmer	"	"	
Mrs. "	36	F	Spinster ?	"	"	
John " & 4 ch.	38	M	Farmer	"	"	
John Thompson	60	M	"	"	"	
Christina "	45	F	Spinster	"	"	
Colin "	23	M	Farmer	"	"	
Sally " & 4 ch.	19	F	Spinster	"	"	
Jane Campbell	26	F	"	"	"	
John Murray	26	M	Farmer	"	"	
Margaret "	30	F	Spinster	"	"	
Mary Newgen	36	F	"	"	"	
George Roy	26	M	Farmer	"	"	
John Handy	30	M	"	"	"	
James Roy & ch.	24	M	"	"	"	
Mary Handy & ch.	20	F	"	"	"	
John Baigham	44	M	Farmer	"	"	
Julia " & 7 ch.	44	F	Spinster	"	"	
John Conroy	40	M	Farmer	"	"	
Thomas O'Neill	30	M	Miner	"	"	

Names of passengers	Age	Sex	Occupation	Country to which they belong	Country of which they intend becoming inhabitants	Ship or vessel with the name of the master or commander
BALTIMORE						
Q. E. Sept. 30, 1822						
W. Sheffield	45	M	Farmer	England	U. States	Brig Mechanic.
J. "	40	M	"	"	"	
J. Shaw	30	M	Shoemaker	"	"	
J. Lossack	21	M	Printer	"	"	
W. Lindsay	29	M	Farmer	"	"	
R. O. Rourke (O'Rourke)	30	M	Printer	Ireland	"	
R. Sands	55	M	Gent.	England	"	
J. Hallam	35	M	Farmer	"	"	
M. Bratt	36	M	Foundry man	"	"	
C. Sheffield	40	F		"	"	
W. Williams	24	M	Foundry man	"	"	
A. Drew	22	F	Milliner	Ireland	"	Sch. Baltimore
E. Humphrey	21	F	"	"	"	
J. O'Neal	26	M	Labourer	"	"	
J Larkin	35	M	"	"	"	
J. Brown	24	M	Weaver	"	"	
J. Morris	22	M	"	"	"	
B. " & 3 ch.	23	F		"	"	
B. McEvoy	21	F		"	"	
J. Henry	50	M	Merchant	"	"	
E. " & 2 ch.	22	F		"	"	
P. McCain *	33	M	Weaver	"	"	
M. " & 2 ch.	28	F		"	"	
J Malone	24	M	Weaver	"	"	
C. Mecar	22	M	"	"	"	
--- Ebzler	32	M	Shoemaker	"	"	Ship Wabash.
W Byers	24	M	Farmer	"	"	Brig Fabius
C. " & ch.	54	F	Spinster	"	"	
J. Smith	50	M	Farmer	Ireland	"	
J. Smyth	26	M	"	"	"	
W. "	24	M	"	"	"	
A. "	22	M	"	"	"	
D. " & 2 ch.	50	F		"	"	
A. Kennedy	40	M	Farmer	"	"	
J Townley	20	M	Clerk	"	"	
S. Andrews	23	M	Farmer	"	"	
M. Wilson & ch.	36	F	Spinster	"	"	
J. McIntire & 3 ch.	26	M	Farmer	"	"	
G. Harvey	25	M	"	"	"	
R. Spear	19	M	"	"	"	
A. "	20	F	Spinster	"	"	
J. Graham	24	M	Farmer	"	"	
W. Orr	18	M	"	"	"	
J. Smith	28	M	Merchant	"	"	

Names of passengers	Age	Sex	Occupation	Country to which they belong	Country of which they intend becoming inhabitants	Ship or vessel with the name of the master or commander
BALTIMORE Cont						
Q. E. Sept. 30, 1822						
J. Smith & child	21	F		Ireland	U. States	
M. Waring	25	F	Spinster	"	"	
M McIntire	19	M	"	"	"	
E. McReynolds	15	F	"	"	"	
H. Kennedy	33	M	Merchant	"	"	
W Eckle	28	M	"	U States	"	Sch. La Plata.
P D. Garert *	40	M	"	"	"	
G. H. Muller	35	M	"	Germany	"	
J. C. H. Weinbrumer	35	M	"	Sweden	"	
G. W. Sweeny	25	M	"	U. States	"	Sch. King Soloman.
G. Green	40	M	"	"	"	Sch. Express.
C. Gauntt	28	M	Off. of Navy	"	"	Sch. Experiment.
E. Marshall	18	M	"	"	"	
T. Claroe	30	M	Mechanic	Cape Haytien	"	
S. Million & ch.	40	M	Carpenter	"	"	
T. D. Johnson	21	M	Merchant	U. States	"	
W. Howell Jr.	25	M	"	"	"	Sch. Lapwing.
J. Dashiel	26	M	"	"	"	
W. Mackler	27	M	"	"	"	
B. Phale	28	M	"	"	"	
D. Monsarrat	29	M	"	"	"	
A. Wade	30	M	Mariner	"	"	
J. Jarvis	31	M	"	"	"	
C. Plecre	35	M	Baker	Panama		Sch. Freeman.
P. Cambesedgh	30	M	Soldier	France		
C. Drigan	30	M	"	"		
T. Berthain/Bertham	27	M	"	"		
A. Gudot	24	M	"	"		
C. Schmidt	28	M	"	Germany		
J. Boutarie	33	M	"	France		
A. Duvraur	25	M	"	Prussia		
T. W Bett	28	M	Merchant	U. States	U. States	
J. Brown	34	M	"	"	"	
W. V. Dreys	54	M	"	France	"	Sch. Harriet.
F. Meyers	54	M	"	Germany	"	
C. W. Storey	30	M	"	U. States	"	Sch. Iris.
F. Adams	28	M	"	"	"	
T. Daniel	35	M	"	"	"	
P. Baldwin	40	M	Mariner	"	"	
S. J. Millin/Miller *	40	M	"	"	"	
E. N. Schaeffer	24	M	Merchant	"	"	Brig Nicholas.
E. Cleveland	25	M	"	"	"	
G. H. Kunst	24	M	Gent.	Germany	"	Ship Jupiter.
A. H. Abraham	21	M	"	"	"	

Names of passengers	Age	Sex	Occupation	Country to which they belong	Country of which they intend becoming inhabitants	Ship or vessel with the name of the master or commander
BALTIMORE Cont.						
Q. E. Sept. 30, 1822						
C. Nine	24	M	Musician	Germany	U. States	
L. Schroeder	23	M	Labourer	"	"	
J. G. Topelman	20	M	Merchant	"	"	
A. D. Quans & 3 ch.	36	F		"	"	
H. A. Tilge	21	M	Hatter	"	"	
C. Welker	42	M	Farmer	"	"	
C. " & 5 ch.	38	F		"	"	
L. Kessler	36	M	Millwright	"	"	
E. " & 3 ch.	24	F		"	"	
P. B. "	34	M	Shoemaker	"	"	
A. " & 2 ch.	30	F		"	"	
F. Sibborne	34	M	Clerk	"	"	
J. Haeseman	36	M	Gent.	"	"	
J. H. Westram	26	M	Blacksmith	"	"	
P. A. Karthams	27	M	Merchant	U. States	"	
E. Wilson	21	M	Collar mkr.	England	"	Ship Mary.
J. Calder	25	M	Grocer	"	"	
W. Fawke	21	M	Farmer	"	"	
W. Delmore	22	M	"	"	"	
C. Pope	33	M	"	"	"	
J. "	27	M		"	"	
J. Jenkins	30	M		"	"	
J. "	24	F		"	"	
R. "	28	F		"	"	
C. " & ch.	26	F		"	"	
J. Page	25	M	Farmer	"	"	
W. Naylor	42	M	"	"	"	
T. Jones	27	M	"	"	"	
R. Parkes	17	M	"	"	"	
G. "	20	M	"	"	"	
W. Spence	20	M	"	"	"	
R. Atkinson & 5 ch.	54	M	"	"	"	
J. Baird	37	M	"	"	"	
E. " & 4 ch.	37	F		"	"	
R. Jones	35	M	Farmer	"	"	
S. " & 3 ch.	36	F		"	"	
J. Davis	42	M	Farmer	"	"	
M. " & 3 ch.	41	F		"	"	
G. Denmas	60	M	Farmer	"	"	
J. Webster	46	M	"	"	"	
M. " & 4 ch.	47	F		"	"	
J. Caldwell	21	M	Labourer	"	"	
G. Wainwright	45	M	Farmer	"	"	
C. " & 4 ch.	46	F		"	"	

Names of passengers	Age	Sex	Occupation	Country to which they belong	Country of which they intend becoming inhabitants	Ship or vessel with the name of the master or commander
BALTIMORE Cont.						
Q. E. Sept. 30, 1822						
G. Stitchcomb	35	M	Mariner	U. States	U. States	Sch. Lady's Delight.
J. McLaughlin	40	M	Farmer	G. Britain	"	Brig Azores.
S. " & 4 ch.	38	F		"	"	
M. Gwinn	21	M	Weaver	"	"	
M. "	60	F		"	"	
M. "	58	F		"	"	
W. Kirker	60	M	Farmer	Ireland	"	Brig Gleaner.
J. "	20	M	Shoemaker	"	"	
W. Lucis	27	M	Clerk	"	"	
M. A. "	18	F	Milliner	"	"	
D. Kirker	55	F	Spinster	"	"	
Mrs. Compte	40	F		U. States	"	Sch. Nancy.
Mrs. Corner	40	F		"	"	
M. Hipkins	16	F		"	"	
W. Hunter	45	M	Merchant	G. Britain	"	Ship Oryza.
G. W. Ellis	23	M	"	U. States	"	Sch. Genl. Stricker.
J. J. Myer	23	M	"	"	"	
J. G. Jose	22	M	"	Porto Rico	Porto Rico	
J. A. Gilas *	40	M		"	"	
--- Ford	35	M	Butcher	U. States	U. States	Sch. Eliza.
H. Woodward	29	M	Tavernkeeper	"	"	
G. Linkswilder	26	M	Farmer	"	"	Sch. Charles Sydney.
J. Dewer	29	M	"	"	"	
G. Lione	31	M	Merchant	"	"	Sch. Rosalie.
W. Beatty	16	M		"	"	
M. Betram	24	M	Currier	Italy	"	Brig Mars.
M. Campbell	38	M	Labourer	Ireland	"	Brig Brutus.
J. McCarperty	32	M	"	"	"	
J. Steel	22	M	"	"	"	
J. Derigen	21	M	"	"	"	
J. Caspey	22	M	Weaver	"	"	
J. Jackson	25	M	Labourer	"	"	
D. McKee	25	M	"	"	"	
H. Clark	30	M	Mason	"	"	
P. Ginnins	29	M	Hatter	"	"	
N. Verner	25	M	Labourer	"	"	
M. Inderson	20	M	"	"	"	
E. Campbell	22	M	"	"	"	
J. McCaferty & infant	20	F		"	"	
G. Robinson	35	M	Merchant	U. States	"	Sch. Sterling.
R. Elliot	23	M	"	"	"	
G. Phillips	19	M	Blacksmith	"	"	
J. Campbell	28	M	"	"	"	
G. Henney	42	M	Labourer	England	"	Ship Balloon.

Names of passengers	Age	Sex	Occupation	Country to which they belong	Country of which they intend becoming inhabitants	Ship or vessel with the name of the master or commander
BALTIMORE Cont.						
Q. E. Sept. 30, 1822						
J. Henney & 7 ch.	43	F		England	U. States	
R. Glassur	28	M	Draper	"	"	
L. C. Boudman	70	M		U. States	"	Ship William.
F. " & 2 ch.	21	M	Locksmith	Germany	"	
C. Rouff	34	M	"	"	"	
J. Edwald	32	M	"	"	"	
L. Kearne	22	M	Tailor	"	"	
E. Springhorn	43	M	Bell founder	"	"	
G. Lower	29	M	Baker	"	"	
P. Sander	33	M	Farmer	"	"	
H. Kern	52	M	"	"	"	
T. Snyder	33	M	Shoemaker	"	"	
C. Koblack, wife & ch.	32	M	Weaver	"	"	
C. Clennen	65	F		"	"	
J. Blenn	42	M	Farmer	"	"	
Mrs. " & 2 ch.	42	F		"	"	
N. Housan	41	M	Farmer	"	"	
Mrs. " & 5 ch.	34	F		"	"	
H. J. Winter	42	M	Farmer	"	"	
Mrs. " & 4 ch.	42	F		"	"	
T. Winder	48	M	Butcher	"	"	
Mrs. " & 4 ch.	48	F		"	"	
J. Mosier, wife & 4 ch.	33	M	Weaver	"	"	
E. Milland	76	F		"	"	
M. Springer	17	F		"	"	
J. Inoter & ch.	30	M	Baker	"	"	
C. Knoblock & ch.	23	F		"	"	
C. Blinn & 2 ch.	23	F		"	"	
E. Housen & 5 ch.	33	F		"	"	
A. M. Winter	29	F		"	"	
E. " & 4 ch.	22	F		"	"	
C. Poor	32	M	Merchant	U. States	"	Sch. Mary Caroline.
C. Schee	35	M	Consul U. S.	"	"	Sch. Nephele.
R. W. Garrison	35	M	Merchant	"	"	Brig Canada.
A. Ashburn	28	M		"	"	Brig Virginia.
J. McCanghay	22	M	Weaver	Ireland	"	Brig Maria.
H. "	22	F		"	"	
J. Keefe	32	M	Tailor	"	"	
B. " & 2 ch.	32	F		"	"	
C. Ryan & ch.	45	F		"	"	
E. Lasby	20	M		"	"	
J. Warghar	28	M	Tailor	"	"	
J. Blakely	27	M	Professor	"	"	
S. Spratt	30	M	Watchmaker	"	"	

Names of passengers	Age	Sex	Occupation	Country to which they belong	Country of which they intend becoming inhabitants	Ship or vessel with the name of the master or commander
BALTIMORE Cont.						
Q. E. Sept. 30, 1822						
J. Spratt & ch.	30	F		Ireland	U. States	
J. McKnight	50	M	Mariner	U. States	"	Sch. Hornet.
C. Roberts	41	F		"	"	
J. "	32	M	Mariner	"	"	
J. Ouldman	25	M	Merchant	Sweden	"	Brig Fredrica Charlotte.
W. Higgins	25	M	Farmer	Ireland	"	Sch. Larch.
M. " & 2 ch.	24	F		"	"	
M. Clark	30	M		"	"	
P. Brann	20	M		"	"	
N. Halley	18	F		"	"	
B. Currey	20	F		"	"	
J. H. Cushing	25	M	Merchant	U. States	"	Sch. Jane.
J. Hancock	40	M	"	England	"	Brig Belvedere.
J. Heron	40	M	"	"	"	
L. Heytsman	30	M	Mechanic	Wertemberg	"	Ship Genl. Lingan.
G. Emrick	35	M	Miller	"	"	
S. Emrick & 3 ch.	26	F		"	"	
P. Morganstern & 3 ch.	47	M	Farmer	"	"	
H. Klein & 4 ch.	35	M	Cooper	"	"	
Mrs. "	26	F		"	"	
T. Probsting	34	M	Merchant	Prussia	"	
C. Brent & 2 ch.	33	M	"	U. States	"	
S. Fitch	30	M	Engineer	"	"	Sch. Junius.
D. J. Antonio	25	M	Merchant	"	"	
J. Phillips	34	M	Mariner	"	"	Brig Homer.
W. Bunce	36	M	"	"	"	Brig Orestes.
J. W. McFaden	28	M	Merchant	"	"	
G. Atkinson	24	M	Baker	England	"	
M. Ayre & 6 ch.	36	F		"	"	
R. Potter	27	M	Gent.	"	"	Brig Edward.
J. Hindekoper *	19	M	Farmer	Holland	"	
J. Dedale	30	M	Saddler	"	"	
J. McMahon	25	M	Farmer	Ireland	"	Sch. Director.
A. Hogg	40	M	Clockmakr.	Germany	"	Ship Athens.
J. Friday	43	M	Farmer	"	"	
P. Sunderland	24	M	Tailor	Ireland	"	Sch. Decatur.
W. Bond	50	M	Farmer	"	"	
A. "	20	M	"	"	"	
S. McAppee	19	M	"	"	"	
M. "	21	F	Seamstress	"	"	
J. "	21	F	"	"	"	
E. Brown	40	F	"	"	"	
J. Hastings	50	M	Farmer	"	"	
S. "	19	F	Seamstress	"	"	

Names of passengers	Age	Sex	Occupation	Country to which they belong	Country of which they intend becoming inhabitants	Ship or vessel with the name of the master or commander
BALTIMORE Cont.						
Q. E. Sept. 30, 1822						
J. Hastings	20	M	Farmer	Ireland	U. States	
W. " & ch.	30	M	"	"	"	
A. Black & child	26	F	Seamstress	"	"	
J Hastings	22	M	Farmer	"	"	
M. Sprawl	20	F		"	"	
J. Cunningham	25	M	Farmer	"	"	
J. Craig	31	M	"	"	"	
E. " & 2 ch.	28	F		"	"	
A. McCarney	21	F	Seamstress	"	"	
T. Ewent	20	M	Farmer	"	"	
J. "	25	F	Seamstress	"	"	
G. Coulter	20	M	Farmer	"	"	
T. Hamilton	30	M	"	"	"	
M. Denning	44	M	"	"	"	
H. " & 7 ch.	40	F		"	"	
H. McCusker	32	M	Farmer	"	"	
J. Crusier	22	M	Farmer	"	"	
P. Collins	22	M	"	"	"	
J. Houghry	18	M	"	"	"	
C. Graham	20	M	"	"	"	
J. Moss	42	M	"	"	"	
M. " & 3 ch.	40	F		"	"	
D. Conley	30	M	Farmer	"	"	
P. "	20	M	"	"	"	
J. "	25	M	"	"	"	
G. "	24	M	"	"	"	
J. Lowry	20	M	"	"	"	
J. Sloan	22	M	"	"	"	
C. McDeivit	24	F	Seamstress	"	"	
B. McCann	22	M	Farmer	"	"	
F. Linn	22	M	"	"	"	
C. Dougherty	25	M	"	"	"	
J. Mitchell	30	M	"	"	"	
T. Bell & 2 ch.	49	M	"	"	"	
A. Megahy	26	F	Seamstress	"	"	
J. Hamilton	36	M	Farmer	"	"	
J. "	26	F		"	"	
D. Boyle & ch.	55	M	Farmer	"	"	
H. Ewing	25	M	"	"	"	
M. "	25	M	"	"	"	
J. Frail	20	M	"	"	"	
J Moore	21	M	"	"	"	
H. McAvoy	20	M	Tailor	"	"	
R. Hunter	21	M	Weaver	"	"	

Names of passengers	Age	Sex	Occupation	Country to which they belong	Country of which they intend becoming inhabitants	Ship or vessel with the name of the master or commander
BALTIMORE Cont.						
Q. E. Sept. 30, 1822						
J. Hunter & ch.	20	F		Ireland	U. States	
J. Gibbon	25	M	Weaver	"	"	
M. "	24	F		"	"	
M. Wilson & 2 ch.	24	F		"	"	
J. Coyle	18	M	Labourer	"	"	
W. Kelly	19	M	Carpenter	"	"	
B. "	22	F		"	"	
J. McGuire	27	M	Farmer	"	"	
A. " & ch.	22	F		"	"	
S. Kelly	50	F		"	"	
O. Dunn	23	M	Farmer	"	"	
B. Demoray	23	F		"	"	
P. Meagher & ch.	35	M	Farmer	"	"	
G. Giudera	38	M	"	"	"	
J. Saunders	23	M	"	"	"	
T. Crawley (Crowley)	37	M	"	"	"	
M. " " & 3 ch.	35	F		"	"	
M. " "	20	M	Farmer	"	"	
J. Kavanagh	30	M	Baker	"	"	
G. Byly	23	M	Carpenter	G. Britain	"	Sch. Napoleon.
M. McMillen	28	M	"	"	"	
G. Moore	25	M	"	"	"	
M. Mollern	26	M	"	"	"	
E. Byly & 2 ch.	19	F		"	"	
C. Johnson	50	M	Mariner	"	"	
A. McTier	25	M	Merchant	U. States	"	Sch. Colin Ramsay.
W. Browning	25	M		Ireland	"	Ship Amazon.
Mrs. Johnson & 2 ch.	25	F		"	"	
J. Donavan	36	M	Farmer	"	"	
M. " & 4 ch.	30	F		"	"	
E. Welsh	22	F		"	"	
J. Foye	21	M	Tailor	"	"	
M. Brown	22	F		"	"	
C. Donaven	20	M		"	"	
Wm. Chirn *	46	M		"	"	
E. F. Trichul *	35	M	Tailor	"	"	Brig Lady Monroe.
A. R Kleppisch & 2 ch.	45	F		Germany	"	
B. Burger	32	M	Mariner	U. States	"	
C. F. Kalkman	40	M	Merchant	"	"	
A. Higham	29	F		England	"	Ship Arethusa.
W. Flint	21	M	Merchant	"	"	
T. Medford	42	M	"	"	"	
E. " & ch.	21	F		"	"	
A. Westerman & 2 ch.	47	F		"	"	

Names of passengers	Age	Sex	Occupation	Country to which they belong	Country of which they intend becoming inhabitants	Ship or vessel with the name of the master or commander
BALTIMORE Cont.						
Q. E. Sept. 30, 1822						
E. Roberts	19	F		England	U. States	
J. "	17	F		"	"	
L. Doyle & 2 ch.	50	F		"	"	
E. Dollard	26	F		Ireland	"	
M. Brown & ch.	23	F		"	"	
P. Furley	25	M		England	"	
M. Murray & 2 ch.	30	F		"	"	
B. Kilduff	30	F		"	"	
M. Kelly & ch.	20	F		"	"	
J. Burns & 3 ch.	27	F		"	"	
W. Korne	23	M		"	"	
E. Fitzpatrick & 3 ch.	27	F		"	"	
G. Lawson	43	M	Supercargo	U. States	"	Brig G. P. Stevenson.
P. Roderigues	49	M	Merchant	Ireland	"	Sch. Paragon.
R. E. Gerper	45	M	"	"	"	Brig Oswego.
J. Galvin	22	M	"	"	"	
N. Peterson	22	M	Merchant	U. States	U. States	
F. X. De Ealo	30	M	"	Spain	"	Sch. Iris.
J. Cotaso	16	M		"	"	
L. Hewitt	28	M	Merchant	France	"	Sch. Sally & Polly.
W. Bias	21	M	Cooper	Ireland	"	
R. Graham	33	M	Farmer	U. States	"	Sch. Nancy.
W. Parker & ch.	54	M	Merchant	G. Britain	"	Sch. Abarilla.
W. Orr	39	M	Weaver	Ireland	"	Sch. Clothier.
E. C. Orr & 3 ch.	42	F		"	"	
J. Brown	28	M	Surgeon	"	"	
J. Lappin & 2 ch.	67	M	Cordwainer	"	"	
T. Webster	19	M	Smith	"	"	
H. Conigan	23	M	Carpenter	"	"	
E. Leison	25	M	Stonecutter	"	"	
J. Smith	65	M	Planter	St. Croix	St. Croix	Brig Panopea.
D. Walker	49	M	Merchant	U. States	U. States	Sch. Experiment.
J. Waln	39	M	"	"	"	
--- Carvello	30	M	"	Cape Haytien	"	
M. O. La Port	45	M		"	"	
M. Torres	25	M		"	"	
P. W. Mariner *	64	M	Mariner	U. States	"	Sch. Fame.
R. W. Kellow	31	M	"	"	"	
J. Wharton	22	M	"	"	"	
W. Kellow	18	M	"	"	"	
P. Finn	20	M	"	"	"	
R. Haye	37	M	Merchant	"	"	
J. R. Thompson	27	M	Mechanic	"	"	Sch. Anna.
J. C. Herwig	23	M	Merchant	"	"	

Names of passengers	Age	Sex	Occupation	Country to which they belong	Country of which they intend becoming inhabitants	Ship or vessel with the name of the master or commander
BALTIMORE Cont.						
Q. E. Sept. 30, 1822						
J. F. Leghtner	27	M	Merchant	U. States	U. States	Sch. Virginia.
F. Caron	36	M		Ireland	"	
C. Henderson	21	M	Weaver	"	"	
B. Burdey	21	M	"	"	"	
J. Black	20	M	"	"	"	
J. Duffee	46	M	Shoemaker	"	"	
D. Tawler	21	M		"	"	
J. Anderson	31	M	Weaver	"	"	
M. " & 4 ch.	30	F		"	"	
J. Gardner	30	M		"	"	
M. " & 2 ch.	28	F		"	"	
T. Rutherford	50	M	Weaver	"	"	
N. "	45	F		"	"	
J. "	26	M		"	"	
S. "	19	F		"	"	
P. McDormatt	27	F		"	"	
R. Mc " & ch.	27	M		"	"	
J. Dorothy	23	M	Labourer	"	"	
E. Gillaspy	22	F		"	"	
W. Mant	30	M	Weaver	"	"	
J. Wood	20	M	"	"	"	
J. Heton	21	M	"	"	"	
A. McLennon	28	M	Farmer	Ireland	"	Ship Cora.
J. Johnson	20	M		"	"	
H. Kennedy	28	M	Shoemaker	"	"	
R. Parton & 2 ch.	51	M	Farmer	"	"	
R. Phillips	60	M	Labourer	"	"	
W. Smith	37	M	Merchant	"	"	
M. Kind or Rind & 4 ch.	45	F		"	"	
Mrs. Willis & ch.	23	F		"	"	
P. Bell	20	F		"	"	
S. Howard	24	M	Farmer	"	"	
J. O. Drain	25	M	"	"	"	
J. Brown	26	M	Clerk	"	"	
R. Connell	27	M	Farmer	"	"	
J Carson	28	M	Shoemaker	"	"	
S. "	28	F		"	"	
W. Biddle	23	M	Farmer	"	"	
J Stewart	30	M	"	"	"	
W Martin	56	M	"	"	"	
J. McFillen	37	M	"	"	"	
D. " & child	34	F		"	"	
N. Watts	22	F		"	"	
E. Mackey	34	F		"	"	

Names of passengers	Age	Sex	Occupation	Country to which they belong	Country of which they intend becoming inhabitants	Ship or vessel with the name of the master or commander
BALTIMORE Cont.						
Q. E. Sept. 30, 1822						
J. McFea	22	M	Farmer	Ireland	U. States	
W. Dinsmere	35	M	"	"	"	
S. Brown	26	M	"	"	"	
M. "	24	F		"	"	
E. McFarline	45	M	Farmer	"	"	
E. " & 4 ch.	45	F		"	"	
W. Ansley	50	M	Farmer	"	"	
A. Donaho	28	M	Mariner	U. States	"	
J. D. Johnson	22	M	Merchant	"	"	
T. Connell	37	M	Shoemaker	Ireland	"	Ship Massasoit.
E. "	25	F		"	"	
W. Carkill	35	M	Tailor	"	"	
J. " & 4 ch.	35	F		"	"	
E. Kinew	24	F		"	"	
W. G. Malin	20	M	Farmer	"	"	
J. Hyde & ch.	28	F		"	"	
C. Gillanders	75	F		"	"	
T. Myer	22	M	Musician	"	"	
J. Briggs	24	M		"	"	
J. C. B. Knopple	25	M		"	"	
J. H. Grossener	21	M	Merchant	U States	"	Ship Dumfries.
NEW YORK						
Q. E. Dec. 31, 1822						
Raymond Matos	18	M	Merchant	Spanish Main	U. States	Sch. Diana. Kimbal.
A. Hernandes	24	M	"	"	"	
Eliza. Record & 4 ch.	30	F	Lady	U. States	"	Brig Margt. & Sarah. Lewis.
John McConnochy	29	M	Merchant	Scotland	Scotland	Sch. Lovely Hope. Lincoln.
John Havison	28	M	Smith	England	U. States	Brig Patriot. Fairchild.
Mary Ann " & ch.	22	F		"	"	
Eliz. Freeman	24	M	Seamstress	"	"	Ship James. Garrison.
D. G. Boritoget	23	M	Merchant	Spain	"	Sch. Leonidas. Bedford.
Geo. Robinson	29	M	"	G. Britain	"	Ship Zodiac. Burns.
J. Pearman	40	M	Farmer	"	"	
John Eames	21	M		"	"	
Ann Ealing & ch.	25	F		"	"	
John Hawsnell	21	M		"	"	
Sarah "	52	F		"	"	
Mary " & ch.	40	F		"	"	
William Mulligan	45	M		"	"	
Wm. Grogen	30	M	Labourer	"	"	
Isaac Mear	30	M	"	"	"	
Henry Willis or Welles	20	M	Farmer	"	"	

Names of passengers	Age	Sex	Occupation	Country to which they belong	Country of which they intend becoming inhabitants	Ship or vessel with the name of the master or commander
NEW YORK Cont.						
Q. E. Dec. 31, 1822						
R. Hay	25	M	Farmer	Scotland	U. States	Brig Minerva. Henderson.
R. Mill	26	M		"	"	
David Dunlop	18	M		"	"	
J. Anderson	39	M		"	"	
M. " & 6 ch.	38	F		"	"	
Wm. Clark	21	M		"	"	
C. P. Monro	29	M		"	"	
John Cookworthy	30	M	Farmer	G. Britain	"	Ship Ulysses. Aurey.
Jane " & 7 ch.	32	F		"	"	
Nancy McLean	21	F		"	"	
Samuel Jones	28	M	Farmer	"	"	
H. Masters	45	M	Merchant	England	England	Ship Vermont. Custer.
W. Leavet	25	M	"	St. Johns	St. Johns	Sch. Rambler. Howard.
D. Adams	40	M	"	U. States	U. States	Sch. Nancy. Crowell.
Jas. Johnston	40	M	"	England	"	
Henry Porter	20	M	"	"	"	
Wm. Hookmulin	25	M	"	"	"	
Peter Omaney	25	M	"	Ireland	"	
Mary Willet & 2 ch.	35	F	"	"	"	
Margt. Lee	22	F	"	"	"	
Joseph Dayley	23	M	Labourer	"	"	
John Cloud	25	M	"	"	"	
Thomas Durant	24	M	"	"	"	
Ann "	22	F		"	"	
Catharine Carton	25	F		"	"	
Nancy Brady	30	F		"	"	
Ann "	28	F		"	"	
John Magrath	25	M	Labourer	"	"	
Arthur Lary	22	M	"	"	"	
Arthur Ferguson	40	M	"	"	"	
Eliz. " & 2 ch.	38	F		"	"	
James Thompson	25	M	Weaver	"	"	
Nancy "	22	F		"	"	
G. Gowen & 2 ch.	40	F		"	"	
Charles B. Shaw	22	M	Merchant	U. States	"	Brig Fanny. Baker.
C. B. Hawkins	20	M	"	"	"	
Joseph Barriero	30	M	"	Spain	Spain	Sch. Neptune. Argino.
Guillaume Lumotte	25	M	"	France	France	
M. Nolingshead	34	M	"	U. States	U. States	Brig Mermaid. Pompter.
M. Braden	30	M	"	"	"	
Bernard Hendrick	41	M	Doctor	Montreal	Montreal	Ship Seine. Williams.
Geo. Monk	35	M	Merchant	U. States	U. States	
Wm. Road	27	M	Mechanic	"	"	
Mrs. " & 2 ch.	32	F		"	"	

Names of passengers	Age	Sex	Occupation	Country to which they belong	Country of which they intend becoming inhabitants	Ship or vessel with the name of the master or commander
NEW YORK Cont. Q. E. Dec. 31, 1822						
Joseph Karns	33	M	Farmer	U. States	U. States	
P. Ingleman	24	M	Baker	"	"	
P. Reider	25	M	Distiller	"	"	
D. Soper	44	M	Farmer	"	"	
N. Futaly	53	M	"	Switzerland	"	
E. " & 3 ch.	52	F		"	"	
A. Rickebock	27	F		"	"	
F. "	22	F		"	"	
D. Ashelman	48	M	Farmer	"	"	
Eliza. " & ch.	38	F		"	"	
H. Rickebock & ch.	54	M	Farmer	"	"	
M. Wonderly	30	M	Saddler	"	"	
Jacob Manget	25	M	Farmer	"	"	
Mary "	26	F		"	"	
John Mabuck	21	M	Farmer	"	"	
John Darly	25	M	Cooper	"	"	
J. Spalter	23	M	Farmer	"	"	
J. Seal	44	M	Cooper	U. States	"	
F. Clark	24	M	Merchant	"	.	Sloop Valiant. Calvin.
Hannah Sanger	22	F		"	"	Ship Oscar. Sanger.
John Clark	25	M	Joiner	England	"	
George Morton	25	M	Merchant	Scotland	"	
Francis Chistle *	28	M	Tailor	G. Britain	"	Ship Orizimbo. Nichols.
Mary " & ch.	21	F		"	"	
John Burrows	71	M	Farmer	"	"	
Francis Steel	31	M	"	"	"	
Jane " & 3 ch.	24	F		"	"	
James Briton	27	M	Shoemaker	"	"	
James Fernside	21	M	Farmer	"	"	
Ann " & 2 ch.	21	F		"	"	
Thomas Jones	24	M	Merchant	"	"	
Mrs. " & ch.	24	F		"	"	
Ann Hamilton	27	F		"	"	
Chester Andrews	20	M	Merchant	U. States	"	
John N. "	25	M	"	"	"	
John McParlin	23	M	Labourer	G. Britain	"	
Ann " & 2 ch.	20	F		"	"	
Wm. Bowers	40	M	Merchant	"	"	
John Gordon	25	M	Labourer	"	"	
Alexr. Cameron	18	M	"	"	"	
Samuel McPherson	17	M	"	"	"	
R. Humphrey	64	M		"	"	Sch. Mt. Vernon. Davison.
Wm. Hutching	28	M		"	"	
John "	26	M		"	"	

Names of passengers	Age	Sex	Occupation	Country to which they belong	Country of which they intend becoming inhabitants	Ship or vessel with the name of the master or commander
NEW YORK Cont.						
Q. E. Dec. 31, 1822						
George Hutching	22	M		G. Britain	U. States	
B. Bird	28	M		"	"	
John Thatcher	31	M		"	"	
Joseph Burns	48	M		"	"	
John Nowland	26	M		"	"	
Sarah Faulkner & 3 ch.	48	F		"	"	
Jane Wallis & 4 ch.	30	F		"	"	
Joseph Scatleburgh	29	M		"	"	
Samuel "	22	M		"	"	
Joseph Bovit *	52	M		"	"	
Sarah " & 4 ch.	50	F		"	"	
Joseph Walker	26	M		"	"	
Sophia "	22	F		"	"	
Wm. Mont	27	M		"	"	
Agnes " & 2 ch.	27	F		"	"	
Thomas Licester	24	M		"	"	
Edwd. Davis	33	M		"	"	
Mrs. " & 2 ch.	33	F		"	"	
Wm. Lewis	53	M		"	"	
Ann " & 8 ch.	49	F		"	"	
Evan Evans	45	M		U. States	"	
Jane " & 6 ch.	43	F		"	"	
John Lamb	47	M	Gent.	"	"	Ship Howard. Holdridge.
Samuel "	36	M	Merchant	"	"	
Mrs. "	21	F	Lady	"	"	
W. B. Lawrence	22	M	Gent.	"	"	
F. Salmon	25	M	Merchant	"	"	
L. Bornnefoux	31	M	"	France	"	
G. Lacort	46	M		U. States	"	
Mrs. " & 3 ch.	31	F		"	"	
J. P. Bond	27	M	Merchant	"	"	
F. W. Primrose	37	M	Barrister	"	"	
J. Chandler	29	M	Merchant	"	"	
J. Crane	34	M	"	"	"	
J. P. Lamartie	21	M	"	France	"	
Richd. M. Sadler	24	M	"	U. States	"	Brig Francis Jarvis. Stenman.
J. Dias	38	M	Hatter	"	"	
J. Tate	35	M	Shoemaker	"	"	
Mary Roberts & ch.	25	F		"	"	
J. Campbell	45	M	Gent.	England	England	Sch. Etheldred. Clement.
R. Montages	48	M	Merchant	"	"	
M. Cottrel	20	M	Gent.	"	"	
C. Morgan & 2 ch.	36	M	"	"	"	
John Hard	65	M	Accountant	Barbadoes	"	Ship Illinois. Finch.

Names of passengers	Age	Sex	Occupation	Country to which they belong	Country of which they intend becoming inhabitants	Ship or vessel with the name of the master or commander
NEW YORK Cont.						
Q. E. Dec. 31, 1822						
D. Jones	44	M	Farmer	England	U. States	
Michael O'Connor	29	M	Hatter	Ireland	"	
B. Duggs	38	M	Mariner	U States	"	Brig Rebecca & Sally.
J. M. Lopez	22	M	Merchant	Spain		Brig Fair American.
F. Castalis	20	M	"	"		
A Bellamy	37	M	"	"		
A. R. Myra & ch.	27	M	Gent.	Govt. of Columbia	U. States	Brig Charles. Young.
John Haway	35	M	"	Gvt Britain	"	Ship Criterion. Sebor
Joseph Mackwell	25	M	Farmer	"	"	
D. Hicks	27	M	"	"	"	
M. Smith	31	M	Mariner	Ireland	"	
R. Wardilow	50	M	Hatter	"	"	
J. Dolph	34	M	Mariner	"	"	
R. Holt	23	M	Mechanic	"	"	
Mary Holt & child	25	F		"	"	
Robt. Thompson & ch.	50	M	Merchant	U. States	"	Sch. Jas. Cropper. Marshall.
J. F. Randolph	45	M	"	"	"	
A. Clark	40	M	"	"	"	
D. Allen	40	M	"	"	"	Sloop Falcon. Post.
G. W. Davenport	21	M	"	"	"	
A. J. Hill	25	M	"	"	"	
A. J. Pierson	30	M	"	"	"	
W. Wood	30	M	"	"	"	
G. Clark	30	M	Mechanic	England	"	Ship Hanover Adamson.
S. Morison	40	M	"	"	"	
J. James	27	M	"	"	"	
J. Wright	27	M	"	"	"	
Wm. Scarborough	41	M	Merchant	U. States	"	Ship Hector. Gillender.
G. U. M. Fairlane	26	M		Scotland	"	
Wm. Carnes	33	M		U. States	"	
Wm. Hill	34	M		"	"	
Thomas Davidson	40	M	"	"	"	
Wm. Walker	24	M	Merchant	G. Britain	"	Ship Atlantic. Taylor.
Wm. Wise	25	M	"	"	"	
Jas. Richard	33	M	Gent.	U. States	"	
Andw. Taylor	28	M	"	"	"	
Eliza Smith & 2 ch.	30	F		"	"	
Wm. Rider	45	M	Farmer	G. Britain	"	
Eliza. "	40	F		"	"	
Jos. Slocum	37	M	Merchant	U. States	"	Sch. Nile. Aldrich.
John Bourn	45	M	"	"	"	Brig Transit. Gillet.
F. V. E. de Camere Pustilli		M	Consul genl.	Portugal	U. States	Barque Sarah Louisa. Colver
A. P. Silva Vaccos		M	Secretary	"	"	

Names of passengers	Age	Sex	Occupation	Country to which they belong	Country of which they intend becoming inhabitants	Ship or vessel with the name of the master or commander
NEW YORK Cont.						
Q. E. Dec. 31, 1822						
V. J. Silva		M		Portugal	U. States	
Vict. A. Silva		M		"	"	
J. G. Seal		M		"	"	
John Fraser	23	M	Merchant	G. Britain	"	Ship Bengal. Pearce.
Wm Roberts	25	M	Clerk	"	"	
G. Bamister *	24	M	Cab. Maker	"	"	
T. Lawrence	44	M	Gent.	"	"	
C. J. C. de Figeneu						
Demona	24	M	Consul	Portugal	"	Ship Emulous. Selden.
Madame " " & ch.	20	F	"	"	"	
Abel Roberts	33	M	Physician	France	"	
S. C. Allen	45	M	Merchant	Spain		Brig David Moffet. Cullen.
A. Wolfe	40	M	"	U. States		
Samuel Johnston	45	M	Shoemaker	England	U. States	Brig Resign. Clement.
Charlotte "	44	F		"	"	
Robt. Thompson	30	M	Farmer	"	"	
John Dixon	32	M		"	"	
Mary " & 3 ch.	24	F		"	"	
John Mays	25	M	Ship carptr.	"	"	
Ann " & 2 ch.	26	F		"	"	
Francis Middleton	28	M	Farmer	"	"	
Robert Peat	24	M	Cab. Maker	"	"	
H. J. Roberts	23	M	Merchant	Cadiz		Ship Romulus. Allen.
T. B. Tilden	23	M	"	U. States	"	
James Wallace	50	M	Brewer	England	"	Brig Elizabeth. Smails.
H. M. Kenmer	28	M	"	Ireland	"	
Wm. Roberts	60	M	Carpenter	England	"	
Mrs. "	39	F		"	"	
Wm. Burgoyne & 2 ch.	42	M	Merchant	U. States	"	Ship Panther. Bennett.
H. W. Hills	36	M	"	"	"	
James Williams	52	M	Gent.	England	"	
B. C. Bremmer *	30	M	Merchant	U. States	"	
Wm. Graham	35	M	Mariner	"	"	
Wm. Adams	23	M	Merchant	England	"	
H. Spooner	27	M	"	"	"	
Robt. Bailey	45	M	Farmer	"	"	Ship William. Noyes.
Jane " & 6 ch.	43	F		"	"	
Betsey Burding	40	F	Spinster	"	"	
Alexr. Hutchinson & 9 ch.	40	M	Farmer	Ireland	"	
Ebenezer Ashley	44	M	Cab. maker	England	"	
Catharine " & 5 ch.	50	F		"	"	
H. Forrest & 5 ch.	31	F	Spinster	"	"	
Wm. Mandeth	45	M	Mason	"	"	

Names of passengers	Age	Sex	Occupation	Country to which they belong	Country of which they intend becoming inhabitants	Ship or vessel with the name of the master or commander
NEW YORK Cont.						
Q. E. Dec. 31, 1822						
Wm. Potters	28	M		Ireland	U States	
J. M. Gonness	21	M	Farmer	"	"	
Bryan Flanagan	23	M	Tailor	"	"	
Martin McIntyre	40	M		"	"	
W. S. Clark	32	M	Ship master	U. States	"	Ship Juno. Doak.
James Day	40	M	"	"	"	
H. J. Finn	34	M	Gent.	G. Britain	"	
Samuel Gregory	35	M	"	"	"	
Jas. A. Bell	21	M	Merchant	"	"	
Hugh Carnes	29	M	Cooper	"	"	
Mary " & 3 ch.	26	F		"	"	
Samuel Wells	45	M	Labourer	"	"	
John Conway	23	M	Student	"	"	
B. Corvenaugh	22	M	"	"	"	
R. Dunke	30	M	Labourer	"	"	
John Cooke	22	M	"	"	"	
Stephen Beale	26	M	"	"	"	
John Charles	26	M	Merchant	Ireland	"	Ship Hannibal. Wilkinson.
Mary "	25	F		"	"	
John Broadbent	22	M		England	"	
Thomas Shepherds	38	M		"	"	
Henry Fisher	40	M		"	"	
J. Cockburn	42	M		"	"	
James Stephens	37	M	Merchant	Scotland	"	Ship William. Manners.
Mrs. " & 3 ch.	36	M	"	"	"	
Richd. A. Baley	24	M	Painter	England	"	
Michael Cayan	30	M	"	"	"	
W. Haffain	24	M	Tailor	"	"	
Patrick Mandin	22	M	Shoemaker	"	"	
James Hollingshead	30	M	Druggist	"	"	
Mary "	25	F		"	"	
Martin Bailey	45	M	Stay maker	"	"	
Philip "	50	M	"	"	"	
Sarah " & 5 ch.	40	M		"	"	
John Timens	22	M	Merchant	"	"	Sch. Martha Schelchley.
Francis "	21	M		"	"	
Jas. Delaney	38	M		"	"	
Mary "	28	F		"	"	
Henry Temmins	24	M		"	"	
Jno. W. Pane	25	M		"	"	
John Cox	28	M		"	"	
H. Passart	33	M	Merchant	U. States	"	Ship Stephania. Smythe.
Stephen Berage	26	M	"	France	"	
S. Maynin	22	M	"	"	"	

Names of passengers	Age	Sex	Occupation	Country to which they belong	Country of which they intend becoming inhabitants	Ship or vessel with the name of the master or commander
NEW YORK Cont.						
Q. E. Dec. 31, 1822						
T. Plottard	24	M	Merchant	France	U. States	
Daniel Frederick	23	M	"	"	"	
Joseph "	21	M	"	"	"	
Amos Scovell	34	M	"	U. States	"	Ship Maria. Fowler.
John Wood	57	M	"	"	"	
Elias Livy	19	M	Physician	England	"	
James Hunter	21	M		"	"	
J. Clause	24	M	Merchant	France	"	
J. Caude	36	M	Attorney	Mexico	Mexico	
Charles Manly	27	M	Painter	England	U. States	
Charlotte " & 3 ch.	27	F		"	"	
John Sutton	26	M	Carpenter	"	"	
Elizabeth Sutton & ch.	22	F		"	"	
David "	26	M	Farmer	"	"	
J. Renard	30	M	Merchant	France	"	Brig Washington. Barstow.
Geo. N. Waite	50	M	Gent.	U. States	"	Ship Cincinnatus. Champlin.
Wallace Eastburn	49	M		G. Britain	"	
John F. Foote	42	M	Farmer	"	"	
Isabella "	40	F		"	"	
Sarah Newill & ch.	30	F		"	"	
Augustus Berthlet	33	M	Farmer	"	"	
R. A. King	30	M	"	"	"	
W. N. Blam *	22	M	"	"	"	
Robt. G. Hirving	27	M	"	"	"	
George Wilds	23	M	Farmer	U. States	"	
James Jaffrey	29	M	"	"	"	
Thos. Brennard	30	M		"	"	
Michael Buckly	60	M	Glazier	"	"	
Susan "	54	F		"	"	
John Wacker	31	M	Teacher	"	"	
George "	29	M	Tinman	"	"	
Daniel "	25	M	Musician	"	"	
Wm. Mott	27	M	Painter	"	"	
John Bailey	23	M	Farmer	"	"	
Wm. Byrne	20	M	Bleacher	"	"	
Phillip Bacon	38	M	Carpenter	"	"	
John Sneeds	46	M	Farmer	"	"	
Charles Hammock	21	M	Cutler	"	"	
Amelia Jones	19	F		"	"	
Abraham Offer	18	M	Shoemaker	"	"	
Thomas Nicholson	29	M	Miller	"	"	
Jno. Langrige	35	M	Farmer	"	"	
Lydia " & 2 ch.	27	F		"	"	
Stephen Ford	45	M	Farmer	"	"	

Names of passengers	Age	Sex	Occupation	Country to which they belong	Country of which they intend becoming inhabitants	Ship or vessel with the name of the master or commander
NEW YORK Cont.						
Q E. Dec. 31, 1822						
Sophia Ford & ch.	24	F		U. States	U. States	
Ann Ellingham & 3 ch.	33	F		"	"	
Christopher Carnes	27	M	Farmer	U. States	"	
John Thorn	25	M		G. Britain	"	
Mary "	27	F		"	"	
John Biden	38	M		"	"	
Sarah " & 5 ch.	39	F		"	"	
Joseph Bertine	23	M	Merchant	Guardaloupe	St Domingo	Sch. Leo. Knight.
Charles Lowhill	27	M	"	St. Domingo	"	
M. D. Thompson	30	M	"	U. States	"	Brig Neptune's Barge.
W. Crimmond	40	M	"	England	"	
A. B. Dufair	45	M	"	France	"	
F. Cabanet	34	M	"	"	"	
Alfred Seaton	25	M	"	"	"	Sch Edgar. Johnson.
Robert Ludlow	22	M	"	"	"	
R. Durzec	26	M	"	"	"	
J. J. Siggs	30	M	"	Switzerland	"	Ship Bellona. Holdridge
A. Regand	25	M	Physician	France	"	
Reuben Howland	52	M	Mariner	U. States	"	Brig John. Barber.
F. Benort	30	M	"	France	"	
Joseph B. Norris	30	M	Merchant	U. States	"	Brig Matteawan. Coffin.
R. W. Folger	32	M	"	"	"	
George H. Johnston	22	M	"	"	"	Ship Robt Fulton. Holdridge.
John Rayner	22	M	Merchant	U. States	U. States	
Jane Allen & 2 ch.	35	F		G. Britain	"	
R. Peck	32	M	Mechanic	"	"	
James Amos	29	M	"	"	"	
W. Weston	23	M	"	"	"	
E. Rellink	27	M	Planter	"	"	
John Flemming	29	M	"	U. States	"	
Wm. Frean	35	M	Merchant	"	"	
Don Antonio	26	M	"	Canary Isles	"	Brig San Bunto. Legais.
Rhoda Boggs	53	F		U. States	"	Ship Packet. Boggs.
Sarah " & ch.	23	F		"	"	
John M. Barry	32	M	Merchant	"	"	Brig Georgetown Packet.
Saml. Croes	32	M	"	"	"	
Wm. Woodside	30	M	"	"	"	
Robt. Waite	22	M		"	"	Brig Mary. Burnes.
Geo. Simpson	28	M		"	"	
D. Smith	20	M		"	"	
Thos. M. Bond	30	M		"	"	
Jas. D. Jones	18	M		"	"	
D. Forrest	25	M		"	"	
E. N. Fry	32	M		"	"	

Names of passengers	Age	Sex	Occupation	Country to which they belong	Country of which they intend becoming inhabitants	Ship or vessel with the name of the master or commander
NEW YORK Cont.						
Q. E. Dec. 31, 1822						
Francis Baez	47	M	Merchant	France	Porto Rico	Sch. Concordia. Badey.
Eugene Duval	27	M	"	"	"	
Jos. Martino	27	M	"	"	"	
Isaac Means	30	M	"	U. States	"	
Mary Bush & 2 ch.	26	F		Ireland	U. States	Ship Alexr. Mansfield.
Mary Spratt	25	F		"	"	
Mary Auchinleck	40	F		"	"	
Ann Humphries	40	F		"	"	
Anabella O. Mullen	20	F		"	"	
Ann Pountany	20	F		"	"	
Wm. Maxwell	41	M		"	"	
Rachel " & 6 ch.	35	F		"	"	
John Wilson	20	M	Weaver	"	"	
Margt. Teale	40	F		"	"	
Robt. Burgess	20	M		"	"	
Margt. Kelman	20	F		"	"	
Nancy Falls & 3 ch.	30	F		"	"	
John Gordon	30	M	Watchmaker	"	"	
John Toale	24	M		"	"	
Jno. Stuart	30	M		"	"	
Danl. McLaughlin	30	M		"	"	
John O'Brian	20	M		"	"	
George Tenent	30	M		"	"	
Wm. Smith	20	M		"	"	
A. McKee	24	M	Farmer	"	"	
Wm. Rabb	24	M	Weaver	"	"	
Samuel Boyd	30	M		"	"	
Wm. Milligan	30	M	Farmer	"	"	
Wm. Fraser & ch.	47	M	Merchant	U. States	"	Ship Robt. Edwards.
M. Bailey	30	M	Farmer	G. Britain	"	
M. English	30	M	Gent.	"	"	
M. Whinns	25	M	Comedian	"	"	
M. Benoby	31	M	Gent.	France	"	
M. Willis	52	M	Manufactr.	G. Britain	"	
Mrs. " & 2 ch.	56	F		"	"	
Mrs. Cheeseman & 5 ch.	40	F		"	"	
Mrs. Traille	38	F		"	"	
M. "	28	M	Shoemaker	"	"	
M. Debil	22	M	Chairmaker	"	"	
M. King	21	M	Miller	"	"	
M. Denick	25	M	Sugar baker	Germany	"	
M. Rofferst *	25	M	"	U. States	"	
C. Burgman	24	M	"	Germany	"	
M. Harburg	24	M		"	"	

Names of passengers	Age	Sex	Occupation	Country to which they belong	Country of which they intend becoming inhabitants	Ship or vessel with the name of the master or commander
NEW YORK Cont. Q. E. Dec. 31, 1822						
George Nankins	23	M		Germany	U. States	
M. Stork	36	M		"	"	
Mrs. "	30	F		"	"	
M. Madac	22	M	Silversmith	"	"	
John Randolph	48	M		U. States	"	Ship New York.
F. Luchise	40	M		Naples	"	
Antonio Mecaluse	50	M		"	"	
George Glen	40	M	Lawyer	U. States	"	
Thomas Shorthouse	49	M	Merchant	"	"	
Wm. Stuart	27	M		G. Britain	"	
J Ogden	37	M		"	"	
Robt. Dayson & 2 ch.	38	M		"	"	
Ann Dalrymple & ch.	35	F		"	"	
Silas E. Wier	45	M		"	"	
James Russell	31	M	Mechanic	U. States	"	
R. Shepherd	30	M	Merchant	"	"	
G. M. Waldburge	31	M		"	"	
Wm. Masery *	27	M		"	"	
Thomas Smith	23	M		"	"	
A. Thompson	23	M		"	"	
Wm. Davis	21	M		"	"	
H. "	17	M		"	"	
A. C. Stanbury	42	M	Teacher	"	"	Ship Luna. Rich.
M. Elhandorf	35	M	Physician	France	"	
John Shepherd	35	M	Merchant	U. States	"	Brig Henrietta.
Lewis Disague *	25	M	"	"	"	
C. R. Roberts	21	M	"	"	"	
C. Van Brunt	27	M	"	"	"	Brig Lydia. Prince.
L. A. Port	22	M	"	Bremen	"	Brig Constitution
Fred. Bember	55	M	Coachmakr.	"	"	
H. Richells	32	M	Grocer	"	"	
John Stenker	16	M	Sugar baker	"	"	
John Hat	18	M	"	"	"	
L. Paster	33	M	Mariner	Spain	Teneriffe	Brig Hannah. Mason.
A. Thorndike	30	M	Merchant	U. States	U. States	Ship Draper. Smith.
F. D. Silva & ch.	46	M	"	Spain	Havana	
Edwd. Proyby	53	M	Farmer	England	U. States	Ship Exchange. Brown.
Thomas Behen & ch.	36	M	"	"	"	
Wm. Davis & ch.	46	M	Tradesman	"	"	
Asahel Chittenden	24	M	Farmer	"	"	
R. Robinson	21	M		"	"	
Wm. Toulder *	26	M		"	"	
James Pavoy	31	M		U. States	"	
Jane Gaither & ch.	32	M		"	"	Brig Brisk. Hutchinson.

Names of passengers	Age	Sex	Occupation	Country to which they belong	Country of which they intend becoming inhabitants	Ship or vessel with the name of the master or commander
NEW YORK Cont.						
Q. E. Dec. 31, 1822						
A. Marshall & ch.	52	F		U. States	U. States	Ship ?
W. G. Williams	21	M	Cadet	"	"	
N. C. Rapine	36	M	Merchant	Switzerland	"	
P. Pauls	31	M	"	Germany	"	
T. C. Duncan	23	M	"	England	"	Ship Hercules. Gardiner.
J. Wright	35	M	Clergyman	"	"	
John Brown	28	M	Gent.	"	"	
J. B. McIlvaine	32	M	Mechanic	U. States	"	Ship Susquehanna. Collinson
H. Kauffman	23	M	Merchant	"	"	Ship Virginia. Reeves.
Don Jose Regulas	27	M	"	Spain	Spain	Brig Vigilant. Harper.
John Stance	23	M	Carpenter	U. States	U. States	
John F. Fortin	25	M	Gent.	"	"	
Wm "	20	M	"	"	"	
Ben. T. Conklin	21	M	"	"	"	
Edwd. Bartlett	58	M	"	G. Britain	"	Sch. Hope & Esther. Bears.
James Canteli	58	M	Gunsmith	"	"	
Mary "	54	F		"	"	
R. McDonald	33	M		"	"	
Moses Nowlan	24	M		"	"	
Eliza Hayward	20	F		"	"	
C. Nolles & 2 ch.	23	M		"	"	
Wm. B. Webster	23	M	Studt. of med	N. Scotia	"	Sch. Nancy. Allen.
Wm. Harrison	25	M	Innkeeper	U. States	"	
George Harrison	25	M	Stonecutter	N. Scotia	U. States	
John Little	24	M	"	"	"	
Henry Francis	21	M	Weaver	"	"	
J. Kitchurn	20	M	Farmer	England	"	Ship Manchester Packet.
R. Hitts	30	M	Ship master	"	"	
E. Turft & 2 ch.	60	M		"	"	
C. Overton	26	M		"	"	
E. " & child	21	F		"	"	
J. Kirkwood	23	M		"	"	
J. Dougherty	23	M		"	"	
C. Ruthwood & ch.	30	M		"	"	
M. Ick	38	M	Merchant	"	"	Ship Elias Burger. Disney.
S. Abbot	34	M	Planter	"	"	
J. Jones	36	M	Mariner	U. States	"	
T. Hiller	24	M	"	"	"	
C. Anspeck	28	M	Merchant	"	"	
G. Patten	29	M	Pilot	"	"	
T. Davis	23	M	Shoemaker	"	"	
A. Apelin	27	M	Merchant	Havana	"	Brig Mary Joan. Arnold.
M. Pedro Vena	28	M	"	Portugal	"	Sch. Dart. Vandene.
John D. Nully	32	M	"	Denmark	"	Ship Chase. Baxter.

Names of passengers	Age	Sex	Occupation	Country to which they belong	Country of which they intend becoming inhabitants	Ship or vessel with the name of the master or commander
NEW YORK Cont.						
Q. E. Dec. 31, 1822						
D. Olmsted	19	M	Merchant	U. States	U. States	Brig Columbia. Bradford.
G. Meyer	45	M	"	"	"	Ship Columbia. Rogers.
F. Forms	42	M		G. Britain	"	
R. Irvin	22	M		"	"	
Wm. McLeod	24	M		U. States	"	
F. M. Lubrin	25	M		"	"	
J. Dixon	19	M		G. Britain	"	
J. W. Wallack	28	M	Comedian	"	"	
Wm. Sennis •	32	M	Merchant	"	"	
Wm. Miller	26	M	"	"	"	Brig Eliza. Burgess.
Mrs. " & ch.	25	F		"	"	
--- Saver	49	M	Merchant	France	"	Brig Charles Coffin.
S. Henry & 2 ch	37	M		Ireland	"	
Samuel Norton	45	M	Merchant	U States	"	Brig Rebecca. Parrot.
George Gardiner	36	M	Gent.	"	"	Sch Henry Davis.
John Gasden	38	M	Officer	G Britain	G Britain	Sch. Nancy Crowell.
Mary "	35	F	Lady	"	"	
W. Simpson	40	M	Merchant	U. States	U. States	
Wm. Hunt	40	M	Physician	G. Britain	G. Britain	
Danl V. Burton	32	M	"	"	"	
S. Bayard	20	M	"	"	"	
Jas. H Ray	20	M	Merchant	"	"	
J. D. Arnly or Amly	25	M	"	"	"	
Wm. H. Holly	27	M	Merchant	U. States	U. States	
H. N. Arnold	23	M	Preacher	G. Britain	G. Britain	
G. Robertson	24	M	Merchant	"		
Wm. Wilson	27	M	"	"		
Wm. Seally/Scally	27	M	"	"		
M. Ann Denison & 2 ch.	30	F	Lady	"		
Samuel Lenox	50	M	Farmer	"		
Sarah " & 7 ch.	50	F		"		
Thos M. Ray	25	M	Labourer	"		
R. Dunn	20	M	"	"		
Wm Porter	22	M	"	"		
J Waters	24	M	"	"		
L. "	22	M	"	"		
M. McDermott	27	M	"	"		
Mary Kent	33	F		G. Britain	G. Britain	Ship London. Gardly.
S. Powers	38	M		"	"	
M. Kensitt	25	M		"	"	
E. Chandler	35	M		"	"	
Caroline Bollman & 4 children	23	F		"	"	
Ann Matthews	20	F		"	"	

Names of passengers	Age	Sex	Occupation	Country to which they belong	Country of which they intend becoming inhabitants	Ship or vessel with the name of the master or commander
NEW YORK Cont.						
Q. E. Dec. 31, 1822						
Jane Byrne	22	F		G. Britain	G. Britain	
G. Spring & ch	37	M	Minister	U. States	U. States	
John D. Wills	23	M	Physician	England	"	
G. H. Snelling	21	M	Gent.	"	"	
G. Ogden	30	M	Merchant	"	"	
J J. Mansom	33	M	"	Florence	"	
W. H Wilson	25	M	"	U States	"	
A. Delofine	25	M	"	"	"	
Samuel Alvey	31	M	"	"	"	
Benj. Pike	45	M	Optician	"	"	
Thomas Tefft *& 5 ch.	37	M		"	"	
J. Browne	34	M		"	"	
Francis Browne	25	M		"	"	
Wm. Neale	49	M	Gardner	"	"	
Sarah " & 8 ch.	49	F		"	"	
John Essex	45	M	Merchant	England	U. States	
John C. Kerr	41	M	"	"	"	Ship Corties. De Cost.
M. Bailey	24	M	Dentist	"	"	
H. F. Rogers	35	M	Merchant	"	"	
M. Broadfoot	38	M		"	"	
R. Wilson	35	M		"	"	
H. M. P. Wallis	23	M	Merchant	"	"	
Wm. Brown	40	M	"	U. States	"	Ship Nestor. Lee.
R. Powers	40	M	"	"	"	
S. Hiles *	32	M	"	"		
G. Leadbater	39	M	Farmer	G. Britain	U. States	Brig Favourite Gardiner.
R. "	22	F		"	"	
Edwd Crumney	22	M	Butcher	"	"	
Wm. Thin *	30	M	Farmer	"	"	
James McFarlan	30	M	Mariner	"	"	
L. Davidson	33	M	Farmer	"	"	
John Ross *	55	M	Architect	Italy	"	Brig Ann. Ashford.
J. Matthews	32	M	Merchant	U. States	"	Sch. Jane. Gibbs.
J. Copeland	20	M	"	"	"	
Jose Pache	48	M	"	France	"	Brig Jos. F. Lewis
B Nones	22	M	"	Spain	"	
D Frisnedo	18	M	"	"	"	
Silas E. Burrow	28	M	"	U. States	"	Brig Port.
John Dempsey	60	M	"	Ireland	"	Sch. Ariadne. Aymor.
John H. Fasy	30	M	"	Demerara	"	
Chas. H. Babug	21	M	"	Holland		
Jacob Medler	60	M	Farmer	U. States	"	Brig Exertion.
S. Raymond	23	M	Mechanic	"	"	
C. H. Johnson	32	M	Mariner	"	"	Brig Jane. Fowler.

Names of passengers	Age	Sex	Occupation	Country to which they belong	Country of which they intend becoming inhabitants	Ship or vessel with the name of the master or commander
PLYMOUTH Q. E. Dec. 31, 1822						
John Canady	45	M	Mariner	U. States	U. States	Sch. Olive Branch Finney.
B. Robinson	35	M	"	"	"	
NANTUCKET Q. E. Dec. 31, 1822						
George Clark	19	M	Mariner	U. States	U. States	Brig Urchin. Chadwick.
Reuben "	23	M	"	"	"	
PETERSBURG Q. E. Dec. 31, 1822						
H. A. Cohors	24	M	Merchant	Hanover	U. States	Vessel not mentioned
G. Borghaus	20	M	Physician	"	"	
D. Hundercook *	33	M	Lawyer	"	"	
H. Fisher	19	M	Blacksmith	"	"	
David Halliday	35	M	Merchant	U. States	"	Ship Scipio.
James "	16	M	Yeoman	"	"	
Thomas Small	30	M	"	"	"	
ALEXANDRIA Q. E. Dec. 31, 1822						
David Owens	25	M	Yeoman	England	U. States	Sch. Almira
NEW BEDFORD Q. E. Dec. 31, 1822						
Alexander Jenkins	42	M	Mariner	U. States	U. States	Brig Elizabeth. Blackmore
J. Patten & child	48	M	Merchant	"	"	
Wm. Coffin	16	M	Mariner	"	"	
Henry Jones	30	M	"	"	"	
Jeremiah Winslow	41	M	Merchant	"	"	Ship Bourbon. Paddock.
Sarah Norris	26	F	Teacher	France	"	
Henry Homes	22	M	Merchant	U. States	"	Brig Ospray. Howland.
NEWBURYPORT Q. E. Dec. 31, 1822						
Zebulon Brown	34	M	Tobacconist	U. States	U. States	Vessel not mentioned
Mrs. "	28	F		"	"	
Widow " & 2 ch.	58	F		"	"	
John Burton	30	M	Labourer	Ireland	"	
John Francis	22	M	Stone cutter	"	"	

Names of passengers	Age	Sex	Occupation	Country to which they belong	Country of which they intend becoming inhabitants	Ship or vessel with the name of the master or commander
NEWBURYPORT Cont.						
Q. E. Dec. 31, 1822						
Robert Francis	30	M	Stone cutter	Ireland	U. States	
William "	19	M	"	"	"	
Arabella " & ch.	57	F	Spinster	"	"	
NEW ORLEANS						
Q. E. Dec. 31, 1822						
Robert E. Kerr	23	M	Clerk	Ireland	U. States	Ship Justina. Almy.
John Curtoys	27	M	"	England	"	
Elizabeth "	20	F		"	"	
John Dunn	35	M	Grocer	"	"	
Mr. Wilman	25	M		U. States	"	Brig Admittance Moody
Mrs. "	45	F		"	"	
Joseph Leclair	15	M	Carpenter	"	"	Sch. James. Blunt.
C. Alexander	35	M		"	"	
Frederick Furst	23	M	Merchant	Hamburg	"	Ship Daphne Kohler.
Charles Duranco	21	M	"	"	"	
James Falls	28	M	"	Ireland	"	Ship Edwd Downes. Russell.
Samuel Bigger	28	M	"	"	"	
John Matthews	22	M	"	"	"	
Samuel Beck	50	M	"	"	"	
Anne " & 2 ch.	20	F		"	"	
James Porter	28	M	Attorney	"	"	
Eliza. "	20	F		"	"	
Sophia "	19	F		"	"	
J. L. Buck	28	M	Merchant	"	"	
Gilbert Vance	35	M	"	"	"	
George Andrews	25	M	Farmer	"	"	
Eliza "	25	F		"	"	
Thomas Chambers	25	M	Farmer	"	"	
J. McKinty	40	M	"	"	"	
James McBride	35	M	Merchant	"	"	
Samuel Hall	23	M	"	"	"	
Gerard Irvin	44	M	Farmer	"	"	
John Shaw	24	M	"	"	"	
Baptist Bernard	40	M	Merchant	U. States	"	Ship Prince Regent Wright.
John George	26	M	Sugar refiner	England	"	
John Vaughan	20	M	Clerk	" "	"	
Jno. Ryan	50	M	Merchant	U. States	"	Sch. Union. Mayo.
F. Perault	45	M	"	"	"	
L. Delachavix	22	M	"	"	"	
J. Chavane	23	M	Cab. Maker	"	"	
J. Henrund *	28	M	Printer	"	"	
L. Marceau	32	M	Merchant	France	"	

Names of passengers	Age	Sex	Occupation	Country to which they belong	Country of which they intend becoming inhabitants	Ship or vessel with the name of the master or commander
NEW ORLEANS Cont.						
Q. E. Dec. 31, 1822						
Joseph Patterson	21	M	Shoemaker	U. States	U. States	
--- Fletcher	29	M	Clerk	England	"	Sch. Kennebeck. Gale.
G. Rollins	53	M	Mariner	U. States	"	Sch. Three Sisters. Scott.
James Brown	34	M	Merchant	"	"	Ship Lord Whitworth. McLain.
Ann "	20	F		"	"	
John Fawcett	21	M		England	"	
David Pepper	18	M		"	"	
John Somers	24	M	Cooper	U. States	"	Brig Atlantic. Bailey.
Wm. H. Phillips	22	M	"	"	"	
Henry Johnson	25	M	Engraver	"	"	Brig Aurilla. Howland.
Joseph Patuzze	28	M	Musician	"	"	
Mrs. "	28	F		"	"	
M. Armand	30	M	Play Actor	France	"	
Mrs. " & ch.	30	F		"	"	
A. Bataille	28	M		"	"	
--- Duvall	30	M		"	"	
--- Make	45	M		"	"	
J. J. Hintz	45	M		"	"	Ship Andw. Jackson.
Peter Young	20	M	Blacksmith	Breman	"	
--- Goinsue	38	M	Merchant	France	"	Brig Mississippi. Johnson.
Felix Barriere	25	M		"	"	
P. Dufan	55	M		"	"	
Mittayer	45	M		"	"	
--- Cazlaux	21	M	Cooper	"	"	
--- Mande	28	M	Tailor	"	"	
Lucas *	26	M	"	"	"	
Louis Brunel	42	M	Physician	"	"	Brig Com. Barry. Lyle.
D. Havers	27	M	Merchant	"	"	Brig Alabama. Hall.
Daniel Burnes	60	M	Mariner	G. Britain	"	
Wm. Smith	30	M	Merchant	"	"	Barque Diana. Jackson
Mrs. "	30	F		"	"	
John Quinn	28	M	Tailor	"	"	
A. Vincent	24	M	Mariner	"	"	
Edwd. Doyle	22	M	Merchant	Ireland	"	Brig Olive & Sarah
Bernd. McGann	24	M	"	"	"	
George Couree	28	M	Carpenter	"	"	
Geo. Welch	30	M	Merchant	"	"	Brig Betsey.
--- Coulon	27	M	Span. officer	Spain	"	Sch. Bee. Barron.
--- Lovalet *	30	M	Merchant	France	"	
--- Martinez	28	M	Tailor	"	"	
--- Cotar	22	M	Span. officer	Spain	Spain	
-- Costellano	27	M	Barber	"	"	
-- Marini	20	M	Carpenter	"	"	
B. Duplantier	31	M	Physician	France	U. States	Brig Hannah.

Names of passengers	Age	Sex	Occupation	Country to which they belong	Country of which they intend becoming inhabitants	Ship or vessel with the name of the master or commander
NEW ORLEANS Cont.						
Q. E. Dec. 31, 1822						
T Correbois	28	M	Actor	France	U. States	
Heloise Anbourg	29	F	Actress	"	"	
Le Blanc "	65	M		"	"	Ship Factor.
C. Chapelle	45	M	Merchant	"	"	
Mrs. " & ch.	40	F		"	"	
P. H Tuys	23	M	Merchant	"	"	
Louis Gillet	36	M	Mechanic	"	"	
N. Broutin	30	M	Trader	"	"	
Mrs. "	26	F		"	"	
Mr Enault	48	M	Butcher	"	"	
Agatha " & 3 ch.	45	F		"	"	
M. Murphy	30	F	Ursuline Nun	"	"	
M. L. Mathurin	30	F	"	"	"	
Lewis Livingston	35	M	Gent.	U. States	"	Ship Jane.
John J. Stoche *	35	M	"	"	"	
Wm. Kenny	37	M	Cooper	"	"	Brig Rogue. Seaver.
Wm Mackey	23	M		England	"	Brig Nicholas. Athey.
Mrs. " & ch.	21	F		"	"	
Mrs. Day	27	F		"	"	
John Nilden & 2 ch.	40	M	Planter	"	"	Ship Gov. Griswold. Rhodes.
R. Hawley	28	M	"	"	"	
John Anduguy	34	M	Mechanic	France	"	
Justus Riley	50	M	Merchant	U. States	"	
Wm. Threlfall	54	M	Farmer	England	"	Brig Eliza. Bragg.
M. A. Bribes	23	M	Attorney	France	"	Ship Jerome. Langburne.
P. Mirimont	17	M	Blacksmith	"	"	
Lewis Gentin	62	M	Watchmaker	"	"	
Mrs. "	55	F		"	"	
P. Brou	21	M	Attorney	"	"	
F. H. Brisblane	31	M	Planter	"	"	
Mrs. " & 2 ch.	22	F		"	"	
Clementine Foitin	17	F		"	"	
G. Flanjac	40	M	Planter	"	"	
Lewis Lazaret	35	M	Merchant	"	"	
Michael Leypolt	40	M	Mariner	"	"	
L. E. Bernard	38	M	Merchant	U. States	"	
J. Rowian *	18	M	Clerk	France	"	
J. Mauberut & 2 ch.	54	F		"	"	
J. Villate	64	M		"	"	
L. Gaumon	52	M	Clerk	"	"	
M. Ray & 5 ch.	45	F		"	"	
G. De Rigueburg	22	M		"	"	
J. P. Roglin	22	M		"	"	
J. J. Bauan	26	M		"	"	

Names of passengers	Age	Sex	Occupation	Country to which they belong	Country of which they intend becoming inhabitants	Ship or vessel with the name of the master or commander
NEW ORLEANS Cont.						
Q. E. Dec. 31, 1822						
J. Labatut	27	M	Physician	France	U. States	
M. Lessonde	28	M	Clerk	"	"	
J. B Labatut	66	M	Merchant	"	"	
M. " & 2 ch.	56	F		"	"	
M. Commerey & 3 ch.	36	F		"	"	
Mrs Maul & ch.	36	F		"	"	
A. D. Lougoume	19	M	Clerk	"	"	
J. M. Conte	50	M	Minister of ?	"	"	Ship N. York Packet.
Joseph Tournes	33	M	Sp. Officer	Mexico	Mexico	
G. "	28	M		"	"	
J. Cuellan	30	M	Civil "	"	"	
J. Guildern *	21	M	Merchant	France	France	
G. de Larnau *	22	M	Planter	"	"	
M. Duga * & ch.	33	F		"	"	
Clarissa Duga & 2 ch.	21	F		"	"	
Anthony Sloane	18	M	Clerk	G. Britain	U States	Brig Wm. Pitt. Stonehouse.
J. Raymond	38	M	Cooper	France	"	Sch. Rebecca. Ellis.
J. B. Duchisne	44	M	"	"	"	
L. Benguise *	25	M	Farmer	"	"	Ship Jason. West.
L. Arnaud	35	M	"	"	"	
A. P. St. Amand	33	M	Merchant	"	"	Ship Schuylkill. Hardie.
L. "	20	M	Farmer	"	"	
W. B. Davis	33	M	Mariner	U. States	"	Sch. Caravan. Lindsay.
E. H. Stow	23	M	Merchant	"	"	
Thomas Barrett	25	M	"	"	"	Ship Orleans Groves.
B. Ville	40	M	"	"	"	
J. Armand	35	M	"	"	"	
M. Richards	35	M	"	"	"	Brig Wm. Tell. Brau.
M. Sighers & 2 ch.	26	M	Lawyer	Germnay	"	
D. Marsta	26	M	Merchant	U. States	"	Brig Florida.
Fredk. Parmly	19	M	"	"	"	
F. H. Kitting	45	M	"	Germany	"	Brig Restitution. Spark.
M Tinman	28	M	Clerk	"	"	
A. Ceday *	25	M	Merchant	France	"	Sch. Packet. Means.
Antonio Montesino	24	M	"	Spain	"	) Sch. San Juan. Frisbee.
R. Cardeus	17	M	Mariner	"	"	) Died in coming up the river,
Jose de Truida *	44	M	"	"	"	) the boat having been struck
						by a log.
Antonio Quindel	22	M	Merchant	"	"	
J. Aulet	38	M	"	"	"	
George Welch	30	M	"	Ireland	"	Sch. Ceres Manson.
Joseph Roney	29	M	"	"	"	
George Miller	50	M	"	"	"	Sch. Anson. Kellog.
A. Chapin	25	M	"	"	"	

Names of passengers	Age	Sex	Occupation	Country to which they belong	Country of which they intend becoming inhabitants	Ship or vessel with the name of the master or commander
NEW ORLEANS Cont. Q. E. Dec. 31, 1822						
M. Fauchet	21	M	Coachmakr.	Ireland	U. States	
Thomas Abraham	30	M	Merchant	U. States	"	Brig Felicity.
A. Cobb	20	M	Sailmaker	"	"	Sloop Polly. Boardman.
NANTUCKET Q. E. Dec. 31, 1822						
George Clark Jr.	19	M	Mariner	U. States	U. States	Brig Urchin. Chadwick.
Reuben Clark	23	M	"	"	"	
NEW HAVEN Q. E. Dec. 31, 1822						
Henry Tucker	52	M	Merchant	England	England	Sch. Betsey. Tyler.
Samuel Maltley	34	M	Merchant	U. States	U. States	Brig Underhill. Trowbridge.
Joseph Gardner	40	M	Mechanic	England	England	
Samuel Trott	22	M	Merchant	"	"	Sloop Albion. Vail.
MARBLEHEAD Q. E. Dec. 31, 1822						
Edmund Ryan	29	M	Fisherman	Ireland	U. States	Sch. Cherub.
John W. Haland	24	M	Cooper	"	"	
B. Smith	28	M	Fisherman	"	"	
Geo. Wittern/Witlem	22	M	"	England	"	
D. Senlin *	23	M	"	Ireland	"	
Patrick Malonie	25	M	"	"	"	
BOSTON Q. E. Dec. 31, 1822						
Mary Ross	35	F	Milliner	U. States	U. States	Sch. Cherub. Andrew.
Mary Rum	40	F	"	"	"	
C. "	19	F	"	"	"	
R. Lord	45	M	Clergyman	Halifax	Halifax	
Jas. Ward	50	M	Farmer	U. States	U. States	
Wm. Foster	30	M	Blacksmith	"	"	
C. White	40	M	Merchant	"	"	
J. Thompson	42	M	"	"	"	
John Story	32	M	"	"	"	
Joseph Sewall	32	M	"	"	"	
Jas. Madrath	27	M	"	"	"	
Mary Porter	24	F	Tailoress	"	"	
Andw. Clay	23	M	Labourer	"	"	

Names of passengers	Age	Sex	Occupation	Country to which they belong	Country of which they intend becoming inhabitants	Ship or vessel with the name of the master or commander
BOSTON Cont.						
Q. E. Dec. 31, 1822						
Wm. Trinell	20	M	Labourer	Halifax	U. States	
John Whalin	24	M	"	"	"	
Wm. "	22	M	"	"	"	
Danl. Conway	27	M	"	"	"	
Pat. Dismale	26	M	"	"	"	
B. Morgan	23	M	"	"	"	
Dennis Cowes	28	M	"	"	"	
Wm. Beck	27	M	"	"	"	
Wm. Hyde	27	M	"	"	"	
Christopher Scott	50	M	Merchant	Scotland	Scotland	Sch. Genl. Greene. Rogers.
Ephraim Willard	35	M	"	"	U. States	
Daniel Faris	40	M	Mariner	"	"	
Mr. Allern	25	M	Teacher	"	"	
Paul Hayes	24	M	Mariner	U. States	"	Sch. Eliza. Stevenson.
Jacob Brown	30	M	"	"	"	
A. Analogoz	30	M	Secy. Russn. Legation	Russia	"	Brig Duxbury.
Eudoxia	32	M		"	"	
H. Keil	27	M	Shoemaker	"	"	
John F. Vacion	38	M	Gent.	Portugal	Portugal	Brig Planter. Lapland.
Edwd. Holden	53	M	Merchant	U. States	U. States	Sch. Eliza. Hopkins.
Samuel L. Page	45	M	Mariner	"	"	Brig Beaver. Groves.
H. C. Nory •	50	M	"	"	"	
J A. Wilkinson	31	M	Gent.	U. States	England	Ship Factor Bassay.
Wm Cripps	24	M	Merchant	England	"	
M. Christie	31	M	"	Scotland	U. States	
Michael Doyle	22	M	Staymaker	Ireland	"	
Samuel Robertson	38	M	Minister	U. States	"	Brig Jason. Lorin.
Mary F. C. Wallis	20	F		"	"	Brig Ruby. Phillips.
F. Stevenson	28	F		"	"	
P. Spofferd	26	M	Merchant	"	"	
J. Wheelwright	41	M	Mariner	"	"	Brig Sword. Sarton.
James Jackson	35	M	"	"	"	
Antonio Ramos	16	M		Portugal	"	Brig Seneca. Gray.
Domingo Silvia	18	M		"	"	
A. Snow	33	M	Mariner	U. States	"	
Francisco J. Almeda	25	M	"	Portugal	"	
Richard Prith & ch.	34	M	"	U. States	"	Brig Calista. Almott.
Wm. J. Apthorp	22	M	Lawyer	"	"	Brig Palmer. Miller.
John Bell	22	M	Physician	"	"	
Peter Madden	41	M	Blacksmith	"	"	Brig Hamilton. Lane.
L. J. Holla	30	M	Jeweller	Paris	"	
J. Masters	35	M	Mariner	U. States	"	Ship Paragon. Brown.
J. Bragg	33	M	"	"	"	

Names of passengers	Age	Sex	Occupation	Country to which they belong	Country of which they intend becoming inhabitants	Ship or vessel with the name of the master or commander
BOSTON Cont.						
<u>Q. E. Dec. 31, 1822</u>						
Wm. G. Holmes	21	M	Mariner	U. States	U. States	
R. Eldred	26	M	"	"	"	
James Ervin	19	M	"	"	"	
--- Dubois	42	M	Traveller	France	France	Ship Imperial. Holmes.
-- Guilhoshes	22	M	"	"	"	
William Austin	22	M	Merchant	U. States	U. States	Brig Falcon. Low.
Wm. P. Carter	19	M	"	"	"	
John Kennet	13	M	"	"	"	
Jose Jachin Zaranto	40	M	Consul Genl.	Portugal	"	Brig Planter. Soule.
Diego M. Gallard	44	M		"	"	
D. Antonio Fernandez	32	F	Lady	"	"	
Abel Greer & ch.	26	M	Carpenter	England	"	Brig Plant. Williams.
John Miller	42	M	Shoemaker	"	"	
Joseph Kiddir	30	M	Merchant	U. States	"	Sch. Billow. Barker.
Thomas "	29	M	"	"	"	
George Lisle	25	M	Baker	Halifax	Halifax	
John Knight	26	M	Labourer	U. States	U. States	
Michael Mortgoney	31	M	"	Ireland	"	
Bridget "	25	F		"	"	
James Harris	18	M	Labourer	"	"	
James Powers	28	M	"	"	"	
Edwd. Gillat	26	M	"	"	"	
James Fox	21	M	"	"	"	
Timothy Wirter *	28	M	Merchant	U. States	"	Ship Madison. Norris.
George Mury *	27	M	Mariner	"	"	
Geo. H. Rollins	40	M	"	"	"	Brig Can?
N. Merrill	28	M	"	"	"	
Moses "	23	M	"	"	"	
Henry "	20	M	"	"	"	
Francis Jones	23	M	Tailor	"	"	Brig Samaritan. Brown.
A. Brumley	23	M	"	"	"	
Stephen Robson	40	M	Coppersmith	"	"	Ship Thomas. Carole.
John Ridgway	36	M	Merchant	England	"	Ship Jasper. Crocker.
Anthony Langdon	40	M	"	"	"	
Edwd. L. Coffin	39	M	Mariner	"	"	Sch. Brilliant. Kindsy.
D. Washburn	19	M	"	"	"	
T. Wormwood	23	M	"	"	"	
Francis Bayley	37	M	Merchant	Cape Hayti	Cape Hayti	Brig Ferox. Patten.
Patrick Neal	24	M	Labourer	England	U. States	Sch. Alfred. Haines.
James "	18	M	"	"	"	
Thomas Power	24	M	Shoemaker	"	"	
Richard Newton	29	M	Labourer	"	"	
Philip Ford	25	M	"	"	"	
John Murphy	24	M	"	"	"	

Names of passengers	Age	Sex	Occupation	Country to which they belong	Country of which they intend becoming inhabitants	Ship or vessel with the name of the master or commander
BOSTON Cont.						
Q. E. Dec. 31, 1822						
James Walsh	24	M	Labourer	England	U. States	
Patrick Connelly	27	M	"	"	"	
John Sinnot	27	M	"	"	"	
Geo. Hatchett/ell	29	M	Coachmakr.	Ireland	"	
Andw. Dollard	30	M	Labourer	"	"	
Wm. Mackay	26	M	"	"	"	
James Young	30	M	Currier	"	"	
Mrs. "	30	F		"	"	
C. Read	29	M	Labourer	"	"	
Mrs. "	27	F		"	"	
Wm. Whelan	26	M	Labourer	"	"	
John Kelby	24	M	"	"	"	
Richd. Darton	26	M	"	"	"	
L. "	26	M	Tailor	"	"	
Richd. Kelly	22	M	Mason	"	"	
Thomas "	36	M	Labourer	"	"	
James Ryan	27	M	"	"	"	
Mrs. "	24	F		"	"	
Wm. Carelly *	24	M	Shoemaker	"	"	
John Murphy	25	M	Labourer	"	"	
Ann Burnes	29	F	Spinster	"	"	
D. Dellen	29	F	"	"	"	
Benj. Ruggles	31	M	Trader	"	"	
M. Deblois	40	M	Merchant	Halifax	Halifax	Sch. Packet Billow. Barker.
M. Gregory	27	M	"	"	"	
M. Allen	26	M	"	"	"	
M. Allison	26	M	"	"	"	
M. "	21	M	"	England	"	
M. Fraser	21	M	"	"	England	
M Curran	21	M	"	"	"	
B. Shaw	26	M	Baker	Ireland	U. States	Sch. Comet.
Mrs. "	24	F	Tailoress	"	"	
Joseph Eny or Esy	30	M	Merchant	U. States	"	Sch. Cherub. Andrews.
Wm. Nock	32	M	"	"	"	
Wm. Walker	32	M	"	"	"	
B. T. Gardner	28	M	Currier	Ireland	"	
Michael Graham	27	M	Labourer	"	"	
Robt. Campbell	35	M	"	"	"	
J. Patterson	28	M	"	"	"	
Joseph Cushing	37	M	"	"	"	
D. Cooper	29	M	"	"	"	
Samuel Cooper	25	M	"	"	"	
Wm. Lemon	24	M	"	"	"	
R. Golap	49	M	"	"	"	

Names of passengers	Age	Sex	Occupation	Country to which they belong	Country of which they intend becoming inhabitants	Ship or vessel with the name of the master or commander
BOSTON Cont. Q. E. Dec. 31, 1822						
Wm. Webster	22	M	Merchant	Halifax	Halifax	
Mary "	19	F		"	"	
Mary Perkins	35	F		"	"	
Polly "	28	F		"	"	
N. "	24	M	Merchant	"	"	
John Hafner	42	M	Butcher	Germany	U. States	Brig Volant. Keeling.
Benj. Dunning	21	M	Mariner	U. States	"	Brig Perseverence. Bowen.
C. B. Higgins	19	M	"	"	"	
J. Wallace	24	M	"	"	"	
F. Vasindi	30	M	Merchant	Vera Cruz	Vera Cruz	Brig Fanny. Brown.
N. Anibarzo	34	M	"	"	"	
D. J. Abbot	32	M	"	U. States	U. States	Brig Zephyr. Cleveland.
G. D. Carter	35	M	"	"	"	Brig Hope. Mann.
John Leving	48	M	"	England	"	Brig Favorite. Wells.
EDGARTOWN Q. E. Dec. 31, 1822						
Thomas Walley	21	M	Merchant	U. States	U. States	Brig Packet of Boston. Doughty.
Fitton Newcomb	41	M	Mariner	"	"	Barge Curlew. Wells.
Wm. Kirnick	23	M	"	"	"	Brig Liberty. Titcomb.
Titus Thomas	30	M	"	"	"	
John Kaly & 4 ch.	50	M	Labourer	Ireland	"	Sch. Essex. Upton.
Richd. Murphy	24	M	"	"	"	
Daniel Gannon	25	M	"	"	"	
Andrew Brian	23	M	"	"	"	
Elizabeth Brown & 5 ch	32	F		U. States	"	Sch. Venus. Emery.
Jon. Pitcher	45	M	Farmer	"	"	
Elijah G. Parsons	23	M	Shoemaker	"	"	
Samuel N. Crosby	21	M	Farmer	"	"	
Kimbal Fuller	28	M	Carpenter	"	"	
Philip Lumb	26	M	Goldsmith	"	"	
Margt. Harbell	30	F		"	"	
John Blanningburg	19	M	Farmer	N. Brunswick	"	
Joseph Hitchey	19	M	Chairmaker	"	"	
Wm. Griffith	23	M	Mariner	Scotland	"	
George McDonald	20	M	Shoemaker	"	"	
ST. AUGUSTINE Q. E. Dec. 31, 1822						
E. Gomez & ch.	40	M	Spanish offcr	Cuba	" on a visit	Sch. Frolic. Cranstone.
Fernands M. Anedondo	35	M	Planter	"	"	

Names of passengers	Age	Sex	Occupation	Country to which they belong	Country of which they intend becoming inhabitants	Ship or vessel with the name of the master or commander
PASSAMAQUODDY Q. E. Dec. 31, 1822						
John Reed	30	M	Tailor	Ireland	U. States	Sch. Independence Haynes.
James Cullem	24	M	Confectionr.	"	"	
John Richard	30	M	Cab. maker	"	"	
Michael Bryne	20	M	Tailor	"	"	
Mary Moony & 3 ch.	25	F		"	"	
Paul Hogan	60	M	Farmer	"	"	
R. "	60	F	Spinster	"	"	
C. McCue	40	M	Cooper	"	"	
Ann " & 4 ch.	25	F		"	"	
Wm. Dair	40	M	Farmer	"	"	
Mary " & 2 ch.	25	F		"	"	
Thomas Scott	60	M	Farmer	"	"	
George "	35	M	"	"	"	
Ann " & 3 ch.	35	F		"	"	
Cath. McCulloch & 2 ch.	24	F		"	"	
C. Long	40	M	Farmer	"	"	
Cath. Long & 6 ch.	40	F		"	"	
Daniel McDermot	18	M	Cooper	"	"	
Andw. Murphy	24	M	Weaver	"	"	
John Aiken	50	M	Farmer	"	"	
Jane " & 8 ch.	40	F		"	"	
Francis Green	26	M	Cab. maker	"	"	
Mary "	20	F	Spinster	"	"	
Mrs. Mott & child	30	F		U. States	"	Sch. Loire. Bassett.
John Gaton	21	M	Mariner	"	"	
Wm. Fitzgerald	26	M	Tailor	N. Brunswick	"	
Wm. Cooper	21	M	Mariner	"	"	
CHARLESTON Q. E. Dec. 31, 1822						
M. Sarrazen & ch	70	F		Havana	"	Sch. Eudora.
P. Packet	40	M	Tailor	"	"	
Mrs. "	40	F		"	"	
M. Fernandez	45	M	Mariner	"	"	
John M. Hopkins	55	M	Merchant	U. States	"	Ship Bayard.
Wm. Timmond	50	M	"	"	"	
Wm. McKenzie	55	M	"	G. Britain	"	
Robert Horrey & ch.	24	M		"	"	
Daniel Nicholson	20	M	Farmer	"	"	
John Nevill	45	M	Merchant	"	"	Sch. Col. G. Armstead.
Joseph Sampson	28	M	"	"	"	Brig Leopold.
N. Cohen	15	M	"	"	"	

Names of passengers	Age	Sex	Occupation	Country to which they belong	Country of which they in- tend becoming inhabitants	Ship or vessel with the name of the master or commander
CHARLESTON Cont. Q. E. Dec. 31, 1822						
J. Lee	18	M	Merchant	G. Britain	U. States	
John Lowden	35	M	"	"	"	Ship Corsair
Ann "	33	F		"	"	
Alexr. Black	33	M		"	"	
Eliza "	30	F		"	"	
Seth Watson	25	M		"	"	
J. J. Vaughan	18	M		"	"	
J. Howe	20	M		"	"	
Elisha Larnerd	25	M	Mechanic	"	"	Sch. Eliza & Polly.
J. D. Hamilton	24	M	Merchant	"	"	
James Brown	21	M		"	"	Ship Roger Stewart.
James Smith	22	M	Clerk	"	"	
Wm. Anderson	22	M	Sawyer	"	"	
Wm. Kennedy	19	M	Clerk	"	"	
Jno. B. Thompson	23	M	"	"	"	
Alexr. Campbell	30	M	Farmer	"	"	
Dougald McIntire	28	M	"	"	"	Ship Plantaginet.
Letty " & 2 ch.	23	F		"	"	
Geo. W. Frost	25	M	Merchant	"	"	
Hugh Wilson	45	M	Farmer	"	"	
Jennet " & 3 ch.	45	F		"	"	
Y. Isnaga	18	M	Planter	Trinidad	"	Sch. Louisa.
M. Mucci	35	M	Painter	Havana	"	Sch. Comet.
M. Theadore	30	M		U. States	"	
Catharine Pritchard	25	F		"	"	Sch. Mary.
John Smith	30	M	Mariner	"	"	
James Emilly	28	M	Planter	France	"	
Urban Grain	28	M	Mariner	"	"	
J. P. Lavencendrie	28	M	Merchant	"	"	
P. Casson	32	M	"	G. Britain	"	Sch. Felix.
--- Cork	45	M	"	"	"	
--- Kesler	30	M	"	"	"	
S. B. Benorst	54	M	Trader	France	"	Ship Portia.
Mrs. " & ch.	22	F		"	"	
M. Petit	28	M	Merchant	"	"	
Mrs. "	23	F		"	"	
James Tinmouth	38	M	Merchant	G. Britain	U. States	Ship Newbury.
Mary " & 2 ch.	38	F		"	"	
John George	25	M	Mariner	"		Sch. Swift.
Margt. McAllister & 2 ch.	25	F		"	"	Ship James Bailey.
Hans "	25	M	Farmer	"	"	
Elizabeth Elliott	18	F	Spinster	"	"	
John Reid	27	M	Farmer	"	"	

Names of passengers	Age	Sex	Occupation	Country to which they belong	Country of which they intend becoming inhabitants	Ship or vessel with the name of the master or commander
CHARLESTON Cont.						
Q. E. Dec. 31, 1822						
Robert Kidd	22	M	Farmer	G. Britain	U. States	
John Caldwell	24	M	"	"	"	
Thomas Palmer	22	M	"	"	"	
Hugh Kelly	30	M	"	"	"	
George Ferguson	19	M	"	"	"	
Andw. McGill	36	M	"	"	"	
Agnes " & 2 ch.	25	F		"	"	
Francis Joseph	26	M	Trader	U. States	"	Brig If.
Philip Martinet	25	M	"	"	"	
John Woodrop	69	M	Merchant	G. Britain	"	Ship S. Carolina.
C. Fitzimmons	22	M	"	"	"	
Wm. Gibson	38	M	"	"	"	
James Moodie	23	M	"	"	"	
Robert Chisolm	25	M	"	"	"	
A. Hutchins	43	M	"	"	"	
C. Todd	35	M	Mariner	U. States	"	Sch. Comet.
Wm. Cobbs	35	M	"	"	"	
Eliza Theus	27	F	Servant	G. Britain	"	Ship Mary Beach.
Isabella Perry	70	M	Midwife	"	"	
James Maggee	25	M	Merchant	"	"	
John Kerr	21	M	"	"	"	
Robert Alexander	28	M	"	"	"	Brig Laura.
John Reside	22	M	"	"	"	
Robert Gunning	25	M	"	"	"	
John McKelvan	25	M	Farmer	"	"	
Thomas Williamson	45	M	"	"	"	
James McLarklin	18	M	"	"	"	
John Russell	18	M	"	"	"	
Wm. Burtin	30	M	"	"	"	
Wm. McWhinney	28	M	"	"	"	
Mrs. "	20	F		"	"	
Margt. Duffey & 3 ch.	30	F		"	"	Ship Cleveland.
Thomas Collard	32	M	Farmer	"	"	
Thomas Jones	63	M	"	"	"	
Robert Burrell	66	M	"	"	"	
Edwd. "	46	M	"	"	"	
M. Morgan	45	M	"	"	"	
J. Berlaut	60	M	Merchant	France	"	Brig Catharine.
Thomas Germaine	40	M		G. Britain	"	Ship Caledonian.
John Campbell	20	M		"	"	
Thomas Scott	16	M		"	"	
George Hunter	16	M		"	"	
George Scott	20	M		"	"	
Robert Small	25	M		"	"	

PASSENGERS WHO ARRIVED IN THE U.S. SEPTEMBER 1821 - DECEMBER 1823

Names of passengers	Age	Sex	Occupation	Country to which they belong	Country of which they intend becoming inhabitants	Ship or vessel with the name of the master or commander
CHARLESTON Cont.						
Q. E. Dec. 31, 1822						
Ann Small	20	F		G. Britain	U. States	
James Stewart	24	M	Clerk	"	"	
John McBride	20	M	"	"	"	
McAdam Smith	20	M	"	"	"	
Henry Bell	20	M	"	"	"	
John Wright	18	M	"	"	"	
John Robinson	19	M	Farmer	"	"	
James Miller	30	M	"	"	"	
Wilson Dalrymple	25	M	"	"	"	
Robt. Hutchinson	24	M	"	"	"	
Daniel Finn	24	M	"	"	"	
Alexander McGrady	19	M	"	"	"	
John Divlin	35	M	"	"	"	
James Smith	32	M	"	"	"	
Thomas Caulfied *	30	M	"	"	"	
Mary A. " & ch.	23	F		"	"	
Geo. Johnson	20	M	Farmer	"	"	
Eliza " & ch.	23	F		"	"	
David Watson	17	M	Farmer	"	"	
Thomas Castles	40	M	"	"	"	
Mary " & ch.	28	F		"	"	
Wm. Willis	21	M	"	"	"	
John Greenlees	23	M	"	"	"	
Geo. Stewart	23	M	"	"	"	
Thomas Neilson	45	M	"	"	"	
Jane " & ch.	36	M		"	"	
Adam Crawford	41	M	"	"	"	
Mary " & ch.	35	F		"	"	
Saml. Duncan	45	M	"	"	"	
Samuel Pearson	50	M	"	"	"	
Mary " & 6 ch.	45	F		"	"	
Robt. Biggs	19	M	"	"	"	
Jno. Smith	22	M	"	"	"	
Andw. Orr	28	M	"	"	"	
Hugh Logan	23	M	"	"	"	
David Henderson	25	M	"	"	"	
James Robinson	22	M	"	"	"	
John "	20	M	"	"	"	
PHILADELPHIA						
Q. E. Dec. 31, 1822						
J. Brownson	29	M	Book keeper	G. Britain	U. States	Ship Lancaster.
Mrs. " & 3 ch.	26	F		"	"	

Names of passengers	Age	Sex	Occupation	Country to which they belong	Country of which they intend becoming inhabitants	Ship or vessel with the name of the master or commander
PHILADELPHIA Cont.						
Q. E. Dec. 31, 1822						
Mrs. Westerman	45	F		G. Britain	U. States	
Mr. O. Serry *	25	M	Chemist	"	"	
James Savel	19	M	Manfactr.	"	"	
C. Berry	42	M	Mariner	"	"	
F. Kolman & ch.	40	M	"	Germany	"	
Samuel Spofford	42	M	"	U. States	"	Brig Lawrence.
Jos. M. Foster	35	M	Merchant	"	"	
Robert S. Tatem *	31	M	U. S. Navy	"	"	
Chas. W. Gay	18	M		"	"	
Lewis Branchine	25	M	Mariner	"	"	
Amos Blanchard	35	M	"	"	"	
Joseph Marlet	35	M	"	"	"	
Wm. Fenwick	28	M	"	"	"	
Benj. Norcross	28	M	"	"	"	
Imlah Haines	27	M	"	"	"	
John Barker	25	M	"	"	"	
George Simpson	27	M	"	"	"	
Mrs. Hodgson & 6 ch.	45	F		"	"	Ship Delaware.
Abigail Ward	30	F		"	"	
P. A. Sandoz	35	M	Jeweller	"	"	Ship Hope. Shippen.
Victor Droz	23	M	Watchmakr.	"	"	
Cornelius Wagner	40	M	Mariner	"	"	
Wm. Hawkins	29	M	Merchant	"	"	
James Donaghy	26	M	Farmer	Ireland	"	Brig Collector.
Pat. Quinn	30	M	Weaver	"	"	
Mary "	21	F		"	"	
Bernard Coulan	28	M	Farmer	"	"	
John Meatly *	24	M	"	"	"	
John McKenna	24	M	Weaver	"	"	
James Maclan *	24	M	"	"	"	
John Mohoon	25	M	"	"	"	
Peter Maguigan	18	M	Farmer	"	"	
Thomas Lomis	30	M	"	"	"	
George Hay	50	M	"	"	"	
Edwd. Brady	30	M	"	"	"	
Jno. Skiffington	25	M	"	"	"	
Daniel Milton/Mellon	25	M	Weaver	"	"	
Francis Gallagher	19	M	Farmer	"	"	
A. Wallace	17	M	"	"	"	
Peter Donally	20	M	"	"	"	
Neal Lanigan	24	M	"	"	"	
Cath. McConnell & 3 ch	35	F		"	"	
John O'Hara	28	M	Farmer	"	"	

Names of passengers	Age	Sex	Occupation	Country to which they belong	Country of which they intend becoming inhabitants	Ship or vessel with the name of the master or commander
PHILADELPHIA Cont.						
Q. E. Dec. 31, 1822						
Wm Ferguson	29	M	Farmer	Ireland	U. States	
B. Ann " & ch.	28	F	"	"	
M. Queen	35	M	Surveyor	"	"	
Mary " & ch.	30	F		"	"	
James Bean	23	M	Shoemaker	"	"	
Wm. Downey	20	M	Tailor	"	"	
Leonora Thompson	26	F		England	"	Ship Venus.
Richd. Booth	60	M	Gent.	"	"	
M. Garrard	40	M	Farmer	"	"	
Mrs. " & 5 ch.	32	F		"	"	
John Fees	43	M	Cab. maker	"	"	
Mrs. " & 6 ch.	41	F		"	"	
James Cole	52	M	Tailor	"	"	
George Cooper	30	M	Brazier	"	"	
Archibald Campbell	21	M	Mariner	"	"	
Mary McDonald & 4 ch.	30	M		"	"	
Thomas Powers	39	M	Draper	"	"	
Wm Anderson	56	M	Cordwainer	"	"	Ship Tuscarora. Sewell.
Mary " & 3 ch.	50	F		"	"	
Simon Cullen	20	M	Merchant	"	"	
D. Burr	25	M	"	"	"	
Robt. Clark & ch.	37	M		"	"	
Wm. Mackay	30	M	"	"	"	
James Adgar & 2 ch.	43	M		"	"	
Wm. Bones	36	M	"	"	"	
Wm. Wyatt	35	M	Clergyman	U. States	"	
Joseph Welsh	27	M	Merchant	"	"	
Saml. Smithman	46	M	Nailer	G. Britain	"	Ship Jane. Ferguson.
Mary " & ch.	36	F		"	"	
James Wraith	30	M	Druggist	"	"	
Robt. Dorin	40	M	Tailor	"	"	
Arthur Renney	22	M	Weaver	"	"	
Joseph Farrow	22	M	Tailor	"	"	
Nixon Scott	26	M	Joiner	"	"	Ship Dido.
Alice " & 2 ch.	22	F		"	"	
Bridget Carroll & ch.	37	F		"	"	
Margt. Kennedy & 2 ch.	28	F		"	"	
Mary Bell & 2 ch.	29	F		"	"	
Eliz. Ray & 4 ch.	30	F		"	"	
--- Scheer	27	M	Musicl. Inst. Maker	Germany	"	Brig Minerva. Gates.
--- Santifaller	40	M	Merchant	"	"	
--- Oppeneiger	50	M	"	"	"	

PASSENGERS WHO ARRIVED IN THE U.S. SEPTEMBER 1821 - DECEMBER 1823

Names of passengers	Age	Sex	Occupation	Country to which they belong	Country of which they intend becoming inhabitants	Ship or vessel with the name of the master or commander
PHILADELPHIA Cont.						
Q. E. Dec. 31, 1822						
--- Valentine	23	M	Merchant	Germany	U. States	
-- Pollock	36	M	"	"	"	
James Briscoe	22	M	Mechanic	U. States	"	Brig Richd & Sally.
Antonio Mora	30	M	Mariner	Spain	"	Sch. Lively. Thurston.
Arnold Halback	35	M	Merchant	U. States	"	Ship Columbia Kurtz.
Caroline "	21	M		"	"	
H. Reitrop *	70	M	Merchant	"	"	
C. Van Gonderen	67	M	"	"	"	
S. C. Caldwell & ch.	35	M		"	"	
J. De Young & 2 ch.	45	F		"	"	
Thomas Wright	35	M	Carpenter	G. Britain	"	Brig Penelope. Chisholm.
Ann "	29	F		"	"	
Thomas Jones	45	M		"	"	
John Bogie *	21	M		"	"	
Andw. Lockart	36	M	Merchant	U. States	"	Ship Bengal. Thockam.
Robt. N. Johnson	32	M	"	"	"	
C. Halsey	35	M	"	"	"	
James McFadden	36	M	Farmer	G. Britain	"	Ship Warren. Webb.
Letitia " & 7 ch.	30	F		"	"	
John McCrew	26	M	Farmer	"	"	
Benj. Duffin	20	M	"	"	"	
Richd. Downing	22	M	Mechanic	"	"	
Mary Leffcock & ch.	44	F		"	"	
Mary Mawdesley & 2 ch.	44	F		"	"	
Susanna Denton & 2 ch.	21	F		"	"	
John Taylor	30	M	Manufactr.	"	"	
Martha "	24	F		"	"	
George English	40	M	Weaver	"	"	
Ann "	40	F		"	"	
A. McDonough	24	M	Trader	"	"	
A. Kelly	21	M	"	"	"	
Richd. Cochran	26	M	Joiner	"	"	
Isabella "	25	F		"	"	
Edwd. Hodges	28	M	Painter	"	"	
Francis Westerman	18	M	Farmer	"	"	
Michl McGinnis	24	M	Labourer	"	"	
Joseph Grossup	18	M	"	"	"	
Jno. Bove *	21	M	Farmer	"	"	
John Friere	22	M	Merchant	Spain	"	Brig Happy Return.
Antonio Burino	24	M	"	"	"	
P. Gommas	23	M	"	"	"	
John Landsman	25	M	Mechanic	Germany	"	
James Walsh	28	M	Weaver	Ireland	"	Sch. Susanna.

Names of passengers	Age	Sex	Occupation	Country to which they belong	Country of which they intend becoming inhabitants	Ship or vessel with the name of the master or commander
PHILADELPHIA Cont.						
Q. E. Dec. 31, 1822						
Eliz. Walsh & 2 ch.	24	F		Ireland	U. States	
Adam Shannon	26	M	Farmer	"	"	
Betsey " & ch.	24	F		"	"	
Francis Peretz	40	M	Merchant	Spain	"	Ship Medora.
N Frazier	21	M	"	U. States	"	
George Bellmer	56	M	"	Germany	"	Ship Janus. Wendt.
J H. Reinecke	23	M	Farmer	"	"	
C.H Gundclach	46	M	Merchant	"	"	
Wm. J. Palmer	40	M	Mariner	U. States	"	
James D. Snow	45	M	"	"	"	
Mrs. Gudcluch & 2 ch.	42	F		Germany	"	
John Marston	23	M	U. S. Navy	U. States	"	Brig Rebecca. Towes.
J. H. Lusby	26	M		"	"	
Francis Harrison	24	M	Mariner	"	"	Brig Philadelphia. Groves
F. Tulan	18	M	Bookbinder	"	"	Ship Sophia. Desseres.
J Delauny	19	M	Farmer	France	"	
H. Snyder	36	M	Merchant	U. States	"	Brig Jas. Murdoch. Smith.
Jno. Halberstadt	27	M	Supercargo	"	"	
R. Cochran	32	M	"	"	"	Brig Sarah Ann. Moliere.
Jno. Holdridge	37	M		"	"	
G. P. Philipps	30	M	Merchant	"	"	Brig Pocahontas. Payne.
Caroline "	23	F		"	"	
Richd. Smith	36	M	Merchant	"	"	
A. Crawford	35	M	Planter	G. Britain	"	Ship Manchester.
W. Singleton	50	M	Merchant	"	"	
Eliz. McConnel & 6 ch.	39	F		"	"	
Arthur "	24	M		"	"	
Thos. Marshall	22	M	Draper	"	"	
J. Smith	28	M		"	"	
J. Pickering	28	M		"	"	
M. Read & 3 ch.	30	M		"	"	
Eliz. Thorp & 2 ch.	21	F		"	"	
Mary Willis	23	F		"	"	Ship Halcyon. Wooster.
Betsey Adams	40	F		"	"	
James Brady	32	M	Labourer	"	"	
Thomas "	30	M	"	"	"	
James Johnson	21	M	"	"	"	
Thomas Leary	23	M	"	"	"	
F. Fayall	24	M	"	"	"	
John Baxter	25	M	"	"	"	
T. Humphreys	46	M	Tailor	"	"	
F. " & 2 ch.	40	F		"	"	
Saml. Blackwood	24	M	Merchant	U. States	"	Brig Eliz. Ann. Brooks.
Manuel Lion	20	M	"	Spain	"	

Names of passengers	Age	Sex	Occupation	Country to which they belong	Country of which they intend becoming inhabitants	Ship or vessel with the name of the master or commander
PHILADELPHIA Cont.						
Q. E. Dec. 31, 1822						
Jose Guerrese	22	M	Merchant	Spain	U. States	
Janis E. Brookes	25	M	"	U. States	"	
Despar Delgardo	30	M	"	Spain	"	Sch. Three Daughters
George Thomas	30	M		G. Britain	"	Brig Aurora. Cavan.
Mrs. "	28	F		"	"	
J. Owen	25	M		"	"	
Lewis Gonanego	35	M	Mariner	U. States	"	Brig Edw. D Douglass.
H. H. Ford	30	M	"	"	"	
James McCuskey	35	M	Weaver	G. Britain	"	Sch. Shamrock. McGrath.
N. Sweeny	35	M	"	"	"	
Joseph Frame	22	M	"	"	"	
James Martin	23	M	"	"	"	
Alexr. Scott	18	M	"	"	"	
James Rolson	23	M	"	"	"	
James Adams	22	M	"	"	"	
R. Scott	21	M	"	"	"	
M. Aiken	60	M	Merchant	U. States	"	Brig Rising Sun. Jones.
J. Pierre	24	M	"	Spain	"	
Wm. Sloan	19	M	"	U. States	"	
P. Saunders	31	M	"	"	"	Sch. Hector. Gage.
M. Strager *	22	M	"	"	"	
John Delmonico	30	M	"	"	"	
J. B. Contear	19	M	"	"	"	
M. Mahon	25	M	"	"	"	Sch. Iris. Bancroft.
Bernard Payne	23	M	Mariner	"	"	
J. S. Thomas	41	M	Merchant	"	"	
George Green	17	M	Saddler	"	"	
James Davidson	18	M	"	"	"	
Jas. C. Dettrome	42	M		Italy	"	Ship Reaper.
James Humphrey	36	M		England	"	
H. Hodge	23	M		U. Indies	U. Indies	Sch. Eagle. King.
John F. Ohle	32	M	Merchant	U. States	U. States	Brig Mary Ann. Carey.
S. F. Coit	35	M	"	"	"	
Pedro Martines	25	M	"	Spain	"	
Thomas "	40	M	"	"	"	
Pedro Blanco	30	M	Mariner	"	"	
Francisco Gomez	35	M	Merchant	"	"	
Wm. De la Roach	35	M	"	G. Britain	"	Sch. Kitty & Susan. Casson.
Fredk. Cobb	22	M	"	U. States	"	Sch. O. H. Perry.
B. Shoemaker	70	M	Mariner	"	"	
Obadiah Dacoster	27	M	Merchant	G. Britain	"	Ship Tobacco Plant. Reed.
Wm. P. Grey	28	M	"	"	"	
B. "	20	M	"	"	"	
P. Galbraith	57	M	Farmer	"	"	

Names of passengers	Age	Sex	Occupation	Country to which they belong	Country of which they intend becoming inhabitants	Ship or vessel with the name of the master or commander
PHILADELPHIA Cont.						
Q. E. Dec. 31, 1822						
Thomas Jones	42	M	Farmer	G. Britain	U. States	
Thomas Nicholson	33	M	"	"	"	
John Everatt	21	M	Lawyer	"	"	
G. W. Tatem *	38	M	Mariner	U. States	"	Sch. Mary Washington.
John Wightman	28	M	"	"	"	
T. Madoskey	30	M		Italy	"	
F. Araguti	25	M		"	"	
S. Malsan	28	M	Supercargo	U. States	"	
F. Gastlumendi	22	M	Merchant	"	"	Brig James Coulter.
F. Mazas	24	M	"	Spain	"	
M. Vigre	35	M	"	"	"	
R. Schoelt	20	M	Mariner	"	"	
J. Julambois *	40	M	Physician	"	"	
James Lopez	22	M	Merchant	"	"	Sch. Sisters. Hill.
A. Pelayo	23	M	"	"	"	
J. R. Lawrence	30	M	Supercargo	U. States	"	Ship Pennsylvania.
Wm. H. Oswald	27	M		"	"	
John Patrick	22	M	Merchant	"	"	Brig Alabama. Hall.
Mrs. Charzes & 3 ch.	30	F		"	"	
Charles Verona	22	M	"	"	"	
Andw. Wood	25	M	"	"	"	
James Robertson	28	M	Weaver	Ireland	"	Sch. Independence.
Jane " & ch.	20	F		"	"	
Barney Murphy	30	M	Farmer	"	"	
Samuel Mullen	30	M	Tailor	"	"	
Sarah " & 2 ch.	30	F		"	"	
James Gillespie	23	M	Weaver	"	"	
Hugh Sweeny	19	M	Farmer	"	"	
Margaret "	26	F		"	"	
James Rice	28	M	Farmer	"	"	
Hugh McLean	26	M	"	"	"	
Nancy "	20	F		"	"	
Henry Galler	18	M	Farmer	"	"	
Thomas Lowry	18	M	"	"	"	
James Kelly	28	M	Weaver	"	"	
S. "	21	F	Seamstress	"	"	
James Bourd	24	M	Farmer	"	"	
James Tassey	40	M	Weaver	"	"	
John Hastings	24	M	Merchant	"	"	
Robt. McNaught	27	M	Weaver	"	"	
James "	21	M	"	"	"	
John Higgins	25	M	Farmer	"	"	
S. Floyd	25	M	"	"	"	
Andw. Bustard	21	M	Shoemaker	"	"	

Names of passengers	Age	Sex	Occupation	Country to which they belong	Country of which they intend becoming inhabitants	Ship or vessel with the name of the master or commander
PHILADELPHIA Cont.						
Q. E. Dec. 31, 1822						
Robt. Turner	25	M	Farmer	Ireland	U. States	
Hugh Tilley	29	M	Bookbinder	"	"	
James "	50	M	"	"	"	
James Johnson	70	M	Farmer	"	"	
Walter Allen	25	M	"	"	"	
Robert Turner	24	M	"	"		
Leopold Bess	42	M	Merchant	France	"	Ship Hunter. Davis.
L. Lafitte	55	M	"	"	"	
B. Strofeld	38	M	"	"	"	
J. Bousguet	24	M	"	"	"	
Geo. Coggshill	38	M	Mariner	U. States	"	Brig Margaret.
Joseph Racuez	36	M	Merchant	Spain	"	
Wm. Frazier	17	M	Mariner	U. States	"	
Robert Clark	40	M	Merchant	"	"	Sch. Lydia. Fortescue.
F. La Sero	22	M	"	France	"	Sch. Favourite. Coquin.
Joseph Johnson	28	M	"	G. Britain	"	Sch. Leo. Claxton.
R. Phipper	45	M	Farmer	"	"	Brig Milo. Young.
Mary " & 5 ch.	39	F		"	"	
J Loverett	30	M	"	"	"	
Eliza " & 4 ch.	28	F		"	"	
Gideon Fairman	45	M	Artist	U. States	"	Ship Moss. Tusley.
D. " & ch	40	F		"	"	
John Spencer	33	M		"	"	
A. Bull	32	M	Architect	"	"	
Augustine Lessam	30	M	"	Guernsey	"	
John Howarth	40	M	Merchant	England	"	
James Clark	30	M	"	"	"	
Edwd. Carey	18	M	"	"	"	
James Cleaver	30	M	Teacher	"	"	
John Ruse	30	M	Baker	"	"	
Ann Cowell & 3 ch.	40	F		"	"	
Ann Lewis & 3 ch.	32	F		"	"	
Jane Hazelhurst & 3 ch.	36	F		"	"	
Edwd. Simmons & ch.	34	M	Merchant	U. States	"	Sch. Columbia. Singer.
F. Braithwaite	45	M	Farmer	G. Britain	"	Ship Liverpool Packet.
Susan " & 4 ch.	45	F		"	"	
John B. Greenwood	45	M	Cordwainer	"	"	
Fanny "	30	F		"	"	
Richd. Williams	33	M	Labourer	"	"	
Morris Jones	30	M	"	"	"	
John Evans	28	M	"	"	"	
Martha Davis & 2 ch.	40	F		"	"	
John Edwards	40	M	Farmer	"	"	
Ann " & 2 ch.	40	F		"	"	

Names of passengers	Age	Sex	Occupation	Country to which they belong	Country of which they intend becoming inhabitants	Ship or vessel with the name of the master or commander
PHILADELPHIA Cont. Q. E. Dec. 31, 1822						
David Workman	25	M	Saddler	G. Britain	U. States	
Wm "	25	M	Cab. maker	"	"	
Thomas Pownal	28	M	Farmer	"	"	
Thomas Williams	28	M	Labourer	"	"	
John Owen	30	M	Mariner	"	"	
Richd. Marshall	30	M	"	"	"	
Wm. Simmons	33	M	"	"	"	
Wm. White	32	M	"	"	"	
Ann " & ch.	30	F		"	"	
Thomas Edwards	36	M	Tailor	"	"	
Gilbert Molony	27	M	Farmer	"	"	
James "	22	M	"	"	"	
Thomas James	44	M	"	"	"	
S. Chapman	53	M	Pedlar	"	"	
M. Lawrence	33	M	Cab. maker	U. States	"	Sch. Maid of the Mill.
Alex. Locust	22	M	Merchant	Spain	"	Brig Alabama. Hall.
Francis Melizet	40	M	"	"	"	
Jose M. Urquiola	16	M	"	"	"	Brig Harp. Sandgram.
George Walters	30	M	Cooper	U. States	"	
G. Antoinette	35	M	Tinker	Germany	"	Brig Mero. Holz.
Wm. Chandler	55	M	Physician	U. States	"	Brig Sarah. Blackstone.
Mrs. "	50	F		"	"	
H. Romer *	45	M	Merchant	Germany	"	Brig Eliz. Ann. Brooks.
J. R. Warder	34	M	"	U. States	"	
J. E. Brooks	23	M	"	"	"	
D. Manlove	32	M	Mariner	"	"	
BARNSTABLE Q. E. Dec. 31, 1822						
George Graham	30	M	Weaver	England	U. States	Sch. Loire. Bassett.
John "	28	M	"	"	"	
Edwd. Reddley	28	M	"	"	"	
Mary " & ch.	21	F		"	"	
Richard Hind	28	F	"	"	"	
Mary " & ch.	25	F		"	"	
Robert Conley	51	M	"	"	"	
Mary " & ch.	30	F		"	"	
Peter Darwin	40	M	"	"	"	
John McReady	26	M	"	"	"	
Stewart Elliott	47	M	"	"	"	
Margt. " & 6 ch.	46	F		"	"	
George "	27	M	"	"	"	
John "	23	M	"	"	"	

Names of passengers	Age	Sex	Occupation	Country to which they belong	Country of which they intend becoming inhabitants	Ship or vessel with the name of the master or commander
BARNSTABLE Cont.						
Q. E. Dec. 31, 1822						
Robert Elliott	21	M	Weaver	England	U. States	
Dinah "	19	F		"	"	
Sarah " & 3 ch.	25	F		"	"	
Francis Patterson	50	M	Silversmith	"	"	
Jane " & 2 ch.	40	F		"	"	
M. Pattison	33	M	Lieut. B. M. Service			
Mrs. " & ch.	25	F				
Edmund McSweeny	24	M	Bootmaker	Ireland	U. States	Sch. Genl. Jackson. Hallet.
Thomas B. Katkin	21	M	Shopkeeper	N. Scotia	"	
John Reeves	63	M	Miller	"	"	
John "	19	M	Mariner	"	"	
George "	17	M	"	"	"	
Foster Rhodes & 2 ch.	28	M	Shipwright	"	"	
Wm. P. "	47	M		"	"	
Cath. " & 3 ch.	23	F		"	"	
Ann " & ch.	29	F		"	"	
Martha M. Reeves & ch.	29	F		"	"	
Eliz. Brenner	24	F		Ireland	"	
Bridget Power & ch.	26	M		"	"	
John Kelly	23	M	Clerk	England	"	
James Dooland •	24	M	Farmer	"	"	
James Rawark	26	M	"	"	"	
Michael Gafney	28	M	"	"	"	
John "	24	M	"	"	"	
James Cody & ch.	44	M	Labourer	Ireland	"	Sch. Victory. Howes.
Judy "	28	F		"	"	
Ann Kenchal	28	F		"	"	
Thomas Trump	28	M	"	England	"	
John Lane	33	M	"	"	"	
Samuel Cole	25	M	Fisherman	"	"	
Thomas Simmot	36	M	Labourer	"	"	
Peggy " & ch.	23	F		"	"	
Philip Kennedy	30	M	"	Ireland	"	
Michael "	28	M	"	"	"	
Wm. Flood	32	M	"	"	"	
Wm. Culleton	24	M	"	"	"	
Andw. Walsh	24	M	"	"	"	
Michael Poor	21	M	"	"	"	
Philip Ryan	21	M	"	"	"	

Names of passengers	Age	Sex	Occupation	Country to which they belong	Country of which they intend becoming inhabitants	Ship or vessel with the name of the master or commander
FRENCHMAN'S BAY						
Q. E. Dec. 31, 1822						
John Cooper	25	M	Labourer	Ireland	U. States	Sch. Julia. Higgins.
Henry Dunn	26	M	"	"	"	
Paul Hannon	22	M	"	"	"	
Robt. Gin	30	M	"	"	"	
Jane Dickey	28	F		"	"	
Owen Caffrey	48	M	"	"	"	
Betsey " & ch.	25	F			"	
Wm. Miller	26	M	"	"	"	
Robt. Scott	20	M	"	"	"	
Francis Loughrie	40	M	"	"	"	
F. Rafferty	32	M	"	"	"	
Pat. Leckeredge	26	M	"	"	"	
Stephen Fox	36	M	"	"	"	
Margt. " & 2 ch.	28	F		"	"	
James Boyd	28	M	"	"	"	
John Dempsey	26	M	"	"	"	
Richd. O'Brien	30	M	"	"	"	
John Brown	36	M	"	"	"	
NORFOLK & PORTS-						
MOUTH						
Q. E. Dec. 31, 1822						
J. Johnson	52	M	Ship master	U. States	U. States	Sch. Pilot Banks.
Joseph Legasa	30	M	Merchant	Cuba	Cuba	Sch. La Plata. Cataramont.
John "	22	M	"	"	"	
N. Delapain	30	M	Miller	U. States	U. States	Brig Eliza Reily. Small
Alexr. Barclay	43	M	Merchant	"	"	Brig Liverpool. Nash.
C. W. Parnell	20	F		"	"	Ann Maria. Summers.
P. Deboice	35	M	Ship master	Domingo	Scotland	
Wm. Bruce	34	M	Merchant	U. States	U. States	Brig Hirum. Collins.
A Tarentella	57	M	Showman	"	"	Sch. Frances. Seaward.
L. J. Butler	25	M		"	"	Brig Only Daughter. Wilkinson.
Lewis Conain	32	M	Merchant	"	"	Sch. Pilot. Banks.
Alexr. Bell	18	M		"	"	Brig Mary Wright. Rooke.
Thomas Smith	25	M	Mariner	"	"	Brig Decatur. Rudder.
NEWPORT						
Q. E. Dec. 31, 1822						
Simon J. Osman	20	M	Planter	France	France	Ship Newport. Burroughs.
John D. Wolf	42	M	Merchant	U. States	U. States	Ship Genl. Jackson. Gonsalve.
Charles Pinkney	25	M	Secy. of Legation	"	"	

Names of passengers	Age	Sex	Occupation	Country to which they belong	Country of which they intend becoming inhabitants	Ship or vessel with the name of the master or commander
NEWPORT Cont. Q. E. Dec. 31, 1822						
Edwd. Spalding	30	M	Merchant	U. States	U. States	
John W. Douglass	34	M	Watchmaker	"	"	Sch. Ephraim. Briggs.
Danl. H. Pallis	17	M		"	"	
SAVANNAH Q. E. Dec. 31, 1822						
Robt. Dreghorn	30	M	Merchant	G. Britain	U. States	Ship Three Sisters. Bell.
Wm. McKinnan	18	M	Clerk	U. States	"	
George Brown	41	M	Farmer	G. Britain	"	
M. Gowen	25	M	Merchant	Scotland	"	--- Blucher. Potter.
M. Hutchinson	15	M		Ireland	"	
James Nuttall	40	M	Surgeon	England	"	--- Lady Gallaton. Harris.
Pat. McCarty	40	M	Labourer	"	"	
Robt. Isaac	45	M	Merchant	U. States	"	Ship Emily. Babcock.
Lucy " & 2 ch.	28	F		"	"	
Fanny "	20	F		"	"	
J. Clark & 2 ch.	20	F		"	"	
Geo. G. Johnston	22	M	Merchant	"	"	
G. Chisolm	25	M	"	"	"	
John Miller	50	M		"	"	

1823

Names of passengers	Age	Sex	Occupation	Country to which they belong	Country of which they intend becoming inhabitants	Ship or vessel with the name of the master or commander
ALEXANDRIA Q. E. March 31, 1823						
Thomas Key	22	M	Clerk	U. States	U. States	Sch. Rose in Bloom. Sowle.
NEW ORLEANS Q. E. March 31, 1823						
Jno. S. Apthorp	19	M	Gent.	U. States	U. States	Brig Geo. Washington. Rhodes.
John Cole	30	M	Carpenter	"	"	Brig Genl. Jackson. Eaton.
Daniel Geraud	35	M	Merchant	"	"	Sch. John & Mary. Brayton.
PROVIDENCE Q. E. March 31, 1823						
James Napier	28	M	Mariner	U. States	U. States	Sch. Experiment. Steele.
Charles Johnson	26	M	"	"	"	
PORTLAND Q. E. March 31, 1823						
John Whitten	34	M	Mariner	U. States	U. States	Brig Melford. Weeks.
James Graves	36	M	"	"	"	
Henry Jeleson	23	M	"	"	"	
Littleton G. Morgan	44	M	"	"	"	Brig Maine. Oxnard.
James Dunbar	37	M	"	"	"	
Saml. Larrabie Jr.	30	M		"	"	
Thos. Patterson	23	M		"	"	
James Snowman	40	M		"	"	
Benj. Dunbar	21	M		"	"	
Jesse Powell	15	M		"	"	
Andw. Bartlett	17	M		"	"	
Saml. Rogers	19	M		"	"	

Names of passengers	Age	Sex	Occupation	Country to which they belong	Country of which they intend becoming inhabitants	Ship or vessel with the name of the master or commander
NEWBERRYPORT						
Q. E. March 31, 1823						
James Marr	22	M	Mason	U. States	U. States	Sch. Maria.
Edward Burgess	34	M	Farmer	N. Brunswick	Carolina	
James McLeod	32	M	"	"	"	
Eliza Doyle	20	F	Spinster	"	"	
Mary Kooney & ch.	30	F	"	Ireland	"	
R. Hacket	25	F	"	"	"	
Nancy Casgrow	23	F	"	"	"	
Wm. McNever	22	M	Labourer	"	"	
M. MacGorman	16	M	Tailor	"	"	
Barney Cane	15	M	Labourer	"	"	
John Gault	24	M	Carpenter	"	"	
Saml. Mason	25	M	"	N. Brunswick	N. Brunswick	
Francis George	28	M	"	England	"	
James Graham	30	M	"	Scotland	"	
Henry Darah	23	M	Tailor	Ireland	"	
Wm. Clark	23	M	Gent.	N. Brunswick	N. Brunswick	
Josiah Webster	46	M	Mariner	U. States	U. States	Sch. Roseway.
Joseph Robinson	20	M	"	"	"	
George C. Wilson	21	M	"	"	"	Sch. Lady Brookes.
Alexis Wilkes	22	M	"	"	"	
Edwd. Scores	25	M	"	"	"	Sch. Lydia.
James Nichols	19	M	"	"	"	
S. CAROLINA						
Q. E. March 31, 1823						
James Gracia	30	M	Mariner	St. Barts.	U. States	Brig Centurion.
Edwd. Goware	35	M	Merchant		Spain	Sch. Horatio.
John Rodriguez	32	M	Mariner		"	
E. Bordier	35	M	Merchant	Geneva	U. States	Ship Bingham.
Jean Baptist	22	M	Painter & glazier	"	"	
Joseph Markilola	23	M	"	"	"	
--- Gardner	35	M	Mariner	U. States	"	Brig Rachel & Sally.
--- Urban	28	M	Trader	France	"	
Wm. Holetear	22	M	"	"	"	
John Brown	30	M		G. Britain	"	Ship Corsair.
B. Young	30	M	Military	Columbia	Columbia	Sch. Maid of the Mill.
James B. Clough	38	M	Merchant	G. Britain	G. Britain	Ship Perfect.
Mrs. " & 4 ch.	28	F		"	"	
Mary Marshall	39	F		"	"	
Ann Bennet	19	F		"	"	
Thos. H. Hindley	43	M	Merchant	"	"	
Alexr. Adam	21	M	"	"	"	

Names of passengers	Age	Sex	Occupation	Country to which they belong	Country of which they intend becoming inhabitants	Ship or vessel with the name of the master or commander
S. CAROLINA Cont.						
Q. E. March 23, 1823						
Isaac Silliman & ch.	32	M	Officer	U. States	U. States	
Henry Goldsmith	18	M	Trader	"	"	Sch. Abigail.
Henry Brown	35	M	Merchant	Germany	"	Sch. Col. Armstead
Isabella "	38	F		"	"	
Joseph Lopez	35	M	Merchant	Portugal	"	
Joseph Matthews	40	M	"	Spain	"	
Nathanl. Lopzey *	32	M	Planter	"	"	
Thos. Marld	45	M	Merchant	"	"	
J Gonsales	35	M	Lawyer	"	"	
H. Ferrester	20	F	Milliner	U. States	"	Sch. Eliza & Polly.
Ann Wilson	25	F	"	"	"	
Diego Maris or Marso	27	M	Military	Chile	Chile	Sch. Bellona.
John Herspool	30	M	Merchant	U. States	U. States	Sch. Sarah Ann.
John Crosbie	55	M	Farmer	G. Britain	"	Ship Hannah.
John Pierce	28	M	"	"	"	
Saml. McCullough	55	M	"	"	"	
John G. Beale	26	M	Mariner	"	"	
John Thompson	22	M	Farmer	"	"	
Wm. Rowland	21	M	Surveyor	"	"	Bark Jane.
James Maloney	35	M	Farmer	"	"	
John Williams	19	M	Clerk	"	"	
Charles Maghim	43	M	Merchant	France	"	Sch. Mechanic.
M. Lorent	30	M	"	"	"	
F. Caura	30	M	"	Spain	"	
John Calabra	30	M	"	"	"	
John Caladara	20	M	"	"	"	
Geo. Lowe	33	M	Col. Officer	Columbia	Columbia	Sch. Nancy & Felix.
John Findlay	21	M	Merchant	G. Britain	U. States	Brig Rosina.
Jane McMoran & ch.	45	F		"	"	
Wm. B. Hall	32	M	"	"	"	Brig Charles.
J S. Russell	25	M	"	"	"	
Sally Vincent & ch.	40	F		Guadaloup	"	Sch. Midas
L. Sproll	20	M	Farmer	G. Britain	"	Brig Ann.
Moses Sproll & 3 ch.	21	M	"	"	"	
R. McColum	40	M	"	"	"	Brig Sally & Hope.
Benj. Chapman	42	M	"	"	"	
A. Henry	24	M	"	"	"	Sch. Felix.
David Canter	40	M	Merchant	"	"	
J. Ross	37	M	"	"	"	
Wm. Humble	22	M	"	"	"	Brig Francis.
Martin Long	45	M	Merchant	"	"	Sch. Phenix.
John McGowan	45	M	"	"	"	Brig Pilgrim.
D. Monet	44	M	Physician	U. States	"	Sch. Marion.
Mrs "	16	F		"	"	

PASSENGERS WHO ARRIVED IN THE U.S. SEPTEMBER 1821 - DECEMBER 1823

Names of passengers	Age	Sex	Occupation	Country to which they belong	Country of which they intend becoming inhabitants	Ship or vessel with the name of the master or commander
S. CAROLINA Cont.						
Q. E. March 31, 1823						
R. Fontinroy	24	M	Planter	U. States	U. States	
J. Denace	24	M	Merchant	Italy	"	
J. Sperow	20	M	Trader	Spain	"	
Francis Joseph	30	M	"	Portugal	"	Sch. Eliza & Polly.
Charles Lowry	50	M	Tailor	U. States	"	Sch. Swift.
Henry Austin	41	M	Merchant	"	"	Ship St. Peter.
A. Putman *	41	M	"	"	"	
John Ward	32	M	"	G. Britain	"	Ship Mary Catharine.
NEW ORLEANS						
Q. E. March 31, 1823						
also June 30, 1823						
Louis Bousaque	26	M	Physician	U. States	U. States	
E. Flemming	24	M	Planter	"	"	
B Benjamin	26	M	Printer	"	"	
Charles Moulton	22	M	"	"	"	
Joseph Lullin	30	M	Merchant	"	"	
Louis Amelia	40	M	Labourer	"	"	
John Fisher	28	M	Merchant	Scotland	"	Brig Patriot. Johnson.
P. Bougel	50	M	Offr. Span. Army	Spain	"	Brig Margaret Toole.
J. F. Lanier	50	M	Merchant	France	"	
Diego Morphy	30	M	"	U. States	"	Brig Sarah Ann. Girandel.
S. Blanco	37	M	Mariner	France	"	
Anto. Anciles	22	M	"	Spain	"	
P. Caillaure	22	M	Cooper	France	"	
Saml. Walker	58	M	Merchant	England	"	
Alexr. Miller	28	M	"	"		
John Crocker	40	M	"	"		
G. Roderiguez	38	M	Mariner	Spain		
Joseph Swiler *	27	M	Merchant	U. States	U. States	Sch. Surprize. Bradley.
Robt. Mussenberg	28	M	Mexn. offcr.	Mexico		
P. Balis *	27	M	Farmer	U. States		
P. T. Parker	30	M	"	"		
Jas. McDonald	34	M	"	"		
D. Dusard	30	M	Physician	France		Brig Parker & Sons. Hodgson.
J. B. Passement	28	M	Merchant	"		Sch. Tartar. Williams.
F. Alzena	23	M	Mariner	Spain		
J. J. Mingual	38	M	"	"		
A. Riata	38	M	"	"		
M. Badia	20	M	Carpenter	U. States		
D. Peck	30	M	Mariner	"		
Robt. Shaw	36	M	Merchant	Ireland	N. Orleans	Ship Allerton. Ekin.

Names of passengers	Age	Sex	Occupation	Country to which they belong	Country of which they intend becoming inhabitants	Ship or vessel with the name of the master or commander
NEW ORLEANS						
Q. E. March 31, 1823						
also June 30, 1823						
Eliz. McIntire & 6 ch.	45	F		England	N. Orleans	
John Weston	22	M	Mechanic	England	U. States	
Mrs. "	22	F		"	"	
Juan Grenier	48	M	Planter	U. States	"	Sch. Meried. Salina.
J. B. Foreada	52	M	Danc. Mstr.	France	"	
Jose Maria	26	M	Mariner	"	"	
J. S. Chauvin	41	M	Baker	"	"	
A. Mispaulibe	50	M	Mariner	"	"	
P. F. Desire	45	M	Carpenter	"	"	
F. Boudel	22	M	Mariner	"	"	
J. Minary	26	M	"	"	"	
J. B. Varnier	30	M	Stone cutter	"	"	
Samuel Gordon	19	M	Merchant	England	"	Brig Elizabeth. Armstrong.
John Cox	35	M	Farmer	"	"	
Ann " & 3 ch.	30	F		"	"	
Sarah George	26	F		"	"	
A. Gaubut	25	M	Merchant	France	"	Sch. Prince Oscar. Gaument.
Mrs. "	18	F		"	"	
Mrs. Dulue & ch.	36	F		"	"	
Mrs. Wilkinson	21	F		England	"	Brig Isabella. Daguer.
John Davis	50	M		U. States	"	Ship Cecilia. Liberal.
--- Levin/Serin	25	M	Merchant	France	"	
--- Fogliarde	29	M	Printer	"	"	
J Cazelard	21	M	Architect	"	"	
--- Lepure	36	M	Machinist	"	"	
--- Goa	40	M	"	"	"	
Mrs. " & ch.	22	F		"	"	
--- Deschamps	25	M	Play actor	"	"	
Mrs. " & ch.	22	F	"	"	"	
--- Olivier	20	F	"	"	"	
V. Racon	30	M	"	"	"	
Mrs. " & ch.	28	F	"	"	"	
J. F. Shatell	28	M	Tailor	Germany	"	Sch. Philip. Caslagholn.
P. V. Bertrand	28	M	Merchant	U. States	"	Sch. Little Sally. Lafite.
Jean Bourdin	32	M	"	"	"	
Jaqu. Challeron	23	M	"	France	"	
S. Carvet	30	M	"	"	"	
J. Naw *	32	M	"	"	"	
F. Thorn	28	M	"	"	"	
Th. Dow	35	M	"	U. States	"	
D. Martinez	29	M	"	Spain	"	
--- Perin *	50	M	Mariner	France	"	
James Morgan	32	M	"	U. States	"	Sch. Huntress. Conte.

Names of passengers	Age	Sex	Occupation	Country to which they belong	Country of which they intend becoming inhabitants	Ship or vessel with the name of the master or commander
NEW ORLEANS Cont. Q. E. March 31, 1823 also June 30, 1823						
J. Chardow & 3 ch.	66	M		France	U. States	
Saml. Blair	22	M	Merchant	U. States	"	
P. H. Chatelaine	24	M	Clerk	France	"	
J. Alphonso	21	M		"	"	
M. de Piya	34	M		Spain	"	
Robt. Crady	23	M	Carpenter	U. States	"	
Joseph Basque	27	M		"	"	Sch. Elizabeth.
B. "	25	M		"	"	
--- Balloch	30	M	Tailor	Scotland	"	
--- Pironi	30	M	Merchant	Italy	"	
--- Duplessis	25	M	Mariner	France	"	
E. Nathan	33	M	Merchant	U. States	"	
Wm. Finiday	27	M	"	England	"	Ship Ganges.
James Cole	48	M	Mechanic	"	"	
Henry Freeman	23	M	Gardner	"	"	
Thos. Sutcliff	35	M	Turner	"	"	
F. Molineur	18	M	Merchant	"	"	
Elizabeth Lowes	54	F		"	"	Ship Laura Ann.
Frances " & 3 ch.	28	F		"	"	
F. Mora	30	M		U. States	"	Sch. Time.
A. McClusky	45	M	Tailor	"	"	
Joseph Galley	40	M	Musician	Italy	"	
F. Baster	59	M	Merchant	"	"	
W. "	19	M	"	"	"	
F. Carri	27	M	"	France	"	Sch. ?
A. Marlat	32	M	"	"	"	
C. Flutas	27	M		"	"	
M. Lubiage	22	M	Mariner	Spain	"	
Wm. Smith	36	M	"	U. States	"	
John Anderly	34	M	"	"	"	Sch. Resource.
Wm. Young	27	M	Merchant	"	"	
Louis Guisnard & ch.	44	M	"	"	"	Brig Jerome.
Victor Bastien	25	M	"	France	"	
Louis Cornie	34	M	Tailor	"	"	
D. Lecut *	39	M	Merchant	"	"	
N. Tennieres	21	M	"	"	"	
L. Gerard	30	M	"	"	"	Brig Robt. Read.
E. Dickinson	32	M	"	U. States	"	
John F. Olivier	22	M	"	"	"	Brig S. Carolina.
L. "	18	M	"	"	"	
M. Guinot	22	M	"	France	"	
J. B. Stevenson	18	M	"	U. States	"	
Mrs Fox & ch.	38	F		Ireland	"	Ship Lady Gordon.

Names of passengers	Age	Sex	Occupation	Country to which they belong	Country of which they intend becoming inhabitants	Ship or vessel with the name of the master or commander
NEW ORLEANS Cont.						
Q. E. March 31, 1823						
aos June 30, 1823						
Wm. Provaw	24	M	Physician	Scotland	U. States	
P. Nugent	20	M	Clerk	Germany	"	
G. Godshalk	32	M	"	"	"	
Wm. McIntire	38	M	Pilot	Scotland	"	
A. Carries	28	M	Merchant	U. States	"	Sch. Helen. Lardy.
L. Cage	40	M		"	"	
Bernard Riaes *	50	M		Spain	U. States	
B. Penn	20	M	Mariner	U. States	"	Brig Hannah & Elizabeth.
Wm. Hunstock	23	M	Merchant	Bremen	"	Brig Resolution.
F. A. Kitting	42	M	"	Hamburg	Hamburg	
Mrs. "	32	F		"	"	
Baron de Hohenburg	24	M		Germany	U. States	Ship Highlander. Welch.
M. Myer	25	M	Farmer	"	"	
F. Superoze	39	M	Merchant	"	"	Brig Washington. Chase.
S. T. Tennant	22	M	"	G. Britain	"	
A. Leroux	36	M	"	France	"	
S. Foucher	35	M	Cab. maker	"	"	Sch. Servilia. Bellille.
J. B. Riviere	26	M	Tailor	"	"	
C. Foucher	24	M	Cab. maker	"	"	
J. B. Labaye	23	M	Cooper	"	"	
F. Hardy	25	M	Tailor	U. States	"	
J. B. Blanden	30	M	"	"	"	
C. Desburguez	30	M	Cab. maker	"	"	
P. Denis	30	M	Tailor	France	"	Sch. Servilia.
P. Baufen & ch.	35	M		"	"	
L. Sijour	35	M	Cab. maker	"	"	
Isaac Smith	30	M	Merchant	U. States	"	Sch. Columbus. Ross.
Richd. Bowdoin	22	M	"	"	"	
G. Bibb	22	M	"	"	"	
D. Leduc	40	M	Physician	"	"	
Chas. Poor	32	M	Merchant	"	"	Sch. Mary Caroline. Schoolfield.
--- Sallow	45	M	"	"	"	
Thos. Millo	24	M		"	"	
Madame Duchesne	40	F		"	"	Sch. Two Sisters.
John Gosse	25	M	Mechanic	"	"	Sch. Eliza.
Wm. Bates	27	M	Merchant	England	"	
J. Passment	28	M	"	France	"	Sch. Tartare.
A. Lefeume	32	M	"	"	"	
Jos. Cruzart & son	28	M	"	"	"	Brig Sarah. Giraudel.
Greg. Roderiguez	34	M	Mariner	"	"	
--- Depine	28	M	Mechanic	"	"	
--- Gouffero (or ert)	26	M	"	"	"	
Vincent Lena	30	M		Italy	"	

PASSENGERS WHO ARRIVED IN THE U.S. SEPTEMBER 1821 - DECEMBER 1823

Names of passengers	Age	Sex	Occupation	Country to which they belong	Country of which they intend becoming inhabitants	Ship or vessel with the name of the master or commander
NEW ORLEANS Cont. Q. E. March 31, 1823 also June 30, 1823						
J. Branguel	22	M	Mariner	Spain	U. States	
J. D. Colorine	50	M	Cook	France	"	
Mrs. Hernandez & 2 ch.	22	F		Spain	"	
Mrs. Jena & ch.	30	F		"	"	
Wm. Monroe	26	M	Mariner	U. States	"	
M. Alain	48	M	Merchant	Spain	"	Sloop Express. Radcliffe.
M. De Crusoit	45	M	"	France	"	
A. Pedro	35	M	"	"	"	
Wm. Paches	30	M	Mechanic	U. States	"	
J. Shurry	25	M	"	"	"	
Alexr. Miller	25	M	Farmer	"	"	
Philip Dordez •	44	M	Merchant	"		Sch. Five Sisters. Radcliff.
B. Collet	33	M	Mechanic	"		
Francis Durals	46	M	"	"		
Anto. Hardy	26	M	"	"		
Jacob Barnes	28	M	Merchant	"		Sch. Huntress. Conte.
A. W. D. Obenem	26	M	"	France	"	Sch. Jealous. Ballot.
M. French	40	M	"	U. States	"	
A. Durand	46	M	Sail maker	"	"	
M. Power	40	M	Merchant	"	"	
Chas. Fault	31	M	Farmer	Germany	"	Sch. Kennebec Trader. Gale.
George Taylor	36	M	Mariner	U. States	"	
Mrs. Knight & 3 ch.	22	F		"	"	Sch. Segunda. Anobas.
Wm. Burnham	25	M	Merchant	"	"	
--- Gleasson	30	M	"	"	"	
P. Ellien	32	M	"	"	"	Brig Nymph. Moore.
A. Moro	30	M	"	Spain	"	
J. F. Magowan	30	M	Clerk	Ireland	"	
R. Pelote	20	M	Cooper	U. States	"	
John Golue	24	M	"	"	"	
Thos. McGiven	30	M		"	"	
James Cutler	35	M	Merchant	"	"	Brig Warbler. Chaffee.
A. Regismuset	29	M	"	France	"	Brig L'Augoute. Dudon.
P. A. Delas	65	M		"	"	Ship Adela & Julie.
C. F. Leret	45	M	Labourer	"	"	
C. A. S. Dessonviller	20	M	Merchant	"	"	
M. Baudoin	45	M		"	"	
J. B. Leclerc	46	M	Merchant	"	"	
Henry Pinet	29	M	"	"	"	
F. E. Dupsey	23	M	Farmer	"	"	
F. J. Juit	20	M	Merchant	"	"	
A. Pitaird & 2 ch.	20	F		"		
W. Bogart	31	M	Merchant	U. States	"	Sch. Geo. Washington. Hunter.

Names of passengers	Age	Sex	Occupation	Country to which they belong	Country of which they intend becoming inhabitants	Ship or vessel with the name of the master or commander
NEW ORLEANS Cont.						
Q. E. March 31, 1823						
also June 30, 1823						
Simon Urel & 2 ch.	45	M		U. States	U. States	Brig Elizabeth. Shankland.
Thos. Yates	25	M		England	"	Sch. Jas. Lawrence. Smith.
Saml. Sheares	30	M	Mariner	U. States	"	
Nicholas Oberay	35	M	"	"	"	
Joseph B. Pariente	40	M		Spain	"	
John Baker	25	M		England	"	
John Wood	71	M	Farmer	"	"	Brig Ceres. Branther ?
John Wood Jnr.	23	M	"	"	"	
Thomas Holmes	20	M	"	"	"	
Jacob "	20	M	"	"	"	
Robt. Cathcart	35	M	"	Ireland	"	
Jane " & 4 ch.	35	F		"	"	
Robt. Mumford	27	M	Merchant	U. States	"	Brig Alonzo. Gold.
Jno. T. Gaubert	31	M	"	France	"	Ship Angelica. Harsen.
Lewis Davis	22	M		England	"	
A. Wanworth & ch.	28	F		France	"	
J. B. J. Jobert	31	M		"	"	
Adela "	24	F		"	"	
James H. Depre	18	M		"	"	
F. Gorlier	67	M		"	"	
C. Samson	44	M	Merchant	"	"	
A. D. Aldrich	25	M	"	U. States	"	Sch. Wm. & Emeline. Springer
Saml. Fountain	35	M	Farmer	"	"	
Robt. Williams	21	M	Mariner	"	"	
--- Lowry	24	M	"	"	"	
Jno. Parson	40	M	"	"	"	
J. F. Dubois	37	M	Merchant	France	"	Brig Mississippi. Johnson.
F. Desboge	19	M	Sugar refinr.	"	"	
F. M. Normand	32	M	Physician	"	"	
M. Briden	21	M	Sugar refinr.	"	"	
A. Godard	23	M	Farmer	"	"	
A. Beurest *	20	M	"	"	"	
Jno. G. Clamageran	45	M	Merchant	"	"	
Jno. Ollerise	48	M		"	"	
L. D. Dagardenis	30	M	Engineer	"	"	
H. L. Dufour	27	M	Jeweller	"	"	
Adolphe Flous	27	M	Merchant	"	"	
N. Ducommun	29	M	Watchmaker	Switzerland	"	
Edwd. Barie	24	M	Merchant	France	"	
P. Joubert	27	M	Druggist	"	"	
Thos. Banks	45	M	Merchant	U. States	"	Ship Unicorn. McKown.
Hugh McAdam	33	M	"	Ireland	"	
Andw. Curel *	30	M	"	"	"	

Names of passengers	Age	Sex	Occupation	Country to which they belong	Country of which they intend becoming inhabitants	Ship or vessel with the name of the master or commander
NEW ORLEANS Q. E. March 31, 1823 also June 30, 1823						
A. Moren	45	M	Merchant	U. States	U. States	Ship Edmond.
F. Gondrar	20	M	Planter	France	"	
J. Dufart	26	M	Physician	"	"	
D. Fessel & 2 ch.	40	M	Merchant	"	"	
M. Hustet * & 2 ch.	21	F		"	"	
M Kanderlendim & ch.	25	F		"	"	
M. Cadouc *	33	F		"	"	
Sabine Cavalier	30	M		"	"	
B. Border	27	M		"	"	
A. Bordere	21	M		"	"	
M. Narboune	26	M	Tailor	"	"	
M. Gordon	26	M	Merchant	U. States	"	Ship America. Steele.
F. Frey	28	M	"	Bremen	"	Brig Rein Deer. Maskell.
M. Monachan	22	M	"	Switzerland	"	
Maria B. John	21	F		France	"	
Henry Deag *	17	M		England	"	
L. M. Neure	33	M		France	"	
Victor Massun	28	M		"	"	Sch. Franklin. Dexter.
Anthony Fernandez	28	M		"	"	
James Gibson	28	M	Mariner	U. States	"	
L. Legar	21	M	"	"	"	
John Barnard	24	M	"	"	"	
John Miller	28	M	"	"	"	Brig Prometheus. Don.
John N. Burns	28	M	Farmer	"	"	
N. Coquille	40	M	Mariner	"	"	Sch. Good Friends. Wheeler.
Bernard Lasua	50	M	"	France	"	
V. Cochian	31	M	"	"	"	Brig Feliciana. Brown.
R. Sarynas	24	M	Merchant	"	"	
John Martin	28	M	Mariner	"	"	
Stephen Wood	24	M	Merchant	U. States	"	
John Finker *	33	M	Mason	France	"	
B. Johner	32	M	Carpenter	"	"	
Gaspar Rufia	23	M	Mariner	Catalonia	Spain	
Jno. P. Garcia	22	M	Merchant	Spain	U. States	Sch. Traveller. Frost.
Samuel Harris	35	M	"	G. Britain	"	Ship N. York Packet.
M. " & ch.	33	F		" .	"	
M. de Gueran	35	F	Milliner	France	"	
Philip Aregno & ch.	35	M	Merchant	Italy	"	
M. Bertrand	23	M	"	U. States	"	
Dominique Brossie	27	M	Blacksmith	France	"	
M. Maurin	36	M	Officer	"	"	Ship Jerome.
M. Dubois	20	M		"	"	
M. St. Cyr	20	M	Architect	"	"	

Names of passengers	Age	Sex	Occupation	Country to which they belong	Country of which they intend becoming inhabitants	Ship or vessel with the name of the master or commander
NEW ORLEANS Cont.						
Q. E. March 31, 1823						
also June 30, 1823						
F. S. Corregoles	25	M	Architect	France	U. States	
M. Lombard	25	M	Druggist	"	"	
M. Fabre	48	M		"	"	
Mad. " & 3 ch.	49	F		"	"	
F. Baulos	45	M	Merchant	"	"	
James Buckley	23	M	"	U. States	"	Brig Syren. Slatt.
Moses Campbell	38	M	Mariner	"	"	
F. Glavarie	55	M	"	"	"	Sch. Genl. Jackson.
P. J. Tuyes	28	M	Merchant	France	"	Ship Roman. Michel.
H. Andry	28	M	Planter	"	"	
M. Munnoiry *	36	M	Merchant	"	"	
L. A. Byotal *	27	M	"	"	"	
Thomas Barrett	25	M	"	Ireland	"	Brig Patriot. Johnson.
N. Caufield	30	M		"	"	Sch. Leos. Clarkson.
Charlotte Caufield	19	F		"	"	
M. Rance	45	M	Merchant	France	"	Sch. Milo. Aldrick.
J. Valdez	40	M	Mariner	Spain	"	Sch. Dorothy. Valsey.
M. Nubeling	21	M		Germany	"	Brig Forland. Vessels.
G. H. Bukel *	16	M		"	"	
U. St. Amand	30	M	Merchant	U. States	"	Brig If. Jones.
Jos. Churchhill	40	M	Mariner	"	"	
Wm. Wilson	30	M	Farmer	"	"	
Samuel Allers	46	M	Physician	Ireland	"	
Augustus Bleaher	36	M		Germany	"	
Edmond Hansten	40	M	Saddler	"	"	
Thos. Ridgley	30	M	Merchant	U. States	"	Sch. Emigrant. Barney.
John Clark	25	M	"	"	"	
Benj. Freeman	34	M	"	"	"	
Jon. Carleton	44	M	"	"	"	
Dixon Morehead	20	M	Mechanic	"	"	
Benj. Burns	25	M		"	"	
James McKenzie	35	M	Farmer	Scotland	"	
Alexr. Baron	34	M	Mariner	U. States	"	Sch. Bee. Deberge.
F. Brunette	42	M	"	"	"	
F. Curre	30	M	Merchant	France	"	
Martin Holle	23	M	"	"	"	
G. Lagrange	22	M	"	"	"	
A. Borie *	38	M	"	"	"	
A. Lasinague	50	M	"	Spain	"	
N. Garra	25	M	"	"	"	
F. Pache	60	M	"	"	"	
F. M. Deserifra & 2 ch.	30	F		"	"	
Joseph Jewell & ch.	52	M	Farmer	U. States	"	Sch. Kennebunk Trader. Gale.

Names of passengers	Age	Sex	Occupation	Country to which they belong	Country of which they intend becoming inhabitants	Ship or vessel with the name of the master or commander
NEW ORLEANS Cont.						
Q. E. March 31, 1823						
also June 30, 1823						
A. Andrews	22	M	Farmer	U. States	U. States	
John Pratt	32	M	"	"	"	
James Taylor	28	M	"	"	"	
Chas. Bradshaw	38	M	Seaman	"	"	
J. Tubiago	23	M	Merchant	Mexico	Mexico	Sch. Volatora. Bazallo.
F. Callico	37	M	"	"	"	
Joseph Casees or Caxes	37	M	"	"	"	
J. Rarness	28	M	"	"	"	
Jose Cimo	25	M	"	"	"	
A. Rodriguez	31	M	"	"	"	
M. Lubrago	18	M	"	"	"	
F. Ruis	40	M	Merchant	"	"	
J. B. Passement	25	M	"	France	U. States	Sch. Tartare.
W. Williams	28	M	Mariner	U. States	"	
John Lee	34	M	"	"	"	
Jno. Lawrence	60	M	"	"	"	
Israel Dickinson	33	M	Merchant	"	"	Brig Robt. Reade. Smith.
Benj. Ashley	40	M	Carpenter	"	"	Brig Belvedere. Robinson.
Morgan Day	33	M	Mariner	"	"	
Wm. Mitchell	24	M		"	"	
John Grace	37	M	Merchant	"	"	Sloop Regulator. Brien.
Cath " & 6 ch.	37	F		"	"	
Margt. Reed	22	F		Ireland	"	
R. M. Pierce	30	M	Merchant	U. States	"	
Sarah " & 3 ch.	25	F		"	"	
Peter McCartney	36	M	Merchant	Ireland	"	
Joseph Channings	35	M	Mariner	U. States	"	
--- Gildmaster	27	M	Merchant	Germany	"	Sch. Eliza. Martique.
--- Belaume	33	M	Engraver	U. States	"	Brig Atlantas. Richards.
John Collins	48	M	Mariner	"	"	
L. Martin	40	M	"	France	"	Sch. 8th of Jany. Quere.
J. Boy	24	M	Merchant	"	"	
Jno. F. Coison	49	M	Planter	"	"	Sch. Mary Washington.
Madame "	24	F		"	"	
L. Bergamo	38	M	Merchant	Italy	"	
F. Munana	25	M	"	"	"	
J. "	50	M	Planter	"	"	
M. Sossart	35	M	Merchant	France	"	Sch. Barracoa. Jones.
G. Snure	50	M	Planter	Germany	"	Sloop Cherub. Mash.
J. Miller	25	M	Merchant	"	"	--- Belle Dolores.
M. Bresas	30	M	Mariner	"	"	
Benj. Phillips	27	M	Ship carpentr.	U. States	"	Brig Perseverence. Pattison.
Saml. Alloway	27	M	Cooper	"	"	

Names of passengers	Age	Sex	Occupation	Country to which they belong	Country of which they intend becoming inhabitants	Ship or vessel with the name of the master or commander
NEW ORLEANS Cont.						
Q. E. March 31, 1823						
also June 30, 1823						
Wm. Alberson	25	M	Blacksmith	U. States	U. States	
Alexr. Shepherd	27	M	Cooper	"	"	
Jno. Claiborne	30	M	Mariner	"	"	
Wm. Jones	29	M	Wheelwright	"	"	
John Boggs	25	M	Ship carpentr	"	"	
Sarah Spear & 2 ch.	40	F		Ireland	"	Ship Edwd. Downey. Russel.
James McCean/McCan	23	M	Farmer	"	"	
James Dunn	20	M	"	"	"	
Henry Hull	30	M	"	"	"	
Saml. Hunter	50	M	Labourer	"	"	
Francis Davis	50	M	Farmer	"	"	
Jane " & 3 ch.	40	F		"	"	
George Little	25	M	Farmer	"	"	
Ann "	22	F		"	"	
Ann Clerk	25	F		"	"	
Susan " & ch.	25	M		"	"	
Pat. Donahoe	20	M	Farmer	"	"	
Pat. "	20	M	"	"	"	
Alexr. Cumming	21	M	"	"	"	
Michl. Savage	22	M	"	"	"	
James McCammon	33	M		"	"	
Danl. Pigot	50	M		"	"	
C. Magennis	21	M		"	"	
--- McCasker	60	M	Farmer	"	"	
Baron Hosenburg	27	M	Nobleman	Germany	Germany	Brig Sarah Ann.
Chas. Goduhu	29	M	Servant	Poland	"	
G. Rodriguez	36	M	Mariner	Spain		
A. Armstead	26	M	Merchant	U. States	U. States	
S. Audifrom	31	M	Planter	France	"	
Wm. Smith	26	M	Mariner	U. States	"	
S. Sargeant	25	M	"	"	"	
P. Ferand	28	M	"	France	"	
J. A. Chardon	18	M	"	"	"	
John Mallet	28	M	Confectionr.	"	"	Sch. Mermaid. Landan.
P. Obagshide	34	M		Netherlands	"	Ship Montgomery. Weston.
T. Bolens	32	M	Merchant	"	"	Brig Hannah. Wetherby.
Peter Rich	36	M	Carpenter	"	"	Ship Maria.
Anna " & ch.	30	F		"	"	
J. Hortz	40	M	Mason	Germany	"	
Mrs. " & 4 ch.	45	F		"	"	
Peter Rin	38	M		"	"	
A. Henderson	26	M	Slater	U. States	"	Sch. Two Sisters. Kellog.
Dominique Gruze	47	M	Merchant	France	"	Sch. Ghent. Folger.

Names of passengers	Age	Sex	Occupation	Country to which they belong	Country of which they intend becoming inhabitants	Ship or vessel with the name of the master or commander
NEW ORLEANS Cont. Q. E. March 31, 1823 also June 30, 1823						
Saml. Caldwell	35	M	Merchant	U. States	U. States	Sch. Wm. & Emeline. Springer.
Saml. King	30	M	Carpenter	"	"	
P. Francisco	45	M	Mariner	"	"	
Wm. Gow	20	M	Carpenter	"	"	
Jno. Hurtel	25	M	Planter	"	"	Sch. Huntress. Conter.
Philip Venst	39	M	"	France	"	
Fred. Berkly	25	M	Mariner	U. States	"	
Charles Jones	23	M	Carpenter	"	"	
Geo. Joure	20	M	Mariner	"	"	
John Baptiste	49	M	"	"	"	
M. Valentine	34	M	Merchant	France	"	
L. H. Lubrice	24	M	"	"	"	Brig Lycurgus. Jowry.
J. Duckworth	20	M	"	England	"	
Fred Furst	24	M	Merchant	Germany	"	Brig Sally. Willrock.
F. Grasmyer	22	M	"	"	"	
Manuel Garcia	56	M		Spain		Ship Govr. Griswold.
J Riley	54	M	"	U. States	"	
John Kerman	34	M	"	Ireland	"	
James Glenny	25	M	Mason	England	"	
James Curnings	22	M	"	"	"	
--- McLogan	22	M	Labourer	Ireland	"	
Joseph Caffarana	21	M	Mariner	Italy	"	Brig Wm. & Jas. Green.
Hugh Curley	22	M	Carpenter	U. States	"	
Mr. Bumpton	45	M	Merchant	"	"	Sch. Ceres. Brown.
M. Rouson	30	M	Planter	Spain	Cuba	
Mr. Logan	25	M	Merchant	U. States	U. States	
Eugene Lusson	18	M	"	"	"	Sch. Louisiana. Mailer.
C. Maximilian & 2 ch.	36	F		"	"	
M. A. Pillas	35	M	Merchant	France	"	Ship Crisis. Bramly.
Robt. Jacobs	30	M	"	U. States	"	Sch. George Stackpole.
Peter Mornel	45	M	Mariner	"	"	
Christopher Graham	30	M	Physician	"	"	Sch. Gen. Washington. Wilson.
Arch. Brooks	26	M		"	"	
Mr. Porteau	50	M	Mariner	France	"	
Joseph Pinez	27	M		Spain	"	Sch. Unity.
EDGARTOWN Q. E. March 31, 1823						
Wm. Howe	23	M		U. States	U. States	Brig Nestor. Weeks.
Joseph Knopp	20	M		"	"	Brig New Packet. Bright.
Joseph Magans	32	M	Mariner	Spain	Spain	Brig Alexr. Mackay.
Joseph Fernandez	42	M	"	"	"	

Names of passengers	Age	Sex	Occupation	Country to which they belong	Country of which they intend becoming inhabitants	Ship or vessel with the name of the master or commander
EDGARTOWN Cont.						
Q. E. March 31, 1823						
Joseph Saabradra *	40	M	Mariner	Spain	Spain	
Gregoria Freira *	25	M	"	"	"	
Philip Domingo	30	M	"	"	"	
R. Fuentes	22	M	"	"	"	
Antonio Fredrico	19	M	"	"	"	
P. Mackay	18	M		"	"	
Timothy Davis	25	M	"	"	"	Brig Carib of Boston.
Anthony Knapp	25	M	"	"	"	Sch. Beluga. Emery
Mary M. Taylor	21	F		"	"	Brig William. Lapham.
Wm. Pressren	48	M	Mariner	"	"	Brig Neutrality.
John Robertson	31	M	"	"	"	
Thomas Sherman	17	M	"	"	"	
John Miller	45	M	"	"	"	
ST. AUGUSTINE						
Q. E. March 31, 1823						
Wm. H. Williams	18	M		Florida	Florida	Sloop Susan.
Eliza "	16	F		"	"	
Mrs. Mannings & 2 ch.	45	F		N. Providence	"	on a visit.
R. Fuentes	68	M	Druggist	Florida	Havana	Sloop Leopard.
L. Lopez	48	M	S. Officer	"	"	
N. Rodriguez	61	M	Planter	"	"	
Ignacio Anedando	25	M	Merchant	"	"	
Jno. A. Cavado	24	M	Scrivener	"	"	
Jose Sanclier	21	M	Labourer	"	"	
Juan Suarez	23	M	"	"	"	
PLYMOUTH, N. C.						
Q. E. March 31, 1823						
Thomas Wicks	25	M	Mariner	U. States	Havana	Sch. Washington. Bozman.
James L. Lewis	26	M	"	"	"	
James Nelson	28	M	"	"	"	
David Higgins	19	M	"	Ireland	"	Sch. Betsey. Groser.
NEW YORK						
Q. E. March 31, 1823						
Wm. Fleming	34	M	Merchant	Canada	U. States	Brig Wm. & Nancy. Hardy.
Chas. Quigly	30	M		"	"	
Fred. L. Folger	57	M	"	U. States	"	Brig Matteawan. Coffin.
J. C. Gelston	27	M	"	"	"	
Fred Clark	20	M	"	?	"	Ship Valiant. Waldrich.

Names of passengers	Age	Sex	Occupation	Country to which they belong	Country of which they intend becoming inhabitants	Ship or vessel with the name of the master or commander
NEW YORK Cont.						
Q. E. March 31, 1823						
George Thompson	32	M	Merchant	G. Britain	U. States	Ship William. Thompson.
Ellen " & 2 ch.	28	F		"	"	
Mrs. E. H. Cox & ch.	40	F	Spinster	U. States	"	
John Banister	21	M	Merchant	G. Britain	"	
Henry Todd	40	M	"	U. States	"	
A. Tessant	36	M	"	France	"	
E. Monaghan	21	M	Mechanic	G. Britain	"	
Henry Grasset	48	M	Surgeon	"	Canada	Ship Acarta. Griswolde
Edwd Martin	52	M	Gent	"	U. States	
Joseph Robert	22	M		"	"	
John Finch	30	M		"	"	
H. Howard	30	M		"	"	
Fred. Dowing	22	M		"	"	
E. Fisher & 2 ch.	25	F		"	"	
Mary Wallace	26	F		"	"	
A. C. Clark	37	M	Farmer	"	"	
H. Loan	40	M		"	"	
Susan Loan & 4 ch.	40	F		"	"	
Jno. Strong & 2 ch.	45	M		"	"	
Jno. Brady	22	M		"	"	
Wm Young	27	M	Farmer	Scotland	"	
Chas. H. Beschenbush	32	M	Silversmith	Germany	"	
Spencer Selms	21	M	Farmer	England	"	
Peter Berry	47	M	Gunsmith	"	"	
Richd. Ban	39	M	Blacksmith	"	"	
S. Tyhert	52	M	Gunsmith	U. States	"	
Wm. Bottemy	32	M	"	England	"	
Wm. Parker	22	M	"	"	"	
Edwd. Shiel	34	M	Merchant	U. States	"	Sch. Sanford. Williams.
Jos. Woollsey	22	M	"	"	"	
Thos. Hamson	38	M	"	"	"	
James Babcock	36	M	"	"	"	Brig Frederick.
Wm. Bryan	28	M	"	"	"	
W. Merrill	30	M	Mariner	"	"	
S. A. Lewis	20	M	Merchant	"	"	
A. J. Perriadasa	21	M	"	Portugal	"	
L. Renaue •	31	M	"	France	"	Brig Olive & Sarah. Blackman.
F. Mars	22	M	Mechanic	"	"	
A. M. Areos	49	M	Merchant	Spain	"	
Thos. Boyd	22	M		U. States	"	
Thos. Martini	49	M		Spain	"	
A. Gignazo	28	M		Italy	"	
Thos. Plommer	30	M	Merchant	U. States	"	Sch. Nancy. Crowell
H. Plant	25	M	"	"	"	

Names of passengers	Age	Sex	Occupation	Country to which they belong	Country of which they intend becoming inhabitants	Ship or vessel with the name of the master or commander
NEW YORK Cont.						
Q. E. March 31, 1823						
Wm. Finlay	32	M	Baker	Ireland	U. States	
Wm. Rasse * & ch.	40	M	Farmer	"	"	
R. Sheardon & 2 ch.	40	F		"	"	
Michael Sheal	22	M		"	"	
Bernard Jounby	24	M		"	"	
H. Dooley & child	22	F		"	"	
C. Halsey	39	M	Merchant	U. States	"	Sch. Maine.
Thos. Homes	25	M	"	"	"	
P. Morin	29	M	"	"	"	Brig Jno. Barber.
P. Sidney	30	M	Mechanic	"	"	
J. Bell *	40	M	Mariner	"	"	
W. Atkinson	36	M	"	"	"	
W. Lewis	30	M	Merchant	"	"	Sch. James Monroe. Marshall.
A. Milne	36	M	"	"	"	
P. Bedshall	33	M	Labourer	England	"	
J. C. Cortays *	28	M	"	"	"	
Wm. Grey	28	M	Merchant	U. States	"	Brig Nestor. Whitney.
M. Matahel/bel	45	M	"	France	"	Sch. Retrieve. Theobald.
C. O. Donnell	21	M	Clerk	G. Britain	"	Ship Dominica. Johnson
J. Manfield	33	M	Labourer	"	"	
Jno. Palmer	35	M	Teacher	"	"	
S. Reed	35	M	Farmer	"	"	
John Craddock	23	M	Grocer	"	"	
M. Canning	24	M	Farmer	"	"	
J. M. Colligan	27	M	Merchant	"	"	
Robt. Butler	34	M	Farmer	"	"	
Wm. Woodless	29	M	Cooper	"	"	
J. McEvoy	30	M	"	"	"	
Robt. Fathan	60	M		"	"	
Ann " & 2 ch.	52	F		"	"	
Jas. Morgan	32	M	Mariner	U. States	"	Brig Copernican. Spears.
S. Foster	28	M	"	"	"	Sch. Harmony. Pratt
G. Hoffman	45	M	Coachmaker	Holland	"	
Geo. Zinshams	31	M	Butcher	"	"	
G. Dobleman	21	M	Merchant	Prussia	"	
C. F. Welhelm	24	M		Holland	"	
A. Weishall	26	M	Farmer	Germany	"	Brig Maria Elizabeth.
C. Wish	35	M	"	Denmark	"	
Maria Wish	32	F		"	"	
H. Brown	28	M		"	"	
H. Manch	31	M	Surgeon	Prussia	"	
C. Schroeder & 2 ch.	37	M	Merchant	Germany	"	
F. Rown	24	M	Farmer	"	"	
C. Shepherd	43	M	Mariner	U. States	"	Sch. Exchange. Davis.

PASSENGERS WHO ARRIVED IN THE U.S. SEPTEMBER 1821 - DECEMBER 1823

Names of passengers	Age	Sex	Occupation	Country to which they belong	Country of which they intend becoming inhabitants	Ship or vessel with the name of the master or commander
NEW YORK Cont.						
Q. E. March 31, 1823						
James Mattley	43	M	Mariner	England	U. States	
James Lion	19	M		"	"	
James Savage	40	M	Lawyer	U. States	"	Brig Cuba. Cushing
Mrs. Lincoln & 2 ch.	30	M		"	"	
John N. Smith	45	M		"	"	
John Jacobs	30	M	Merchant	England	"	
Jno. J. Thibaud	50	M	"	U. States	"	Ship Ontario.
Chas. D. Busson	25	M	Clerk	France	"	
J Robinson	29	M	Merchant	U. States	"	
H. O. Marshall	38	M	Shipmaster	"	"	
J. M. Jolivet	22	M	Jeweller	France	"	
C. Toupet	20	M	Clerk	"	"	
A. D. Baffiniere	26	M	"	"	"	
C. L. Williamson	24	M	U. S. Navy	U. States	"	Brig L. M. Pelham Hatch.
P. Proal	64	M	"	"	"	
Mr. Woodward	31	M	Manufactr.	England	"	Sch. Mercator. Allen.
W. Turner	25	M	Surgeon	"	"	Sch. Jas. Cropper. Marshall.
A. Stevenson	35	M	Manufactr.	"	"	
E. M. Powell	33	M	Farmer	"	"	
Wm. Cambell	42	M	Merchant	Scotland	"	
J. Bellsborough	18	M	"	England	"	
M. Scott	25	M	Farmer	"	"	
J. Taylor	44	M	"	"	"	
J. " & 4 ch.	38	F		"	"	
Mary Withers & 5 ch.	40	F		"	"	
Jas. M. Renney	27	M	Labourer	"	"	
F. Arreno	22	M	Merchant	Havana	"	Brig Fair American.
Don Jose Regulus	26	M	"	Spain	Spain	Brig Vigilant. Harper.
C. Revero	28	M	Mariner	"	"	
N. Bicher	44	M	"	U. States	U. States	Brig Anna Elizabeth. Hamilton.
Mr. Phelps & 2 ch.	32	M	Merchant	"	"	Ship Florida. Brown.
John Roberts	24	M	"	"	"	
F. H. Hedge	18	M	"	"	"	Ship Eagle. Adams.
Jas. Henderson	37	M	Draper	G. Britain	"	Ship Albion. Swanson.
Benj. Tytler	48	M	Printer	"	"	
Jno. Palmer	20	M	Cab. maker	"	"	
J. W. Beswict *	24	M	Gent.	"	"	
Robt. Jackson	45	M	Farmer	"	"	
N. D. Ellenwood	19	M	Merchant	U. States	"	Ship Beaver. De Peyster.
N. C. Harris	24	M	Printer	"	"	Sch. Cath. & Jane. Stasey.
J. Finley	34	M	Merchant	"	"	Sch. St. Helena Pitner
C. Bakeman	23	M	Mariner	"	"	
P. Ovecoux *	30	M	"	"	"	
John Brown	62	M	"	"	"	

Names of passengers	Age	Sex	Occupation	Country to which they belong	Country of which they intend becoming inhabitants	Ship or vessel with the name of the master or commander
NEW YORK Cont.						
Q. E. March 31, 1823						
Owen Sullivan	45	M		U. States	U. States	
J. Steele	23	M		"	"	
L. Goodsill	28	M	Gent.	U. States	U. States	Brig Radius. Granger.
Thos. Emerson	18	M		"	"	
J. Moore	42	M		"	"	
A. Buchet	30	M	Merchant	France	"	Brig Maria. Chadwick.
Mrs. "	28	F		"	"	
Wm. Tell	46	M	Teacher	G. Britain	"	Sch. F. Henrietta. Dickinson.
Mary " & 2 ch.	25	F		"	"	
George Blany	42	M	Farmer	Ireland	"	
Edwd. " & 2 ch.	25	M		"	"	
Robt. Kirkpatrick	30	M	"	"	"	
Sarah "	23	F		"	"	
Robt. Anderson	36	M		"	"	
Jno. Wilkinson & ch.	22	M		"	"	
John Murray	25	M	Merchant	"	"	Brig Mazzingho. Thatcher.
Thos. Shaw	30	M	"	"	"	Brig Hibernia. Watteling.
H. D. Mandeville	35	M	"	U. States	"	Ship Wm. & Jane. Bartlow.
A. Varron	32	M	"	Italy	"	Sloop Masedora. Smith.
D. Zaredon	28	M	"	"	"	
Peter Mewetts	36	M	"	Switzerland	"	
L. Brachmin	35	M	Mechanic	France	"	
J. Della Tork	41	M	Merchant	U. States	"	Brig Packet. Dougherty.
Jas. Arno •	48	M	"	"	"	
Andw. Webster	32	M	Labourer	Scotland	"	Brig Ariel. Boag.
D. McLaughlin	24	M	Merchant	"	"	
R. A. Cook	25	M	"	U. States	"	Sloop Pauline Julia. Tooke.
D. Louise	30	F		St. Domingo	"	Sch. Fair Play. Kimball.
D. Bellamin	30	M	Merchant	"	"	
W. Baartscher	52	M	Mariner	U. States	"	
Jas. H. Keating	30	M	Merchant	"	"	
C. Cotterell	25	M	Mariner	"	"	
W. R. Jones	25	M	Coachmakr.	"	"	
D. Leavitt	30	M	Merchant	"	"	
J. R. Kane	22	M	"	"	"	
N. S. L. Hoffman	24	M	Physician	"	"	
Stephen Davis	30	M	Mechanic	"	"	Sch. Elizabeth. Ballard.
J. J. Wallen	26	M	"	"	"	
J. Green	25	M	"	"	"	Brig Mary. Noyes.
Mrs. "	24	F		"	"	
Wm. Graves	35	M	Merchant	"	"	Ship Amity. Maxwell.
Mary "	38	F		"	"	
Wm. Hollingsworth	45	M	"	"	"	
Jno. Fayer	28	M	..	Ireland	"	

Names of passengers	Age	Sex	Occupation	Country to which they belong	Country of which they intend becoming inhabitants	Ship or vessel with the name of the master or commander
NEW YORK Cont.						
Q. E. March 31, 1823						
M E. Hersant	28	M	Sec. French Ambassador	France	U. States	
T. Schmidtt	22	M	Merchant	Germany	"	
James Bourne	31	M	Gent.	U. States	"	Sch. Albany Packet.
Jno. G. Taytor	24	M	"	"	"	
John McGillery	50	M	Merchant	Scotland	"	Sch. Olive Branch. Boyce
Daniel Gibbs	26	M	"	U. States	"	Sch. Geo. Henry Thacher.
H. A. Coit *	24	M	"	"	"	Sch. Swan. Storer.
G. B. Curtis	40	M	Mechanic	"	"	Brig Columbia. Bradford.
Geo. Reed	22	M	"	"	"	
James Rhodes	25	M	"	"	"	
Stephen Corigdon	23	M	"	"	"	
Jas. Westcott	22	M	"	"	"	
E. Farrier	22	M	"	"	"	
W. Rola	19	M	"	N. Orleans	"	
H. Combs	38	M	"	"	"	
Joseph Lambert	23	M	"	U. States	"	Brig Mechanic. Godfrey.
Peter Tarquand *	45	M	Commissr. Brit. Service	England	Canada	Brig Mentor. Martin.
Wm. Shaler	22	M	Consul at Algiers	U. States	U. States	Ship Ontario. Collins.
F. Naghel	42	M	Mariner	"	"	Brig Bordeaux. Bulman.
C. Napier	40	M	"	"	"	Brig Cuba. Cushing.
H. S. Grace	25	M	Farmer	England	"	
U. Barnes	22	M	Clerk	U. States	"	Brig Rebecca. Morrison.
M. Stinman	35	M	Mariner	"	"	Brig Enterprise. Hawley.
John Bailey	22	M	"	"	"	
John M. Southgate	26	M	Merchant	"	"	Ship Constitution. McKee.
G. M. Sloan	27	M	"	"	"	
Chas. Bradford	55	M	Mariner	"	"	
Andw. Davids	43	M	"	"	"	
H. Henry	40	M	"	"	"	
B. Wilson	35	M	Merchant	"	"	Ship Lord Wellington. Pollock.
L. Cochran	27	M	Surgeon	G. Britain	"	
Robt. "	34	M	Merchant	"	"	
Eliza " & 2 ch.	30	F		"	"	
W. P. Hamilton	43	M	Gent.	"	"	
Robt. Spear	23	M		"	"	
Bernd. O. Hauton	30	M	Labourer	"	"	
John Pore	36	M	"	"	"	
John Augustine	44	M	Merchant	Italy	"	Sch. Hannah & Amy. Stone.
Mrs. " & 4 ch.	28	F		"	"	
Wm. Hall	23	M	Mariner	U. States	"	
Thomas Prentice	42	M	"	"	"	Ship Commerce. Gardiner.

Names of passengers	Age	Sex	Occupation	Country to which they belong	Country of which they intend becoming inhabitants	Ship or vessel with the name of the master or commander
NEW YORK Cont.						
Q. E. March 31, 1823						
Benj. Burn	22	M	Saddler	U. States	U States	
Geo P. Lloyd	28	M	Druggist	G. Britain	"	
Jas. Brown	31	M	Merchant	"	"	
A. Fish	44	M	Farmer	"	"	
James Steele	58	M	Shoemaker	"	G. Britain	
Jas. Martin	35	M	Farmer	"	"	
James Bates	40	M	Joiner	"	"	
Wm. "	31	M	"	"	"	
Geo. "	14	M	"	"	"	
Richd Davis	41	M	Mariner	U. States	"	Ship Amphion. Blinn.
Jos. Roberts	14	M	"	"	"	
John Stewart	34	M	Merchant	"	"	Sch. Convoy. Chapman.
W. J. Wellesey	27	M	"	"	Jamaica	
Mrs. "	23	F		"	"	
Mrs. Lydon	31	M		Ireland	U. States	
S. C. Nowell	22	M	Merchant	U. States	"	Sch. Wm. & Henry. Colven
R. Longman	24	M	Mechanic	England	"	Ship Anna Maria. Gall.
Mrs. " & ch.	19	F		"	"	
Wm. Collyer	38	M	Merchant	"	"	
M. Taffey	22	M	Labourer	"	"	
J. Drake	24	M	Printer	"	"	
M. Wilson	23	M	Merchant	"	"	
M. Doughty	21	M	Clerk	"	"	
M. Morrow	25	M	Labourer	"	"	
Mr. York	22	M	"	"	"	
M. Watson	23	M	"	"	"	
A. P. Gibson	31	M	Gent.	U. States	"	Ship Panther. Bennett.
Mary Ketgal *	21	F	Lady	"	"	
Nancy Bennett	26	F	"	"	"	
E. George Jr.	27	M	Merchant	"	"	Brig Margaret. West.
Edwd. Hodges	35	M	"	"	"	
John Dewar	19	M	"	Scotland	"	Barque Spartan. Ward.
James Brash	30	M	"	"	"	
John Williams	32	M	"	"	"	
Wm. Mitchell	35	M	Farmer	"	"	
H. Briant	28	M	Mechanic	Ireland	"	Ship Bayard. Van Dyson.
Sarah "	22	F		"	"	
Thos. Smittman	27	M	Jeweller	England	"	
Spencer Selmet	46	M	Farmer	"	"	
H. Batling	22	M	Cooper	Germany	"	Brig Howard. Perkins.
Baron Tuylle *	40	M	Russian Minister	Russia	"	Ship N. York. Maxwell.
J. Wallenstein	32	M	Secretary	"	"	
A. Taylor	24	M	Merchant	G. Britain	"	

Names of passengers	Age	Sex	Occupation	Country to which they belong	Country of which they intend becoming inhabitants	Ship or vessel with the name of the master or commander
NEW YORK Cont.						
Q. E. March 31, 1823						
G. Monroe	43	M	Merchant	G. Britain	U. States	
Sarah " & 2 ch.	31	F		"	"	
A. Reggia *	55	M		"	"	
W. Wilson	43	M		"	"	
Wm. Key	26	M		"	"	
Henry Richards	50	M	Mariner	U. States	"	Brig Abeona. Lester.
Eliza Ferrington	35	M	Mechanic	"	"	
J. Scheffelin	27	M	Merchant	"	"	
Benj. Ferrington	26	M	Mechanic	"	"	
L. Rugh *	27	M	"	"	"	
Thos. Graves	41	M	Ship master	"	"	Brig Lark. Noyes.
Charles Simon	29	M	Merchant	"	"	Brig George. Harris.
Geo. Felix	25	M	Physician	Germany	"	
Edwd. Magorman	26	M	Merchant	Ireland	"	
C. Thomas	34	M	Mariner	England	"	Brig Union. Cotten.
Isabella Gray & ch.	23	F		"	"	
Wm. Aikins	21	M	Labourer	Ireland	"	
Wm. Moore	21	M	Hatter	"	"	
R. Adams	50	M	Farmer	"	"	Brig Greenhow. Gray.
A. " & 2 ch.	40	F		"	"	
Thomas Plunket	30	M	"	"	"	
M. Mead	22	M	"	"	"	
Jno. Poice	40	M		"	"	
Wm. "	38	M		"	"	
Elisha Francis	48	M	Tanner	"	"	Ship Orbit. Macy.
Jno. F. Gandard	29	M	Merchant	France	"	
John Watt	29	M	"	G. Britain	"	
Danl. Carroll	49	M	Farmer	"	"	
John Johnson	25	M	Clothier	"	"	
J. Shofield	21	M	"	"	"	
Jno. F. Richmond	22	M	Farmer	"	"	
John Andre	28	M	Storekeeper	"	"	
Edwd. Clinton	35	M		"	"	
Jno. Saxon	52	M	Farmer	"	"	
Chas. " & 2 ch.	48	M	"	"	"	
Wm. Copeland	24	M	"	"	"	
Mary " & ch.	22	F		"	"	
John Dennis	25	M	Supercargo	U. States	"	Sloop Windham. Brown.
M. Stocking	20	M	Mariner	"	"	
Mrs. Russell & 2 ch.	27	F		"	"	Brig Fame. Ross.
J. L. Francine *	39	M	Merchant	Spain	"	Brig Hippomanes. Bourne.
A. Kelly	40	M	"	Ireland	"	Brig New Speculation.
Jacob Gabat	35	M	Mechanic	France	"	Sch. Curlew. Stinman.
Joseph Williams	30	M	Barber	U. States	"	

Names of passengers	Age	Sex	Occupation	Country to which they belong	Country of which they intend becoming inhabitants	Ship or vessel with the name of the master or commander
NEW YORK Cont.						
Q. E. March 31, 1823						
Wm. Davidson	50	M	Merchant	England	U. States	Ship Comet Moore.
Ann " & 7 ch.	40	F		"	"	
James Taylor	55	M	Farmer	"	"	
Mary " & 4 ch.	30	F		"	"	
Geo. Abbot	35	M	Shoemaker	"	"	
Alexr. Stone	21	M	Labourer	"	"	
John Norton	39	M	Baker	"	"	
James Webster	28	M	Watchmaker	"	"	
Samuel "	29	M		"	"	
Edmund Humber	32	M	Painter	"	"	
R. Roberts	32	M	Cab. maker	"	"	
Eliz. " & ch.	33	F		"	"	
Joseph Whyers	22	M	Baker	"	"	
Robt. Buist	23	M	Gardner	"	"	
Joseph Mildwaters	28	M	Joiner	"	"	
Charlotte " & 2 ch.	28	F		"	"	
James Abbott	40	M	Shoemaker	"	"	
Ann " & 2 ch.	50	F		"	"	
Aaron "	38	M	Farmer	"	"	
Martha " & 6 ch.	39	F		"	"	
John Knight	25	M	"	"	"	
John Sutton	33	M	Teacher	"	"	
John Partridge	21	M	Farmer	"	"	
BOSTON						
Q. E. March 31, 1823						
Edmd. Fowle	26	M	Merchant	U. States	U. States	Brig Ant. Lane.
John Young	23	M	Mariner	"	"	Brig Clio. Constant.
Jon. Mumsnell	25	M	"	"	"	
Margt. Nash	20	F		"	"	Sch. Billow. Barker.
Edmd. Jourdan	24	M	Planter	"	"	
Jno. Horner	41	M	Mariner	"	"	
S. Corning	38	M	Grocer	"	"	Sch. Genl. Jackson. Hallet.
H. Smith	29	F		"	"	
R. J. Offley	22	M	Merchant	"	"	Brig Niger. Luce.
M. Harrod	29	M		"	"	
Wm. Ford	27	M	Mariner	"	"	
Mr. Allen	23	M	"	"	"	Sch. Billow. Barker.
Mr. Hume	25	M	Labourer	Scotland	"	
Mr. Darius	25	M	"	"	"	
Mr. Caldwell	20	M	"	"	"	
John Gillan	26	M	Stonecutter	"	"	Ship Falcon. Ashton.
R. A. Jones	20	M	Weaver	"	"	

Names of passengers	Age	Sex	Occupation	Country to which they belong	Country of which they intend becoming inhabitants	Ship or vessel with the name of the master or commander
BOSTON Cont.						
Q. E. March 31, 1823						
John Higgins	30	M	Farmer	Scotland	U. States	Brig Lucy Ann.
Susan "	18	F		"	"	
W. Ford	40	M	Preacher	Halifax	"	Sch. Cherub. Andrew
Mary Ford & 4 ch.	38	F		"	"	
James Ward	19	M	Farmer	"	"	
Wm. Brown	35	M	Merchant	"	"	
Danl. Coy	24	M	"	"	"	
Danl. Bousitt	22	M	"	"	"	
Wm. Morgan	30	M	Mariner	"	"	Eliza & Nancy. Amos
David Hagerston	20	M	Gardner	G. Britain	"	
Joshua Nash	49	M	Mariner	U. States	"	Sch. John Brown.
Jno. G. Nazan *	23	M	Merchant	"	"	
M. Gage	29	M	Physician	"	"	
John Daniels	16	M		England	"	Ship Fortitude. Gibson
C. "	26	M	Shoemaker	"	"	
Jno. Peat	28	M	Mariner	"	"	
M. Castello	25	M	Gent.	Cuba	Cuba	Sch. Florida
Francis Chapean	37	M	Merchant	France	U. States	Ship Hope. Manor
Mrs. Annoes	30	M		Halifax	Halifax	Sch. Billow. Barker.
Mr. Ward	22	M	Merchant	U. States	U. States	
Mr. Fodridge	28	M	"	Halifax	Halifax	
Mr. Dart	25	M	Tailor	"	"	
Mr. Fraser	26	M	Labourer	"	"	
Mr. Shea	27	M	Tailor	"	"	
Mr. Abbott	23	M	Tinman	"	"	
BALTIMORE						
Q. E. March 31, 1823						
R. Evans	24	M	Farmer	U. States	U. States	Vessel not mentioned
P. Castle	40	M	Labourer	Ireland	"	
B. Victor	18	M	Farmer	"	"	
Geo. Robertson	28	M	Merchant	"	"	
S. Gibson	24	M	"	"	"	
Peter Goverts	50	M	"	"	"	
Charles M. Pratt	22	M	"	U. States	U. States	
R. E. Rich	24	M	"	"	"	
James Templeton	34	M	"	"	"	
Jno. B. Smith	26	M	Supercargo	"	"	
H. Fulford	32	M	Merchant	"	"	
Jno. Benedict	45	M	Mariner	"	"	
M. Defosset	36	M	Officer	France	"	
J. B. Andrews	31	M	Mariner	U. States	"	
Christopher Coleman	40	M	"	"	"	
				"		

Names of passengers	Age	Sex	Occupation	Country to which they belong	Country of which they intend becoming inhabitants	Ship or vessel with the name of the master or commander
BALTIMORE Cont.						
Q. E. March 31, 1823						
H. Didier	41	M	Merchant	U. States	U. States	
John Burnham	18	M	"	"	"	
Chas. Berpham	25	M	"	"	"	
B. B. Basso	24	M	"	Buenos Ayres	"	
Jno. W. Ward	28	M	"	U. States	"	
Joseph Learacle *	50	M	"	Surinam	Surinam	
Thos. Johnson	24	M	"	U. States	U. States	
Peter Burt	60	M	Shipwright	England	"	
J. McFaddon	25	M	Merchant	U. States	"	
W. S. Woodsides	28	M	"	"	"	
Jno. Renno	22	M	"	"	"	
Robt. C. Marn	34	M	"	"	"	
J. M. de Zozay *	45	M	Ambassador Mexico	Mexico	"	
J. Torrens	35	M	S. Legation	"	"	
Juan Ignacio Villasenor	50	M	Padre	Mexico	"	
Francisco de Paula Tamarez	20	M	Officer	"	"	
Manuel Villesener	17	M	"	"	"	
Andw. Zoyaze	25	M	"	"	"	
Wm. B. Gates	38	M	Mariner	U. States	"	
John McPherson	26	M	Gent.	"	"	
John Murphy	30	M	Mason	"	"	
E. B. Babbit	35	M	U. S. Navy	"	"	
Joseph F. Lewis	22	M	Merchant	St. Jage de Cuba	"	
Mary "	16	F		"	"	
Thos. Vickery	25	M	Supercargo	U. States	"	
Wm. Howell	32	M	"	"	"	
H. W. Cottrell	35	M	Mariner	"	"	
D. M. Miles	32	M	"	"	"	
C. P. Darrell	27	M	"	"	"	
M. T. Wortle *	40	M	"	"	"	
Michael Callaghan	21	M	"	"	"	
A. Comett *	26	M	Merchant	"	"	
F. J. Coffin	40	M	"	"	"	
Geo. Beir *	28	M	"	"	"	
Pat. Galleger	25	M	"	"	"	
Wm. G. Bolgiano	23	M	"	"	"	
Maria "	16	F		"	"	
Wm. Ellenburg	44	M	Carpenter	"	"	
D. Philory	30	M	Merchant	"	"	
J. W. G. Wharton	32	M	"	"	"	
M. C. Bergman	28	F	Cook	Germany	"	

Names of passengers	Age	Sex	Occupation	Country to which they belong	Country of which they intend becoming inhabitants	Ship or vessel with the name of the master or commander
BALTIMORE Cont.						
Q. E. March 31, 1823						
Christina M. Myers *	19	F	Cook	Germany	U. States	
C. Ernest	20	F	"	"	"	
F. Gutenburg	21	F	"	"	"	
C. A. Heinicker	25	M	Merchant	"	"	
Fred. Essenwerie	35	M	"			
ALEXANDRIA						
Q. E June 30, 1823						
George H. Dalrymple	23	M	Merchant	Barbadoes	Barbadoes	Brig Jesse. Donaldson.
David Harding	36	M	Groom	"	"	
Mathias Vanna & ch.	43	M	Merchant	U. States	U. States	Sch. New Prescillia. Bacon.
Wm. Godwin	37	M	Mariner	"	"	
John Lymbam/burn	33	M	"	"	"	Brig Frederick. Barrett.
Mary McDevett & 2 ch.	28	F		Ireland	"	Ship Pioneer. Crabtree.
Bryan McLaughlin	24	M	Farmer	"	"	
RICHMOND						
Q. E. June 30, 1823						
Daniel Adams	23	M	Ship master	Virginia	U. States	Virginia Packet.
Briaut *	22	M	"	France	"	
John Walker	27	M	Merchant	U. States	"	Ship Rassalas.
John Stewart	17	M	Clerk	"	"	
NEWBURYPORT						
Q. E. June 30, 1823						
John A. Shaw	27	M	Mariner	U. States	U. States	Ship not mentioned.
Daniel Dill	27	M	"	"	"	
John Chase	22	M	"	"	"	
Daniel Carney	30	M	Commissary Genl.	G. Britain	G. Britain	
George W. Morse	55	M	Ship master	U. States	U. States	
PROVIDENCE						
Q. E. June 30, 1823						
Amos M. Vinton	24	M	Merchant	U. States	U. States	Ship Asia. Holden.
John Thornton	28	M	Physician	Scotland	England	Sch. Enterprize. Paine.
Isaac Bowen Jr.	46	M	Merchant	U. States	U. States	Brig Mary Ann. Tew.
N. W. Bowen	17	M	Clerk	"	"	
Timothy W. Barnes	37	M	Mariner	"	"	Sch. Dollar. Hall.
Benj. Marshall	22	M	Cooper	"	"	Brig Fame. Parker.

Names of passengers	Age	Sex	Occupation	Country to which they belong	Country of which they intend becoming inhabitants	Ship or vessel with the name of the master or commander
PROVIDENCE Cont. Q. E. June 30, 1823						
Caleb Corey	22	M	Cooper	U. States	U. States	
George Ferand	25	M	Merchant	France	"	Brig Pegasus. Greene.
BRISTOL AND WARREN Q. E. June 30, 1823						
Isaac Packard	45	M	Merchant	U. States	U. States	Ship Ann. D. Wolf.
Augusta "	18	F	Seamstress	"	"	
John Grace	35	M	Merchant	Cuba	Cuba	
John F. Mansing	38	M	"	U. States	U. States	
Jeremiah Studson *	28	M	Carpenter	"	"	Sch. Serena. Carter.
Jane A. Brand	19	F	Seamstress	"	"	
A. B. Terrill	40	M	Mariner	"	"	Sch. Adeline. Gibbs.
Martin Salsbury	36	M	Cooper	"	"	
N. Hood	38	M	"	"	"	Brig James. Cole.
Thos. Forbes	35	M	Merchant	"	"	Brig Bodowin. Carr.
Charles Allen	25	M	Mechanic	"	"	
Matthew "	23	M	"	"	"	
W. Vaughan	22	M	"	"	"	
Bowen "	24	M	"	"	"	
George "	26	M	"	"	"	
Christopher Vaughan	25	M	"	"	"	
Saml. C. Smith	29	M	"	"	"	
James D. Herrick	23	M	"	"	"	
Thomas Swan	40	M	Mariner	"	"	Sch. Catharine. Linger.
MARBLEHEAD Q. E. June 30, 1823						
Wm. Van Buskirk	34	M	Gent.	N. Scotia	N. Scotia	Brig Nancy.
Jacob G. Hogman	43	M	Mariner	U. States	U. States.	
NEWPORT Q. E. June 30, 1823						
John Wood	53	M	Gent.	U. States	U. States	Brig Mary. Dunwell.
Rebecca " & 5 ch.	51	F		"	"	
Henry Bartlett	35	M	Merchant	"	"	Brig If. Bull.
Gertrude Harper	15	F		"	"	
Hannah Rodgers	28	F		"	"	

PASSENGERS WHO ARRIVED IN THE U.S. SEPTEMBER 1821 - DECEMBER 1823

Names of passengers	Age	Sex	Occupation	Country to which they belong	Country of which they intend becoming inhabitants	Ship or vessel with the name of the master or commander
BOSTON						
Q. E. June 30, 1823						
Wm. Olive	43	M	Tailor	U. States	U. States	Brig Favorite. Webster.
S. Ashman	28	M	"	"	"	
Elizabeth Thurston *	24	F		"	"	Ship London Packet. Curtis.
D. Joy	45	M	Mariner	"	"	
Mrs. McCarty & 2 ch.	33	F		"	"	
D Saunders	24	M	Mariner	G. Britain	"	
Mrs. "	21	F		"	"	
Mark Thomas	28	M	Painter	"	"	
T. Bentinck	29	M	Lace mnfr.	U. States	"	
John Bruder	45	M	Cooper	"	"	
John S. Gossler	45	M	Merchant	Hamburg	"	Ship Emerald. Fox.
Matthew Pinton	22	M	"	England	"	
W. Mitchell	38	M	Farmer	"	"	
Wm. Thomas	28	M	"	"	"	
Thos. Popkin	20	M	Merchant	U. States	"	Brig Favorite. Shipley.
Jno. S. Petty	23	M	Planter	Bahama	Bahama	Sch. Jerry. Clark.
Jno. F. Craven	50	M	Merchant	France	U. States	Ship Delphos.
Chas. "	37	M	"	"	"	
James Castinet	22	M	Carpenter			
W. Lolly	31	M	Farmer	N. Britain	N. Britain	Sch. Celia & Nancy. Ames.
John Lockney	25	M	Merchant	"	"	
Cath. "	20	F		"	"	
Nancy Colson	28	F		U. States	"	
B. Douring * & 3 ch.	27	F		"	U. States	
Enos B. Balch	25	M	Student	"	"	Brig Charles. Summers.
J. Walker	36	M	Mariner	"	"	
S. Rowden	25	M	"	"	"	
W. B. Smith	20	M	"	"	"	
D. Powers	21	M	"	"	"	
John Quirk	35	M	Laborer	Ireland	"	Sch. Billow. Barker.
John McLane	27	M	"	"	"	
Mrs. "	29	F		"	"	
John Carr	24	M	"	"	"	
Joseph Faden	20	M	"	"	"	
Joshua Pool	32	M	Mariner	U. States	"	Bark American. Brown.
Robt. Smith	40	M	Gardner	Scotland	"	Sch. Cherub. Athearn.
D. Davidson	24	M	Mariner	"	"	
Wm Brothers	22	M		"	"	
John Leary	24	M	Gardner	Ireland	"	
Nicholas Hart	22	M	Butcher	"	"	
W. McDegan	30	M	Laborer	"	"	
Pat. Power	27	M	"	"	"	
John Ross	25	M	"	"	"	
David Chapman	50	M	Merchant	U. States	"	Sch. Albert. Shack.

Names of passengers	Age	Sex	Occupation	Country to which they belong	Country of which they intend becoming inhabitants	Ship or vessel with the name of the master or commander
BOSTON						
Q. E. June 30, 1823						
James Peters & 2 ch.	35	M	Merchant	U. States	U. States	
Philip Silva	26	M	"	"	"	
Chas. A. Prince	27	M	"	"	"	Ship Lucilla. Candler
Wm. Lengthlin *	24	M		Ireland	"	
F. Fannell *	24	M	Labourer	"	"	
Mary "	18	F		"	"	
C. A De Rundance *	36	M	Baker	Surinam	"	Brig Telemachus. Crosby
J. A. Welsh	30	M	Merchant	U. States	"	Brig Wanderer Picket.
Geo. Ray	22	M	Clerk	"	"	
Hugh H. Kendall	23	M	Merchant	"	"	
L. Chase	22	M	Carpenter	"	"	Sch. Lucretia. Holmes.
Henry Horner	33	M	Merchant	"	"	Brig Albion. Jones
Peter Doyle	36	M	"	England	"	Ship Pallas. Johnston.
W. Gardner	30	M	Carpenter	U. States	"	Sch. Ostrich. Bings.
J. Paulins	49	M	Merchant	Cape de Verd	Cape de Verd	Brig Hazard Blackman
John Dedrick	34	M	Mariner	U. States	U States	
W. Stanwood	22	M	Merchant	"	"	Brig Abeona. Eaton.
David Bennett	54	M	Cooper	"	"	
James Smith	35	M	Tailor	"	"	Brig Osprey. Ellis.
John Porter	16	M	"	"	"	
W. Scott	31	M	Mariner	England	England	Brig Margt Hodges.
Edwd. Cheves	39	M	"	U. States	U. States	
Henry Porter	26	M	"	"	"	Ship Sally Ann. Edes.
Wm Barr	26	M	Mariner	"	"	Bark Leopard Crafts.
James Crouther	30	M	"	England	England	Ship Jasper. Crocker.
J. Rodgers	25	M	Labourer	"	U. States	
Edwd. "	19	M	"	"	"	
John Johnston & ch.	40	M	"	"	"	
Robt. Turner	30	M	Farmer	Scotland	"	Ship Columbia. Woodward.
Mary " & 2 ch.	25	F		"	"	
James Sargent	28	M	Merchant	U States	"	Brig Chas. & Ellen. Berry.
B. F. Hohn	24	M	"	"	"	Brig Champion
W. W. Coleman	21	M	"	"	"	
Jno. A. Roberts	21	M	"	"	"	
Jno. Clark	45	M	"	Halifax	N Scotia	Sch. Billow. Barker.
J. B. Haffleton	30	M	"	"	"	
M. Miller	32	M	"	"	"	
Jas. McGrath	29	M	"	"	"	
W. Jones	28	M	Trader	"	"	
John Thomas	24	M	"	"	"	
John Donnett	23	M	"	"	"	
James Lynch	22	M	"	"	"	
Jas. Ekstrom	30	M	"	"	"	
Edwd. Upton	33	M	"	"	"	

Names of passengers	Age	Sex	Occupation	Country to which they belong	Country of which they intend becoming inhabitants	Ship or vessel with the name of the master or commander
BOSTON						
Q. E. June 30, 1823						
John Dodge	39	M	Merchant	U. States	U. States	Brig Victory. Keating.
Danl Johnston	39	M	Labourer	"	"	
Josiah Lockart	21	M	Merchant	"	"	Brig Franklin. Bodfish
B. M Clipp	20	M	"	"	"	Brig Cherub. Munson.
C. W. Apthorp	27	M	Mariner	"	"	Brig Henry. Atwood.
K. Martell	42	M		"	"	Sch. Planet. Dyer
Robt. C. Mackey	25	M	Merchant	"	"	Brig Orien. Crawford.
Thos Dunn	34	M	"	"	"	Brig New Packet. Bright.
W. Rayne	40	M	"	"	"	Sch. Franklin. Fisher.
Mrs. Cummings & 4 ch.	46	F		England	"	Brig Milo. Ord.
Jno. L Payson	26	M	"	U. States	"	Brig Cyprus. Chaddock.
F. Taylor & ch.	22	F		"		
S. Moreau	30	F		"		
Joseph Brand	26	M	"	St. Johns	St. Johns	Sch. Enterprize Vaughan.
John Ritchie	22	M	Weaver	"	U. States	
Wm. Campbell	22	M	Farmer	"	"	
P. Landrigan	40	M	Merchant	Ireland	"	Sch. Cherub. Athean.
M. Degan	29	F		"	"	
M. Quirk	24	F	Mantua mkr.	"	"	
D. Sweeney	22	M	Laborer	"	"	
Chas. "	26	M	"	"	"	
John Carroll	24	M	"	"	"	
H. Brown	18	M	Shoemaker	"	"	
Dennis Keshan	25	M	Farmer	"	"	
James Lick	32	M	"	"	"	
B. Fitzpatrick	16	M	"	"	"	
Michael Kelly	27	M	"	"	"	
James Husson	25	M	"	"	"	
Thomas Milligan	26	M	Carpenter	"	"	Sch. Mary Ann. Byelow.
M. Murphy	27	M	"	"	"	
John Welch	27	M	Mariner	U. States	"	Sch. Felicity. Gray.
A. Wolcott	24	M	"	"	"	
John Stone	26	M	"	"	"	
Jos. Malage	32	M	Merchant	France	France	Brig Nimrod. Alden.
Chas. Pargnet	52	M	"	"	"	Brig Byron. Bradbury.
Joseph Guest	40	M	Mariner	U. States	U. States	Ship Mercury. Nichols.
Thos. Poole	24	M	Shoemaker	"	"	
Peter Doyle	52	M	Labourer	England	"	
W. Way	23	M	Merchant	"	"	Sch. White Oak. Hammond
John O. Reilley	25	M	Clerk	Ireland	"	
Peter Stafford	27	M	"	"	"	
H. Marsh & child	28	F		"	"	Brig Zodiac. Cais.
Geo. Gordon	28	M	Farmer	"	"	
Mrs. " & ch.	36	F		"	"	

Names of passengers	Age	Sex	Occupation	Country to which they belong	Country of which they intend becoming inhabitants	Ship or vessel with the name of the master or commander
BOSTON Cont						
Q. E. June 30, 1823						
John O'Neal	35	M	Weaver	Ireland	U. States	Sch. Eliza Ann Ames.
Margt. " & 3 ch.	31	F		"	"	
Mary Rutter & ch.	25	F		"	"	
S. Sanders	25	M	Carpenter	"	"	
D. McGowan	40	M	Merchant	Scotland	"	Sch. Infant. Tupper.
M. Hatch	24	M	"	U. States	"	
David Upham	30	M	Farmer	N. Scotia	"	Sch. Geo & Henry. Lakin.
Danl. Canady	34	M	"	"	"	
John Ruddock	30	M	Carpenter	Ireland	"	
Mary " & 3 ch.	56	M ?	"	"	"	
Mary Ann Klour	56	M ?		Germany	"	
John Smith & ch.	50	M	Mariner	U. States	"	Mary & Eliza. Ellis
Thomas Dixon	40	M	Merchant	England	"	Brig Active. Low.
Mrs. " & 3 ch.	28	F		"	"	
M. P. B. Judson	23	M	Physician	U. States	"	
J. W. Parker	32	M	Merchant	"	"	
Jno. Beeting & ch.	30	M	Silk dyer	Scotland	"	Brig Atlas. Adams.
Gilbert Crury *	20	M	Blacksmith	"	"	
A. J. B. Demisquiter	27	M	Merchant	Surinam	Surinam	Brig Susanna Mary. Kidd.
Moses Dias	31	M	Clerk	England	"	Sch. Midas. Williams.
J. M. Hawes	40	M	Merchant	U. States	U. States	Sch. Ontario. Davis.
Benj. Brewer	50	M	Mariner	"	"	
Thomas Morrison	53	M	"	"	"	Brig Caroline. Jones.
E. Choet *	24	M	"	"	"	
J. Warner	22	M	Merchant	"	"	
Thomas Sinclair	50	M	Cooper	"	"	Brig Hammet. Hinchman.
T. Shaknigle *	35	M	Printer	Germany	"	Sch. Geo. Henry. Lakin.
Richd. Bent	37	M	Mechanic	"	"	Sch. Janus. Holmes.
Richd. Allen	22	M	Merchant	U. States	"	Sch. Plato. Treadwell.
Thos. Kenney	27	M	Cooper	Halifax	Halifax	Sch. Cleopatra. Coffin.
Peter Welch	42	M	Mason	"	"	
Mary Lewis	58	F		Wales	U. States	Ship Grand Turk. Higgins.
L. "	22	M	Turner	"	"	
Griffith Jones	29	M	"	"	"	
Richd. "	27	M	Farmer	"	"	
John Thomas	21	M	"	"	"	
Evan Hughs	46	M	"	"	"	
Abraham Howland	44	M	"	"	"	
Jane " & 7 ch.	44	F		"	"	
Robt. Morris	32	M	"	"	"	
David Stephens	52	M	"	"	"	
Jane " & ch.	32	F		"	"	
Griffith Thomas	24	M	"	"	"	
David Roberts	20	M	"	"	"	

Names of passengers	Age	Sex	Occupation	Country to which they belong	Country of which they intend becoming inhabitants	Ship or vessel with the name of the master or commander
BOSTON Cont.						
Q. E. June 30, 1823						
Joseph Mountfort	37	M	Cooper	U. States	U. States	Brig Cumberland. Judson.
Thos. Searle	28	M	Merchant	"	"	Brig Globe. Smith.
George Bell	23	M	Mariner	"	"	Brig Ohio. Ellingwood.
S. Barnett	16	M	"	"	"	
P. Bangor *	36	M	Merchant	St. Domingo	St. Domingo	Sch. Deborah. Henry.
Edwd. Holden	50	M	"	U. States	U. States	
W. Shannon	33	M	Merchant	"	"	Sch. Ceres. Rogers.
C. M. Lampson	27	M	"	"	"	
H. Brown	60	M	Weaver	England	"	
M. Moore	20	M		U. States	"	Ship Pearl. Coombs.
J. Fenton	28	M	Mason	Ireland	"	
Margt. Fenton & ch.	29	F		"	"	
John Lines	26	M	Farmer	U. States	"	Brig Sarah Cole.
A. Shaw & child	34	M	Ship master	"	"	
H. Dryden	23	M	Mariner	"	"	
Ephraim Dushin	25	M	"	"	"	
Thos. Sanders	28	M	"	"	"	
NEW YORK						
Q. E. June 30, 1823						
James P. Carroll	45	M	Merchant	England	U. States	Ship Hudson. Champlin.
Mary " & 7 ch.	38	F		"	"	
Isaac S. Clason	26	M		U. States	"	
S. Cuffy & ch.	28	F		"	"	
Edwd. Ming	23	M		"	"	
Jno. Hastings	38	M		"	"	
Philander Seline & 11 ch	43	M		"	"	
Thomas Pope	54	M	Mechanic	"	"	
Joseph Goodcask	27	M	"	"	"	
Nathan Bates	25	M	Farmer	"	"	
Edw. Conelly	18	M	"	"	"	
Wm. Stamp	20	M	"	"	"	
Saml. "	60	M	"	"	"	
Joseph "	35	M	"	"	"	
Sophia " & 2 ch.	28	F		"	"	
Saml. Croneh *	27	M	"	"	"	
Nancy " & 2 ch.	24	F		"	"	
James Heath	23	M	Mechanic	"	"	
James Gardner	26	M	Farmer	"	"	
Dorcas " & 3 ch.	29	F		"	"	
Wm. Gardner	22	M	"	"	"	
Richd. Cutney	22	M	"	"	"	
Wm. Sweeter	52	M	"	"	"	

Names of passengers	Age	Sex	Occupation	Country to which they belong	Country of which they intend becoming inhabitants	Ship or vessel with the name of the master or commander
NEW YORK Cont.						
Q. E. June 30. 1823						
Elizabeth Sweeter	31	F		U. States	U. States	
Edwd. Rouvet	55	M	Merchant	France	"	Ship Malabar. Orme.
John Mansan	35	M	Mechanic	Ireland	"	
James Jamison	38	M	Farmer	Scotland	"	Ship Ben Lomond.
Wm. Ireland	39	M	Mariner	U. States	"	Brig Jane. Fowler.
Wm. Chauncy	30	M	Merchant	"	"	
Geo. Barry	28	M	"	"	"	
Theodore Nicolet	32	M	"	France	"	
Alfred Robinson	38	M	"	England	"	
Robert Owens	22	M	"	Wales	"	
E. Dayly	19	M	"	U. States	"	Brig Cato. Rawson.
J. E. Zunigo *	49	M	"	France	"	Brig Pomona. Bright.
Pedro Jose Tuciba	34	M	"	Spain	"	
Carlos Fernandez	38	M	"	"	"	
Joseph Canet	32	M	"	"	"	
A. Dawson	35	M	"	England	"	
A. J. Hill	24	M	"	"	"	Sch. Ariadne. Aymar.
Salvador Chappells	35	M	"	U. States	"	Brig Betsy. Bates.
Thomas Cooper	28	M	"	"	"	
A. Anders	38	M	Mechanic	"	"	
Matthew Paterson	34	M	Merchant	Dominica	Dominica	Sch. Adno. Woodberry.
J. Bigby	30	M	"	G. Britain	Canada	Sch. Columbia. Rogers.
Robt. Hill	26	M	"	"	"	
John Wilson	20	M	"	"	"	
H. Stephens	20	M	"	"	"	
Saml. Butcher	27	M	"	"	U. States	Sch. Cortes. Ogden.
Jno. Richardson	25	M	Physician	"	"	
Jas. Sibell	30	M	Merchant	U. States	"	
M. Geraud	26	M	"	"	"	Sch. Gov. Tomkins. Brown.
W. R. Freeman	19	M	"	"	"	Sch. Maria Ann.
A. Emerson	30	M	"	"	"	
Thos. Fagan	28	M	Planter	Demerara	"	Sch. Anderson.
T. H. Mitchell	30	M	Merchant	U. States	"	Sch. Fly. Bayer.
Pat. Hayes	54	M	Mariner	"	"	
Wm. M. Queen	27	M	Merchant	"	"	
George Lyman	27	M	"	"	"	
Bernd. Salaza	15	M	Servant	Vera Cruz	"	
Wm. Brittan	83	M	Merchant	U. States	"	Ship Aug. & Jno. Hanson.
J. F. Budy *	28	M	Farmer	Ireland	"	Brig Wilson. Britton.
M. "	23	F		"	"	
Catherine Budy &2 ch.	56	F		"	"	
B. Britton	24	M		"	"	
George Y. Robertson	25	M	Surgeon	U. States	"	
Robt. Hogan	23	M	"	"	"	

PASSENGERS WHO ARRIVED IN THE U.S. SEPTEMBER 1821 - DECEMBER 1823

Names of passengers	Age	Sex	Occupation	Country to which they belong	Country of which they intend becoming inhabitants	Ship or vessel with the name of the master or commander
NEW YORK Cont						
Q E. June 30, 1823						
H. J. Tuthill	22	M	Merchant	Ireland	U. States	
Wm. Tansey	26	M	Farmer	"	"	
Mary "	36	F		"	"	
James Gallagher	30	M	"	"	"	
Jas. Byrne	36	M	Butcher	"	"	
Margt. "	34	F		"	"	
Owen Smyth	35	M	Farmer	"	"	
Catharine Smyth	25	F		"	"	
Margt. "	30	F		"	"	
Mary Freeman & ch.	26	F		"	"	
P. Doyle	45	M	Farmer	"	"	
Catharine Philips	19	F		"	"	
J. Bartlett	45	M	Mariner	U. States	"	
C. M. Coffin	42	M	"	"	"	Ship Hercules. Gardiner
J. L. Patterson	30	M	"	"	"	
George Lapsley	37	M	Farmer	"	"	
John Davis	23	M	"	"	"	
C. Jenkins	52	M	"	"	"	
Edwd. "	22	M	"	"	"	
Jno. Reynolds	26	M	"	"	"	
Jno. Beck	23	M	"	"	"	
Thomas Steele	21	M		"	"	
Wm. Woodle & ch.	42	M		"	"	
Thos. Wellington	50	M		"	"	
Margt. Camington & ch.	28	F		"	"	
John Nickley	35	M	Merchant	"	"	Sch. Mercator Allen
Wm. Canterbridge	23	M	Mariner	"	"	
J. Angers	28	M	Merchant	"	"	Sch. Natches. Barnard.
J Ponton	20	M	"	"	"	
Charles Bissett	40	M	Mariner	"	"	Brig Aginora. Mitchell.
Mrs. "	34	M		"	"	
Joseph Lockwood	28	M	Clerk	England	"	
Mary Ann Russell	25	F		"	"	
Robt. Brewster	32	M	Farmer	"	"	
Mary "	32	F		"	"	
Jas Templeton	30	M	Merchant	Scotland	"	Sch. Combine. Duncan.
Benj. Foot	36	M	Mechanic	U. States	"	Sch. Henry Davis.
Wm. Johnston	30	M	"	"	"	
Chas. J. Gilbert	20	M	Merchant	Bermuda	"	
Wm. Saltus	30	M	"	"	"	
John Bull	44	M	"	U. States	"	Sch. Lady Hunter. Desbrow.
Z. Fowler	22	M	"	St. Johns	"	
Wm. Mills	25	M	Mariner	Ireland	"	

Names of passengers	Age	Sex	Occupation	Country to which they belong	Country of which they intend becoming inhabitants	Ship or vessel with the name of the master or commander
NEW YORK Cont.						
Q. E. June 30, 1823						
Ann Mills & 4 ch.	30	F		Ireland	U. States	
John Kennedy	30	M		"	"	
Catharine " & 2 ch.	25	F		"	"	
Edwd K. Collar	21	M	Merchant	U. States	"	Brig Bee. Wilson.
Mary M. Cannon	28	F		"	"	Sch. Abigail.
Saml. Hinkley	38	M	Merchant	"	"	
Wm. Watson	28	M	"	England	"	
John Young	25	M	"	U. States	"	Brig Caravan. Dill.
R. B. Rhodes	24	M	"	"	"	Sch. Havana. Holdridge
C. Combe	36	M	"	France	"	
T. Norman	24	M	"	U. States	"	
J. A. Dupray & ch.	32	M	"	France	"	Brig Grampus. Bangs.
O. G. Baue *	25	M	"	U. States	"	Sch. Genl. Lorellette
Nathanl. Saule *	56	M	Mariner	"	"	Brig Sarah. Hinch.
George Trevy *	30	M	"	"	"	
Wm. W. Bollings	20	M	"	"	"	
W. T. Shepperd	33	M	Merchant	G. Britain	"	Ship Meteor. Cobb.
Wm. Caffrey	23	M	"	"	"	
George Witherspoon	26	M	"	"	"	
Saml. C. Denansit	23	M	"	"	"	
Eliz. "	22	M	"	"	"	
George Peck Jr.	27	M	Stone cutter	"	"	
Elizabeth " & 4 ch.	33	F		"	"	
A. Lesaundre	40	M	Merchant	France	"	Ship William. Gardiner.
A. Tosenta	23	M	"	Malanzas	Malanzas	
E. Dagger	25	M	Carpenter	U. States	"	
E. Lattimore	24	M	"	"	"	
Saml. W. Cole	23	M	"	"	"	
Theo. Nevit	25	M	"	"	"	
Nathan Edwards	35	M	Cooper	"	"	
J. Hess	26	M	Merchant	Switzerland	U. States	Brig Kanawa. Lee.
James Baker	36	M	"	U. States	"	
Thos. Watson	30	M	Shoemaker	"	"	Brig Cabbosse. Jackson.
Aaron McCartny	29	M	Carpenter	"	"	
T. Camment	29	M	Shoemaker	"	"	
J. Whitehead	38	M	Mariner	"	"	
J. P. Fogg	37	M	Merchant	"	"	
E. Lowrey	45	M	"	"	"	
J. L. Maller	40	M	"	Denmark	"	Sch. Elias Burger Densey.
Mrs. " & 3 ch.	20	F		"	"	
A. C. Barnsbeam	25	M	"	U. States	"	
Anthony Williams	22	M		"	"	
Ann Bennett	55	M ?	Lady	G. Britain	England	Sloop Jay. Page.
Thos. Cathway	24	M	Merchant	"	"	

Names of passengers	Age	Sex	Occupation	Country to which they belong	Country of which they intend becoming inhabitants	Ship or vessel with the name of the master or commander
NEW YORK Cont.						
Q. E. June 30, 1823						
G. Gray	25	M	Merchant	G. Britain	England	
Alexr. C. Kitchell	31	M	"	U. States	U. States	
C. Ross	27	M	"	"	"	
R. C. Brien	27	M	Farmer	G. Britain	"	
G. Johnston	50	M	Blacksmith	U. States	"	
D. D. Patterson	41	M	Merchant	"	"	Brig Albert. Wallach.
E. Hedding	70	M	"	"	"	Sloop Protector. Wills.
W. Kelly	22	M	"	Ireland	"	Sch. Wm. Barker. Nichols
Jno. McDormon	40	M	"	U. States	"	Brig Echo. Blanchard.
D. W. Ridgway	35	M	"	"	"	
Jno. A. Parker	23	M	"	"	"	
John Bridge	23	M	"	"	"	
Gen. D. Tucker	25	M	"	"	"	Sch. Mary Margaret
A. Bennett	20	F		"	"	Sch. Southern Trader Kelly.
F. Clark	22	M	Merchant	"	"	
C. Saloun *	33	M	Mariner	France	"	Brig Transit. Gillet.
John Young	45	M	"	U. States	"	
D. Perez	50	M	Merchant	Spain	"	Brig Packet Dougherty.
Gabriel	25	M	Mariner	"	"	
M. Rodrigues	35	M	Merchant	"	"	
J. Regulas	30	M	"	"	"	
Charlotte Baker	26	F	Lady	U. States	"	Ship William. Manus.
J. O. Callghan	40	M	Clergyman	Ireland	"	
Patrick Cowley	20	M	Labourer	"	"	
John Sullivan	26	M	"	"	"	
Mary " & ch.	20	F		"	"	
Eliza Speahan & ch.	26	F		"	"	
Jno. Baines	35	M	Shipwright	"	"	
Mary Ann Baines & 3 ch	30	F		"	"	
Jno. Higgins	28	M	Farmer	"	"	
Jeremiah "	25	M	"	"	"	
J. Kenaway	27	M	"	"	"	
Jas. Murphy	24	M	"	"	"	
M. Rierdan	20	M	"	"	"	
Mary Butler & ch.	22	F		"	"	
Ch. Ivory	58	M	Labourer	"	"	
Margt. " & 3 ch.	40	F		"	"	
Stephen Toomy & ch.	28	M	Farmer	"	"	
Margt. "	26	F		"	"	
Jno. Shuby	24	M	Butcher	"	"	
Thos. Laughlin	20	M	"	"	"	
Ellen Shuby	25	F		"	"	
Mary Hawley & ch.	40	F		"	"	
L. Mosses	34	M	Carpenter	U. States	"	Brig Planter. Pratt.

Names of passengers	Age	Sex	Occupation	Country to which they belong	Country of which they intend becoming inhabitants	Ship or vessel with the name of the master or commander
NEW YORK Cont.						
Q. E. June 30, 1823						
J. Cape	29	M	Carpenter	U. States	U. States	
J. Mexey	22	M	"	"	"	
B. De Forest	24	M	Mercht.	"	"	
Thos. West	28	M	"	"	"	
R. C. Woods	24	M		"	"	Brig Gleaner. Smith.
S. Grant	22	M	Carpenter	"	"	
Jno. Gilmore	23	M	Blacksmith	"	"	
H. Fox	26	M	Cooper	"	"	
Soloman Fox	26	M	"	"	"	
Jas. Robertson	18	M	Clerk	Scotland	"	Ship Camillus. Peck.
J. McCulloch & ch.	45	F		"	"	
Janett Hanson & ch.	30	F		"	"	
A. Williams	35	M	Merchant	England	England	Ship Florida. Matlock.
John Berry	40	M	Baker	"	"	
F. Stead	25	M	Merchant	"	U. States	Ship Jas. Cropper. Marshall.
M McGreenoch	24	M	"	"	"	
J. Davis	41	M	"	"	"	
Jas. Bird	48	M	"	"	"	
S. Black	40	M	"	Scotland	"	
P. S. Ogden	35	M	"	Canada	Canada	
C. Grant	25	M	"	"	"	
James Chamberlain	23	M	"	England	U. States	Brig Susanna. Stevens.
Joseph Smith	32	M	Farmer	"	"	
Sophia " & 4 ch.	32	F		"	"	
John Sandford	36	M	"	"	"	
Elizabeth " & 4 ch.	30	F		"	"	
P. Fanning	24	M		"	"	
John Smith	19	M		"	"	
Jno. Miller	21	M		"	"	
Jno. Hall	36	M		"	"	
George Robb	23	M	Supercargo	U. States	"	Sch. Roxana.
Michael Anderson	36	M	Mariner	"	"	
John Hitchcock	40	M	Merchant	"	"	Brig Four Sons.
E. "	35	F		"	"	
Mrs. Freeland	40	F		"	"	
Rachel Waterbury	30	F		U. States	"	Sch. Nancy. Crowell.
Francis Ludlow	30	M		"	"	
Wilford Simpson	40	M	Merchant	"	"	
Saml. Kirkpatrick	25	M	Labourer	Ireland	"	
Jeremiah Lane	15	M	"	"	"	
John Hagarty	18	M	"	"	"	
Peter Kirk	20	M	"	"	"	
Peter O'Hara	22	M	"	"	"	
Peter Tegart	24	M	"	"	"	

Names of passengers	Age	Sex	Occupation	Country to which they belong	Country of which they intend becoming inhabitants	Ship or vessel with the name of the master or commander
NEW YORK Cont.						
Q. E. June 30, 1823						
Mary Tegart & 2 ch.	26	F	Labourer	Ireland	U. States	
Christopher Coulter	25	M	"	"	"	
Wm. "	22	M	"	"	"	
Mr. Paney	28	M	Merchant	France	"	Sch. Grey Hound.
Marie "	22	M		"	"	
S. Bouviard	49	M	"	U. States	"	Sch. Robt. Burns.
Henry Wood	21	M	"	Ireland	"	
James Reid	25	M	"	"	"	
James Morrison	28	M	Morocco Dresser	"	"	
Hugh "	24	M	Coppersmith	"	"	
James Gamble	23	M	Farmer	"	"	
Jane " & 2 ch.	30	F		"	"	
Henry Lyons	36	M		"	"	
Ann Walker	66	F		G. Britain	G. Britain	Sch. Lady Hunter. Prindell.
James Hunt	54	M		"	"	
Nancy Carroll & 2 ch.	57	F		"	"	
Owen O'Neal	32	M	Cooper	"	"	
Cath. " & 2 ch.	30	F		"	"	
John Duncan	32	M	Mason	"	"	
Mary " & ch.	35	F		"	"	
Joseph Riggs	28	M	Mariner	"	"	
Bridget " & ch.	22	F		"	"	
Ann Beatry * & 3 ch.	38	F		"	"	
Joseph Hunt	41	M	Currier	"	"	
Bernard Lapham	28	M	Cooper	"	"	
Jno. McCallum	22	M	Labourer	"	"	
Dennis McCarty	21	M	"	"	"	
John Fisher	25	M	Merchant	Bermuda	"	Sloop Alpha. Algate
B. Algate	23	M	Mechanic	"	"	
A R Poole	25	M		England	"	Sch Radius. Farmington.
E. Haggerson	24	M	"	"	"	
W Brittan	31	M	Officer	St. Johns	"	
W Andrews	23	M	Mechanic	U States	"	Brig Rebecca. Parrott.
J. Brague	21	M	"	"	"	
Lambert Berdine	41	M	Merchant	Guadaloupe	"	Sch. Henry ?
Ursule " & 5 ch.	37	M	"	St. Eustatia	"	
M. Perrott	36	M	"	France	"	Sch. La Guadaloupe.
Mrs. "	23	F		"	"	
Hugh Dougherty	68	M	Farmer	Ireland	"	Sch. Gleaner. Pease.
Eliz. " & 5 ch.	64	F		"	"	
Archibald Smith	19	M	Clerk	"	"	
Alexr. Connelly	23	M	Farmer	"	"	
Nathaniel "	23	M	"	"	"	

PASSENGERS WHO ARRIVED IN THE U.S. SEPTEMBER 1821 - DECEMBER 1823

Names of passengers	Age	Sex	Occupation	Country to which they belong	Country of which they intend becoming inhabitants	Ship or vessel with the name of the master or commander
NEW YORK Cont.						
Q. E. June 30, 1823						
John Hadden	23	M	Farmer	Ireland	U. States	
Wm. Cochran	37	M	"	"	"	
Ann " & 3 ch.	35	F		"	"	
H. P. Down	24	M	Merchant	U. States	"	Brig Abeona. Lester.
S. Volin	24	M	Saddler	"	"	
R. Roveesa	26	M	Merchant	"	"	
A. Graves	54	M	Mariner	"	"	
M. Machand	23	M	Merchant	Havana	"	
Wm. Clark	30	M	"	U. States	"	Brig Delmarnock.
Eliza " & 3 ch.	20	F		"	"	
Thomas Wall	30	M	Teacher	"	"	
Jas. Rinmont	25	M	"	"	"	
Jane Lamb & child	24	F		"	"	
R. Ghiliovise	30	M	Merchant	Italy	"	Sch. Logan. Dennison.
F. Rachael	25	M	Professor	England	"	Ship Elizabeth. Smith.
J. F. Hance	36	M		"	"	
F. A. Baules	23	M	Merchant	Spain	"	
G. Franchant	35	M	"	"	"	
C. " & ch.	28	F		"	"	
J. Bourcloes * & ch.	45	M		"	"	
P. Tapart	36	M		"	"	
M. "	28	M		"	"	
L. Shannon	50	M	Mariner	U. States	"	Sch. Douglass. Brown.
M. A. De Wolfe	22	M	Gent.	"	"	Brig Alabama. Hall.
Mrs. " & ch.	20	F		"	"	
Joseph Seymore	25	M	Clerk	"	"	
J. Warwick	30	M	Merchant	"	"	
Edwd. C. Donnell	30	M	Mechanic	"	"	
Jno. R. Lattimore	29	M	Merchant	"	"	Ship Superior. Dowder.
Jas. E. Withall	24	M	"	"	"	
James Dowall	28	M	Farmer	Ireland	"	
G. Greenfield	22	M	Weaver	"	"	
John Brady	19	M	Farmer	"	"	
Hugh Stephenson	35	M	Merchant	"	"	
Mrs. "	30	F		"	"	
Jacob Harvy	25	M	"	"	"	
Jno. Taylor	25	M	"	"	"	
W. F. Laughton	20	M	"	"	"	
Barnard Duffee	23	M	Labourer	G. Britain	"	Mt. Vernon. Rawson.
Mary "	22	F		"	"	
James Gollard	30	M	Brass founder	"	"	
John Moore	29	M	"	"	"	
Wm. Maybourne	32	M	Mason	"	"	
Wm. Walboff	33	M	Farmer	"	"	

239

Names of passengers	Age	Sex	Occupation	Country to which they belong	Country of which they intend becoming inhabitants	Ship or vessel with the name of the master or commander
NEW YORK Cont.						
Q. E. June 30, 1823						
C. Steward & ch.	44	M	Confectionr.	G. Britain	U. States	
Jno. Hutchinson	20	M	Labourer	"	"	
Jas. Woods	57	M	Merchant	Ireland	"	Brig Commerce. Langden.
Jno P. Kiernan	22	M	"	"	"	
R. Gaba & child	45	F		Jamaica	"	Sloop Essex ? Rogers.
W. Linton	43	M	Farmer	England	"	Sch. Braganza.
Mrs. " & ch.	33	F		"	"	
C. Webster	23	M	Merchant	Canada	Canada	
R. Porter	30	M	Mariner	U. States	U. States	Sch. Daphne. Kohler.
P. Proctor	45	M	"	"	"	
A. Stanley	45	M	"	"	"	
M. H. Percival	45	M	Collectr. of Quebece	England	Canada	Sch. Amity. Maxwell.
J. P. Tappan	27	M	Merchant	U. States	U. States	
M. De Rheim	37	M	"	"	"	
W. E. Logan	29	M	Merchant	"	"	
Jno. Robb	32	M	"	"	"	
Jas. Walcher	28	M	"	"	"	
Wm. Benson	28	M	Farmer	England	"	
R. "	28	M	"	"	"	
Thomas Harper	27	M	"	"	"	
Joseph Durand	29	M	Storekeeper	"	"	
Martha " & 5 ch.	25	F		"	"	
J. R. Salmond	20	M	Merchant	U. States	"	Brig Mary. Noyes Jr.
Saml. "	34	M		"	"	
Jonah Tathnall	30	M	Offcr. Navy	"	"	
A. Lullins •	35	M	Merchant	"	"	
Jas. Goff	40	M	"	"	"	
Robt. W. Yates	32	M	Capt. R. Navy	England	England	Ship Cincinnatus. Sebor.
John Small	70	M	Gent.	"	"	
James "	30	M	"	"	"	
Thomas West	43	M	Farmer	"	"	
Jemima " & 6 ch.	31	F		"	"	
Mary " & 2 ch.	40	F		"	"	
Wm. "	47	M		"	"	
Edwd. "	29	M		"	"	
Chas. Brakefield	33	M		"	"	
Mrs. " & 5 ch.	31	F		"	"	
Thos. Quarf •	32	M		"	"	
Henry Brown	21	M		"	"	
Thos. "	26	M		"	"	
Benj. Wimble	30	M		"	"	
Jas. Holdgate	28	M		"	"	
Richd. Needs	32	M		"	"	

Names of passengers	Age	Sex	Occupation	Country to which they belong	Country of which they intend becoming inhabitants	Ship or vessel with the name of the master or commander
NEW YORK Cont.						
Q. E. June 30, 1823						
A. Rankin	29	M		Scotland	England	
Janett "	30	F		"	"	
James Hattie *	34	M	Farmer	England	"	
Eliz. " & 4 ch.	30	F		"	"	
Anthony Fuller	30	M		"	"	
Esther " & 4 ch.	26	F		"	"	
Richd. "	32	M		"	"	
Mary " & 5 ch.	26	F		"	"	
Domil Lynch	28	M		Ireland	"	
Robt. Swan	34	M	Trader	Canada	"	Sch. Hunter. Sears.
Sarah "	33	F		"	"	
M. Benbridge	23	M	Shoemaker	"	"	
Peter Henderson	71	M		G. Britain	"	Ship Leeds. Stodart.
M. J. Tobias	43	M	Merchant	"	"	
N. Bethune	34	M	"	"	"	
Wm. Peddie	34	M	"	"	"	
G. B. Hutchins	31	M	Lieut. R.Nvy.	G. Britain	U. States	
H. Heycock	21	M	Merchant	"	"	
A. McGull	21	M	"	"	"	
J. H. Post	34	M	Mariner	U. States	"	
E. Hotchkiss	45	M	Merchant	"	"	Brig Shepherdess. Storer.
R. Randall	30	M	"	"	"	
S. Rentz	24	M	Baker	Russia	"	
J. Buttman	20	M	"	Switzerland	"	
John Warnock	24	M	Clergyman	Ireland	"	Alexr. Mansfield. Bunch.
Jane "	24	F		"	"	
Alexr. Stuart	20	M	Merchant	"	"	
Jno. McDowell	24	M	Labourer	"	"	
Sarah "	22	F		"	"	
John Wallace	25	M	Clergyman	"	"	
Cornelius Reilley	17	M	Farmer	"	"	
Jno. Ward	18	M	"	"	"	
Stewart Wharton	30	M	Weaver	"	"	
Edwd. Sweeny	20	M	"	"	"	
Jas. McKean	20	M	"	"	"	
Archibald Mitchell	25	M	Cooper	"	"	
Jas. McGifford	20	M	Farmer	"	"	
Edwd. Hazlton	33	M	Weaver	"	"	
Moses Wilson	30	M	Tanner	"	"	
Jas. Campbell	20	M	Weaver	"	"	
Albert Sanders	25	M	Mariner	U. States	"	Brig Cicero. Johnston.
Fred. Sawyer	20	M	"	"	"	
Charles Murich	30	M	"	"	"	Brig Nancy. Matthews.
Wm. Waddington	43	M	Farmer	England	"	Ship Magnet. Mount.

Names of passengers	Age	Sex	Occupation	Country to which they belong	Country of which they intend becoming inhabitants	Ship or vessel with the name of the master or commander
NEW YORK Cont.						
Q. E. June 30, 1823						
Wm. D. Slater	20	M	Clerk	England	U. States	
Jno. Thomas	23	M	Farmer	"	"	
Cath. "	22	F		"	"	
R. Jones	22	M	"	"	"	
C. "	26	F		"	"	
W. Prichard	24	M	"	"	"	
M. Williams	22	M	Shoemaker	"	"	
H. Allen	32	M		Ireland	"	
Ann " & 7 ch.	30	F		"	"	
Henry Lee/Lea	20	M		"	"	
W. W. Chester	35	M	Merchant	U. States	"	Ship Wm. Thompson.
Mrs. "	24	F		"	"	
G. S. Fox	26	M	Merchant	"	"	
Alfred Brooks	21	M	"	"	"	
Wm. Lynch	50	M	Merchant	"	"	
Andw. Mitchell	23	M	"	"	"	
J. Robinson	29	M	Secy. to Leg. to Spain	"	"	
John Milderburger	28	M	Merchant	"	"	Sloop Charles. Coffin.
Danl. Boucouse	27	M	"	"	"	Brig Peruvian. Russell.
Peter D. Baithe	19	M	Student	"	"	
J. Abeille	25	M	Doctor	France	"	Sch. Union. Titcombe.
Jno. A "	23	M	Merchant	"	"	
W. Stewart	30	M		Ireland	"	Sch. Jno. Dickinson.
James & child	50	M		"	"	
Andw. Simpson	24	M		U. States	"	
Robt. "	24	M		"	"	
M. Lalehise •	32	M	Priest	France	"	Brig Monroe. Handly.
Jno. Baptiste	22	M		Spain	"	
M. Puget	32	M	Merchant	"	"	
G. S. Morgan	21	M	"	"	"	
T. Valdore	35	M	"	"	"	Sch. Col. Geo. Armstead.
G. Jacobus	27	M	"	U. States	"	Sch. Nile. Aldrich.
C. F. Russoo •	22	M	"	"	"	
Robt. Hagan	38	M	"	"	"	Sch. Atilla. Adams.
Nathanl. Dill	38	M	Mariner	"	"	Brig Anna. Daniels.
Manuel Jaques	40	M	Merchant	Spain	Spain	Brig Margt. Harwood.
James Hill	29	M	"	Scotland	U. States	Ship Favourite. Bears.
E. Chappell	30	M	"	"	"	
John S. Ellery	45	M	"	U. States	"	Ship Maria. Fowler.
Charles E. Pierson	33	M	Physician	"	"	
Ann M. " & 2 ch.	29	F		"	"	
Mary E. Hibberd	22	F		"	"	
Margt. Colvert	21	M		"	"	

PASSENGERS WHO ARRIVED IN THE U.S. SEPTEMBER 1821 - DECEMBER 1823

Names of passengers	Age	Sex	Occupation	Country to which they belong	Country of which they intend becoming inhabitants	Ship or vessel with the name of the master or commander
NEW YORK Cont.						
Q. E. June 30, 1823						
Wm. Blake	38	M	Cloth dresser	England	U. States	
Sarah " & 5 ch.	32	F		"	"	
Saml. Whiting	46	M	Bricklayer	"	"	
Sarah " & 6 ch.	42	F		"	"	
Michael Aschroft	35	M	Innkeeper	"	"	
Sarah "	30	F		"	"	
John Britten	28	M	Cloth dresser	"	"	
Sarah "	26	F		"	"	
Betsey Band & 4 ch.	26	F		"	"	
James Abraham	47	M	Carpenter	"	"	
Jacob Barling	32	M	Labourer	"	"	
James "	29	M	"	"	"	
Stephen "	25	M	"	"	"	
Jno. Stretten	47	M	"	"	"	
Wm. Dorson	25	M	"	"	"	
Edmund Mortimer	18	M	Blacksmith	"	"	
Jno. Franks	40	M	Merchant	U. States	"	
Joseph Nash	28	M	Cloth dresser	England	"	
John Gibbs	29	M	Dyer	"	"	
Luke Wilks	31	M	Tailor	"	"	
Francis Cranin *	28	M	Tanner	Ireland	"	
John Sharpe	65	M	Gent.	England	England	Ship Manhattan.
Jane "	66	M		"	"	
Richd. Pettit	35	M	Merchant	"	"	
Elizabeth "	38	F		"	"	
John Saddler	51	M		Ireland	"	
Eliz. "	58	F		"	"	
T. B. Wraggs	23	M	Merchant	England	"	
Joseph Brown	23	M	"	"	"	
Robt. Phillips	34	M	"	"	"	
Mary Brown & 3 ch.	35	F		"	"	
Wm. F. Partridge	52	M	Grocer	"	"	Ship Euphrates. Sprague
Diana " & 2 ch.	32	F		"	"	
Wm. Blanchall	58	M	Farmer	"	"	
Thos. "	53	M		"	"	
Mary " & 3 ch.	55	F		"	"	
John Thomas	36	M	Farmer	"	"	
Jacob Davis	29	M	"	"	"	
Mary " & 3 ch.	25	F		"	"	
Charles Jones	42	M	Shoemaker	"	"	
John "	20	M	Surgeon	"	"	
Matthew Coad *	55	M	Merchant	Ireland	"	
Benj. Davis	21	M	Shoemaker	"	"	
Edwd. White	26	M	Farmer	"	"	Brig L. M. Pelham. Hatch.

Names of passengers	Age	Sex	Occupation	Country to which they belong	Country of which they intend becoming inhabitants	Ship or vessel with the name of the master or commander
NEW YORK Cont.						
Q. E. June 30, 1823						
Bridget White & 7 ch.	36	F		Ireland	England	
Danl. Madegon	27	M	Farmer	"	"	
P. Donnelson	30	M		"	"	
H. " & 2 ch.	30	M		"	"	
Andw. McMahon	28	M		"	"	
Mary " & ch.	29	F		"	"	
James Hatch	30	M		"	"	
Mary " & 2 ch.	30	F		"	"	
Francis Murphy	27	M		"	"	
Wm. Doherty	21	M		"	"	
Bridget Powell & 3 ch.	30	F		"	"	
Thos. Pollock & 2 ch.	42	M	Farmer	"	"	Ship Friends. Choates.
Wm. Boyd	22	M	"	"	"	
A. Frasier	43	M	Labourer	Scotland	"	
Cath. " & child	32	F		"	"	
David McArthur	23	M	Farmer	"	"	
John Clack	26	M		"	"	
Agnes " & ch.	27	F		"	"	
Wm. Davis	22	M		"	"	
David Biset *	24	M		"	"	
David Bremen	22	M	Shoemaker	?	?	
C. Ferguson & child	28	F		Ireland	U. States	
John Swaine	40	M	Carpenter	Scotland	"	
R. Kier	26	M	Merchant	"	"	
Margt. Robinson & 3 ch.	42	F		"	"	
Wm. Frazier	45	M	Labourer	"	"	
Eliz. " & 4 ch.	45	F		"	"	
George Beaton	24	M	Farmer	"	"	
Wm. Mitchell	37	M	"	"	"	
M. A. Babcock	19	M	Merchant	U. States	"	Ship Chase. Baxter.
J. C. "	24	M	"	"	"	
John Gill	35	M	Mechanic	Ireland	"	
M. McKinsley	46	M	Merchant	U. States	"	Brig Radius. Granger.
J. Riley	26	M	"	"	"	
F. Vassieur	25	M	"	Cuba	"	
C. Marshall	32	M	Clergyman	U. States	"	Sch. Rolla. Vaughan.
George Griswold	22	M	Student	"	"	
P. Sidney	35	M	Merchant	"	"	Brig John. Barber.
C. Tuarigue *	37	M	"	"	"	
J. Davis & ch.	35	F		"	"	
M. Welch & ch.	48	F		Ireland	"	Ship Ganges. Tompkinson.
J. O. Cross	27	M	Merchant	England	"	N. Y. Packet. Stone.
L. Hopkins	26	M	Farmer	"		
E Thomas	56	M	"	"		

Names of passengers	Age	Sex	Occupation	Country to which they belong	Country of which they intend becoming inhabitants	Ship or vessel with the name of the master or commander
NEW YORK Cont.						
Q. E. June 30, 1823						
Wm Price	34	M	Carpenter	England		
Thos. Lyne	17	M	Mariner	"		
Richd Taughem	20	M	Merchant	U States	U. States	
A Commeson	29	M	Farmer	England	"	
Z. Maclachlan	22	M	Merchant	U. States	"	Sch James. De Boot.
M Smith	45	M	"	"	"	Sch. Ploughboy. De Manlove.
Geo. W. Sturgis	30	M	"	"	"	Ship Huntress. Lavender.
C. H Gordon	26	M	"	"	"	
J. B. Dufan	39	M	"	"	"	Brig New Packet Chase.
C. Howell	25	M	"	"	"	
P. Parmanstau *	23	M	"	France	"	
A. Bertram	28	M	"	"	"	
Manuel Garcie	16	M		Vera Cruz	"	
J. Cortes	19	M		Havana	"	
Richd Birnee	25	M	Merchant	Ireland	"	Sch. Dublin Packet. Newccmb.
Jno. H. Toluson	26	M	Farmer	"	"	
B. Reilley & 2 ch	46	F	Spinster	"	"	
Andw. Walsh	23	M		"	"	
Philip Kennedy	22	M	Farmer	"	"	
James Bryan	20	M	"	"	"	
P. Scarlet	23	F		"	"	
James Fay	24	M	Farmer	"	"	
James Stewart	28	M	Merchant	"	"	
Joseph O'Neil	22	M	Labourer	"	"	
Wm. Martin	21	M	Merchant	"	"	
Jno. Reilly	24	M	"	"	"	
Danl. Donahue	46	M	"	"	"	
Nancy "	20	F		"	"	
Mary "	23	F		"	"	
P Masther	23	M	Farmer	"	"	
Richd. Barney	25	M	Tailor	"	"	
Wm. Gracie	35	M	Merchant	U. States	"	Ship Lewis Skiddy.
Eugene McCarthy	39	M	"	France	"	
Luke Pischin	34	M	"	"	"	
George Alanx	45	M	"	"	"	
H. Longduplan	29	M	"	"	"	
Wm Munden	31	M	Shoemaker	England	"	
Mrs. " & 5 ch.	30	F		"	"	
George Duff	32	M	Merchant	"	"	
Jos. Blanden	52	M	Carpenter	"	"	
Walter Bates	40	M	Merchant	St. Johns	St. Johns	Sch. Nancy. Crowell.
Gilbert M. Drake	23	M	"	"	"	
Wm. F. Williams	28	M	"	"	"	
Jane Patterson	35	F		"	"	

Names of passengers	Age	Sex	Occupation	Country to which they belong	Country of which they intend becoming inhabitants	Ship or vessel with the name of the master or commander
NEW YORK Cont.						
Q. E. June 30, 1823						
Ann M. Smith	35	F		St. Johns	St. Johns	
John Hasting	24	M	Merchant	"	"	
Jacob Wilson	22	M	Labourer	Ireland	(U. States)	
J. Haschell	25	M	"	"	"	
Jno. Kilchrist	24	M	"	"	"	
James Hallett	24	M	"	"	"	
Mary "	25	F		"	"	
Thos. Mackafee	25	M	Labourer	"	"	
Lydia "	22	F		"	"	
Mary Swaney & 2 ch.	25	F		"	"	
Thos. Huxley	38	M	B. Army	England	"	Ship Corinthian. Davis.
Jno. Nesbitt	24	M	Merchant	"	"	
Jno. Brown	48	M	Trader	"	"	
James Turnbull	21	M	Farmer	"	"	
Wm. Kinnett	21	M	Draper	"	"	
Jno. B. Pinot	32	M	Merchant	France	"	Sch. Ann Eliza Jane. Abeille.
Samuel Langshaw	35	M	"	England	"	
James Turner	25	M	Baker	"	"	
C. Delfoza	45	M	Merchant	U. States	"	Ship Areosta. Haines.
G. J. Gilburn	25	M				Sch. Ice Plant. Bunker.
Robt. Duncan & child	44	M	"	G. Britain	G. Britain	Sch. Endeavour. Kemp.
W. J. Marshall	25	M	Merchant	Barbadoes	Barbadoes	Brig Wm. & Nancy. Hardy.
W. Tate	42	M	Planter	"	"	
Mr. Tappan	40	M	"	"	"	
M. Berbeck	50	M	"	"	"	
M. Bowers	35	M	"	"	"	
M. Martindate	37	M	"	"	"	
M. Boynest & 3 ch. *	40	M	Planter	Guadaloupe	Guadaloupe	Brig Orono. Gordon.
M. Cellivan	30	F		U. States	U. States	
Jno. Forsyth	40	M	Envoy U.S. to Spain	"	"	Sch. Othello. Lambert.
Mary " & 5 ch.	35	F		"	"	
A. Toulelot *	40	M	Merchant	France	"	
Dilbos	20	M	"	"	"	
W. Rodrique	24	M	"	"	"	
Jno. Pignan	40	M	"	"	"	
W. Eayrs	34	M	"	U. States	"	Sch. Hope. Clark.
Mary Clark	24	F		"	"	
C. Desmousins	30	M		France	France	Sch. Hope Return. Downes
G. Actonis *	45	M		Hayti	Hayti	
W. Driver	25	M	Mariner	England	U. States	Brig Edwd. D. Douglass. Hallet.
A. Goure	25	M	Merchant	Spain	"	Brig Pocahontas. Cooke.
James Sindon	28	M	"	"	"	
P. M. Pedro	24	M	"	"	"	

Names of passengers	Age	Sex	Occupation	Country to which they belong	Country of which they intend becoming inhabitants	Ship or vessel with the name of the master or commander
NEW YORK Cont.						
Q. E. June 30, 1823						
F. Oasques	40	M	Merchant	Spain	U. States	
G. Smith	25	M	"	"	"	
T. Martiner * & ch.	49	M	"	"	"	
S. Brookes	19	M	Clerk	England	"	Sch. Louisa Matilda. Stony.
W. Johnston	45	M	Farmer	"	"	
J. Robinson	35	M	Merchant	U. States	"	Sch. Eliza Barker. Alley.
F. Harris	65	M	Gent.	England	"	British Brig Mt. Vernon. Fulford.
F. " Jr.	27	M	"	"	"	
Sarah Ann Harris	32	F		"	"	
Betsey Loch *	23	F		"	"	
John "	29	M		"	"	
David Griffith	24	M	Farmer	Wales	"	
Wm. Jenkins	40	M	"	"	"	
Catharine "	50	F		"	"	
S. Peters	40	M	"	"	"	
Edwd. Griffith	35	M	"	"	"	
Thos. Brown	24	M	"	"	"	
Eliz. Kingdom & ch.	29	F		"	"	
Wm. "	29	M		"	"	
Henry Read	40	M	Joiner	"	"	
Wm. Malbone	24	M	Gent.	"	"	
Elizabeth "	24	F		"	"	
Henry Davis & ch.	42	M	Mechanic	England	"	Ship Criterion. Day.
F. Dederick & ch.	32	M	Farmer	"	"	
G. Henry	35	M	Merchant	"	"	Brig Rover. Lindsay.
A. Gladen	30	M	"	Martinique	"	
S. Gurand	19	M	"	S. Domingo	"	
James Rangely	50	M	"	England	"	Ship Jno. Wells. Harris.
Mary " & 5 ch.	40	F		"	"	
Wm. Strang	20	M	"	Scotland	"	
Joseph Lindsay	17	M	"	England	"	
P. J. Elmash	42	M	Farmer	"	"	
Thos. Cole	28	M	"	"	"	
Jane " & 2 ch.	27	F		"	"	
Nathan Smith	43	M	Currier	"	"	
Ann "	26	F		"	"	
Edwd. Pooley	40	M	Farmer	"	"	
Maria " & 5 ch.	35	F		"	"	
Wm. Garrett Jr.	23	M	Mechanic	U. States	"	
Aaron James	29	M	Merchant	Ireland	"	Ship Concordia. Bastly.
Wm. Johnson	38	M		"	"	
Samuel Wadle	22	M		"	"	
B. McNally	22	M	Labourer	"	"	
Wm. Crossley	19	M	Weaver	"	"	

NEW YORK Cont.
Q. E. June 30, 1823

Names of passengers	Age	Sex	Occupation	Country to which they belong	Country of which they intend becoming inhabitants	Ship or vessel with the name of the master or commander
Bernard Largy	29	M	Weaver	Ireland	U. States	
Mary " & 2 ch.	30	F		"	"	
Agnes Rutland	22	F		"	"	
Betsey Johnson	20	M		"	"	
John Caldwell	24	M	Farmer	"	"	
John Rush	20	M	Weaver	"	"	
Mary Duffee & 2 ch.	30	F		"	"	
Ann McLaughlin	25	F	Spinster	"	"	
Jno. Hood	22	M	Merchant	"	"	
John Delsee	52	M	Carpenter	"	"	
James Campbell	29	M	"	"	"	
Charles A. Dale	37	M	Gent.	U. States	"	Brig Day. Boree.
Mrs. " & 3 ch.	35	F		"	"	
G. Marcello	25	M	Tutor	Italy	"	
Josiah Lovett	35	M	Ship master	U. States	"	
S. E. de Punoy & 6 ch.	36	F		S. America	"	Sch. Eclipse. Hathaway.
M. Echesima	39	F		"	"	
J. V. Echezima	26	M	Merchant	"	"	
Christopher Hughes	36	M	Ch. Affrs. Sweden	U. States	"	Ship Jno. Cropper. Marshall.
Wm. Thornton	33	M	Farmer	England	"	
Thomas Ward	24	M	Mechanic	"	"	
J. Cotton & son	51	M	Clerk	"	"	
John Connell	40	M	Merchant	U States	U. States	Sch Marmion Hawkins.
Rachel "	36	F		"	"	
Eliza Lorondon & ch	40	F		"	"	
Sarah Milne & 2 ch.	40	F		"	"	
Wm. Orme	23	M	Merchant	"	"	
James Robbins	27	M	"	"	"	
Wm. "	21	M	"	"	"	
C Rouinage *	40	M	"	"	"	
M Desjardins & 2 ch	40	F		France	"	
James Kelly	30	M	Merchant	G. Britain	"	Sloop Sarah's Delight Fisher
Jno. Fisher	40	M	"	"	"	
S. Nicholson	24	M	"	Ireland	"	Sch. Xenophon. Hillman.
T. Moore	25	M	Tanner	"	"	
Clarissa Moore	18	F		"	"	
Andw. Armstrong	32	M	Farmer	"	"	
M. C. Wood	18	M	"	"	"	
Asa Gordell	34	M	Mechanic	U. States	"	Sloop Stranger. Rogers.
John Brown	36	M	Ship master	"	"	Sch. Little Wm. Evans.
Mrs. "	30	F		"	"	
Jacob Ball	35	M	"	"	"	
Robt. Simpson	25	M	Merchant	"	"	

Names of passengers	Age	Sex	Occupation	Country to which they belong	Country of which they intend becoming inhabitants	Ship or vessel with the name of the master or commander
NEW YORK Cont. Q. E. June 30, 1823						
John Cryder	22	M	Merchant	U. States	U. States	
Robt. Wilson	30	M	Farmer	England	"	Brig Chas. Hamilton. Kendall.
David Miller	35	M	Baker	Scotland	"	Sch. Sally. Liscombe.
Rufus Jordan	21	M	Farmer	U. States	"	
H. Woolbridge	27	M	Stone cutter	Hayti	"	Sch. Curlew. Stenman.
C. Bale	27	M	Merchant	"	"	
G. G. House	35	M	"	"	"	
J. Morance	50	M	"	"	"	
Thos. Lewis	30	M	"	"	"	
B. Fowler	24	M	"	England	"	Brig Wilton. Herring.
R. Tapley	28	M	Farmer	N. Brunswick	Canada	Ship Susan Morton. Sutton.
H. " & 2 ch.	22	F		"	"	
Alexr. Campbell & 3 ch.	25	M		"	"	
John "	22	M		"	"	
Nathanl. "	50	M		"	"	
D. Ernesto	34	M	Officer	Portugal	Portugal	Sch. Diana. Mott.
D. Cardazo	43	M	"	"	"	
C. F. Plump *	22	M	Merchant	Germany	U. States	Brig Sophia.
Jno. Badge	30	M	Farmer	G. Britain	U. Canada	Brig Horsely Hill. Hunter.
Margt. "	20	F		"	"	
Geo. Avery	28	M	Farmer	"	U. States	Sch. William. Moffat.
Wm. Rowland	25	M	Carpenter	"	"	
Thos. Davis	26	M	Currier	"	"	
Jno. "	24	M	"	"	"	
E. Morgan	26	M	Carpenter	England	"	
Charles E. Wilson & ch	24	M	Planter	U. States	"	Brig Prize. Talbot.
Jas. Brown	20	M	Cooper	"	"	
Wm. F. Carwood Jr.	28	M	Merchant	G. Britain	Canada	Sch. Canada. Macy.
Stephen Hills	51	M	Architect	U. States	U. States	
Elizabeth "	29	F		"	"	
Jno. Nielson	47	M	Merchant	"	"	
P. McGill	32	M	"	G. Britain	Canada	
Duncan Kennedy	38	M	"	U. States	U. States	
Horace Cunningham	26	M	"	"	"	
Joseph Cecil Jr.	27	M		G. Britain	G. Britain	
H. Blood & ch.	26	F		"	"	
Wm. Atkinson	25	M	"	"	"	
Jno. Lawrence	36	M		"	"	
Jno. Robinson	31	M		"	"	
E. " & ch.	29	F		"	"	
Jas. Clapham	49	M	Merchant	"	"	
D. M. Bunker	24	M	Mariner	U. States	U. States	Ship Indian Chief. Humphrey.
Wm. King	23	M	Goldsmith	Ireland	"	

Names of passengers	Age	Sex	Occupation	Country to which they belong	Country of which they intend becoming inhabitants	Ship or vessel with the name of the master or commander
NEW YORK Cont.						
Q. E. June 30, 1823						
Susanna King & ch.	25	F		Ireland	U. States	
Thos. Covenales & ch.	54	M	Farmer	England	"	
John Peacock	32	M	Tailor	"	"	
Eliz. " & 4 ch.	30	F		"	"	
John Fisher	33	M	Farmer	"	"	
Anne " & 3 ch.	27	F		"	"	
R. Heprustall •	21	M	Currier	"	"	
James Welch	27	M	Tailor	Ireland	"	
Jane "	25	F		"	"	
Jno. Robinson	32	M	Butcher	England	"	
Betsey "	20	F		"	"	
Wm. Moffat	23	M	Weaver	"	"	
Margt. "	32	F		"	"	
Jas. Graham	23	M	Reedmaker	Ireland	"	
Ann " & ch.	23	F		"	"	
Thos. Peacock	30	M	Farmer	England	"	
Ann. " & ch.	36	F		"	"	
Thomas Bumstead	19	M	"	"	"	
Mary " & 4 ch.	47	F		"	"	
Thos. Allen	33	M	"	"	"	
Wm. Williams	21	M	"	"	"	
James Thomas	41	M	Coal miner	Wales	"	
Richd. Davis	59	M	Hairdresser	England	"	
Thos. Owens	24	M	Labourer	"	"	
Peter "	22	M	"	"	"	
Christopher Salmon	21	M	Carpenter	"	"	
Thos. Monkman	23	M	Farmer	England	"	
Thos. Jennings	65	M	Gardner	Ireland	"	
John Costar	29	M	Smith	"	"	
Peter Cosgred	24	M	Labourer	"	"	
Edwd. Adams	40	M	"	"	"	
Wm. Brown	19	M	Farmer	"	"	
Jno. Patterson	23	M	Soap boiler	"	"	
Jno. Kelly	24	M	Labourer	"	"	
P. Egan	24	M	"	"	"	
Pat. Roche	28	M	"	"	"	
Jno. Graham	30	M	"	"	"	
Jno. Divan	24	M	"	"	"	
J. O'Brien	27	M	"	"	"	
B. Archpole	24	M	Coal miner	Wales	"	
Simon Jones	24	M	Farmer	Scotland	"	
Simon Baxter	19	M		Poland	"	
E. Herschel	19	M	Instrmt.mkr.	"	"	
J. Herman	28	M	Farmer	Russia	"	

Names of passengers	Age	Sex	Occupation	Country to which they belong	Country of which they intend becoming inhabitants	Ship or vessel with the name of the master or commander
NEW YORK Cont.						
Q. E. June 30, 1823						
Wm. Robinson	26	M	Labourer	England	U. States	
Jas. McMan	22	M	Stone cutter	Scotland	"	
James Loughlin	31	M	Shoemaker	Ireland	"	
Thomas Briggs	30	M	Labourer	England	"	
George Kimball	35	M	Merchant	U. States	"	Sch. Wonomtogus. Hill.
Mrs. " & ch.	36	F	"	"	"	
N. Janett	30	M	"	"	"	
Francis Penniston	35	M	"	Bermuda	"	
E. Meade	32	M	"	"	"	
W. W. Yardley	21	M	"	U. States	"	
Seth Hall	28	M	Mariner	"	"	
Jno. Nonan	30	M	"	"	"	
Charles Groves	30	M	"	"	"	
A. Sayers	28	M	Merchant	"	"	
M. J. Hall	22	M	"	"	"	Brig Caroline. Midlen.
M. F. Julien	59	M	"	"	"	
R. Gonzales	22	M	"	Spain	"	
C. Harris	24	M	Ship master	U. States	"	
D. Coudry	28	M	Mariner	"	"	
B. C. Clark	28	M	Merchant	"	"	
M. Thompson	34	M	"	"	"	Sch. Romeo. Barclay.
Mrs. " & 2 ch.	25	F	"	"	"	
Thos. Owen	22	M	Merchant	"	"	
J. P. Skinner	22	M	Farmer	"	"	
John Adams	22	M	Clerk	"	"	Brig Hippomanes. Bourne.
John Salagar	48	M	Merchant	Spain	"	
John Buchford	22	M	Mariner	U. States	"	Sch. Galatea. Goldthwaite.
S. Chappell	22	M	Merchant	"	"	
A. Macross	19	M	"	Spain	Spain	
A. McMahon	35	M	"	"		
Jos. Posancas	32	M	"	Cuba	Spain	
Antonio Albindo	34	M	"	"	"	
M. Martin & 6 ch.	42	F		Ireland	U. States	Sch Constitution Stanley.
Phillip Robins	48	M		U. States	"	Brig Ann Elizabeth. Hamilton.
Wm. F. Hodge	28	M	"	"	"	
Joseph B. Nones	28	M		"	"	
C. Julian	26	M		France	France	
Albert Gallatin	60	M	Ambassador	U. States	U. States	Sch. Montano. Smith.
Mary "	50	F		"	"	
Francis "	18	F		"	"	
James "	26	M	Merchant	"	"	
J. M. Meerst	39	M	"	Brussels	"	
Wm. R. Smith	27	M	"	U. States	"	
P. L. Passavant	46	M	"	"	"	

Names of passengers	Age	Sex	Occupation	Country to which they belong	Country of which they intend becoming inhabitants	Ship or vessel with the name of the master or commander
NEW YORK Cont.						
Q. E. June 30, 1823						
F. Magnus	37	M	Merchant	U. States	U. States	
J. Dryfaus	32	M	"	France	"	
Edwd. F. Dupenchal	31	M	Mechanic	"	"	
Peter L. Veque	23	M	"	"	"	
Wm. B. Vanderwoorst	18	M	Merchant	U. States	"	
Mary Legal & ch.	60	F		France	"	
Danl. H. Hall	24	M	Baker	U. States	"	
Jno. Byrne	69	M	Clergyman	G. Britain	"	Ship London. Candler.
Eliza. Sharp	26	F		"	"	
W. Chipman	35	M		"	"	
Mrs. "	30	F		"	"	
L. Ashburn & 4 ch.	49	M		"	"	
Thos. Stanton	30	M		"	"	
Martha "	22	F		"	"	
Geo. Tingle	33	M	Merchant	"	"	
Mary "	31	F		"	"	
Geo. Dawell	28	M	Merchant	"	"	
Eliza "	25	F		"	"	
G. S. Gilfilbin	25	M	Merchant	"	"	
W. Willis	55	M		U. States	"	
Wm. McKinstry	60	M	Clergyman	"	"	
Geo. Barclay	32	M	Merchant	"	"	
Matilda "	30	F		"	"	
Wm. Thompson	30	M	"	G. Britain	"	
Geo. Wildon	48	M	"	"	"	
Cath " & ch.	30	F		"	"	
Thos. G. Loddington	27	M	Merchant	G. Britain	"	
Mary Ellen & 3 ch.	24	F		"	"	
Francis Campbell	32	M	Auctioneer	"	"	
James Page	25	M	Farmer	"	"	
David Hughes	24	M	"	"	"	
W. R. Man	28	M	Bricklayer	"	"	
A. Nunn	20	M		"	"	
Wm. French	25	M	Miller	"	"	
Eliza " & ch.	22	F		"	"	
Jas. Jennings	30	M	Farmer	"	"	
Ann " & 5 ch.	25	F		"	"	
Wm. Howe	30	M		"	"	
H. Hill	27	M		"	"	
Ann "	25	F		"	"	
J. Wheeler	30	M		"	"	
James Otway & 5 ch.	40	M		"	"	
Wm. "	27	M		"	"	
Thos. Ranger	25	M		"	"	

Names of passengers	Age	Sex	Occupation	Country to which they belong	Country of which they intend becoming inhabitants	Ship or vessel with the name of the master or commander
NEW YORK Cont.						
Q. E. June 30, 1823						
F. Davis	35	M		G. Britain	U. States	
Jane " & 7 ch.	32	F		"	"	
Philip Harns	25	M	Farmer	"	"	
Edwd. Wilson	44	M	"	"	"	
Mary " & 3 ch.	40	F		"	"	
Stephen Hicks	25	M		"	"	
Mrs. Franks & 2 ch.	28	F		"	"	
Mrs. Moore	25	F		"	"	
Benj. Hall	26	M		"	"	
S. S. Langworthy	22	M	Merchant	U. States	"	Brig Genl. Jackson. Vermilge.
Wm. Bryden	38	M	"	Jamaica	Jamaica	Sloop Active. Jones.
Wm. J. Ramage	31	M	Physician	U States	U. States	
J. Hallowell	25	M	Lawyer	"	"	
James Drake	57	M	Merchant	Spain	Cuba	Brig Jas. Barron. Fisher.
Mrs. " & 5 ch.	39	F		"	"	
Jno. Cardenas	38	M	"	"	"	
J. C. Tennant	23	M	"	"	"	
C. Hayes	23	M	"	U. States	U. States	
P. Lewis	38	M		"	"	
M. D. Favignon & 2 ch.	32	F		France	"	Sch. Careassina. Robinson.
H. Patterson	25	M	Merchant	U. States	"	
C. Beguet	24	M	"	"	"	
P. Arlez & ch.	27	M	"	"	"	
Jno. G. Bailey	24	M	"	"	"	Brig Velocipede. Kirtland.
D. Marcucia	22	M	"	France	"	
Lewis Renard	35	M	"	"	"	
F Adams	30	M	"	U. States	"	Sch. Blue Eyed Mary.
W. W. Saltenstall	28	M	"	"	"	
D. Reverall	35	M	"	Cuba	Cuba	
Dan. F. Debille & ch.	40	M	"	"	"	
James Robson	46	M	Clergyman	Halifax	Halifax	Sch. Hope & Hester.
Maria McDonald	25	F		U. States	U. States	
Geo. C. Gary	25	M		"	"	Ship Favourite. Bunker.
W. Halkworth	25	F		"	"	
Domingo Piera	40	M	Merchant	Portugal	"	Sch. Richard. Harvey.
J. Coltan	32	M	Printer	U. States	"	
Thos. Foote	23	M	Mason	"	"	
B. D. Nelson	34	M	Merchant	G. Britain	"	Brig Aginona. Gay.
Jos. Dodson	43	M	Mariner	U. States	"	
Saml. Nichols	40	M	Merchant	St. John	"	Sch. Nancy. Crowell.
Sarah Gregory	48	F		"	"	
Samuel Peters	32	M	"	"	"	
Wm. B. Cox	22	M	"	"	"	
E. Peacock & 4 ch.	35	F		Ireland	"	

Names of passengers	Age	Sex	Occupation	Country to which they belong	Country of which they intend becoming inhabitants	Ship or vessel with the name of the master or commander
NEW YORK Cont. **Q. E. June 30, 1823**						
Chas. Canel	25	M	Labourer	Ireland	U. States	
A. Fry & child	30	F		"	"	
Pat. McKinter	22	M	"	"	"	
A. Cocker	25	M	"	"	"	
Geo. Morrow	24	M	"	"	"	
Jane Wilson & ch.	28	F		"	"	
Eliza Given & 2 ch.	30	F		"	"	
Dennis Duffee	24	M		"	"	
James Strong	28	M		"	"	
Mary Darety & 3 ch.	28	F		"	"	
Mrs. Fulford & 2 ch.	33	F		G Britain	"	
Abraham Holmes	30	M	Mariner	"	"	
Sidney "	20	F		"	"	
H. Graham	50	M	Grocer	Ireland	"	Ship Susquehanna. Stewart.
Cath. "	55	F		"	"	
R. Patterson	28	M	Merchant	"	"	
Margt. " & 3 ch.	28	F		"	"	
B. Caraway	30	M	"	"	"	
Andw. McGowan	25	M	Labourer	"	"	
Jas. Hyon *	24	M	"	"	"	
Jno. Laughlem	24	M	"	"	"	
P. Kilkenny	22	M	"	"	"	
Margt. Fersian & 4 ch.	37	F		"	"	
Sarah McMilly & 3 ch.	30	F		"	"	
W Bergiven/Bergwen	41	M	Merchant	"	"	
F. Barnard	50	M	"	"	"	
Samuel Grant	21	M	Clerk	Scotland	Canada	Sch. Honduras Packet.
W. S. Cooper/Coopes	40	M	Merchant	U. States	U. States	Sch. Bengal. Conyngham.
W. H. Whitehead	35	M	"	"	"	
C. Robert & ch.	32	F		Holland	"	Brig Martha. Bernard.
Jno. Reichart	41	M	Farmer	U. States	"	
Geo. L. Baker	29	M	"	"	"	
Wm. Killinger	23	M	Carpenter	Germany	"	
G. Burkle	30	M	Farmer	"	"	
Jacob Stark	28	M	"	"	"	
Adam Bergdolf	27	M	Tailor	"	"	
Danl. Kaffer	36	M	Shoemaker	U. States	"	
Jacob Spismen	35	M	Baker	Germany	"	
Philip Gordon	29	M		"	"	
H. Bulenfelt	35	M		"	"	
Tobias Smith	53	M	Blacksmith	"	"	
Cath. " & 8 ch.	44	F		"	"	
Jacob Schnieder	36	M	Carpenter	"	"	
Magdelina " & 4 ch.	52	F		"	"	

Names of passengers	Age	Sex	Occupation	Country to which they belong	Country of which they intend becoming inhabitants	Ship or vessel with the name of the master or commander
KENNEBUNK Q. E. June 30, 1823						
T. Marais	34	M	Merchant	France	U. States	Brig Sabat. Pope.
Joseph Claude	40	M	"	"	"	
PORTLAND Q. E. June 30, 1823						
Don L. Marois	20	M	Merchant	St. Domingo	U. States	Sch. Jas. Monroe.
Abner Pratt	21	M	"	"	"	
N. LONDON Q. E June 30, 1823						
Gilbert Georges	45	M	Merchant	France	France	Brig Merchant. Blin.
A. Bourier & 4 ch.	70	M	"	"	"	
E. R. Coueler	47	M	"	"	"	
Charles Calard	45	M	"	"	"	
L. Rorey	42	M	"	"	"	
NEW HAVEN Q. E. June 30, 1823						
Alexr. Hall	23	M	Labourer	England	U. States	Sch. Union. Gibbs.
James Burns	23	M	"	"	"	
Catharine Hall	55	F		"	"	
Matthew Patrick	20	M	"	"	"	
Wm. McGown	19	M	"	"	"	
John Doyle	35	M	"	"	"	
Catharine Doyle & 2 ch	35	F		"	"	
Sarah McMacken & 2 ch.	40	F		"	"	
Alexr. McClacherly	23	M	"	"	"	
John Burns	18	M	"	"	"	
Owen Flanigan	55	M	"	"	"	
Rose " & 4 ch.	55	F		"	"	
Margt. McGiven	30	F		"	"	
Rose Burns & ch.	30	F		"	"	
SALEM & BEVERLY Q. E. June 30, 1823						
John Quick	22	M	Waiter	Ireland	U. States	Sch. Amazon. McKenzie.
John Campbell	26	M	Labourer	"	"	
John Shea	19	M	Nailer	"	"	
John Burke & 3 ch.	36	M	Distiller	"	"	

PASSENGERS WHO ARRIVED IN THE U.S. SEPTEMBER 1821 - DECEMBER 1823

Names of passengers	Age	Sex	Occupation	Country to which they belong	Country of which they intend becoming inhabitants	Ship or vessel with the name of the master or commander
SALEM & BEVERLY Cont. Q. E. June 30, 1823						
Eliza Burke & ch.	30	F		Ireland	U. States	
Walter Sheppard	17	M		"	"	
Richd. Power	40	M		"	"	
James Malone	21	M	Horse doctor	"	"	
Michael Hifle •	48	M	Labourer	"	"	
Mary "	46	F		"	"	
Catharine "	26	F		"	"	
John "	24	M	Labourer	"	"	
Mary " & 3 ch.	24	F		"	"	
Wm. Taylor	22	M	"	"	"	
Francis F. Wood	28	M	"	"	"	
Philip Kennedy	26	M	"	"	"	
John Franklin	45	M	"	"	"	
Charles Quigley	40	M	"	"	"	
Cornelius Kennedy	28	M	"	"	"	
Jno. O'Donell	36	M	"	"	"	
Daniel Donevan	30	M	Carpenter	"	"	
Mary Quigley & ch.	30	F		"	"	
John Powell	23	M	Labourer	"	"	
John Hoar	28	M	"	"	"	
SAVANNA Q. E. June 30, 1823						
John C. Buchanan	22	M	Merchant	Scotland	W. Indies	Ship Sally.
Asa Goodall	34	M	Manufactr.	U. States	U States	Sch. Romeo. Barclay.
Lucy "	21	F		"	"	
E. Foster	25	M	Cab. maker	"	"	
Thomas Robinson	22	M	Joiner	G. Britain	"	Ship Factor. Haskell.
Wm. Gillespy	59	M	Miller	"	"	
Wm. McIncrom •	25	M	Farmer	Ireland	"	
Edmd. O'Donnell	27	M	Priest	"	"	
NORFOLK AND PORTSMOUTH Q. E. June 30, 1823						
Thomas Madigan	30	M	Merchant	G. Britain	U. States	Sch. Rising Sun. Bradford.
Danl. Aldgate	25	M	"	Bermuda	Bermuda	Sloop Alpha. Aldgate.
Wm. Bruce	35	M	"	"	"	Sch. Francis. Newbold.
Amanda Smith	20	F		U. States	U. States	Sloop Roxana. Smith.
James Taylor	35	M	Farmer	England	"	Ship Glide. Pierce.
Henry Hasbon	23	M	"	"	"	

Names of passengers	Age	Sex	Occupation	Country to which they belong	Country of which they intend becoming inhabitants	Ship or vessel with the name of the master or commander
NORFOLK AND PORTSMOUTH Cont. Q. E. June 30, 1823						
John Curtis	25	M	Farmer	England	U. States	
Michael Kelly	30	M	"	"	"	
Thomas Fagan	25	M	"	"	"	
Francis "	27	M	"	"	"	
Edwd. Rogers	33	M	"	"	"	
Stephen Stapley	45	M	"	"	"	
Mary Curtis & 2 ch.	23	F		"	"	
John R. Beves	40	M	Merchant	Dominica	Dominica	Sch. Selina. White.
Henry L. Weiderholdt	55	M	Ship master	U. States	U. States	Brig Eliza Betsey. Small.
John Herron	24	M	Naval Offcr.	"	"	
James Cunningham	22	M	Supercargo	"	"	Sch. Princess Ann. Banks.
Margt. Gaven & 5 ch.	40			Ireland	"	
CHARLESTON, S. C. Q. E. June 30, 1823						
John Ward	32	M	Merchant	England	"	Ship Mary.
John Donaughan	45	M	"	"	"	Brig Clarissa Ann.
John Routiers	25	M		Holland	"	Ship Thalia.
D. McGinn	36	M	Physician	"	"	Brig Chas. Coffin.
Mrs. " & 2 ch.	24	F		Spain	Spain	
Christophe Castino	32	M	Merchant	Portugal	U. States	
Antonio Aimar *	28	M	Trader	"	"	
Peter Dordelay	23	M	Mariner	Germany	"	
D. Smith	30	M		G. Britain	"	Sch. Favourite.
Mrs. " & ch.	30	F		"	"	
M. Samporac	30	M	Merchant	France	"	Brig Caroline Ann.
Mariane Pala	22	F		Spain	Spain	Sch. Leopard.
J. Harrizle	22	M		"	"	
Ann Henderson	32	F		G. Britain	G. Britain	Brig Minerva.
John Ross	20	M	Labourer	"	U. States	Brig Columbia.
Antonio Cabal	48	M		France	"	Brig Alexr. Le Grand.
F. Sasmento	32	M		"	"	
A. Couffon	30	M	Merchant	"	"	
R. Danviers	24	M	"	"	"	
Henderson Ferguson	60	M	Planter	U. States	"	Sch. Swift.
Mrs. "	50	F		"	"	
Theodore Gaillard	50	M	Factor	U. States	"	
L. Watkins	28	M	"	"	"	
Sextus Gaillard	26	M	"	"	"	
John Warner	50	M	Commercl. Agent	"	"	Sch. Jane.
Charles Starr	23	M	U. S. Navy	"	"	

PASSENGERS WHO ARRIVED IN THE U.S. SEPTEMBER 1821 - DECEMBER 1823

Names of passengers	Age	Sex	Occupation	Country to which they belong	Country of which they intend becoming inhabitants	Ship or vessel with the name of the master or commander
CHARLESTON Cont.						
Q. E. June 30, 1823						
D. Belt	28	M	U. S. Navy	U. States	U. States	
Francis Marshall	52	M	Planter	"	"	Sch. Harriet.
Thos. D. Loughany	35	M	Merchant	"	"	Sch. Wicker.
Isaac Suthram	44	M	Manufactr.	"	"	Sloop Providence
John Murphy	22	M	Merchant	"	"	
L. R. Strong	27	M	"	"	"	
Mrs. Jove & child	39	F		"	"	Brig Catharine.
M. Galuchat	35	M		France	"	
A. Schutt	27	M	Planter	"	"	
La Maitre	25	M	Merchant	"	"	
--- Urban	40	M	"	"	"	
--- Gaillard	35	M	"	"	"	
Peter Macalette *	45	M	Mariner	U. States	"	Sch. Hornet.
Walter Wilkie	33	M	Trader	"	"	
John Shuburke	27	M	Mariner	"	"	
Henry Little	48	M	Farmer	"	"	
Joan " & 8 ch.	30	F		G. Britain	"	Brig Phoebe.
Joseph Espina	50	M	Merchant	Spain	"	Brig Rachael & Sally.
Stephen Anderson	25	M	"	U. States	"	
Anthony Purdy	35	M	"	"	"	
Stephen Burrows	32	M	"	"	"	
John Morriston	27	M	"	"	"	
M. Aiken	30	M	"	"	"	
T. Tomaison	48	M	Mariner	France	"	Sloop Norfolk.
Charles O. Sullivan	32	M	Painter	G. Britain	"	Brig Chas. Coffin.
Mrs. " & 3 ch.	23	F		"	"	
Anthony Aymar *	30	M	Trader	Italy	"	
Madam Delorme	55	M		France	"	
Peter Dordelly	24	M		"	"	
J. B. Zegniags	23	M		"	"	
John Stoddard	26	M		"	"	
C. Martinelle	35	M	Mariner	"	"	
Wm. Kerr	40	M	Merchant	G. Britain	"	
Jesse Livingston & ch.	32	M		"	"	Ship Roger Stewart.
Mrs. Lowe & 2 ch.	35	F		"	"	Ship Isabella.
M. Somerville	32	M	Butcher	"	"	
M. Halman	25	M	Sugar baker	Germany	"	
James Magill	22	M	Farmer	G. Britain	"	Ship Phaeron.
E. "	21	M		"	"	
Francis La Rouselier *	33	M	Merchant	France	"	Brig Fanny.
Joseph Barrick	21	M	"	"	"	
James Gordall	29	M	"	"	"	
M. Mendoza	35	M	"	Spain	"	
Mrs. " & 3 ch.	25	F		"	"	

Names of passengers	Age	Sex	Occupation	Country to which they belong	Country of which they intend becoming inhabitants	Ship or vessel with the name of the master or commander
CHARLESTON Cont.						
Q. E. June 30, 1823						
Mrs. Rosetta	28	F		Spain	U. States	
S. E. Lightburn	37	M	Merchant	Britain	"	Sch. Dolphin.
James Griese	30	M	"	"	"	
H. Junge	22	M	"	U. States	"	Sch. Return.
M. Brown	48	M	"	"	"	Brig Catharine.
M. Cloth	35	M	"	Germany	"	
J. Tholos	30	M	"	France	"	
A. Forsythe	55	M	Mariner	"	"	Sch. Eliza.
R. F. Martin	28	M	Trader	"	"	Sch. Aurora.
Wm. Barton	34	M	"	"	"	
NEW BERNE						
Q. E. June 30, 1823						
John Gerry	55	M	Merchant	France	France	Sloop Constitution,
Joseph Emerson	24	M	"	U. States	U. States	
BARNSTABLE						
Q. E. June 30, 1823						
Patrick Kelly	31	M	Merchant	Ireland	U. States	Sch. Loire. Possett.
Hugh Maguire	26	M	Servant	"	"	
Jane Donald	24	F	"	"	"	
Francis McCarthen	23	M	Labourer	"	"	
Mary Griffin	18	F		"	"	
Wm. McGuntly & ch.	25	M	Farmer	"	"	
John Devine	22	M	"	"	"	
Pat. Nugent	23	M	"	"	"	
Richd. Devine	22	M	"	"	"	
Charles Galegar	19	M		"	"	
James Quagly	19	M	Shoemaker	"	"	
Andw. Irvin	22	M	Farmer	"	"	
Samuel Roulston	21	M	"	"	"	
Wm. Goulden	21	M	"	"	"	
James McBride	18	M	"	"	"	
Pat. Havlen	21	M	"	"	"	
Mary "	16	F		"	"	
Mary Mitchell	21	F		"	"	
William Ellis	32	M	Carpenter	"	"	
E. McClaskey	16	M	"	"	"	
Bryan "	24	M	Haridresser	"	"	
U. "	24	F		"	"	
Alexr. McCallaston	38	M	Farmer	"	"	
Nancy " & 6 ch.	36	F		"	"	

Names of passengers	Age	Sex	Occupation	Country to which they belong	Country of which they intend becoming inhabitants	Ship or vessel with the name of the master or commander
BARNSTABLE Q. E. June 30, 1823						
Edwd. Coaks	40	M	Gent.	Ireland	U. States	
Betsey "						
M. "	31	M	Labourer	"	"	
Elisha Hand	30	M	Merchant	N. Brunswick	"	
Robert Gay	30	M	Farmer	"	"	
BALTIMORE Q. E. June 30, 1823						
James Bossure	25	M	Mariner	U. States	U. States	Vessel not mentioned.
Eliza "	17	F		"	"	
R. Mathas	16	M		Hayti	Hayti	
Alexr. Finir	45	M	Supercargo	U. States	U. States	
Mrs. Wallace	34	F		"	"	
Eli Buker	27	M	Merchant	"	"	
Oliver Ruggles	55	M	"	"	"	
W. R. Audling	35	M	Mariner	"	"	
Wm. H. Goodwin	26	M	Supercargo	"	"	
Joseph Meade	34	M	"	"	"	
George Dysart	26	M	Cooper	"	"	
John Patrick	24	M	Supercargo	"	"	
Chas. G. Snow	34	M	Mariner	"	"	
Saml. Hancock	25	M	Labourer	"	"	
Elizabeth " & ch.	27	F		"	"	
M. Killikelly	19	M	Student	Ireland	"	
Thos. Moran	28	M	Tutor	"	"	
John McAlister	30	M	Labourer	"	"	
Jno. Murphy	24	M	"	"	"	
Mary Baker & 2 ch.	18	F		"	"	
Bridget Neal	34	F		"	"	
Hannah Ambler	28	F		"	"	
Wm. Myer	35	M	Merchant	"	"	
W. Hennickson	21	M	Clerk	"	"	
J. Reece	20	M	Carpenter	"	"	
H. Schroeder & ch.	27	M	Merchant	"	"	
A. O. Verbeck	21	M	Tailor	"	"	
Danl. Jordan	25	M	Merchant	"	"	
Isaac Mays	28	M	"	"	"	
Hugh Dick	27	M	"	Jamaica	"	
Edmd. Peale	18	M	"	U. States	"	
D. B. Nones	45	M	"	"	"	
A. Fisk	40	M	Mariner	"	"	
S. Vanhorn	30	M	"	"	"	
Jno. Clayton	30	M	Carpenter	"	"	

Names of passengers	Age	Sex	Occupation	Country to which they belong	Country of which they intend becoming inhabitants	Ship or vessel with the name of the master or commander
BALTIMORE Cont.						
Q. E. June 30, 1823						
Jno. R. Thompson	25	M	Merchant	U. States	U. States	
M. G. Ford	35	M	"	"	"	
Jno. Morris	22	M	"	"	"	
Simon Moses	29	M	"	"	"	
R. A. Denny	45	M	"	"	"	
Chas. Hausewolf	35	M	"	"	"	
Jno. Day	40	M	"	England	"	
F. Cassiner	14	M		"	"	
Joseph Saville	45	M	"	U. States	"	
Jemima " & ch.	21	F		"	"	
Jas. Forbes	45	M	Physician	"	"	
Moses Ingle	22	M	Merchant	"	"	
A. Graham	30	M	"	"	"	
P. Leonard	26	M	Iron mftr.	"	"	
B. "	24	M	"	"	"	
Thomas Russell	26	M	Weaver	England	"	
Isaac Fitton	26	M	"	"	"	
Wm "	24	M	"	"	"	
A. F. Lubohn	40	M	Merchant	U. States	"	
Jno. Garnard *	35	M	"	"	"	
Jno. Taylor	27	M	"	"	"	
Charles Harrison	13	M		"	"	
John Boadly	35	M	Mariner	"	"	
Alexr. McCormick	28	M	Planter	Spain	"	
John Peraz	25	M		"	"	
Chas. Luta	35	M	Barber	"	"	
H. Bell	24	M	Mariner	U. States	"	
G. B. Gill	28	M	Merchant	"	"	
Samuel Walker	45	M	"	"	"	
Alexr. Hosack	25	M	U. S. Navy	"	"	
Wm. S. Sangston	21	M	U. S. Navy	"	"	
Daniel Riffel	50	M	Carpenter	"	"	
David "	20	M	"	"	"	
A. "	50	M	"	"	"	
John Parker	25	M	"	"	"	
John Nunon	26	M	Merchant	"	"	
E. Kenrick	22	M	"	"	"	
Wm. Frisbee	40	M	Mariner	"	"	
D. Keath	45	M	Physician	Kingston	"	
A. C. Perchota	40	M	Merchant	"	"	
Mrs. " & 4 ch.	40	F		"	"	
F. Brown	35	M	Clerk	Germany	"	
Geo. G. Smith	25	M	Ship master	U. States	"	
M. Edwards	30	M	Mariner	"	"	

Names of passengers	Age	Sex	Occupation	Country to which they belong	Country of which they intend becoming inhabitants	Ship or vessel with the name of the master or commander
BALTIMORE Cont.						
June 30, 1823						
Josiah Porter	18	M	Farmer	U. States	U. States	
Thos. Short	21	M	Weaver	Ireland	"	
Chas. "	23	M	Carpenter	"	"	
Mary " & ch.	20	F		"	"	
Charlotte Gilky & ch.	30	F		"	"	
E. Johnston & 6 ch.	40	F		"	"	
H. McLeary	21	M	Farmer	"	"	
Wm. McKenna	21	M	"	"	"	
W. H. Iglehart	23	M	Merchant	U. States	"	
P. O. Brenan	21	M	"	"	"	
C. W. Story	35	M	"	"	"	
P. Fisher	45	M	"	"	"	
A. G. Raneler *	40	M	"	"	"	
G. W. Arasmends	25	M	"	"	"	
Francisco Domanes	21	M	"	Spain	"	
Richd. Adams	25	M		U. States	"	
Thos. O. Howell	18	M	Clerk	" "	"	
James Armstrong	25	M	"	"	"	
G. Wortman	39	M	Merchant	Germany	"	
Charles Gallwitz	23	M	Painter	"	"	
Joseph Grunick	21	M	Jeweller	"	"	
W. Miller	30	M	Brewer	"	"	
John Scott	22	M	"	"	"	
Theodore Miller	21	M	"	"	"	
George W. Dault	29	M	"	"	"	
Gasper Schol	55	M	Farmer	"	"	
B. Stuler	57	M	"	"	"	
S. Walter	21	M	"	"	"	
C. Hartman	30	M	"	"	"	
Theodore Gober	32	M	Merchant	"	"	
M. Gober & 2 ch.	19	F		"	"	
Ellen Gibson & 3 ch.	30	F		Ireland	U. States	
M. McCay & 5 ch.	36	F		"	"	
Robt. Taylor	24	M		"	"	
Jane " & ch.	26	F		"	"	
John Cowan	18	M	Farmer	"	"	
Jane March & 2 ch.	50	F		"	"	
Martin Duffey	25	M	"	"	"	
Margt. Ennis & ch.	40	F		"	"	
R. Wilkinson	25	M		"	"	
Jno. H. Wood	28	M	Mariner	"	"	
Thos. D. Johnson	22	M	Merchant	U. States	"	
Wm. Palmer	23	M	"	"	"	
John Christy	28	M	"	"	"	

Names of passengers	Age	Sex	Occupation	Country to which they belong	Country of which they intend becoming inhabitants	Ship or vessel with the name of the master or commander
BALTIMORE Cont.						
Q. E. June 30, 1823						
Fred. Dawson	21	M		U. States	U. States	
Joohn Block	43	M	Grocer	Germany	"	
Hugh Gallagher	24	M	Officer	U. States	"	
Geo. Robinson	33	M	Merchant	"	"	
E. Mathieu	26	M	"	France	"	
F. A. Kramer	55	M	"	"	"	
N. McKane	27	M	"	"	"	
Alexr. Thompson	17	M	Clerk	"	"	
P. C. Green	25	M	Mariner	"	"	
James Moss	40	M	Merchant	"	"	
Harriet " & child	38	F		"	"	
H. E. Hunter	36	M	"	"	"	
M. Robert	50	F		St. Domingo	"	
Rosine "	22	F		"	"	
W. Bivoaler	23	M	"	"	"	
Henry Lewis	28	M	Carpenter	U. States	"	
OSWEGATCHIE						
Q. E. Sept. 30, 1823						
Joseph Elden	29	M	Farmer	England	U. States	Vessel not mentioned.
Wm. Freeman	23	M	"	"	"	
John Burman	22	M	"	"	"	
Wm. Ralph	18	M	Lawyer	"	"	
John Mann	21	M	Farmer	"	"	
Mary Barman	18	F		"	"	
Hugh Curge	29	M	"	Ireland	"	
Eliza " & 3 ch.	26	F		"	"	
George McWha	29	M	"	"	"	
Henry Rollins	32	M	"	England	"	
Ann " & 6 ch.	30	F		"	"	
Wm. Brown	24	M	Stone mason	Ireland	"	
Jane " & 2 ch.	25	F		"	"	
Hugh McBride	28	M	Weaver	"	"	
Margaret Finlay	27	F	Seamstress	"	"	
NEWPORT						
Q. E. Sept. 30, 1823						
Ramon R Gonzalez	21	M	Merchant	Spain	U. States	Sch. Rolla. Vaughan.
John Cruickshank	25	M	Mariner	England	England	Brig Quill. Lewis.
Robert Merose *	15	M	Mariner	England	England	
Charles Clinton	38	M	Gent.	"	"	Ship Boy. Greene.

Names of passengers	Age	Sex	Occupation	Country to which they belong	Country of which they intend becoming inhabitants	Ship or vessel with the name of the master or commander
ALEXANDRIA						
Q. E. Sept. 30, 1823						
Joseph Levy	25	M	Merchant	England	U. States	Sch. Rose in Bloom. Soule.
Abraham Barnett	23	M	"	"	"	
William Hargus	50	M	Farmer	"	"	Ship Boston. Fenley.
Edward Lloyd	37	M	Shoemaker	"	"	
Charles "	24	M	Labourer	"	"	
Thomas Leath	39	M	Shoemaker	"	"	
Thomas King	34	M	Tailor	"	"	
Margaret "	31	F		"	"	
Thomas Milligan	31	M	Teacher	"	"	
Margt. " & ch.	32	F		"	"	
John Matthews	27	M	Miller	"	"	
Nehemiah "	21	M	Labourer	"	"	
Wm. Grearly	21	M	"	"	"	
Wm. Peake	30	M	Carpenter	"	"	
John Steele	29	M	Labourer	"	"	
Thos. Clemens	21	M	"	"	"	
John Donahoe	22	M	"	Ireland	"	
Matthew Waite	69	M	Bricklayer	"	"	
Jane "	62	F		"	"	
Hannah "	18	F		"	"	
Matthew "	30	M	Bricklayer	"	"	
Sarah " & ch.	35	F		"	"	
John Huddlestone	41	M	Joiner	"	"	
Elizabeth " & 4 ch.	34	F		"	"	
John Simpson	33	M	Labourer	"	"	
Mary " & 5 ch.	33	F		"	"	
J. B. Bascome	23	M	Clerk	"	"	Brig Hope. Wilson.
MARBLEHEAD						
Q. E. Sept. 30, 1823						
William Hughs	30	M	Carpenter	Ireland	U. States	Sch. Good Exchange.
Archibald Kenedy	46	M	Farmer	U. States	"	Sch. Mary.
BRISTOL						
Q. E. Sept. 30, 1823						
Samuel Spink	22	M	Carpenter	U. States	U. States	Brig Brothers. Green.
Jesse Cottrell	23	M	"	"	"	
E. N. Harking	35	M	Mariner	"	"	Brig Matilda. Smith.
E. Hinkley	28	M	"	"	"	
Darius Clapp	22	M	Merchant	"	"	
Henry Wight	34	M	"	"	"	Brig Jacob. Eddy.

Names of passengers	Age	Sex	Occupation	Country to which they belong	Country of which they intend becoming inhabitants	Ship or vessel with the name of the master or commander
PROVIDENCE						
Alexr. McGregor	23	M	Mason	Scotland	U. States	Sch. Enterprize. Paine.
James Lumsden	25	M	"	"	"	
John More	28	M	Physician	U. States	"	Brig Traveller.
J. W. Lovett	30	M	Carpenter	"	"	
Samuel Beall	35	M	"	"	"	
Mason Morse	26	M	Merchant	"	"	Brig Beaver. Ruggles.
Ebenezer Wade	22	M	"	"	"	Ship Columbia. Hatch.
John Conway	50	M	"	"	"	Ship Providence. Bowers.
John Debeman	27	M	"	"	"	
R. C. Geyer	24	M	Merchant	"	"	
James Perkins	34	M	Mariner	"	"	Brig Aginorea, Bacon.
George W. Olney	32	M	Merchant	"	"	Sch. Enterprize. Mowey.
Edwin Mowey	24	M	"	"	"	
James Casey	32	M	Labourer	Ireland	"	
John Maharogan	19	M	Mariner	"	"	
Josiah Rhodes	26	M	Mariner	U. States	"	Brig Enterprize. McLane.
NEWBURYPORT						
Q. E. Sept. 30, 1823						
Daniel Knight	49	M	Mariner	U. States	U. States	Brig Margaret.
John Peterson	40	M	"	"	"	
Ebenezer Wilson	50	M	Farmer	"	"	Sch. Hope.
Samuel Bell	27	M	Physician	Nova Scotia	"	Sch. Comet.
Jane " & 2 ch.	25	F		"	"	
NANTUCKET						
Q. E. Sept. 30, 1823						
George Clark	52	M	Mariner	U. States	U. States	Sch. First Attempt. Robinson.
Samuel Rea	41	M	"	"	"	Brig Juliana. Bradshaw.
Wm. Jenkins	23	M		"	"	Brig Commerce. Longfellow.
Wm. Snow	24	M		"	"	
O. Goodwin	28	M	Supercargo	"	"	Ship Acaster. Cloutman.
B. B. Barker	28	M	Clerk	" "	"	
S. Brooks	21	M	"	"	"	
John Plucket	18	M		England	"	Ship Juno. Rich.
Mary Burns	35	F		"	"	
Charles Day	40	M		"	"	
Thomas Everhare	34	M		"	"	
Susan Evans	47	F		U. States	"	Ship Mercury. Nichols.
Sarah Whitcroft	28	F		England	"	
Robt. Wood	44	M		"	"	
Ann Philips	31	F		"	"	Ship Greenhow. Gray.
Saml. Hodges	39	M		"	"	
Ann Rubles & ch.	25	F		"	"	

Names of passengers	Age	Sex	Occupation	Country to which they belong	Country of which they intend becoming inhabitants	Ship or vessel with the name of the master or commander
NANTUCKET Cont.						
Q. E. Sept. 30, 1823						
Dorothy Robinson & 5 ch.	35	F		England	U. States	
Joseph Clifton	70	M	Cordwainer	U. States	"	Sch. Lady Washington. Haskell.
E. Ferguson	24	F		"	"	
George Black	19	M	Printer	Scotland	"	Brig Alexander. Barker.
Thomas Crosby	35	M	Glass maker	G. Britain	"	
Ann " & 2 ch.	30	F		"	"	
Joseph "	30	M	"	"	"	
Wm. Hayley	38	M	"	"	"	
Mrs. "	35	F		"	"	
B. Price	24	M	"	"	"	
H. R. Warner	35	M	Mariner	U. States	"	Brig Somers. Lord.
Wm. Tinker	35	M	Merchant	England	"	Brig Venus. Saunders.
Hannah "	21	F		"	"	
John C. Baker	28	M	Mason	U. States	"	Sch. Lucretia. Palmer.
Jno. W. Booth	35	M	Merchant	"	"	Ship Topaz. Callender.
James "	25	M	"	"	"	
Thos. Winterbotham	42	M	"	"	"	
M. Browning	32	M	"	England	"	Sch. London Packet.
Lucy " & 2 ch.	26	F		"	"	
John R. Amery	21	M	"	"	"	
Wm. G. Tory	26	M	"	"	"	
Charlotte Burke	39	F		"	"	
John Elliott	27	M	Mechanic	U. States	"	
Henry Dickens	36	M	Farmer	"	"	
John Williams	33	M	"	"	"	
Susanna "	27	F	"	"	"	
J. Currie & 5 ch.	35	M	"	"	"	
Jos. Augu. Casar	39	M	Physician	Hayti	Hayti	Brig William Ross
E. Jenkins	31	M	Mariner	U. States	U. States	
Robt. Burns	24	M	"	"	"	Brig Hero. Kinsman.
J. C. Whitman	31	M	Merchant	"	"	Brig St. Clair. Whitmore.
Jane Britton	31	F	Lady	Ireland	"	
Catharine Wheelwright	20	F	"	"	"	
Cath. Young & 3 ch.	40	F	"	U States	"	
W Goddard	39	M	Army	Halifax	Halifax	Brig Geo. Henry. Laken.
Jacob Alman	23	M	Carpenter	U. States	U States	
Saml. Hopkins	16	M		"	"	
Davis Murphy	22	M	Mariner	Ireland	"	
M. Devarde	28	M	Blacksmith	U. States	"	
Richard "	25	M	"	"	"	
Rebecca Campbell & 2 ch.	30	F		"	"	
H. Raintid	30	M	Mariner	Holland	"	Brig Argus. Loraif

Names of passengers	Age	Sex	Occupation	Country to which they belong	Country of which they intend becoming inhabitants	Ship or vessel with the name of the master or commander
NANTUCKET Cont.						
Q. E. Sept. 30, 1823						
Henry Larcor	46	M	Mariner	U. States	U. States	Brig Clio. Brown.
B. F. Johnston	26	M	"	"	"	
Charles Falham	27	M	"	"	"	
A. A. F. Lopez	18	M	Merchant	S. America	S. America	
Saml. Hodges Jr.	30	M	Consul	U. States	U. States	Brig Oswego. Wightman
M. W. "	26	F		"	"	
John Thompson	32	M	Mariner	"	"	
W. A. " & ch.	22	F		"	"	
M. Alcantara	35	M		S. America	Portugal	
Hannah Marshall	23	F	Spinster	U States	U. States	Sch. Lucy. Marshall.
Wm. Rhodes	35	M	Merchant	England	England	Ship Emerald Fox.
Sarah Fox	22	F		U. States	U. States	
Thos. Pristin	26	M	Glass blower	England	England	
John Scott	24	M	"	Ireland	U. States	
M. Murphy	39	M	"	"	"	
Thos. Gillas	21	M	"	"	"	
Susan Dougherty & 4 ch.	36	F		"	"	
J. D Rundame	26	M	Barber	Surinam	"	Brig Telemachus. Crosby.
Daniel Turns *	50	M	Soap boiler	Ireland	"	Sch. Hope. Haskell.
Margt " & 5 ch.	50	F		"	"	
Thos. H. Alleyne	32	M	Planter	U. States	"	Sch. Two Sons.
Thos. H. Perkins	36	M	Merchant	"	"	Ship Amethyst. Bussey.
Wm. E. Channing	43	M	Clergyman	"	"	
Mrs. "	38	F		"	"	
B. A. Cobbs	33	M	Merchant	"	"	
Mrs. Cobbs	28	F		"	"	
J. Wells	26	F		"	"	
Andw. Ritchie	39	M	Lawyer	"	"	
Joseph Coolidge Jr.	24	M	"	"	"	
Henry Lewis	32	M	"	"	"	
Thomas Woodford	36	M	Carpenter	"	"	
Margt. Maguire & 3 ch.	30	F		"	"	
Harnet Everston & ch.	25	F		"	"	
Mary Wordhull & 5 ch.	39	F		"	"	
Edmund Don	25	M	Merchant	"	"	
N. B. Richardson	39	M	"	"	"	Brig Echo. North.
Isaac McCary	17	M	Trader	"	"	
P. Crowell	52	M	Ship master	"	"	Sch. Boxer. Mayo.
Mrs. "	31	F		"	"	
P. Woodhouse	35	M	Brit. Officer	G. Britain	G. Britain	Sch. Geo. Henry. Laken.
Geo. H. Horton	30	M	"	"	"	
James Pennoyer	29	M	Merchant	N. Orleans	U. States	
John Hawes	38	M	"	U. States	"	
E. Gannetts	25	M	"	"	"	

Names of passengers	Age	Sex	Occupation	Country to which they belong	Country of which they intend becoming inhabitants	Ship or vessel with the name of the master or commander
NANTUCKET Cont. Q. E. Sept. 30, 1823						
Wm. Bancroft	29	M	Blockmaker	U. States	U. States	
Eliza. " & 6 ch.	29	F		"	"	
Geo. W. Otis	23	M	Physician	"	"	Brig Oak. Weeks.
Leonard Cotton	23	M	Mechanic	"	"	Brig Mary & Eliza. Ellis.
C. Thomas	36	M	Mariner	England	"	Sch. Billow. Basko.
M. Bromly	50	M	Labourer	Halifax	"	
James Archibald	57	M	Carpenter	"	"	
Jas. C. Brien	29	M	"	"	"	
Jas. Blake	25	M	"	"	"	
Thos Wilson	21	M	"	"	"	
Timothy Claxton	33	M	Artificer	England	"	Brig Independence. King
Ann "	28	F	"	"	"	
Richard Fellows	42	M	"	"	"	
Wm. Wass	20	M	Farmer	Germany	"	Brig Ramble.
F. W. Ellis	24	M	Merchant	U. States	"	Sch. Rover. Lincoln.
Charles I. Staff	19	M	"	Germany	"	Brig Eliza. Burgess.
L. Buckholtt	29	M	Mariner	"	"	
Jno. Allen	28	M	Merchant	England	"	Sch. Thomas. Miller.
M. Cogenell	45	M	"	U. States	"	Brig Samosel. Bartlett.
Jos. Perkins	42	M	Mariner	"	"	Brig Anna Maria. Brown.
Wm. McClennon Jr.	29	M	Rigger	"	"	Sch. Geo. Henry. Laken.
A. Dechian	30	M	Tinner	Halifax	Halifax	
James Magrath	32	M	Trader	"	"	
John Brookman	23	M	Carpenter	"	"	
John Cummings	27	M	Trader	"	"	
Charles Reach	31	M	Farmer	"	"	
W Welsh	28	M		"	"	
Eleanor " & 4 ch.	38	F		"	"	
Patrick Denis	20	M	Weaver	"	"	
G. B. Potts	42	M	Merchant	U. States	"	Sch. Felicity. Hopkins.
John Moreno	23	M	Labourer	Havana	"	Brig Phoenix. Shaw.
Thomas Wescott	23	M	Merchant	England	England	
James Douglas	25	M	Physician	"	"	
John Lewis	25	M		U. States	U. States	Sch. Caravan.
Henry Call	16	M	Cooper	"	"	
D. Strong	45	M	Surgeon	G. Britain	G. Britain	Sch. Billow. Barker.
M. B. Long	19	M	Printer	Halifax	Halifax	
M. Chichester	21	M	Officer	U. States	U. States	
Mrs. Fales & ch.	50	F		"	"	
W. W. McErry	21	M		"	"	
M. McDonald	25	M	Tobacconist	Halifax	Halifax	
M. Bailey	30	M	Farmer	"	"	
M. Galloway	55	M	"	"	"	
M. Sewall	25	M	"	"	"	

Names of passengers	Age	Sex	Occupation	Country to which they belong	Country of which they intend becoming inhabitants	Ship or vessel with the name of the master or commander
NANTUCKET Cont.						
Q. E. Sept. 30, 1823						
M. Beckley	25	M	Farmer	Halifax	Halifax	
M. Wild	25	M	"	"	"	
M. Long	30	M	"	"	"	
M. Smith	38	M	"	"	"	
M. Martin	40	M	"	"	"	
Wm. Owens	25	M	Cordwainer	G. Britain	U. States	Ship Fortitude Gibson.
Ella " & 2 ch.	26	F		"	"	
Alfred Richardson	32	M	Merchant	U. States	"	Ship Parthian. Brewster
P. P. Hargoien	48	M	'	S. America	S. America	
Robt. Barton	25	M	Surgeon	England	England	
H. L. Seymore	15	M	Mariner	"	"	
Samuel Conant	40	M	Shipmaster	U. States	U. States	Ship Liverpool Packet.
James M. Manis *	26	M	Merchant	"	"	
Neil McLeod	36	M	"	Canada	Canada	Brig Emerald. Gray.
Jane "	30	F		"	"	
Wm. Sayere	45	M	Mariner	U. States	U. States	Sch. Wm. & Emeline. Springer.
E. Dickinson	30	M	Merchant	"	"	
Joseph Hastings	38	M	Tallow chdlr	"	"	Sch. Vigilant. Balson.
Ambrose Brindoir	46	M	Merchant	France	France	Brig Ohio. Lunt.
Ann "	43	F		"	"	
W. R. Smith	23	M	Mariner	U. States	U. States	
Dudley Leavitt	30	M	Farmer	"	"	Sch. Geo. Henry. Lakin.
Edward Cleary	25	M		England	Uncertain	
Michael Hogan	24	M	Butcher	U. States	U. States	
Bridget "	18	F		"	"	
Eliza Ruckley	25	F	Spinster	"	"	
Wm. Deblois	32	M	Merchant	N. Scotia	N. Scotia	Sch Billow. Barker.
George C White	34	M	"	"	"	
Mrs. "	28	F		"	"	
Thomas Ellis	23	M	Merchant	U. States	U. States	
James Don	50	M	"	"	"	
C. Ferly	35	M	Mariner	"	"	
P. M. Gordon	34	M	"	"	"	
M. Duffee	34	M	"	"	"	
James "	35	M	"	"	"	
Edward Donelly	36	M	"	"	"	
NEW YORK						
Q. E. Sept. 30, 1823						
Wm. Equonton	35	M	Mechanic	U. States	U. States	Ship Eolus. Geer.
John Sapell	42	M	Farmer	"	"	
Thomas Taylor	50	M	"	"	"	
Jane " & ch.	44	F		"	"	

Names of passengers	Age	Sex	Occupation	Country to which they belong	Country of which they intend becoming inhabitants	Ship or vessel with the name of the master or commander
NEW YORK Cont.						
Q. E. Sept. 30, 1823						
M. Oddy	21	M	Merchant	England	England	Sch. Edgar. Johnson.
Mrs. Bolton & 2 ch.	35	F	"	"	"	Brig Jas. & Margt. Milne.
M. Anderson	25	M	"	Scotland	U. States	
Mrs. Peltier	22	F		France	"	
A. Gurdalicone *	45	M	Preacher	Turkey	"	Sch. Douglass Brown.
Walter Culton *	41	M	Merchant	U. States	"	Brig American. Dominick.
John Dudley	34	M	Ship master	"	"	
L. B. Hensques *	38	M	Merchant	France	France	Sch Brandt. Hunbrennet
Joseph Clark	28	M	"	Scotland	U. States	Sch. Jacolinia P Alney
Mary Ann " & 4 ch.	28	F		"	"	
James Blackburn	33	M	"	England	"	
Edwd. Raynols	32	M	"	"	"	
James Brown	55	M	Farmer	"	"	
Thomas Dickson	30	M	"	"	"	
Ann " & 2 ch.	32	F		"	"	
Charles Gibson	45	M	"	"	"	
Hannah " & 4 ch.	38	F		"	"	
John Mastermaid	30	M	Labourer	Ireland	"	
L. Luby *	25	M	"	"	"	
F. Cown	32	M	"	"	"	
David Williams	42	M	Farmer	"	"	
Eliza " & 4 ch.	37	F		"	"	
Wm. Bruse	22	M	"	"	"	
Martha "	21	F		"	"	
Abraham Evans	28	M	"	"	"	
James Grannon *	35	M	"	"	"	
Wm. McDowell	24	M	Farmer	"	"	
Archibald "	23	M	"	"	"	
John "	36	M	"	"	"	
Jane " & 6 ch.	50	F		"	"	
Wm. Colsan	34	M	"	"	"	
Ann " & 3 ch.	30	F		"	"	
Joseph Armstrong	66	M	"	"	"	
Wm "	23	M	"	"	"	
P. Hughes	35	M	"	"	"	
Bridget "	22	F		"	"	
Jno. McCanny	28	M	"	"	"	
James Wilson	25	M	"	"	"	
Ann " & ch.	23	F		"	"	
H Duyer *	25	M	"	"	"	
Wm. Jorden	25	M	"	"	"	
M. Fitzsimmons	25	M	"	"	"	
H. Ward	25	M	"	"	"	
Jno. Griffith	22	M	"	"	"	

Names of passengers	Age	Sex	Occupation	Country to which they belong	Country of which they intend becoming inhabitants	Ship or vessel with the name of the master or commander
NEW YORK Cont. Q. E. Sept. 30, 1823						
Jane Griffith	25	F		Ireland	U. States	
Edwd. Phillips	25	M	Farmer	"	"	
Jno. Robertson	34	M	"	"	"	
Thomas Babel	35	M	"	"	"	
Gracio Gonzales	33	M	Merchant	Porto Rico	Porto Rico	Sch George. Nixon.
Joseph Danby	27	M	"	England	U. States	
Frs. Banetti & ch.	60	M	"	U. States	"	Brig Hopes Delight. Baker.
D. Douglass	24	M	"	G. Britain	"	Sch. Ann Maria. Tan.
Richd. Shepherdson	50	M	Farmer	U. States	"	
Mary " & ch.	47	F		"	"	
Wm. Parkin & 2 ch.	42	M	Miller	G. Britain	"	
Wm. Shepherdson	45	M	Farmer	"	"	
Eliza " & 6 ch.	42	F		"	"	
Wm. Bonfry	24	M	"	"	"	
George Ellis	50	M	"	"	"	
Henry Catby	25	M	"	"	"	
John Gaunt	54	M	"	"	"	
Ann " & 7 ch.	48	F		"	"	
Jas. Bearcloft	30	M	"	"	"	
Jane "	21	F		"	"	
Thomas Burton	27	M	"	"	"	
Sarah " & 3 ch.	27	F		"	"	
Thos. Bates	44	M	"	"	"	
Eliza " & 2 ch.	44	F		"	"	
F. Natrivia	25	M	Merchant	U. States	"	
Wm. McLuke	25	M	Taylor	G. Britain	"	
Owen Early	30	M	Labourer	"	"	
Patrick Moore	22	M	Labourer	"	"	
P. Morgan	25	M	"	"	"	
Eliza Lynch	22	F		"	"	
Rose Mullen	25	F		"	"	
Michael Hadden	26	M	"	"	"	
Andw. Farrell	26	M	"	"	"	
L. Evans	31	M	"	"	"	
Mary " & 4 ch.	40	F		"	"	
Richd. Wheeler	29	M		"	"	
Rebecca " & 3 ch.	28	F		"	"	
Wm. Wriley	35	M		"	"	
Ellen "	24	F		"	"	
Wm. Wheeler	33	M		"	"	
Catharine "	26	F		"	"	
Wm. May	30	M		"	"	
Mary "	28	F		"	"	
Alexr. Moore	30	M		"	"	

PASSENGERS WHO ARRIVED IN THE U.S. SEPTEMBER 1821 - DECEMBER 1823

Names of passengers	Age	Sex	Occupation	Country to which they belong	Country of which they intend becoming inhabitants	Ship or vessel with the name of the master or commander
NEW YORK Cont.						
Q. E. Sept. 30, 1823						
L. Hargraves	28	M	Farmer	G. Britain	U. States	
Thos. Riceton	23	M	"	"	"	
Wm. Archbold	42	M	Labourer	"	"	
Wm. Gobby	22	M	"	"	"	
A. Petrie	19	M	"	"	"	
Margt. "	25	F		"	"	
A. Donald	26	M	"	"	"	
John Maackady	22	M	"	"	"	
Wm. Mecuvia & ch	24	M	Weaver	Ireland	"	Sch. Atlantic. Cousins.
Peter McCasta	24	M		Scotland	"	
John Nellis	20	M		Ireland	"	
Edwd. Kelly	40	M		"	"	
Ann " & 4 ch.	33	F		"	"	
Joseph Wilson	23	M		"	"	
Wm. Brathaust	23	M		"	"	
Jno. G. Walterling	60	M	Merchant	Demerara	"	Sch. Susan. Ivey.
Maria J. " & ch.	30	M		"	"	
W. J. Renney	39	M	Mechanic	"	"	
Alfred King	23	M	Merchant	"	"	
H. A. Pitt	22	M	"	"	"	Brig Horizon. Clark.
Henry Askin *	23	M	Cordwainer	G. Britain	"	
M. Hurley & 2 ch.	24	F		"	"	
Wm. H. Baldwin	32	M	Merchant	England	"	Brig Cato. Boyer.
Jno. F. David	30	M	"	U. States	"	
G H. Goodwin	26	M	"	"	"	
Emily Dunn & ch.	28	F		"	"	
H. J. Taney	27	M	"	"	"	Brig Lady's Delight.
J. R. Pola *	25	M	"	"	"	
John Bunder *	30	M	Mariner	"	"	
Robt. G. Mitchell	30	M	Merchant	"	"	Sch. Diana. Higgins.
A. C. Lancilot	60	M	Planter	France	"	
P. Le Roux	31	M	"	"	"	
L. Dubois	29	M	"	"	"	
H. Black	36	M	"	England	"	
George Jackson & 4 ch.	37	M	British commissr.	"	"	Brig Columbia. Rogers.
Ann Braithwaite	38	F		"	"	
Cath. Brandt	26	F		"	"	
Elizabeth Cooke	30	F		"	"	
George Parish	42	M		"	"	
John Fethuston	27	M		"	"	
Isaac Stephenson	57	M	Miller	"	"	
Wm. Shepherd	37	M	Merchant	"	"	
George Tartar	25	M	"	"	"	

Names of passengers	Age	Sex	Occupation	Country to which they belong	Country of which they intend becoming inhabitants	Ship or vessel with the name of the master or commander
NEW YORK Cont.						
Q. E. Sept. 30, 1823						
George Johnson	19	M	Merchant	England	U. States	
Jno. Watts	70	M		"	"	
Thos. Irvin	59	M	Merchant	U. States	"	
A. Bethulot	46	M	Attorney	G. Britain	G. Britain	
Benj. "	24	M	Physician	"	"	
John Chilcot	38	M	Clerk	"	"	
M. Ashworth	23	M	"	"	"	
Stephen Chase	53	M	Farmer	"	"	
Benj. Adams	52	M	Merchant	Wales	"	Ship Orozembo. Nichols.
Mary Brown & 2 ch.	25	F		Scotland	"	
Thomas Preston	33	M	Farmer	England	"	
Janet " & 2 ch.	26	F		"	"	
Jas. Skenozo *	31	M	"	"	"	
Ann "	25	F		"	"	
Wm. "	26	M	"	"	"	
Elias Evans	25	M	Labourer	Wales	"	
Wm. Roberts	21	M	"	"	"	
Richd. Williams	55	M	"	"	"	
Owen Humphreys	51	M	Farmer	"	"	
Mary " & 5 ch.	52	F		"	"	
Wm. Richard	40	M	Farmer	"	"	
Louisa " & 5 ch.	40	F		"	"	
Wm. Jones	25	M	"	"	"	
John Griffith	24	M	"	"	"	
Richd. "	24	M	"	"	"	
Wm. Lewis	26	M	"	"	"	
Evan Parry	23	M	"	"	"	
Jane "	21	F		"	"	
Wm. Griffiths	39	M	Labourer	"	"	
Eliza Griffiths & 3 ch.	39	F		"	"	
Wm. Norden	26	M	Mariner	U. States	"	
A. B. Gillies	33	M	Millwright	Scotland	"	
Evan Rees	34	M	Shoemaker	Wales	"	
Mary " & 5 ch.	36	F		"	"	
Patrick Reilly	36	M	Farmer	"	"	
Mary "	27	F		"	"	
George Grant	27	M	"	"	"	
John Thomas	28	M	Labourer	"	"	
Thomas Collins	60	M		"	"	
Jane " & ch.	33	F		"	"	
John Reed	26	M		"	"	
David Roberts	26	M		"	"	
Catharine " & 4 ch.	24	F		"	"	
Evan Thomas	70	M	Tanner	"	"	

Names of passengers	Age	Sex	Occupation	Country to which they belong	Country of which they intend becoming inhabitants	Ship or vessel with the name of the master or commander
NEW YORK Cont.						
Q. E. Sept. 30, 1823						
Margt. Thomas	68	F		Wales	U. States	
Wm. Roberts	23	M	Labourer	"	"	
Griffith Evans	30	M	Tanner	"	"	
Rebecca " & 2 ch.	25	F		"	"	
Catharine Richards	24	M		"	"	
D. Laughton	56	M	Book keeper	Scotland	"	
J. Atkinson & 2 ch.	55	M	Farmer	Wales	"	
Peter Susan	47	M		"	"	
Thomas Davies	28	M		"	"	
J. Jones	28	M		"	"	
Catharine Jones	21	F		"	"	
John Young	24	M	Dyer	"	"	
H. Thompson	21	M	"	"	"	
Wm. Williams	43	M	Farmer	"	"	
E. " & ch.	45	F		"	"	
James Griffith	34	M	"	"	"	
Jane " & 4 ch.	32	F		"	"	
H. Kennedy	57	M	Merchant	U. States	"	Ship James Monroe.
Henry Babad	26	M	"	"	"	
Jno. Rittenhoven	43	M		France	"	
Wm. B. Napier	25	M	"	U. States	"	Ship Cortes De Cost
D. Teale	40	M	"	G. Britain	"	
E. Allen	25	F		"	"	
Jno. Poffer & 3 ch.	37	M	"	U. States	"	
Harnet "	28	F		"	"	
Wm. Schmidts	36	M	"	G. Britain	"	Brig Rovina. Lettigon.
John Dougal	45	M	Farmer	"	"	
Thos. Schick	26	M	Labourer	"	"	
Margt. " & 2 ch.	28	F		"	"	
David McDougal	31	M	Farmer	"	"	
M. Strong & 8 ch.	35	M		"	"	
Anthony Sara	32	M	Merchant	Corsica	"	Sch Tartar Kevans.
James K. Davies	22	M	Mariner	U. States	"	Ship Trident. Coffin.
C. Easton	23	M	Merchant	"	"	Brig South Carolina. Johnson.
Wm. K. Benny	26	M	"	"	"	
Robert Orr	26	M	"	Scotland	Scotland	
Ann M. Lowry	25	F		Jamaica	England	Sloop Jay. Boggs.
Wm. Walker	25	M	Merchant	"	"	
S. Trowbridge	42	M	Mariner	U. States	U. States	Sch. Levant Baker.
Wm. Tyson	27	M	"	"	"	
L. August	25	M	"	"	"	
Wm. Hall	22	M	"	"	"	
Jno. Savage & ch.	32	M	Planter	Jamaica	"	Sch. Nile. Aldrick.
J. T. Lawrence	34	M	"	"	"	

Names of passengers	Age	Sex	Occupation	Country to which they belong	Country of which they intend becoming inhabitants	Ship or vessel with the name of the master or commander
NEW YORK Cont.						
Q. E. Sept. 30, 1823						
Mary Anderson	26	F		Jamaica	U. States	
Jno. Vandeveir	38	M		U. States	"	
T. Dwight	21	M	Merchant	"	"	Brig Eagle. Tollis.
Richd. James	34	M	Tailor	Ireland	"	Ship Angelica. Harsen.
Sarah " & 4 ch.	33	F		"	"	
John Morgan	44	M	Labourer	Wales	"	
Thos. Leak	30	M	"	"	"	
Lewis Richards	33	M	leather drssr.	"	"	
E. Davies	42	M	Weaver	"	"	
Ann " & 3 ch.	43	F		"	"	
Samuel Salter	30	M	Shoemaker	England	"	
Edwd. Quinlan	32	M	Farmer	Ireland	"	
Jas. Crowes	22	M	"	"	"	
Thos. Kelly	32	M	Clerk	"	"	
Edwd. Moore	30	M	Farmer	"	"	
Robt. Major	48	M	Butcher	"	"	
Pat. Murry	50	M	Blacksmith	"	"	
Ann " & 5 ch.	47	F		"	"	
Geo. Sinclair	24	M	Butcher	Scotland	"	
Geo. Rinnier	40	M	Shoemaker	Ireland	"	
Ellen " & ch.	34	F		"	"	
Richd. Loyd	30	M	Joiner	"	"	
Jno. Edward	25	M	Shoemaker	"	"	
A. Clarkson	24	M	Farmer	"	"	
Jno. McShaffry	35	M	Tobacconist	"	"	Sch. Leader. Cousins.
Mary " & 3 ch.	36	F		"	"	
Christopher Prince	31	M	Farmer	N. Scotia	"	
John Allen	26	M	Mariner	U. States	"	Brig Gervis.
Martin S. Wood	22	M	Merchant	"	"	Brig Florida. Woodbury.
J. M. Espardo	28	M	Commercl. agent for ?	"	"	Sch. Favourite. Lefevour.
C. Denoniller	34	M	Merchant	France	France	
E. Gazour	39	M	Shipmaster	"	"	
P. Lemoine	42	M	Merchant	"	"	
W. Bryan	39	M	Planter	Antigua	U. States	Sch. Betsey. Tilton.
Elizabeth & child	24	F		"	"	
Rebecca Elliot	50	F		"	"	
Thos. Dawson	26	M	Carpenter	England	"	Sch. Grand Turk. Taber.
Jane "	29	F		"	"	
Francis Taveran & ch.	41	M	Merchant	U. States	"	Ship Cadmus. Whilock.
H. Chevolat	23	M	"	France	"	
A. J. S. Amabrie *	26	M	"	"	"	
F. B. Daguet	40	M	Gardner	"	"	
Jas. Lasquoyas	46	M	Upholsterer	U. States	"	Brig Nassau. Welden.

PASSENGERS WHO ARRIVED IN THE U.S. SEPTEMBER 1821 - DECEMBER 1823

Names of passengers	Age	Sex	Occupation	Country to which they belong	Country of which they intend becoming inhabitants	Ship or vessel with the name of the master or commander
NEW YORK Cont.						
Q. E. Sept. 30, 1823						
Ann Lasquoyas	32	F		U. States	U. States	
Mary Ann Benson	24	F		"	"	
G. Peaver	45	M	Carpenter	"	"	Sch. Pactolus. Rilby.
Jno. Bruce	41	M	Tobacconist	"	"	
Geo. Stint	21	M	"	"	"	
Charles Yates	25	M	Gun smith	G. Britain	"	Sch. Cicero. Johnson
John Marklot	56	M	Merchant	U. States	"	Sch Manchester. Meek.
Mrs. " & 4 ch.	34	F		"	"	
F. Gonzales	36	M	"	Spain	"	
G. Fersands	23	M	"	France	"	
Eliza Sinclair & ch.	28	F		England	"	Sch. Elias Burger.
R. "	28	M	Planter	"	"	
Samuel Abbot	54	M	"	"	"	
C A. Davies	25	M	Merchant	U. States	"	Sch New Priscilla. Crowell.
Thos. Hill	40	M	"	"	"	
Henry Morris	20	M	"	"	"	
R. Casagenes	25	M	"	Spain	"	
F. Cogshall	30	M	Mariner	U. States	"	
E. Spaulding	28	M	Merchant	"	"	Sch. Blue Eyed Mary. Gardner.
B. H. Meakings	22	M	"	"	"	
H. Fugiman	30	M	"	Hamburg	"	Brig Nancy. Matthews.
Peter Stelfox	25	M	"	England	"	Sch. Minerva Wilson.
Jno. Lauton	30	M	"	"	"	
Wm. Whitehead	28	M	"	"	"	
Chas. Comstock	23	M	Farmer	U. States	"	
Jno. Lansdale	42	M	"	Scotland	"	
John Hudson	28	M	Merchant	U. States	"	Sch. Meteor Cobb
Thos. Newbold	26	M	"	"	"	
J. Bowman	45	M	Farmer	Scotland	"	Brig Statora. Patten.
Jane " & 2 ch.	45	F		"	"	
Wm. Clark	55	M	"	"	"	
Eliza " & 6 ch.	40	F		"	"	
Joseph Butler	46	M	"	"	"	
Sarah " & 5 ch.	32	F		"	"	
W. L. Palmer	49	M	Gent.	U. States	"	Sch. Howard. Holdridge.
C. " & 5 ch.	39	F		"	"	
Ruth Richey	36	F		Halifax	"	Sch. Wm. Basker. Nichols.
Fanny Riley	26	F		Ireland	"	
Marg. Brown & ch.	22	F		"	"	
Jas. McLaughlin	20	M		"	"	
J. Woodward	25	M	Merchant	Halifax	N. Scotia	Ship Andw. Jackson. Gold.
E. Pauvert	21	M	"	U. States	U. States	
John Richardson	20	M	Clerk	G. Britain	"	Sch. Broke. McCulloch.
Robt. "	21	M	"	"	"	

Names of passengers	Age	Sex	Occupation	Country to which they belong	Country of which they intend becoming inhabitants	Ship or vessel with the name of the master or commander
NEW YORK Cont.						
Q. E. Sept. 30, 1823						
Robert Cunningham	30	M	Tailor	G. Britain	U. States	
Helen "	32	F		"	"	
Jane Hunter	23	F		"	"	
Wm. Mackay	62	M	Teacher	"	"	
Margt. " & ch.	38	F		"	"	
J. Moreland & 3 ch.	40	F		"	"	
James Temple & 2 ch.	24	M	Farmer	"	"	
A. Russell	19	M	Clerk	" "	"	
Danl. Mitchell	40	M	Shoemaker	"	"	
Margt. "	21	F		"	"	
Geo. Richardson & 2 ch.	41	M	Merchant	"	"	
James Fisher	60	M		"	"	
Thomas "	30	M	Labourer	"	"	
Ann "	24	F		"	"	
Susan "	22	F		"	"	
P. Fleming & 5 ch.	35	M		"	"	
Alexr. Frasier	35	M	Mason	"	"	
C. Anderson	20	M	"	"	"	
James Stewart	38	M	Merchant	U. States	"	Sch. Maria. Mather.
R. Lewis	32	M	Mariner	"	"	Sch. Nimrod. Sterling.
James Babcock	34	M	Merchant	"	"	Brig Frederick. Stillman.
Chas. Rey	23	M	"	"	"	Sch. Industry. Jenkins.
Jno. W. Bumtin	17	M		"	"	Sloop Thos. & Eliza. Wallace.
Chas. Zeitter	25	M		Germany	"	Brig Louisa. Colus.
E. Muluman	21	M		"	"	
E. Segui *	24	M	Planter	France	"	Brig Andromache. Andrews.
O. Goodrich	27	M	Mechanic	U. States	"	
John Moore	26	M	Merchant	"	"	Brig Blooming Rose. Betts.
Jas. Montadevert	32	M	"	"	"	
A. Villiers	25	M	"	France	"	
J. Frasier	29	M	Farmer	U. States	"	Brig Yamacian. Clark.
Mrs. " & child	23	F		"	"	
H. Conway	22	F		Ireland	"	Sch. Nestor. Lee.
S. P. Riven/Rivers *	36	M	Merchant	Holland	"	
Andw. Britton	34	M	"	Ireland	"	
Wm. Wallace	22	M	Labourer	England	"	
Samuel Fox	25	M	"	"	"	
R. P. Whimple	21	M	"	"	"	
Wm. McGillivary & 2 ch.	50	M	Merchant	Scotland	"	Sch. Hannibal. Watkinson.
Wm. Peacock	56	M		"	"	
Mary "	22	F		"	"	
A. B. Butterworth	24	M	Accountant	G. Britain	"	Brig Minerva. Anderson.
Jno. Gibson	24	M	Farmer	"	"	

Names of passengers	Age	Sex	Occupation	Country to which they belong	Country of which they intend becoming inhabitants	Ship or vessel with the name of the master or commander
NEW YORK Cont.						
Q. E. Sept. 30, 1823						
Mary Gibson & ch.	32	F		G. Britain	U. States	
Wm. Johnston	29	M	Farmer	"	"	
Jane " & 3 ch.	28	F		"	"	
Jno. Fitzgerald	23	M	"	"	"	
Wm. Gib	29	M	Painter	"	"	
D. McRory	28	M	Upholsterer	"	"	
Jno. Collins	40	M	Merchant	"	"	
Samuel C. Reid	38	M	Mariner	U. States	"	Sch. Jane. Rice.
J. A. Arongo	23	M	Lawyer	Cuba	Spain	
J. M. Pastenero	24	M	Merchant	"	"	
A. Thompson	44	M	Mariner	U. States	U. States	
Wm. Rilly	22	M	Merchant	Ireland	"	Sch. Eliza Ann. Barstow.
Jno. "	30	M	Tobacconist	"	"	
James Faley *	26	M	"	"	"	
B. Duncan	22	M		"	"	
C. Weldon	23	M		"	"	
P. Conway	25	M		"	"	
F. Frayman	21	M		"	"	
J. Dolan	45	M		"	"	
Moses Tryon	40	M	Merchant	U. States	"	Brig Radius. Granger.
L. Lavellette	25	M	Planter	Spain	"	
J. Yalseur	30	M	"	"	"	
C. Castro	30	M	"	"	"	
Jno E. Glean	42	M	Merchant	U. States	"	Sch. Diligence. Eustis.
Robt. Kerr	45	M	"	G. Britain	"	
H. A. Hardy	37	M	"	U. States	"	Brig Prince Edward. Sears.
C. D. Hoffman	25	M	Physician	"	"	
S. Swain	40	M	Mariner	"	"	
J. H. Barry	36	M	Merchant	"	"	
J. A. Dolbie	27	M	Carpenter	G. Britain	"	
Charles R. Lawrence	37	M	Merchant	U. States	"	
J. A. Tom	21	M	Mariner	"	"	
Fred. Beahr	50	M		Germany	"	Brig Constitution.
Geo. Hoake	24	M	Printer	"	"	
B. Meyers	34	F		"	"	
C. Richers & child	23	M		"	"	
Fred. Schusler/Schuster	22	M	Sugar baker	"	"	
C. Baschin	24	M	"	"	"	
C. D. Sabeck	29	M	"	"	"	
H. Cornwall	30	M	B. Army	England	Halifax	Ship Stephania. Macy.
Mrs. "	25	F		"	"	
S. V. S. Wilder	42	M	Merchant	"	"	
Mrs. E. " & 4 ch.	25	F		"	"	
G. De Wolfe	48	M	"	U. States	U. States	

Names of passengers	Age	Sex	Occupation	Country to which they belong	Country of which they intend becoming inhabitants	Ship or vessel with the name of the master or commander
NEW YORK Cont.						
Q. E. Sept. 30, 1823						
L. Halbut	19	M	Student	France	France	
J. Benvagnan	15	M	"	"	"	
F. L. Duplessis	20	M	Physician	England	U. States	
P. Teaguett	50	M	Planter	U. States	"	Ship Romulus. Allen.
Jno. Moreland	34	M	Merchant	"	"	
Wm. Burnham	30	M	"	"	"	
J. Gomar	50	M	"	"	"	
J. Tague *	32	M	"	"	"	
J. Magotin	19	M	"	"	"	
Fred Williams	19	M	"	"	"	
Jno. Campbell	30	M	"	"	"	
Louisa Moore	25	F		Ireland	"	Brig Howard. Stocking.
Ann Keen	20	F		"	"	
Thos. W. Clark	23	M	Lawyer	U. States	"	
Jas. Burkett	48	M	Mariner	Ireland	"	
Thos. W. Cullinane	35	M	Farmer	"	"	
Jas. Cornell	40	M	"	"	"	
Wm. Baker	44	M	"	"	"	
G. Roche	25	M	"	"	"	
Wm. Rogers	46	M	Clerk	"	"	
Margt. "	36	F		"	"	
Jas. Brown	34	M	Labourer	"	"	
Bridget "	28	F		"	"	
G. Patten	25	M		"	"	
Jon. Fitzgerald	36	M	Farmer	"	"	
M. Sheehan	20	M	"	"	"	
J. Fitzgerald	22	M	"	"	"	
J. Murphy	38	M		"	"	
M. Swift	20	M		"	"	
Susan Reed	36	F		"	"	
Jno. Barry	25	M		"	"	
Danl. McMarah	22	M		"	"	
Jno. O. Sullivan & ch.	40	M		"	"	
P. Fowler	28	M		"	"	
Jno. Barrett	22	M		"	"	
Wm. Power	25	M		"	"	
P. Malony	25	M		"	"	
D. Cellin	28	M		"	"	
Edwd. Dunn	47	M		"	"	
Peggy "	34	F		"	"	
Wm. Norris	22	M		"	"	
Thos. O. Bryan	20	M		"	"	
Johanna "	20	F		"	"	
Allen Pitman	38	M		"	" "	

Names of passengers	Age	Sex	Occupation	Country to which they belong	Country of which they intend becoming inhabitants	Ship or vessel with the name of the master or commander
NEW YORK Cont.						
Q. E. Sept. 30, 1823						
Martin Greely	22	M	Farmer	Ireland	U. States	
Jno. Taylor	21	M	"	"	"	
Thos. Barrett	22	M	"	"	"	
G. FitzGerald	23	M	"	"	"	
Eliza " & 5 ch.	22	F		"	"	
Thos. Haw	32	M	Labourer	"	"	Sch. Weser. Stodell.
Owen McLowen	20	M	"	"	"	
Jno. Kimball	18	M	"	"	"	
P. McCallie	22	M	"	"	"	
P. Ward	31	M	"	"	"	
W. Sheridan	18	M	"	"	"	
P. Baxter	19	M	"	"	"	
Robt. Rogers & 2 ch.	35	M		"	"	
Edwd. Nichols	25	M		"	"	
P. Duffey	26	M		"	"	
E. Jones	36	M		"	"	
Thos. Jones & 4 ch.	30	M		"	"	
Rose McLowen & 2 ch.	26	F		"	"	
Jane Rogers & 3 ch.	27	F		"	"	
A. M. Pumanto & 3 ch.	32	F		France	"	Sch. Acaster. Griswold.
Ann Ridley	26	F		England	"	
Jos. Stammers	52	M	Farmer	"	"	
Mary Ann " & 8 ch.	44	F		"	"	
C. Bailey & 3 ch.	25	F		"	"	
Robt. Cutting	31	M	Farmer	"	"	
Thos. "	24	M	"	"	"	
S. Newman	52	M	Mariner	"	"	
P. J. Nicholls	29	M	Surveyor	"	"	
Sarah "	31	F		"	"	
S. Langridge	41	M	Farmer	"	"	
Francis "	36	M	"	"	"	
Eliza "	17	F		"	"	
Thos. D. Franklin	24	M	"	"	"	
Joseph Corben	24	M	"	"	"	
Danl. Silcocks	37	M	"	"	"	
Wm. Blake	45	M	"	"	"	
Eliza " & 4 ch.	43	F		"	"	
Thos. Sanders	73	M	"	"	"	
A. Patten	37	M	"	"	"	
Wm. Britten	23	M	"	"	"	
Thos. Roofe *	35	M	"	"	"	
Sarah " & 5 ch.	31	F	"	"	"	
Thomas Thorncraft	24	M	"	"	"	
J. Granger & ch.	38	M	"	"	"	

Names of passengers	Age	Sex	Occupation	Country to which they belong	Country of which they intend becoming inhabitants	Ship or vessel with the name of the master or commander
NEW YORK Cont.						
Q. E. Sept. 30, 1823						
Thos. Everden & 2 ch.	55	M	Farmer	England	U. States	
C. Hepty	25	M	Mechanic	Switzerland	"	
Susan Strong & 2 ch.	40	F		England	"	
A. Quaife & ch.	29	F		"	"	
Wm. Laird	60	M	Farmer	"	"	
Cath. "	58	F		"	"	
Saml. Weslan/Weslau	41	M	"	"	"	
Ann " & 9 ch.	30	F		"	"	
Sarah Evans & ch.	38	F		"	"	
Richd. Braiser	30	M	Farmer	"	"	
Sarah " & 6 ch.	40	F		"	"	
Thomas Butcher	39	M		"	"	
Jno. Millson	64	F		"	"	
Martha "	52	F		"	"	
Jno. Tribley	28	M		"	"	
Eliza Neine	54	F		"	"	
Hannah E. Neine	21	F		"	"	
H. Woodwith & 5 ch.	33	F		"	"	
Joseph Taylor *	25	M	Mechanic	"	"	
A. "	26	F		"	"	
John Sands	62	M	Farmer	"	"	
Henry Lewis	21	M	"	"	"	
Henry Williams	26	M	Victualler	England	"	Ship Oscar. Morris.
Jane " & ch.	23	F		"	"	
Edwd. Jenkins	47	M	Farmer	"	"	
Margt. " & 11 ch.	44	F		"	"	
Wm. Harrison	28	M	"	"	"	
Robt. Abbot	35	M	Physician	U. States	"	Sch. Chase. Baxter.
F. McGilvary	40	M	Planter	G. Britain	"	
P. P. Delapaine	33	M	Merchant	U. States	"	
O. Leward	35	M	Mechanic	"	"	Brig Robt. Read. Smith.
Jas. Edwards	24	M	Shoemaker	G. Britain	"	Sch. Mentor. Brown.
Ann Leonard	30	F	"	"	"	
P. Welsh	34	M	Weaver	U. States	"	
Hugh Beattie	26	M	Surgeon	Demerara	"	Brig Visitor. Lewis.
Samuel Lyon	30	M	Merchant	Curracoa	"	Brig Rebecca & Sally. Auger.
Frs. Dupier	19	M	"	"	"	
David Riddie	40	M	Mechanic	Scotland	"	Brig Hiram. Morpen.
E. Ludlow & 5 ch.	34	F		U. States	"	Sch. Bayard. Vandyke.
L. E. Crufot & 2 ch.	28	F		France	"	
L. D. Angeran	23	M	"	"	"	
Helen Young	27	F		"	"	
N. M. Britton	24	M	Merchant	"	"	Brig Aspasia. Everitt.
F. H. Goodwin	25	M	"	England	"	

Names of passengers	Age	Sex	Occupation	Country to which they belong	Country of which they intend becoming inhabitants	Ship or vessel with the name of the master or commander
NEW YORK Cont. Q. E. Sept. 30, 1823						
Jas. Low	24	M	Merchant	U. States	U. States	
A. Vickars	28	M	Engineer	England	"	
P. Magalet	47	M	Ship master	U. States	"	
A. Mancu *	37	M	Painter	Italy	"	
F. Manter	40	M	Merchant	Spain	"	
J. A. Rinark	21	M	"	"	"	
A. Gouguard	40	M	"	"	"	
David Thompson	22	M	Farmer	Scotland	"	Sch. Commerce. Ritchie.
Eliza "	23	F		"	"	
John "	22	M	Merchant	"	"	
Jno Simpson	22	M	"	"	"	
D. M. Robinson	18	M	Farmer	"	"	
Hugh Neil	25	M	"	"	"	
Robt. Hitchen & 3 ch.	50	M	"	"	"	
Jas. "	25	M	"	"	"	
Alexr. Ribby	46	M	"	"	"	
Eliza " & 3 ch.	40	F		"	"	
Chas. Anderson	32	M	Baker	"	"	
Wm. Chambers	22	M	Farmer	"	"	
Francis "	17	M	"	"	"	
O. Wingate	23	M	"	"	"	
David Crawford	22	M	Merchant	"	"	
D. Glen	21	M	Farmer	"	"	
John McGibbin	38	M	"	"	"	
Edwd. Cockburn	30	M	Merchant	"	"	
Jane "	35	F		"	"	
B. Bunkin	24	M	Farmer	"	"	
Robt. Sanderson	25	M	"	"	"	
N. Stusly *	27	M	"	"	"	
Jno. Buckram	18	M	"	"	"	
Jno. McFadon	26	M	"	"	"	
A. Milay	24	M	Teacher	"	"	
Mary "	30	F		"	"	
Jas. Gibson	36	M	Merchant	"	"	
Jas. Scott	25	M	Farmer	"	"	
Wm. Walker	18	M		"	"	
David Boyle	45	M		"	"	
D. Forbes	22	M		"	"	
D. Glen	60	M		"	"	
Ann " & 5 ch.	50	F		"	"	
T. Pater	40	M		"	"	
Jno. Zigmen	30	M		"	"	
James McEwen	25	M	Merchant	"	"	
John Downes	18	M	"	"	"	

Names of passengers	Age	Sex	Occupation	Country to which they belong	Country of which they intend becoming inhabitants	Ship or vessel with the name of the master or commander
NEW YORK Cont.						
Q. E. Sept. 30, 1823						
Jno. Ferguson	18	M	Merchant	Scotland	U. States	
Henry T Woodward	37	M	Farmer	Ireland	U. States	Sch. Panther. Bennett.
L. S. " & 5 ch.	37	F		"	"	
Francis Mughan	36	M	Merchant	"	"	
Henry McCardle	20	M	"	"	"	
Jno. Cartwright	42	M	"	England	"	
Jno. Berwick	45	M	"	"	"	
Thos. C. Lowndes	22	M	"	U. States	"	
A. G. Balston	25	M	"	"	"	
M. Whitting	25	M	"	"	"	Sch. Dart. Allen.
Henry Todd	52	M	"	Bermuda	Bermuda	Sloop Alpha. Algate.
W. Shikelford	32	M	"	U. States	U. States	
D. C. Algate	25	M	"	"	"	
Lafond Chanopin	30	M	Planter	Guadaloup	France	Brig Elizabeth. Gardner.
Maria A. "	20	F		"	"	
Maria Venus	50	F		"	"	
Edmd. Neale	42	M	Planter	"	"	
H. Tomlinson	26	M	Merchant	U. States	U. States	Brig George. Knight.
L. Garnier	40	M	"	"	"	
L. Angino	40	M	Farmer	"	"	
Jno. H. Parker	23	M	Accountant	Ireland	"	Sch. Triton. Wilkinson.
Jno. Wilson	56	M		"	"	
Wm. "	19	M		"	"	
Jno. " Jr.	21	M		"	"	
Mary Ann Wilson	54	F		"	"	
Martha " & 2 ch.	25	F		"	"	
Elizabeth Moore	25	F		"	"	
Isabella "	21	F		"	"	
Wm. Brown	62	M	Farmer	"	"	
Rebecca "	62	F		"	"	
Jno. Long	18	M		"	"	
Thos. Lowther	23	M		"	"	
Andw. Moffat	25	M		"	"	
Wm. Rector	25	M		"	"	
L. Scott	23	M		"	"	
Eliza Scott	17	F		"	"	
Wm. Harper	25	M		"	"	
Mary " & 2 ch.	25	F		"	"	
Mary Kelso	22	F		"	"	
Robt. Lover	60	M	Farmer	"	"	
Saml. "	30	M	"	"	"	
A. Embden	30	M	Merchant	Hamburg	"	Sch. Enterprise. Black.
Cath. Anderson	50	F		U. States	"	
S. S. Penroy	40	M	Merchant	Spain	Spain	Sch. Genl. Marion. Allen.

Names of passengers	Age	Sex	Occupation	Country to which they belong	Country of which they intend becoming inhabitants	Ship or vessel with the name of the master or commander
NEW YORK Cont.						
Q. E. Sept. 30, 1823						
E. Hidden	32	M	Mechanic	U. States	U. States	
Patrick Brine	25	M		N. Foundland	"	Sch. Mariner. McAllister
Mary "	25	F		"	"	
Thos. Casey	30	M	Cooper	"	"	
D. Scallon	55	M	Physician	"	"	
P. Shelly	28	M	Merchant	"	"	
B. Eymar	30	M	"	France	"	Brig Charles. Coffin.
J B. Tignaige	23	M	"	"	"	
Jno. Buariard	23	M	Mechanic	"	"	
Charles Atkinson	27	M	Officer	England		Sch. Exchange. Arnold.
Ann " & ch.	28	F		"		
Wm. M. Curry	22	M		"		
M. Metcalf	36	M		"		
Neil McLane	32	M	Labourer	"		
Jane "	29	F		"		
Robt. Potter	33	M	"	"		
B. "	33	M		"		
Jno. Rorke	29	M	"	"		
Peter Hood	28	M	"	"		
Pat. Welden	37	M	Baker	"		
Margt. " & 6 ch.	37	F		"		
Pat. McFarlan	40	M	Labourer	"		
Michael "	34	M	Carpenter	"		
Andw. Evans	32	M	Grocer	Wales	U. States	Sch. Frances Henrietta. Dickinson
N. H. Doge	25	M	"	Ireland	"	
Michael Short	30	M	Labourer	"	"	
Jas. "	24	M	"	"	"	
Bryan "	22	M	"	"	"	
Thos. McIntire	30	M	"	"	"	
L. Welch	27	M	"	"	"	
Robt. McEvans	50	M	Mariner	"	"	
Robt. Moore	21	M	"	"	"	
Thos. Harris	57	M	"	"	"	
Thos. " Jr.	18	M	"	"	"	
Eliza " & 3 ch.	55	F		"	"	
John "	27	M	Farmer	"	"	
George Lovell	27	M	"	"	"	
Esther " & 2 ch.	28	F		"	"	
Thos. J. Cork *	26	M	"	"	"	
Ann " & 5 ch.	26	F		"	"	
Joseph Webb	26	M	"	"	"	
Sarah "	24	F		"	"	
Henry Churchill	36	M	"	"	"	
Saml. Hallington	21	M	"	"	"	

Names of passengers	Age	Sex	Occupation	Country to which they belong	Country of which they intend becoming inhabitants	Ship or vessel with the name of the master or commander
NEW YORK Cont.						
Q E. Sept. 30, 1823						
H. Phipps	21	M	Farmer	Ireland	U. States	
Wm Watt	22	M	Baker	"	"	
John Pearson	20	M	Labourer	"	"	
Wm Jobson	20	M	Farmer	"	"	
John Humphries	55	M	Draper	U. States	"	Ship New York. Maxwell.
Jane "	52	F		"	"	
Arthur Baker	52	M	Tailor	"	"	
Harriet " & 2 ch.	28	F		"	"	
Robt. Everett	33	M	Clergyman	"	"	
Eliza " & 2 ch.	27	F		"	"	
Wm. Hall	34	M	Merchant	"	"	
H. Pressam & ch.	30	F		"	"	
Thos. Everett	27	M	Merchant	"	"	
Mary " & 2 ch.	30	F		"	"	
Richd. Jones	27	M	Farmer	"	"	
R. J. Haynes	54	M	Planter	England	"	
Eliza B. " & 3 ch.	47	F		"	"	
Thos. "	29	M		"	"	
Wm. Nelson	46	M	Merchant	"	"	
Jno. Clemenson	27	M	Farmer	"	"	
Jas. Sanderson	38	M	Merchant	"	"	
Jesse Jones	40	M	Clergyman	"	"	
L. Lewis	19	M	Farmer	"	"	
M. Le Peltibin	40	M		France	"	Brig Packet. Doughty.
A. Pelayo *	22	M	Merchant	Spain	Spain	
Jno. Mazuge	25	M	"	"	"	
Frs. Angle	52	M	"	"	"	
John Earle	34	M	"	G. Britain		Sch. Robt. Fulton. Graham.
Frances "	24	F		"		
Edwd. Mallard	28	M	"	"		
C. Cumming	42	M	"	"		
Alexr. Scott	22	M	Farmer	"		
Wm. W. Good	27	M		"	U. States	Sch. Caravan. Sparrow.
Michael MaGuire	30	M	"	"	"	
Nancy "	24	F		"	"	
Jno. Cabell *	33	M	"	"	"	
J. Hanlieu *	24	M	"	"	"	
Richd. F. Simmons	24	M	"	"	"	
M. Donelly	26	M	Tailor	"	"	
P. Magrath	27	M	Farmer	"	"	
Jno. Donnahoe	25	M	"	"	"	
Matthew Owens	25	M	"	"	"	
Jos. Spiller	21	M	Clerk	"	"	
Wm. Duane	63	M		U. States	"	Sch. Quito. Baldwin.

Names of passengers	Age	Sex	Occupation	Country to which they belong	Country of which they intend becoming inhabitants	Ship or vessel with the name of the master or commander
NEW YORK Cont.						
Q. E. Sept. 30, 1823						
Elizabeth Duane	22	F		U. States	U. States	
S. Larich	33	M	Consul Genl.	Sweden		
Richd. Back	27	M	Offcr U. S. A	U. States	"	
Jno. Gaither	28	M	Merchant	"	"	
Jno. R. Picard	25	M	"	Cuba	Cuba	
Robt. Mann	30	M	"	England	England	Sloop MacDonough. Baker.
B. J. Tucker	30	M	"	Barbadoes	Barbadoes	
Jno. Bairie	45	M	"	U. States	U. States	Brig Marcia. Bigly.
Seth Talbot	47	M	"	"	"	
D. Noble	32	M	Mariner	"	"	Brig Aurella. Howland.
Jno. R. Cheeks	32	M	Merchant	Barbadoes	"	Sch. Rambler. Boardman.
John White	45	M	"	"		Brig Superb. Burr.
F. Edey	40	M	"	"	"	
Saml. P. Tudor	32	M	"	"		
Saml. Whitney	25	M	"	"		
D. Dummell	20	M	"	"		
Jno. Alleyne	30	M	"	"		
J. K. McConney	32	M	"	" "		
Geo. Humphrey	20	M	"	"		
Jno. Huth	30	M	"	"		
Thos. Baldoron	30	M	"	"		
Edwd. Morgan	25	M	"	"		
Joseph Yates	48	M	Farmer	St. Johns	U. States	Sch. Lady Hunter. Palmiter.
James Flintoff	53	M	"	"	"	
Jas. Muneline *	28	M	"	"	"	
H. " & 2 ch.	26	M	"	"	"	
Jno. Bell	24	M	"	"	"	
Sarah " & 2 ch.	20	F		"	"	
Wm. Cochran	19	M	Labourer	"	"	
Jas. Hughes	23	M	Weaver	"	"	
Jas. Bruce	20	M	Labourer	"	"	
Jane Cather & 3 ch.	50	F		"	"	
Wm. Jamieson	35	M	"	"	"	
Saml. "	30	M	"	"	"	
N. Russell	25	F	Seamstress	"	"	
M. "	22	F	"	"	"	
E. Ellen	24	F	"	"	"	
B. Rodwick	55	M	Merchant	U. States	"	Sch. Hope. Lewis.
A. Maissir	22	M	"	France	"	Sch. Asia. Minigh.
W. Hanns/Hanut	34	M	"	"	"	
Wm. Taylor	55	M	Farmer	"	"	
Mrs. " & 3 ch.	30	F		"	"	
A. Handieside	20	M	Mechanic	England	"	Sch. London Packet. Benedict.
B. Ducass	35	M	Mariner	France	"	Brig Emeline. Rawlings.

Names of passengers	Age	Sex	Occupation	Country to which they belong	Country of which they intend becoming inhabitants	Ship or vessel with the name of the master or commander
NEW YORK Cont.						
Q. E. Sept. 30, 1823						
Jno. Runny	42	M	Physician	Spain	U. States	
Danl. Geraud	38	M	Merchant	U. States	"	
G. Sanmukelli	26	M	"	Rome	"	Sloop Betsey. Eddy.
G. T. Matheson	23	M	"	England	England	Sch. Citizen. Hughs.
Alexr. McGee	20	M	Mariner	"	"	Sch. Esperanza.
Richd. Farrell	30	M	Merchant	Ireland	U. States	Brig Jubilee. Waterhouse.
John Camp	20	M	Mechanic	Halifax	"	Sch. Penobscot. Staples.
C. Fennell	35	F		U. States	"	
E. Ferris	35	F		"	"	
Sarah Hubard	40	F		"	"	
Wm. Small	47	M	Mariner	"	"	Sch. Moxa. West.
C. Larochelle	25	M	Merchant	Hayti	"	Sch. Pedlar. Gerrish.
C. Buxheda	31	M	"	Spain	Spain	Sch. Charlestown Packet. Mansfld.
Jno Seward	26	M	Farmer	England	U. States	Sch. Jno. Dickinson. Burras.
Robt. Arthur	20	M	Tanner	"	"	
A. Griffith & 6 ch.	35	F		"	"	
R. "	32	M	Farmer	"	"	
W. Hughes	33	M	Labourer	"	"	
Ann Clark & 3 ch.	36	F		"	"	Sch. St. Michael. Tucker.
Geo. Barnard	31	M	Architect	"	"	Sch. Maria. Fowle.
J. Balek	41	M	Ship master	U. States	"	
J. Jackson	41	M	Glass blower	England	"	
J. Prentiss	25	M	Tanner	U. States	"	
Wm. Senior	30	M		"	"	
Catharine " & 5 ch.	26	F		"	"	
Thos. Gough	22	M	Labourer	"	"	
C. Cannon & 4 ch.	30	F		"	"	
C. Abrahams & 2 ch.	34	F		"	"	
Wm. Tilley	24	M	Glass blower	"	"	
Alexr. Gun & 2 ch.	49	M		"	"	
B. Molan	38	M	Officer	G. Britain	"	Sch. Elizabeth. Smith.
F. J. Heon	24	M	Professor of Languages	Prussia	"	
Catharine Heon	24	F		"	"	
J. B. De Lamotte	24	M		France	"	
J. W. Post	22	M		U. States	"	Ship Marmion. Hawkins.
W. T. Worthington	20	M		"	"	
Robt. Greenhow	23	M		"	"	
T. Stoble	26	M	Merchant	"	"	
Ann Betterton	35	F		"	"	Sch. Margaret. Mounts.
Jno. M. Turner	45	M		"	"	
J. Stroker	22	M		"	"	
J. Garrett	17	M	Labourer	"	"	
W. Stanman	25	M	"	England	"	

PASSENGERS WHO ARRIVED IN THE U.S. SEPTEMBER 1821 - DECEMBER 1823

Names of passengers	Age	Sex	Occupation	Country to which they belong	Country of which they intend becoming inhabitants	Ship or vessel with the name of the master or commander
NEW YORK Cont.						
Q. E. Sept. 30, 1823						
Wm. Nichols	30	M	Locksmith	England	U. States	
Chas. Franks	26	M		"	"	
John Woodman	24	M	Baker	"	"	
M. Jackson	26	M	Merchant	G. Britain	"	Sh. Leeds. Stodard
B. " & 3 ch.	23	F		"	"	
Ellen Craig	21	F		"	"	
Peter Jackson	28	M	Farmer	"	"	
E. Greaves	44	M	Merchant	"	"	
W. W. Greenup	25	M		"	"	
E. Holden	28	M		"	"	
J. Rankin	34	M		"	"	
T. Ferris	32	M		"	"	
A. Richards	50	M		"	"	
C. W. Woolsey	21	M		"	"	
M. Doufoux	26	M	Merchant	France	"	Sch. Maria Ann. Mayrick.
--- Languille	20	M	"	"	"	
--- Amant	21	M	Mariner	"	"	
--- Pediage	42	M	Baker	Spain	"	
--- Cochin	31	M	Mariner	"	"	
--- Chauchie	32	M	"	"	"	
C. Chesman	41	M	"	"	"	
--- Moile	26	M	"	"	"	
B. Charchellet	23	M		"	"	Ship Adonis. Rocharde.
L. Jacobs	26	M	Lawyer	France	"	
Thos. Brown	45	M	Manufactr.	England	"	Sch. Cane. Halliday.
Betsey & 8 ch.	48	F		"	"	
Samuel Lawrence	21	M	Tanner	"	"	
M. Colston	15	M	"	"	"	
P. Spaclan	48	M	"	"	"	
Eliza " & 6 ch.	51	F		"	"	
Jno. Reed	48	M	"	"	"	
Mary " & 4 ch.	48	F		"	"	
Jno. Webber	27	M	"	"	"	
Gideon Dodge	30	M	Mechanic	U. States	"	Sch. Repartee. Waite.
Wm. Donnan	26	M	Teacher	Scotland	"	Sch. Commerce. Whiting.
Richd. Gypsin	27	M	Farmer	England	"	
Wm. Wilson	26	M	Mariner	Ireland	"	
Robt. Beattie	22	M	Farmer	"	"	
P Rock	36	M	Teacher	"	"	
John Quinn	48	M	Farmer	"	"	
John Dankes	32	M	Miner	"	"	
Ann " & 2 ch.	24	F		"	"	
James Farrell	30	M	Teacher	England	"	
P. Malstay	28	M	Farmer	Ireland	"	

Names of passengers	Age	Sex	Occupation	Country to which they belong	Country of which they in-tend becoming inhabitants	Ship or vessel with the name of the master or commander
NEW YORK Cont.						
Q. E. Sept. 30, 1823						
Edwd. Larkin	30	M	Labourer	Ireland	U. States	
H. Sherwood	23	M	Baker	"	"	
Edwd. Brennan	25	M	Farmer	"	"	
W. Steward	36	M	"	"	"	
Wm. Coleburn	33	M		England	"	
Chas. " & ch.	30	M		"	"	
Bridget Clark	26	F		Ireland	"	
John Bain	38	M	Millwright	"	"	
John Harrison	29	M	Clerk	"	"	
Eliza Gillard & 4 ch.	30	F		"	"	
Mary Moore & 4 ch.	30	F		"	"	
Margt. Renny & 3 ch.	26	F		"	"	
M. Washburn & 1 ch.	35	F		England	"	Sch. Dublin Packet. Newcombe.
Anthony McDonald	50	M	Merchant	U. States	"	
D. R. Moorehead	27	M	Physician	Ireland	"	
John Taylor	20	M		"	"	
J. Allen	30	M		"	"	
E. Eccleston	24	M		"	"	
J. Kearns	45	M	Tanner	"	"	
Ann " & ch.	45	F		"	"	
Jno. Layd	30	M		"	"	
J. " Jr.	25	M		"	"	
Thos. "	22	M		"	"	
Sarah Terry * & 3 ch.	30	F		"	"	
J. M. McDonald	28	M	Farmer	"	"	
James Connan	24	M	"	"	"	
Nancy " & ch.	27	F		"	"	
P. Moore	28	M	"	"	"	
M. Farrell & ch.	27	F		"	"	
M. McCabe	22	M		"	"	
Jno. Recanes *	30	M	Farmer	"	"	
Saml. McFadden	24	M	"	"	"	
Jas. Hosier	20	M	"	"	"	
Wm. Montgomery	22	M	"	"	"	
John Connor	22	M	"	"	"	
J. B. Perot	21	M	Merchant	France	"	Sch. Ann Eliza Jane. Labousse.
Alexr. Stewart	31	M	Farmer	G. Britain	"	Ship Union. French.
Isabella " & 2 ch.	25	F		"	"	
Jno Bennett	31	M	"	"	"	
Francis Thompson	25	M	Physician	"	"	
Evan James	30	M	Carpenter	"	"	
M. Cann	28	M	Labourer	"	"	
Elias Richards	28	M	"	"	"	
E. Burrow	27	M	Farmer	"	"	

Names of passengers	Age	Sex	Occupation	Country to which they belong	Country of which they intend becoming inhabitants	Ship or vessel with the name of the master or commander
NEW YORK Cont.						
Q. E. Sept. 30, 1823						
Jno. Smith	28	M	Gardner	G. Britain	U. States	
Edwd. Fallon	28	M	Merchant	"	"	
Jno. McRee	34	M	"	"	"	
Geo. Clifton	28	M	Farmer	"	"	
P. Waters	21	M	"	"	"	
Edwd. Connor	37	M	Book keeper	"	"	
John Gaston	36	M	Merchant	U. States	"	Sch. Amity. Maxwell.
James N. Nevin	21	M	"	"	"	
Isaac Y. Howell	38	M		Amsterdam	"	
C. Mackiar	45	M		Demerara	"	
John Johnson	45	M	Merchant	England	"	
Wm. Rose	27	M	"	"	"	
Jas. Anderson	26	M	"	"	"	
Geo. Ralph	33	M	"	"	"	
C. W. Rockwell	24	M	"	"	"	
S. Hyde	54	M	"	"	"	
Thos. Sands	33	M		"	"	
M. Morgan & 4 ch.	38	F		"	"	
John Doin	26	M	Tailor	Ireland	"	
Y. Billsborough	23	M	Farmer	"	"	
Wm. Morris	36	M	Merchant	G. Britain	"	Sch. Friends. Choate.
Eliza "	27	F		"	"	
John Findlay	23	M	Clerk	"	"	
A. Carton	25	M	"	"	"	
Wm. Taylor	54	M	Farmer	"	"	
Samuel Wood	50	M	"	"	"	
Eliza " & ch.	24	F	"	"	"	
W. Rillock	25	M	"	"	"	
Ann " & 2 ch.	25	F		"	"	
Donald Smith	22	M	Labourer	"	"	
Jas. Cunningham	20	M	"	"	"	
R. Cullen & 4 ch.	50	F		"	"	
Wm. Gibson	55	M	Farmer	"	"	
James "	22	M	Merchant	"	"	
Edwd. Conley	36	M	Mechanic	Ireland	"	Sch. Four Sisters. Spauling.
B. "	30	F		"	"	
Jos. M. Buvesier *	30	M	Merchant	Spain	"	Sch. Admittance. Pittsbury.
Antonio Piniton	35	M	"	"	"	
James Eylerna	28	M	"	England	"	Sch. Manhattan. Rickelson.
T. Reale	28	M	B. Navy	"	"	
Thos. A. Powers	28	M	Merchant	U. States	"	
J. Dickinson	45	M	"	"	"	
W. Reed	25	M	"	"	"	
T. W. Delmour	28	M	"	"	"	

Names of passengers	Age	Sex	Occupation	Country to which they belong	Country of which they intend becoming inhabitants	Ship or vessel with the name of the master or commander
NEW YORK Cont.						
Q. E. Sept. 30, 1823						
John Buckey	30	M	Farmer	England	U. States	
Mrs. "	30	F		"	"	
F. O. Miara	30	M	"	"	"	
Mary " & 4 ch.	28	F		"	"	
Edwd. Cotter * & 4 ch.	35	M	"	"	"	
Jno. O'Brian	52	M	Shipmaster	U. States	"	
Jane " & 7 ch.	45	F		"	"	
J. Thompson	22	M	Saddler	"	"	Sch. Emigrant. Barnes.
Wm. Herbert	35	M	Planter	"	"	
Jno. Y. Machetts	32	M	Merchant	"	"	
Jno. Semonton	45	M	"	"	"	Sch. Chase. Pinkney.
G. E. Pendegrass	40	M	"	"	"	
J. Fenno	29	M	"	"	"	
W. Lawrens	30	M	Mariner	"	"	
P. B. Carman	32	M	"	"	"	Sch. Packet Margt. Harden.
James Croft	48	M	Merchant	England	"	Sch. Persia Minchee
M. Ryan	37	M	"	"	Barbados	Sch. Falcon. Morrell.
Chas. Hasken	28	M	"	Ireland	U. States	
Jas. Carnes	22	M	Mariner	U. States	"	
Samuel Mitchell	50	M	Merchant	"	"	Sch. Sperm. Clark.
H. Moore	21	M	Mechanic	"	"	Sch. Almira. Doane.
Chas. M. Smith	25	M	"	"	"	
N. Johnson	23	M	Mariner	"	"	
Margt. McIntosh	50	F		Scotland	" "	Sch. Camillus. Peck.
James "	21	M	Farmer	"	"	
Donald "	18	M	"	"	"	
Ann " & 3 ch.	20	F		"	"	
David Thompson	22	M	"	"	"	
Mrs. Ferguson	45	F		"	"	
John "	20	M	Weaver	"	"	
A. Minton	25	M	Lawyer	"	"	
A. J. Clinton	22	M	"	"	"	
Thos. Hutchinson	27	M	Cab. maker	"	"	
Margt. "	23	F		"	"	
Wm. Bradley	60	M		"	"	
Catharine " & 4 ch.	60	F		"	"	
James Kincaid	55	M	Farmer	"	"	
Jas. Towait	19	M	Goldsmith	"	"	
Jas. Grant	21	M	Farmer	"	"	
John Murray	27	M	Mechanic	"	"	
Margt. Wilson & ch.	23	F		"	"	
Janet Ainsley & 5 ch.	30	F		"	"	
Wm. Hutton	22	M	Labourer	"	"	
D. Davis	22	M	Merchant	Wales	"	Sch Constitution. Ward.

Names of passengers	Age	Sex	Occupation	Country to which they belong	Country of which they intend becoming inhabitants	Ship or vessel with the name of the master or commander
NEW YORK Cont.						
Q. E. Sept. 30, 1823						
Wm. Yunor *	23	M	Merchant	Wales	U. States	
J. Lindsay	20	M	Farmer	Scotland	"	Brig Hannah. Martin.
W. J. Harmony	20	M	Merchant	Spain	"	Sch. Halsey. Small.
Richd. Synar *	23	M	"	England	"	Sch. Alexr. Mansfield. Baush.
Jno. King	32	M	Weaver	Ireland	"	
Jno. Baven	39	M	Labourer	England	"	
Joseph Parke	50	M	"	"	"	
Jno. Wim *	49	M	Farmer	Uppr. Canada	U. Canada	
David Dunlop	30	M	Merchant	"	"	
Nicholas Findlay	25	M	Labourer	Ireland	"	
Jno. Andrews	20	M	Tinman	Switzerland	"	
M. Bushby	36	M	Merchant	St. Croix	St. Croix	Sch. S. Carolina Packet. Knapp.
L. Greenwood	35	M	"	"	"	
Mrs. Bushby	26	F		"	"	
Maj. Moody	42	M	Officer	"	"	
M. White	55	M	Planter	G. Britain	G. Britain	Sch. Aurora. Ring
F. L. Folger	31	M	Merchant	U. States	U. States	
M. T. Heard	40	M	"	"	"	Wm. Thompson. Crocker.
Saml. D. Bradford	25	M	"	"	"	
E. Wooton	24	M	"	"	"	
G. A. Shepherd	30	M	"	"	"	
N. Rich	24	M	Mechanic	England	Canada	Sch. Trimmer. Nagel.
Thos. Rich	21	M	"	"	"	
Wm. Patton	25	M	Merchant	U. States	U. States	Sch. Carolina Ann. Baush.
Jno. Barcroft	25	M	"	"	"	
J. Malcomson	24	M	"	Ireland		
James Stewart	25	M	Farmer	"	"	
Robt. Brooks	45	M	"	"	"	
Mary " & 4 ch.	42	F		"	"	
Maria Grevan & 2 ch.	30	F		"	"	
J. Little	55	M	"	"	"	
Mary Little	50	F		"	"	
Wm. "	22	M		"	"	
H. Hamilton	44	M	Farmer	"	"	
Mary Ann & 5 ch.	40	F		"	"	
Jno. McBride	22	M	"	"	"	
Andw. Dunlop	22	M	"	"	"	
F. Bacchus & ch.	40	M	Merchant	"	"	
J. F. Smith	43	M	Mariner	U. States	"	Sch. Harmony. Starbuck.
M. H. Sergeant	25	M	"	"	"	
P. Sidney	40	M	"	"	"	
Chas. Bonaparte	20	M		Rome	"	Sch. Falcon. Eames.
S. "	20	F		"	"	
Jno. Stochoe	46	M	Physician	England	"	

Names of passengers	Age	Sex	Occupation	Country to which they belong	Country of which they intend becoming inhabitants	Ship or vessel with the name of the master or commander
NEW YORK Cont.						
Q. E. Sept. 30, 1823						
P. Riccioli	48	M		Rome	U. States	
T. Vedeli	39	M		"	"	
G. Roselli	30	M		"	"	
A. Paus	48	M		Brussells	"	
Thos. C. Smith	25	M	Merchant	U. States	"	Brig Romp. Scudder.
H. Wolfe	56	M	Mechanic	"	"	Brig Ann. Ashford.
J. B. Durand	45	M	Merchant	"	"	Sch. Paris. Robinson.
Mrs. " & ch.	49	F		"	"	
S. Saul	30	M	Physician	"	"	
Mrs. "	17	F		"	"	
J. Aimelen *	28	M	"	"	"	
B. De Ruyter	32	M	Merchant	Holland	"	
A. Hoguet	45	M	"	"	"	
P. Julian	60	M	"	"	"	
A. G. Thomasson	32	M	Blacksmith	U. States	"	
H. D. Pattel	27	M	Merchant	France	"	Sch. Lewis. Skwaley.
Mrs. "	24	F		"	"	
Thos. Brannan	42	M	Mechanic	Ireland	"	Sch. Convoy. Currey.
D. "	45	M	Merchant	"	"	
Mary " & 5 ch.	38	F		"	"	
A. B. Carrington	28	M	Merchant	U. States	"	Sch. Mary. Fuller.
R. W. Norfor	38	M	Mariner	England	"	Sch. Imposter. Rian.
D. W. C. Oliphant	35	M	Merchant	U. States	"	
J. W. Archibald	25	M	"	"	"	Brig Com. Porter.
L. Duvall	27	M	Gilder	"	"	Brig Alexr. the Grand. Faven.
M. Hartman	24	M	Tailor	"	"	
C. Spinney	22	M	Mariner	"	"	
C. Lambson	22	M	"	"	"	
J. Bynieux	34	M	Merchant	St. Domingo	St. Domingo	Sch. Fair Play. Kimball.
J. R. Smith	32	M	Mariner	U. States	"	Sch. Concordia. Bailey.
L. Hany	45	M	"	"	"	
M. Blanden	31	M	Merchant	Spain	Cuba	Sch. Constitution. Berrian.
M. Saidler	25	M	"	U. States	U. States	
H. J. Magrath	23	M	"	England	England	Sch. Hope's Return. Baker.
P. Savan	40	M	"	France	France	
J. H. Gilberts	25	M	"	Bermuda	G. Britain	Sch. Two Brothers. Kimble.
N. S. Dill	36	M	"	"	"	
F. Beattie	44	M	"	G. Britain	Canada	Sloop Ariana. Pearce.
Geo. Foster	25	M		"	"	Ship Hudson. Champion.
A. Groves	26	M	"	"	"	
W. Dowson	36	M	Clergyman	"	"	
E. J. " & 3 ch.	28	F		"	"	
H. Hurst	23	M	Merchant	"	"	
P. Patterson	52	M	"	"	"	

Names of passengers	Age	Sex	Occupation	Country to which they belong	Country of which they intend becoming inhabitants	Ship or vessel with the name of the master or commander
NEW YORK Cont.						
Q. E. Sept. 30, 1823						
Mary F. Thomas & ch.	28	F		G. Britain	Canada	
Geo. Kimboch	37	M	Merchant	"	"	
Charlotte " & 2 ch.	22	F		"	"	
M. M. Clarke & 2 ch.	32	F		"	"	
E. Minns	22	F		"	"	
J. "	22	M	Mechanic	"	"	
Thos. "	24	M	"	"	"	
Richd. O. Hardy	24	M		England	"	
Thos. Wright	25	M	Surgeon	"	"	
W. Barnstable	16	M		"	"	
Charles Jones	37	M	Merchant	"	"	
O. Wilder	39	M	"	U. States	U. States	
F. Rutledge	22	M	"	"	"	
J. M. Bellamy	42	M	Farmer	England	England	
Stephen Watson	32	M	"	"	"	
Eliza " & 7 ch.	33	F		"	"	
James Howe	27	M	"	"	"	
Isabella "	25	F		"	"	
G. R. Joseline	25	M	"	"	Canada	
R. Gowen	35	M	"	"	"	
L. P. H.	30	M	Tailor	"	"	
Jno. Brooks	25	M	"	"	"	
Edwd. Hilyar	25	M	"	"	"	
Wm. Bassett	24	M	Merchant	"	"	
Chas. Chapman	20	M	Tanner	"	"	
H. Boots & ch.	23	M	Farmer	"	"	
Mary Ann Boots	20	F		"	"	
Mr. Canfield	32	M	Merchant	"	"	
David Dolberg	29	M	Shoemaker	Sweden	U. States	Sch. Oscar. Hockut.
M. Frazier	23	M	Merchant	U. States	"	Brig Dick. Woodhouse.
L. Borchers	24	M	"	France	"	Ship Harriet. Williams
H. Dyer	22	M	Mechanic	"	"	
J. Garrene *	20	M	"	"	"	
V. Dancangut	18	M	"	"	"	
M. Laimir	36	M	"	"	"	
Jno. Helveston	23	M	"	U. States	"	Sch. Gipsey. Fogler.
Wm. Blinkhorn	57	M	Farmer	England	Canada	Sch. Pedlar. Larrabie.
Ann " & 7 ch.	54	F		"	"	
J. Croft	34	M	"	"	U. States	Sch. Euphrates. Sprague.
Margt. Croft & 3 ch.	49	F		"	"	
H. North	24	M		"	"	
Mary "	21	F		"	"	
D. Poor	37	M	Merchant	U. States	"	Brig John. Howland.
T. R. Thorbuck	36	M	"	Germany	"	

Names of passengers	Age	Sex	Occupation	Country to which they belong	Country of which they intend becoming inhabitants	Ship or vessel with the name of the master or commander
NEW YORK Cont.						
Q. E. Sept. 30, 1823						
L. Giles	60	M	Tailor	U. States	U. States	
G. Forrest & ch.	28	M	Labourer	"	"	
S. Hardyear	20	M	Teacher	England	"	Brig Matilda. McKown.
A. Hunardy & ch.	23	M	Merchant	Havana	"	Brig Hero. Collins.
B. Gaston	35	M	"	"	"	
N. G. Ingraham	36	M	"	U. States	"	
J. L. Brewster & ch.	38	M	"	"	"	
D. L. Peugnet	30	M		France	Canada	Brig Olympia. Souther.
H. "	29	M		"	"	
H. Boit	55	M		"	"	
Mrs. " & 4 ch.	55	F		"	"	
Robt. Beveridge	29	M	Merchant	U. States	"	Sch. Orbit. Tinkham.
Richd. Smarte	33	M	"	"	"	
Saml. Parker	40	M	"	"	"	
Jane "	35	F		"	"	
Thos. Pemberton	45	M	"	England	"	Sch. Corinthian. Davis.
Maria "	33	F		"	"	
Jno. Bradbury	33	M	"	"	"	
Esther "	27	F		"	"	
Geo. W. Wallis	25	M	"	"	"	
Thos. Rhodes	25	M	"	"	"	
Joseph Cooker	27	M	"	"	"	
V. Lovell	37	M	Farmer	"	"	Ship Florida. Matlock.
F. " & 9 ch.	37	F		"	"	
Wm. Vasey	40	M	"	"	"	
Jane " & 3 ch.	32	F		"	"	
Geo. Spink & 5 ch.	49	M	"	"	"	
Richd. Hickes	27	M	"	"	"	
Wm. Watson	21	M	"	"	"	
F. "	27	M	"	"	"	
A. Malbouch	24	M	"	France	"	Brig Factor Gray.
T. Freis	45	M	Merchant	Switzerland	"	
Eliza " & 7 ch.	32	F		"	"	
D. Havistock	34	M	Carpenter	"	"	
Mary "	28	F		"	"	
Saml. Lusher	46	M	Farmer	"	"	
Mary " & 7 ch.	40	F		"	"	
Hannah Willoughby	40	F		U. States	"	Sch. Nancy. Crowell.
George Harris	35	M	Distiller	"	"	
Huldah "	32	F		"	"	
Geo. Escher	18	M	Baker	"	"	
Wm. Walker	25	M	"	"	"	
J. Graham	30	M	Labourer	"	"	
Matthew Graham	28	M	"	"	"	

Names of passengers	Age	Sex	Occupation	Country to which they belong	Country of which they intend becoming inhabitants	Ship or vessel with the name of the master or commander
NEW YORK Cont.						
Q. E. Sept. 30, 1823						
P. Doroty	20	M	Labourer	U. States	U. States	
N. Rodden	22	M	"	"	"	
Thos. Bonton	27	M	"	"	"	
Jno. Irvin	22	M	Tailor	"	"	
Wm. Patterson	32	M	Labourer	"	"	
Margt. " & 2 ch.	29	F		"	"	
P. Mulligan	27	M	"	"	"	
Owen Gomley	25	M	"	"	"	
Wm. McCawly	24	M	"	"	"	
Jas. Downy	28	M	Tailor	"	"	
Frs. Osburn	27	M	Labourer	"	"	
Jno. Gallagher	30	M	"	"	"	
Mary " & 4 ch.	28	F		"	"	
Jno. Somerville	20	M	Clerk	"	"	
Samuel Osborn	36	M	Farmer	G. Britain	"	Sch. Rufus King. Badger.
Mary " & 7 ch.	37	F		"	"	
Thos. Roe	42	M	Farmer	"	"	
Anna " & 7 ch.	38	F		"	"	
James Salmon	55	M	Priest	"	"	
James Ryan	28	M	Brick layer	"	"	
Dorothy " & ch.	25	F		"	"	
Wm. R. Forrester	31	M	Tobacconist	"	"	
Robt. N. Rowe	28	M	Clerk	"	"	
L. Milwood	25	M	"	"	"	
James Ellis	40	M	Farmer	"	"	
Ann " & 5 ch.	40	F		"	"	
James Macky	28	M	Clerk	"	"	
Daniel Knight	49	M	Mariner	U. States	"	Brig Margt.
CHARLESTON, S. C.						
Q. E. Sept. 30, 1823						
Dominic Divison	28	M	Merchant	Spain	U. States	
Madam Mulando	28	F		"	"	Sch. Mary.
M. Dordelly	26	M	Tobacconist	U. States	"	
Alexr. Banniton	24	M	Merchant	"	"	
Hugh Bowley	22	M	"	"	"	Ship Hunter.
A. Hernandez	25	M	"	Spain	"	Sch. Adeline.
Jno. Finiochi *	28	M	"	"	"	
Isaac Martin	30	M	Cooper	U. States	"	
Joseph Jewett	24	M	"	"	"	
John Benesille *	28	M	Mariner	"	"	
John M. Hardy	23	M	"	"	"	Sch. Swift.
David Canter	45	M	"	"	"	Sch. Marion.
			"			

Names of passengers	Age	Sex	Occupation	Country to which they belong	Country of which they intend becoming inhabitants	Ship or vessel with the name of the master or commander
CHARLESTON Cont.						
Q. E. Sept. 30, 1823						
John Oates	60	M	Mariner	U. States	U. States	
Don A. Zeno Saldaner	34	M	"	Spain	"	
Francis C. Black	30	M	Merchant	U. States	"	
L. Frisbie	27	M	"	"	"	
D. Thompson	50	M		G. Britain	"	Sch. Fish Hawk.
Wm. J. Rowe	30	M	Lawyer	"	"	
John Douglass	25	M	Merchant	"	"	
Wm. Ascoot	30	M	Clerk	"	"	
Thomas Budd	30	M	Mariner	U. States	"	Sch. Eliza & Polly.
Thomas Hatch	34	M		"	"	
Jno. P. Barrie	28	M	Trader	"	"	
Antonio Domingo	28	M	"	"	"	
Wm. Oates	19	M	"	"	"	Sch. Dolphin.
Joseph Penera	25	M	"	"	"	
Saml. Philbrick	30	M		"	"	Sch. Eliza & Maria.
Silvester Murphy	29	M		"	"	
Wm. R. Peyton	26	M		"	"	
John Stone	35	M		"	"	
Charles Prevost	40	M	Physician	"	"	Sch. MacDonough.
John Hambelton	26	M	Carpenter	"	"	
B. McGinn	24	M	Farmer	"	"	
John Clark	50	M	Mariner	"	"	Sloop Norfolk.
Geo. Armstead	30	M	"	"	"	
Thos. Jackson	26	M	"	"	"	
Chil. Magnice *	25	M	Merchant	"	"	Sch. Marion.
Francis Deval	21	M	"	"	"	
Jno. Fabrack	50	M	Mariner	"	"	
Joseph Sylvia	28	M	"	"	"	
Joseph Johnson	30	M	"	"	"	Sch.
Chas. Lowry	40	M		"	"	Sch. Oleander.
Wm. P. Young	20	M		"	"	
H. A. "	24	M		"	"	
Arthur Oconnon *	20	M		"	"	Sch. Return.
Mrs. "	18	F		"	"	
Jno. La Fontaine	28	M		"	"	
Joseph A. Allen	44	M		"	"	
Benj. Briton	31	M		"	"	
Thos. Sinclair	42	M		"	"	
A. Lyon	28	M		"	"	Ship Fame.
Peter Lawrence	60	M		"	"	Brig Commerce.
Geo. Sutton	37	M	Mariner	"	"	Sch. Eliza & Polly.
Emanuel Orban	28	M	"	"	"	
E. Stephens	35	M	Minister	"	"	Ship Perfect.
Jon Lutz	44	M	Physician	"	"	Ship Ceres.

Names of passengers	Age	Sex	Occupation	Country to which they belong	Country of which they intend becoming inhabitants	Ship or vessel with the name of the master or commander
CHARLESTON Cont						
Q. E. Sept. 30, 1823						
A. Wishuby	18	M	Merchant	U. States	U States	
Ab. Buckin *	58	M	Labourer	"	"	
Hodge Pinkney	50	M	Planter	"	"	
Wm. Peat	30	M	Mariner	"	"	Brig Ann.
Elias Wilkins	40	M	Farmer	"	"	Sch Experiment.
Joshua Walker	35	M	"	"	"	
Robt. Beck & ch.	35	M	Joiner	"	"	
John Turnbull	50	M	Farmer	"	"	
Benedict Mispert	60	M	Cutler	Switzerland	"	Ship Eolus. Geer
Jacob "	23	M	"	"	"	
Samuel "	25	M	Carpenter	"	"	
Lewis "	22	M	Cutler	"	"	
Mary "	26	F		"	"	
Jacob Shelburn	27	M	Carpenter	"	"	
Jacob Hasches	21	M	Shoemaker	"	"	
John Buanard/Busnard	24	M	"	"	"	
--- Karns	38	M	Clockmaker	"	"	
--- Sigman	39	M	Shoemaker	"	"	
Charles Napier	30	M	"	"	"	
Fred. Shults	20	M	Farmer	"	"	
Joseph Spirer	23	M	Nailer	Germany	"	
B. Leshin	45	M	Hosier	"	"	
F. Narden	42	M	Miller	"	"	
L. " & 9 ch.	41	F		"	"	
David "	41	M		"	"	
John Claude	23	M	Shoemaker	"	"	
C. Jaques	56	M	Farmer	"	"	
Mrs. " & 7 ch.	42	F		"	"	
John Schimanke	44	M	"	"	"	
Mrs. " & 6 ch.	36	F		"	"	
M. Nicherde	43	M	Carpenter	"	"	
Mrs. " & 4 ch.	43	F		"	"	
NEW HAVEN						
Q. E. Sept. 30, 1823						
J A. Anderson	28	M	Merchant	England	U. States	Brig Underhill. Clarke.
Geo. Mardenburgh	50	M	Planter	"	"	Brig Charles. Glenny.
Mary " & 2 ch.	45	F		"	"	
John Guijer *	30	M	Merchant	"	"	
M Divine	29	M	Farmer	"	"	Sch. Union. Gibbs.
Geo. Dougherty	20	M	"	"	"	
Wm. Gallagher	25	M	"	"	"	
Mary Flinn & ch.	28	F		"	"	

Names of passengers	Age	Sex	Occupation	Country to which they belong	Country of which they intend becoming inhabitants	Ship or vessel with the name of the master or commander
NEW HAVEN Cont.						
Q. E. Sept. 30, 1823						
J. Harrigan	30	F		England	U. States	
M. McAnnon & ch.	30	F		"	"	
Z. Celly & child	31	F		"	"	
Francis Collins	32	M	Weaver	"	"	
Rose "	28	F		"	"	
H. McAnder	22	F		"	"	
Eliz. Ferrell & ch.	25	F		"	"	
P. "	23	M	Weaver	"	"	
Jno. Glaney	18	M	Shoemaker	"	"	
Jas. McGill	30	M	Weaver	"	"	
Chas. Hart	25	M	"	"	"	
Sally " & 3 ch.	23	F		"	"	
Michael Dykers	54	M	Merchant	W. Indies	"	Sch. Julia & Laura. Hansen.
Joanna "	48	F		"	"	
Jno. H. " & 2 ch.	22	M	"	"	"	
Isaac Garcia	24	M		"	"	
Jonah Prindle	48	M	"	"	"	
Henry R. Snow	36	M	"	"	"	
NORFOLK						
Q. E. Sept. 30, 1823						
John Danell	24	M	Attorney	Bermuda	Bermuda	Brig Luna. Knox.
Anthony J. Peniston	24	M	Merchant	"	"	
Eliz. Tucker & ch.	35	F		"	"	
John W. Langdon	25	M	Mariner	U. States	U. States	Sch. Ceres. Brown.
Jno. Owen	18	M	"	"	"	
Robt. Jaques	34	M	"	Cuba	"	
J. L. De Aranzamond	23	M	"	Columbia	"	
James Mooney	35	M	Farmer	Ireland	"	Brig Abegail. Goodday.
Michael Kenny	30	M	"	"	"	
Patrick Turner	30	M	"	"	"	
Peter Mullen	27	M	Weaver	"	"	
T. Gorman	24	M	"	"	"	
John Finegan	27	M	Blacksmith	"	"	
Thos. Halfpenny	34	M	Farmer	"	"	
Michael Burant	34	M	"	"	"	
Jane " & ch.	31	F		"	"	
Patrick Fanekin	24	M	"	"	"	
Christopher Conway	23	M	Baker	"	"	
John Nuttle	30	M	Gardner	"	"	
John Fallon	36	M	Farmer	"	"	
M. Wright	24	M	Weaver	"	"	
Mary Beats	42	F		Scotland	"	

Names of passengers	Age	Sex	Occupation	Country to which they belong	Country of which they intend becoming inhabitants	Ship or vessel with the name of the master or commander
NORFOLK Cont.						
Q. E. Sept. 30, 1823						
J. McClean	25	F		Scotland	U. States	
Jos Almeida	18	M		U. States	"	Brig Oscar.
J. B. Ardoin	16	M	Clerk	St. Barts	"	
RICHMOND						
Q. E. Sept. 30, 1823						
Robert Spear	45	M	Clerk	U. States	U. States	Vessel not mentioned.
Thomas S. Frost	23	M	Baker	"	"	
Wm. Gray	30	M		"	"	
Archibald Armstrong	23	M		Ireland	"	
Benj. Shaw	25	M	Merchant	England	"	
John Taylor	70	M		U. States	"	
BALTIMORE						
Q. E. Sept. 30, 1823						
M. Bauer	32	M	Merchant	Bremen	U. States	Vessel not mentioned.
Edwd. Beher	19	M	Clerk	Hamburgh	"	
Charles Jamer	31	M	Tailor	Brunswick	"	
A. " & 4 ch.	39	F		"	"	
Jno. C. Eggers	37	M	"	Hanover	"	
Charlotte " & 4 ch.	46	F		"	"	
Charles Wride	23	M	Surgeon	"	"	
H. Rodeman	31	M	Sugar baker	"	"	
Christian Leaze *	25	M	Turner	Germany	"	
Ch. Wohner *	46	M	Weaver	"	"	
Jno. Groll	23	M	Gardner	"	"	
C. D. Rhodes	33	M	Merchant	"	"	
Richd. Stubs	28	M	"	"	"	
F. Bence *	35	M	"	"	"	
S. Hill	29	M	Farmer	U. States	"	
--- Poursman	32	M	"	"	"	
Thos. Hanegan	26	M	Labourer	Ireland	"	
Wm. Gillis	24	M	Carpenter	Scotland	"	
D. Milvy/Miloy	21	M	Farmer	Ireland	"	
Saml. Johnson	37	M	"	"	"	
M. Linnett	28	M	"	" "	"	
W. Monroe & ch.	42	M		Scotland	"	
J. Howard & ch.	26	M	"	England	"	
Samuel Gilchrist	29	M	"	Scotland	"	
P. Doyle	29	M	"	Ireland	"	
P. Yarnet	31	M	"	"	"	
Mary Lanman & ch.	30	F		"	"	
	60	M				

Names of passengers	Age	Sex	Occupation	Country to which they belong	Country of which they intend becoming inhabitants	Ship or vessel with the name of the master or commander
BALTIMORE Cont.						
Q. E. Sept. 30, 1823						
James Lawler	60	M	Farmer	Ireland	U. States	
Richd. Wright	28	M	"	"	"	
Wm. Pettit	19	M	"	"	"	
P. Brennan	25	M	"	"	"	
Samuel Wilson	16	M	"	"	"	
R. Ferin	28	M	"	"	"	
Wm. Quinn	24	M	"	"	"	
S. Baker	32	M	"	"	"	
M. " & 2 ch.	26	F		"	"	
Abraham Anberg	22	M	Merchant	Germany	"	
M. Baum	18	M	"	"	"	
H. Klinebergh	26	M	"	"	"	
N. Mier	36	M	Farmer	England	"	
M. E. Moore	28	F		"	"	
F. Bright	30	M	Merchant	N. Orleans	"	
Wm. Trowbridge	25	M	Mechanic	U. States	"	
V. Sement	30	M	Physician	France	"	
R. Defourneaux *	32	M	Merchant	"	"	
P. Giuchard	28	M	Shoemaker	"	"	
G. Dunan	22	M		"	"	
C. Bless	25	M	Mariner	U. States	"	
E. Abell	30	M	"	"	"	
Jno. Maloy	50	M	"	"	"	
Wm. Day	40	M	Mariner	"	"	
J. A. Silliman	20	M	"	"	"	
John Town	20	M	Mariner	"	"	
J. Tince *	38	M	"	Havana	"	
F. Ricant & ch.	40	M	Merchant	"	"	
F. Squires	30	M	"	"	"	
George Clark	32	M	"	U. States	"	
J. Davis	25	M	Labourer	Wales	"	
M. Casty	27	M	"	"	"	
P. Fullem	28	M	"	Ireland	"	
J. Mummey	29	M	"	"	"	
M. Cooney	30	M	"	"	"	
J Smith	25	M	Farmer	Scotland	"	
Jas. Dalon	28	M	Labourer	Ireland	"	
M. Bean	31	M	"	"	"	
Mary " & 2 ch.	27	F		"	"	
A. Fowler	28	M	Supercargo	U. States	"	
Wm. Cooper	34	M	Farmer	Ireland	"	
M. " & 3 ch.	34	F		"	"	
G. Buchnan	30	M	Merchant	"	"	
J Chayter	15	M	Mariner	"	"	

PASSENGERS WHO ARRIVED IN THE U.S. SEPTEMBER 1821 - DECEMBER 1823

Names of passengers	Age	Sex	Occupation	Country to which they belong	Country of which they intend becoming inhabitants	Ship or vessel with the name of the master or commander
BALTIMORE Cont.						
Q. E. Sept. 30, 1823						
F. Snow	40	M	Mariner	Ireland	U. States	
Thos. Grady	50	M	Farmer	"	"	
John Galvin	27	M	"	"	"	
Jas. Purcell	26	M	"	"	"	
Thos. "	23	M	"	"	"	
R. "	25	M	"	"	"	
Jas Doyle	25	M	"	"	"	
E. Commerford	25	M	"	"	"	
Jno. Fitzgerald	35	M	"	"	"	
J F. "	37	M	"	"	"	
J "	26	M	"	"	"	
Judith "	26	F		"	"	
Wm. Manning	27	M	"	"	"	
Edmund "	19	M	"	"	"	
James Byrne	18	M	"	"	"	
John Whelan	24	M	"	"	"	
Mary "	25	F		"	"	
M. Hackett	24	M	"	"	"	
E. Kenock	20	M	"	"	"	
Wm. Bryan	24	M	"	"	"	
Wm. D. Harris	25	M	Supercargo	U. States	"	
James Geddes	28	M	Coppersmith	"	"	
Geo. W. Sweeny	25	M	Supercargo	"	"	
Peter Taylor	35	M		"	"	
John Ryan	55	M	Priest	G. Britain	"	
George Ross	35	M	Mariner	"	"	
H. Champayne	29	M	Farmer	U. States	"	
T. C. Vitter	45	M	"	"	"	
Wm. Saifan *	24	M	Joiner	Germany	"	
Maria Vozzy	28	F		"	"	
Christina Walter	29	F		"	"	
David Reser	55	M	Shoemaker	"	"	
Louisa " & ch.	22	F		"	"	
John Rotlinger	30	M	Farmer	"	"	
Margt. "	25	F		"	"	
John Jest	28	M	Cooper	"	"	
George Sauer	55	M	"	"	"	
Maria " & 4 ch.	50	F		"	"	
David Seilor	46	M	Farmer	"	"	
Mary " & ch.	40	F		"	"	
M. Kline	45	M	Merchant	"	"	
C. Woofyaarde	28	M		"	"	
J. Dikin	45	M	Planter	"	"	
J. Bosiances	30	M	Merchant	"	"	

Names of passengers	Age	Sex	Occupation	Country to which they belong	Country of which they intend becoming inhabitants	Ship or vessel with the name of the master or commander
BALTIMORE Cont.						
Q. E. Sept. 30, 1823						
P. M. Piabea	27	M	Merchant	Germany	U. States	
J. M. Bolle	25	M	"	"	"	
B. Amegarda *	25	M	"	"	"	
John Monge	25	M	"	"	"	
Wm. Burne	45	M	Mariner	"	"	
W. P. Brely	22	M	Merchant	U. States	"	
Jacob Gordell	47	M	Blacksmith	Holland	"	
Elizabeth " & 4 ch.	22	F		"	"	
P. Coward	33	M	Gardner	"	"	
R. Goodrich	35	M	Supercargo	U. States	"	
J Rhia	45	M	Farmer	Scotland	"	
E. "	45	F		"	"	
Wm. "	25	M	Teacher	"	"	
E. " & 2 ch.	22	F		"	"	
Jno. Cummings	45	M	Teacher	"	"	
Margt. " & 5 ch.	40	F		"	"	
S. Harret & 10 ch. *	42	F		"	"	
Wm. McKinny	47	M	Teacher	"	"	
Martha " & 5 ch.	35	F		"	"	
Mary Gales	27	F		"	"	
C. Michales	35	M	Merchant	Germany	"	
W. Duzther	30	M	"	"	"	
M. Flint	26	M	Sugar baker	"	"	
Jesse Buss	25	M	Farmer	"	"	
M. Gilbert	24	M	Carpenter	"	"	
John Simpson	25	M	Sugar baker	"	"	
Henry Ellis	25	M	Farmer	"	"	
John Gunnett	45	M	Farmer	England	"	
Mrs. " & 7 ch.	45	F		"	"	
Samuel Hope	35	M		"	"	
Mrs. " & 10 ch.	35	F		"	"	
Wm. Williams	40	M	Farmer	"	"	
Mrs. " & ch.	33	F		"	"	
James Buss	28	M	"	"	"	
Edward Bates	25	M	"	"	"	
Mrs. " & 2 ch.	24	F		"	"	
Wm. Spier	26	M	"	"	"	
Mrs. " & ch.	24	F		"	"	
John Johnson	26	M	"	"	"	
Bernard O'Brien	22	F	"	"	"	
C. Keefe	25	M	"	"	"	
Mr. Vansylbury	30	M	"	"	"	
John P. Ford	34	M		"	"	
Wm. P. Matthews	30	M	Supercargo	U. States	"	

Names of passengers	Age	Sex	Occupation	Country to which they belong	Country of which they intend becoming inhabitants	Ship or vessel with the name of the master or commander
BALTIMORE Cont.						
<u>Q. E. Sept. 30, 1823</u>						
Jno. Reeves	50	M	Mariner	U. States	U. States	
Wm. Davidson	45	M	"	"	"	
John Cross	29	M	Carpenter	"	"	
John C. Dunle •	24	M	Merchant	Germany	"	
James Stewart	31	M	"	U. States	"	
C. M. Waring	30	M	"	"	"	
J. Boggs	40	M		"	"	
A. Williams	25	M		"	"	
Wm. J. Sangston	23	M	"	"	"	
M. Jones	35	M	"	"	"	
Jas. Taylor & 2 ch.	42	M	Clergyman	"	"	
Robt. Dunwoody	60	M	Farmer	"	"	
Mary " & 7 ch.	40	F		"	"	
C. Patterson	30	M	"	"	"	
Mary " & 5 ch.	30	F		"	"	
Samuel Potts	20	M	Weaver	"	"	
Cath. Malcomb & ch.	26	F		"	"	
O. Robinson	45	M	Farmer	"	"	
E. " & 2 ch.	47	F		"	"	
John Jackson	25	M	Carpenter	"	"	
Jas. Lindsey	23	M	"	"	"	
Robt. Sprout	23	M		"	"	
Robt. Hall	20	M	Physician	"	"	
Saml. McMaster	21	M	Weaver	Ireland	"	
Jno. Sterling	44	M	"	"	"	
Mary " & 5 ch.	34	F		"	"	
John Borling	25	M	Carpenter	"	"	
John Domagin	28	M	"	"	"	
A. "	23	M		"	"	
Patrick Donelly	16	M		"	"	
B. "	17	F		"	"	
John Hunter	26	M		"	"	
James Gibby	21	M		"	"	
Elizabeth "	21	F		"	"	
Robt. Humphries	27	M		"	"	
Mary "	22	F		"	"	
Wm. Tirgut	24	M		"	"	
Jno. O'Connor	25	M		"	"	
Wm. Donelly	26	M		"	"	
Wm. Donagh	22	M		"	"	
Mary " & 2 ch.	20	F		"	"	
B. Marshall & 4 ch.	31	F		"	"	
B. Bela	39	M	Merchant	"	"	
Chas. Blisse	40	M	"	Italy	"	

Names of passengers	Age	Sex	Occupation	Country to which they belong	Country of which they intend becoming inhabitants	Ship or vessel with the name of the master or commander
BALTIMORE Cont.						
Q. E. Sept. 30, 1823						
D. Benoitt	27	M	Merchant	Italy	U. States	
R. M. Miles	26	M	Mariner	U. States	"	
M. W. Pringle	39	M	Merchant	"	"	
J. Jessop	36	M	"	"	"	
H. Dougherty & 2 ch.	32	F		"	"	
Jane Kemp	50	F		"	"	
L. Cox & ch.	32	F		"	"	
L. McDermot	26	F		"	"	
P. Kerr	20	M	Farmer	G. Britain	"	
M. McGarry	27	M	Grad of T. College ?	"	"	
Robt. Boyd	22	M	Labourer	"	"	
J. R. Parkinson	29	M	Farmer	"	"	
Ebenezer Hunter	19	M	Tailor	"	"	
P. Malcom	32	M	Merchant	"	"	
Simon Fagan	28	M	Book keeper	"	"	
Andw. Hook	34	M	Merchant	"	"	
Thomas Glass	22	M	Clerk	"	"	
Wm. Flint & ch.	22	M	Merchant	"	"	
Edwd. Brady	33	M	Farmer	"	"	
E. " & 2 ch.	30	F		"	"	
M. Coleman	35	M	Teacher	Ireland	"	
Michael Ryan	30	M	Farmer	"	"	
R. Atkinson	28	M	Tailor	"	"	
J. B. Gill	28	M	Supercargo	U. States	"	
Michael Callaghan	50	M	"	"	"	
James Caregan	28	M	Carpenter	"	"	
H. Kohler	22	M	Merchant	Hanover	"	
John Halmn *	35	M	Farmer	Wales	"	
Michael Free	38	M	Shoemaker	England	"	
Mrs. "	36	F		"	"	
Henry Kirkman	36	M	Shoemaker	"	"	
V. Foulk	24	M	Farmer	Wales	"	
John McGinnis	21	M		Ireland	"	
P. Connel	28	M	Mechanic	"	"	
John Fallon	30	M	"	"	"	
Percy Bryant	25	M	"	"	"	
BARNSTABLE						
Q. E. Sept. 30, 1823						
Joseph Hanson	42	M	Shoemaker	Halifax	U. States	Sch. Alert. Pearse.
Betsey "	46	F		"	"	
Mary Lane & ch.	35	F		"	"	

Names of passengers	Age	Sex	Occupation	Country to which they belong	Country of which they intend becoming inhabitants	Ship or vessel with the name of the master or commander
BARNSTABLE Cont.						
Q. E. Sept. 30, 1823						
Mary Brown	40	F		Halifax	U. States	
Timothy Deany	24	M	Farmer	"	"	
Thos. Carey	50	M	"	"	"	
Michael "	48	M	"	"	"	
Patrick "	24	M	"	"	"	
Cath " & 2 ch.	20	F		"	"	
Edwd. Greenhurst	22	M	Labourer	"	"	
T. P. Pruer	24	M	Printer	Quebec	"	
Richd. Daniel	24	M	Labourer	Halifax	"	
John Gill	26	M	"	"	"	
Sarah "	30	F		"	"	
Michael Carney	30	M	"	"	"	
B. Hart	24	M	"	"	"	
James McGerald	21	M	Shoemaker	"	"	
Jacob Killum	49	M	Cordwainer	"	"	Sch. Hope. Lewis.
Susan " & 8 ch.	39	F		"	"	
Fred. K. Tuel	26	M	Hatter	"	"	Sch. Madeira Packet. Baker.
Wm. Charles Moore	52	M		"	"	Brig Monroe. Trapp.
A. Williams	30	M	Merchant	"	"	
John Gore	22	M	Watchmakr.	"	"	
Mary Devin	35	F		"	"	
Mary Whittle	32	F		England	"	Sch. Hope & Esther. Bourse.
Jeremiah O'Connor	28	M	Labourer	"	"	
Simon Ward	25	M	"	"	"	
George Gunnison	26	M	Tailor	"	"	
William Church	19	M	Merchant	G. Britain	"	Sch. Loire. Passett.
Jane "	18	F		"	"	
John Menon	22	M	"	"	"	
John Quire	24	M	Labourer	"	"	
Maria Gallighan	22	F		"	"	
A. Rutherford	35	M	Weaver	"	"	
Ann "	30	F		"	"	
Daniel Duffee	20	M	Labourer	"	"	
Daniel Peple	30	M	"	"	"	
C. "	20	F		"	"	
Daniel Monhegan	24	M	Clerk	"	"	
M. Doretty	20	M	Labourer	"	"	
David Wilson	24	M	Labourer	G. Britain	"	
James McCarvers	18	M	"	"	"	
Edwd. Duffee	24	M	"	"	"	

Names of passengers	Age	Sex	Occupation	Country to which they belong	Country of which they intend becoming inhabitants	Ship or vessel with the name of the master or commander
OSWEGATCHIE Q. E. Sept. 30, 1823						
William Laning	27	M	Farmer	G. Britain	U. States	
Frances " & 2 ch.	27	F		"	"	
John Dolton	23	M	"	"	"	
Elizabeth Ashton	65	F		"	"	
Moses Call	50	M	"	Ireland	"	
Jane "	50	F		"	"	
John Scott	55	M	Carpenter	"	"	
Robert "	22	M	Farmer	"	"	
Thomas "	24	M	"	"	"	
Andw. "	21	M	"	"	"	
Nancy Baty	55	F	Spinster	"	"	
Patrick "	30	M	Farmer	"	"	
Thomas "	21	M	"	"	"	
Robert Thompson	28	M	"	"	"	
Mary " & 2 ch.	18	F	Spinster	"	"	
Andw Philpot	63	M	Farmer	"	"	
Wm. Martin	23	M	Weaver	"	"	
Jane " & ch.	25	F		"	"	
James McKee	25	M	Labourer	"	"	
Margt. " & ch.	20	F		"	"	
Sally Philpot	29	F	Spinster	"	"	
John Grier	22	M	Farmer	"	"	
Robert Clark	20	M	Labourer	"	"	
NEW ORLEANS Q. E. Sept. 30, 1823						
A. Poncil	33	M	Fencing mstr	France	N. Orleans	Sch. Ligern. Rivers.
--- Jeanly	45	M	Mariner	"	"	
Batiste	40	M	"	"	"	
--- Cadet	35	M	"	"	"	
Francis Paullet	53	M	Merchant	U. States	U. States	Sch. Victor. Vennard.
Benj. Schoolfield	35	M	Mariner	"	"	
Wm. Bunce	35	M	"	"	"	Brig Prestes.
John Farmer	40	M	Merchant	"	"	Sch. Sarah Ann. Rudd.
Antonio Rodreguy	65	M	Farmer	"	"	
John Kisler/Kister	55	M	"	"	"	Sch. Tassell. Wilcox.
Charles Savignac	23	M	"	France	"	Sch. Traveller. Frost.
John Englader	28	M	Cooper	"	"	
Joseph Johns	33	M	Merchant	U. States	"	
J. Anderson	30	M	"	"	"	Sch. Time. Tucker.
J. M. Lesgate	27	M		Spain	"	Sch. Nancy. Nelson.
E. Laca	23	M	"	"	"	
A. Merritt	23	M	"	U. States	"	

Names of passengers	Age	Sex	Occupation	Country to which they belong	Country of which they intend becoming inhabitants	Ship or vessel with the name of the master or commander
NEW ORLEANS Cont.						
Q. E. Sept. 30, 1823						
O. W. Spitta	30	M	Merchant	Bremen	U. States	
Jean Cassa	28	M		France	"	Sch. Suprema. Salin
G. Ramoe	40	M		Spain	"	
J. C. Gardetti	25	M	Dentist	U. States	"	
Peter Wakefield	30	M	Farmer	"	"	
R. Gonalungo	26	M	Mariner	Spain	"	
M. Dinarich	28	M	"	Italy	"	
L. Bont	46	M	"	France	"	
Joseph	35	M	"	"	"	
George Wilcock	28	M	Farmer	U. States	"	Sch. Kennerbeck Trader.
Wm. Somerinson	30	M	"	"	"	
A. Rian	45	M	"	"	"	
M. Orbe	28	M	"	"	"	
J. M. Undarze	26	M	Merchant	Spain	"	
R. Redondilla	40	M	"	"	"	
J. L. Endura	35	M	"	"	"	
J. Rubio	22	M	"	"	"	
Y. Arladi	26	M	"	"	"	
M. L. de Quirtans/tano	50	M	"	"	"	
F. Callico	32	M	"	"	"	
J. Montanat	25	M	Printer	U. States	"	
A. Chesholm	28	M	Merchant	"	"	Two Sisters. Lawrenson.
James Diggins	40	M		England	"	Sch. Marquis. Wellington.
Mrs. " & 4 ch.	25	F		"	"	
Wm. Henderson	30	M	Merchant	"	"	
Joseph Montanos	23	M	Printer	U. States	"	Sch. Hope & Polly.
B. Caller	40	M	Merchant	"	"	
J. Parson	30	M	Butcher	"	"	
C. Duncan & 2 ch.	34	F		"	"	
B. Buscatti	30	M	Merchant	"	"	
James Musk	30	M	"	"	"	
N. Martinstein	23	M	"	"	"	Brig Carolina. Moling.
F. Lewis	48	M	"	"	"	
H. Laurelle	23	F		"	"	
Basil Brian	30	M	Mechanic	"	"	
P. Rosseau	34	M	"	"	"	
James B. Wallace	30	M	"	"	"	Morgiana. Shankland.
E. M. Henry	25	M	"	"	"	
Wm. S. Leger	25	M	"	"	"	
Wm. Lambert	23	M		"	"	
M. Laurens	55	M	Merchant	"	"	Ship America. Chew.
F. Gareau	21	M	"	France	"	
John Dickenson	35	M	"	U. States	"	Sch. Emigrant. Barney.
F. Castillo	22	M	"	Havana	"	

Names of passengers	Age	Sex	Occupation	Country to which they belong	Country of which they intend becoming inhabitants	Ship or vessel with the name of the master or commander
NEW ORLEANS Cont.						
Q. E. Sept. 30, 1823						
A. Payne	23	M	Merchant	Havana	U. States	
Charles Johnson	24	M	Mariner	U. States	"	Sloop Chems. March.
Henry Bagert	24	M	"	"	"	
J. Lubragu	35	M	Merchant	Spain	Mexico	Sch. Segund Galligo. Maurin.
Jose Ponez	39	M	"	"	"	
J. Romera	35	M	"	"	"	
J. Allis •	25	M	"	"	"	
P. J. Fusti	30	M	"	"	"	Sch. Voladora. Bassolos.
F. Rodriguez	28	M	"	"	"	
Z. Martinez	18	M	"	"	"	
Eliza Brunet	21	F		U. States	U. States	Sch. L'Aimable Caroline.
Wm. Easton	19	M	Mechanic	England	"	Brig Jesse Boag.
B. Passment	23	M	Merchant	U. States	"	Brig Louisiana. Rugan.
Antoine Lefebre	27	M	"	"	"	
Joan Millet	28	M	"	Spain	Spain	Brig Polacre. Millet.
Augustine Figurola	29	M	Baker	"	"	
B. Grole	40	M	Physician	France	U. States	Sch. Jealous. Tardy.
L. Arnaud	20	M		"	"	
Jno. McMillan	45	M		Ireland	"	
F. Challiot	26	M		France	"	
F. Juanille	40	M	Mariner	"	"	
James Blood	25	M		U. States	"	
J. Morgan	35	M	"	"	"	Sch. Wm. & Emeline.
A. G. Aldridge	27	M	Merchant	"	"	
A. Boy	16	M		"	"	
Alexander Brown	33	M	Mariner	"	"	Sch. Bee. Deberge.
F. Brunetti	42	M	"	"	"	
M. Gourch	30	M	Carpenter	France	"	
P. Amezaga	40	M	Merchant	Mexico	Mexico	Sch. Dorothy Massicot.
P. Amoretto	45	M	"	"	"	
J. Anosell	43	M	"	"	"	
N. Gana	24	M	"	"	"	
F. Sorasabell	45	M	"	"	"	
J. Suro	30	M	"	"	"	
Antonio Rodriguez	35	M	"	"	"	
Antonio Manuel	20	M	Mariner	"	"	
Joseph Pepperel	45	M	Mariner	U. States	"	
Baptiste Hardy	59	M	Butcher	"	"	Brig Belvedere. Sampson.
M L Dupare	45	F		"	"	
M Hardy & 2 ch	21	F		"	"	
F. Perault	42	M	Merchant	"	"	
H " & 4 ch.	32	F		"	"	
Louise Durvier & ch.	65	F		"	"	
G. Duvall & 3 ch.	27	M	Mason	"	"	

Names of passengers	Age	Sex	Occupation	Country to which they belong	Country of which they intend becoming inhabitants	Ship or vessel with the name of the master or commander
NEW ORLEANS Cont.						
Q. E Sept. 30, 1823						
S. Villers	37	M	Carpenter	U. States	Mexico	
Theresa Minor *	24	F		"	"	Brig Belvedere.
J Rousseau	37	M	Mechanic	"	"	
Dorsey McCarty	24	M	Mechanic	U. States	U. States	
S. O'Brien	35	M	Merchant	"	"	
Rosella Bran	55	F		"	"	
A. " & ch.	23	F		"	"	
Wm. Bounce	40	M	Mariner	"	"	Brig Orestes. Mutis.
T. Vine	27	M	Mason	"	"	Brig Irene.
S. Ray	26	M	Mechanic	"	"	
F. Venier	40	M	"	"	"	Ship Seine. Williams.
M Heurtin	35	M	Farmer	France	"	
Mrs. " & 2 ch.	25	F		"	"	
Fred. L. Folger	32	M	Merchant	"	"	Brig Mattewan. Coffin.
Edwd. G. Gardner	26	M	"	U. States	"	
A. Lesseps	30	M	Planter	France	"	Brig Mexico. Stanwood.
A. Hanson & 2 ch.	40	M	Carpenter	U. States	"	
S. T. Gallaghan	66	M	Clergyman	"	"	Sch. McDonough. Ryan.
John Runian	27	M	Farmer	"	"	
J. H. Redant	26	M	Mariner	"	"	
Jas. Webster	24	M	Merchant	England	"	Sch. Sea Flower. Dupalt.
Jno. Morin	50	M	Mechanic	France	"	
M. Calbo	30	M	"	"	"	
Mrs. " & ch.	25	F		"	"	
Thomas Barrett	26	M	Merchant	U. States	"	Sch. Triumph. Lee.
Wm. Johnston	23	M	Mechanic	"	"	
James Finlay	21	M	"	"	"	
J. Lauriente	32	M	"	France	"	
Stephen Donaldson	34	M	Merchant	U. States	"	Sch. Terise. Carmon.
R. Preston	35	M	"	"	"	
P. McCartney	33	M	"	"	"	
Th. A. Gordon	22	M	Farmer	"	"	
G. B. L. Bush	26	M	Physician	"	"	
Joseph Jonas	29	M	Merchant	"	"	Sch. Time. Tucker.
M. Febrell	29	M	"	"	"	
J. J. Cruizat	30	M	"	Spain	"	Sch. Louisiana.
M. "	27	M	"	"	"	
S. Blanc	30	M	"	U. States	"	
Robert Lynd	14	M	Mechanic	"	"	
D. Bovelli	46	M	Mariner	Sardinia	"	Ship Mars. Mitchell.
James Faset or Faret	55	M	Merchant	U. States	"	Ship Balize. Harding.
John Malline	37	M	Mariner	"	"	
Joseph Beraud	59	M	"	"	"	
G. Bedan	55	M	"	"	"	

Names of passengers	Age	Sex	Occupation	Country to which they belong	Country of which they intend becoming inhabitants	Ship or vessel with the name of the master or commander
NEW ORLEANS Cont.						
Q. E. Sept. 30, 1823						
J. L. Jauffray & ch.	56	M	Mariner	U. States	U. States	
W. Lerang	22	M	Planter	France	"	
--- Francilian	24	M	Merchant	Switzerland	"	
James Fenno	30	M	Merchant	U. States	"	Sch. Geo. Washington. Hunter.
R. Benedict	23	M	"	"	"	
J. M. Nadle	25	M	"	France	"	
Francis Puhon	35	M	Mariner	Italy	"	
W. Bogart	31	M	Merchant	U. States	"	
Robert Caller	35	M	"	"	"	Sloop Agent. Brooks.
H. B. Allen	36	M	"	"	"	
M. Gentums	28	M		"	"	
John Vincent	30	M		"	"	
William Morris	26	M		"	"	
E. Peabody	23	M	Mariner	"	"	
N. Puerto	35	M	Merchant	Spain	"	Brig Mariner. Garcia.
S. Chauvet	32	M	"	France	"	
F. Michaud	31	M		"	"	
J. B. Hespy	26	M		"	"	
J. Rugier	25	M		"	"	
D. Martinez	30	M		"	"	
J. Cameron	28	M		"	"	
J. Gomez	35	M		"	"	
S. Caracos *	50	M		"	"	
Antonio Angelito	28	M		"	"	
Raymond Lafer	32	M		"	"	
F. Maningomat	20	M	Merchant	"	"	Ship Edward. Howard.
F. Cantavell *	19	M		"	"	
J. Pereira	20	M	"	"	"	
E. Lopez	20	M	"	Spain	"	Sch. Josepha. Quintenella.
D. Poincy *	23	M	"	"	"	
L. " & 3 ch.	28	F		"	"	
J. Lessier	48	M	"	U. States	"	Ship Imperial.
P. "	23	M	"	"	"	
Robt. Puys	29	M	"	France	"	
E. Holagray	21	M		"	"	
Mrs. Turcas	59	F		U. States	"	
M. " & 3 ch.	40	F		"	"	
C. Eyman	57	M	Merchant	"	"	
J. B. Cloutier	27	M	Planter	"	"	
R. Franknaught	35	M	Merchant	"	"	Sch. Sarah Ann Buddes
Saml. Thirsans	37	M	"	"	"	
J. J. Gautier	32	M	"	"	"	
D. Chukins *	25	M	"	"	"	
J. O'Conner	30	M	"	"	"	

Names of passengers	Age	Sex	Occupation	Country to which they belong	Country of which they intend becoming inhabitants	Ship or vessel with the name of the master or commander
NEW ORLEANS Cont.						
Q. E. Sept. 30, 1823						
C. Linnbourgh	45	M		U. States	U. States	Sch. Emigrant. Barney.
F. Bermudoz	60	M		Spain	"	
Dennis Dermiren	35	M	Gardner	Ireland	"	
Thomas Dick	22	M	Merchant	U. States	"	
M. Howard & 2 ch.	35	F		"	"	Brig Parker & Son. Hodgson.
Henry Ross	35	M		Ireland	"	
L. Lopez	40	M		Havana	Havana	
Antonio Narcio	35	M	Merchant	Spain	Cuba	Brig Bien Bendo. Escula.
F. Finners	30	M	"	"	"	
M. Arbeo	28	M	"	"	"	
J. Crispo	35	M	"	"	"	
F. Audinot	32	M	"	"	"	
Domingo Cocki	34	M	"	"	"	
Pedro Cabe	36	M	"	"	"	
Gilberd Andre	60	M		"	"	Brig Sarah Ann. Cassaigau.
M. V Durell	24	M	"	U. States	U. States	
John Parker	35	M	"	England	"	
G. Cruan	35	M	"	France	"	
R. S. Bowie	40	M		U. States	"	
Mrs. " & 3 ch.	33	F		"	"	
J. B. Ducos	50	M	Mariner	France	"	
F. Roger	34	M	"	"	"	
J. Gano	40	M	"	"	"	
M. Delano	20	M		U. States	"	
S. Baldwin	17	M		"	"	Sch. Dorothy. Massuit.
A. Lefeure	33	M	Mechanic	France	"	
J. B. Passement	25	M	Merchant	"	"	
P. Lanusse	23	M	"	"	"	
J. B. Gravacos	35	M	"	"	"	
B. Robinson	40	M	"	U. States	"	
J. C. Osborn	25	M	"	"	"	Sloop Intrepid. Holmes.
A. Berman	28	M	"	France	"	
Mrs. " & ch.	20	F		"	"	Sch. Thorn. Arnoux.
A. Chesse	26	M	Mechanic	"	"	
C. Hibart	20	M	"	"	"	
H. Benitt	25	M	"	"	"	
J. P. Berty	35	M	"	U. States	"	
Jaques Virgile	35	M	"	"	"	
Victor Massia *	28	M	Merchant	"	"	Sch. Helen. Ferrand.
--- Vanbrenner	40	M	"	Germany	"	
--- Andre	17	M	"	France	"	
G. Walter	17	M	Clerk	U. States	"	Brig Brothers. Hill.
J. N. Melinder	38	M		Mexico	Mexico	Sch. Jane. Corson.
M. Gonzalez	15	M		"	"	

Names of passengers	Age	Sex	Occupation	Country to which they belong	Country of which they intend becoming inhabitants	Ship or vessel with the name of the master or commander
NEW ORLEANS Cont.						
Q. E. Sept. 30, 1823						
J. Callico	27	M		Mexico	Mexico	
S. Drioche	25	M		U. States	U. States	Brig Two Marys. Coffin.
J. B. Defer	45	M	Merchant	France	"	Ship Courier. Lithgow.
Mrs. " & 2 ch.	35	F		"	"	
J Corbet	25	M	"	"	"	Sch. Louisa. Newbury.
--- Mour	22	M	Mechanic	U. States	"	
John Sazar	17	M		Porte au Prince	"	
P. Bruera *	52	M	Planter	U. States	"	
Elizabeth Roche	50	F		"	"	
Antonio Hidell	27	M	Mechanic	Germany	"	Ship Columbus. Folger
Augustine Jenfrean	31	M	Sugar refinr.	France	"	
J. Labacre	24	M	Butcher	"	"	
D. Machesette	33	M	Tanner	Italy	"	
G. Buckham	40	M	Mechanic	England	"	
C. Maynelle *	38	M		France	"	Ship Highlander. Welsh.
H. Lominet	45	M	Mariner	"	"	Ship Harriet. Stiles.
John Onott	22	M	"	"	"	
P. Juan	38	M	Spain	"	"	Sch. Juanita. De Vegu.
--- Gildbuster	30	M	Merchant	Germnay	"	Sch. Eliza. Nartique.
--- Fabiani	31	M	"	France	"	
J. Ducoin	42	M	Mechanic	"	"	Sch. Louisiana.
J. Alux	29	M	Mariner	Spain	"	
J. Gras	20	M		"	"	
S. Montin	35	M		France	"	
--- Frascher	25	M	Baker	"	"	
J. Dillon	33	M	Merchant	U. States	"	Sch. Caroline. Benzon.
J. McMaster	27	M	"	"	"	
J. Shane	30	M	"	"	"	
S. Riddle	26	M	"	"	"	
J. Bradshaw	25	M	"	"	"	
Charles Menial	61	M	Planter	"	"	Brig Intelligence. Godfrey.
Mrs. Salas & 2 ch.	44	F		"	"	
Henry Bloodze	40	M	Farmer	"	"	Sch. Victory. Green.
Saml. Moore	32	M		"	"	
J. McGlown	25	M		Ireland	"	
John Rathman	35	M		Germany	"	
R. Deganate	28	M	Merchant	Mexico	"	
A. Klepenburgh	32	M		Germany	"	
S. F. Dorvall	34	M	Merchant	U. States	"	
J. Smith	30	M	Mariner	"	"	
John Porter	35	M	"	"	"	
G. Bell	35	M	Merchant	"	"	Sch. Jas. Madison. Smith.
L. Salun *	27	M		"	"	Sch. Jealous. Tardy.
A. Robles	34	M	"	"	"	

Names of passengers	Age	Sex	Occupation	Country to which they belong	Country of which they intend becoming inhabitants	Ship or vessel with the name of the master or commander
NEW ORLEANS Cont.						
Q. E. Sept. 30, 1823						
J. B. Morgan	34	M	Merchant	U. States	U. States	
J. Ballot	32	M	Mariner	France	"	
H. Fessart	35	M	Merchant	"	"	Sch. Betsey. Hallet.
J. Edina	28	M	"	Spain	"	Sch. Valadora Bassallos.
A. Chastaqua	38	M	Mechanic	St. Domingo	"	
J. Casse	24	M	Merchant	France	"	
J. Rambeaud	30	M	Mariner	France	"	
A. Abrier	40	M	Merchant	Havana	"	
C. Caillon	21	M	Mechanic	"	"	
C. Caille	32	M	"	Germany	"	
J. Carrick	39	M	Merchant	Scotland	"	
Wm. Boothe	40	M	"	U. States	"	Ship Ann. McPherson.
B. Tontmales	25	M	"	Spain	"	
J. B. Pasement	26	M	"	U. States	"	Sch. Leander. Garido.
Wm. Williams	28	M	Mariner	"	"	
S. J. Lovegrool	27	M		"	"	
E. Deterand	28	M	Merchant	Spain	"	Sch. Little Sally. Lafitte.
J. B. Vanier	30	M	Mechanic	France	"	
A. Sony	23	M	"	U. States	"	Sch. Prince Oscar. Gallimin.
F. Bosse	35	M	"	"	"	
SAVANNAH						
Q. E. Dec. 31, 1823						
Admiral Greaves	60	M	Mariner	G. Britain	G. Britain	Ship Hesperus. McCorckill.
M. De Forgiers	50	M	Consul U. S.	France	France	
M. Jose *	30	M	Merchant	U. States	U. States	
M. Dennis	42	M	Carpenter	"	"	
John Mitchell	25	M	Accountnt.	G. Britain	G. Britain	Brig Caledonia. Lindsay.
George Perry	22	M	Tin smith	"	"	
Wm. Scott	17	M	Clerk	"	U. States	Brig Eliza Ann. Baird.
Arch. Smith	30	M	Bricklayer	"	"	
James Wood	40	M	Carpenter	U. States	"	Ship Georgia. Varnum.
D. Macleod	40	M	Merchant	"	"	
J. A. Hylly *	20	M	Attorny	"	"	
M. Rogers	30	M	Painter	England	"	
Mrs. " & ch.	25	F		"	"	
M. Sloan	30	M		Ireland	"	
Mrs. "	25	F		"	"	
Jacob Wolf	48	M	Labourer	Poland	"	Brig Helen. Erskin.
Alexr. Galloway	30	M	Tailor	Scotland	"	
Mrs. "	24	F	Tailoress	"	"	
Alexr. Miller	18	M	Clerk	"	"	
John Bar	24	M	"	"	"	Ship Three Sisters. Bell.

Names of passengers	Age	Sex	Occupation	Country to which they belong	Country of which they intend becoming inhabitants	Ship or vessel with the name of the master or commander
NORFOLK						
Q. E. Dec. 31, 1823						
Robt. Purchase	40	M	Merchant	Barbadoes	Uncertain	Brig James Barron. Robertson.
J. S. Wainwright	28	M	"	"	W. Indies	Brig Commerce. Burns.
John Stowe	20	M	"	"	"	
John Boyce	47	M	Wheelwright	"		Ship Glide. Pierce.
Jane " & 8 ch.	45	F		"		
Francis Franklin	25	M	Carpenter	England	U. States	
H. Copeland	22	M	Miller	"		
Ann "	20	F		"		
Jno. Lewin	30	M	Shoemaker	"		
Ann " & 3 ch.	30	F		"		
David McDowell	38	M	Merchant	"		
Jannet "	39	F		"		
Robt. McIntosh	20	M	Navy officer	"	England	
John Wiley	28	M	Baker	U. States	U. States	Brig Hunter. Bisset.
A. J. Pemston & ch.	25	M	Merchant	Bermuda	"	
Noah Jewett	39	M	"	U. States	"	Brig Samuel. Phelan.
Elizabeth "	39	F		"	"	
Wm. Roberts	26	M	"	England	"	Brig Unison. Hufbuck.
Edwd. de Schack	34	M		"	"	
Richd. J. Jenny	27	M	Attorny	"		
Alexr. Freeman	22	M	Mariner	U. States	"	Sch. Hero. Martin.
J. M. Lucas	19	M	"	"	"	
John Savage	50	M	"	"	"	
E. Dinsley	20	M	"	"	"	
Danl. Tubbs	22	M	"	"	"	
Benj. Brush	37	M	"	"	"	
Jas Stephenson	32	M	Carpenter	England	"	Sch. Dover. Jeffares.
G. Purcell	19	M	Midshipman	U. States	"	Sch. Princess Ann. Banks.
F. W. Robinson	21	M	Merchant	W. Indies	"	Sch. Regulator. Patterson.
ALEXANDRIA						
Q. E. Dec. 31, 1823						
Francis Ward	30	M	Surveyor	Ireland	U. States	Ship Pioneer. Crabtree
A. Wersen	26	M	Merchant	Sweden	"	Brig Eliz. Sturgis. Larrimore.
Samuel Whitney	48	M	"	Barbadoes	"	Sch. Rose in Bloom. Sowle.
Thomas Baldson	38	M	"	"	"	
P. Da Coriascai	28	M	Gent.	Brazil	"	Sch. Dash. Bacon.
NEWPORT						
Q. E. Dec. 31, 1823						
John Goffe	40	M	Farmer	G. Britain	U. Canada	Ship Robinson Potter. Waite.
Sarah " & 9 ch.	33	F		"	"	

PASSENGERS WHO ARRIVED IN THE U.S. SEPTEMBER 1821 - DECEMBER 1823

Names of passengers	Age	Sex	Occupation	Country to which they belong	Country of which they intend becoming inhabitants	Ship or vessel with the name of the master or commander
NEWPORT Cont.						
Q. E. Dec. 31, 1823						
Mary Williams & 5 ch.	40	F		U. States	U. States	
James O'Donnel	40	M	Merchant	G. Britain	"	
Henry Edwards	30	M	"	"	"	
M. Morgan	45	M	Farmer	"		
Wm. "	54	M	"	"		
Daniel Thomas	45	M	"	"		
M. Roberts & ch.	21	F		"		
F. Callaghan	24	M	Farmer	"		
PROVIDENCE, R. I.						
Q. E. Dec. 31, 1823						
Lewis Quintin	21	M	Mariner	France	U. States	Brig Pomona. Aborn.
Rod. B. Chisholm	25	M	Merchant	U. States	"	Sch. Enterprise. Paine.
James Jackson	22	M	"	"		
NEWBURYPORT						
Q. E. Dec. 31, 1823						
Sarah Caton	39	F	Spinster	U. States	U. States	Sch. Olive Branch.
George Forsyth	26	M	Merchant	"	"	
Thos. Curtin	40	M	Fisherman	N. Foundland	"	Sch. Genl. Putnam.
Mary " & ch.	40	F		"	"	
John Hawkins	30	M	"	"	"	
Michl. Murphy	25	M	"	"	"	
Daniel Floyd	20	M	"	"	"	
Michael Brown	30	M	"	"	"	
Daniel Lari	40	M	Fisherman	"	"	Brig Fame.
Michael Foly	40	M	"	"	"	
T. Pickett	55	M	Merchant	France	France	Brig America.
Oliver Keating	60	M	Mariner	U. States	U. States	Sch. Planet.
Edward Goodrich	30	M	"	"	"	
PORTLAND						
Q. E. Dec. 31, 1823						
Mary Cothen & 5 ch.	40	F		St. Johns	U. States	Sch. Leander. Jones.
John Cockering	37	M	Trader	"	"	
Carlo Lucciani	27	M	Painter	Italy	Italy	Sch. James Monroe. Gerts
M. Chapman	45	F		U. States	U. States	Sch. Reporter. Waite
M. Stevens	35	F		"	"	
H. McCaulin	20	M	Hosier	Ireland	"	
Wm. Earley	20	M	Labourer	"	"	
Ebenezer Correy	30	M	Baker	U. States	"	

Names of passengers	Age	Sex	Occupation	Country to which they belong	Country of which they intend becoming inhabitants	Ship or vessel with the name of the master or commander
PORTLAND Cont.						
Q. E. Dec. 31, 1823						
Jas. Gordon	20	M	Baker	U. States	U. States	
H. Smith	20	F		"	"	
John Brady	25	M	Farmer	Ireland	"	
Catharine Brady	24	F		"	"	
James "	26	M		"	"	
Susan "	23	F		"	"	
Thomas Bell	45	M		"	"	
Thomas Fagan	40	M		"	"	
John Merne	28	M		"	"	
Sarah Sherwood	22	F		"	"	
Betsey Gilligan	21	F		"	"	
Stephen James	27	M	Merchant	St. John	St. John	Sch. Experiment. Miller.
George Chadwick	29	M	Mechanic	"	"	
Andw. Sallion	24	M	"	Ireland	U. States	
Catharine "	20	F		"	"	
Jno. McCausland	42	M	Farmer	"	"	
Eliza "	30	F		"	"	
Jane " & 5 ch.	59	F		"	"	
Wm. "	30	M		"	"	
E. Sprague	29	M	Painter	"	"	
Charles P. Bell	26	M	Merchant	U. States	"	Sch. Jane. Chandler.
Benj. Babb	26	M	Mariner	N. Scotia	"	
NEW ORLEANS						
Q. E. Dec. 31, 1823						
M. C. Villiers	70	M	Officer	Spain	Havana	Sch. Louisiana. Mailes.
P. Gilchrist	47	M	Planter	England	U. States	
M. Riviere	20	M		France	"	
M. Piernas	25	M		"	"	
A. Hermant	23	M	Missionary	"	"	Brig Colomba. Amazoga.
Angelo Oliva	50	M	"	Naples	"	
J. Sargiano	20	M	"	Piedmont	"	
J. Chighisola	38	M	Merchant	Genoa	"	
G. LaGrange	35	M	"	France	"	Sch. Rimera Gallega.
Jos. Grassotte	52	M	Cook	"	"	
E. Gararie	20	M	Shoemaker	France	"	Sloop Susan. Newman.
S. Picaul	18	M		"	"	
P. Misseon	53	M	Pedlar	"	"	
J. McCain	32	M	Farmer	U. States	"	
J. Robert	40	M	Merchant	"	"	Sch. Eliza. Nartogue.
Joseph Bosque	26	M	"	France	"	
Victor Bashen	22	M	"	"	"	
D. Warburg	30	M	"	Germany	"	

Names of passengers	Age	Sex	Occupation	Country to which they belong	Country of which they intend becoming inhabitants	Ship or vessel with the name of the master or commander
NEW ORLEANS Cont.						
Q. E. Dec. 31, 1823						
Martin Hasle	22	M	Merchant	France	U. States	
J. Laurent	33	M	"	"	"	
A. Poulain	32	M	"	"	"	
F. Picoud/Picond	32	M	"	"	"	
M. Adame	15	M		Mexico	"	
T. O. Sprigg	33	M		U. States	"	
--- Herpen	20	M		France	"	
D. Tixegale	25	M	Merchant	Spain	"	Brig Flor de St. Juan. Ulloa.
John Jones	35	M	Bricklayer	U. States	"	Sch. Union. Mayo.
Louis Sajour & ch.	36	M	Merchant	"	"	Sch. Louisa. Newberry.
B. Broadball	26	M	Distiller	England	"	
Antonio Punan & ch.	22	M	Grocer	U. States	"	
F. Esclasoes	17	M	Tailor	"	"	
Valcose Burel *	24	M	Carpenter	U. States	"	
Alfred Martin	20	M	Cab. makr.	"	"	
J. Mahe	48	M	Mariner	"	"	
John Marie	39	M	Carpenter	"	"	
James Everton	32	M	Mariner	"	"	
J. A. Subjaga	25	M	Merchant	Mexico	"	Sch. Orleans. Paillet.
A. Courbet	32	M		France	Mexico	
M. Echarly	22	M		Mexico	"	
M. Subiaga	19	M		"	"	
M. Andarbo	28	M		"	"	
Jose Alvarez	20	M		"	"	
H. S. Abal	40	M		"	"	
H. Fernandez	23	M		"	"	
S. Gomez	30	M		"	"	
S. Romero	25	M		"	"	
V. Gauye	25	M		"	"	
F. Brunette	45	M		"	"	
L. Furneaux	25	M		France	U. States	Brig Fox. Parker
F. Pailler	20	M	Baker	"	"	
J. Daughuly	27	M	Gardner	Ireland	"	
Jas. Fitzgerald	31	M	Mariner	"	"	
John Bates	28	M	"	"	"	
F. G. Boismanu *	40	M		France		Sch. Leander Gaslanoga.
S. P. Arnaud	30	M		"	"	
J. B. Passement	26	M	Merchant	"	"	
U. Williams	28	M	Mariner	U. States	"	
P. Lanusse	24	M		France	"	
F. E. Wedekind	25	M	Merchant	Germany	"	Sch. Kennebeck Trader. Brothers.
E. R. Rosenberg	30	M	"	"	"	
A. Carbonette	25	M	Mechanic	U. States	"	
J. A. Boltcher	45	M	Merchant	Germany	"	

Names of passengers	Age	Sex	Occupation	Country to which they belong	Country of which they intend becoming inhabitants	Ship or vessel with the name of the master or commander
NEW ORLEANS Cont.						
Q. E. Dec. 31, 1823						
Nancy Boltcher & ch.	35	F		Germany	U. States	
R. O'Brian	28	M	Mariner	U. States	"	
John Harding	30	M	"	"	"	
U. Nasen	35	M	"	"	"	
H. Thompson	29	M	"	"	"	
R. Barney	27	M		"	"	
A. Barret	20	M	Carpenter	England	"	Ship Unicorn. McKown.
Jas. Byrnes	56	M		"	"	
H. Speiring	30	M	Mariner	"	"	
Edwd. Farmer & 2 ch.	63	M	"	"	"	
Mary Speiring & 2 ch.	25	F		"	"	
J. R. Welsh	24	M	Clerk	"	"	
M. Prados	30	M	Merchant	U. States	"	Sch. Louisiana. Mailes.
M. T. Thompson	25	M	"	"	"	
M. Harel	28	M	"	France	"	
M. Rodriguen	40	M	"	Spain	"	
J. Quiren	40	M	"	U. States	"	
M. Guilhin	24	M	"	"	"	Brig Casket. Tracy.
M. Soubercaze *	40	M		"	"	
M. Chenou	44	M		France	"	
M. Rion	55	M	Merchant	"	"	
Jean Borce	50	M	Carpenter	France	"	
B. B. Gray	26	M		U. States	"	Ship American Hero. Knox.
D. M. Agarreo	35	M	Merchant	Spain	"	Brig Crosthwaite. Jones.
Jose Velaces	28	M	"	"	"	
Pablo Pon	30	M	Apothecary	"	"	
W. H. Cowan	40	M	Physician	England	"	Brig New Century. Cowlson.
James Sutch *	40	M	Planter	"	"	
Gabl. Gerome	62	M		U. States	"	Sch. McDonough. Ryon.
M. "	35	F		"	"	
M. Foster	23	M	Tailor	"	"	
V. Pear	28	M		"	"	
D. Shambau	56	M		"	"	
E. Doyle	22	M		Ireland	"	
Chas. Barthoud	45	M	Jeweller	France	"	Sch. Betsy & Peggy.
Mrs. " & 3 ch.	40	F		"	"	
Fanny Dumornay	30	F		"	"	
Louisa Jornazon	18	F		"	"	
--- Champmela	40	M	Tanner	"	"	
Robt. Preston	35	M		Scotland	"	
M. J. Gleerson	20	M		Ireland	"	
Jno. Garnier	40	M	Merchant	U. States	"	Ship American. Chew.
Peter Sauve	19	M	Planter	"	"	
J. Matossy	30	M	Confectionr.	"	"	

PASSENGERS WHO ARRIVED IN THE U.S. SEPTEMBER 1821 - DECEMBER 1823

Names of passengers	Age	Sex	Occupation	Country to which they belong	Country of which they intend becoming inhabitants	Ship or vessel with the name of the master or commander
NEW ORLEANS Cont.						
Q. E. Dec. 31, 1823						
J. Goldenbow	50	M		U. States	U. States	
Mrs. "	22	F		"	"	
Prosper Dubart	28	M		France	France	
J. Toxit	29	M		"	"	
B. De Marigny	38	M		"	"	
M. " & 5 ch.	28	F		"	"	
M. Frances	60	F		"	"	
M. Pappet	25	F		"	"	
George Valmer & ch.	36	M	Butcher	Germany	"	
Martin "	16	M	"	"	"	
Dorothea Frostin	18	F	Seamstress	"	"	
Catharine Schucloan	20	F	"	"	"	
Auguste Vellon	23	M	Watchmaker	"	"	
Fred. Prusch	23	M	Baker	"	"	
B. Friaca	23	M	Confectionr.	"	"	
T. Bavet	24	M	Farmer	France	"	
C. Gerard	28	M	"	"	"	
E. Larogue	20	M	Clerk	U. States	"	Brig Hollen. Leslie
Mary "	45	F		"	"	
H. Delfosse	48	F		"	"	
J. Lamariane	21	M	Clerk	"	"	
N. Visinier	50	M	Teacher	"	"	Brig Roxana. Miller.
John F. Cuaset	40	M	Merchant	"	"	
Wm. Morgan	30	M	Pilot	"	"	Ship Mary. Wilson.
Wm. Williams	25	M	Joiner	Wales	"	
A. C. Felke	45	F		France	"	Brig South Carolina. Thornton.
A. Julin	18	F		"	"	
Casar Courts	20	M		"	"	
C. Combier	20	M		"	"	Sch Nancy. Coller.
D. W. Dobbs	25	M		U. States	"	
--- Dowling	22	M	Tanner	Ireland	"	
B. C. Brian	32	M	"	"	"	
M. Webber	60	M	Mariner	U. States	"	
D. Blanco	30	M		Portugal	"	
D. Bradshaw	40	M		Italy	"	
--- Benjamin	22	M	Printer	U. States	"	
--- Montgomery	25	M	Mariner	"	"	
Nicholas	40	M	"	Germany	U. States	
--- Sardoforry	30	M	"	Italy	"	
Isaac Stone	26	M	Merchant	U. States	"	Sch. Hamilton & Hiram. Tucker.
A. Wood	19	M	"	"	"	
Soloman Saltus	27	M	"	"	"	
Jas. Inerasily	50	M	Planter	Cuba	Spain	
Anthony Arnud *	34	M	Merchant	U. States	U. States	

Names of passengers	Age	Sex	Occupation	Country to which they belong	Country of which they intend becoming inhabitants	Ship or vessel with the name of the master or commander
NEW ORLEANS Cont.						
Q. E. Dec. 31, 1823						
J T. Oliver	25	M	Merchant	U. States	U. States	
U. Moreau	28	M	"	Spain	"	Brig Union. Gale
S. S. "	25	M	"	"	"	
B. Regurda	35	M	Shoemaker	U. States	"	
S. Chase	28	M	Merchant	"	"	
C. Rockwood	35	M	Carpenter	"	"	Sch. Director. Hamilton.
Wm. Mills	40	M	"	Scotland	"	Sloop Volant. Carrier.
Mrs. "	30	F		"	"	
George Rolling	45	M	Mariner	U. States	"	
S. Madroso	45	M	"	Spain	Mexico	Sch. Dorothy. Massicot.
Antonio Pimpinel	30	M	Merchant	"	"	
M. Garner *	24	M	"	"	"	
Joseph Sinro	25	M	"	"	"	
F. Basuclo	20	M	"	"	"	
A. de la Torre *	28	M	"	"	"	
Ant. Rodrigues	30	M	"	"	"	
Juan Garcia	32	M	"	"	"	
Cyprian Gross	45	M	Physician	France	U. States	Ship Emulous. Selden.
M. "	32	F		"	"	
D. Dupuys	40	M	Planter	U. States	"	
M. "	20	F		"	"	
A. Brunel	38	M	Planter	"	"	
John Cumming	18	M		"	"	
F. Labitut	19	M		"	"	
P. Lanusse Jr.	19	M		"	"	
F. Auguste	16	M		"	"	
C. Aldrick	35	M	Merchant	"	"	Brig Hyperion. Richard.
S. S. Goodwin	35	M	Professor	"	"	
David Beach	30	M	Merchant	"	"	
J. C. Everett	30	M	Mason	"	"	
J. Brier	25	M	Mariner	"	"	
C. T. Hehen	35	M	"	Germany	"	
T. Bougie	30	M	Baker	France	"	
J. B. Espy	26	M	Merchant	"	"	Sch. Little Sally. Lafitte.
J. Dansac	25	M	"	"	"	
J. Laurens	30	M	"	"	"	
J. Fernandez	25	M	"	"	"	
J. C. Tanner	28	M		"	"	
J. Ferrand	30	M		France	"	
--- Prieffel	30	M		"	"	
A. Froman	30	M		Germany	"	
D. Halay	35	M		"	"	
Wm. Miller	28	M		"	"	
J. Foster	28	M		"	"	

Names of passengers	Age	Sex	Occupation	Country to which they belong	Country of which they intend becoming inhabitants	Ship or vessel with the name of the master or commander
NEW ORLEANS Cont.						
Q. E. Dec. 31, 1823						
J. D. Bein	21	M	Merchant	England	U. States	Ship Jane. Holmes.
James Jenkinson	15	M	Clerk	"	"	
--- Bradford	40	M	Merchant	U. States	"	Brig Hope. Spears.
Stephen Pennington	34	M	"	"	"	Brig Hercules. Johnson.
John George	35	M	"	England	"	Brig Isabella. Cameron.
David Allen	30	M	"	"	"	
Owen Jones	35	M	"	"	"	
N. Duchenin	16	F		U. States	"	Sch. Harriet. Rogers.
F. Hesergue	31	M	Baker	"	"	
T. V. Kettel & ch.	48	M	Merchant	"	"	
Saml. Rickler	23	M	"	"	"	
Fredk. Furst	24	M	"	Germany	"	Ship Rebecca. Wheaton
James Black	30	M	"	Scotland	"	Ship King George. Smith.
P. Marquess	45	M	Upholsterer	U. States	"	Brig Holly. Hammond.
Isaac Nicholas	34	M	Carpenter	Hayti	"	
J. Mouton	16	M	Clerk	U. States	"	
R. Deni	26	M	Cab. maker	Hayti	"	
Wm. Moore	45	M	Merchant	U. States	"	Sloop Intrepid. Holmes.
J. McRay	30	M	"	"	"	
B. Cutter	30	M	"	"	"	
Richd. Pierce	35	M	"	"	"	
C. Briell *	45	M	Mariner	"	"	
J. Gonzales	30	M	Merchant	Mexico	"	
B. Godfrey	30	M	Mariner	U. States	"	
F. Thun	30	M	Merchant	Mexico	"	
Jno. W. Noble	24	M	Mariner	U. States	"	
--- Johnson	25	M	"	"	"	
Oliver Woolley	25	M		"	"	
Chas. Mitchell	30	M	"	Sweden	"	Brig Oscar. Aliveda
P. Johnson	35	M	"	"	"	
C. Jourdan	67	M	Bookseller	France	"	Ship Edward. Howard.
Anthony Nuckett	46	M	Teacher	"	"	
T. Porche	28	M	Planter	Holland	"	
R. Hotten	30	M	Mariner	"	"	Brig Mexico. Howard.
J. G. Tool	35	M	"	"	"	
H. C. Schuving	23	M	"	"	"	
Erig Shoff	43	M	"	"	"	
J. B. Kouithoff	21	M	"	"	"	
James Jones	23	M	Merchant	"	"	Sloop Susan. Newman.
John Lopez	40	M	Painter	"	"	
Mary "	26	F		"	"	
A. Leveto	28	M	Merchant	Austria	"	
Jas Lopez	25	M	Painter	Spain	"	
Ant. "	21	M	Merchant	"	"	

Names of passengers	Age	Sex	Occupation	Country to which they belong	Country of which they intend becoming inhabitants	Ship or vessel with the name of the master or commander
NEW ORLEANS Cont						
Q. E Dec. 31, 1823						
David Heidle	24	M	Trader	U. States	U. States	
F. Cheh •	41	M	Merchant	Spain	Spain	Sch Constitution
J. J. Corbo	40	M	"	"	"	
A. Venero	25	M	"	"	"	
J. Naveda	23	M	"	"	"	
M. M. Guiterron	40	M	"	"	"	
J. Carbonel	40	M	"	"	"	
J. Finenci	28	M	"	"	"	
J Cladio	21	M	"	"	"	
J. Cavallero	22	M	"	"	"	
J. Cañet •	22	M	"	"	"	
J Sanaga	21	M	"	"	"	
A. Buerbo	54	M	"	"	"	
A. P. Bonilla	30	M	"	"	"	
F. Farina •	24	M	"	"	"	
J Luama	45	M	"	"	"	
J. Mestero	20	M	"	"	"	
M. Gomen	32	M	"	"	"	
M. Poraga	18	M	"	"	"	
D. Mier	28	M	"	"	"	
J. Compo	60	M	"	"	"	
F. Higues	46	M	"	"	"	
J. de la Buisco	22	M	"	"	"	
J. Lopez	26	M	"	"	"	
A. Lombo	45	M	"	"	"	
C. Camelion	42	M	"	"	"	
J. A. Lerdo	40	M	"	"	"	
George Lloyd	30	M	"	England	U. States	Ship Jno. Thomas. Roberts.
E. Freret •	18	F		U. States	"	
Wm. "	20	M		"	"	
Thos. Roddick	19	M		Scotland	"	
Fred Salked	16	M		England	"	
Benj. Frasier	30	M		"	"	
M. Berinandez	50	M	Merchant	Cuba	Cuba	Sch. Geo. Hand. McPherson.
George Beck	53	M		Germany	Denmark	Brig Monroe. Howland.
Clemt. Julien	26	M		France	U. States	Ship Virgin. De la Roche.
Lawrence Rosseter	49	M		Ireland	"	
Pat. Egan	32	M	Farmer	"	"	
Mrs. " & 2 ch.	28	F		"	"	
E. Hawkins	20	M	U.S.N.Offcr.	U. States	"	Sch. Hamilton. Tucker.
--- Olivier & ch.	30	M	Play actor	France	"	
--- Rousset	28	M	"	"	"	
M. "	20	F		"	"	
Jno. Pressis	30	M	Merchant	Spain	"	

Names of passengers	Age	Sex	Occupation	Country to which they belong	Country of which they intend becoming inhabitants	Ship or vessel with the name of the master or commander
NEW ORLEANS Cont.						
Q. E. Dec. 31, 1823						
M. Augel	30	M	Merchant	Spain	U. States	
M. Arcos	43	M	Mariner	"	"	
--- Domingo	32	M	Merchant	"	"	
--- Fernandez	33	M	Mariner	"	"	
Jno. Hase	35	M	Trader	U. States	"	
Joseph Scran	28	M	Hairdresser	France	"	Sch. Geo. Washington. Baron.
P. Joutz	39	M		Italy	"	
P. Allair	25	M		U. States	"	Sch. Eliza. Nartigue.
A. Guirot	21	M		"	"	
BALTIMORE						
Q. E. Dec. 31, 1823						
P. Oldfield	23	M	Merchant	U. States	U. States	Vessel not mentioned.
C. H. Foster	28	M	"	"	"	
J. Thompson	23	M	Farmer	Halifax	"	
Jane " & ch.	24	F		"	"	
Matthew Kelly	37	M	Mariner	U. States	"	
Jno. McFadon	30	M	Merchant	"	"	
George Muscroft & ch.	38	M	Culler		"	
Wm. Alexander	24	M	Weaver	Ireland	"	
Elizabeth Graham	18	F		"	"	
Adam Harris	25	M	Farmer	"	"	
Susanna Boyd	25	F		"	"	
Robt. Graham	20	M	Weaver	"	"	
P. Heron	16	M	Labourer	"	"	
Isabella Harris	60	F		"	"	
Elizabeth Silbour	56	F		"	"	
Alexr. Cortes	25	M		"	"	
F. W. Hink	45	M	Merchant	U. States	"	
Augustus Wagner	26	M	Physician	Germany	"	
J. Solomon	26	M	Pedlar	U. States	"	
Rachel " & ch.	20	F		"	"	
Mary Ballow & 2 ch.	20	F		"	"	
John Vangulder	26	M	Butcher	"	"	
Rose " & ch.	26	F		"	"	
Edwd. Stoler	20	M	Merchant	Hamburg	"	
P. G. Chavatte	35	M	"	"	"	
John W. Hodges	30	M	"	U. States	"	
John Thompson	30	M	Carpenter	"	"	
Jacob B. Garet	25	M	Painter	"	"	
Wm. Baker	23	M		England	"	
Jno. H. Offley	21	M	Merchant	U. States	"	
P. C. Green	24	M	Mariner	"	"	

Names of passengers	Age	Sex	Occupation	Country to which they belong	Country of which they intend becoming inhabitants	Ship or vessel with the name of the master or commander
BALTIMORE Cont.						
Q. E. Dec. 31, 1823						
G. W. Mitchell	28	M	Merchant	England	U. States	
Antonio Vigo	45	M	Mariner	Spain	Temporary	
Jabez Boothroyd	45	M	Merchant	Hayti	St. Domingo	
Alexr. Dunker	44	M	"	"	"	
M. Zives & 4 ch.	35	M		"	"	
Wm. Palmer	36	M	Merchant	U. States	"	
Wm. Burtcher	52	M	Mariner	"	"	
Joseph Jones	34	M	Watchmakr.	"	"	
Henry L. Clive	29	M	"	"	"	
George Banks	38	M	Merchant	"	"	
Thomas Dukehart	33	M	Mariner	"	"	
Wm. Eddy	24	M	Farmer	"	"	
Margt. " & ch.	18	F		"	"	
Prudence McKenzie & 5 ch.	52	F		N. Scotia		
John M. Kanky	22	M	Merchant	U. States	"	
Lewis Davint	36	M	Mariner	"	"	
Joseph Delile	30	M	"	"	"	
D Chester	28	M	Merchant	"	"	
--- Nogare	38	M	"	Santa Cruz	"	
Wm. Ross	20	M	Baker	England	"	
Sarah " & 2 ch.	22	F		"	"	
Joseph Beardly	42	M	Butcher	"	"	
W. Bendy	34	M	Farmer	"	"	
K. " & 2 ch.	27	F		"	"	
J. Curtin & 5 ch.	47	F		"	"	
H. Schaffer	42	M	Farmer	Holland	"	
Margt " & 6 ch.	32	F		"	"	
Conrad Weanker	35	M		"	"	
Mrs. " & 4 ch.	35	F		"	"	
Alexr. Kirkland	33	M	Merchant	U. States	"	
Don Nicholas	35	M	"	Spain	"	
Don Felix	28	M	"	"	Temporary	
J. Sullivan	40	M	"	U. States	U. States	
F. Verines	25	M	"	Spain	Temporary	
Juan Maria Spence *	27	M	"	"	"	
J. M. "	24	M	"	"	"	
N. Soarer	30	M	"	"	"	
Isabel Ferram	45	F		"	"	
Juliana Cano	25	F		"	"	
O. Carpenter	30	M	Merchant	U. States	"	
Thos. W. Wharton	20	M	"	"	"	
P. Sargeteau	22	M	Mariner	Bordeaux	"	
Raymond Roy	35	M	"	"	"	

Names of passengers	Age	Sex	Occupation	Country to which they belong	Country of which they intend becoming inhabitants	Ship or vessel with the name of the master or commander
BALTIMORE Cont.						
Q. E. Dec. 31, 1823						
John Lama	24	M	Merchant	Spain	Temporary	
Joseph Gray	25	M	"	"		
James Stansbury	28	M	Mariner	U. States	U. States	
M. Machado	35	M	Span. offcr.	Neiuvetos	"	
H. Costana	40	M	Merchant	"	"	
Peter Areas	25	M	Span offcr.	"	"	
Jno. W. Massey	30	M		U. States	"	
Thos. A. Lane	40	M	Mariner	"	"	
W. Massicot	46	M	"	"	"	
John Haining	25	M	Merchant	England	Jamaica	
James Phillips	56	M	Supercargo	U. States	U. States	
Danl. Powers	25	M		"	"	
Saml. T. Burk	24	M	Traveller	England	"	
V. B. Lawrence	35	M	Merchant	U. States	"	
Jno. Cordon	29	M	"	"	"	
Joseph Cana	20	M	"	"	"	
Matthew Rive	40	M	Mariner	"	"	
Thomas Coward	38	M	"	"	"	
C. H. Eirinbrandt	33	M	Merchant	Bremen	"	
G. H. Fruise	26	M	"	"	"	
C. F. Offensandt	20	M	"	"	"	
B. Mayer	25	M	"	"	"	
M. Mirnay •	24	M	Labourer	England	"	
P. Wenon •	30	M	"	"	"	
Geo. Glascott	22	M	Attorney	"	"	
Chas. F. Singleton	25	M	Merchant	U. States	"	
Thos. Erving	30	M	Doctor	"	"	
Thos. Adderton	45	M	Mariner	"	"	
F. Addors	40	M	Jeweller	"	"	
G. G. Atkinson	26	M	Supercargo	"	"	
James Chaytor	50	M	Mariner	"	"	
Wm. S. Woodside	28	M	Merchant	"	"	
Edwd. Butler	25	M	"	"	"	
Saml. Tinion	30	M	Mariner	"	"	
P. C. Green	35	M	"	"	"	
R. Ambos	25	M	"	"	"	
W. G. Bolgiano	25	M	Merchant	Havana	"	
J. F. Didier	21	M	"	"	"	
Chas. P. Deborre	24	M	"	Mexico	"	
John Mantusa	35	M	"	"	"	
Jose Garcia & ch.	24	M	"	"	"	
Peter Petilonis	30	M	"	"	"	
John Leonard	30	M	Musical Ins. Maker	U. States	"	

Names of passengers	Age	Sex	Occupation	Country to which they belong	Country of which they intend becoming inhabitants	Ship or vessel with the name of the master or commander
PASSAMAQUODDY						
Q. E. Dec. 31, 1823						
M. Denny	30	F		Ireland	U. States	
Jane Gray	37	F		"	"	
Martha "	21	F		"	"	
Alexr. Rogers	31	M	Labourer	"	"	
Ann "	27	F		"	"	
Edwd McFerly	39	M	Farmer	"	"	
John Wheelan	18	M	Labourer	"	"	
Robt. Lundy	26	M	"	"	"	
M. "	23	M		"	"	
Alexr. Long	31	M	"	"	"	
Ann Magreedy	21	F		"	"	
P. McGunnigall	23	M	"	"	"	
Wm. Dougherty	31	M	"	"	"	
Rose " & 3 ch.	31	F		"	"	
Alexr. Reiley & ch.	23	M	Farmer	"	"	
T. Nixon	16	M	Labourer	"	"	
Alexr. Smith	17	M	"	"	"	
Robt. "	15	M	"	"	"	
John McGlen	20	M	"	"	"	
Alexr. "	23	M	"	"	"	
Jane "	19	F		"	"	
Fanny Loughery	20	F		"	"	
Catharine McSoully	37	F		"	"	
Joseph Long	57	M	Labourer	"	"	
Felix Boyle	62	M	Farmer	"	"	
John Hurley	19	M	"	"	"	
Francis Ledden	23	M	"	"	"	
John Roden	28	M	"	"	"	
Robert Steele	30	M	"	"	"	
Joseph McLane	30	M	Labourer	"	"	
Samuel Smith	25	M	"	"	"	
Alexr. Long	20	M	Cloth printer	"	"	
Ann Rogers	25	F	Cook	"	"	
Nancy McFaly	19	M		"	"	
John Wheelan	40	M	Farmer	"	"	
James Stewart	36	M	Weaver	"	"	
Danl. McCauley	27	M	Farmer	"	"	
Alexr. Long	20	M	"	"	"	
P. McGunnigall	20	M	Weaver	"	"	
Thos. McComen	24	M	Labourer	"	"	
Wm. Dougherty	20	M	Shoemaker	"	"	
F. Nunan *	20	M	Weaver	"	"	
Abner Smith	20	M	"	"	"	
Robt. Ling	40	M	"	"	"	

Names of passengers	Age	Sex	Occupation	Country to which they belong	Country of which they intend becoming inhabitants	Ship or vessel with the name of the master or commander
PASSAMAQUODDY Cont. Q. E. Dec. 31, 1823						
B. McLoughter	25	M	Farmer	Ireland	U. States	
F. L. Alden	23	M	"	"	"	
Danl. McGline	23	M	Farmer	"	"	
Joseph Donaldson	24	M	"	"	"	
Patrick Owens	45	M	"	"	"	
Charles Boyle	23	M	"	"	"	
John Macadon	20	M	"	"	"	
John McClear	20	M	"	"	"	
Alexr. Helps	24	M	"	"	"	
Joseph Long	23	M	"	"	"	
James Mooney	18	M	"	"	"	
Edwd. McCablee	28	M	"	"	"	
Thos. Whary	25	M	Weaver	"	"	
Patrick McCurnick	24	M	Gardner	"	"	
Jas. McLean	24	M	Teacher	"	"	
Charles Tully	35	M	Weaver	"	"	
Wm. Mills	21	M	Teacher	"	"	
Jas. McEuhill	27	M	Labourer	"	"	
Richd. McGunner	20	M	"	"	"	
Alexr. Smith	20	M	"	"	"	
John "	18	M	"	"	"	
Andw. Williamson & 4 ch.	41	M	Farmer	"	"	
Patrick Harson	28	M	"	"	"	
Andw. Husney	23	M	"	"	"	
Michael Crowley	20	M	"	"	"	
Andw. Williamson	25	M	"	"	"	
Andw. McKainy	23	M	Labourer	"	"	
Lawrence Kennedy	23	M	"	"	"	
John Morian	22	M	"	"	"	
John O'Donnell	21	M	Farmer	"	"	
Dominick "	26	M	"	"	"	
Ann "	22	F	Spinster	"	"	
Ann Goodwin	24	M	"	"	"	
R. Cunningham	18	M	Weaver	"	"	
Owen McGlade	24	M	Farmer	"	"	
Francis Murray	25	M	Labourer	"	"	
Francis Douchy	30	M	Weaver	"	"	
Catharine "	25	M	Spinster	"	"	
John Donelly	24	M	Cordwainer	"	"	
Robert Smith	32	M	Farmer	"	"	
James "	34	M	"	"	"	
Michael Morris	24	M	"	"	"	

Names of passengers	Age	Sex	Occupation	Country to which they belong	Country of which they intend becoming inhabitants	Ship or vessel with the name of the master or commander
PASSAMAQUODDY Cont. Q. E. Dec. 31, 1823						
Mary Morris & child	22	F		Ireland	U. States	
James Donelly	23	M	Labourer	"	"	
Robt. McBryant	22	M	Weaver	"	"	
Sarah "	19	F		"	"	
John Dunell	20	M	Farmer	"	"	
Joseph Rogers	21	M	"	"	"	
Wm "	19	M	"	"	"	
Isaac Gardner	20	M	"	"	"	
H. Gibson	19	M	"	"	"	
Adams Span	24	M	"	"	"	
Joseph Workman	20	M	"	"	"	
David Hilearty *	21	M	"	"	"	
James Armstrong	21	M	"	"	"	
Samuel Goen *	24	M	"	"	"	
Wm. Eustis	20	M	"	"	"	
Wm. McGlauphin	23	M	"	"	"	
Robert Nixon	23	M	"	"	"	
Robt. McMurray	25	M	"	"	"	
Wm. McMurray	23	M	"	"	"	
Sampson Graham	23	M	"	"	"	
Wm. Smith	23	M	"	"	"	
Samuel Scott	46	M	"	"	"	
Margt. "	45	F	"	"	"	
Philip "	22	M	"	"	"	
Robert Edwards	24	M	"	"	"	
John "	19	M	"	"	"	
Robt. "	54	M	Weaver	"	"	
Ann "	54	F		"	"	
Elizabeth "	26	F		"	"	
E. Campbell	19	F		"	"	
James Hedick	22	M	Weaver	"	"	
John M. Clarrel *	24	M	"	"	"	
Robert Lemont	20	M	Labourer	"	"	
James "	18	M	"	"	"	
John "	14	M	"	"	"	
Jane Denny & 2 ch.	40	F		"	"	
James Coyd	25	M	"	"	"	
James Moore	26	M	"	"	"	
Alice "	22	F		"	"	
Thos. McCebin	22	M	"	"	"	
David McFarland	22	M	"	"	"	
John Dunlop	22	M	"	"	"	
Joseph Patterson	24	M	Farmer	"	"	

PASSENGERS WHO ARRIVED IN THE U.S. SEPTEMBER 1821 - DECEMBER 1823

Names of passengers	Age	Sex	Occupation	Country to which they belong	Country of which they intend becoming inhabitants	Ship or vessel with the name of the master or commander
PASSAMOQUOODY Cont. Q. E. Dec. 31, 1823						
Thos. Bell	21	M	Farmer	Ireland	U. States	
Thomas Patterson	56	M	"	"	"	
Rachel " & ch.	40	F		"	"	
Matthew Murphy	45	M	Weaver	"	"	
James Mills	20	M		"	"	
Wm. Pratt	30	M	Weaver	"	"	
James Nickerson	30	M	Farmer	"	"	
Mary " & 2 ch.	28	F		"	"	
Richd. Dendy	53	M	Farmer	"	"	
Alice "	51	F		"	"	
Robt. Johnston	40	M	"	"	"	
Margt. " & ch.	40	F		"	"	
Francis Alice	35	M	"	"	"	
Jane " & 3 ch.	28	F		"	"	
Wm. Brimstone	21	M	"	"	"	
Margt. "	18	F		"	"	
Ellen Speott *	20	F		"	"	
George Hiller	22	M	"	"	"	
Alexr. Lettea	55	M	Weaver	"	"	
Wm. "	26	M	"	"	"	
Andw. Sprout	22	M	"	"	"	
Samuel Gray	16	M	"	"	"	
Mary Souther	26	F		"	"	
David Graine	50	M	Farmer	"	"	
James Taylor	41	M	Preacher	"	"	
Catharine " & 3 ch.	26	F		"	"	
Robt. Dinwiddie	64	M	Weaver	"	"	
Mary " & 8 ch.	40	F		"	"	
Wm. McCharty	24	M	Shoemaker	"	"	
Alexr. McCambridge	19	M	Labourer	"	"	
Wm. Brines	23	M	"	"	"	
Margt. Divit & 2 ch.	26	F		"	"	
Danl. McAllister	40	M	"	"	"	
Hugh Brown	27	M	"	"	"	
Elizabeth " & 2 ch.	20	F		"	"	
George McElho	30	M	Baker	"	"	
Catharine " & 4 ch.	24	F		"	"	
John Rogers	45	M	Labourer	"	"	
Ann " & 2 ch.	45	M		"	"	
Matthew Riddle & 6 ch.	50	M	"	"	"	
Thomas Moore	25	M	"	"	"	
John Beck	20	M	"	"	"	
Robt. McCinnachi	23	M	"	"	"	

Names of passengers	Age	Sex	Occupation	Country to which they belong	Country of which they intend becoming inhabitants	Ship or vessel with the name of the master or commander
PASSAMAQUODDY Cont. Q. E. Dec. 31, 1823						
Robt. Given	19	M	Labourer	Ireland	U. States	
Arthur McEwens	22	M	"	"	"	
James McFillen	23	M	"	"	"	
Wm. Straney	30	M	"	"	"	
John McUfe *	25	M	"	"	"	
James McElke *	24	M	"	"	"	
James Rose	27	M	"	"	"	
C. Patterson & ch.	34	M	Farmer	"	"	
Samuel Potts	20	M	"	"	"	
Mary Patterson & 5 ch.	30	F		"	"	
Oswald Robertson	45	M	"	"	"	
Eliz. " & 2 ch.	47	F		"	"	
Robt. Sproul	22	M		"	"	
Maria "	19	F	Spinster	"	"	
John Jackson	25	M	Carpenter	"	"	
James Lindsey	23	M	Labourer	"	"	
Thomas McKown	29	M	"	"	"	
Michael Crilley	23	M	"	"	"	
Michael Conelly	24	M	"	"	"	
Robt. McDoll	30	M	Shoemaker	"	"	
Mary Conelly	26	F	Spinster	"	"	
Nancy Crilly *	22	F	"	"	"	
Bernard McIntire	14	M	Weaver	"	"	
John McDonald	17	M	Cooper	"	"	
S. Sullivan	30	M	Bricklayer	"	"	
James O'Brien	31	M	"	"	"	
John Doherty	25	M	Labourer	"	"	
John Coylen	25	M	"	"	"	
Judith Sullivan & 2 ch.	30	F	Spinster	"	"	
Cath. O'Brien & ch.	29	F	"	"	"	
Mary Doherty & ch.	25	F	"	"	"	
Maria Strane	26	F		"	"	
John Allison	30	M	Farmer	"	"	
H. Shewut *	28	M	Carpenter	"	"	
John Daley	20	M	Farmer	"	"	
James Raferty	24	M	"	"	"	
Mary " & ch.	22	F	Spinster	"	"	
Margt. Ramsey	24	F	"	"	"	
Thos. McGunnigle	32	M	Farmer	"	"	
Margt. Black	24	F	Spinster	"	"	
Eleanor "	22	F	"	"	"	
Robt. Harris	20	M	Paper maker	"	"	
James Lutter	21	M	Farmer	"	"	

Names of passengers	Age	Sex	Occupation	Country to which they belong	Country of which they intend becoming inhabitants	Ship or vessel with the name of the master or commander
PASSAMAQUODDY Cont. Q. E. Dec. 31, 1823						
Wm. Ellis	20	M	Farmer	Ireland	U. States	
Thomas Ellis	74	M	"	"	"	
Joseph Hamilton	32	M	"	"	"	
Ann "	28	F	Spinster	"	"	
Margt. McDole & ch.	26	F	"	"	"	
Mary Carlin & 2 ch.	26	F	"	"	"	
Rose Linch & 2 ch.	24	F	"	"	"	
Robt. Steel	26	M	Farmer	"	"	
Margt. " & 3 ch.	26	F		"	"	
Robt. Steel	26	M	Farmer	"	"	
John Shilock	26	M	"	"	"	
John Steel	26	M	"	"	"	
Mary Shilock	20	F	Spinster	"	"	
Jane Rickson & 3 ch.	36	F	"	"	"	
Hannah Campbell & child	30	F	"	"	"	
Catharine McBride	34	F	"	"	"	
Samuel Rumsey	28	M	Farmer	"	"	
John Barnwell	24	M	Weaver	"	"	
Jane Campbell	22	F	Spinster	"	"	
James McClintock	25	M	Labourer	"	"	
Daniel Warde	50	M	Farmer	"	"	
Alexr. McArthur	36	M	Carpenter	"	"	
Benj. Burns	25	M	Farmer	"	"	
P. McGrail	24	M	"	"	"	
C. Clark	25	M	"	"	"	
Danl. McGarvick	36	M	"	"	"	
Patrick Quinn	35	M	"	"	"	
Margt. "	18	F	Spinster	"	"	
Rose McNeil	20	F	"	"	"	
Margt. Gibson	40	F	"	"	"	
Thomas Bourn	21	M	Saddler	"	"	
Ann "	50	F		"	"	
M. McCaffan & 3 ch.	48	F		"	"	
Ellen Lehon & 3 ch.	30	F		"	"	
B. F. Simmons	40	M	Carpenter	"	"	
Patrick "	31	M	Cooper	"	"	
Henry "	30	M	Labourer	"	"	
B. McDonald	26	M	"	"	"	
Alexr. Hamitt *	22	M	"	"	"	
John Clary	30	M	"	"	"	
Mary " & 3 ch.	25	F	Spinster	"	"	
Chas. McManners & 3 ch.	50	M	Labourer	"	"	

Names of passengers	Age	Sex	Occupation	Country to which they belong	Country of which they intend becoming inhabitants	Ship or vessel with the name of the master or commander
PASAMAQUODDY						
Cont.						
Q. E. Dec. 31, 1823						
Wm. Newell	60	M	Cooper	Ireland	U. States	
Mary "	22	F	Spinster	"	"	
H. "	18	M	Cooper	"	"	
Simon Nelson	30	M	"	"	"	
L. "	60	M	"	"	"	
John "	34	M	"	"	"	
Flora "	28	F	Spinster	"	"	
Jane "	28	F	"	"	"	
James "	15	M	Labourer	"	"	
Robt. McElroy	21	M	"	"	"	
Wm. Boyd	18	M	Weaver	"	"	
Francis Clark	50	M	Farmer	"	"	
Pat. "	20	M	"	"	"	
John "	16	M	"	"	"	
Michael " & 2 ch.	26	M	"	"	"	
Catharine "	50	F	Spinster	"	"	
Peggy "	20	F	"	"	"	
Simon Gardner	44	M	Mariner	"	"	
D. "	44	F	Spinster	"	"	
John Miller	20	M	Mariner	"	"	
John Molzae *	14	M	"	"	"	
Wm. Golder	70	M	Farmer	"	"	
James "	31	M	"	"	"	
John Powers	20	M	"	"	"	
Hugh Matthews	27	M	"	"	"	
U. Powers	22	M	Labourer	"	"	
James "	20	M	"	"	"	
James Daley	24	M	Merchant	"	"	
Calvin Gibbs	30	M	"	"	"	
--- Stevens	36	M	Baker	"	"	
EDGAR TOWN						
Q. E. Dec. 31, 1823						
George L. Young	21	M		U. States	U. States	Sch. Morgiana. Sears.
M. J. G. Boste	28	M	Merchant	Portugal	Portugal	Sch. Boston. Freeman.
J. P. Dos Quinos	28	M	"	"	"	
--- George	20	M	Servant	"	"	
Benjamin Descoins	33	M	Merchant	France	St. Thomas	Sch. Strong. Jaques.
Edward Holden	51	M	"	U. States	U. States	Died on the passage.
John Adderton	20	M	Mariner	"	"	Ship Ontario. Bunker.
Enoch Preble	60	M	"	"	"	Brig Washington. Collogan.
Wm. Crawford	26	M		Scotland	Scotland	

PASSENGERS WHO ARRIVED IN THE U.S. SEPTEMBER 1821 - DECEMBER 1823

Names of passengers	Age	Sex	Occupation	Country to which they belong	Country of which they intend becoming inhabitants	Ship or vessel with the name of the master or commander
BOSTON						
Q. E. Dec. 31, 1823						
Richd. W. Green	34	M	Mariner	U. States	U. States	Ship C. Cain. Wilkes.
Abraham Swain	39	M	"	"	"	
Henry Parsons	50	M	"	"	"	
A. G. Craft	37	M	"	"	"	
Thomas Robinson	35	M	Merchant	"	"	
Wm. Green	24	M	Mariner	"	"	
Wm. Warner	24	M	"	"	"	
Charles H. Lowe	15	M	"	"	"	
Charles Searle	18	M	"	"	"	
Geo. G. Gary	23	M	Ship master	"	"	Ship Panther. Austin.
Wm. Hawkins	29	M	Merchant	"	"	
Charles Moore	34	M	"	"	"	
Danl. S. Ralston	22	M	"	"	"	
Wm. G. Cutter	25	M	Coach mkr.	"	"	
Geo. F. Weaver	23	M	Offcr. U.S. Navy	"	"	
Wm. Martin	38	M	Mariner	"	"	
James Williams	23	M	"	"	"	
Wm. Drury	21	M	"	"	"	
Wm. L. Hudson	28	M	Officer of U.S. Navy	"	"	
Ethniel ? S. Key	23	M	Carpenter	"	"	Sch. Fame. Goodwin.
M. Witham	42	M	Merchant	Halifax	"	Sch. Geo. & Henry. Lakin.
Miss "	21	F		"	"	
Mr. Gray	22	M		Ireland	Ireland	
Mr. Shadduck	24	M		"	"	
Mr. Minhead	25	M	Merchant	U. States	U. States	
Mr. Osborne	21	M	"	Halifax	Halifax	
F. Upham	33	M	"	Ireland	U. States	
B. Carroll	30	M	"	"	"	
James Frazier	76	M	"	Montreal		Sch. Providence. Nolen.
Wm. Morrisey	29	M	"	N. Scotia	N. Scotia	Sch. Billow. Barker.
Jno. Cummins	27	M	"	"	"	
James Foley	21	M	Printer	"	"	
C. Childs	34	M	Carpenter	England	"	
Jno. Wright	26	M	Coachman	U. States	"	
Michael Harney	27	M	Labourer	N. Scotia	"	
Thos. Steward	26	M	Shoemaker	"	"	
Jno. Valentine	43	M	Labourer	U. States	"	
M. Senion	33	M	Minister	Poland	U. States	Sch. Janus. Holmes.
D. Prinker	28	M	Physician	Germany	"	
M. Manchon	30	M	Merchant	France	"	
Geo. M. Siscomb	21	M	"	U. States	"	Sch. Genl. Macomb. Hiscock.
F. Manpair *	32	M	Planter	France	"	Brig Harriet. Hinchman.

Names of passengers	Age	Sex	Occupation	Country to which they belong	Country of which they intend becoming inhabitants	Ship or vessel with the name of the master or commander
BOSTON Cont.						
Q. E. Dec. 31, 1823						
J. F. Puppan	25	M	Planter	France	U. States	
Harriet Tufts	20	F		U. States	"	Ship Jasper. Crooker.
Wm. Rice	35	M	Mariner	"	"	
R. Rogers	40	M	"	"	"	
Francis Evileth	27	M	Merchant	"	"	
Wm. J. Loring	27	M	"	"	"	Ship Athens. Curtis.
Joseph Budger	40	M	"	"	"	Brig Golden Age. Blair.
Stephen Gallaty	15	M	To be edu-cated	?	"	
P. "	13	M	"	"	"	
E. De Roya Costa	26	M	Merchant	Portugal	"	
Fernando Massa	26	M		Sicily	"	
G. Allinelle	20	M		"	"	
Joseph Halstad	32	M	Carpenter	U. States	"	Brig Ruby. Phillips.
Eleazar Phelps	50	M	Cooper	"	"	Sch. Tantamount. Allen
Jane Young	20	F		"	"	
Nicholas Lileyuen *	40	M	Mariner	Sweden	"	Ship Bramin. McGlathlen.
John Allen	25	M	Trader	Halifax	Halifax	Sch. Geo. Henry. Lakin.
Mrs. Henry & 3 ch.	36	F		U. States	U. States	
James L. Levett *	20	M	Merchant	"	"	Ship Pearl. Marble.
George Hammond	27	M	"	"	"	
Elisha Merrian	25	M		Cab. maker	"	Sch. Charles. Chase.
Wm. H. Reany	19	M	Merchant	"	"	
Mrs. A. Connars	40	F		Halifax	Halifax	Sch. Billow. Barker.
Mrs. Johnson	29	F		"	"	
Edmd. Flint	22	M	Mechanic	"	"	
Wm. Martin	21	M	"	"	U. States	
Henry Brissonnet	20	M	Merchant	France	France	Brig Cornelia. Low Jr.
Thos. S. Winslow	35	M	Mariner	U. States	U. States	Ship Pocahontas. Howland.
James Harris	32	M	Merchant	"	"	Brig Forester. Soule.
John Greely	25	M	Mariner	England	"	Ship Warren. Webb.
Chester Dickenson	38	M	"	U. States	"	Ship Galatea. Goldwhaite.
Wm. Allen	36	M	"	England	England	
John Lay *	35	M	Merchant	U. States	U. States	
E. Ederkin	44	M	Ship mstr.	"	"	Brig H. Gardner.
Benj. Prince Jr.	21	M	Supercargo	"	"	Brig Lynn. Brown.
Edwd. Austin	20	M	Merchant	"	"	Brig Adriana. Austin.
Joseph Mathias	28	M	"	Holland	"	
James Taylor	50	M	Mariner	England	England	Sch. Geo. Henry. Lakin.
Wm. J. Orr	30	M	Merchant	Jamaica	Jamaica	
Robt. Mann	35	M	"	England	U. States	
Robert Stuart	24	M	"	Canada	Canada	
John Folonnar	21	M	"	England	England	
Henry Freeman	35	M	"	Canada	Canada	

Names of passengers	Age	Sex	Occupation	Country to which they belong	Country of which they intend becoming inhabitants	Ship or vessel with the name of the master or commander
BOSTON Cont.						
Q. E. Dec. 31, 1823						
James Perley	34	M	Mariner	. U. States	U. States	
Sarah Cowley	43	F		"	"	
Jane Neace *	24	F		"	"	
Ann M. Kewse	20	F		Halifax	"	
James Landerkin	29	M	Planter	"	"	
Elizabeth " & 2 ch.	29	F		"	"	
Richd. Morrisey	30	M	Merchant	England	"	
John Reddy	30	M	"	"	"	
Thomas Morrison	30	M	"	Ireland	"	
James Mithled *	21	M	Mason	"	"	
Patrick Brown	23	M	Farmer	"	"	
Thomas Norris	24	M	"	"	"	
John Harfhaty *	23	M	"	"	"	
Mary "	21	M		"	"	
John Sparrow Senr.	55	M	Mariner	Orleans	Orleans	
L. "	25	M	"	"	"	
John " Jr.	23	M	"	"	"	
D. S. "	20	M	"	"	"	
Wm. "	14	M	"	"	"	
M. Moody	18	M	"	"	"	
J. Ellis	22	M	Mariner	"	"	
George Howe	21	M	"	"	"	
Henry Nugent	18	M	"	"	"	
Robert Carter	20	M	"	"	"	
Isaac Kables	20	M	"	"	"	
James Simons Jr.	19	M	"	"	"	
Joseph Markell	20	M	"	"	"	
Otis Pendleton	43	M	"	"	"	
Henry Tinker	26	M	"	"	"	
James Simons	24	M	"	"	"	
Samuel Wrothbone	27	M	"	"	"	
Wm. Carver	17	M	Baker	"	"	
Jose Maria Heredia	19	M		Spain		Brig Galaxy. Harding.
Pat. McAnally	42	M	"	Ireland	U. States	
Benj. Dessoin	30	M		France	France	Sch. Strong. Jaques.
Edward Holden	57	M	Merchant	U. States		
Mr. Hazen	22	M	"	N. Brunwick	St. Johns	Sch. Billow. Barker
Mr. Belyea	22	M	Carpenter	"	"	
Wm. Poor	32	M	Labourer	Ireland	U. States	
Mrs. McCarthy & 3 ch.	27	F		"	"	
Wm. Smith	53	M		England	"	Ship Ruth. Shaw.
Susanna "	48	F		"	"	
John Evans	24	M	Farmer	"	"	
Francis Lopez	25	M		Portugal	Brazil ?	

Names of passengers	Age	Sex	Occupation	Country to which they belong	Country of which they intend becoming inhabitants	Ship or vessel with the name of the master or commander
BOSTON Cont.						
Q. E. Dec. 31, 1823						
Wm. H. Whitwell	34	M	Merchant	U. States	Brazil ?	
James H. Tidmarsh	45	M	"	N. Scotia	N. Scotia	
--- Pilipiny *	35	F	Linen draper	France	U. States	Brig Henry. Atwood.
Samuel Halman	24	M	Tailor	Holland	"	Brig Juniper. Parsons.
Charles Browing	58	M		U. States	"	Sch. George Henry. Laken.
John White & ch.	48	M		Quebec	"	
Paul C. Lang	27	M		"	"	
P. Landergan	50	M		"	"	
James Morris	32	M		"	"	
James McGratt	30	M		"	"	
John Powell	20	M		U. States	"	
James Donaldson	21	M		"	"	
Henry Senett	25	M		"	"	
Edward Ellis	44	M	Tailor	"	"	
James Crall *	19	M	Saddler	"	"	
Michael Nowell	22	M	Watchmaker	Ireland	"	
Shane Rhone	35	M	Carpenter	"	"	
NEW. YORK						
Q. E. Dec. 31, 1823						
E. Feissar	28	M	Merchant	Spain	Havana	Ship Tarantula. Pratt.
B. Magna	23	M	"	"	'	
M. Caino	30	M	Labourer	U States	U States	Sch. Olive Branch. Chesnut.
John Campbell	25	M	Weaver	England	"	
Mrs. Banks	39	F		Ireland	"	
Mary McEnuth	20	F		"	"	
Eliza Devine	21	F		"	"	
Biddy Connell	17	F		"	"	
James Levity & ch.	26	M	Weaver	"	"	
N. " & ch.	23	F		"	"	
Robt. Armstrong	23	M	Labourer	"	"	
Grace McLoughlin	20	F		"	"	
Biddy McMullen	18	F		"	"	
James Martin	22	M	Weaver	"	"	
Dorothy " & 3 ch.	20	F		"	"	
Jacob S. Warner	19	M	Merchant	U. States	"	Sch. Molly. Baxter.
B. De M. Croix	15	M	Physician	"	"	
J Sanchez	46	M	Merchant	Havana	"	Brig Hyperion. Brightman.
J. De Mayter	19	M	"	"	"	
Mrs. Sanchez	22	F		"	"	
Mrs. De Mayter & 3 ch.	33	F		"	"	
Mr. Lesap	60	M	Planter	U. States	"	Ship Seine. Williams.

Names of passengers	Age	Sex	Occupation	Country to which they belong	Country of which they intend becoming inhabitants	Ship or vessel with the name of the master or commander
NEW YORK Cont.						
Q. E. Dec. 31, 1823						
J. P. M. Silva	20	M	Merchant	Portugal	U. States	Brig Pomona. Bright.
Mr. Eyre	32	M	Mariner	U. States	"	Sch. Cicero. Brown.
James Griffin	22	M	"	"	"	
M. Nugent	27	M	Engineer	"	"	Brig Rapid Flyer.
P. Gerif	28	M	Merchant	France	"	
John Picharry	34	M	"	"	"	
M. Arriamac *	58	M	Mechanic	"	"	
Antonio Buria	26	M	Merchant	"	"	
R. Aroxarena	28	M	"	Spain	"	
J. Arogor	32	M	"	"	"	
Rachel Bonnet	22	F		N Brunswick	N Brunswick	Sch. Nancy. Crowell.
Mary "	18	F		"	"	
J. D. Ansley	26	M	Merchant	U. States	U. States	
P. W. Fraser	20	M	"	"	"	
W. B. Webster	26	M	Physician	N. Brunswick	N Brunswick	
C. Bordman	22	M	"	"	"	
James C. Chapman	22	M	"	"	"	
John Hastings	29	M	"	"	"	
C Hawkins	28	F		Ireland	U States	
Susan Stewart	22	F		"	"	
E. Anderson	25	M		"	"	
P. Duncan	26	M	Labourer	"	"	
Thos. Farender	22	M	"	"	"	
B. Snell	47	M	Mariner	U. States	"	Sch. Fly. Huntress
F. Y. Gardere	25	M	Merchant	"	"	
Mary Donelly	28	F	Milliner	Ireland	"	Sch. Astrea. Loring.
John H. Seaward	65	M	Mariner	U States	"	
David Hughes	50	M		Scotland	"	
Wm. Ker	35	M		"	"	
Henry Daniels	27	M		U. States	"	
C. French	40	M	Merchant	"	"	Sch. Culloden. Stinman.
P. D. Clark	51	M	Mariner	"	"	
Chas. W. Therton *	39	M	Merchant	"	"	Brig Hope. Moore.
Robert Gillespie	54	M	Farmer	Scotland	"	
Janet Hough	60	F		"	"	
Elizabeth "	29	F		"	"	
Alfred Seton	30	M	Merchant	U. States	"	Sch. Chas. town Packet.
John B. Contian *	20	M	"	"	"	Ship Weser. Hidell.
Lewis Howard	49	M	"	"	"	
Charles Broust *	47	M	"	"	"	
John N. Corquin	42	M	Mariner	"	"	
Asa C. West	37	M	"	"	"	
C. D. Robert	28	M	Planter	Dominica	Dominica	Sch. Maria. March.
R. Sisson	31	M	Mariner	U. States	U. States	

Names of passengers	Age	Sex	Occupation	Country to which they belong	Country of which they intend becoming inhabitants	Ship or vessel with the name of the master or commander
NEW YORK Cont.						
Q. E. Dec. 31, 1823						
A. Siclief *	39	M	Mariner	U. States	U. States	
J Baubard	19	M	Tailor	Guadaloupe	Guadaloupe	
John Adonis	39	M	Mechanic	St. Johns	St. Johns	Sloop Brothers. Baker.
Jane "	30	F		"	"	
Wm. Corn/Cors/Cox	22	M	Farmer	"	"	
Wm. D. Patten	20	M	Merchant	U. States	U. States	Sch. Live Oak. Blair.
Mrs. Utten	46	F		Jamaica	Jamaica	Sch. Huntress. Morgan.
Mr. Easor	28	M	Planter	"	"	
Mrs. "	28	F		"	"	
Mrs. Morgan & ch.	25	F		U. States	"	
Ann Riley	22	F		Ireland	U. States	
J. Graham	46	M		Scotland	"	
Peter Campbell	26	M	Planter	"	"	
J. D. Drinker Jr.	26	M	Merchant	U. States	"	Sch. Plough boy. Manlove.
Antonio Eymar	35	M	"	Spain	Spain	
Wm. McKaller	50	M	Naval offcr.	England	England	Ship John Wells. Harrow.
Thos. Barraclouch	19	M	Merchant	"	"	
W. Gray	18	M	"	U. States	U. States	
S. "	23	M	"	"	"	
John Swainson	20	M	"	"	"	
John A. Grace	35	M	"	England	England	
Joseph Milne	25	M	"	"	"	
Jas. "	20	M	"	"	"	
Wm. Cripps	24	M	"	"	"	
A. Agassus	26	M	"	"	"	
Thomas Fanning	30	M	"	"	"	
John R. Bainard	36	M	Mariner	St. Domingo	St. Domingo	
Eliza A. Stevens	16	F		England	England	
Joseph Smart	21	M	Farmer	"	U. States	Ship N. York Packet. Stone.
John Hallett	37	M	"	"	"	
Eliza " & 8 ch.	34	F		"	"	
Evan Reeze	27	M	"	Wales	"	
Ann "	20	F		"	"	
Geo. W. Worrell	22	M		U. States	"	Brig Brutus. Bradley.
Francis Lamin	40	M	Merchant	Spain	Spain	Ship Victory. Kingsbury.
E. Livingston	22	M	"	U. States	U. States	
Nathaniel Paine	30	M	Farmer	England	"	Brig Joseph. Holdridge.
Eliz. " & ch.	37	F		"	"	
James Read	24	M	Surgeon	"	"	
Francis Lear	37	M		"	"	
John Thomas	42	M		"	"	
Elizabeth " & 7 ch.	37	F		"	"	
Sarah Cliff & 6 ch.	36	F		"	"	
J Story	30	M	Mariner	"	"	Brig Packet. Doughty.

Names of passengers	Age	Sex	Occupation	Country to which they belong	Country of which they intend becoming inhabitants	Ship or vessel with the name of the master or commander
NEW YORK Cont.						
Q. E. Dec. 31, 1823						
Robt. Strong	36	M	Mariner	England	U. States	
John K. Wright	22	M	"	"	"	
Wm. Burton	24	M	"	"	"	
L. C. Zeulfeboff	30	M	Officer	Germany	"	Brig Margaret. West.
Robt. Young	20	M	Merchant	England	England	Sch. Mercator. Allen
P. S. Judson	20	M	"	U. States	U. States	
Samuel Wheaton	30	M	Mariner	"	"	
Wm. Way	25	M	Merchant	"	"	Sch. Marke. Small.
James Smith	36	M	"	G. Britain	"	Ship Bahama. Wood.
Mary " & 3 ch.	30	F		"	"	
John Magin	24	M		"	"	
David Lawrence	43	M	Farmer	"	"	
Ann " & 7 ch.	43	F		"	"	
James Abel	48	M	Butcher	"	"	
Mary " & 7 ch.	38	F		"	"	
Wm. Dodd	44	M	Farmer	"	"	
Mary " & 5 ch.	35	F		"	"	
Wm. Morris	30	M	"	"	"	
Mary " & 2 ch.	32	F		"	"	
James Burnly	50	M	Manufactr.	"	"	
Thomas Evans	30	M	Baker	"	"	
Wm. Arnold	28	M	Shoemaker	"	"	
Samuel Wilmot	24	M	Butcher	"	"	
George Robinson	31	M	Brewer	"	"	
Elizabeth " & 2 ch.	35	F		"	"	
Mary Lawton	20	F		"	"	
Richard Perrin	22	M	Cab. maker	"	"	
S. E. Krok	30	M	Merchant	Sweden	"	Ship India. Hatch.
Geo. Paterson	21	M	"	Denmark	"	
L. Lethelins	36	M	"	"	"	
John Graham	22	M	"	England	Jamaica	Brig Favorite. Dyer.
Robert Swan	18	M	"	Scotland	U. States	
Manuel Pierol *	30	M	"	Guatemala	"	
Pedro Aycinena *	25	M	"	"	"	
Robert Hamilton	25	M	Mariner	"	"	
Thomas Hindman	80	M	Merchant	Ireland	"	Ship Favorite. Bearnes.
Alexr. Bonner	35	M	"	U. States	"	
John Taite	20	M	"	"	"	
James J. Lewis	23	M	Farmer	"	"	
Robert Wilson	21	M	"	Ireland	"	
Samuel Wood	17	M	"	"	"	
John Clark	66	M	"	"	"	
P. J. Trimble	24	F	Spinster	"	"	
Biddy Downest *	16	F	"	"	"	

Names of passengers	Age	Sex	Occupation	Country to which they belong	Country of which they intend becoming inhabitants	Ship or vessel with the name of the master or commander
NEW YORK Cont.						
Q. E. Dec. 31, 1823						
Walter Bell	25	M	Farmer	Ireland	U. States	
Patrick Derlin	26	M	Weaver	"	"	
N. Major	15	M	"	"	"	
Richd. McKay	20	M	Farmer	"	"	
John McGeugon	21	M	"	"	"	
James Borland	25	M	"	"	"	
M. Kausman	35	M	Paper mkr.	Germany	"	Ship Orion. Abendroth.
Mrs. " & ch.	28	F		"	"	
Mr. Boseker	32	M	Merchant	"	"	
Lewis Folson & ch.	40	M	Mariner	U. States	"	Sch. Essex. Upton.
Edward Glenn	30	M	Mechanic	England	"	Sloop Alpha. Algate.
Richard Fisher	18	M	Merchant	Bermuda	Bermuda	
Geo. Thos. Hone	50	M	Physician	England	U. States	Ship James Cropper.
Thos. "	20	M		"	"	
Elizabeth " & 2 ch.	45	F		"	"	
Thos. Blakeley	31	M	Merchant	"	"	
Joseph Sharpe	29	M		"	"	
Geo. H. Busher	27	M	"	"	"	
James Ponsford	45	M	"	"	"	
Geo. G. Johnston	23	M	"	"	"	
Samuel Wright	29	M	"	"	"	
Jas. G. King	32	M	"	"	"	
Wm. D. Woolsley	23	M	"	"	"	
Jas. Stewart	43	M	Advocate	"	"	
Elizabeth "	27	F		"	"	
George Bingley	29	M	Merchant	"	"	
Hannah Sharpe	27	F		"	"	
James Bishop	20	M	Mariner	U. States	"	Brig Rebecca & Sally.
John Stimpson	24	M	Merchant	"	"	Brig Lydia. Prince.
Nicholas Lawrence	23	M	Coachmkr.	"	"	
Justice Bradley	52	M	Shoemaker	"	"	
Geo. H. "	18	M	"	"	"	
Wm. A. Paloner	28	M	"	"	"	
John H. Shaw	52	M	Mariner	"	"	
James Garetson	42	M	Hatter	"	"	
M. Loiges	43	F		France	France	Brig Hesper. Hubbard.
Miss "	20	F		"	"	
Z. Lamson	30	M	Mariner	U. States	U. States	
James French	32	M	"	"	"	Ship Briganza. Allen.
Geo. Griffith	40	M		"	"	
Biddy Johnston	27	F		"	"	
Joshua Davis	40	M	Planter	England	"	Sch. Zion. Hoodless.
Robt. Hillard	40	M	Mariner	U. States	"	Brig Morning Star. Waring.
Thomas Giffet	30	M	"	"	"	

Names of passengers	Age	Sex	Occupation	Country to which they belong	Country of which they intend becoming inhabitants	Ship or vessel with the name of the master or commander
NEW YORK Cont.						
Q. E. Dec. 31, 1823						
J. Ghilome	25	M	Merchant	France	France	
Wm. Frean	40	M	"	U. States	U. States	Sch. Midas. Bennett.
E. W. Huntington	30	M	"	"	"	
A. Pool	50	M	"	G. Britain	"	
M. De Guerro	50	M		Spain	Spain	Brig Catharine Rogers.
Miguel Sauch	50	M	Physician	"	"	
J. J. Jones	30	M		"	"	
E. C. Rutlege	24	M		"	"	
H. Ceron	22	M	Merchant	France	"	Sch. Pacification. Sheeds.
W. Thompson	28	M	Mechanic	U. States	"	
B. Renshaw	30	M	Merchant	"	"	Brig Harriet & Lucy.
E. Wambersie	60	M		"	"	
Mrs. " & 2 ch.	47	F		"	"	
Fred. D. Spalding	19	M		"	"	
John McGregor	30	M	Cook	Scotland	"	
Thomas Gray	32	M	Merchant	Ireland	"	Ship Chase. Baxter.
Mrs. " & ch.	23	F		"	"	
James McClucken	37	M	Planter	"	"	
John Vitter	33	M	"	St. Eustatia	"	
Robt. Dubon	17	M	Merchant	France	"	Sch. Margaret. Harraden.
M. Eutrope	30	M	"	"	"	
Silas Brownell	25	M	Carpenter	U. States	"	
John Colbran	44	M	Farmer	England	"	Brig Commerce. Bates.
George Twinner	37	M	"	"	"	
Hugh Mathers	21	M	"	"	"	
Laurence "	23	M	"	"	"	
James Kennedy	28	M	"	"	"	
Henry Hodgins	20	M	"	"	"	
Margaret "	27	F		"	"	
James "	22	M	Farmer	"	"	
George Kendrick	20	M	"	"	"	
David Williams	56	M	"	"	"	
David Moody	26	M	"	"	"	
Thomas Armstrong	60	M	"	"	"	
Henry Gibson	60	M	"	"	"	
Margt. "	20	F		"	"	
Jane " & ch.	18	F		"	"	
Alexr. Montgomery	26	M	"	"	"	
James O'Brian	22	M	"	"	"	
Mary " & ch.	29	F		"	"	
T. J. Lanyan	20	M	"	"	"	
Margt. Gibson	24	F		"	"	
Isaac Patterson	25	M	"	"	"	Brig Trent. Barstow.
Ann "	18	F		"	"	

PASSENGERS WHO ARRIVED IN THE U.S. SEPTEMBER 1821 - DECEMBER 1823

Names of passengers	Age	Sex	Occupation	Country to which they belong	Country of which they intend becoming inhabitants	Ship or vessel with the name of the master or commander
NEW YORK Cont.						
Q. E. Dec. 31, 1823						
James Sears	25	M	Gardner	England	U. States	
Elizabeth Kelly	43	F		U. States	"	Brig Abeona. Harper.
J. Devotion	23	F		"	"	
James Renshaw	35	M	N. Officer	"	"	
D. Thompson	35	M		"	"	
Diego Real	40	M		"	"	
Francisco Maria	26	M		"	"	
Wm. Glenthworth *	19	M		"	"	
Wm. Johnston	25	M		"	"	
Lewis Brandes	25	M	Secy.to Dan. Legation	Denmark	"	Ship Baltic. Bunker.
H. Justin	38	M	Merchant	Bayonne	"	Brig Liberty. Hatch.
Joseph Williams	42	M	"	Port au Prince	"	
John Mastinborough	39	M	"	U. States	"	
S. Fairbank	37	M	"	"	"	Ship Canada. Macy.
H. Beck	23	M	"	"	"	
Wm. Pearman	27	M		England	England	
James Gordon	28	M	"	"	Jamaica	
J. H. Marshall	23	M	"	"	U. States	
M. Moult	35	M	"	"	"	
S. Marze	22	M	"	Switzerland	"	
J. Duckworth	23	M	"	England	"	
Wm. Langsdon	33	M	"	"	"	
J. Mariet *	22	M	"	Switzerland	"	
Robt. Wilson	38	M	"	Scotland	"	
G. Scott	40	M	"	"	"	
A. Thompson	42	M	"	"	"	
Charles Rivers	40	M	"	England	"	
Eliza "	24	F		"	"	
Wm. Moult	17	M	Clerk	"	"	
Jas. C. Buchanan	22	M		U. States	"	
Sarah Knock & ch.	23	F		N. Scotia	"	Sloop McDonough. Baker.
Catharine Dorane	34	F		"	"	
Maria Stamper	27	F		"	"	
Margt. Holstock	17	F		"	"	
Jas. A. Dean	32	M		"	"	
P. L. De St. Croix	20	M		"	"	
Allen Campbell	30	M	Blacksmith	Scotland	"	
Mary " & 4 ch.	26	F		"	"	
Grace "	21	F		"	"	
Robert Dowall	22	M		"	"	
Fanny Johnston	68	F		U. States	"	
M. Broucard	65	M		France	"	Sch. Curlew. Keating.
Miss "	21	F		"	"	

Names of passengers	Age	Sex	Occupation	Country to which they belong	Country of which they intend becoming inhabitants	Ship or vessel with the name of the master or commander
NEW YORK Cont.						
Dec. 31, 1823						
Wm. Gordon	34	M		U. States	U. States	
A. Crosby	36	M	Saddler	"	"	
L. T. Haywood	30	M	Merchant	"	"	
Wm. Graves	23	M	"	"	"	Ship Douglas. Bourne.
B. P. Cruger	45	M	"	"	"	Ship Mentano. Smith
Anna C. Sauvalle & 2 ch.	30	F		"	"	
C. V. Lematni	18	F		"	"	
Jno. B. "	22	M	"	"	"	
G. Lomez *	26	M	"	Spain	"	
B. Menendez	25	M	"	"	"	
John Paddon	48	M	"	England	"	
James "	21	M	"	"	"	
V. J. Wilmer	44	M	Priest	Switzerland	"	
Felix "	23	M	Butcher	"	"	
J. De Ayerman *	36	M		Mexico	Mexico	Ship Othello. Lambert
R. " "	27	F		Spain	"	
J. De Castro & 6 ch.	30	F		"	"	
F. Kino	34	M	Farmer	"	"	
J. Corago	48	M	Mariner	Portugal	"	
J. J. Duponvillon	25	M	Merchant	France	U. States	
W. W. Billings	21	M		U. States	"	
W. Hall Jr.	21	M		"	"	
Geo. W. Codwin	34	M	"	"	"	Sch. Boston. Cox.
D. S. Skatts	33	M	"	"	"	Ship Robt. Fulton. Marshall.
P. Pierson	65	M	"	"	"	
Wm. S. Scott	28	M	Surgeon	G. Britain	Canada	
Geo. E. Wilson	18	M	"	U. States	U. States	
R. A "	24	M	Farmer	"	"	
P Lange & 4 ch.	36	F		Copenhagen	"	Ship Frikston. McCander
M. Datinhoff	25	M	Cab. maker	"	"	
M. Sichon	25	M	"	"	"	
Francis Zellinger	29	M	Mariner	France	France	Brig Charlotte Corday Russell.
C. Penigal	29	M	"	"	"	
J. Q. Mortis	28	M	Merchant	St. Domingo	St. Domingo	
D. Edmi *	30	M	Physician	France	France	
Jno. H. Albers	26	M	Merchant	Denmark	U. States	Ship Cumberland. Odom
Wm. Stenson	26	M	"	England	"	
J. A. Solzs *	24	M	Clerk	Prussia	"	
R. C. Plucker	25	M	"	"	"	
Eliza P. Bramley	33	F		U. States	"	Ship Crisis. Brumley.
A. G. Dalman	52	M		Stockholm	"	
Z. F. Johnston	20	M	Mariner	U. States	"	Brig Commerce. Hayward.
H. Shefferts	21	M	"	England	"	

Names of passengers	Age	Sex	Occupation	Country to which they belong	Country of which they intend becoming inhabitants	Ship or vessel with the name of the master or commander
NEW YORK Cont.						
Q. E. Dec. 31, 1823						
Mrs. Gomez & 3 ch.	28	F		Spain	Havana	Sch. Lady Tompkins. Russell.
J. W. L. Spinola	38	M	Merchant	Portugal	U. States	
S. Boda	35	M	"	France	Havana	
W. Davenport	28	M	"	Bermuda	Bermuda	Sch. William. Dexter.
Mrs. Murphy & 5 ch.	35	F		U. States	U. States	Brig Ambuscade. Knight.
Rebecca Dunkin	39	F		Jamaica	Jamaica	
P. Pensek	50	F		"	"	
Saml. Hassart	20	M	Student	U. States	U. States	
Durand P. Andre	46	M	Consul Genl.	France	"	Ship Bayard. Dyke.
Mrs. Durand & 5 ch.	31	F		"	"	
Elizabeth Curran	45	F		St. Domingo	"	
Sarah Vandyke	23	F		U. States	"	
Mrs. De Yanah	51	F		Switzerland	"	
Mrs. Camex	35	F		France	"	
Mrs. Viglians	50	F		"	"	
Mrs. Nevon & 2 ch.	35	F		U. States	"	
James Allam	24	M	Merchant	"	"	
N. Villings	23	M	"	Switzerland	"	
Thomas Rogers	24	M	"	U. States	"	
P. Perrin	39	M	"	"	"	
E. Brisguard	24	M	"	"	"	
H. Roberts	70	M	"	"	"	
Antonio Vitra	65	M	"	"	"	
Edward Chardon	21	M	"	"	"	
Francis Delpesch	30	M	"	France	"	
Chas. Juquot	28	M	"	"	"	
J. Fumet	23	M	"	"	"	
M. Carpentiere	50	M	"	"	"	
F. Labournie	19	M	"	"	"	
Michael Petin	24	M	"	"	"	
Caroline Gautiere	23	F		"	"	
Victoria Demont	30	F		"	"	
Elizabeth Small	26	F		U. States	"	
F. Maria & ch.	30	F		"		
John Montgomery	35	M	Merchant	G. Britain	U. States	Ship Diamond. Macy.
John Roulston	46	M	"	U. States	"	
Matthew Kelly	43	M	Mariner	"	"	
Edwd. Kenzie	36	M	"	G. Britain	"	
Andw. Murray	23	M	Merchant	"	"	
Geo. Bisber	26	M	"	U. States	"	
John Cannon	25	M	"	"	"	
F. Ropp *	25	M		Havana	"	
Philip Duff	25	M		"	"	
Lewis Brunet	45	M	Merchant	Spain	"	Brig Transit. Gillet.

Names of passengers	Age	Sex	Occupation	Country to which they belong	Country of which they intend becoming inhabitants	Ship or vessel with the name of the master or commander
NEW YORK Cont.						
Q. E. Dec. 31, 1823						
A. Harandus	25	M	Merchant	Cuba	Spain	
Jos. M. Arragora	24	M		"	"	
Mr. Hortwright *	41	M	"	St. Croix	St. Croix	Brig Commerce. Clements.
Mrs. " & ch.	32	F		"	"	
Thos. Dean	23	M	"	England	U. States	Ship Panthea. Bennett.
? Igolsby	25	M	"	Ireland	"	
Saml. Butcher	23	M		England	"	
R. Hudson	38	M	Lawyer	U. States	"	
T. W. Fisher	22	M	Merchant	England	"	
S. H. Smith	23	M	Physician	"	"	
James Brown	23	M	Clerk	"	"	
James Stewart	38	M		"	"	
Hugh Gillan	60	M	Carpenter	"	"	
Jane "	60	F		"	"	
Luke Berry	30	M	Priest	U. States	"	
H. McKean	30	M		Ireland	"	
James Bauder	30	M	Merchant	U. States	"	Ship Nestor. Lee.
John Baring	25	M	"	G. Britain	"	
Wm. Heycock	25	M	"	"	"	
J. Hulbrow	30	M	"	Germany	"	
Chas. Devoe	30	M	"	G. Britain	"	
Fredk. Samuel	22	M	"	"	"	
David "	20	M	"	"	"	
W. Lawrence	45	M	"	France	"	
Thos. H. Chalmers	31	M	Grocer	U. States	"	Indian Chief. Humphries.
Daniel Wright	55	M	Farmer	Scotland	"	
Mr. Bomisher	26	M	Merchant	Germany	"	Ship Cotton Plant. Gregory.
J. "	24	M	Merchant	"	"	
Cath. Kiebs & 2 ch.	48	F		U. States	"	
Thos. W. Ludlow	28	M	Lawyer	"	"	Ship New York. Maxwell.
Barnard Bayley	30	M	Merchant	"	"	
V. De Camp	20	M	Comedian	"	"	
George Jones	23	M		"	"	
Wm. Cooper	25	M		"	"	
John Ridgley	33	M		"	"	
Henry Williams	21	M		"	"	
John Waln	38	M	Merchant	"	"	
W. R. Waring	30	M	Physician	"	"	
R. Higgins	32	M	Merchant	"	"	
John Davidson	37	M	"	"	"	
Lewis Rapeneau	36	M	Advocate	Montreal	"	
F. W. Des Beviers	29	M	"	"	"	
Richard Tylnerst	30	M	Farmer	England	"	
Thomas Smith	24	M	Merchant	U. States	"	

Names of passengers	Age	Sex	Occupation	Country to which they belong	Country of which they intend becoming inhabitants	Ship or vessel with the name of the master or commander
NEW YORK Cont.						
Q. E. Dec. 31, 1823						
Charles Wilkins	59	M		U. States	U. States	
Henrietta "	19	F		"	"	
Ann "	22	F		"	"	
D. Colden	27	M		"	"	
Frances "	27	F		"	"	
Wm. Pope	24	M	Merchant	"	"	
Alexr. Palaini	40	M	"	Montreal	"	
James D. Ogden	33	M	"	U. States	"	
John Wilson	20	M	"	"	"	
Henry Delias	20	M	"	Bremen	"	
James McKinly	23	M	Labourer	Ireland	"	Ship Minerva. Mayell.
Alexr. Thompson	30	M	"	"	"	
John Marshall	29	M	"	"	"	
James Patterson	32	M	Farmer	Scotland	"	
Wm. Wright	40	M	"	Ireland	"	Ship Farmer. Collins.
J. C. Davis	26	M	"	England	"	
Thomas Hitchie	32	M	"	Ireland	"	
Michael Baker	35	M	"	"	"	
Thomas Gray	24	M	"	"	"	
Anna "	27	F		"	"	
P. P. Waite	23	M	"	"	"	
Charles "	17	M	"	"	"	
Mary C. "	20	F		"	"	
Eliza Leonard	22	F	Spinster	"	"	
Cath. McManners & 2 ch.	24	F	"	"	"	
F. Vanderbilt •	50	M	Merchant	Germany	"	Sch. Catharine. Cruise.
Jno. Dallet	15	M		U. States	"	Brig Georgetown Packet. Rathbone.
E. L. Shannon	19	M		"	"	
J. Riverio & ch.	40	M	"	Spain	"	
M. Castro & 4 ch.	40	M	"	"	"	
B. Gordiles	25	M		"	"	
C. Maury	30	M	"	"	"	
F. Rosa	30	M		Spain	"	
P. Purde	30	M	Tailor	"	"	
A. Roberts	20	M		U. States	"	
J. St. John	18	M	Merchant	Havana	"	Brig Nancy. Naghel.
B. Blauntt •	25	M	"	"	"	
Edwd. Bell	34	M	"	U. States	"	Sch. Antelope. Blanvelt.
D. Caherty	26	M	"	Ireland	"	Ship Malabar. Orne.
M. R. Cotton	23	M	"	U. States	"	Brig Charity. Goodrich.
Henry Hatiger	36	M	"	"	"	
P. Stuart	30	M	Planter	Scotland	"	Brig Superior. Tilley.
Geo. W. Wilson	30	M	Merchant	England	Canada	Sch. Exchange. Davis.

Names of passengers	Age	Sex	Occupation	Country to which they belong	Country of which they intend becoming inhabitants	Ship or vessel with the name of the master or commander
NEW YORK Cont.						
Q. E. Dec. 31, 1823						
J. J. Rainburga	40	M	Mariner	U. States	U. States	
H. Bolland	40	M		England	"	Ship Criterion Day
Jas. Raynor	23	M		"	"	
F. Parke	21	M		"	"	
Jno Canada	25	M		"	"	
Sarah "	20	F		"	"	
Mrs. Haly	42	F		"	"	
Miss "	18	F		"	"	
Wm. Mann	35	M	Jeweller	"	"	
Sarah "	-					
Chas. Upjohn	40	M	Tailor	"	"	
Mary " & 4 ch.	35	F		"	"	
Sarah Point	40	F		U. States	"	
J Wilson	20	M		England	"	
D. C. McKeizie	39	M	N. Officer	"	Canada	Ship Congress. Derby.
W. West	35	M	Merchant	"	U. States	
Mrs. " & child	18	F		"	"	
James Dorsey	17	M		U. States	"	
James O'Reiley	33	M		Ireland	W Indies	
Mrs. Haley & 2 ch.	35	F		"	"	
Mrs. Clark	40	F		U. States	U. States	
Wm. Bassett	30	M	Farmer	England	"	
Mrs. " & ch.	25	F		"	"	
Wm. Whirlin	56	M	Carpenter	"	"	
Wm. " Jr.	16	M	Farmer	"	"	
R. Smith	30	M		"	"	
Mary " & 2 ch.	30	F		"	"	
A. Baker	35	M	Farmer	"	"	
J. Smith	45	M	Weaver	"	"	
James Smith	32	M	Tailor	"	"	
Daniel Gerard	40	M	Merchant	U. States	"	Brig Emeline. Noyes.
Wm. R. Blake	21	M	Comedian	Halifax	G. Britain	Sch. Nile. Morgan.
Lewis Roache	40	M	Merchant	Ireland	U. States	Sch. Nancy. Crowell
Helena " & 6 ch.	38	F		"	"	
George Robinson	23	M	Merchant	"	"	
Mary Davis	35	F		"	"	
Mary Buchanan	25	F		"	"	
Elizabeth Wilson & ch.	22	F		"	"	
James Smith	40	M		"	"	
Wm. Beachly & 2 ch.	26	M	Shoemaker	"	"	
Fred. Crawford	24	M	"	"	"	
Alexr Morehead	20	M	"	"	"	
James Holland	30	M	"	"	"	
Catharine Barlow	20	F		G. Britain	"	Sch Lady Hunter Palmetter.

Names of passengers	Age	Sex	Occupation	Country to which they belong	Country of which they intend becoming inhabitants	Ship or vessel with the name of the master or commander
NEW YORK Cont.						
Q. E. Dec. 31, 1823						
George Wallace	27	M		G. Britain	U. States	
Mrs. " & 2 ch	24	F		"	"	
James Hurley	20	M		"	"	
Michael Sullivan	21	M	Carpenter	"	"	
Charles Riley	22	M	Mason	"	"	
Wm. Shurdon	23	M	Tailor	"	"	
James Shannon	24	M		"	"	
John Quirk	40	M	Carpenter	"	"	
Thomas Righ	30	M	Labourer	"	"	
James Hogan	29	M	"	"	"	
Abm. Marsh	19	M	"	"	"	
James Sullivan	21·	M	"	"	"	
James W. Sampson	28	M	Merchant	"	"	Ship Cortes. De Cost.
Prince Murat	21	M		Holland	"	
S. R. Pitman	26	M		U. States	"	
W. H. Wardly	22	M	"	"	"	Brig South Carolina. Johnston.
Mrs. Newton & child	40	F		England	"	Ship William. Moffat.
Geo. Halbrook & ch.	40	M	Joiner	"	"	
Francis Banks	27	M	Tailor	"	"	
Charles Stanly	20	M	"	"	"	
James Bird	25	M	Labourer	"	"	
Jno. Sinait *	24	M	"	"	"	
Wm. Solman	21	M	"	"	"	
P. Maren *	45	M	Mariner	U. States	"	
M. Jones	18	M		Wales	"	
Joseph Monterro	49	M		Spain	"	Sch. Rampart. Paine.
F. Chuvard	38	M		France	"	
Josiah Hassal	27	M	Merchant	Ireland	"	Ship Hector. Gallinder
Ann "	26	F		"	"	
Wm. S. Capper	23	M	"	England	"	
A. Ewing	35	M	"	Ireland	"	
Daniel Walton	26	M	Brewer	England	"	
Thomas Townshend	22	M	"	"	"	
E. P. Capper	25	M	Merchant	"	"	
Geo. A. Underhill	21	M		W Indies	"	
J. C. De la Houssee *	30	M	Major	England	England	Sch. Monroe. Webber.
Mrs. " "	28	F		"	"	
John Living	40	M	Merchant	U. States	"	
P. McGregor	35	M		England	U. States	
A. Cox	40	M	"	U. States	"	Brig U. States. Hopkins.
Wm. Cheyne	21	M	Surgeon	Scotland	"	
E. Philips	20	M	Merchant	England	"	
Mrs. Cox	30	F		U. States	"	
C. Halsinbech	27	M	"	Hamburg	"	Ship Robert Burns. Coffin.
L. L. Near	35	M	Physician	"	"	

Names of passengers	Age	Sex	Occupation	Country to which they belong	Country of which they intend becoming inhabitants	Ship or vessel with the name of the master or commander
NEW YORK Cont.						
Q. E. Dec. 31, 1823						
F. L. Vase	35	M	Mechanic	Hamburg	U. States	
James Anderson	28	M	Merchant	Scotland	"	
G. McMusdrell	22	M	"	"	"	Brig Dutchess of Gloucester.
A. Atchinson	38	M	"	"	"	
John Steer	28	M	Farmer	"	"	
Helen "	26	F		"	"	
Sophronia Baxter	25	F		"	"	Brig Clio. Baxter.
Sarah Nichols & ch.	29	F		U. States	"	Ship Orozimbo. Nichols.
Charles Gibbs	28	M		England	"	
John Whitworth	23	M	Manufactr.	"	"	
Sarah "	21	F		"	"	
Robert Burris	26	M	"	"	"	
G. Jones	35	M	Farmer	"	"	
Mary " & 4 ch.	35	F		"	"	
James Donaldson	21	M		U. States	"	Ship Columbia. Rogers.
R. S. Cleveland	50	M	Merchant	"	"	
R. Laurie	41	M	"	"	"	
W. A. Conway	34	M	Comedian	G. Britain	"	
W. D. Lillington	26	M	Merchant	"	"	
J. Rudge	39	M	Shoemaker	"	"	
J. Thwaite	56	M	Labourer	"	"	
H. Hadley	38	M	Farmer	"	"	
Henry Elliot	25	M	"	"	"	Brig Brutus. Holdridge.
A. Furst	22	M		"	"	
Peter Paris	25	M	Merchant	France	Honduras	Sch. Alabama.
C. Francis	35	M	Mariner	"	"	
G. Palma	22	M	"	"	"	
James Faderelle •	25	M	Merchant	"	"	
Edward Menna	50	M	Tailor	Ireland	U. States	Brig Hibernia Watteling.
Margaret Connor	19	F	Spinster	"	"	
James Ryan	21	M		"	"	
W. C. Coleman	25	M	Mariner	U. States	"	Sch. Baltimore. Hubbard.
M. Evense	30	M	Merchant	England	"	
Mrs. Deneman	45	F		U. States	"	
W. A. Curry	30	M	Merchant	"	"	Brig John. Howland
Wm. Shannon	34	M	"	"	"	
Wm. M. Roache	38	M	Baker	Barbadoes	"	
P. A. Comes	40	M	Merchant	U. States	"	Brig Laura Ann. Huntington.
W. Whelon	21	M	"	"	"	
Wm. P. Morris	48	M	Farmer	England	"	Ship Frances Henrietta.
Nelly " & 6 ch.	42	F		"	"	
Wm Pease	19	M	"	"	"	
H. Goodchild	23	M	Organist	"	"	
J. Duke	22	M	Shoemaker	"	"	

Names of passengers	Age	Sex	Occupation	Country to which they belong	Country of which they intend becoming inhabitants	Ship or vessel with the name of the master or commander
NEW YORK Cont						
Q. E. Dec. 31, 1823						
S. Lawson	32	M	Labourer	England	U. States	
S. Kippax	37	M	Farmer	"	Canada	Ship William.
J. C. Sullivan	40	M	Merchant	U. States	U. States	Ship Genl. Brown. Skidely.
M. Clark	34	M	"	"	"	
J. D. McIlvain	33	M	"	"	"	
J. Lavina	27	M	Span. Navy	Cadiz	Spain	
J. McMendes *	45	M	Curate	Mexico	Mexico	
B. O. Bregan	45	M	Deputy to Cortes	"	"	
C. Jarque *	32	M	Jeweller	Spain	Spain	
P. Aleantara	34	M	Lawyer	"	"	
Mrs. " & ch.	33	F		"	"	
Wm. Wilson	18	M		U. States	U. States	Ship Florida. Wilson.
P. Sparkman	28	M	Farmer	G. Britain	U. Canada	
Wm. Patton	42	M		"	"	
Nancy " & 5 ch.	37	F		"	"	
Robt. Brooksbank	45	M	Farmer	"	"	
J. Paget	55	M	"	"	"	
J. Trimmer	56	M	"	"	"	
G. Ebbett	22	M	Clerk	"	"	
E. Brady	36	M	Merchant	"	"	
J. Stewart	37	M	Farmer	Ireland	U. States	Sch. Lincoln. Johnson.
B. " & 5 ch.	26	F		"	"	
R. McCutcher	32	M	Weaver	"	"	
Mrs. " & 4 ch.	31	F		"	"	
Wm. Armstrong	27	M	Farmer	"	"	
J. "	24	F		"	"	
Madame De Carné	45	M	Lady	France	"	Ship Lima. O'Hara.
J. L. Joindre	23	F		"	"	
Alfred Delarue	20	M		"	"	
J. Bertrand	20	F	Attendant	"	"	
M. S. B. Smith	38	M	Student	U. States	"	
C F Le Roux	35	M	Merchant	Switzerland	"	
Henry Fremont	45	M	"	France	"	
John H. Linn	38	M	"	U. States	"	
Thomas Hunt	21	M		England	"	Ship Acasta. Griswold.
Eliz. Loring & 5 ch.	44	F		"	"	
Ann Maria Cutting	40	F		"	"	
Henry " & 7 ch.	36	M		"	"	
Moses Anstia/Austin	28	M	Merchant	"	"	
S. B. Hatfield	21	M	Painter	"	"	
Mary Henkin & ch.	39	F		"	"	
Sarah Ransom & 4 ch.	37	F		"	"	
C. Fay	31	M	Priest	France	Canada	Ship Cadmus. Whitlock.

Names of passengers	Age	Sex	Occupation	Country to which they belong	Country of which they intend becoming inhabitants	Ship or vessel with the name of the master or commander
NEW YORK Cont.						
Q. E. Dec. 31, 1823						
S. B. Rawle	36	M	Merchant	U. States	U. States	
E. Pennington	23	M	"	"	"	
W. McFarlane	20	M	"	"	"	
A. Colombel	22	M	"	"	"	
E. Bringeon	43	M	"	France	"	
E. Rousseau	40	M	"	"	"	
J. Vesse	46	M	Rope maker	Germany	"	
Cath. "	53	F		"	"	
B. Stageman	25	M	Merchant	"	"	
Chas. Cooper	26	M	"	U. States	"	Brig Fenelon. Lee.
Wm. Bruce	35	M	"	"	"	Sch. Hella. Wright.
Lewis Bewait	30	M	Musician	"	"	Sch. Fair Play. Kimball.
Mrs. " & 2 ch.	30	F		"	"	
Fredk. L. Folger	35	M	Merchant	"	"	Brig Mattiwan. Coffin.
Wm. Holland	24	M	"	England	"	Ship Hannibal. Watkinson.
Robt. Pryor	53	M	Farmer	"	"	
H. Wilkinson	22	M	Merchant	"	"	
J. C. De Costa	21	M	"	U. States	"	
M. Randolph	25	M	"	"	"	
Job Wragg	25	M	Book keeper	England	"	
R. Simmons	33	M	Merchant	Ireland	"	
M. Rider	45	M	Brewer	England	"	
J. Sibbold	28	M	Book keeper	Ireland	"	
J. Gilbert	43	M	Shop keeper	England	"	
D. Kinnard	18	M	"	Ireland	"	
Robt. Young	36	M	Farmer	England	"	
H. Kelly	21	M	Book keeper	Ireland	"	
Don F. Verda •	30	M		Spain	Cuba	Ship Draper. Thorndike.
Don T. Guia	48	M		"	"	
Don L. S. Suders •	28	M		"	"	
John Tarr	25	M	Planter	Antigua	U. States	Brig Spartan. Delane.
Jno. Hoggard	34	M	"	"	"	
F. G. Tucker	29	M	Merchant	"	"	
Clarissa Bailey & 2 ch.	22	F		U. States	"	Sloop William. Prince.
John Baptist	40	M	Doctor	"	"	
Betsey Chancey	20	F	Cook	"	"	
J. W. Meeker	25	M	Merchant	"	"	Sch. Paulina Julia. Tooker.
Isaac Milner	25	M	"	"	"	
Peter Kunel	55	M	Mariner	Germany	"	Brig Bancon. Barstow.
R. R. Hunter	36	M	Am. consul	U. States	"	Ship London. Allyn.
M. S. "	24	F		G. Britain	G. Britain	
H. Hartly	22	M	B. Army	"	"	
Wm. McCord	20	M		Canada	Canada	
A. Lanfear	32	M	Merchant	"	"	

Names of passengers	Age	Sex	Occupation	Country to which they belong	Country of which they intend becoming inhabitants	Ship or vessel with the name of the master or commander
NEW YORK Cont.						
Q. E. Dec. 31, 1823						
J. Winslow	23	M	Merchant	Canada	Canada	
Wm. Learne	24	M	Physician	"	"	
James Hayne	48	M	Mariner	U. States	"	
Wm. Kershaw	22	M	"	"	"	
Thos. "	25	M	Student	"	"	
M. A. Bellamy & 6 ch.	40	F		G. Britain	"	
S. Newly	26	M	Grocer	"	U. States	
V. Gabriella	46	M	Merchant	U. States	"	
J. Tuckey	55	M	Farmer	G. Britain	"	
C. "	21	F	"	"	"	
Jno. Symes	31	M	"	"	"	
Jno. Nighan	31	M	Leather dyer	G. Britain	"	
Jno. Niggins	17	M	Clerk	"	"	
Wm. Edwards	34	M	Jeweller	"	"	
Wm. Hayne	15	M	Student	U. States	"	
M. Dominguez	25	M	Merchant	Spain	"	Brig Abeona. Harper.
Jose de Regules	26	M	"	"	"	
G. Sotres	33	M	"	"	"	
S. Chapple	35	M	"	"	"	
Dionisio de Verguosso	33	M	"	"	"	
B. M. Navarro	22	M	"	"	"	
Chas. M. Glatham	45	M	Mariner	Scotland	"	Brig Nassau. Wilsen
S. V. Sipkins	40	M	"	Holland	"	Brig Prince Edwd. Russell.
C. K. Lawrence	40	M	"	U. States	"	
Thomas Bell	38	M	Merchant	"	"	
H. Blokriel	28	M	Mariner	Holland	"	
Henry Kains	46	M	Farmer	U. States	"	Brig Martha. Barber.
P. Burinker	30	M	Carpenter	Switzerland	"	
Mrs. "	30	F		"	"	
P. Macelito	50	M	Mariner	Italy	"	Brig Packet. Doughty.
Antonio Buria	25	M	Merchant	Spain	Havana	
Thomas Martin	49	M	"	"	U. States	
Joseph Hailoma	25	M	Mariner	"	"	
B. Constant	33	M	Merchant	Maragalante	"	Sch. Mary. Hurd.
D. Ravend	29	M	"	"	"	
C. B. Scovelli	35	M	"	U. States	"	Brig Wm. Henry. Lester.
John McKittera	28	M	"	"	"	
Henry Roper	32	M	Merchant	"	"	Ship Orbit. Tinkham.
Charles Boyet	26	M	"	Holland	Holland	
Mrs. "	28	F		"	"	

ADDENDA

Where vessel is not stated, refer back to text.

Names of passengers	Age	Sex	Occupation	Country to which they belong	Country of which they intend becoming inhabitants	Ship or vessel with the name of the master or commander
p. 51 After Thomas Barnwell R James	28	M	Glazier	G Britain	U. States	
p. 76 Under S. Macomb Mrs. " & 4 ch.	35	F		Cuba	Cuba	
p 76 After James Wood John Sheridan	24	M		England	U. States	
p. 80 After B. F. Willard W Salstansall	25	M	Merchant	U. States	U. States	
p. 90 After Edwd. Faraby Wm. Cranch	23	M	Farmer	G. Britain	U. States	
p. 92 After M. Gill James O'Neil	26	M	Labourer	Ireland	U. States	
p. 105 After Wm. Hitchey L. C. Lambert	20	M		England	U. States	Sch. Catharine. Costelly.
p. 152 After C. Mecar J. R. Dredge	22	M	Merchant	U. States	U. States	Ship Wabash.
p. 161 After J. Heton G. Hippsley	28	M	Officer	England	U. States	Sch. Fox

Names of passengers	Age	Sex	Occupation	Country to which they belong	Country of which they intend becoming inhabitants	Ship or vessel with the name of the master or commander
p. 173 After Mary Canteli Mary S. "	36	F		G. Britain	U. States	
p. 178 After B. Duplantier P. Blandain	48	M	Physician	France	U. States	
p. 204 Before Louis Bousaque Francis Larassetur	32	M	Merchant	U. States	U. States	Sch. Five Sisters. Radcliffe.
p. 214 After Arch. Brooks James Fenno	29	M	Mariner	U. States	U. States	
p. 215 After P. Mackay James Cunningham	21	M		U. States	Spain	Brig Carib of Boston.
p. 221 After A. Fish Mrs. " & 3 ch.	30	F		G. Britain	U. States	
p. 233 After Geo. Barry Geo. Harden	23	M	Merchant	U. States	U. States	
p. 239 After R. Roveesa A. Roberts	34	M	Merchant	U. States	U. States	
p. 239 After Jas. E. Withall James Jelly	24	M	Farmer	Ireland	U. States	
p. 258 After M. Halman M. Fickman	20	M	Labourer	Germany	U. States	
p. 270 After M. Anderson M. Lamount	25	M	Merchant	Scotland	U. States	
p. 272 After H. J. Taney P. Dastie	40	M	Merchant	Cuba	U. States	

Names of passengers	Age	Sex	Occupation	Country to which they belong	Country of which they intend becoming inhabitants	Ship or vessel with the name of the master or commander
p. 287 After Jno. Seward Thos. Gibson	20	M	Teacher	England	U. States	
p. 313 After J. Dillon J. Vandum	25	M	Merchant	U. States	U. States	
p. 319 After M. Soubercaze M. Guivolet	62	M		France	U. States	
p. 330 After Matthew Murphy Ann " & 3 ch.	45	F		Ireland	U. States	
p. 335 After John Allen T. Debresay	22	M	Student of Medicine	Halifax	Halifax	Sch. Geo. Henry. Lakin.
p. 48 Omit Robert Fletcher						
p. 258 McMilly should read: McMilly/McNulty						

INDEX OF VESSELS

The vessels are arranged in alphabetical order, followed by the name of the captain, where known, and the type of vessel; i.e. ship, brig, schooner (sch) etc. At first sight, there may appear to be some duplicated entries, since there are many ships of the same name Sometimes, a vessel of the same name, with the same captain may be designated a brig, ship or schooner; and although this may or may not be an error, they have been put in separately, as perhaps the captain did in truth command a different vessel of the same name on his next voyage The captains' names are frequently not given, or where given, quite illegible. Where they appear several times, they are often spelled in several different ways, so where it is obvious that the same man is meant, the abbreviation "and var ", meaning variations of spelling, has been used Occasionally there appears the same ship on apparently the same voyage, with a different captain, and for this there seems no explanation Note additions to the index on p 427.

359

CYGNET. Kimbal. Sch. 66
CYPRUS. Chaddock. Brig. 230
CYPRUS. Dickson Brig 40, 60

DALMANOCK. Cummings. Brig 91
  See also DELMARNOCK.
DAPHNE. Kohler. Sch. 240
DAPHNE. Kohler or Koler. Ship. 134, 177
DART. Sch. 56
DART. Allen. Sch. 283
DART. Van Dine or Dene, Vandine or dine.
  Sch. 18, 71, 124, 173
DASH. Bacon. Sch. 315
DASH. Cunningham. Sch 58
DAVID MOFFET. Cullen. Brig 167
DAY. Boree. Brig. 248
DEBBY & ELIZA. Ship. 126
DEBORAH. Fleming Ship. 59
DEBORAH. Gray. Ship. 39
DEBORAH. Henry. Sch. 232
DECATUR. Sch. 6, 157
DECATUR. Ballard. Sch. 51
DECATUR. Bell. Brig. 142
DECATUR. Brownell. Brig. 46
DECATUR. Rudder. Brig. 199
DELAWARE. Ship. 190
DELEGATE. Davis. Brig. 100
DELMARNOCK. Brig. 239. See also
  DALMANOCK.
DELPHOS. Ship. 228
DESPATCH. Uram. Ship. 16
DEUX FRERES. Brig. 55
DIAMOND. Macy. Ship 345
DIOMIDE. Harris. Brig. 65
DIOMIDE. Snow. Sch 63
DIANA ? Sch. 32
DIANA. Higgins. Sch. 272
DIANA. Jackson. Barque. 178
DIANA. Kimbal. Sch. 162
DIANA. McPherson. Sch. 86, 125
DIANA. Mott. Sch 249
DICK. Sch. 56
DICK. Woodhouse. Brig 294
DIDO Ship. 191
DILIGENCE. Eustis 278
DILIGENCE. Jones. Brig. 44
DIRECTOR. Sch. 157
DIRECTOR. Hamilton. Sch. 321
DOLLAR. Hall. Sch 226
DOLLAR. Mayo. Sch 60
DOLPHIN. Sch. 259, 297
DOLPHIN. Blanchard. Sch 42
DOLPHIN. Colby. Sch 92
DOLPHIN. Nichols. Sch. 72
DOLPHIN. Tissett Brig 121
DOMINICA Johnson. Ship 217
DORIS. Brig 57
DOROTHY Massicot or Massuit Sch
  309, 321, 312
DOROTHY. Valsey Sch 211
DORSET. Dixon. Ship 35 70
DOUGLAS. Bourne Ship 344

DOUGLASS Brown(e). Sch. 239, 270
DOVER Jeffares. Sch. 315
DRACO Atwood Brig. 44
DRACO Bishop. Brig 105
DRAPER Cary Ship. 80
DRAPER Smith. Ship 172
DRAPER Thorndike Ship 352
DUBLIN PACKET. Newcomb(e) Sch 122.
  245, 289
DUBLIN PACKET. Newcomb Ship. 22
  74
DUCLETT. Williams. Sch 47
DUCTILE Williams Ship 131
DUMFRIES Ship. 162
DUTCHESS OF GLOUCESTER. Brig. 350
DUXBURGH. Drew Brig 63
DUXBURY. Brig. 182

EAGLE. Adams Ship 218
EAGLE. Davis Ship. 40
EAGLE. King. Sch. 15, 194
EAGLE. Mix Ship 112
EAGLE. Soule. Sch 12
EAGLE Tollis. Brig. 275
ECHO. Blanchard. Brig. 236
ECHO. Jordan Brig. 68
ECHO. North Brig 267
ECHO. Thompson. Brig 102
ECLIPSE. Hathaway. Sch. 248
EDGAR. Johnson Sch 170, 270
EDMOND. Ship. 210
EDWARD. Brig. 157
EDWARD. Clark. Brig 52
EDWARD Howard or Hayward. Ship. 51,
  311, 322
EDWARD D DOUGLAS Brig. 144 194
EDWARD D DOUGLAS. Morgan. Brig. 13
EDWARD D DOUGLAS. Hallet Brig. 246
EDWARD DOWNEY or DOWNS. Russel
  Ship. 177, 213
EIGHTH OF JANUARY. Quere Sch. 212
ELBE. Syme Ship 123
ELECTRA Robinson Ship 8, 51
ELIAS BURGER Sch 276
ELIAS BURGER Densey Sch 235
ELIAS BURGER Disney. Ship 119, 173
ELIAS BURGER Jennings. 33
ELIZA. Sch 7, 155 207, 259
ELIZA. Bowen Brig 63
ELIZA. Bragg Brig. 179
ELIZA. Burgess. Brig. 174, 268
ELIZA Folger. Brig. 114
ELIZA. Griffith. Brig. 103
ELIZA. Hopkins Sch. 104, 182
ELIZA. Martique, Nartique and var Sch.
  136, 212, 313, 317, 324 See also
  ELIZABETH.
ELIZA. Nelson. Sch 133
ELIZA Stevenson. Sch. 182
ELIZA. Waring. Brig 20
ELIZA & ABBY Drummond. Ship. 96
ELIZA & MARIA. Sch. 297

ELIZA & NANCY. Amos. 224
ELIZA & POLLY. Sch. 53, 68, 69, 145, 187
  203, 204, 297 (2)
ELIZA ANN. Ames. Sch. 231
ELIZA ANN. Baird. Brig. 314
ELIZA ANN. Barstow. Sch. 278
ELIZ. ANN. Brooks. Brig. 193, 197
ELIZA BARKER Alley. Sch 247
ELIZA BETSEY. Small. Brig. 257
ELIZA JANE. Burger. Ship. 115
ELIZA JANE. Pearson. 43
ELIZA JANE. Weldon. Sch. 24
ELIZA PIGET or PIGOTT. Waterman. Sch.
  20, 45 75
ELIZA REILY. Small. Brig 199
ELIZABETH. Sch. 206
ELIZABETH. Armstrong. Brig. 205
ELIZABETH. Bakenor. Sch. 99
ELIZABETH. Ballard. Sch. 219
ELIZABETH. Blackmore. Brig. 176
ELIZABETH. Clark. Sloop. 29, 134
ELIZABETH. Delano. Ship. 117
ELIZABETH. Fougard. Sch. 14
ELIZABETH. Gardner. Brig. 283
ELIZABETH. Hasle. Sch. 135
ELIZABETH. Lapham. Sch. 16
ELIZABETH. Nartique Sch 67
  See also ELIZA.
ELIZABETH. Sebor. Ship. 31
ELIZABETH. Shankland. Brig. 209
ELIZABETH. Smail(s). Brig. 91, 167
ELIZABETH. Smith Sch. 287
ELIZABETH. Smith Ship 239
ELIZABETH. Williams. Brig. 87
ELIZ. STURGIS. Larrimore Brig. 315
EMELINE. Sch 68
EMELINE. Noyes Brig. 348
EMELINE. Rawlings. Brig. 286
EMERALD. Sch. 3
EMERALD. Bradford. Sch. 51
EMERALD Fox. Ship. 228, 267
EMERALD Gray. Brig 143, 269
EMIGRANT. Baker. Brig 111
EMIGRANT. Barney or Barnes. Sch 211,
  291, 308, 312
EMILY Sch 5
EMILY Sloop. 55
EMILY Babcock. Ship. 200
EMMA. Fosdick. Brig 72, 80
EMULOUS. Selden or Selvin Ship. 47,
  167, 321
ENDEAVOUR. Sloop. 145
ENDEAVOR. Carter Ship 70
ENDEAVOUR. Kemp. Sch. 246
ENDORA. Sch. 6
ENDYMION. Hathaway. Sch. 49, 89
ENTERPRISE. Black. Sch. 283
ENTERPRISE. Hawley Brig 220
ENTERPRISE. Mater. Sch. 61
ENTERPRISE. Morton. Sch. 62
ENTERPRIZE. Paine. Sch. 226, 265, 316
ENTERPRIZE Shaw. Sch 46
ENTERPRIZE. McLain. Brig. 265
ENTERPRIZE. Vaughan. Sch 230

GEORGIA. Varnum. Ship. 35, 70, 314
GEORGIANA. Cornick. Ship. 106
GERVIS. Brig. 275
GHENT. Folger. Sch. 213
GIPSEY Fogler. Sch. 294
GLEANER. Brig. 155
GLEANER. Pease. Sch. 238
GLEANER. Saunders. Sch. 74, 112
GLEANER. Smith. Brig 237
GLENTHORNE. K. Lewis. Ship 126
GLIDE. Adams. Ship. 38
GLIDE. Pierce. Ship. 256, 315
GLOBE. Brittan Ship. 33
GLOBE. Hill Sch. 91
GLOBE. Smith. Brig. 232
GOLDEN AGE. Blair. Brig. 335
GOOD EXCHANGE. Sch. 264
GOOD EXCHANGE Leran. Sch. 35
GOOD FRIENDS. Sch. 142
GOOD FRIENDS Wheeler. Sch. 210
GOOD HOPE. Hague Sloop. 66
GOOD INTENT. Weightman. Sloop. 135
GOVR. BROOKS. Snow. Sch. 105
GOVR. BROOKS. Brig. 53
GOVR. GRISWOLD. Ship. 214
GOVR. GRISWOLD. Rhodes. Ship. 179
GOVR. GRISWOLD. Snow. Ship. 49
GOVR. HAWKINS. Bowen. Ship. 13
GOVR HENCK. 61
GOVR. HOPKINS. Wilkinson. Brig. 98
GOVR KNIGHT. Sloop. 42
GOVR TOMKINS. Brown. Sch. 233
GOWAN. Mearns Brig. 133
GRAFF ZENZENDARFF. Ship. 56
GRACE. Sch. 54
GRAFF KATCHRUSTH. Salin. Brig. 136
GRAMPUS. Bangs. Brig. 235
GRAND TURK. Higgins. Ship. 231
GRAND TURK. O'Hara. Ship. 33
GRAND TURK. Taber. Ship. 275
GREENHOW. Gray. Brig. 222
GREENHOW. Gray. Ship. 265
GREYHOUND. Sch. 238
GREYHOUND. Peck. Sch. 35, 62

H. GARDNER. Brig 335
H. MORE. Heinn. Brig. 63
HAL. Grant. Brig. 12
HALCYON. Wooster. Ship. 12, 193
HALSEY. Small. Sch. 292
HAMILTON. Lane. Brig. 182
HAMILTON. Tucker. Sch. 323
HAMILTON & HIRAM. Tuckey. Sch. 320
HAMMET. Hinchman. Brig. 231
HANNAH. Brig. 178
HANNAH. Ship. 203
HANNAH. Cullen. Brig. 25
HANNAH. Martin. Brig. 292
HANNAH. Mason. Brig. 49, 112, 172
HANNAH. Wetherby. Brig. 213
HANNAH & AMY. Stone. Sch. 220
HANNAH & ELIZABETH. Brig. 207

HANNAH & SUSAN. Jaque. Sch. 3
HANNIBAL. Watkinson or Wilkinson. Sch.
  or ship. 87, 168, 277, 352
HANOVER. Adamson. Ship. 166
HAPPY RETURN. Brig. 192
HARMONY. Brig. 5
HARMONY. Lewis Brig. 129
HARMONY. Pratt. Sch. 217
HARMONY. Starbuck. Sch. 292
HARMONY. Thomas. Sch. 20
HARP. Sandgram Brig. 197
HARRIET. Brig. 56
HARRIET. Sch 153, 258
HARRIET. Clark. Brig 144
HARRIET. Hinchman. Brig. 334
HARRIET. Kennard. Sch. 99
HARRIET. Rogers. Sch. 93, 322
HARRIET. Stiles. Ship. 313
HARRIET. Williams. Ship. 294
HARRIET & LUCY. Brig 342
HARRIET SMITH. Tofts. Brig. 21
HAVANA. Holdridge Sch 235
HAVRE PACKET. Miller Brig. 98
HAYTIAN Smith Sch. 82
HAZARD. Blackman. Brig 229
HAZARD. Higgins. Sch 113
HECTOR. Gage. Sch. 194
HECTOR. Gillander and var. Ship. 137,
  166, 349
HELECON. Johnson Brig. 33
HELEN. Erskin. Brig. 91, 314
HELEN. Ferrand Sch. 312
HELEN. Lardy. Sch. 207
HELEN. Patterson. Brig. 48
HELICON Dayton. Brig. 110
HELLA. Wright. Sch. 352
HENRIETTA. Brig. 172
HENRY ? Sch. 238
HENRY. Atwood. Brig. 105, 230, 337
HENRY. Davis. Sch. 174. 234
HENRY CLAY. Fosdick Brig. 75
HERALD. Fox. Ship. 64, 105
HERCULES. Cobb. Ship. 22
HERCULES. Gardiner Ship. 47, 114, 173,
  234
HERCULES. Johnson. Brig. 322
HERO. Burr or Beers. Sch. 63, 102
HERO. Collins Brig 295
HERO. Kinsman. Brig. 266
HERO. Martin. Sch. 315
HERTON. Webster. Brig 112
HESPER. Hubbard. Brig. 341
HESPERUS. McCorckill. Ship. 314
HIBERNIA. Hutchinson Brig. 10
HIBERNIA. Wattling Brig. 28, 219, 350
HIGHLANDER. Gibson. Sch. 137
HIGHLANDER. Moor. 137
HIGHLANDER. Welch or Welsh. Ship.
  14 207, 313
HIND. Boyal Brig. 45
HIND. Prince. Brig. 107
HIPPOMANES. Bourne or Bounce Brig.
  30, 50, 80, 119, 222, 251
HIRAM. Easton. Brig. 97

HIRAM. Morpen. Brig. 281
HIRUM Collins. Brig. 199
HOLLEN Leslie. Brig 320
HOLLY Hammond. Brig 322
HOMER Brig. 56, 157
HONDURAS PACKET. Sch. 254
HOPE. Sch. 265
HOPE. Clark. Sch 246
HOPE. Haskell. Sch 267
HOPE Hatch. Brig 29
HOPE Lassell. Sch 100
HOPE Lewis Sch 19, 20, 286, 306
HOPE Mann. Brig. 185
HOPE Manor. Ship. 224
HOPE. Moore. Brig 338
HOPE Shippen Ship. 46, 190
HOPE Spears. Brig. 322
HOPE. Wilson Brig. 264
HOPE & ESTHER. Bears or Bourse 173,
  306
HOPE & HESTER. Sch. 253
HOPE & POLLY. Sch. 308
HOPE & POLLY. Vaughan. Brig 62
HOPE RETURN Downes. Sch 246
HOPE'S DELIGHT. Baker Brig 271
HOPE'S RETURN. Baker. Sch 293
HORACE. Hatch 87
HORATIO. Sch. 202
HORATIO. Hallett Sch. 137
HORIZON. Clark Brig 272
HORIZON. Smith. Brig. 134
HORNET. Ship. 6, 157, 258
HORNET. Page Brig 64
HORSELY HILL. Hunter. Brig. 249
HOTSPUR. Bragg. Brig. 67
HOWARD. Ship. 10
HOWARD. Blackner. Brig 62
HOWARD. Holdridge. Sch 276
HOWARD. Holdridge. Ship. 165
HOWARD. Perkins Brig. 221
HOWARD. Stocking. Brig 279
HUDSON. Champlin or Champion. Ship.
  232, 293
HUGH WALLACE. McClure. Brig 15
HULDAH & JUDAH Thomas Sch 80,
  110
HUNTER. Ship. 5, 296
HUNTER. Bisset. Brig. 315
HUNTER. Davis. Ship. 12, 142, 196
HUNTER. Doggitt. Brig. 106
HUNTER. Sears. Sch. 25, 94, 124, 147
  241
HUNTRESS. Conte(r) Sch 205, 208, 214
HUNTRESS. Morgan. Sch. 30, 50, 87, 339
HURON Graham. Boat 34
HYPERION Brightman Brig 337
HYPERION. Richard. Brig 321

ICEPLANT. Bunker Sch. 139, 246
IDRIS Evans. Brig. 65
IF. Brig 188
IF. Bull. Brig 227

SELINA. White Sch 257
SENECA. Dutch. Brig 72
SENECA. Gray Brig 182
SERENA. Carter. Sch. 227
SHAMROCK. McGrath Sch. 194
SHANMEL. Luce Brig. 62
SHEPHERDESS Frink. Sch. 57
SHEPHERDESS. Storer or Stores. Brig. 92, 241
SISTERS. Dobie Brig. 137
SISTERS Hill. Sch. 195
SIX BROTHERS. Williams. Sch. 84
SOLDADE ESPARD. Tarquin Brig. 116
SOLDADO. Montu. Brig. 52
SOLON. Johnson. Sch. 107
SOLON. Joy. Ship. 134
SOMERS. Lord. Brig. 266
SOPHIA. Brig. 249
SOPHIA. Desseres. Ship. 193
SOUTH BOSTON. Ship. 5
SOUTH BOSTON. Campbell. Ship. 105
SOUTH CAROLINA. Brig. 206
SOUTH CAROLINA. Ship. 145, 188
SOUTH CAROLINA. Cartwright. Ship. 80, 121
SOUTH CAROLINA. Johns(t)on. Brig. 124, 274, 349
SOUTH CAROLINA. Thornton. Brig. 320
SOUTH CAROLINA PACKET. Cartwright. Ship. 49
SOUTH CAROLINA PACKET. Guill. Ship. 25
SOUTH CAROLINA PACKET. Knapp. Sch. 292
SOUTHERN TRADER. Kelly Sch. 236
SOUTHERN TRADER. Sampson. Sch. 3
SPARTAN. Chapman. Brig. 51
SPARTAN Delane Brig. 352
SPARTAN. Mastigue. Sch. 135
SPARTAN Ward. Barque. 221
SPERM Clark. Sch. 291
SPRIGHTLY. Canon Brig. 81
SPRING. Brig. 19
STANDARD. Brig. 55
STAR. Bacci. Sch. 96
STAR. Lawrence. Sch. 42
STATORA. Patten. Brig. 276
STEPHANEA. Burke Ship 74
STEPHANIA. Macy. Ship. 278
STEPHANIA. Smythe Ship. 168
STEPHANIAN. Bunker. Ship. 1
STERLING, Sch. 155
STORK. Bray. Sch. 60, 104
STRANGER. Fisher. Ship 140
STRANGER. Rogers. Sloop. 248
STRONG. Jaques. Sch. 333, 336
SUKEY. Haskall. Sch. 82
SUPERB. Burr. Brig. 286
SUPERB. Conner. Brig. 18
SUPERB. Ham(ilton). Brig. 21
SUPERIOR. Dixon. Brig. 12
SUPERIOR. Dowder. Ship. 239
SUPERIOR. Mavorach. Brig. 99
SUPERIOR. Snow. Ship. 98

SUPERIOR. Tilley. Brig. 347
SUPREMA. Salin. Sch. 308
SURPRIZE. Bradley. Sch. 204
SUSAN. Sloop. 215
SUSAN Ivey. Sch. 272
SUSAN. Newman Sloop. 317, 322
SUSAN. Rogers. Sloop. 135
SUSAN. Wallis. Ship. 64
SUSAN & SARAH. Robinson. Brig. 68
SUSAN MORTON. Sutton. Ship. 249
SUSANNA. Sch 192
SUSANNA. Stevens. Brig. 237
SUSANNA MARY Kidd. Brig. 231
SUSQUEHANNA. Collinson. Ship. 173
SUSQUEHANNA. Stewart. Ship. 254
SWAN Skinner. Sch. 26
SWAN. Storer. Sch. 220
SWIFT. Sch. 187, 204, 257, 296
SWIFTSURE. Baker. Brig. 61
SWORD Sarton. Brig. 182
SYREN. Slatt. Brig 211

TANTAMOUNT. Allen. Sch. 75, 335
TARANTULA. Pratt. Ship 337
TARTAR. Dennett. Sch. 66, 134
TARTAR. Kevans. Sch. 274
TARTAR. Williams. Sch 204
TARTARE. Sch 207, 212
TASSELL Wilcox. Sch 307
TELEGRAPH. Blanchard. Sch. 51
TELEMACHUS. Crosby. Brig 267, 229
TERISE. Carmon. Sch. 310
THALIA. Ship. 257
THAMES. Marshall Ship. 23, 88
THETIS. Newcombe. Sch. 3, 36
THOMAS. Burgess. Sch. 104
THOMAS. Carole. Ship. 183
THOMAS. Miller Sch 268
THOMAS. Sampson Brig 122
THOMAS & ELIZA. Wallace. Sloop 277
THOMAS & SARAH. Gay. Sch. 119
THOMAS GELSTON. Ship. 5
THORN. Arnoux Sch. 312
THORN Greaves Sch. 135
THORNTON. Holmes. Brig 14
THREE BROTHERS. Young. Sch. 60
THREE DAUGHTERS. Sch. 194
THREE SISTERS. Bell. Ship. 36, 200, 314
THREE SISTERS. Scott. Sch. 178
TIMANDRA. Yamall. Brig. 141
TIME. Sch. 206
TIME. Tucker. Sch. 307, 310
TOBACCO PLANT. Reed Ship. 194
TOM. Spear. Brig. 101
TOM SHIELDS. Saxton. Sch. 135
1OPAZ. Callender. Ship 266
TRAFALGAR. Henderson. Brig. 84
TRANSIT. Gillet Brig 78, 166, 236, 345
TRANSIT. Greig. Ship. 14
TRAVELLER Brig. 265
TRAVELLER. Frost. Sch. 116, 210, 307
TRAVELLER Goldie. Brig. 70

TRENT. Barstow Brig. 342
TRIDENT. Bunham. Brig. 45
TRIDENT. Coffin. Ship. 274
TRIMMER. Nagel Sch. 292
TRITON Ship. 69
TRITON Bassey Ship 38, 103
TRITON. Wilkinson. Sch. 283
TRIUMPH. Lee. Sch 310
TROJAN. Ship 55
TRUE BLUE. Brig 56
TRYALL. Farnsworth Ship. 107
TURK. Rice. Brig 105
TUSCARORA. Sewell. Ship. 191
TUSCARORA. West. Ship. 13, 144
TWO BROTHERS. Henchman Ship. 39
TWO BROTHERS. Kimble. Sch 293
TWO BROTHERS. Tuckey. Brig 36
TWO BROTHERS. Webber Sch 66
TWO BROTHERS Young. Sch. 102
TWO FRIENDS. Adams Sch 89
TWO FRIENDS. Chote. Brig. 65
TWO FRIENDS. Laker Sch. 37
TWO FRIENDS. Snow. Brig 134
TWO MARYS Coffin. Brig 313
TWO SISTERS. Sch 207
TWO SISTERS. Kellog. Sch 213
TWO SISTERS. Lawrenson and var 41, 308
TWO SONS. Sch. 267

ULYSSES. Aurey. Ship. 163
ULYSSES. Stone. Ship 93
UNDERHILL. Clarke. Brig 298
UNDERHILL. Trowbridge. Brig. 181
UNICORN. McKown. Ship 141, 209, 319
UNION Cotton. Brig 222
UNION. French. Ship. 289
UNION Gale. Brig 321
UNION. Gibbs. Sch. 255, 298
UNION. Mayo Sch. 177, 318
UNION. Patterson. Sch. 84
UNION Titcombe Sch 242
UNISON. Hufbuck. Brig 315
UNITED STATES. Hopkins. Brig 349
UNITY. Sch 214
UPTON. Sampson Brig 125
URCHIN Chadwick Brig 176, 181

VALADORA. Bassallos. Sch. 314
VALIANT. Calvin. Sloop. 164
VALIANT. Waldrich. Ship 215
VANCOUVER. Leach. Brig 38
VELOCIPEDE. Kirtland. Brig 253
VENUS. Sch. 96
VENUS Ship 191
VENUS. Atwood. Brig 60
VENUS Chandler. Ship. 18
VENUS. Emery. Sch. 108, 185
VENUS Ferris. Brig. 79
VENUS Mount Sch 73

INDEX OF PERSONS

Andry, H , 211
Anduguy, John, 179
Anedando, Ignacio, 215
Anedondo, Fernands M., 185
Angelito, Antoni, 311
Angell, I. R , 121
Angeno, L., 283
Angeran, L. D , 281
Angers, J , 234
Angle, Frs , 285
Aniago -, 134
Anibarzo, N , 185
Anna, Francis, 46
Anners, Ann, 130
    James, 130
Annoes, Mrs., 224
Anosell, J , 309
Ansley, J D., 338
    W , 162
Anspeck, P., 173
Anstia/Austin, Moses, 351
Anthony, John, 53
Antoinette, G , 197
Antonio, D J , 157
    Don, 170
Apelin, A., 173
Appleton, John J , 55
Apps, James, 87
Apthorp, C. W., 230
    Jno S., 201
    Wm. J., 182
Aquilar, Nicholas, 55
Araguti, F., 195
Arans, Joseph, 65
Arasmends, G. W , 262
Arbeo, M., 312
Arbuckle, James, 23
Archbald, James, 268
Archbold, Wm., 272
Archibald, A., 44
    J W., 293
    James, 92
Archpole, B., 250
Arcos, M., 324
Arcost, A M., 50
Ardoin, J B., 300
Areas, Peter, 326
Aregno, Philip, 210
Areos, A M., 216
Areos, Martin, 116
Arey, Samuel, 140
Arguillous, Jose Maria, 31
Arladi, Y., 308
Arlez, P., 253
Armand, J., 180
    M., 178
Armed, James, 37
Armour, M., 142
Armstead, A., 213
    Geo , 297
Armstrong, Andrw., 248
    Archibald, 300
    Cath., 149
    Danl., 49
    E., 2

Armstrong, cont.
    Ellen, 95
    Henry, 56
    J., 351
    James, 262, 329
    Jane, 9
    John, 121
    Joseph, 270
    Margt., 95
    Robt., 95, 337
    Samuel, 125
    Saml. J., 40
    Sidney, 95
    Susan, 101
    Thomas, 95, 342
    Wm., 95, 149, 270, 351
Arnaud, J. D., 134
    J.P., 318
    L, 180, 309
Arne, E., 56
Arnly/Amly, J. D., 174
Arno, Jas., 219
Arnold, H. N., 174
    Philip, 82
    Wm., 340
Arnud, Anthony, 320
Arogor, J., 338
Arolly, F., 3
Arongo, J. A., 278
Aroxarena, R., 338
Arragota, Jos. M., 346
Arratt, D., 76
Arreno, F., 218
Arriamac, M., 338
Arrott, James, 19
    Robt., 86
Arsenaux, Mrs., 67
Arsola, H., 141
Arthur, John, 145
    Robt., 287
Arundell, Eliz., 27
    W., 27
Aschroft , Michael, 243
    Sarah, 243
Ascoot, Wm., 297
Ashburn, A., 156
    L., 252
Ashelman, D., 164
    Eliza., 164
Ashely, Benj., 212
    Catharine, 167
    Ebenezer, 167
Ashman, S., 228
Ashmuth, John, 64
Ashton, Elizabeth, 307
Ashworth, M., 273
Askin, Henry, 272
    Jno., 126
    Joseph, 39
Aslo, James, 72
Asser, Saml., 79
Astor, J.J., 77
Atchinson, A., 350
Atkinson, Ann, 284
    Charles, 79, 284

Atkinson, cont.
    G., 157
    G.G., 326
    J.T., 57
    James, 93
    J., 274
    John, 93
    R., 154, 305
    Richd., 23
    Thomas, 144
    W., 217
    Wm., 24, 85, 249
Auchinleck, Mary, 171
Audifrom, S., 213
Audinot, F., 312
Audling, W. R., 260
Augel, M., 324
Aughworthy, S. S. J., 133
August, L , 274
    F., 321
Augustine, Henry, 19
    John, 220, 125
Aulet, J., 180
Auriane, Lewis, 59
Austin, D , 92
    Edwd., 335
    Henry, 204
    J., 31
    Moses, 351
    P., 45
    Susanna, 83
    William, 183
Avellar, J. S. D., 134
Avery, Geo., 249
Avice, Francis J., 97
Avila, I. S. D , 39 (See Avellar)
Aycinena, Pedro, 340
Aykerora, Joseph, 140
Aymar, Anthony, 5, 258
Ayre, M., 157
Azar --- , 14

Baartscher, W., 219
Babad, Henry, 274
Babb, Benj., 317
Babbit, E. B , 225
Babel, Thomas, 271
Babcock, Amos, 119
    Cath., 119
    J. C , 244
    James, 216, 277
    M A , 244
Babug, Chas H , 175
Bacchus, F , 292
Bacci, S J., 106
Back, Richd., 286
Backhuse, Andw., 148
    Mary, 148
Backus, F R , 141
    Thomas, 71, 117
Bacon, Nathan, 54
    Phillip, 169

Bacon cont.
    Wm , 19
Baden, Nicholas, 12
Badge, Jno . 249
    Margt . 249
Badia, M , 204
Baez, Francis, 171
Baffiniere, A D., 218
Bagert, Henry, 309
Baggs, Alexr., 150
    Archibald, 150
    Isaac, 150
    Mary, 150
    Rachel, 150
    Susan, 150
Baigham, John, 151
    Julia, 151
Bailey, C , 280
    Clarissa, 352
    Hannah, 13
    John, 58, 169, 220
    Jno. G., 253
    Jane, 167
    M., 171, 175, 268
    Martin, 168
    Moses, 18
    Philip, 168
    Robt , 167
    Sarah, 168
    Thomas, 13
Baillie, S., 115
Bailley, Richd , 18
Bain, John, 289
Bainard, John R , 339
Baines, Jno., 236
    Mary Ann, 236
Baird, E., 154
    J., 154
    James, 85, 142
    Samuel, 147
    Thomas, 73
Bairie, Jno., 286
Baithe, Peter D , 242
Bakeman, C , 218
Baker, A., 348
    Arthur, 285
    C., 54
    Charlotte, 236
    Geo. L., 254
    Harriet, 285
    J.S., 29
    James, 235
    John, 11, 209
    John C., 266
    M , 125, 301
    Mary, 112, 260
    Michael, 347
    P., 117
    S., 301
    Thomas, 112, 125
    Wm., 279, 324
Balano, J., 73
Balch, Enos B , 228
    J., 287

Cullen, cont.
  Simon, 191
Culleton, Wm , 198
Cullinane, Thos. W. , 279
Culling, Mary, 47
  Richd. , 47
  Thomas, 47
Culton, Walter, 270
Cully, Edwd. , 40
Cumin, Francis, 22
Cumming, Alexr. , 213
  C. , 285
  J , 119
  John, 321
Cummings, Mrs. , 230
  Ann, 147
  Charles, 110
  John. 268, 303
  Margt. , 303
  Robt. , 128
Cummins, Hugh, 147
  Jno. , 334
  Robt. , 12
Cunin, Joseph, 78
Cunningham, Charles, 60
  Helen, 277
  Horace, 249
  J. , 158
  James, 98, 257, 290, 356
  Jane, 73
  John, 2
  M. , 61
  Patrick, 79
  R. , 328
  Robert, 277
Curel, Andw. , 209
Curge, Eliza, 263
  Hugh, 263
Curley, Hugh, 214
Curran, Elizabeth, 345
Curran, M. , 184
Curnings, James, 214
Curre, F. , 211
Currey, B. , 157
  Wm. , 68
Currie, George, 2
  J. , 266
  Robt. , 106
  Wm. , 106
Curry, W. R. , 350
  Wm. M. , 284
Curtin, J. , 325
  Mary, 316
  Thos. , 316
Curtis, Mr. , 105
  G. B. , 220
  Jacob, 77
  James, 37
  John, 257
  Joseph, 96
  Mary. 96, 257
  Robert, 108
Curtoys, Elizabeth, 177
  John, 177

Cusha, Matthias, 62
Cushing, J.H. , 157
  Joseph, 184
  Thomas, 41, 63
Cutchen, W.H. , 86
Cutler, James, 208
Cutney, Richd. , 232
Cutter, B. , 322
  Wm. G. , 334
Cutting, Ann Maria, 351
  Henry, 31, 351
  Robt. , 280
  Thomas, 280

Da Coriascai. P. , 315
Dacoster, Obadiah, 194
Dagardenis, L. D. , 209
Dagget, E , 235
Dagie, John, 99
Daguet, F. B. , 275
Dailey, James, 133
Dair, Mary, 186
  Wm. , 186
Dale, Charles A. , 248
Dale, Hugh, 23
  Robt. , 143
Daley, James, 333
  John, 331
  Michael, 22
  V. , 84
Dalgell, Robt , 99
Dall, Alexr , 74
  Helen, 74
Dallet, Jno. , 347
Dalman, A.G. , 344
Dalon, Jas. , 301
Dalrymple, Ann, 172
  George H. , 226
  Wilson, 189
Dalton, Mrs. , 5
  John, 105
Daly, B. , 81
  Thos. , 81
Damey, H.J. , 110
  Henry, 110
Damon, John, 53
  Richd. F. , 113
Dana, Nicholas L. , 62
  Patrick, 99
Danby, Joseph, 271
Dancangut, V. , 294
Danell, John, 299
Danford, George, 80
Danhorke, Peter, 146
Daniel, Judith, 71
  Richd , 306
  T. , 153
  Wm. , 104
Daniels, C. , 224
  Henry, 338
  Isaac, 19
  J. D. , 56

Daniels, cont.
  John, 224
Dankes, Ann, 288
  John, 288
Danney, Louis, 14
Danny, Allan, 148
  John, 148
  Timothy, 148
Dansac, J. , 321
Dantillac, Victor, 93
Danton, Robt. , 41
Danviers, R. , 257
Daquin, Louis, 17
Darah, Henry, 202
Darby, Chas. W. , 60
  Robt. , 76
Darety, Mary, 254
Dargor, C.C , 99
Darick, Danl. , 61
Darius, Mr. , 223
Darly, John, 164
Darrach, Wm. , 48
Darrell, C.P , 225
Dart, Mr. , 224
Darton, L , 184
  Richard, 184
Darwin, Peter, 197
Dash, John, 52
Dashiel, J , 153
Dastie, P. , 356
Datinhoff, M. , 344
Daubut, J. B. , 14
Daughuly, J , 318
Daulby, W. W. , 118
Dault, George W. , 262
Daunas, Nicholas, 37
Davelin, Sally, 4
Davenport, G. W. , 166
  John, 95
  W. , 345
David, John, 132
  Jno. T. , 272
Davids, Andw. , 220
Davidson, Alexr. , 118
  Ann, 223
  D , 228
  James, 194
  John, 346
  L , 175
  Margt , 7
  Thomas, 166
  W. , 119
  Wm. , 223, 304
Davies, Ann, 275
  C.A. , 276
  E , 275
  James K. , 274
  Thomas, 274
Davint, Lewis, 325
Davis, Benj. , 243
  D. , 45, 291
  Edwd. , 165
  Eustace, 141
  F. , 253

Davis, cont.
  Francis, 213
  H. , 172
  Henry, 109, 247
  Henry A. , 107
  J. , 154, 237, 244, 301
  J C. , 347
  Jacob, 243
  Jane, 213, 253
  John. 86, 145, 205, 234, 249
  Joshua, 341
  Lewis, 209
  M , 154
  Martha, 196
  Mary. 86, 95, 149, 243, 348
  Richd , 221. 250
  Samuel, 94
  Stephen, 219
  T , 173
  Thomas, 10, 67, 93, 249
  Thomas H. , 91
  Timothy, 215
  W. B. , 180
  Wm. , 95, 149, 172 (2). 244
Davy, Albert, 86
Dawell, Eliza. 252
  Geo. , 252
Dawes, Nathan, 109
Dawson, A. , 233
  C. , 128
  Fred. , 263
  Jane, 275
  Lucy, 91
  Thos. , 275
  Wm. , 92, 111
Day, Mrs. , 179
  James, 168
  John, 115, 261
  Morgan, 212
  Wm. , 301
Dayly, E. , 233
Dayley, Joseph, 163
Dayson, G. , 17
  Robt. , 172
Dayton, G. , 88
Deag, Henry, 210
Deagan, H. , 85
  Wm , 85
Dealy, Joseph, 128
Dean, Jas. A. , 343
  Thos. , 346
  Wm P. , 94
De Andivago, Chev, 19
Deansfield, John A. , 79
Deany, Timothy, 306
De Aranzamond, J. L. , 299
Dearmand, James, 94
De Armas, F. , 136
Death, Charlotte, 83
  Elizabeth, 83
  John, 83
De Ayerman, J. , 344
  R. , 344
Debal, H. , 68

Dixon, cont.,
  Thomas, 231
Doase, Mary, 88
  Vincent, 88
Dobbin, Robert, 8
Dobbs, D. W., 320
  Wm., 88
Dobleman, G., 217
Dodd, Henry, 84
  Margt., 84
  Mary, 340
  Wm., 13, 340
Doddy, Peter, 2
Dodge, Gideon, 288
  John, 230
  Joseph, 115
Dodgson, Mary, 144
Dodson, Jos., 253
  Thomas, 143
Doge, N. H., 284
Doherty, John, 331
  Mary, 331
  Wm., 244
Doin, John, 290
Dolan, Alexr., 150
Dolan, F., 278
  Thos., 142
Dolberg, David, 294
Dolbie, J. A., 278
Dolever, George, 64
Dollard, Andw., 184
  E., 160
Dollen, Ann, 133
  Chas., 133
Dolph, J., 166
Dolton, John, 307
Domagin, A., 304
  John, 304
Domanes, Francisco, 262
Dominberg, G. L., 57
Domingo, ---, 324
  Antonio, 297
  Philip, 215
  S., 6
Dominguez, M., 353
Dominick, F. W., 84
Dominique, ---, 136
  John, 55
Don, Edmund, 267
  James, 269
Donagh, Mary, 304
  Wm., 304
Donaghy, James, 190
  Sarah, 129
Donaho, A., 162
Donahoe, D., 93
  John, 79, 264
  Pat., 213 (2)
Donahue, Danl., 245
  Mary, 245
  Nancy, 245
Donald, A., 272
  Benj., 31
  Danl. C., 133

Donald, cont.
  Elizabeth, 63
  Jane, 259
  Martin, 80
Donaldson, James, 350, 337
  Joseph, 328
  Stephen, 310
Donally, Peter, 190
Donathan, Thomas, 5
Donaughan, John, 257
Donaven, C., 159
Donelly, B., 304
  Edward, 269
  James, 329
  John, 328
  Lawrence, 11
  Mary, 338
  M., 285
  Michael, 11
  Patrick, 304
  Wm., 304
Donevan, Daniel, 256
Donnahoe, Jno., 285
Donnan, Wm., 288
Donnell, C. O., 217
  Edwd. C., 239
Donnelly, Henry, 139
Donnelson, H., 244
  P., 244
Donnett, John, 229
Donop, Fred., 57
Donougher, John, 137
Donovan, Ann, 32
  J., 159
  Johanna, 32
  M., 159
  Thos. B., 32
Donover, Eleanor, 138
  Pat., 138
Dool, Andw., 8
Dooland, James, 198
Dooley, H., 217
Doran, E., 79
  J., 79
Dorane, Catharine, 343
Dordelay, Peter, 252
Dordelly, M., 296
  Peter, 258
Dordez, Philip, 208
Doretty, M., 306
Dorin, Robt., 191
Dorothy, Mrs., 132
  J., 161
Doroty, P., 296
Dorrivigney, F., 136
Dorsett, Geo. W., 99
Dorsey, James, 348
  Mary, 134
Dorshaw, Mary, 104
  Th., 104
Dorson, Wm., 243
Dortoli, Diego, 72
Dorvall, S. F., 313
Doubretier, Henry, 65

Douchy, Catharine, 328
  Francis, 328
Doufoux, M., 288
Dougal, John, 274
Dougherty, Ann, 138
  C., 158
  Eliz., 238
  Geo., 298
  H., 9, 305
  Hugh, 238
  J., 173
  Jane, 9
  Morgan, 74
  Rose, 327
  Susan, 267
  Wm., 327 (2)
Doughty, M., 221
Douglas, James, 268
Douglass, Campbell, 5
  Chas., 120
  D., 271
  John, 297
  John W., 200
  Maria, 6, 120
  W., 83
  Wm., 33, 111
Dounam, John, 118
Douring, B., 228
Douthwrait, Jas., 149
Dow, Richd., 97
  Thos., 205
Dowall, James, 239
  Robert, 343
Dowing, Fred., 216
  J., 118
Dowling, ---, 320
Down, H. P., 239
Downes, John, 282
Downest, Biddy, 340
Downey, Alexr., 41
  Wm., 191
Downing, Richd., 192
Downs, Hugh, 74
  James, 74
Downy, Jas., 296
Dowson, E. J., 293
  W., 293
Doyle, Ann, 102
  Catharine, 102, 255
  E., 319
  Edwd., 178
  Eliza, 202
  James, 38, 102, 302
  John, 22, 104, 255
  L., 160
  Lawrence, 37
  Michael, 182
  P., 234, 300
  Patrick, 102
  Peter, 229, 230
  Simon, 31
  Thomas, 31
Drain, J. O., 161
Drake, Gilbert M., 245

Drake, cont.
  J., 221
  James, 253
  Thomas, 117
Draper, Lorenzo, 63
  Thomas, 61
Dredge, J. R., 355
Dreffren, Henry, 55
  Maria, 55
Dreghorn, John, 36
  Robt., 200
Drelawn, C. S., 18
Drew, A., 152
  George, 52
Dreys, W V., 153
Drigan, C., 153
Driggs, S., 112
Drigham, Wm., 18
Drinker, J D. Jr, 339
Drioche, S., 313
Driscoll, Dennis, 9
Driver, W., 246
Drobble, James, 27
Droz, Victor, 190
Drum, Pat, 129
  Thomas, 84
Drury, Wm., 334
Dryden, H., 232
Dryfaus, J., 252
  Joseph, 1
Duane, Elizabeth, 285
  Wm, 285
Duant, J G, 31
Dubart, J. K., 136
  Prosper, 320
Du Berceau, Lavielle, 87
  W. Matilda, 87
Duboas, Theodore, 108
Dubois, ---, 183
  J F., 209
  L., 272
  M., 210
Dubon, Robt., 342
Ducan, P., 338
Du Canarc(r)y, Lewis, 20
Ducass, B., 286
Duchenin, N, 322
Duchesne, Madame, 207
Duchisne, J B., 180
Duckworth, J, 214
Ducommun, M., 209
Duclese, G, 123
Duclose, ---, 66
Ducoin, J, 313
Ducos, J B, 312
Dudley, John, 270
Dufair, A. B., 170
Dufan, J B, 245
  P., 178
Duff, Ab., 64
  George, 245
  Philip, 345
Duffee, Barnard, 239
  Daniel, 306

Emerson, cont.
  Thos., 219
Emery, SamL., 98
Emilly, James, 187
Emrick, G., 157
  S., 157
Emsham, Geo., 82
Enault, Mr., 179
  Agatha, 179
Endura, J.L., 308
Englader, John, 307
Engles, Fred., 134
English, Ann, 192
  George, 192
  M., 171
Ennis, M., 126
  Margt, 262
  Patrick, 58
Emteria, Francisco, 105
Enuigh, B., 84
Eny or Esy, Joseph, 184
Equenton, Wm., 269
Ernest, C., 226
Ernesto, D., 249
Ernin, A., 136
Ervin, James, 183
  Thomas, 21
Erving, James, 126
  Thos., 326
Erwin, John, 138
Erwing, Saml, 138
Escher, Geo., 295
Esclasoes, F., 318
Escondon, ---, 29
Esler, Ann, 138
  David, 138
Esnard, Chas., 137
Espardo, J.M., 275
Espenville, D., 31
Espina, Joseph, 258
Espy, J.B, 321
Essenwerie, Fred., 226
Essex, John, 175
Essom, Mrs., 105
Estano, G., 18
Esteban, Sebastian, 67
Esy. See Eny.
Eudoxia, 182
Eules, F., 97
Eustis, Wm., 329
Eutrope, M., 342
Evans, Abraham, 270
  Andw., 284
  Elias, 273
  Evan, 165
  F., 86
  Griffith, 274
  Jacob, 107
  Jane, 165
  John, 196, 336
  L., 271
  Mary, 271
  Owen, 119
  R., 224

Evans, cont.
  Rebecca, 274
  Rufus, 127
  Sarah, 281
  Susan, 265
  Thomas, 126, 340
Evense, M., 350
Everand, Thomas, 22
Everatt, John, 195
Everden, Thos., 281
Everett, Eliza, 285
  J.C., 321
  Mary, 285
  Robert, 285
  Thos., 285
Everhare, Thomas, 265
Everhart, Wm., 126
Everston, Harnet, 267
Everton, James, 318
Evileth, Francis, 335
Ewart, Samuel, 7
Ewent, J., 158
  T., 158
Ewing, A., 349
  Christiana, 84
  H., 158
  Judith, 78
  M., 158
  Thomas, 84
  Wm., 84
Eylerna, James, 290
Eyman, C., 311
Eymar, Antonio, 339
  B., 284
  H., 68
Eyre, Mr., 338
  George M., 9

Faber, H.J., 69
  Wm. R., 55
Fabiani, ---, 313
Fabrack, Jno, 297
Fabre, M., 211
Faddlington, James, 85
Faden, Joseph, 228
Faderelle, James, 350
Fagan, Francis, 257
  Simon, 305
  Thos., 233, 257, 317
Faggan, John, 86
Fairbank, S., 343
Fairfield, John, 109
Fairlane, G.W.M., 166
Fairman, D., 196
  Gideon, 196
Falerty, Andw., 102
Fales, Mrs., 268
Faley, James, 278
Falham, Charles, 267
Falio, Francis, 69
Fallen, Mary, 92
Fallon, Edwd., 290

Fallon, cont.
  John, 299, 305
Falls, James, 177
  Nancy, 171
Fanekin, Patrick, 299
Fannell, Ellen, 58
  F., 229
  Joseph, 58
  Mary, 229
Fanning, P., 237
  Thomas, 339
Fapp, Wm., 73
Faraby, Edwd., 90
Faret See Faset
Farina, F., 323
Farender, Thos., 338
Farington, Elijah, 72
Faris, Daniel, 182
Farley, Thos., 122
Farmer, Edwd., 319
  James, 4
  John, 132, 307
Farney, James, 147
Farrar, Thomas, 77
Farrell, Andw., 271
Farrell, James, 288
  M., 289
  Richd., 287
Farrier, E., 220
Farrow, Joseph, 191
  Mary, 120
  M., 120
Faset/Faret, James, 310
Fasy, John H., 175
Fathan, Ann, 217
  Robert, 217
Fauchet, M., 181
Faulkner, Sarah, 165
Fault, Chas., 208
Favignon, M.D., 253
Fawcett, John, 178
Fawke, W., 154
Fay, C., 351
  James, 245
Fayall, F., 193
Fayer, Jno., 219
Feagan, Cath., 133
  Thos., 133
Featherston, Chas., 133
Febrell, M., 310
Feder, Mr. L., 49
Fees, John, 191
Feissar, E., 337
Felix, Don, 325
  Geo., 222
  P., 135
  S., 18
Felke, A.C., 320
Fellows, Caleb, 66
  Nathanl., 142
  Richd., 268
Feltus, John P., 114
Fennell, C, 287
Fenner, Joseph, 101

Fenner, cont
  Wm., 89
Fenno, J., 291
  James, 356, 311
Fenokea, Jno., 30
Fenton, Ann, 23
  J., 232
  Margt., 232
Fenwick, Wm., 190
Ferand, George, 227
  P., 213
Fergus, David, 129
  Jannit, 129
  Mary, 129
Ferguson, Mrs., 291
  Arthur, 163
  B. Ann, 191
  C., 244
  E., 266
  Eliz., 9, 163
  George, 188
  Henderson, 257
  Isabella, 120
  J., 37
  James, 34
  Jane, 9
  John, 9, 70, 283, 291
  Robt., 47, 73
  Wm., 191
Ferin, R., 301
Ferly, C., 269
Fernade, M., 31
Feranda, John, 115
Fernandez, 324
  Anthony, 210
  Carlos, 233
  D. Antonio, 183
  Edwd, 98
  F., 18
  Francesci, 70
  H., 318
  J., 321
  John, 12
  Joseph, 14, 214
  M., 186
  Manuel, 6
Fernando, Antonio, 72
Fernside, Ann, 164
  James, 164
  Thomas, 34
Ferram, Isabel, 325
Ferrand, F., 321
Ferrel, P., 15
Ferrell. Eliz, 299
  P., 299
Ferrester, H., 203
Ferrian, Margt., 254
Ferriday, Wm., 16
Ferrington, Benj., 222
  Eliza, 222
Ferris, E., 287
  M., 137
  T., 288
Ferry, Charles, 45

Hanut. See Hanns.
Hany, L., 293
Happiday, Pierre, 96
Harandus, A., 346
Harbell, M., 108
   Margt., 185
Harbinson. Betsey. 114
Harburg, M., 171
Harby, T., 102
Hard, John, 165
Harden, Geo., 356
Harding, David, 226
   John, 319
Hardington, W. B., 116
Hardman, Nancy, 137
Hardy, Anty., 208
   Baptiste, 309
   F., 207
   H. A., 278
   John M., 296
   M., 309
   Richd., 294
   Thomas, 119
Hardyear, S., 295
Hardyman, Wm., 39
Hare, Joseph, 143
   Wm., 70
Harel, M., 319
Harfell, John, 40
Harfhaty, John, 336
   Mary, 336
Hargoien, P., 269
Hargraves, L., 272
Hargus, William, 264
Harkin, John, 147
Harking, E. N., 264
Harmony, W. J., 292
Hamey, Michael, 334
Hams, Philip, 253
Harny, ---, 17
Harpen, J. B., 17
Harper, Gertrude, 227
   Jane, 7
   M., 88
   Mary, 137, 283
   Samuel B., 58
   Thomas, 240
   Wm., 283
Harpham, Joseph, 25
Harrel, Victor, 66
Harret, Robert, 55
   S., 303
Harriet, Roger, 53
Harrigan, J., 299
Harriman, Chas. H., 115
Harrington, C., 61
   Dennis, 63
   James, 40
Harris, Abel, 54
   Adam, 324
   C., 251
   Charles, 96
   Eliza, 284
   F., 247

Harris, cont.
   F. Jr., 247
   George, 295
   Huldah, 295
   Isabella, 324
   J. Jr., 93
   James, 122, 183, 335
   John, 77, 284
   M., 210
   Mary, 125
   N. C., 218
   Richd., 125
   Robt., 33, 59
   Samuel, 210
   Sarah Ann, 247
   Thos., 284 (2)
   Wm., 85
   Wm. D., 302
Harrison, Alfred, 24
   Charles, 261
   Francis, 193
   George, 57, 173
   Gustavus, 56
   John, 289
   Joseph, 6
   Robert M., 57
   Lewis, 29
   Wm., 103, 173, 281
Harrizle, J., 257
Harrod, M., 223
Harrold, Revd. D., 13
Harson, Patrick, 328
Hart, B., 81, 306
   Chas., 299
   D., 49
   John, 144
   Nicholas, 228
   Sally, 299
   Thomas, 43, 55
   Wm. B., 81
Hartell, Christian, 42
Hartly, H., 352
Hartman, C., 262
   M., 293
   S., 121
Harvey, G., 152
   H., 85
Harvy, Jacob, 239
Harvick, Charles, 124
Hasbon, Henry, 256
Haschell, J., 246
Hasches, Jacob, 298
Hase, Jno., 324
Hasel, Antonio, 33
   H., 33
Haskell, C., 122
   James, 59
   Richd., 61
Haskin, Chas., 291
Haskett, John, 110
Hasle, Martin, 318
Haslett, James, 7
Haslin, H., 126
Hass, J., 235

Hassal, Ann, 349
   Josiah, 349
Hassart, Saml., 345
Hassinger, David, 11
   John K., 11
Hasteny, Edmund, 100
Hasthers, A., 124
Hasting, John, 45, 246
Hastings, J., 157, 158 (2)
   John, 195, 232, 338
   Joseph, 269
   S., 157
   W., 158
Hat, John, 172
Hatch, James, 244
   M., 144, 231
   Mary, 244
   N. C., 25
   Thomas, 297
Hatchett/ell, Geo., 184
Hatfield, Ann, 88
   Henry, 88
   Peter, 72
   S., 105
   S. B., 351
Hathamon, F., 131
   Richd., 131
Hathrick, Peter, 34
Hatiger, Henry, 347
Hattie, Eliz., 241
   James, 241
Hatwell, Thomas, 112
Haughty, Jane, 70
   John, 70
Hausewolf, Chas., 261
Hauton, Bernd, O., 220
Haver, Wm., 105
Haven, D., 178
Havison, John, 162
   Mary Ann, 162
Havistock, D., 295
   Mary, 295
Havlen, Mary, 259
   Pat., 259
Haw, Thos., 280
Haway, John, 166
Hawes, J. M., 231
   John, 267
Hawkins, A., 116
   Bernard, 55
   C., 338
   C. B., 163
   Charles, 55
   E., 323
   John, 316
   Wm., 190, 334
Hawley, J. G., 67
   Mary, 236
   R., 179
Haworth, B., 141
   Richd., 141
Hawpt, Jacob, 21
Hawsnell, John, 162
   Mary, 162

Hawsnell, cont.
   Sarah, 162
Hawthorn, P., 116
Hay, Eliza, 127
   George, 190
   John, 97, 124
   R., 163
   Richard, 118
   Wm., 127
Hayden, Eliza, 103
Haye, R., 160
Hayes, C., 253
   Pat., 233
   Paul, 182
Hayley, Edwd., 61
   Wm., 266
Hayne, James, 353
   Wm., 353
Haynes, B., 45
   Eliza B., 285
   R. J., 285
   Thos., 285
Hayward, Edward, 8
   Eliza, 173
   Richd. B., 8
Haywood, Danl., 57
   John, 75
   L. T., 344
Hazelhurst, Jane, 196
Hazen, Mr., 336
Hazlton, Edwd., 241
Head, Eliz, 144
   G, 109
   Sarah, 110
Heard M. T., 292
Hearn, Timothy, 148
Hearsay, Wm., 122
Hearson, David, 110
   Eliz, 110
   George, 110
   Thomas, 83
Heath, James, 232
   Wm., 101
Hedding, E, 236
Hedge, F. H, 218
Hedick, James, 329
Hefferman, John, 141
Hegan, Thomas, 128
Hehen, C. T., 321
Heidle David, 323
Heifren, Wm., 36
Height, John, 101
   R H, 125
Heinick, C A, 226
Heinohier, J. G., 21
Helger, L., 13
Helhause, Wm., 57
Helveston, Jno, 294
Hemmernyrway, Thomas, 53
Henchman, G., 64
Henderick, J, 85
   Joanna, 85
Henderson, Mrs, 39, 104
   A, 213

INDEX OF PERSONS

Jones, cont.
   C., 31,242
   Catharine, 274
   Charles, 8, 214, 243, 294
   D., 166
   E., 280
   Edwd., 151
   Eliz., 82
   Frances, 183
   G., 350
   George, 346
   Griffith, 231
   Henry, 176
   J., 173, 274
   J B., 75
   J.J., 342
   James, 322
   Jas. D., 170
   Jeremiah, 89
   Jesse, 285
   John, 61, 76, 151, 318
   John D., 23
   Joseph, 82, 325
   M., 71, 304
   Mary, 27, 122, 350
   Morgan, 69
   Morris, 196
   Owen, 322
   R., 154, 242
   R.A., 223
   Rachel, 13
   Richd., 82, 231, 285
   Robert, 142
   S., 154
   Samuel, 92, 137, 163
   Sarah, 27
   Simon, 250
   T., 154
   Thomas, 5, 70, 73, 164, 188, 192, 195, 280
   W., 229
   W.R., 219
   Wm., 70, 102, 213, 273
Jont, Fred., 123
   P., 123
Jordan, Danl., 260
   Rufus, 249
Jorden, Wm., 270
Jose, Antonio, 108
   J.G., 155
   M., 314
Joseline, G.R., 294
Joseph, 308
   Francis, 64, 188, 204
   Francisco, 35
   Isaac, 51
   Rebecca, 51
Jost, John, 302
Joubert, P., 209
Jounby, Bernard, 217
Jourdan, C., 322
   Edmd., 223
Joure, Geo., 214
Joutz, P., 324

Jove, Mr., 258
Joy, D., 228
   John, 109
   Joseph, 90
   Sarah, 90
Joynt, G.C., 29
   Mary, 29
Juan, P., 313
Juanille, F., 309
Judson, A.H., 117
   M.P.B., 231
   P.G., 80, 117
   P.S., 340
Juit, F.J., 208
Julambois, J., 195
Julian, C., 251
   P., 293
Julien, Clemt., 323
   Francis, 66
   M.F., 251
Julin, A., 320
Julius, A.C., 65
Junge, H., 259
Juquot, Chas., 345
Justin, H., 343
Justine, Thomas, 23

Kables, Isaac, 336
Kaffer, Danl., 254
Kain, John, 74
Kains, Henry, 353
Kalkman, C.F., 159
Kaly, John, 185
Kane, J.R., 219
   L., 15
   Thomas, 102
Kanderlandim, M., 210
Kaney, Philip, 8
Kanky, John M., 325
Karns, Joseph, 164
Karrick, Joseph, 57
Karthams, P.A., 154
Katkin, Thomas B., 198
Kauffman, H., 173
Kaulbach, George, 147
   Sarah, 147
Kausler, Wm.C., 53
Kausman, M., 341
Kavanagh, J, 159
Kaver, Thomas, 11
Kearne, L., 156
Kearns, Ann, 289
   J., 289
   Rosanna, 148
Kearroy, Edmund, 102
Keath, D., 261
Keating, Jas. H., 219
   Oliver, 316
   Richd., 62
Keefe, B., 156
   C., 303
   J., 156

Keely, John P., 30
Keen, Ann, 279
Keil, H., 182
Keith, ---, 56
Kehoe, John, 61
   Lawrence, 75
   Philip, 74
Kelby, John, 184
Kelham, John, 14
Kellog, Silas, 32
Kellow, R.W., 160
   W., 160
Kelly, ---, 37
   A., 192, 222
   Alexr., 147
   Ann, 272
   B., 159
   Biddy, 147
   Charles, 115
   E.D., 101
   Edwd., 138, 272
   Eliz., 127, 343
   Francis, 146
   H., 352
   Hugh, 188
   J.S., 101
   James, 133, 195, 248
   John, 11, 57, 95, 149, 198, 250
   M., 160
   Mary, 147
   Matthew, 57, 324, 345
   Michael, 58, 230, 257
   Patrick, 259
   Richd., 184
   S., 159, 195
   Thomas, 41, 42, 275
   Thomas M., 61
   Timothy J., 97
   W., 159, 236
   Wm., 104
Kelman, Margt, 171
Kelso, Mary, 283
Kelty, B., 102
Kemp, Jane, 305
   John, 47
Ken, Robt., 77
Kenaway, J., 236
Kenchal, Ann, 198
Kendall, Hugh H., 229
Kendrick, George, 342
Kenedy, Archibald, 264
Kenifeck, Daniel, 22
Kenmer, H.M., 167
Kennedy, A., 152
   Andw., 11
   Catharine, 235
   Cornelius, 256
   D.S., 28
   David, 33
   Duncan, 79, 249
   H., 153, 161, 274
   James, 135, 342
   John, 235

Kennedy, cont.
   Lawrence, 328
   Margt., 191
   Mary, 59
   Michael, 198
   Philip, 198, 245, 256
   Richard, 7
   Stephen, 89
   Thomas, 7
   Wm., 7, 187
Kennet, John, 183
Kennett, Wm., 246
Kenney, Margt., 149
   Thos., 231
Kennison, Ann, 99
   Mary, 99
Kenny, Mrs, 119
   F.F., 78
   John, 43
   Michael, 299
   Nancy, 95
   Wm., 133, 179
Kenock, E., 302
Kenrick, E., 261
Kens, Wm., 99
Kensitt, M., 174
Kent, John, 23
   Mary, 174
   Michael, 47
Kentzing, B.H., 144
Kenworthy, J., 118
Ker, Wm., 338
Kerman, John, 214
Kern, H., 156
Kerney, Wm., 22
Kerr, Fredk., 40
   Jas., 47
   John, 64, 188
   John C., 175
   M., 77
   Mary Ann, 122
   P., 305
   Robt., 77, 278
   Robert E., 177
   Robt.,J., 122
   Wm, 258
Kershaw, C., 82
   Thos., 353
   Wm, 353
Keshan, Dennis, 230
Kesler, ---, 187
Kessler, A., 154
   E., 154
   L., 154
   P.B., 154
Ketgal, Mary, 221
Kettel, R.V., 322
Kewse, Ann M., 336
Key, Ethniel ? S., 334
   S., 89
   Thomas, 201
   Wm., 222
Kidd, Robert, 188
   Wm. K., 73

May, John, 101
   Mary, 271
   Wm., 271
Maybourn, Wm., 239
Mayer, B., 326
Maynard, Gabriel, 56
   John, 56
Maynelle, C., 313
Maynin, S., 168
Mayo, Bridget, 104
   James, 104
   Jose, 59
Mays, Ann, 167
   Isaac, 260
   John, 167
   Margt., 29
Mayter, J. De, 337
Mazas, F., 139, 141, 195
   Francis, 12
Mazias, J., 30
Mazuge, Jno., 285
Mea, Ferdinand, 113
Meacon, Ebenr., 50
Mead, M., 222
Meade, E., 251
   Joseph, 260
Meadowcraft, Mary, 23
Meagher, P., 159
Meakings, B.H., 276
Meanans, E., 82
Means, Isaac, 171
Mear, Isaac, 162
Mearandez, Francis, 70
Meatly, John, 190
Mecaluso, Antonio, 172
Mecar, C., 152
Mecel, ---, 137
Mecuvia, Wm., 272
Medlar, Jno., 126
   Saml., 126
   Susan, 126
   Thomas, 126
Medler, Jacob, 175
Medole, Cath., 133
   James, 133
Meeker, J. W., 352
Meerst, J.M., 251
Megahy, A., 158
Megel, Christopher, 135
Megonigal, Jane, 138
   R., 138
Meir, Antonio, 52
Meised, John, 127
Melias, J. F., 92
Melinder, J.M., 312
Melizet, Francis, 197
Mell, James, 85
Melleger, Mary, 121
   Thomas, 121
Melloes, Wm.; 85
Melone, J., 152
Manard, ---, 14
Mendeburn, C., 14
Menders, Joseph, 107
Mendoza, M., 258

Mendoza, Mrs., 258
Menindez, B., 344
Menial, Charles, 313
Menna, Edward, 350
Menon, John, 306
Merchant, James, 57
   Philip, 13
Merino, F., 135
Merlin. See Wm. Martin.
Merne, John, 317
Merose, Robert, 263
Merrian, Elisha, 335
Merrill, Henry, 183
   Moses, 96, 183
   N., 183
   W., 216
Merrit, Nehemiah, 83
Merritt, A., 307
Mestero, J., 323
Mestor, B.M., 52
Metcalf, Ann, 112
   Elizabeth, 112
   Isaac, 112
   Jane, 112 (2)
   John, 83
   M., 284
Mewerts, Peter, 219
Mexey, J., 237
Meyer, G., 174
   David, 5
   J., 21
   Wm. F., 30
Meyers, B., 278
   F., 153
Meyo, Charles, 53
Mezer, A., 49
Miara, F.O., 291
   Mary, 291
Michael, Mary, 105
Michales, C., 303
Michaud. Mnr., 134
   F., 311
Mi(c)helon, A., 26
Michoux, G.M., 14
Micken, Pat., 138
Middleton, Francis, 167
   Henry, 5
   James, 44
   John, 78
Midford, E., 159
   T., 159
Mier, D., 323
   N., 301
Milay, A., 282
   Mary, 282
Milburn, John, 70
Milderburger, John, 242
Mildwaters, Charlotte, 223
   Joseph, 223
Miles, D.M., 110, 225
   R.M., 305
Mill, R., 163
Millain, Thomas, 129
Millan, P, 50
Milland, E., 156

Miller, Alexr., 204, 208, 314
   Asa, 96
   David, 249
   G. W., 142
   George, 109, 180
   Gilbert, 50
   Helen, 120
   Henry, 119
   Hugh, 4
   J, 212
   James, 6, 124, 189
   John, 35, 62, 86, 183, 200,
      210, 215, 237, 333
   Joseph, 99
   M., 229
   Matthew, 123
   Robert, 148
   Robt. H., 107
   S. J. See Millin
   Stephen, 5
   Theodore, 262
   W., 262
   Wm., 22, 43, 174, 199, 321
Millet, Joan, 309
Milligan, Edwd., 144
   John, 106
   Margt., 95, 264
   Samuel, 95, 149
   Susanna, 149
   Thomas, 230, 264
   Wm., 171
Millin/Miller, S. J, 153
Million, S., 153
Millo, Thos., 207
Mills, Ann, 235
   Danl., 41
   Jas., 29, 127, 330
   John, 62
   Jeremiah, 109
   Moses, 2
   Samuel, 109
   Thos. J., 46
   Wm., 234, 321, 328
Millson, Jno., 281
   Martha, 281
Miln, George, 93
Milne, A., 129, 217
   Jas, 339
   Joseph, 339
   Sarah, 248
   Wm., 1
Milner, Isaac, 352
   Jas., 34
   Joshua, 34
Miloy. See Milvy.
Milroy, Wm. M., 56
Milton, Daniel, 190
Milvil, John, 39
Milvy/Miloy, D., 300
Milwain, John, 25
Milwood, L., 296
Minary, J., 205
Minds, Matthew B, 18
Miner, Betty, 8
Ming, Edwd., 232

Mingual, J.J., 204
Minhead, Mr., 334
Minns, E., 294
   J., 294
   Thos., 294
Minor, Jos., 43
   Theresa, 310
Minot, Catharine, 98
Minton, A., 291
Minzies, Christian, 2
   Robt., 2
Mirimont, P., 179
Mirmay, M., 326
Mispaulibe, A., 205
Mispert, Benedict, 298
   Jacob, 298
   Lewis, 298
   Mary, 298
   Samuel, 298
Misseon, P., 312
Mitchell, A., 44
   Alexr., 41
   Andw., 242
   Archibald, 241
   Chas., 57, 322
   Danl., 277
   David, 69
   Francis, 12
   George, 81
   G. W., 325
   Henry, 125
   J., 135, 158
   J.W., 58
   John, 108, 314
   Margt, 277
   Mary, 3, 259
   Robert, 38
   Robt. G., 272
   Samuel, 291
   T.H., 233
   W., 228
   Wm., 212, 221, 244
Mitchen, ---, 67
Mithled, James, 336
Mitlu, T., 16
Mitt, Mr., 100
Mittayer, 178
Mitter, F., 61
Mix, E.H., 72
Moffat, Andw., 283
   L., 5
   Margt., 250
   Wm., 250
Moffett, David, 25
Moggio, Augustine, 24
Mohoon, John, 190
Mohr, Henry, 30
Moile, ---, 288
Molan, B., 287
Moles, Antonio, 116
Molineur, F., 206
Mollyman, Richd., 102
Mollyneux, John, 95
   Thomas, 95
Molony, Gilbert, 197

Pacy, Joseph, 8, 90
Paddon, James, 344
   John, 344
Page, J., 154
   J. F., 60
   James, 252
   John, 110
   N., 150
   Saml., 49
   Samuel L., 182
   T. L., 49
   Theodore, 1
Paget, J., 351
Pailler, F., 318
Paine, Asa, 109
   Eliz., 339
   J., 92
   Nathaniel, 339
Painter, A., 47
Paiz, Joseph, 125
Pala, Mariana, 257
Palaine, Alexr., 342
   C., 276
Palk, Wm., 94
Pallet, H., 48
Pallis, Danl. H., 200
Palma, G, 350
Palmer, George, 19
   Jno., 218
   Jas. W., 217
   R., 128
   Thomas, 188
   W. L., 276
   Wm., 40, 262, 325
   Wm. J., 193
Paloner, Wm. A., 341
Pane, A., 67
   Jno. W., 168
Paney, Mr., 238
   Marie, 238
Pannell, Antonio, 68
Panrin, C., 124
Panson, Jos. R., 72
Papineau. See Papunee.
Pappet, M., 320
Papunee/Papineau, Charles, 94
Par, R., 28
Pargnet, Chas., 230
Pariente, Joseph B., 209
Paris, Peter, 350
Parish, George, 272
Park, John, 2, 13
   Letitia, 2
   Robt., 150
   W., 31
   Wm., 4
Parke, F., 348
   Joseph, 292
Parker, ---, 58
   Geo., 77
   J. W., 231
   Jas. H., 283
   Jane, 295

Parker, cont.
   John, 261, 312
   Jno. A., 236
   M., 29
   P. T., 204
   Robt., 122
   Saml., 295
   Thomas, 106
   W., 160
   Wm., 77, 216
Parkes, R., 154
Parkin, Wm., 271
Parks, John, 82
Parmanstau, P., 245
Parmer, R., 107
Parmley, Eleazer, 26
   J., 26
Parmly, Fredk., 180
Parnell, C. W., 199
Parora, Domingo, 45
Parrent, Levi, 138
   Mary, 138
Parris, Saml., 130
Parry, Evan, 273
   Jane, 273
Parson, J., 308
   Jno., 209
Parsons, Elijah G., 185
   Henry, 334
Parton, R., 161
Partridge, Diana, 243
   John, 223
   Wm. F., 243
Pasquel, Jose Antonio, 29
Pasement, J. B., 314
Passart, H., 168
Passavant, P. L., 251
Pasement, J. B., 204, 212, 312, 318
Passment, John B., 65
   B., 309
   J., 135, 207
Passware, John, 50
Pastenero, J. M., 278
Paster, L., 172
Patchet, James, 147
   Margaret, 147
Pater, T., 282
Paterson, George, 11, 340
   Matthew, 233
Patlin, W. D., 125
Patrick, D F., 102
   John, 56, 148, 195, 260
   Mary, 148
   Matthew, 255
Pattel, H. D., 293
Patten. See Patlin.
Patten, A., 280
   G., 173, 279
   Grace, 101
   J., 176
   Wm., 139
   Wm. D., 339
Patterson, Ann, 78, 342

Patterson, cont.
   C., 304, 331
   D. D., 236
   David, 95
   Francis, 198
   H., 353
   Isaac, 342
   J., 184
   J. L., 234
   James, 347
   Jane, 198, 245
   Janett, 30
   Jno., 6, 41, 87, 139, 250
   Joseph, 178, 329
   Margt., 139, 254, 296
   Mary, 95, 304, 331
   N., 12
   P., 293
   R., 254
   Rachel, 330
   Robt., 78, 127
   T. H., 41
   Thomas, 201, 330
   Wm., 28, 30, 106, 296
   Wm. G., 78
Pattison, 198
Patton, Nancy, 351
   W. D., 21
   Wm., 292, 351
Patuzze, Joseph, 178
Paud, James, 120
Paul, James, 42
   John, 7, 82
Paulins, J., 229
Paullet, Francis, 307
Pauls, P., 173
Paus, A., 293
Pauvert, E., 276
Pavoy, James, 172
Paxon, Richd., 12
   Samuel, 14
Payne, A., 309
   Bernard, 194
   Fred. W., 26
Payor, ---, 101
Paysant, Mad., 65
Payson, Jane, 93
   John, 93
   Jos. L., 230
Peabody, E., 311
   Isaac, 44
   P., 48
Peach, Richd., 116
   Sally, 116
Peacock, Ann, 250
   E., 253
   Eliz., 250
   John, 250
   Mary, 277
   Thos., 250
   Wm., 277
Peake, Wm., 264
Peale, Edmd., 260

Pear, V., 319
Pearl, James, 130
Pearman, J., 162
   Wm., 343
Pearson, John, 285
   Mary, 189
   Samuel, 189
   Wm., 13
Pease, R., 55
   Wm., 350
Peat, Mr., 39
   Jno., 224
   Robert, 167
   Wm., 298
Peau, ---, 66
Peaver, G., 276
Pechin, Peter, 66
Peck, D., 204
   Elizabeth, 235
   George, 235
   R., 170
   Virgil, 25
Pecond, Joseph, 66
   S., 66
Peddie, Wm., 241
Pedesclaud, H., 135
Pediage. ---, 288
Pedro, P. M., 246
   A., 208
Peircy, Joseph, 110
Pelayo, A., 142, 195, 285
Pelcher, Wm, 109
Peldes, J., 12
Pell, Joseph, 3
Pellet, Charles, 114
Pelote, P, 208
Peltier, Mrs., 270
Pemberton, Jas., 128
   Maria, 295
   Thomas, 129, 295
Pemilent, Luke, 25
Pernston, A. J., 315
Pendegrass, G. E., 291
Pendergrass, O, 20
Pendergrast, Edwd, 24
Pendleton, Otis, 336
Pendreas, Joseph, 48
Penera, Joseph, 297
Pengley, John, 148
Penigal, C., 344
Penill, Edwd., 117
Peniston, Anthony J., 299
Penn, B., 207
Pennet, James, 70
Pennington, E., 352
   Stephen, 322
Penniston, Francis, 251
Pennoyer, James, 267
Penny, John, 77
Penroy, S. S., 283
Pensek, P., 345
Peat/Pent, M., 14
Pentland, Wm., 122

Sanderson, P., 41
  Robt., 282
  S., 78
Sandford, Elizabeth, 237
  John, 237
Sandham, George, 80
Sandiford, R., 51
  U., 51
Sandoz, P.A., 190
Sands, John, 281
  Joseph, 122
  R., 152
  Thos., 290
  Wm., 95
Sanger, Hannah, 164
Sangston, Wm.J., 304
  Wm.S., 261
Sanmukelli, G., 287
Santifaller, ---, 191
Sapell, John, 269
Sara, Anthony, 274
  O., 14
Sarah, Nicholas, 111
Sarcher, B., 103
Sardoforry, ---, 320
Sargeant, Mary, 24
  S., 213
Sargeant, Wm., 24
Sargent, James, 229
Sargereau, P., 325
Sargiano, J., 317
Sarpham, James, 141
Sarrazen, M., 186
Sarriague, ---, 135
Sarynas, R., 210
Sasmento, 257
Sate, John, 77
Sauch, Miguel, 342
Sauer, George, 302
  Maria, 302
Saule, Nathanl., 235
Saunders, D., 228
  G., 77
  J., 159
  John, 40
  Joseph, 76
  P., 194
Sauvalle, Anna C., 344
Sauve, Peter, 319
Savage, C., 29, 91
  Gordon, 131
  James, 113, 218
  John, 274, 315
  Michl., 213
  Wm., 57, 76
Savan, P., 293
Savater, Joaquim, 145
Savel, James, 190
Saver, ---, 174
Savignac, Charles, 307
Saville, Jemima, 261
  Joseph, 261
Sawyer, C., 120
  Francis, 50

Sawyer, cont.
  Fred., 241
  S., 120
Saxon, Chas., 222
  Jno., 222
Sayere, Wm., 269
Sayers, A., 251
Sazar, John, 313
Scainsborough, D , 125
  Hannah, 125
Scallack, Wm., 91
Scallon, D., 284
Scally. See Seally.
Scanler, Hugh, 121
Scanlor, James, 138
Scarborough, John, 23
  Wm., 166
Scarlet, P., 245
Scatleburgh, Joseph, 165
  Samuel, 165
Schack, Edwd. de, 315
Schaeffer, E.N., 153
Schaffer, H., 325
  Margt., 325
  Wm., 10
Schale, John, 142
Scharpenter, Martin, 21
Schee, C., 156
Scheer, ---, 191
Scheffelin, J , 222
Schenck, P.R., 119
Schick, Margt., 274
  Thos., 274
Schilk, Joachim, 21
Schimanke, John, 298
Schliephake, H., 144
Schlrip, Wm., 32
Schmidt, C., 153
Schmidts, Wm , 274
Schmidtt, T., 220
Schmidtz, H.G.D., 126
Schneider, F.G., 86
Schnider, George, 87
Schnieder, Jacob, 254
  Magdelena 254
Schoelt, N., 195
Schofield, Abraham, 142
  James, 142
Schol, Gasper, 262
Schoolfield, Abraham, 65
  Benj., 307
Schroeder, C., 217
  H., 260
  L., 154
Schucloan, Catharine, 320
Schult, A., 258
Schuran, P., 49
Schusler, Fred., 278
Schuving, H.C., 322
Scobie, Jane, 111
Scofield, John, 21
Scores, Edwd., 202
Scott, Alexr., 194, 285
  Alice, 191

Scott, cont.
  Andrew, 106, 307
  Ann, 186
  Archibald, 38
  Christopher, 182
  Eliza, 283
  Elizabeth, 110
  Ellen, 8
  G., 343
  George, 93, 186, 188
  J., 141
  James, 71, 110, 282
  John, 89, 262, 267, 307
  Jonathan, 110
  L., 283
  Margt., 329
  Mary, 106
  Nixon, 191
  Philip, 329
  R., 194
  Rebecca, 4
  Robt., 199, 307
  Samuel, 329
  Sarah, 140
  Thomas, 186, 188, 307
  W., 218, 229
  Walter, 91
  Wm., 8, 314, 344
Scovell, Amos, 169
Scovelle, C.B., 353
Scowell, Amos, 23
Scudder, E.G., 105
Sculchi, P.B., 12
Scull, James, 142
Seabrook, Sarah, 3
Seal, J., 164
  J.G., 167
Seally, Wm., 174
Searce, Diana, 83
Searle, A.M., 46
  Charles, 334
  Thomas, 132, 232
Sears, James, 343
  John, 100
  Wm.C., 44
Seas, Madam, 18
Seatley, Wm., 86
Seaton, Alfred, 26, 170
  John, 60
Seavers, F., 32
Seaward, John H., 338
Sebballa, Margt., 113
Segar, A., 53
Segui, E., 277
Sehora, M.D., 62
Seiler, David, 302
  Mary, 302
Seinna, R. De la, 30
Seline, Philander, 232
Seller, R., 61
Selmet, Spencer, 221
Selms, Spencer, 216
Sement, V., 301
Seminall, M., 11

Semonton, Jno., 291
Senecal, A., 17
Senett, Henry, 337
Senion, M., 334
Senior, Catharine, 287
Senniace, R., 136
Senlin, D., 181
Sennis, Wm., 174
Sepman, R.N.J., 77
Seran, Joseph, 324
Sergeant, John, 4
  M.H., 292
Serin/Levin, ---, 205
Serperte, S., 72
Serrin, ---, 15
Serrion, Louis S., 75
Serry, Mr. O., 190
Seton, Alfred, 338
Sewall, George, 99
  Joseph, 181
  M., 268
  Wm., 76
Seward, 287
  O., 281
Sewell, H., 110
Seymore, H.L, 269
  Joseph, 239
Shaaff, Arthur, 89
Shadduck, Mr., 334
Shaffer, John, 39
Shaknigle, T., 231
Shaler, Wm., 220
Shambau, D., 319
Shane, J., 313
Shankey, Catharine, 148
  James, 148
  John, 148
Shannon, Abigail, 43
  Adam, 193
  Betsey, 193
  E.L., 347
  Hugh, 145
  James, 5, 349
  L., 239
  W., 232
  Wm., 91, 350
Shanton, James, 25
Sharp, Eliza, 252
  Henry, 48
  Jane, 243
  Nicholas, 103
  Peter, 5
  Wm., 134
Sharpe, Hannah, 341
  John, 115, 243
  Joseph, 341
  Mary, 115
Shatell, J.F., 205
Shattuck, Ann, 71
Shaw, A., 232
  B., 184
  Benj., 98, 300
  Charles B., 163
  Edmund, 141

417

ADDITIONS AND CORRECTIONS TO INDEXES

OMIT

www.ingramcontent.com/pod-product-compliance
Lightning Source LLC
Chambersburg PA
CBHW050558270326
41926CB00012B/2097